Private
Neighborhoods

and the Transformation
of Local Government

Robert H. Nelson

Private
Neighborhoods

and the Transformation
of Local Government

URBAN INSTITUTE PRESS
Washington, D.C.

9779824

Library of Congress Cataloging in Publication Data

Nelson, Robert H. (Robert Henry), 1944-
    Private neighborhoods and the transformation of local government / Robert H. Nelson.
        p. cm.
    Includes bibliographical references and index.
    ISBN 0-87766-751-9 (pbk. : alk. paper)
    1.   Neighborhood government—United States. 2.   Citizens' associations—United States.   I.   Title.
    JS391.N45 2005
    323'.042—dc22

                                                                                    2005012225

ISBN 0-87766-751-9 (paper, alk. paper)

Printed in the United States of America

10 09 08 07 06 05   1 2 3 4 5

THE URBAN INSTITUTE is a nonprofit, nonpartisan policy research and educational organization established in Washington, D.C., in 1968. Its staff investigates the social, economic, and governance problems confronting the nation and evaluates the public and private means to alleviate them. The Institute disseminates its research findings through publications, its web site, the media, seminars, and forums.

Through work that ranges from broad conceptual studies to administrative and technical assistance, Institute researchers contribute to the stock of knowledge available to guide decision-making in the public interest.

For my parents,
Robert Alfred Nelson and Irene Rauha Palonen Nelson

Contents

Foreword

Private neighborhood associations govern or regulate to some degree half the new housing built in the United States in the 1980s and 1990s. Some 52 million Americans now live in such housing, and the number of private communities—homeowners associations, condominiums, and cooperatives, some of which are the hotly debated gated communities—is rising rapidly. The growing importance of these developments suggests that there is a need to take another comprehensive look—the first being Evan McKenzie's seminal 1994 study, *Privatopia*—at the issues they raise.

As a glance at the contents page reveals, this book is really many books in one. Some sections may be more useful to scholars and students, others to lawyers, and still others to stakeholders in neighborhood associations and local officials. Many readers will appreciate Dr. Nelson's big intellectual tent. The author's fluid history of the evolution of local government and the rise of private neighborhood associations provides grist for serious discussions of how ingrained or pliable the privatization of neighborhoods may be. The extensive legal and economic analyses in *Private Neighborhoods* draw on theories of consumer and collective choice, as well as case law, and zero in on the transformation of traditional zoning regulations and other legal restrictions into contractual covenants. Dr. Nelson rethinks how current law might apply to and within new institutions that are neither private corporations nor local governments as traditionally defined. He also serves up concrete guidelines for crafting neighborhood constitutions.

The final three chapters (part VI) of *Private Neighborhoods* raise issues about how the U.S. Constitution might be construed as it applies to private associations. Building on the work of economists Albert Hirschman and James M. Buchanan, Nelson argues that neighborhood groups should be allowed to secede from municipalities to form their own governance units. This is a controversial view.

In keeping with the Urban Institute Press's commitment to the free play of ideas on public policy, we hope that the many issues Dr. Nelson's exceptional scholarship raises will focus more scholarly and policy attention on the rise of private communities and fuel informed debate about its implications.

Robert D. Reischauer
President
The Urban Institute

Preface

For most of American history, the standard form of living arrangement was a single home or an apartment that was owned or rented by an individual household. Any need for collective action among individual property owners was met by a local government in the public sector. Local governments provided public services and facilities, such as street construction and maintenance, garbage collection, law and order enforcement, and community parks and playgrounds. Once zoning was introduced in 1916, local governments also regulated the interactions among individual property owners, interactions that could influence the quality of the surrounding neighborhood environment.

Since the 1960s, however, local government's role has increasingly been privatized. In 1965 fewer than one percent of all Americans were living in a private community association. By 2004, 18 percent—about 52 million Americans—lived in housing within a homeowners association, a condominium, or a cooperative, and very often these private communities were of neighborhood size.[1] Indeed, since 1970 about one-third of all new housing units in the United States have been built within a private community association. In California at present, 60 percent of all new housing is being built in a community association.[2] People living in these areas are required to join the private association in order to purchase a home or other property there.

This privatizing of the neighborhood over the past 40 years represents a radical new development in the history of American local government. The rise of private neighborhoods, one legal authority writes, is achieving "a large-scale, but piecemeal and incremental, privatization of local government."[3] It is significantly altering the way tens of millions of Americans obtain housing. An expert on homeowner association and condominium law declares that these new forms of housing ownership are creating "a revolution in American housing patterns."[4] Another states more broadly that there is today an ongoing "massive societal transformation represented by restricted-access living" across the United States. Although originally oriented to higher-income groups, private communities are now "found throughout the country and cater to all income levels, including working class citizens."[5]

The rise of the "private neighborhood association"—the term that will be used in this book to describe the several legal forms for private collective ownership of housing—follows the rise of the corporate business ownership of private property in the late 19th century. Both represent fundamental turns away from individual property ownership and toward new collective forms of private property. Indeed, the rise of the private neighborhood association represents the most important property right development in the United States since the creation of the modern business corporation. By 1994 the California Supreme Court would declare that "common interest developments are a more intensive and efficient form of land use that greatly benefits society and expands opportunities for home ownership."[6] In the modern age, new forms of property ownership had to be created to coordinate private economic activity within large organizations—first, private business corporations more than 100 years ago, and now, private residential neighborhood associations.

Revisiting Political Philosophy

Since the 17th century, the leading political philosophies have been founded on the twin concepts of the individual and the nation-state. Among the founders of modern political theory, John Locke was a great defender of the rights of the individual, Thomas Hobbes of the virtues of a powerful state. A private neighborhood association might now be seen as a new kind of political actor, a small powerful jurisdiction that is entered into voluntarily as an exercise of individual choice.

Other types of actors, such as the European Union and the member states to the North American Free Trade Agreement (NAFTA), emerged in the second half of the 20th century. If on a much smaller geographic scale, the self-governing private neighborhood can also be seen as part of the rise of new governmental forms that may dramatically rework the political landscape of the 21st century. It is giving the individual neighborhood, for the first time, a main role in the American governing system. Private neighborhood governance seems likely to become increasingly important to America's overall political arrangements. The rise of the private neighborhood association thus is raising new questions about the structure of American government, questions that may require that we revisit basic issues and arguments in political philosophy.

Neighborhood associations raise tensions among different forms of individual freedom. One freedom is an individual's right to join a group that offers a setting for collective action, such as a church. Yet, within a given group tight limits may be imposed on other individual rights such as speech, assembly, and religion—and in a neighborhood association these limits are imposed throughout a common geographic area. Exclusive groups may also deny other individuals who do not share the same values the right to join the group—and thus to some degree they further limit the individual rights of each such excluded outsider. Identifying the tensions among individual rights is easy; resolving them, however, is more complicated and requires balancing competing goals and values as they are affected by the rise of private neighborhood associations.

Although the United States was founded on a philosophy of individual liberty (expressed politically through the right to vote and economically through the protection of private property), the 20th century saw a significant shift away from the original emphasis on individual freedom. Many American intellectuals sought to manage society toward particular ends, often hoping that applying new methods developed by the social sciences would make this possible, and requiring a more collective social control. Indeed, some hoped for comprehensive social management in all areas by the government; the majority, however, argued for new institutional arrangements of private groups that would then lead to the desired social ends. John Maynard Keynes thus famously contended—in opposition to Marxists and socialists—that the private market should be preserved because society could manage the market process to avoid unemployment and achieve other desirable goals.[7]

More recently, Robert Putnam and others have argued that excessive individualism and a loss of shared values threaten the United States, which is losing its "social capital."[8] One proposed remedy is to encourage stronger private associations that would educate the American people locally in practicing democracy and other aspects of group life, and in this way also help to inculcate stronger values. These values may differ significantly from individual to individual but many advocates of a more vital "civil society" argue that some values are preferable to no values.*

---

*William Galston, a distinguished American political philosopher at the University of Maryland, thus argues that "the greatest threat to children in modern liberal society is not that they will believe in something too deeply, but that they will believe in nothing very deeply at all. Even to achieve the kind of free self-reflection that many liberals prize, it is better to begin by believing something." Civic attitudes in general will be encouraged in American life by wide processes of "rational deliberation" in which it may be more important that "the stakes are meaningful" in each case, rather than the precise character of the issues debated. See William A. Galston, *Liberal Purposes: Goods, Virtues and Diversity in the Liberal State* (New York: Cambridge University Press, 1991), 255.

From this perspective, the critical issue in assessing the future of neighbor-hood associations is not resolving the tension among different forms of indi-vidual freedom. It is instead a question of whether encouraging neighborhood associations, along with other forms of private associational life, will advance the necessary common bonds and otherwise make American society "work better." Will the rise of private neighborhood associations contribute to mak-ing American democratic life more vigorous and enlightened? Will it provide the social capital needed for a political system to succeed and for the economy to prosper? The grounds for judgment here are more utilitarian and less a philosophical resolution of conflicting claims to individual freedom. How to resolve the social and legal status of the private neighborhood association will be an important ground for future debate in American political philosophy.[9]

A Personal Journey

The beginnings of this book go back as far as 1968 when, as a graduate student in the economics department at Princeton University, I completed my course-work for a PhD. At that time the problems of America's urban areas—some of which had burned recently in riots—were at the forefront of public attention. I resolved to become an urban economist and subsequently wrote my PhD the-sis in this area.[10] This interest eventually led to the publication of *Zoning and Property Rights* in 1977, a book that described the "privatization" of zoning over 60 years of land-use regulation.[11] Although this outcome was a large departure from the received theories of zoning, the workings of zoning can be regarded in practice as socially beneficial in the same way that other private property rights generally play a constructive role in encouraging productive efforts in society. In the case of zoning, the de facto private rights promoted building and maintaining attractive residential neighborhoods.

The theme that government regulations, such as zoning, have been captured for private purposes has since become a common argument, often associated with James Buchanan and the "public choice" school of economics, as well as the University of Chicago school of economics. Like zoning, many other regula-tory institutions of American government have intellectual roots in the political and economic thought of the Progressive Era (which historians typically date from 1890 to 1920). In the 1980s and 1990s, many "progressive" systems of regulation in areas such as transportation, energy, banking, communications, and still others were cut back or eliminated. In other nations, such industries were often privatized, as a privatization movement—analogous to the deregu-lation movement in the United States—spread across the world.

Zoning has thus far not been deregulated; the formal institution of zoning is alive and well. However, American neighborhoods have been substantially privatized. Zoning has steadily evolved in practice toward a collective private property right. Many municipalities now make zoning a saleable item by imposing large fees for approving zoning changes. Many Americans seem to prefer a de facto private status for their immediate neighborhood environment— putting the neighborhood in the same category as their automobile, furniture, and other private possessions. The rise of the private neighborhood association, as this book will show, is the culmination of a long process of neighborhood privatization in the United States over the 20th century.

In the late 1970s, after taking a job in the U.S. Department of the Interior in Washington, D.C., my interests shifted to another area of U.S. land policy.* Many of the institutions of the public lands—representing 30 percent of the land in the United States—were also products of the Progressive Era. As I delved further into public land management, I found many parallels between the history of private land zoning and of public land management. In each case, the goal had been comprehensive planning by government of the physical environment—applying methods of scientific management to shape future use of land. In both cases, the outcome had been a privatization of nominally governmental functions.[12] The public "planning" that took place frequently provided a camouflage for the advancement of private interests. The Progressive-Era rhetoric and rationales still lived on in zoning and management of public lands, but the greatest beneficiaries typically were private groups.

In the 1980s my intellectual interests extended to include the study of another Progressive-Era legacy. The American Economic Association was formed in 1885, part of a systematic effort to create professional associations that would provide expert knowledge across many areas of American society. Yet, once again, I found the progressive model flawed; the economics profession had promised more than it could deliver. Indeed, the scientific method— so enormously successful in the study of physical nature— had proven difficult to transfer to human affairs. Despite the contrary view of many fellow economists, the values underpinning economics could not be separated from the scientific elements in either practical applications or basic theory. It was appropriate, as I increasingly came to conclude, to regard American professional economics as one of the new "secular religions" that had become prominent in the modern age.[13]

This book continues my exploration of the practical failures of Progressive-Era political and economic ideas. I first explored this theme in *Zoning and*

---

*In 1975 I joined the Office of Policy Analysis in the Office of the Secretary of the U.S. Department of the Interior. Partly because this office functioned at times in the manner of an in-house think tank for the Interior Department, and afforded considerable opportunity for professional research and writing, I remained there until 1993. At that point I left to join the faculty of the School of Public Affairs at the University of Maryland in College Park.

Property Rights in 1977. While that book focused on zoning, this book describes the rise of the private neighborhood association and the likelihood that it will become a central political institution in America in the 21st century.

A New Area of Study

Economists did not appreciate the full social significance of the corporate ownership of property until long after corporations had become prominent in America. Indeed, it was not until 1932, when Adolf Berle and Gardiner Means showed that the rise of the modern corporation had transformed the relationship between the ownership of business property and the managerial control, that this development gained the wide attention of the American economics profession.[14] Even today, much economic analysis best suits a market framework of atomistic firms with individual owners and decisionmakers. The internal workings of business corporations pose issues of collective choice and action that have more traditionally been studied within the framework of American political science.

Social scientists have also been slow to recognize the rise of the private neighborhood association.* Economists have thus far shown little interest in their professional publications.[15] This is not due to a lack of useful tools that might be applied to the study of private neighborhoods. Since the 1960s, James Buchanan, Gordon Tullock, and others in the "public choice" school have explored collective decisionmaking from an economic perspective.[16] The insights of Mancur Olson in his 1965 classic, *The Logic of Collective Action*, are readily applicable to the functioning of private neighborhood associations.[17] Economists have shown a long-standing interest in the role of private property rights in an economic system.

Following Charles Tiebout's classic article, a substantial economic literature of "fiscal federalism" developed.[18] Tiebout in effect argued that a system of local governments could function like a group of private clubs, acting to align the supply of collective services closely with the demands for these services.

---

*In a recent book, a prominent American social scientist and the director of the Center for American Political Studies at Harvard University, Theda Skocpol, undertakes a broad review of trends in association life in the United States over the past century. She argues that there has been a fundamental shift from membership associations with large numbers of active local chapters—groups such as the Masons and the Knights of Columbus—to new forms of national lobbying and professional associations—groups such as the National Organization for Women and Greenpeace. Yet, remarkably, Skocpol never brings up the subject of private neighborhood associations or addresses the seeming inconsistency of their rapid rise with her main thesis. See Theda Skocpol, *Diminished Democracy: From Membership to Management in American Civic Life* (Norman, OK: University of Oklahoma Press, 2003).

With the rise of the private neighborhood association, the real world of local governance more closely conforms to the assumptions of a Tiebout world. As a leading legal practitioner in the field of neighborhood association law notes, "the assessments of the condominium association can be compared to the taxes of a city," and the ability of the board of directors "to develop and modify rules and regulations is similar to the ability of a municipality to pass and amend ordinances."[19] Yet, the transaction costs of creating and modifying neighborhood associations in response to new economic circumstances—in moving from one economic equilibrium to another—are less than the costs of local government.

In the 1990s, a small group of political scientists began to note the growing social significance of private neighborhood associations. However, they often viewed the private character of the neighborhood association as a step backward from the "progressive" trends of the 20th century.[20] The rise of the neighborhood association was thus seen as a parochial and divisive turn away from the higher ideals of a unified national community. As compared with social scientists, lawyers have paid considerably more attention to the rise of neighborhood associations. Already, more than 4,000 cases involving the actions of private neighborhood associations have ended up in court.[21] Most of the legal literature, however, has narrowly focused on issues of neighborhood associations' authority and range of permissible behavior.

The Plan of the Book

This book will apply a broadly economic framework to explore the rise of the private neighborhood association and its social significance. On the whole, the book will take a positive view.[22] This is not to deny the existence of problem areas. Indeed, the book will present possible changes in the organization of neighborhood associations—how they are legally established, how they are governed, how they conduct their operations, and in general their "constitutional" structure. The goal will be to provide an agenda for future improvements in how private neighborhood associations work.

The intended audience for the book includes land-use professionals with backgrounds in law, urban planning, economics, political science, and other fields. In addition, residents of private neighborhood associations and others with practical concerns relating to their theory, history, and workings may also find the book of value. As in my other works, I seek to write in a manner accessible to professionals and nonprofessionals alike, who may, for whatever reason, have a strong concern in the area addressed.

Part I of the book describes the rise of the private neighborhood association. In the 1960s, state governments enacted new laws to encourage the creation of neighborhood associations. Real estate developers responded with enthusiasm. This was not, however, the first act of asserting collective control over the surrounding neighborhood. That step was taken with the establishment of zoning early in the 20th century. Part II shows how the rise of private neighborhood associations culminated a process of neighborhood privatization that first began with the spread of zoning regulation of land use.

By the 1960s and 1970s, as part of a wider questioning of progressive plans for American government, a neighborhood movement arose to advocate decentralizing local governance. The neighborhood movement was mostly concerned with local governments in the public sector. Yet, the number of new private neighborhood associations has now greatly exceeded the number of new neighborhood public governments. This powerful "private neighborhood movement" will likely do much to shape future local governance in the United States. Part III sets this development in the context of wider political and economic public philosophies in American history.

At present, neighborhood associations can only be created in new housing developments where homebuyers must agree to the association's legal authority as a condition of purchase. However, many established neighborhoods might benefit from a private neighborhood association. In part IV, I propose that an established neighborhood should be able to create a private neighborhood association on the basis of a supermajority vote of current property owners. Gaining more secure control over the surrounding environment would potentially benefit many inner-city neighborhoods that have physically deteriorated and suffer from crime, drugs, and other social problems.

The private status of the neighborhood association gives it an option to experiment more freely with new governing methods. Until now, neighborhood associations have not taken much advantage of this freedom. Most neighborhood associations operate under boilerplate founding documents that real estate lawyers routinely provide. Part V proposes that the "constitutions" of neighborhood associations should be more diverse and more closely tailored to the needs and circumstances of each individual neighborhood. A menu of constitutional options—new methods for electing neighborhood boards of directors (the neighborhood "legislature"), for administering the neighborhood, and for resolving neighborhood legal disputes—is provided for review of interested parties.

Many basic social choices must be made concerning the future role of neighborhood associations in American life. These issues include the permissible legal powers of neighborhood associations to exclude prospective residents, the acceptable voting qualifications in neighborhood association elections, and the terms under and degree to which associations will be legally allowed to withdraw from their existing local government. Part VI explores these areas of current public policy concern.

This book thus provides a comprehensive analysis of the history of private neighborhood associations in the United States, their current circumstances, and the potential future directions for change. The book can be read in its entirety or by selecting portions of particular interest. Readers who are already knowledgeable about the legal arrangements and workings of neighborhood associations, for example, might find part I of less interest. Readers with broader interests in the role of neighborhood associations in the American political economy might well find parts II and III of the greatest benefit. If the extension of neighborhood associations to established neighborhoods holds an appeal, part IV provides a blueprint for implementation. A reader interested in reforming his or her existing neighborhood association might find part V to be of the greatest usefulness. Finally, readers looking for the future desirable political and legal role of private neighborhood associations in American life might find part VI to be of the greatest interest.

NOTES

1. See the web site of the Community Associations Institute, Alexandria, Virginia, http://www.caionline.org/about/facts.cfm.

2. David W. Lyon, "Foreword," to Tracy M. Gordon, *Planned Developments in California: Private Communities and Public Life* (San Francisco: Public Policy Institute of California, 2004), iii.

3. Steven Siegel, "The Constitution and Private Government: Toward the Recognition of Constitutional Rights in Private Residential Communities Fifty Years after Marsh v. Alabama," *William & Mary Bill of Rights Journal* 6 (Spring 1998), 560–61.

4. Robert G. Natelson, "Consent, Coercion, and 'Reasonableness' in Private Law: The Special Case of the Property Owners Association," *Ohio State Law Journal* 51 (Winter 1990), 42.

5. Richard Damstra, "Don't Fence Us Out: The Municipal Power to Ban Gated Communities and the Federal Takings Clause," *Valparaiso University Law Review* 35 (Summer 2001), 542, 530.

6. *Nahrstedt v. Lakeside Village Condominium Association*, 878 P.2d at 1288 (1994). See also Katharine N. Rosenberry, "Home Businesses, Llamas and Aluminum Siding: Trends in Covenant Enforcement," *John Marshall Law Review* 31 (Winter 1998).

7. John Maynard Keynes, *The General Theory of Employment, Interest and Money* (New York: Harcourt, Brace, and World, 1965).

8. Robert D. Putnam, "Bowling Alone: America's Declining Social Capital," *Journal of Democracy* 6 (January 1995); Robert D. Putnam, "Tuning In, Tuning Out: The Strange Disappearance of Social Capital in America," *PS: Political Science and Politics* (December 1995); and Robert D. Putnam, *Bowling Alone: The Collapse and Revival of American Community* (New York: Simon and Schuster, 2000).

9. Nancy L. Rosenblum, *Membership & Morals: The Personal Uses of Pluralism in America* (Princeton, NJ: Princeton University Press, 1998), ch. 4.

10. Robert Henry Nelson, *The Theory of Residential Location* (PhD thesis, Princeton University, 1971).

11. Robert H. Nelson, *Zoning and Property Rights: An Analysis of the American System of Land Use Regulation* (Cambridge, MA: MIT Press, 1977).

12. See Robert H. Nelson, *Public Lands and Private Rights: The Failure of Scientific Management* (Lanham, MD: Rowman & Littlefield, 1995); and Robert H. Nelson, *A Burning Issue: A Case for Abolishing the U.S. Forest Service* (Lanham, MD: Rowman & Littlefield, 2000). On the failings of public land management, see also Robert H. Nelson, *The Making of Federal Coal Policy* (Durham, NC: Duke University Press, 1983).

13. See Robert H. Nelson, *Economics as Religion: From Samuelson to Chicago and Beyond* (University Park, PA: Pennsylvania State University Press, 2001); and Robert H. Nelson, *Reaching for Heaven on Earth: The Theological Meaning of Economics* (Lanham, MD: Rowman & Littlefield, 1991).

14. Adolf A. Berle and Gardiner C. Means, *The Modern Corporation and Private Property* (New York: MacMillan, 1932).

15. There are a few exceptions. See, for example, Donald J. Boudreaux and Randall G. Holcombe, "Government by Contract," *Public Finance Quarterly* 17, no. 3 (1989); Yoram Barzel and Tim R. Sass, "The Allocation of Resources by Voting," *Quarterly Journal of Economics* 105 (August 1990); Fred Foldvary, *Public Goods and Private Communities: The Market Provision of Social Services* (Brookfield, VT: Edward Elgar, 1994); and Donald J. Boudreaux and Randall G. Holcombe, "Contractual Governments in Theory and Practice," in David T. Beito, Peter Gordon, and Alexander Tabarrok, eds., *The Voluntary City: Choice, Community, and Civil Society* (Ann Arbor: University of Michigan Press, 2002).

16. James M. Buchanan and Gordon Tullock, *The Calculus of Consent: Logical Foundations of Constitutional Democracy* (Ann Arbor: University of Michigan Press, 1962).

17. Mancur Olson, *The Logic of Collective Action: Public Goods and the Theory of Groups* (Cambridge, MA: Harvard University Press, 1965).

18. Charles M. Tiebout, "A Pure Theory of Local Expenditures," *Journal of Political Economy* 64 (October 1956); see also Wallace E. Oates, "An Essay on Fiscal Federalism," *Journal of Economic Literature* 37 (September 1999).

19. Peter M. Dunbar, *The Condominium Concept: A Practical Guide for Officers, Owners and Directors of Florida Condominiums, 7th edition* (Tallahassee, FL: Aras Publishing, 2000), 11.

20. Evan McKenzie, *Privatopia: Homeowner Associations and the Rise of Residential Private Government* (New Haven, CT: Yale University Press, 1994).

21. Wayne S. Hyatt and Susan F. French, *Community Association Law: Cases and Materials on Common Interest Communities* (Durham, NC: Carolina Academic Press, 1998).

22. See also, most recently, Robert H. Nelson, "The Rise of the Private Neighborhood Association: A Constitutional Revolution in Local Government," in Dick Netzer, ed., *The Property Tax, Land Use and Land Use Regulation* (Northampton, MA: Edward Elgar with the Lincoln Institute of Land Policy, 2003); and Robert H. Nelson, "The Private Neighborhood," *Regulation* 27 (Summer 2004).

Acknowledgments

I began this book in 1997, after receiving an invitation from professor Steven Eagle of the George Mason University School of Law to prepare a paper on "Freedom of Contract in Property Law" as it related to the American practice of zoning regulation. My paper on "Privatizing the Neighborhood: A Proposal to Replace Zoning with Private Collective Property Rights to Existing Neighborhoods" served as the starting point for the conference discussion (the conference was held in Alexandria, Virginia, with the support of the Donner Foundation). I benefited there from the comments of many attendees with expertise in local land use regulation, including written (and later published) comments by William Fischel, Steven Eagle, and Robert Ellickson. As this conference paper evolved over the next years into a book manuscript, Robert Poole of the Reason Foundation provided valuable advice. I also owe a great debt of gratitude to Lee Anne Fennell who commented valuably on multiple drafts of the book. As the manuscript came closer to completion, Peter Gordon provided additional helpful suggestions. Others who have commented usefully on portions of the manuscript at one or another time include Jonathan Adler, Lincoln Cummings, Albert Foer, and Jesse Walker.

As a member of the faculty of the School of Public Policy of the University of Maryland throughout the period in which this book was written, I thank the School for the supportive environment it provided. The Competitive Enterprise Institute in Washington, D.C., for which I served as a senior fellow from 1995 to 2002, also provided additional support. I also benefited over the period in which this book was under preparation from the support and hospitality of the Centre for Applied Social Sciences in Harare, Zimbabwe (1999); the International Centre for Economic Research in Turin, Italy (2000); and the Faculty of Law of Keio University in Tokyo, Japan (2002). Most recently, I had the opportunity to try out ideas in the book at conferences in Tucson, Arizona, in January 2003, and in Cambridge, Massachusetts, in May 2003, hosted by the Lincoln Institute of Land Policy. Finally, Kathleen Courrier and the Urban Institute Press acted in the old-fashioned role of an editor, making numerous suggestions and otherwise helping significantly to improve the final product.

Introduction

A Constitutional Revolution

In 1988, the U.S. Advisory Commission on Intergovernmental Relations (ACIR) officially announced the arrival of an important new player on the American governmental scene. According to the ACIR, "Traditionally the intergovernmental system has been thought to include the national government, state governments, and local governments of all kinds." It had become necessary, however, to adapt "the concept of intergovernmental relations . . . to contemporary developments so as to take account of territorial community associations that display many, if not all, of the characteristics of traditional local government." As a result, as the ACIR declared, "the governance of local communities in the United States can be said to exist increasingly in two worlds, one public and one private."[1]

Because of the rise in private collective ownership of residential property, the private sector's role in providing local services has increased. An authority on community association law predicts, moreover, that in the future these associations will "perform more community services," such as transportation and education, functions that "were formerly public services." All this will have increasing "legal, political, social, and economic consequences . . . [that will] implicate corporate, municipal, constitutional, and other areas of law as well as social and public policy concerns."[2] Given the different ground rules under which private governments work, these changes amount to at least a small revolution in local government—with potentially even greater consequences in the years to come.

A Divided Society?

Given the degree of social change it represents, it is not surprising that the shift in American society to collective ownership of residential property over the past 40 years is provoking controversy. Political scientist Evan McKenzie, for one, is disturbed by the "astonishing nationwide growth" in private neighborhood associations.[3] He fears that those who live in private neighborhoods will become "increasingly segregated from the rest of society."[4] Furthermore, the newly private character of suburban areas will divert our citizenry from pressing national and international concerns—including poverty, racial discrimination, and other urgent matters.* The severest critics of gated communities go so far as to describe these neighborhoods as "a return to the Middle Ages, to moats and drawbridges (with modern amenities)" or as "a gang way of looking at life" that could ultimately lead to "the end of civilization" as we know it.[5]

From their studies of California neighborhood associations, Stephen Barton and Carol Silverman find a "privatization of the governing process" that strengthens "individualistic and uncivic understandings." Neighborhood associations "have the potential to further weaken people's understanding of public life."[6] The rise of the private neighborhood association has, in fact, become a symbol for broader trends in American life that concern many people. Frederick Skinner, professor of history at the University of Montana, comments, "The resentment I feel" about the presence of a local private neighborhood "is part of a larger bag of resentments I haul around about the increasing privati-

---

*The possibility that the well-off members of society will choose to segregate themselves in private communities is realized in an extreme form in some parts of Brazil. In Sao Paulo, the murder rate is 60 per 100,000 citizens, compared with 7 per 100,000 in the Washington, D.C., metropolitan area and 8 per 100,000 in New York; kidnappings are frequent. Many of the people with the means to do so seek to cut themselves off physically from the rest of society. The richest among them have even taking to flying by helicopter to destinations around the city (also partly to avoid traffic). The *Washington Post* described one of these walled communities in Sao Paulo:

> Alphaville is home to 30,000 of Sao Paulo's most privileged residents. It has three helipads and four entrances and exits, all monitored 24 hours a day.
> Inside the compound, visitors are recorded by cameras at guard checkpoints in residential zones. In the communal areas, children can attend well-guarded schools and enjoy afternoon sports on fenced-in fields watched over by Alphaville's black-clad security guards.
> "The elite have made a decision. Instead of looking to better Brazilian society in general, they are abandoning it and finding their own personal protection behind guarded walls," said Teresa Caldeira, a noted Brazilian anthropologist and author of the book *City of Walls: Crime, Segregation, and Citizenship in Sao Paulo.* "The rich are retrenching, restricting their lives in incredible ways and living their lives in an increasingly paranoid fashion." Anthony Faiola, "Brazil's Elites Fly above Their Fears: Rich Try to Wall Off Urban Violence," *Washington Post,* June 1, 2002.

zation of the West."[7] Law professor Sheryll Cashin laments that the rise of neighborhood associations has "put the nation on a course toward civic secession." The spread of "secessionist attitudes" is promoting a "reduced empathy" for people outside neighborhood association boundaries, a "polarization" within metropolitan areas, and a reduced capacity for "shared sacrifice or redistributive spending" within such areas.[8]

Richard Louv sees an old "America I" being replaced by a new "America II" in which neighborhood associations are prominent. Neighborhood associations represent a "shelter revolution" whose impact "radically changes what it means to be a neighbor."[9] In Louv's view, the ultimate consequences will be harmful:

> Now we are moving into new tribes, into condo communities and urban villages and new small towns. The selectivity of these new tribes ultimately means that a few members have the key to the future. The new tribes operate wonderfully for those who can afford, through money or knowledge, to buy into them. But this privilege comes at a price.
>
> America is fragmenting into subsocieties, regions, sections, information-rich and information-poor, instead of defining what we want—security, economic stability, community, home—and then trying to get that for all the people.[10]

Two hundred years ago, citizens had to own property in order to vote in many American elections.[11] Such practices were gradually abolished, however, as the franchise was extended to almost every American citizen. Universal voting rights are now regarded as a triumph of modern democracy. Yet, private neighborhoods revert to the earlier systems of voting based on property ownership.* As long ago as 1969, Albert Foer contended that "a strong case can be made for the position that . . . the property basis of political participation in [the private] Reston and Columbia [communities] may violate the equal protection clause" of the constitution.[12] Foer turned out to be wrong constitutionally (thus far, at least), but many observers continue to argue that, legal or not, a system of local voting based on property ownership is wrong. Barton and Silverman, in fact, label neighborhood associations as "profoundly undemocratic."[13]

Cornell law professor Gregory Alexander says that "residential associations . . . may represent the dominant aspect of the late 20th century contribution to American residential group life." This social innovation is "fundamentally dif-

---

*Renters thus are disenfranchised in most neighborhood associations. Yet, one 1987 California survey found that in 14 percent of the neighborhood associations studied, renters occupied the majority of the units; the median association had 20 percent of its units occupied by renters. See Steven E. Barton and Carol J. Silverman, *Common Interest Homeowners' Association Management Study* (Sacramento, CA: California Department of Real Estate, 1987).

ferent from both traditional fee ownership of the detached house and apartment living." It seeks "to infuse a social experience of groupness into modern ownership of residential property." Yet, as Alexander assesses the outcome, "the vision of self-governance and participatory democracy within these groups often is illusory." Many residents are uninterested and uninvolved in their associations. Boards of directors often fail to take effective charge of enforcement and service provision. There is a large gap "between the Panglossian image of many residential associations and [the] reality."[14]

Alexander also finds that many residents "experienced coercion in agreeing to association rules and in joining the association itself." In some parts of the United States, neighborhood associations have now become so widespread that they dominate the local housing market; it might be difficult to find any suitable housing not located within a neighborhood association. Moreover, once residents have joined an association, they are often surprised at the extent of collective control. Two attorneys who have worked with California neighborhood associations complain that they "can tax you, control your freedom of expression, limit religious expression, in some states regulate your reproductive rights, impose fines for failing to follow their rules, and tell you what color to paint your house." The results can come to resemble the stuff of "Big Brother fantasies" or even horror stories from "totalitarian regimes."[15] Another legal critic laments that neighborhood associations "are alive and their presence threatens homeowners everywhere" with oppressive rules and other restrictions on their actions imposed by their neighbors.[16]

All in all, as McKenzie argues in *Privatopia*, the ardent defenders of private neighborhoods are the captives of a new kind of "utopian faith" that reflects the current era of widespread privatization around the world.[17] Given all the problems associated with neighborhood associations, "government officials . . . need to make an informed choice about whether to permit more CID [common interest development] construction, and, if so, what kind."[18] Perhaps the rise of the private neighborhood association should be seen as a grand social experiment that has failed, and steps should now be taken to reverse it.

Private Suburbs

Criticisms of neighborhood associations, however, typically neglect a crucial factor. The privatization of the American neighborhood did not begin with, nor has it been confined to, neighborhood associations. Indeed, the rise of suburban zoning first effectively privatized many American neighborhoods. Even in the public sector, residents themselves often see "a small suburban town . . . as little more than a form of homeowners' association."[19] Sociologist David Popenoe writes of the longstanding "privatization of space" in metropolitan areas in the United States,* commenting that the well-off suburb in America has a "deeply private feel" as the households there "live behind the protection of fence, hedge, or wall, venturing forth only within the confines of a motorized enclosed box."[20] Fully half of American municipalities in the public sector have populations of fewer than 1,000 people; three-quarters have fewer than 5,000.[21] Such figures reflect a reality described by another observer as a long-standing "strong cultural preference for local powers" in the United States.[22]

As yet another social commentator argued recently, "the suburb is the last word in privatization."[23] The political analyst William Schneider states that "suburbanites' preference for the private applies to government as well."[24] University of Virginia law professor Richard Schragger finds that the American suburbs in the 20th century have "essentially become privatized," resulting in a new "political economy of privatized local government."[25] All in all, as Popenoe complains,

> It is in the privatization of space, because it is so tangible and visible, that the break-down of the public realm in metropolitan life can most clearly be seen. The American suburb is the extreme case, but privatization is a dominant motif in most of the other ecological zones of the metropolis as well. Streets and sidewalks that once provided public pedestrian interaction and even entertainment have for the most part been abandoned to the utter privacy of the automobile; public parks have fallen into disuse and misuse; town squares have become the mostly ornamental appendages of commercialism. . . . Where is the public space in a Houston or a Los Angeles? It does exist, but is overwhelmed by the dominance of essentially private spheres.[26]

In the legal arena, the courts have often seen the suburban municipality in private terms. In one case, Chief Justice Warren Burger wrote, "I believe that a community of people are—within limits—masters of their own environment" and, as a result, "citizens should be free to choose to shape their community so it embodies their conception of the 'decent life.' "[27] Harvard law professor Gerald Frug notes that "many recent Supreme Court cases suggest that cities can best empower themselves by acting just like property owners." The main purpose of suburban zoning, Frug observes, is "the protection . . . of the private sphere of home and family, property, and community." It is common for cities to be "envisioned, and regulated, like property owners. Both property owners and

---

*The desire for greater privacy would seem to be a luxury good that extends with increasing economic means to many other areas besides exterior living patterns. Fifty years ago, for example, the typical new home had one bathroom; now it has two or three, and in many houses more—according to one report, the greatest single change in American housing design. The buyers of new homes today "want to be alone: That means, if they've got the money, they're not interested in teaching the lessons they learned from their parents about the merits of sharing. They want privacy." As *Better Homes and Gardens* editor Joan McCloskey says, "We all shared a bathroom—parents and five children—when I was a kid, but I have no idea how we did it." Sandra Fleishman, "Builders' Winning Play: A Royal Flush," *Washington Post,* November 24, 2001, H1.

cities can be defined in terms of territory, organized to advance 'parochial interests,' and . . . understood as having a concrete self-interest to promote."[28]

Within this American system of "private" suburbs, zoning functions as a "property right" to the collectively owned environment.[29] If the essence of a property right is the ability to exclude others, zoning then creates this legal authority for suburban communities. University of Illinois law professor Lee Anne Fennell describes a system of "collective property rights created through zoning. Zoning splits property rights between the individual landowner and the local government by vesting a set of collective property rights in the community." The practical effect is that "while traditional notions of nuisance grant the community some power to limit land use, zoning shifts certain additional property rights from the landowner to the community. Thus, under current zoning law, the community's interest in maintaining a particular atmosphere or growth pattern is protected by a property rule."[30]

In a series of law journal articles over the course of the 1990s, Columbia law professor Richard Briffault conducted an authoritative review of the legal arrangements of U.S. local governments.[31] Briffault finds that the actions of local governments follow three basic models: (1) the democratic "polis," (2) the "firm," and (3) "the administrative arm of the state [government]."[32] Zoning represents local government acting in a private "firm" capacity; the "stockholders" are in effect the residents of the municipality.[33] However, it would be almost impossible to establish a collective regime of exclusion in an established neighborhood through voluntary (necessarily unanimous) consent alone. In such places, zoning effectively overcomes the transaction-cost obstacles to collective rights through the use of government coercive powers.

Public zoning, to be precise, is a legal device for overcoming free-rider and holdout problems associated with ordinary private collective action.* As Briffault observes, local government can be a particularly useful device because it can serve as a means of employing "the coercive power of the state for private economic ends."[34] The privatization of local government also advances the public welfare in the same way as a system of private property rights in general. Zoning creates new collective property rights that establish positive incentives for building and maintaining attractive neighborhood environments. According to Patricia Burgess, in Columbus, Ohio, the historic practice of "zoning served the realtors' and land developers' purposes the way [private] deed restrictions did, by helping to determine an area's character" and sustain higher property values.[35]

---

*When one individual is a small part of a large group, his or her actions will have little or no effect on total group outputs. Hence, there will be little private incentive to contribute to group activities, even though the person may benefit from them. However, if every individual behaves in this manner—acting as a "free-rider"—the group will be unable to take effective collective action and no one will realize the benefits.

Protecting the Environment Privately

The exercise of private collective rights differs in important respects, however, from the administration of public zoning. By virtue of their private status, private covenants can be more comprehensive than the usual zoning controls (although historic districts show that comprehensive controls can exist in the public sector as well). Compared with public municipalities, neighborhood associations have, among other features, different voting rules, governance systems, and taxation methods. In general, the constitutional status of "private" actions—including the exercise of collective private rights to property—differs significantly in American law from "public" actions—including the administration of zoning controls over property.[36]

The rise of the private neighborhood association demonstrates that, given private and public alternatives, many Americans prefer the private route. They may be seeking a greater control over their neighbors' actions. One individual commented about the benefits of belonging to a neighborhood association: "Your neighbor will probably be prevented from rebuilding his '57 Chevy in his front yard, or parking his recreational vehicle for six months at a time." A woman in Southern California declared, "I thought I'd never live in a planned unit development, but then I realized I wanted a single-family detached home with some control over my neighbors. I looked at one house without a homeowner association. The guy next door built a dog run on the property line. All night long his Dobermans ran back and forth."[37]

There are many complaints about the "dictatorial" and "arbitrary" actions of neighborhood associations. Nevertheless, a 1999 Gallup poll for the Community Associations Institute found that 75 percent of unit owners were "very or extremely satisfied" with their experience of living in a neighborhood association. Furthermore, 48 percent stated that they planned to live in a neighborhood association in the future.[38] In another survey, 52 percent of unit owners declared that they "mostly agree" and 30 percent that they "completely agree" with the statement "community association homeownership is a satisfactory housing choice." Among these homeowners living in associations, 66 percent agreed that the neighborhood social environment was either "friendly" or "neighborly," while 26 percent found it "distant or private" and 8 percent found it "divided and unfriendly." Among homeowners who had served on association boards of directors, 83 percent reported that they either "completely agree" or "mostly agree" with the statement "serving on an association board of directors has been a good experience."[39]

Although there are numerous critics, neighborhood associations also have many strong defenders.[40] Gerald Korngold, dean of the law school at Case Western Reserve University, finds that the obligation to obey private rules produces "great benefits" for the neighborhood residents. The tight restrictions create environments that frequently serve as "places of renewal" and promote "happiness and peace of mind." Although there will be both "costs and benefits" to any form of group living, Korngold believes that in most cases the restrictions imposed by neighborhood associations serve unit owners' overall interest. These restrictions act to control "spillovers that can harm property values and visual ambience" and thus raise the overall value of neighborhood land and property.[41]

In gated communities, according to Setha Low, many "residents who did not select the community for its gates now would only live behind protective walls." She believes that gated communities reflect a growing unwillingness—unfortunate in her mind—to share a common residential environment with other kinds of people. Fear of crime is a main reason many people live in gated communities. Nevertheless, Low also finds that in many cases "they [community residents] say that they would always choose a gated community again, even if safety was not the basis of their initial decision."[42] Among other things, the security gate stands as a symbol of common values and social bonds.*

The rise of large business corporations also provoked deep social unease in the late 19th and early 20th centuries. Yet Americans have come to accept the positive role of large businesses in American society. Business corporations operate under state charters that prescribe various stockholder rights, disclosure requirements, governance procedures, and other rules for the exercise of ownership rights by the shareholders. Since the 1930s, the federal government has set additional ground rules for business corporations, including the various requirements established by the Securities and Exchange Commission.

Neighborhood associations also operate within a legal framework established by state governments. Florida and California have already modified their statutes for condominiums and homeowners associations many times. Neighborhood associations must comply with federal laws prohibiting racial, age, and other forms of discrimination. Like oversight of the private business corporation, the proper role for government in overseeing the workings of collective ownership of private residential property will be an important subject for public policy debate for years to come.

As in other areas of American life, the courts will no doubt be a leading player in resolving these social issues. They will be called upon, for example, to rule on the permissible manner of privately regulating individual actions within neighborhood associations. In making such rulings, the longstanding

---

*This is not a new development. As one urban historian reports, there was a long time in "earlier centuries when the walls of a community were inviolable, indeed almost sacred. . . . Ramparts not only protected against enemies but formed a spiritual boundary of equal significance, for such barriers preserved those within from the evil outside." Kenneth T. Jackson, *Crabgrass Frontier: The Suburbanization of the United States* (New York: Oxford University Press, 1985), 14.

legal distinction between "public" and "private" will inevitably play an important role. As law professor Gerald Wetlaufer explains a basic assumption in the American legal system, "there is a public sphere and a private sphere, and . . . the state may act legitimately within the public sphere but not within the private sphere" (at least to anywhere near the same extent).[43]

"Public" and "Private" Ambiguities

Yet, given the legal importance of the private-public distinction, it is surprisingly difficult to pin down. One legal authority finds that the doctrine of "state action" has long been regarded as a "conceptual disaster area" in the law, although more recent court arguments have meant that it has been "considerably yet imperfectly narrowed."[44] Another legal commentator finds that "the words public and private may seem distinct enough—and they are used in popular and political discourse as if they were—but they are not."[45]

Law professors and judges aren't the only experts who have trouble defining the difference between "public" and "private." Political scientists, economists, and other students of government find it difficult as well. Some might suggest that "public" could be taken to mean "governmental." However, neighborhood associations are themselves forms of government and yet are private. The small suburban municipality may nominally be "public," but in practice its actions often have a "private" character.

Some might suggest that a feasible way of distinguishing "public" from "private" is in terms of "collective" and "individual"—as one speaks broadly of the collective provision of a "public service." However, from a legal perspective, many actions such as membership in a private golf club are collective and yet not public. Other people might suggest that public and private actions can be distinguished by the motives behind them. A "public" action might be viewed as taken to advance an altruistic motive—as in a "public-spirited" action. A "private" act might reflect a dominant motive to benefit the individual person (or group). However, many people contribute their time and effort to nonprofit organizations, such as soup kitchens for the poor and other charities—organizations that are nonetheless private. Further complicating the matter is the argument—at least as old as Adam Smith—that actions intended for private profit may nonetheless serve a public purpose, even when there is no explicit intent to do so.

Defining "private" as an action taken for monetary gain does not work either. A person might go hiking in the woods as a private act, and that action brings no financial benefit. Some people might suggest—in the spirit of John Locke—that a "public" entity can be distinguished from a "private" entity because the former cannot change the initial contract without unanimous consent. However, like the U.S. Constitution, most public constitutions provide for amendment procedures that fall well short of requiring unanimous consent. The founding documents of most private associations similarly contain procedures for their amendment, and few of these documents require unanimous consent for most types of changes.

Yet another way of defining a public action is by the presence of an element of coercion. Only a government, for example, has the power to put someone in prison. However, many actions that fall in the public category do not involve any degree of coercion. No one is obligated to use food stamps or to drive on a public road. Moreover, private coercion can be deemed legitimate as well— as when someone responds in kind to a direct physical attack on his or her person. A private guard has the legal right to forcibly restrain a person from trespassing on private property.

Only a public government can set the terms for the legitimate use of force in society. In other respects as well, only a government can set the social framework for public and private actions alike. Government is in this respect "foundational" and, short of a system of anarchy, has some unique roles. However, these elements of government represent only a tiny part of the total range of "public" actions.

In short, we may frequently use the terms "public" and "private" in ordinary speech, but often we use them in different ways. Specific usage may depend closely on the social context and may shift with changing conventions of language. It should come as no surprise that the courts have found it difficult to deal with such definitional ambiguities.* With respect to private neighborhood associations, David Kennedy finds that "state courts have reached wildly different conclusions when faced with the argument that a residential association qualifies as a state actor."[46] All in all, as Dan Tarlock has similarly commented, "American law has [traditionally] drawn a distinction between public and private associations to decide how power should be allocated between the state and individual," but private neighborhood associations clearly "strain this distinction."[47]

---

*The court difficulties are illustrated by their confused efforts to say whether a shopping center should be treated as a "public" or a "private" entity. In 1968, the U.S. Supreme Court seemed to declare that shopping centers are for many practical purposes state actors, ruling that they could not prohibit picketing by union members against businesses in the centers. However, four justices, including Justice Hugo Black, dissented. Four years later, the Supreme Court backtracked, allowing a shopping center to exclude protesters against the Vietnam War, declaring that "property [does not] lose its private character merely because the public is generally invited to use it for designated purposes." Then, a few years later, the Supreme Court abandoned its 1968 ruling altogether. In a private shopping center, the court declared, "the constitutional guarantee of free expression has no part to play." For discussion of these and other cases, see Harvey Rishikof and Alexander Wohl, "Private Communities or Public Governments: 'The State Will Make the Call,' " *Valparaiso University Law Review* 30 (Spring 1996), 536–41.

Private Prerogatives

Despite the difficulty in finding generally applicable definitions of "public" and "private," it nevertheless makes a large difference legally how a specific activity in American life is classified. If an action is deemed to be private—however this might have been established—then this determination will often have major implications in terms of the courts' views and expectations. For example, a neighborhood association is legally permitted to engage in a wider set of actions than a municipal government in the public sector (which in concept could be of identical population and geographic size). For example,

1. A private neighborhood association can legally assign voting rights according to the extent of property ownership, or (in concept) on the basis of a wide range of other possible voting eligibility criteria. A general-purpose municipal government is legally required under the constitution—as determined by the U.S. Supreme Court in its 1968 *Avery* decision—to allocate voting rights on the basis of one person/one vote.[48]
2. A private neighborhood association can discriminate in admitting residents to the neighborhood in various ways that most likely would not be legal for a municipal government. For example, a neighborhood association for senior citizens can exclude younger people, including any children, from living there permanently. It is doubtful that a municipality in the public sector could sustain a similar discriminatory entry rule based on the age of potential residents.
3. If it wishes, a private neighborhood association can sell the entry rights into the neighborhood. A municipal government could not similarly sell a zoning change, even though the zoning change might have the identical practical consequence of granting land use. In fact, a direct monetary sale of entry rights—through zoning—would be regarded as a corrupt act of "bribery" or the illegal sale of a public regulation.
4. A private neighborhood association can explicitly enforce precise trespass controls over the numbers and types of visitors allowed into the neighborhood (as long as its actions are not based on race or some other illegal criteria). Entry into a gated community may require official permission—a private "visa" in the manner of entering a nation-state. In determining the number of residents allowed, a private neighborhood association can maintain, in essence, a local "immigration" policy. Such actions in a public setting would very likely represent an unconstitutional infringement on the federal government's exclusive prerogative to control matters of internal and external movement—as determined by the Supreme Court in various interstate commerce, "right to travel," and other decisions.

5. A private neighborhood association can engage in many forms of commercial activities within (or, in concept, outside of) the neighborhood; for example, it can operate a neighborhood grocery store or gas station, publish a neighborhood newspaper, or manage a restaurant. Under most state laws (although these could be changed), it would at present be difficult or impossible for a local government in the public sector to engage in a similar range of commercial activities directly oriented to the general marketplace.

6. A private neighborhood association can commit to undertake future actions that would be legally binding and enforceable in court for the lifetime of the association; a municipal government in the public sector would find it more difficult to similarly bind the future actions of a duly elected municipal legislature.

7. A private neighborhood association can hire a new employee or dismiss an existing employee under the same legal rules as a business corporation or other private firm. In most public jurisdictions, this same action would be subject to different—and typically more exacting—standards of judicial review. Compared with private businesses, governments generally face greater difficulties in firing their tenured civil servants.

8. A neighborhood association of virtually any size or shape can, in principle, be created as an exercise of the private rights of the owner of an appropriate parcel of land (subject to municipal regulatory review and approval). Establishing a new neighborhood government in the public sector—even one falling within exactly the same geographic boundaries as the neighborhood association—would necessarily proceed in a legally and politically more complicated way, and would involve compliance with state laws for municipal incorporation.

Private status, as these examples illustrate, in most cases presents a wider range of possibilities that confer greater flexibility in shaping new institutions of governance. However, private status can also create some obligations and burdens that would not fall on a government in the public sector. A private neighborhood association, for example, typically must pay property and other taxes to municipal governments. On the other hand, a municipal government of neighborhood size would have no such financial obligations to any higher level of government. Furthermore, even if such obligations were constitutionally permissible, the upward transfer of funds to higher levels of government in a way similar to the private tax payment process individuals and associations follow is almost never required of a local government. To the contrary, such governments typically *receive* significant transfers of funds from federal and state governments—transfers that, in most cases, would not be available to private neighborhood associations.

Alternative Constitutional Regimes

On further reflection, then, we can see the best way to think about the distinction between "public" and "private." There is one broad legal framework for the functioning of U.S. local governments that operate as "public" entities. There is another legal framework for local governments that operate as "private" entities. These two legal regimes—often grounded in U.S. constitutional requirements as well as federal and state law—are often markedly different. The chief distinguishing characteristic is the much greater range of options available in the private regime. In most of the areas described above, the options available to a private neighborhood association encompass and then go well beyond those legally allowed to a municipal government in the public sector.* Wayne Hyatt, a legal practitioner in this area, comments, "In the absence of unusual circumstances or perhaps an emotionally driven decision, the U.S. Constitution does not apply in common interest community situations today."[49] As a result, "the community association and the underlying body of community association law provide a legally recognized framework with considerable power and almost infinite flexibility upon which to build the governing process of a real estate development." While current neighborhood associations may have significant failings, they also present "a major chance to innovate in governance." Within neighborhood associations of the future, "governance must be as innovative and as responsive" to members' needs as is the design of the neighborhood's common physical environment.[50]

As we noted earlier, the manner of determining whether an action qualifies for public or private status is not well defined or fixed.[51] Indeed, the method shifts over time with changes in political and economic thinking and with new Supreme Court and other court decisions. Historically, the progressive era in the United States opened up a long period over the course of the 20th century during which many formerly private actions shifted to public status. The Supreme Court initially sought to limit the increasing governmental regulation of private actions, but eventually capitulated in the New Deal years. As a result, formerly private matters, such as the type of clientele acceptable to a restaurant or the type of tenant allowed in an apartment building, have come to be regarded legally as public or state actions. Social practices in the workplace that were formerly regarded as private interactions among fellow employees

---

*The public and private differences extend to the permissible "limitations on First Amendment rights to freedom of speech and association; the right to travel; due process issues raised by the applications of an association's rules to nonmembers; and equal protection questions raised by discrimination on the basis of race or class." In almost every case, the private neighborhood association has wider legal authority. David J. Kennedy, "Residential Associations as State Actors: Regulating the Impact of Gated Communities on Nonmembers," *Yale Law Journal* 105 (December 1995), 790–91.

now are regarded as matters for state oversight under sexual harassment and other workplace laws.

Nevertheless, although the legal significance of a private status has been much diminished in the past century, important differences still remain. The legal authority of a neighborhood association today is similar to that of a private business corporation. Indeed, neighborhood associations are typically organized under state law as a form of nonprofit private corporation.

There is, in fact, almost no area of activity, public or private, that does not operate under some degree of government oversight and control. Even in the area of marriage, traditionally considered among the most private of actions, government requires blood tests and regulates other aspects of entering into (and perhaps later separating from) marriage. Private business corporations must comply with a host of requirements that extend to their basic governing arrangements. However, the private business corporation—and the private neighborhood association—ultimately have a wider scope of operational freedom when it comes to using property without government interference.

Because of the neighborhood association's private status, a private land developer has the flexibility to tailor a system of governance according to the neighborhood's specific needs, just as a business corporation may choose to issue stocks with different voting rights, or choose to issue larger numbers of bonds. In the case of DC Ranch in Scottsdale, Arizona, the developer sought to create "a governance structure as special as the physical qualities the development would offer to community residents. The internal governance system that was created combines a sense of stewardship with enforcement techniques that truly work."[52] Private profit in such circumstances is put at the service of devising a better system of local governance—at least from the viewpoint of the home buyers themselves and their own hopes for better government.

A Constitutional Revolution

The rise of the neighborhood association in American life thus might be described as a grand experiment in local constitutionalism. The specific provisions of each neighborhood's private constitution are contained in its founding documents or, formally, its "declaration." Like a public constitution, the declaration sets out a governing process in the neighborhood, including the method of selection and operating rules for the board of directors, the unit owner voting rules, the legitimate areas of neighborhood responsibility (as reflected partly in covenants), neighborhood appeal procedures, and the steps required to amend the neighborhood constitution. As Hyatt explains, "The declaration is not a contract but, as a covenant running with the land, is effectively a constitution establishing a regime to govern property held and enjoyed in common."[53]

Carl Kress finds similarly that a neighborhood declaration is a "foundational document that creates the development and may be likened to the association's constitution, laying out the rights and responsibilities of owners within the association."[54] Although the jurisdictional boundaries encompass a much smaller area, the neighborhood "governing documents are . . . akin to the constitution that provides the fundamental rules of governance for a country."[55]

Reflecting the constitutional character of the founding documents, law professor Susan French advocates a formal "bill of rights" for neighborhood associations.[56] Even if people have moved into an association with full knowledge of its operating rules, most associations have provisions for changing the rules (usually by a supermajority vote). However, if this potential for change were abused, French says, it could "substantially reduce the value of units to their owners or force them to move." Inattentive or unlucky unit owners could face the prospect that "dreams can turn to nightmares for homeowners who are forced to make a choice of moving or giving up beloved pets, lovers, or even children." To minimize the likelihood of any such unpleasant surprises, French recommends that home buyers receive a formal guarantee that "the majority cannot unite to deprive them of the liberties they are not willing to sacrifice for the advantages of ownership in the community."[57]

Unlike the federal Constitution, which applies the same rules everywhere across the United States, a neighborhood bill of rights might vary from one neighborhood to the next, reflecting local preferences and needs. French recognizes that there is a trade-off to living in a private neighborhood association: "Americans have been willing to give up some degree of freedom to secure the advantages of ownership in common interest communities." The manner of resolving this trade-off could well differ significantly from neighborhood to neighborhood, much as the aesthetic preferences with respect to land use can differ among neighborhoods. As a result, neighborhood constitutions might be written in many different ways to suit the specific needs of individual neighborhoods.

Conclusion

There are now more than 250,000 neighborhood associations in the United States, about ten times the number of general-purpose municipalities. In its founding declaration, each of these associations established a constitutional arrangement for neighborhood governance. The rise of the private neighborhood association amounts to a new exercise in constitution writing on a scale larger than this country has ever seen before. Reflecting their private status, associations' constitutional options are broader than the political options available to local governments in the public sector. As a result, the overall constitutional

status of local government in the United States is in the process of being significantly reworked today.

In order to achieve this kind of constitutional revolution for local governments in the public sector, the Supreme Court would have had to revisit and
reinterpret its past decisions addressing the legal status of these governments.
The tight constitutional constraints on municipal actions—most of them the
result of Supreme Court decisions over the past 150 years—could have been
reconsidered and perhaps some (or many) of them loosened or abolished.
However, any such judicial rethinking of the constitutional status of U.S. local
government would inevitably have been a long and slow process with a very
uncertain outcome. Instead, it has been easier and simpler to shift local government's legal status from "public" (a state actor) to "private" (an exerciser of
private property rights). By means of this device, a constitutional revolution in
local government has been accomplished much more quickly and with much
less stress and strain than the standard route of judicial review and revision of
past court decisions. This book will examine how this constitutional revolution
has been accomplished and how it is working to transform local government
across the United States.

NOTES

1. U.S. Advisory Commission on Intergovernmental Relations, *Residential Community Associations: Private Governments in the Intergovernmental System?* (Washington, DC, 1989), ii, 1.

2. Wayne S. Hyatt, "Common Interest Communities: Evolution and Reinvention," *John Marshall Law Review* 31 (Winter 1998), 307–8.

3. Evan McKenzie, *Privatopia: Homeowner Associations and the Rise of Residential Private Government* (New Haven, CT: Yale University Press, 1994), 11.

4. Ibid., 22.

5. Glen O. Robinson, "Communities," *Virginia Law Review* 83 (March 1997), 304–5 (describing the views of Roger K. Lewis and quoting from Jane Jacobs).

6. Stephen E. Barton and Carol J. Silverman, "Public Life and Private Property in the Urban Community," in Barton and Silverman, eds., *Common Interest Communities: Private Governments and the Public Interest* (Berkeley: Institute of Governmental Studies Press, University of California, 1994), 306, 311.

7. Quoted in Florence Williams, "Behind the Gate," *High Country News* (November 11, 2002).

8. Sheryll D. Cashin, "Privatized Communities and the 'Secession of the Successful': Democracy and Fairness Beyond the Gate," *Fordham Urban Law Journal* 28 (June 2001), 1677, 1685, 1690, 1683, 1686.

9. Richard Louv, *America II* (New York: Penguin Books, 1985), xx.

10. Ibid., 300.

11. Alexander Keyssar, *The Right to Vote: The Contested History of Democracy in America* (New York: Basic Books, 2000), Ch. 1, "In the Beginning."

12. Albert A. Foer, "Democracy in the New Towns: The Limits of Private Government," *University of Chicago Law Review* 36 (Winter 1969), 412.

13. Stephen E. Barton and Carol J. Silverman, "Preface," in Barton and Silverman, eds., *Common Interest Communities,* xii.

14. Gregory S. Alexander, "Dilemmas of Group Autonomy: Residential Associations and Community," *Cornell Law Review* 75 (November 1989), 5, 11, 43, 44–45.

15. Mike Bowler and Evan McKenzie, "Invisible Kingdoms," *California Lawyer* (December 1985), 55.

16. Sharon L. Bush, "Beware the Associations: How Homeowners' Associations Control You and Infringe Upon Your Inalienable Rights!!," *Western State University Law Review* 30 (Spring 2003), 1.

17. McKenzie, *Privatopia,* 24.

18. Evan McKenzie, "Common Interest Housing in the Communities of Tomorrow," paper presented at the Second "Communities of Tomorrow Summit," sponsored by the Community Associations Institute, Washington, D.C., March 21, 2001, 25.

19. Carol J. Silverman and Stephen E. Barton, "Shared Premises: Community and Conflict in the Common Interest Development," in Barton and Silverman, eds., *Common Interest Communities,* 141.

20. David Popenoe, *Private Pleasure, Public Plight: American Metropolitan Community Life in Comparative Perspective* (New Brunswick, NJ: Transaction Books, 1985), 117.

21. Richard Briffault, "Our Localism: Part II—Localism and Legal Theory," *Columbia Law Review* 90 (March 1990), 348.

22. Sheryll D. Cashin, "Localism, Self-Interest, and the Tyranny of the Favored Quarter: Addressing the Barriers to New Regionalism," *Georgetown Law Journal* 88 (July 2000), 1987.

23. Andres Duany and Elizabeth Plater-Zyberk, quoted in William Schneider, "The Suburban Century Begins," *The Atlantic* 270 (July 1992), 37.

24. Schneider, "The Suburban Century Begins," 37.

25. Richard Schragger, "Consuming Government," (Book Review of *The Homevoter Hypothesis,* by William A. Fischel), *Michigan Law Review* 101 (May 2003), 1835, 1852.

26. Popenoe, *Private Pleasure, Public Plight,* 117.

27. *Schad v. Mount Ephraim,* 452 U.S. at 85, 87 (1981). (Burger is dissenting in this opinion.)

28. Gerald E. Frug, "Decentering Decentralization," *University of Chicago Law Review* 60 (Spring 1993), 265, 270.

29. See Robert H. Nelson, *Zoning and Property Rights: An Analysis of the American System of Land Use Regulation* (Cambridge, MA: MIT Press, 1977); William A. Fischel, *The Economics of Zoning Laws: A Property Rights Approach to American Land Use Controls* (Baltimore: Johns Hopkins University Press, 1985).

30. Lee Anne Fennell, "Hard Bargains and Real Steals: Land Use Exactions Revisited," *Iowa Law Review* 86 (October 2000), 16–17.

31. Richard Briffault, "Our Localism: Part I—The Structure of Local Government Law," *Columbia Law Review* 90 (January 1990); Richard Briffault, "Our Localism: Part II—Localism and Legal Theory," *Columbia Law Review* 90 (March 1990); Richard Briffault, "Who Rules at Home?: One Person/One Vote and Local Governments," *University of Chicago Law Review* 60 (Spring 1993); Richard Briffault, "The Local Government Boundary Problem in Metropolitan Areas," *Stanford Law Review* 48 (May 1996); Richard Briffault, "The Rise of Sublocal Structures in Urban Governance," *Minnesota Law Review* 82 (December 1997); and Richard Briffault, "A Government for Our Time?: Business Improvement Districts and Urban Governance," *Columbia Law Review* 99 (March 1999).

32. Briffault, "Who Rules at Home?," 419.

33. See William A. Fischel, *The Homevoter Hypothesis: How Home Values Influence Local Government Taxation, School Finance, and Land-Use Policies* (Cambridge, MA: Harvard University Press, 2001).

34. Briffault, "Who Rules at Home?," 383.

35. Patricia Burgess, *Planning for the Private Interest: Land Use Controls and Residential Patterns in Columbus, Ohio, 1900–1970* (Columbus: Ohio State University Press, 1994), 76.

36. See Lee Anne Fennell, "Contracting Communities," *University of Illinois Law Review* (2004), 829–98.

37. Examples cited in Bowler and McKenzie, "Invisible Kingdoms," 56.

38. Community Associations Institute and Gallup Organization, *National Survey of Community Association Homeowner Satisfaction* (Alexandria, VA: Community Associations Institute, June 23, 1999), 6, 12.

39. Doreen Heisler and Warren Klein, *Inside Look at Community Association Homeownership—Facts, Perceptions* (Alexandria, VA: Community Associations Institute, 1996), 43–46.

40. An early defense is found in Uriel Reichman, "Residential Private Governments: An Introductory Survey," *University of Chicago Law Review* 43 (Winter 1976).

41. Gerald Korngold, *Private Land Use Controls: Balancing Private Initiative and the Public Interest in the Homeowners Association Context* (Cambridge, MA: Lincoln Institute of Land Policy, 1995), 10, 9, 6, 5, 7.

42. Setha M. Low, "The Edge and the Center: Gated Communities and the Discourse of Urban Fear," *American Anthropologist* 103 (March 2001), 55, 52. See also Setha Low, *Behind the Gates: Life, Security and the Pursuit of Happiness in Fortress America* (New York: Routledge, 2003).

43. Gerald B. Wetlaufer, "Systems of Belief in Modern American Law: A View from Century's End," *American University Law Review* 49 (October 1999), 9.

44. David J. Kennedy, "Residential Associations as State Actors: Regulating the Impact of Gated Communities on Nonmembers," *Yale Law Journal* 105 (December 1995), 782.

45. McKenzie, *Privatopia*, 123–24.

46. Kennedy, "Residential Associations as State Actors," 784.

47. A. Dan Tarlock, "Residential Community Associations and Land Use Controls," in Advisory Commission on Intergovernmental Relations, *Residential Community Associations*, 76.

48. *Avery v. Midland County*, 390 U.S. 474 (1968).

49. Hyatt, "Common Interest Communities," 340.

50. Wayne S. Hyatt, "The Evolution in Community Governance," in Adrienne Schmitz and Lloyd W. Bookout, eds., *Trends and Innovations in Master-Planned Communities* (Washington, DC: The Urban Land Institute, 1998), 44, 40. See also Wayne S. Hyatt, "Community Associations: Change and Continuity," ULI Research Working Paper Series, Paper 646 (Washington, DC: The Urban Land Institute, 1995).

51. Clayton P. Gillette, "Mediating Institutions: Beyond the Public/Private Distinction," *University of Chicago Law Review* 61 (Fall 1994), 1375–1441.

52. Hyatt, "The Evolution in Community Governance," 48.

53. Wayne S. Hyatt, "Condominium and Home Owner Associations: Formation and Development," *Emory Law Journal* 24 (Fall 1975), 990.

54. Carl B. Kress, "Beyond Nahrstedt: Reviewing Restrictions Governing Life in a Property Owner Association," *U.C.L.A. Law Review* 42 (February 1995), 840.

55. Marshall E. Tracht, "Co-Ownership and Condominium," in Boudewijn Bouckaert and Gerrit De Geest, eds., *Encyclopedia of Law and Economics, Volume II, Civic Law and Economics* (Cheltenham, UK: Edward Elgar, 2000), 78.

56. Susan F. French, "The Constitution of a Private Residential Government Should Include a Bill of Rights," *Wake Forest Law Review* 27, no. 2 (1992), 345–52.

57. Ibid., 349–50.

PART I
Managing the Neighborhood Commons

Interdependency is a characteristic of modern life. A large business corporation often has tens of thousands of employees working together in a common enterprise. Similarly, urban neighborhoods bring large numbers of people together in settings in which the actions of any one can significantly influence the environmental quality for others. Individuals facing such situations have several options. They can move to a rural area where there is a greater distance between neighbors; they can do nothing and accept the uncertainties that come from close, unregulated contact with many other people; or they can seek greater control over their neighbors' actions—recognizing that this will involve at the same time surrendering some of their own individual freedoms.

There is no one answer for everyone; the solution depends partly on individual resources and preferences. Some people may value their autonomy highly; others may strongly desire to live in a well-controlled neighborhood environment. Urban history shows, however, that the majority of 20th-century Americans preferred to live in close interdependency with others and establish a system of mutual regulation. At first, neighborhood residents looked to local governments and municipal zoning as the principal means for controlling the actions of those living near them. The last third of the 20th century, however, saw a turn to private forms of collective control associated with the rise of the private neighborhood association.

For some people, the phrase "private regulation" may seem an oxymoron. "Regulation" seems by its nature "public." There is, admittedly, a tension in the idea of a private institution imposing a tight form of social control. Many people associate "private" with individual freedom of action; yet, most private neighborhood associations operate in a way that significantly curtails individual freedom. Indeed, the rise of private neighborhood associations in the United States has probably resulted in a greater reduction in individual freedom of action than any other social development of the second half of the 20th century.

Yet, this diminution of individual autonomy is itself the product of individual free choice—an expression of freedom in another respect. Paradoxically, many millions of Americans have chosen of their own free will to live in a local regime of less freedom. They have chosen to be subject to tight regulation by their fellow neighbors in order to gain collective control over the actions of these same neighbors. For some people, such behavior seems hypocritical. One commentator thus writes of "these new fashioned feudalists" living today in neighborhood associations, residents "who are decidedly libertarian concerning the outside world, [but] are surprisingly socialistic concerning the private inside world of their gated minicities." People living in these neighborhoods "willingly accept a wide variety of community regulations that they would challenge as unconstitutional in other contexts—from gun control, to restrictions on exterior paint colors, lawn maintenance standards, and prohibitions on basketball hoops over garages."[1]

Libertarian thought has posed some intriguing questions. Do people have the right to choose not to be free? Can they sell themselves voluntarily into slavery? No answer will be altogether satisfactory. The option of selling oneself into slavery would today be universally rejected. Joining a neighborhood association is not nearly as stark, but involves a related tension. Can people choose freely to associate with a group of people territorially when this may involve severe restrictions on their individual freedoms in the future? Libertarians generally answer that individuals should be free to make such a choice. A key factor here is that, unlike slavery, joining a neighborhood is a reversible choice; an unhappy resident can always choose to move out of an overly oppressive neighborhood—if perhaps at considerable financial and other cost.

Another factor in the individual freedom issue is that the close interdependency of modern urban life may in particular create a strong demand for regulatory controls that must be satisfied one way or another. If there is no private institution available to satisfy this demand, the citizenry will turn to municipal zoning and other forms of public regulation. Indeed, the creation of zoning in the progressive era was a significant step in establishing America's modern welfare and regulatory state. In today's big cities, distant bureaucracies within large governments administer zoning. Private neighborhoods may be all-powerful within their territorial boundaries, but they regulate only a small area. If big government is seen as a threat to individual freedom, private neighborhood associations represent a significant step away from the accumulation of governmental power in any one place. Friedrich Hayek, winner of the 1974 Nobel Prize in economics, thus declared:

Most of what is valid for town planning is, in effect, an argument for making the planning unit for some purposes larger than the usual size of individually owned property. Some of the aims of planning could be achieved by a division of the contents of the property rights in such a way that certain decisions would rest with the holder of the superior right, i.e., with some [private] corporation representing the whole district or region and possessing powers to assess benefits and charges to individual subowners. Estate development in which the developer retains some permanent control over the use of the individual plots offers at least one alternative to the exercise of such control by political authority. There is also the advantage that the larger planning unit will still be one of many and that it will be restrained in the exercise of its powers by the necessity of competing with other similar units.[2]

James Buchanan, a founder of the "public choice" school of economics and winner of the 1986 Nobel prize in economics, argues similarly that voluntary choice includes the option to choose a constitutional regime of reduced personal freedom:

> The justificatory foundation for a liberal social order lies, in my understanding, in the normative premise that individuals are the ultimate *sovereigns* in matters of social organization, that individuals are the beings who are entitled to choose the organizational-institutional structures under which they will live. . . . On the other hand, the normative premise of individuals as sovereigns does not provide exclusive normative legitimacy to organizational structures that—as, in particular, market institutions—allow internally for the most extensive range of separate individual choice. Legitimacy must also be extended to "choice-restricting" institutions so long as the participating individuals voluntarily choose to live under such regimes.[3]

The principle of sustaining market freedom (even the freedom to surrender large elements of freedom) will not achieve a total internalization of interdependencies among land uses because one whole neighborhood almost inevitably will influence other whole neighborhoods. As Hayek thus comments, "It is true that there will always be some factors in planning which only the larger units [beyond the individual development] can consider."[4] Any attempt to incorporate interdependencies at this wide geographic scale will almost inevitably require a government unit in the public sector. Zoning thus may not be necessary to regulate the interactions of individual property owners within a single neighborhood, but public zoning in some form may still be required to regulate interdependencies among the whole neighborhood units themselves.

Another option, however, is to accept that such longer-distance interdependencies will mostly be left out of the social calculation. In an imperfect world, perhaps it is not worth the effort to try to factor them into social planning and decisionmaking. As Hayek commented, an attempt to internalize all land use impacts within one large political jurisdiction inevitably requires a centralized authority that will create problems of a different kind. It will sacrifice the benefits of local knowledge and control; "as the area of unified [town] planning is extended, particular knowledge of local circumstances will, of necessity, be less effectively used." There is no simple solution. For Hayek, the interdependency of land uses, potentially extending in many directions, indicates that "the practical problems which policy raises here are of great complexity, and no perfect solution is to be expected."[5]

In general, the free-market model does not work as simply when real-world geographic and territorial considerations are incorporated. A world in which each firm occupies a different location offers no possibility (even in concept) of the perfectly competitive market found in abstract economic theorizing. In the retail market, for example, many land uses (businesses) demonstrate a significant element of local monopoly power because of their convenient locations (i.e., traveling to another store would involve significant additional costs for nearby homeowners). There is no perfect competitive equilibrium, as commonly described in economics textbooks, in a world with so much spatial differentiation.

The element of voluntary choice is often said to distinguish the private neighborhood association from the local government in the public sector. However, as discussed above, most residents of a municipality have also chosen voluntarily to live in that location. They can leave almost as easily as (and perhaps sometimes more easily than) residents of a neighborhood association. Yet another free-market theorist, Daniel Klein, asserts that national and state governments must not be allowed to "encroach on the principle of liberty," but at "the truly local level" of government matters may be different. Indeed, greater restrictions on individual freedom may be acceptable for a small municipality "because we grant town government the status of a contract, as for a proprietary community." The principles of a minimal state may be difficult to apply at the most local level because "local government services beyond the Nightwatchman functions may occupy a gray area between ordinary contract and State power."[6] When the local community is actually governed privately, as in a neighborhood association, the argument for the defense of local collective rights to control individual actions becomes stronger still.

Tens of millions of Americans in the 20th century voted with their feet to live in a small society of "neighborhood socialism." The rise of the private neighborhood association in the second half of the century did more to decentralize the structures of American governance than probably any other political development. Paradoxically, this new private institution also imposed a tighter degree of government control over the actions of individual Americans than historically they have been willing to accept from any other form of government in the United States. The five chapters of part I will explore the historical background and the general character of this important new political trend in American life.

Chapter 1 reviews briefly the legal and other historical factors that have made collective ownership of housing possible on such a wide scale in the United States. Chapter 2 examines specific regulatory and other administrative means by which neighborhood associations have acted to protect their environmental quality. Chapter 3 describes the political systems through which neighborhood associations carry out their responsibilities. Chapter 4 considers additional constitutional provisions that are typically included in the founding declarations of neighborhood associations. Finally, chapter 5 explores the workings of local democracy in practice as experienced in many thousands of neighborhood associations over the past 40 years.

NOTES

1. Jay M. Shafritz and E. W. Russell, *Introducing Public Administration* (New York: Longman, 1997), 89.

2. Friedrich A. Hayek, *The Constitution of Liberty* (Chicago: Henry Regnery Company, 1960), 351–52.

3. James M. Buchanan, *The Economics and Ethics of Constitutional Order* (1991), reprinted (pages 221–29) in James M. Buchanan, *The Logical Foundations of Constitutional Liberty: Volume 1, The Collected Works of James M. Buchanan* (Indianapolis: Liberty Fund, 1999), 288.

4. Hayek, *Constitution of Liberty,* 352.

5. Ibid., 352, 350.

6. Daniel B. Klein, *Three Libertarian Essays* (Irvington-on-Hudson, NY: Foundation for Economic Education, 1998), 26–28.

1

Collective Ownership
of Housing

In early American history, corporate charters for businesses were issued individually and each charter required the action of a state legislature. The specific terms set by the legislature could vary considerably from one corporation to another. Then, from 1845 to 1875, about half the states moved to abolish this system and to establish general procedures for routinely granting corporate charters. In 1875, New Jersey adopted a general law that contained the broadest and most flexible provisions for business incorporation to that point. Other states quickly followed New Jersey's example.[1]

By the end of the 19th century, modern legal provisions for the collective ownership of business property were found throughout the United States. Only a small number of business corporations existed before the Civil War, but by 1900, almost two-thirds of U.S. manufacturing output was being produced by firms operating under the legal status of a corporation. In the 1960s, that share rose to 95 percent.[2] By 1995, the business corporations listed on the New York Stock Exchange had 155 billion shares with a market value of $6 trillion.

Although neighborhood associations were already being established in the United States in the 19th century, it was not until the 1960s—or about 100 years after the rise of the business corporation—that these associations emerged as a central feature in residential property ownership. Most states passed laws authorizing for the first time the condominium form of housing ownership. In the next few decades, states also enacted legislation to clarify the legal status of homeowners associations. Today, a private neighborhood association is usually organized legally as a form of nonprofit private corporation. Its legal authority to purchase, borrow, loan, and make other contractual commitments is similar to that of an ordinary business corporation. Like a business corporation, the neighborhood association has limited liability; just as the stockholders are liable for no more than the value of their individual holdings of business stock, the unit owners in a condominium or homeowners association are liable for no more than the maximum value of their individual home investments.*

Reflecting in part their common corporate status, both business corporations and neighborhood associations are democracies. The shareholders elect the corporation's board of directors just as the unit owners elect the association's board of directors. In both the corporation and the neighborhood association, the number of votes is proportional to the share of property ownership. So if the owners of many business corporations and many neighborhood associations only slightly influence the actual management of the commonly owned property, it is not for lack of a formal democratic framework of governance. Rather, this situation reflects the large asymmetries of information between the legal owners and the actual managers and the problems of organizing for collective action in the face of free-rider and other obstacles.

The private neighborhood association does not yet, however, dominate American housing to the extent that corporate ownership dominates American business. This is true, in part, because the rate of housing depreciation is less rapid than the typical turnover of business property, resulting in a slower rate of transition for housing stock. Nevertheless, about 50 percent of the new housing built in the United States during the 1980s and 1990s was located in a neighborhood association. The private neighborhood association may yet challenge the business corporation as the most important form of collective property ownership in American life. Just as the rules governing the corporation's shareholder democracy remain an important policy issue for public debate—and have recently been revised subsequent to Enron and other corporate scandals—so, too, the appropriate rules for the democratic governance of private neighborhood associations are sure to command the attention of policymakers in future years.

---

*The actual extent of unit owner liability in the event the neighborhood association declares bankruptcy remains to be fully determined in the law. If the association were regarded legally as an autonomous unit, then some might argue that creditors would be able to recover only the value of the common areas. Others might argue that the association would have an obligation to impose special assessments on unit owners to recover funds owed to creditors, perhaps as part of a bankruptcy settlement. It is also possible that creditors would be able to take possession of all the bankrupt association's neighborhood properties, including the individual units, thereby evicting all the owners in the process. The courts, however, might very well be reluctant to abolish a neighborhood government and throw hundreds or even thousands of unit owners into the street. Such considerations might vary between condominiums and homeowners associations, reflecting the different legal structures under which they are established. It seems likely that state legislatures will be required to address this issue further in the future. See Kristin L. Davidson, "Bankruptcy Protection for Community Associations as Debtors," *Bankruptcy Developments Journal* 20 (2004), 583–632.

Three Types of Neighborhood Associations

There are three main legal forms for the collective ownership of residential property: the homeowners association, the condominium, and the cooperative. In a homeowners association, each person owns his or her home individually, often including a private yard. The homeowners association—which any home buyer is required to join as a condition of purchase in that neighborhood—is a separate legal entity that holds title to the "common areas," such as streets, parks, recreation facilities, and other common property. It also enforces neighborhood covenants with respect to the allowable uses and modifications of homes and properties. The individual owners of neighborhood properties are also automatically the "shareholders" in the homeowners association, collectively owning the assets and controlling the actions of the association. Homeowners associations are often used as the legal instrument for land use management, public service delivery, and the performance of other governmental functions in "planned unit developments."

In a condominium, the individual owners also hold title to their own personal units and, as "tenants in common," automatically share a percentage interest in the "common elements." These common elements can include things like dividing walls, stairways, hallways, roofs, yards, green spaces, golf and tennis clubs, and other neighborhood elements exterior to the individually owned units.[3] Despite their different legal origins and status, homeowners and condominium associations generally are governed in very similar ways.

Cooperatives are less common and are more likely to be a single building. They became popular in New York City in the decades after World War II, partly as a way of avoiding the problems that rent control was posing for owners of apartment buildings. As of 1995, there were 416,000 cooperative apartments in New York City.[4] In a cooperative, the entire property—including the individually occupied housing units—is owned jointly. Individual occupants have legal entitlements to the use of their units but are not, strictly speaking, the owners even of the interior portions. Cooperatives typically exercise the tightest control over new entrants, often closely screening possible unit buyers for their professional background, personal reputation, financial assets, and other issues of concern to cooperative members. Unlike a condominium, the individual members of a cooperative are legally liable for sustaining mortgage payments and other financial obligations for the entire building complex. Thus, by analogy, a cooperative more closely resembles a business partnership, while a homeowners association and a condominium more closely resemble a business corporation.

Some people think that a private community is synonymous with a "gated community." However, gated communities—while they have attracted wide publicity (and much critical commentary)—are but a limited part of the total number of neighborhood associations in the United States. By one estimate, 8 million people lived in 20,000 gated communities nationwide in the late 1990s.[5] Based on this estimate, about 10 percent of neighborhood associations may be gated, and 20 percent of all the residents in neighborhood associations may live in gated communities (because, in part, of the cost of maintaining security, gated communities tend to be larger on average than other neighborhood associations).

Given the growing popularity of gated communities, these percentages are likely to rise. Indeed, gated communities are becoming the norm in Southern California and some other rapidly growing areas. In Orange County, California, for example, about half of the housing in unincorporated areas is located in a gated community. A January 1999 survey showed that 68 percent of the homes available for sale in the county were in gated communities. One commentator unhappy with these trends foresees a future for the Los Angeles area in which "vast, sprawling clusters of gated communities are connected to one another and to fortress buildings, enclosed malls, and sports stadiums by a web of freeways and interchanges."[6] Nevertheless, the real estate industry is in the business of providing what homeowners want. One study in the St. Louis area found that, over a 20-year period, properties inside gated communities sold for about 17 percent more than similar properties outside such communities.[7]

The number of condominiums grew more rapidly in the 1970s, but since the 1980s, the leading instrument of new collective ownership of American housing has been the homeowners association. As shown in table 1.1, in 1998 there were about 10.6 million housing units in homeowners associations and 5.1 million housing units in condominium associations. At present, fully 9 percent of Americans live in a homeowners association.

Table 1.1. *U.S. Housing Units in Neighborhood Associations, by Type and Year, 1970–1998*

Type of association	1970	1980	1990	1998
Condominium	85,000	1,541,000	4,847,921	5,078,756
Homeowners association	265,000	613,000	5,967,000	10,562,964
Cooperative	351,000	482,000	824,000	748,840
Total association housing units	701,000	3,636,000	11,638,921	16,390,560
Total associations	10,000	36,000	130,000	204,882
Total U.S. housing units	69,778,000	87,739,000	102,263,678	111,757,000
Neighborhood association units, as % of U.S. total	1.22	4.14	11.38	14.67

Source: Frank H. Spink, ed., *Community Associations Factbook* (Alexandria, VA: Community Associations Institute, 1999), 19.

Different writers have grouped these forms of collective ownership together under various terms, such as a "residential community association," "common interest community," and "residential private government," among others. As mentioned previously, this book refers to such arrangements of collective housing ownership as a "neighborhood association."* Recognize, however, that not all such collective ownerships are of neighborhood size; some are as small as a single building or as large as a mid-size city.

As of the late 1980s, the Advisory Commission on Intergovernmental Relations estimated that about 80 percent of neighborhood associations had a " 'territorial' scope that [made] them resemble a local community, rather than a high-rise condominium."[8] The average neighborhood association contains about 200 housing units. Some are much larger, however. Reston, Virginia, covers 74,000 acres, has a population of more than 35,000, and comprises 12,500 residential units and more than 500 businesses. The Sun City (Arizona) "neighborhood association" has 46,000 residents and contains ten shopping centers.[9]

The three legal forms of private collective ownership of residential property all have somewhat different histories. All originated outside the United States and were at some point transplanted to these shores. The homeowners association, however, was the first to arrive.

Origins of the Homeowners Association

The homeowners association as a legal entity dates at least as far back as the 18th century and the management arrangements established for some of London's private parks. Lot owners whose properties were adjacent to a park would enter into covenants under which they jointly pledged to support park maintenance. By 1831, these English models had crossed the Atlantic to inspire a common ownership regime for New York City's Gramercy Park, sometimes said to be the first neighborhood association in the United States. Samuel Ruggles, a land developer, set aside and fenced in a park area for the mutual enjoyment of 66 surrounding lot owners. He then deeded the Gramercy Park

---

*The term "neighborhood association" has also frequently been used to refer to a group of neighbors who join together after the neighborhood has been occupied. Such neighborhood groups have no authority to require membership, and members pay any dues or assessments voluntarily. Some members of the neighborhood typically do not join. The purpose of such an association may be to organize events, such as a crime watch or neighborhood barbecue, or to distribute a neighborhood newsletter. In this book, "neighborhood association" is used in a different sense. The term refers to a formal neighborhood legal arrangement in which all the owners are required to join the association as an initial condition of their property purchase, and to agree to the future enforcement of private land use restrictions and to pay association assessments to cover service costs.

area over to the private owners and named them as the trustees in charge of its future maintenance.[10]

The first true homeowners association in the United States, however, was established at Louisberg Square in Boston. A common area had been set aside when the project was built in 1826, but no special arrangements had been made for maintenance. In 1844, the 28 nearby lot owners resolved this problem by signing a joint agreement to establish the Committee of the Proprietors of Louisberg Square, binding themselves and their successors to maintain the park.

By the late 19th century, some of America's leading housing developers were creating large private communities.[11] The developer would lay out the lots and bind the actions of future owners through a system of covenants incorporated into the deeds. Based in part on the advice of Frederick Law Olmsted, such covenants were in 1871 attached to each land parcel in the Riverside development near Chicago. The restrictions specified that each future home built at each site must cost at least $3,000, must be set back 30 feet from the front edge of the yard, and must allow for the front yard area to be kept open.[12] In the 1890s, Edward Bouton used deed restrictions to control the future construction of properties in his Roland Park (Baltimore) development, a legal model that was widely studied and copied in the early 20th century.

However, it was difficult to write covenants that adequately specified future aesthetic concerns. A judge might have to make subjective determinations—for example, whether a new housing design was "compatible" with the existing community motif. Furthermore, covenant enforcement often proved burdensome; it might depend on some individual homeowner willing to shoulder the legal cost for the entire neighborhood. Enforcement posed a typical free-rider problem in that, even though the collective benefit might be large, the expense to any one neighborhood resident might exceed the individual benefit. For these and other reasons, as urban historian David Beito comments, many "covenants . . . suffered from the lack of an effective enforcement mechanism."[13]

Maintaining recreational facilities, open spaces, and other common elements presented another problem for private residential communities. Many developers accepted the responsibility for assuring the upkeep of these areas over the project's lifetime. However, developers often found themselves subject to residents' criticisms and complaints. Residents often protested increases in maintenance fees.

A desire to resolve such operating problems motivated J. C. Nichols—another leading builder of large private communities in the United States—to establish in 1910 the Country Club District Improvement Association in Kansas City. The association of residents in this private community took ownership of the common areas and accepted the responsibility for future management. In this case, membership in the association was voluntary, but in 1914, Nichols pioneered the mandatory homeowners association at the Mission Hills development. As part of the initial terms of purchase, each buyer was required to join the homeowners association and to agree to comply with various requirements of collective ownership within the Mission Hills area. Any subsequent purchaser would also be bound by the same legal requirements. Under the founding provisions of the association, future increases in fee assessments had to be approved by the unit owners with a two-thirds majority vote. Other decisions were made by majority rule. It was important to establish the association in advance of residents moving in because, as Nichols and other community builders had discovered, "it was easier to get people to accept higher costs as part of the initial deal than to present them with the added cost after they had closed the deal."[14] In his Sunset Hills subdivision in Kansas City, for example, Nichols was unable to persuade enough owners to join a voluntary association after he failed to establish a requirement for association membership as an initial condition of purchase.

By the 1920s, the development of large private communities was spreading more widely across the United States.* In 1924, builder Hugh Potter visited the private communities built by Nichols in Kansas City as part of the planning for his new River Oaks development in Houston, Texas. Once developed, membership in the River Oaks homeowners association was mandatory. The association took care of streets, trash removal, tree care, and garbage collection; it also enforced the deed restrictions. In 1929, Clarence Perry published his influential "Regional Survey of New York and Its Environs," declaring that the neighborhood unit should be a starting point for city planning. Perry pointed out the need for the neighborhood association:

> The kind of housing required by child-rearing families is peculiarly and vitally dependent upon the resources and character of the immediate vicinity.

---

*Marc Weiss has described the importance to American land development among the "community builders" of the early 20th century. They established a pattern of "private innovation preceding public action" with respect to urban design and maintaining tight control over future land uses in the community. As one leading planner commented in a 1925 speech, "It is the realtor subdivider who is really planning our cities today, who is the actual city planner in practice." Weiss explains, "The community builders were subdividers who changed the nature of American land development during the early decades of the twentieth century. They did this initially by taking very large tracts of land and slowly improving them, section by section, for lot sales and home construction. Strict long-term deed restrictions were imposed on all lot and home purchasers, establishing uniform building lines, front and side yards, standards for lot coverage and building size, minimum housing standards and construction costs, non-Caucasian racial exclusion, and other features. Extensive landscaping and tree planting were emphasized to accentuate the natural topography and beauty. Public thoroughfares included curved streets, cul-de-sacs, and wide boulevards and parkways. Often special areas were set aside for retail and office buildings, apartments, parks and recreation facilities, churches, and schools. Private utilities and public improvements were coordinated as much as possible with present and future plans for subdivision development and expansion." Marc A. Weiss, *The Rise of the Community Builders: The American Real Estate Industry and Urban Land Planning* (New York: Columbia University Press, 1987), 3, 68, 45.

The cellular city is the inevitable product of an automobile age.

The area to be occupied by a residential community should be just what is required for the nice working of a school, playground, and local shop services.

The developer can surround a new home with a satisfying environment, but it can be preserved, after he has gone, only by the residents themselves. For this purpose, a voluntary property owners' association is an indispensable community mechanism.[15]

In another example, Radburn, New Jersey, designed in the 1920s by progressive reformers seeking to demonstrate the advantages of comprehensive physical and social planning, contained a private governing association whose responsibilities included enforcement of a comprehensive set of deed restrictions.[16] William Worley comments that the importance of mandatory homeowner associations for large developments at that time—and to the present—"cannot be overestimated. They carry out maintenance and improvements on behalf of other homeowners . . . that many residents would not do themselves."[17]

Traditionally, the courts have been skeptical of private deeds mandating tight permanent restrictions on land use. After the passage of a certain amount of time, courts have often refused to enforce deed restrictions, concerned that it is social necessary to allow for future flexibility in land use. The success of private communities, however, has depended on a greater legal acceptance of indefinite binding restrictions. The Ohio Supreme Court took an important step in 1929 in the case of *Dixon v. Van Sweringen Co.* The Van Sweringen Company had developed a private subdivision of around 4,000 lots in Shaker Heights, Ohio, a suburb of Cleveland, and included a set of covenants controlling future land uses. In upholding covenant enforcement, the Ohio Supreme Court declared, "We see no reason for denying the right of these partners to contract between themselves, the result of such contracts being . . . to create a highly exclusive and valuable residential district."[18] As a promotional pamphlet explained to new home buyers, "The ugly residence injures surrounding property values, particularly with relation to possibilities of resale. . . . Against such occurrences the only safeguard is in creating definite standards for home construction. And this is practical only where land is extensively held under single control [of one association] for a long period of time."[19]

The Van Sweringen development was located only a few miles from Euclid, Ohio—the public municipality involved in the famous U.S. Supreme Court case that in 1926 established the constitutionality of municipal zoning. As Gerald Korngold explains, "Just as *Euclid* in 1926 validated public land use controls, [so in] *Dixon* in 1929 [the Ohio Supreme Court] legitimized the newly emerging regime of private land use arrangements."[20] The courts henceforth would act to enforce these restrictions as long as the unit owners in the area collectively wanted them enforced.

Protecting Well-Off Neighborhoods

It was not coincidental that the growing use of deed restrictions coincided closely with the spread of public zoning, introduced in New York City in 1916. Both forms of collective control over surrounding land uses within a neighborhood met much the same needs. Indeed, some students of zoning credit early experiences with private deed restrictions with providing "both the physical and political model for zoning and subdivision regulations."[21] According to one authority on neighborhood associations, the restrictions imposed by present-day neighborhood associations amount to a system of "finely-tuned private zoning measures that make community living possible."[22]

The protections under both public and private zoning are most important to better-off neighborhoods. As Marc Weiss comments, during the 1920s and 1930s, areas with "high property values" required special protective measures.[23] A lower-income housing occupant would often be motivated to try to enter a higher-income neighborhood. Whether by deed restriction or public zoning, higher-income neighborhoods in the suburbs were determined to prevent this from happening. The majority of neighborhood associations today are located in suburban areas.

At one time, deed restrictions had the "advantage" over zoning because private restrictions could be used to exclude blacks and other racial groups. Early in the 20th century, in fact, a number of American cities enacted racial zoning—which amounted to an attempt at local "apartheid"—but the U.S. Supreme Court ruled in 1917 that such racial zoning was unconstitutional.[24] Nevertheless, racially restrictive private covenants remained legal until 1948 when the Supreme Court ultimately declared their use also to be unconstitutional.[25] Racial restrictions—sometimes extended to Jews and Asians as well—had been common in large, private housing developments in both the North and the South during the period between the two world wars. A study in New York State found that 63 percent of new developments containing 20 or more housing units had employed racially restrictive covenants in 1947.[26]

Actively promoted by the federal government through mortgage insurance, tax preferences, highway building, and other methods, individual ownership of homes soared in the United States after World War II. The Urban Land Institute (formed in 1936) and other builder organizations promoted the use of mandatory homeowner associations as a practical way of taking care of green spaces, playgrounds, swimming pools, tennis courts, and other common areas increasingly found in large private developments. During the post-war building boom, the Federal Housing Administration (FHA) encouraged builders to include comprehensive deed restrictions in developments and insisted that they be tightly enforced, in part to ensure that FHA would not be called upon to bail out failing projects. In 1944, the Veterans Administration also created a mortgage guarantee program, adopting policies similar to those of the FHA. Government and industry were working in close partnership to shape the physical, social, and legal environment of the burgeoning American suburbs.[27]

Higher-Density Living

The 1960s witnessed rapid changes in many areas of American life—from the Beatles to escalating crime rates, the movement for coeducation in many colleges, and the rise of a counterculture among young people. It was a period of large changes in American housing patterns as well. Indeed, the timing was not altogether coincidental. The upheavals in American society in the 1960s coincided with baby boomers' rise to adulthood, bringing not only increased demands for housing but also new social values that this generation would soon be advancing.

Less enamored with economic "progress" and more concerned about the "environment" than previous generations, the "boomer" generation fostered new policies that acted to limit housing availability. These policies slowed new highway construction, tightened suburban limits on land use supplies, demanded more and larger open spaces, and exercised greater pressures to limit growth in general. Such factors contributed to a new tightness in metropolitan land markets and rapid escalation in land prices in many areas. In 1948, the cost of land nationwide had averaged 11 percent of the cost of suburban housing; by the 1970s, however, land costs had risen to more than 25 percent of the average cost of an American home.[28]

Rising land and housing prices meant a growing demand for housing at higher occupancy densities. Housing built at higher densities allowed for significant economies of scale in land use, including joint provision of parks, green spaces, and other common facilities. Townhouses became a form of "apartment" dwelling adapted to suit buyers' desire for private ownership and other circumstances of the suburbs. Home buyers were increasingly confronted with a choice: either purchase a home far out in the distant suburbs where land costs were lower, or give up on the idea of an individual lot for personal use. In well-located suburban areas, only households in the higher income brackets could afford a significant amount of their own private space. In 1972, a study of urban trends reported: "The proportion of American families able to afford a single family house . . . has been decreasing."[29]

As many people discovered that they would have to accept higher densities in order to be able to afford a home, they also found themselves living in closer proximity to their neighbors. A stereo system blaring 300 feet away might be barely audible; however, loud music 30 feet away could keep you up all night. The actions of neighbors in general became more important to the enjoyment of a shared neighborhood environment. A greater demand thus arose for collective controls over neighbors' actions, a demand accompanied by a greater willingness to sacrifice elements of individual freedom in order to gain such controls.

Zoning had always been a crude device for maintaining neighborhood quality. It could keep out new industrial and commercial uses, but traditionally had not regulated such aesthetic matters as the house color, shrubbery placement, deck building, and other details of neighborhood landscaping and architecture. If such matters were to be controlled by the neighborhood as well, new forms of land use control—in all likelihood private forms—would be needed. A private set of controls would also have the advantage—in the case, for example, of future complaints—that each resident had already given his or her explicit written consent to the neighborhood rules.

As compared with the standard workings of public municipalities, a higher quality of neighborhood services could also often be attained by purchasing them privately. Many city neighborhoods were required to negotiate with distant urban bureaucracies concerning the manner of and appropriate levels for service delivery. These urban bureaucracies were often unresponsive and insensitive, as well as inefficient in their delivery of services to neighborhoods. A common standard of quality might be imposed on each neighborhood throughout the city, although different neighborhoods might have widely varying preferences. Many neighborhoods concluded they could do better on their own, buying services from private providers operating under the competitive pressures of the marketplace. In fact, after reviewing the results of a large body of research since the 1980s, Jeffrey Greene has concluded that "clearly, if a city wants to save money, privatization (in the form of contracting) is a viable alternative to public provision."[30]

Many neighborhood associations across the United States were built around golf courses as an organizing feature. Compared with the usual municipal golf course, a private association often limited the levels of golfer use more tightly, and maintained a higher standard of upkeep for fairways and greens. Privately maintained parks could plant gardens, mow the lawn regularly, and otherwise maintain attractive facilities seldom seen in their municipal counterparts. Indeed, in the 1970s and 1980s, many park areas in the public sector appeared seedy and run-down; other city properties often suffered from poor maintenance. If garbage collection was being poorly handled, it was easier for a private neighborhood to hire a new firm than for its municipality to improve its public performance. Private police patrols might even be hired to supplement the level of security already being provided by municipal police.

As Marc Weiss and John Watts observe, neighborhood associations thus "continued to enforce deed restrictions, but their essential purposes increasingly reflected two other priorities: the provision of attractive services and the economical maintenance of common property."[31] There could be significant economies in assigning several different tasks—say lawn care, tree pruning, and street cleaning—to the same outside contractor. Rather than mow their own lawns, many residents preferred to turn this task over to the neighborhood association, which could then hire a private crew to do all the neighborhood lawns together. One report for the Community Associations Institute found "an astounding number of people [who] say they chose a community association because someone else would mow the lawn, make sure the place was properly landscaped, and the driveways were paved."[32] Law professor Robert Natelson explains:

> Through its preservation and community enhancement activities, the association offers its members the . . . replacement of high contract costs with lower agency costs. . . . Without an association, the members would have to investigate each of the large number of amenities and services available in modern society, learn enough about each amenity and service to be able to understand its pricing, appraise different services provided by the same supplier (as when a single maintenance person both mows lawns and repairs plumbing), and assess the respective contributions of each participant in a single project. By purchasing a unit in a subdivision governed by a Property Owners Association, the owner receives the entire panoply of services in exchange for one periodic monthly assessment.[33]

New thinking about land use planning and the appropriate design of large housing projects in the suburbs also played a role in the rise of private neighborhood associations. The typical zoning ordinance specified that each home should have its own separate lot; the large lot sizes required under zoning emphasized individual "private" space over the availability of "public" space. Therefore, in a perfect world of zoning, each person would be rich enough to create his or her own "private park," surrounded by other residents of similar incomes and lifestyles.

Jane Jacobs and other urban critics, however, argued that such zoning goals were a prescription for sterile, bland, and, in general, unappealing land use patterns.[34] Zoning emphasized individual autonomy at the expense of opportunities to live in and among the members of a vital community. Suburbanites in residential neighborhoods might have to drive several miles to the nearest convenience store, gas station, dry cleaner, or other service establishment. Like large lot sizes, residents' dependence on the automobile for transport reinforced strict separation from other suburban residents.

The idea of the "planned unit development" was conceived and, from the 1960s, was accepted by many urban planners as an antidote to such concerns. In such a development, mixtures of housing types—including townhouses and single-family homes—may appear in the same neighborhood. In addition, retail and other commercial establishments may be positioned closer to homes. Residents may be able to walk to a corner convenience store or a neighborhood barbershop. There might also be a common area of open space for the whole neighborhood—a "public" (at least for the neighborhood residents) rather than a "private" space. Zoning rules, therefore, had to be changed to accommodate increased mixing of land uses and the provision of common areas available to all residents. In planned unit development, the density of the entire development, not the size of the individual lots, counts toward overall compliance with zoning density controls.

Thus, the changing economics of the land market and shifting preferences in land development during the 1960s created a demand for a new regime of collective property ownership in the United States. The traditional "fee simple" ownership of individual lots and homes was no longer satisfactory for many circumstances. The instrument of the homeowners association was already available, but brand new forms of collective ownership also became desirable. This decade thus witnessed the introduction of a new legal instrument for the collective ownership of American housing—the condominium.

Condominium Ownership

The first condominium in the United States—the Greystoke development—was constructed in Salt Lake City in 1962.[35] Just 30 years later, condominium units would represent 5 percent of all American housing. Condominium ownership offered the basic advantages of other forms of collective ownership, including more efficient land use. In addition, the median price of a condominium unit in the late 1980s was about 10 to 15 percent below the median price of a single-family home, reflecting in part the economies resulting from higher-density housing.[36]

Although relatively new to the United States, condominium ownership has ancient origins. Some early antecedents appeared in Germany in the Middle Ages, where "story property"—the separate ownership of different stories within the same building—was found as long ago as the 1100s.[37] Various European cities including Paris, Milan, Brussels, and Nantes also had "horizontal property" laws, many from the 15th and 16th centuries. France adopted perhaps the first nationwide law governing horizontal property in 1804. This law provided that, among other things, "the main walls and the roof are at the charge of all the proprietors, each in proportion to the value of the story belonging to him."[38] The first statute providing for a full-fledged modern form of condominium ownership was adopted in Belgium in 1924.

Across the Atlantic, Mexico in 1884 adopted a law for the common ownership of a single building by the owners of the separate stories. A modern law of condominium ownership was introduced in Brazil in 1928, based on the Belgian model. Condominiums soon spread to other parts of Latin America.

Influenced by these developments, a rudimentary condominium law was enacted in Puerto Rico in 1951, and the first condominiums in U.S. territories were subsequently built there. As mentioned earlier, however, the condominium form of ownership was unknown on the U.S. mainland until as recently as 1960.

In that year, partly at the request of Puerto Rican representatives, the House and Senate subcommittees on housing conducted hearings on the issue. As a result, the National Housing Act of 1961 made FHA mortgage insurance available to purchasers of individual units in condominiums. The Federal Housing Administration soon took steps to promote wider condominium ownership, including the publishing of a model condominium statute. Based in part on the FHA model, almost every state by 1967 had adopted legislation setting a legal framework for condominium ownership.

In earlier homeowners associations, each housing unit had a separate lot. Condominium ownership, however, began as an arrangement for shared ownership among the owners of the multiple stories of a single building. As a legal instrument, condominium ownership was often better suited to circumstances in which there existed common walls, hallways, patios, and other structural elements that individual unit owners might share in common. Repairs, repainting, and other maintenance and upkeep of the common elements became the joint responsibility of all the unit owners, as undertaken by the condominium association. However, many developments legally organized as condominiums today bring together unit owners not only within a single building, but also among multiple buildings within the same condominium project.

From a starting point of zero percent in 1960, condominiums by 1970 represented 12 percent of all housing units in neighborhood associations. By 1998, this figure had risen to 31 percent. As shown in table 1.2, condominiums have been a rapidly growing part of the housing supply in many states. Condominium units in 1990 had the largest share—21 percent—of the total housing units in Hawaii. They represented 16 percent of the total housing supply in Florida and 8 percent in California. In addition to these two states, condominiums have also been popular in Colorado, Connecticut, Illinois, Massachusetts, New Jersey, New York, Texas, and Virginia. At the other end of the spectrum, condominium units in 1990 represented less than 1 percent of all housing units in Arkansas, Mississippi, South Dakota, and West Virginia. Regionally, condominiums have been slowest to take hold in the Midwest, and most common in the South and West.

In the 1970s and 1980s, high inflation and national economic instability—resulting in severe financial pressures on many state and local governments—fueled the spread of condominium ownership. State and local deficits meant that these governments were less willing to accept new responsibilities for

Table 1.2. *Number of Condominium Units, by State, Region, and Year, 1980–1990*

State	1980	1990	Rank (1990)
California	425,969	856,165	2
Colorado	66,188	124,032	8
Connecticut	38,735	119,935	10
Florida	510,976	944,590	1
Illinois	160,091	242,653	4
Massachusetts	30,953	157,716	7
New Jersey	53,336	222,105	5
New York	106,110	343,825	3
Texas	87,683	203,069	6
Virginia	48,815	122,757	9
All other states	723,979	1,511,074	
Total	2,252,835	4,847,921	
Region			
Northeast	280,527	1,019,382	
Midwest	384,025	676,966	
South	858,794	1,792,879	
West	729,489	1,358,694	

Source: Frank H. Spink, ed., *Community Associations Factbook* (Alexandria, VA: Community Associations Institute, 1999).

street construction and maintenance, garbage collection, and other municipal services. The 1978 voter approval of Proposition 13 limited the ability of California's local governments to raise their property taxes, making it more difficult to cover the costs of land development. Therefore, local governments in California (and in many other states) often granted municipal approval for a large new project on the condition that local services be provided privately through a neighborhood association, thus relieving a portion of the fiscal burden.[39] As law professor James Winokur observes, "There is substantial evidence to suggest that the 'load shedding' of local government fiscal responsibilities onto common interest communities has been a conscious governmental strategy for relieving strain on shrinking resources." Indeed, developers often find that local regulations "either require or encourage them to create commonly owned property managed by community associations."[40]

The mid-1970s witnessed another important milestone when the Federal National Mortgage Association (FNMA) and the Federal Home Loan Mortgage Corporation (FHLMC) included mortgages for housing units in neighborhood associations in the secondary lending market. The purchasers of housing in neighborhood associations were now eligible for virtually all the forms of government assistance that had long been provided for individually owned homes. Market competition among traditional individual ownership and the new collective forms of housing ownership could now take place on a level playing field. As home buyers voted with their feet, the number of housing units in neighborhood associations soared from 1 percent of the total U.S. housing supply in 1970 to 4 percent in 1980, 11 percent in 1990, and 17 percent in 2001.

Growing Pains

Despite the overall popularity of private neighborhood associations, increasing complaints about their management were heard by the 1970s. Developers sometimes did not follow through on their contractual commitments to incoming unit owners, or misrepresented their intentions. Some developers signed long-term management contracts with their own favored outside firms, contracts that bound the neighborhood association many years into the future, extending well beyond the point at which management was turned over to the unit owners.[41] In general, the process of transition from management control by the developer to unit-owner control was often difficult and confusing. Many neighborhood associations experienced difficulties in holding required meetings, keeping adequate records, collecting assessments, and enforcing land use restrictions. A 1973 survey of 1,760 condominium residents found that most were satisfied with their overall condominium experience, but fully 61 percent were unhappy with one or another aspect of their association's management.[42]

In that same year, leaders in the real estate industry joined together to form the Community Associations Institute (CAI), an organization created to improve the quality of neighborhood association management. Since then, CAI (now located in Alexandria, Virginia) has provided technical assistance for many aspects of association management and governance. For example, one CAI document lays out the details for gradually shifting management control of a neighborhood association from the original developer to unit owners.[43] Besides its numerous written materials, CAI also provides a wide range of instructional programs in neighborhood association management.[44]

Many state legislatures also responded to growing public complaints in the 1970s by passing a second generation of condominium statutes. Virginia (in 1972) and then Georgia were among the first to take this action. And after the National Conference of Commissioners on Uniform State Laws published its Uniform Condominium Act in 1977, even more states adopted new condominium laws.[45] Under this model law, the details of neighborhood land use restrictions and required assessments should be fully disclosed to purchasers of units prior to the final closing. It recommends a 67 percent vote of approval for amending a neighborhood association's founding documents. As of 1998, 21 states had enacted legislation following this overall model—though in some cases with considerable modification in the details.

The National Conference on Uniform State Laws also published a Uniform Planned Community Act (later adopted by Oregon and Pennsylvania) and a Model Real Estate Cooperative Act (adopted by Virginia and Pennsylvania). Given the considerable overlap among the various model laws, the Conference presented its consolidated Uniform Common Interest Ownership Act (UCIOA) in 1982 (and an amended version in 1994). The UCIOA contains many recommendations for the legal arrangements and decisionmaking procedures pertinent to neighborhood associations.[46] It suggests, for example, a minimum quorum of 20 percent for attendance at neighborhood meetings of all the unit owners. For board of directors meetings, the recommended quorum is 50 percent. The UCIOA also recommends that the original builder retain management control until 75 percent of the units in a development have been sold. At that point, the majority of voting rights should shift to the unit owners. (However, even then, the members of the neighborhood association would be legally limited in their ability to control the developer's actions in completing the existing project plan.)

Florida and California

As noted above, Florida has long been a hotbed of condominium activity. Today it has an estimated 20,000 condominium associations that are home to more than 2 million people.[47] Perhaps the most famous neighborhood association in the United States is Celebration, Florida, built by the Disney Corporation in the Orlando area in close proximity to Disney World.[48] The first occupants moved into Celebration in 1996, and it is now more of a small city than a neighborhood, occupying 5,000 acres with a population of 20,000. The Disney Corporation intended Celebration to be on the cutting edge of urban design, community living, and local governance—and, as such, it may offer a model for future neighborhood associations across the United States. Celebration's attributes—including the Disney name—have resulted in housing prices 20 to 25 percent higher than similar housing in nearby subdivisions.

In 1990, California was second only to Florida in its number of condominiums. Indeed, Florida and California together host about 40 percent of all the condominiums in the United States. Including all types of neighborhood associations, an estimated six million Californians lived in private communities in 1994.[49] One observer finds that neighborhood associations today "dominate the entire local housing market . . . in the newer suburban areas, particularly of

the South and West," and that they "govern nearly all new residential development" in the more rapidly growing parts of metropolitan areas in California,
Florida, and Texas.[50]

Florida adopted its first condominium legislation in 1963. Various consumer reforms were then enacted in the 1970s, including a 1977 reworking
that still provides the basic framework for Florida condominium law. Further
significant amendments were passed in 1986, and during the 1990s the state
legislature made some changes in the condominium statute almost every year.
One expert in Florida condominium law, Joseph Adams, describes state law in
this area as in almost "a constant state of change." From its original 6 pages in
1963, the Florida condominium law has grown to 47 pages. Indeed, some
observers think things have gone too far, describing the 1990s as "the zenith of
legislative micromanagement for Florida's condominium and cooperative
communities."[51] A Florida state agency, the Bureau of Condominiums (located
within the Division of Florida Land Sales, Condominiums and Mobile Homes
of the Department of Business Regulation), is responsible for administering
the numerous condominium requirements.

Florida condominium law covers many issues. For example, it provides that
a condominium buyer can void the purchase contract without penalty within
15 days of signing. There are numerous disclosure requirements for builders.
The 1991 amendments provide for mandatory, nonbinding arbitration of many
kinds of internal disagreements. Adams finds that "the intricacies of complex or
poorly written statutory provisions are foreign to many trial judges" and that
"harried circuit court judges are often not the best public servants to hear many
condominium disputes." However, private arbitration specialists who work regularly in the area of condominium law "are accustomed to [such] mundane
matters and are also well schooled in some of the subtle complexities of Florida
condominium law," and thus are better suited to handle many cases.[52]

Illustrative of the level of micromanagement in Florida, the state legislature
in 1998 was required to revisit the arrangements for cable television contracts.
The existing law directed that the expenses of a master cable contract should be
shared among the unit owners according to the same formula applied for paying the maintenance costs. Many Florida condominiums allocate maintenance
costs in proportion to the square footage of each housing unit, which thus
resulted in different cable television charges for different units. Florida condominium residents, however, thought that each unit owner should pay the same
amount for the same cable hookup. Just to make this legally possible, the
Florida legislature had to change the state condominium law.

A 1987 study questioned Florida unit owners concerning their reasons for
choosing to live in a condominium. Some of the responses reflected traditional
considerations in real estate, including price (89 percent rated this factor "very
important" or "important"), convenience of location (76 percent), and invest-

ment quality (74 percent). Other factors more specific to group living under collective ownership included recreational opportunities (77 percent), the presence of neighbors with similar values and lifestyles (72 percent), security (85 percent), and the absence of individual maintenance responsibilities (90 percent). The group rules and restrictions that protect investment and lifestyle were important to 93 percent of the respondents.[53]

In 1985 California enacted its basic law for neighborhood associations, the Davis-Sterling Act (a milestone in the political career of Assemblyman Gray Davis, later to become the governor of California). In the years since, this legislation has been amended more than 35 times, resulting in a law described by one student as in a "constant state of flux."[54] The Davis-Stirling Act requires that neighborhood associations invite unit owners to board meetings, prepare and report budgets annually (with appropriate disclosures), establish clear procedures for enforcing association rules, and make meeting minutes available to unit owners.[55] The California law generally seeks to establish a fair and reasonable set of procedures for decisionmaking within neighborhood associations.

In some areas, the Davis-Stirling Act overrides a neighborhood association's governing documents. State law provides, for example, that the board of directors has the authority to increase its association budget by as much as 20 percent in a single year, no matter what the neighborhood constitution may say. The law thus overrode some neighborhood associations that limited budget growth to 10 percent or less in their private constitutions. However, the early 1980s witnessed high inflation rates, and these associations were arguably being prevented from meeting their financial obligations—or, alternatively, were required to obtain a supermajority vote of unit owners to change their constitutional budget restraints. California law also provides that the board of directors can impose a special assessment of up to 5 percent of the annual budget for a nonrecurring expenditure, but approval of any higher special assessments requires a full vote of the association unit owners.

In other areas—similar to Florida's condominium law—the Davis-Stirling Act allows an individual neighborhood association to determine its own governance arrangements if such matters are specifically addressed in the association's founding documents. This law thus may serve as a default standard. The neighborhood association can do what it wants in writing its own neighborhood constitution. If it fails to address some issue, however, the state law acts as a fallback to prevent any confusion that might result from the lack of an established procedure. Some of the older neighborhood associations, for example, never adopted rules for amending the founding documents. The Davis-Stirling Act sets out standards by which amendments can be approved in such associations, including the required supermajority percentage for budget changes.

Neighborhood Associations Today

From 1980 to 1990, the total number of neighborhood associations in the United States rose from 36,000 to 130,000. By 2003, the number had risen further to about 250,000. While the condominium was the most popular form of collective ownership in the 1970s, around 10 million new housing units have been built in homeowners associations since 1980, as compared with 2.5 million new units in condominiums. In all forms of neighborhood associations in the early 1990s, 42 percent of the total housing units were townhouses and 18 percent were single-family homes.[56] Most recently, collective ownership—the new norm for new housing development across the United States—has begun to extend downward to reach the full range of the income scale. The Community Associations Institute reported in 2002 that "private developers and community planners have turned to creating condominiums and planned communities, using equity controls, to provide and maintain low-to-moderate income housing."[57]

Students of neighborhood associations have found that their widespread use is "transforming the urban and suburban landscape, not just physically but also politically."[58] In the suburbs of the Midwest and the Northeast, mostly developed before the rise of the private neighborhood association, tight controls over neighborhood land use typically required a proliferation of small municipalities each with its own public zoning authority. Over much of the southern and western parts of the United States, however, private neighborhood associations increasingly replaced local zoning from the 1960s onward. With their own private controls in place, there was less resistance to annexation laws that favored central city expansion. Now, as Briffault notes, "Southern and Western metropolitan areas generally have fewer municipalities than their Northern and Eastern counterparts."[59] Newer cities, such as Houston and Phoenix, sometimes spread over large geographic areas in which there were many neighborhood associations but few autonomous local municipalities. As part of this newer pattern of local governance, large county governments also typically play a greater role in providing metropolitan services.

The rise of neighborhood associations is thus opening the way for a new manner of organization of local government in the United States. Smaller scale "micro" services, such as garbage collection and street maintenance, and internal neighborhood regulation of land use are undertaken privately through the neighborhood association. The units of local government in the public sector are typically larger and concentrate on "macro" services, such as arterial highways, water systems, and sewer systems that require regional coordination. The larger public governing bodies may also have a role in making those land use regulatory and other decisions that involve a full regional scale of impact. Overall, the rise of the private neighborhood association has amounted to a "quiet revolution in the structure of community organization, local government, land-use control, and neighbor relations" in the United States.[60] Robert Natelson concluded in 1990 that neighborhood associations have "emerged from the legal and social periphery to become a central feature of modern society."[61]

Conclusion

If current trends continue, most Americans at some point in the 21st century might well live under a regime of collective residential property ownership. It would be the most important change in American ownership of private property since the rise of the business corporation at the end of the 19th century. This transformation has not resulted from any grand social plan or comprehensive legal design. The legal framework for collective ownership of housing emerged within the real estate industry in response to its own perceived needs. Its full social significance for local government, housing, and other areas of American life is only now being studied and more widely appreciated.

NOTES

1. See Vicki Been, " 'Exit' as a Constraint on Land Use Exactions: Rethinking the Unconstitutional Conditions Doctrine," *Columbia Law Review* 91 (April 1991), 533–35.

2. Gardiner C. Means, "Testimony on Economic Concentration," reprinted in *Hearings on Economic Concentration,* before the Subcommittee on Antitrust and Monopoly, Committee on the Judiciary, United States Senate, July 1, 1964, 15.

3. David Clurman, F. Scott Jackson, and Edna L. Hebard, *Condominiums and Cooperatives,* 2nd ed. (New York: John Wiley, 1984).

4. Richard J. Kane, "The Financing of Cooperatives and Condominiums: A Retrospective," *St. John's Law Review* 73 (Winter 1999), 103 n. 13.

5. Lois M. Baron, "The Great Gate Debate," *Builder* (March 1998), 94, reprinted in Urban Land Institute, *Gated Communities* (Washington, DC: Urban Land Institute, 2000). See also Edward J. Blakely and Mary Gail Snyder, *Fortress America: Gated Communities in the United States* (Washington, DC: Brookings Institution Press, 1997).

6. Dennis R. Judd, "The Rise of the New Walled Cities," quoted in Richard Damstra, "Don't Fence Us Out: The Municipal Power to Ban Gated Communities and the Federal Takings Clause," *Valparaiso University Law Review* 35 (Summer 2001), 531 n. 42.

7. Damstra, "Don't Fence Us Out," 534 n. 59.

8. "Introduction" to U.S. Advisory Commission on Intergovernmental Relations, *Residential Community Associations: Private Governments in the Intergovernmental System?* (Washington, DC, 1989), 1.

9. Steven Siegel, "The Constitution and Private Government: Toward the Recognition of Constitutional Rights in Private Residential Communities Fifty Years after Marsh v. Alabama," *William and Mary Bill of Rights Journal* 6 (Spring 1998), 479.

10. The early history of homeowners associations is described in Evan McKenzie, *Privatopia: Homeowner Associations and the Rise of Residential Private Government* (New Haven, CT: Yale University Press, 1994), chap. 2.

11. For a history of American housing, see Gwendolyn Wright, *Building the Dream: A Social History of Housing in America* (Cambridge, MA: The MIT Press, 1981).

12. See William S. Worley, *J. C. Nichols and the Shaping of Kansas City: Innovation in Planned Residential Communities* (Columbia: University of Missouri Press, 1990), 139.

13. David T. Beito, "The Formation of Urban Infrastructure through Nongovernmental Planning: The Private Places of St. Louis, 1869–1920," *Journal of Urban History* 16 (May 1990), 283.

14. Worley, *J. C. Nichols and the Shaping of Kansas City*, 172.

15. Clarence Arthur Perry, "The Neighborhood Unit: A Scheme of Arrangement for the Family-Life Community" in *Neighborhood and Community Planning, Regional Survey of New York and Its Environs* (1929), quoted in Howard W. Hallman, "The Neighborhood as an Organizational Unit: A Historical Perspective," in George Frederickson, ed., *Neighborhood Control in the 1970s: Politics, Administration and Citizen Participation* (New York: Chandler Publishing Co., 1973), 9–10.

16. Donald R. Stabile, *Community Associations: The Emergence and Acceptance of a Quiet Innovation in Housing* (Westport, CT: Greenwood Press, 2000), 53–55.

17. Worley, *J. C. Nichols and the Shaping of Kansas City*, 176.

18. *Dixon v. Van Sweringen Co.*, 166 N.E. at 892 (Ohio 1929).

19. Quoted in Gerald Korngold, "The Emergence of Private Land Use Controls in Large-Scale Subdivisions: The Companion Story to *Village of Euclid v. Ambler Realty Co.*," *Case Western Reserve Law Review* 51 (Summer 2001), 626.

20. Ibid., 623.

21. Marc A. Weiss, *The Rise of the Community Builders: The American Real Estate Industry and Urban Land Planning* (New York: Columbia University Press, 1987), 4.

22. Patrick J. Rohan, "Preparing Community Associations for the Twenty-First Century: Anticipating the Legal Problems and Possible Solutions," *St. John's Law Review* 73 (Winter 1999), 14.

23. Weiss, *The Rise of the Community Builders*, 11–12.

24. *Buchanan v. Warley*, 245 U.S. 60 (1917).

25. *Shelley v. Kraemer*, 334 U.S. 1 (1948). Illustrating the legal difficulties and confusions in seeking to define the boundary to separate private from public actions, the Supreme Court was hard pressed to come up with a legal basis for its decision to newly limit the private freedom to practice racial exclusion. In the end, the Court declared that racial covenants had to be enforced by the courts, and this very fact made their legal defense a matter of "state action." However, if such reasoning were extended more broadly, virtually any action in society would be transformed to become a public action. Few legal authorities have doubted that the Court reached a correct conclusion in *Shelley* but there has been wide criticism of its specific argument. See, for example, Shelley Ross Saxer, "Shelley v. Kraemer's Fiftieth Anniversary: 'A Time for Keeping; a Time for Throwing Away'?" *Kansas Law Review* 47 (November 1998).

26. Siegel, "The Constitution and Private Government," 504.

27. For a recent useful survey, see Pietro S. Nivola, *Laws of the Landscape: How Policies Shape Cities in Europe and America* (Washington, DC: Brookings Institution Press, 1999).

28. James L. Winokur, "The Financial Role of Community Associations," *Santa Clara Law Review* 38 (1998), 1137 n. 4.

29. Lynne B. Sagalyn and George Sternlieb, "Introduction," in *Zoning and Housing Costs: The Impact of Land-Use Controls on Housing Price* (New Brunswick, NJ: Center for Urban Policy Research, Rutgers University, 1972), 2.

30. Jeffrey D. Greene, *Cities and Privatization: Prospects for the New Century* (Upper Saddle River, NJ: Prentice Hall, 2002), 148.

31. Marc A. Weiss and John W. Watts, "Community Builders and Community Associations: The Role of Real Estate Developers in Private Residential Governance," in U.S. Advisory Commission on Intergovernmental Relations, *Residential Community Associations*, 101.

32. Jasmine Martirossian, *Decision Making in Communities: Why Groups of Smart People Sometimes Make Bad Decisions* (Alexandria, VA: Community Associations Institute, 2001), 65.

33. Robert G. Natelson, "Consent, Coercion, and 'Reasonableness' in Private Law: The Special Case of the Property Owners Association," *Ohio State Law Journal* 51 (Winter 1990), 47.

34. Jane Jacobs, *The Death and Life of Great American Cities* (New York: Random House, 1961).

35. Carl B. Kress, "Beyond Nahrstedt: Reviewing Restrictions Governing Life in a Property Owner Association," *UCLA Law Review* 42 (February 1995), 842.

36. Clifford J. Treese, ed., *Community Associations Factbook, 1993 edition* (Alexandria, VA: Community Associations Institute, 1993), 18.

37. This history is based in part on Robert G. Natelson, *Law of Property Owners Associations* (Boston: Little, Brown, 1989), 19–32. See also Robert G. Natelson, "Comments on the Historiography of Condominium: The Myth of Roman Origin," *Oklahoma City University Law Review* 12 (Spring 1987).

38. Natelson, *Law of Property Owners Associations,* 24.

39. C. James Dowden, "Community Associations and Local Governments: The Need for Recognition and Reassessment," in Advisory Commission on Intergovernmental Relations, *Residential Community Associations.*

40. James L. Winokur, "The Financial Role of Community Associations," *Santa Clara Law Review* 38 (1998), 1139–40.

41. Jordan I. Shifrin, *Guilt by Association: A Survival Guide for Homeowners, Board Members and Property Managers,* 2nd ed. (Lincoln, NE: Writers Press Club, 2001), 37.

42. Weiss and Watts, "Community Builders and Community Associations," 101.

43. See Amanda G. Hyatt, *Transition from Developer Control,* 2nd ed., GAP Report 3 (Alexandria, VA: Community Associations Institute, 1996).

44. Information concerning CAI and its publications is available at http://www.caionline.org/.

45. Wayne S. Hyatt and Susan F. French, *Community Association Law* (Durham, NC: Carolina Academic Press, 1998), 20–21.

46. The provisions of the UCIOA are discussed in Katharine N. Rosenberry and Curtis G. Sproul, "A Comparison of California Common Interest Development Law and the Uniform Common Interest Ownership Act," *Santa Clara Law Review* 38, no. 4 (1998).

47. Joseph E. Adams, "Community Associations: 1998 Survey of Florida Law," *Nova Law Review* 23 (Fall 1998), 66.

48. See Douglas Frantz and Catherine Collins, *Celebration, USA: Living in Disney's Brave New Town* (New York: Henry Holt, 1999); and Andrew Ross, *The Celebration Chronicles: Life, Liberty, and the Pursuit of Property Value in Disney's New Town* (New York: Ballantine Books, 1999).

49. "The Reasonable Pet: An Examination of the Enforcement of Restrictions in California Common Interest Developments after Nahrstedt v. Lakeside Village Condominium Ass'n Inc.," *Santa Clara Law Review* 36, no. 3 (1996), 793 n. 3.

50. Steven Siegel, "The Constitution and Private Government," 553, 553 n. 488.

51. Adams, "Community Associations," 66–67.

52. Ibid., 90–91.

53. Natelson, "Consent, Coercion, and 'Reasonableness' in Private Law," 74 n. 157.

54. Rosenberry and Sproul, "A Comparison of California Common Interest Development Law and the Uniform Common Interest Ownership Act," 1079.

55. Curtis Sproul, "The Many Faces of Community Associations Under California Law," in Steven E. Barton and Carol J. Silverman, eds., *Common Interest Communities: Private Governments and the Public Interest* (Berkeley: Institute of Governmental Studies Press, University of California, 1994), 65–67.

56. Treese, ed., *Community Associations Factbook, 1993 edition,* 17.

57. Clifford J. Treese, *Introduction to Community Association Management, Governance, and Services* (Alexandria, VA: Community Associations Institute, 2002), 23.

58. Steven E. Barton and Carol J. Silverman, "Common Interest Communities: Private Government and the Public Interest Revisited," in Barton and Silverman, eds., *Common Interest Communities,* 39.

59. Richard Briffault, "Our Localism: Part I—The Structure of Local Government Law," *Columbia Law Review* 90 (January 1990), 81 n. 342.

60. Steven E. Barton and Carol J. Silverman, "Preface," in Barton and Silverman, eds., *Common Interest Communities,* xi.

61. Natelson, "Consent, Coercion, and 'Reasonableness' in Private Law," 42.

2

Neighborhood Environmentalism

The rise of the private neighborhood association, which commenced in the 1960s, coincides with the growth of the environmental movement in the United States. The common timing may not be altogether coincidental. America's concern for environmental quality is not limited to forests, wetlands, and other parts of wild nature. It extends as well to the urban environment where concerned Americans have made heroic efforts over the past 40 years to reduce air pollution, water pollution, exposure to hazardous wastes, and the presence of other potentially harmful substances. Most people spend their time outdoors closer to their homes than anywhere else; therefore, their own neighborhood surroundings figure prominently in their desire for a high-quality environment. In 1974, when environmental concern in the United States was at its peak, the U.S. Supreme Court in its *Belle Terre* decision strongly endorsed the use of local zoning powers to protect neighborhood environmental quality.[1] Justice William Douglas, author of many books and articles in support of environmental protection throughout the nation, wrote the opinion.

The organized environmental movement, admittedly, has paid little attention to the quality of the neighborhood environment over the past four decades. Issues such as wilderness protection and endangered species have commanded much greater interest. However, some environmental thinkers have recently suggested that the environmental movement should reconsider its priorities. William Cronon, author of *Changes in the Land* (the environmental history of New England), declared in a later 1995 book that "any way of looking at nature that encourages us to believe we are separate from nature— as wilderness tends to do—is likely to reinforce environmentally irresponsible behavior." We must develop a new attitude toward nature, he suggests, recognizing that "the tree in the garden is in reality no less other, no less worthy of our wonder and respect, than the tree in an ancient forest that has never known an ax or a saw." The environmental movement, Cronon argues, must begin to devote greater attention to "the part of nature we intend to turn toward our own ends . . . asking whether we can use it again and again and again—sustainably—without its being diminished in the process."[2]

For the environmental movement, it may have seemed that there was less reason to be concerned for neighborhood environments because people were willing to pay good money for high quality in their immediate surroundings. A real estate developer could make a large profit in this way. Developers thus would have strong private incentives to become skilled in creating attractive neighborhoods. The environmental movement also typically looked to government to accomplish its objectives. A form of environmental protection that could be accomplished privately was less appealing for fund raising and in general less suited to the methods of environmental activism. Perhaps another factor was that, as Cronon suggests, a neighborhood environment was not considered a "natural" setting, and the environmental movement sought above all to separate humans from nature—to protect "wild" nature from human intrusion.

Nevertheless, the rise of the private neighborhood association in the late 20th century produced yet another side to the American movement for environmental quality. Like many environmental policies, this "neighborhood environmentalism" was a response to a problem of the commons. Within a neighborhood, the private incentive is for less desirable uses to move into sites now occupied by more desirable uses, thus benefiting from their surroundings and raising the welfare of the new entrants. Individual landowners, moreover, will be willing to sell lots for such redevelopment at much higher densities with cheaper housing. One apartment house in a neighborhood of low-density homes will enrich the owner. However, if each landowner behaves in this fashion, the overall result will be a deterioration of the neighborhood environment. As Garrett Hardin famously argued in 1968, whether it is open grazing lands or urban neighborhoods, a solution to "the tragedy of the commons" requires either a system of government regulation or a system of private property rights.[3] Zoning represented the public regulatory option, the private neighborhood association the property right approach.

Private Restrictions

Neighborhood associations typically maintain tight restrictions on how property within their boundaries is used. These restrictions (the "covenants, conditions, and restrictions," or "CC&Rs") are specified in the property deeds

and described in the founding document (the "declaration," or political constitution of the neighborhood). These restrictions are designed to exclude
many land uses in order to protect the neighborhood environment's existing
character. As James Winokur observes, "concern for segregation of land uses,"
or providing protection from "industrial, commercial and even multi-family
residential uses," is a prime objective of most neighborhood associations.[4]

These protections also usually include elements that go well beyond conventional zoning in the public sector.[5] Any significant exterior modification of
a property, such as the installation of a new roof, the construction of a fence,
or the planting of shrubbery, is likely to require collective approval. In northern Virginia, art teacher Peggy Nigon "likes that the home colors" in her
neighborhood association mostly "all match." There is a pair of "bright teal
houses" that she drives past on the way to work, and she wonders "how that
happened."[6] Millions of other unit owners in neighborhood associations across
the United States share her opinion and have acted together to control strictly
the exterior colors of homes in their neighborhoods. Some neighborhood
associations regulate the placement of basketball hoops, or prohibit their
installation altogether. In Maryland, the Middlebury Homeowners Association
allows the construction of in-ground swimming pools, but rules out above-
ground pools.

Some of these rules seem excessive, although many unit owners support
even the tightest controls. In Colorado the South Creek Eight Homeowners
Association demanded that a unit owner remove a hot tub. The Plantation
Walk Homeowners Association in Tennessee regulates the grass height and
edging style used in mowing lawns. Other associations regulate such details as
the color of swing sets or even the size (to the 1/16th of an inch) of screws used
for balcony railings. The Sunstream Homeowners Association in San Diego
prohibited a unit owner from attaching a ceramic sign with the family name to
the outside of the owner's entry door. According to the rules of the association,
the hanging or placement of any signs in the common areas—including every
part of a property's exterior—requires association approval.

Neighborhood association rules frequently limit the way individual properties are used. Some associations stipulate that garage doors must be kept closed
when not in use. Associations often specify the types of motor vehicles allowed
in the neighborhood—prohibiting house trailers, larger trucks, or even any
kind of truck at all—and the manner of parking permitted on neighborhood
streets and driveways. In proposing "sample rules," an industry leader, Lucia
Trigiani, suggests, "No playing or lounging shall be permitted, nor hall baby
carriages, velocipedes, bicycles, playpens, wagons, toys, benches, chairs, or
other articles of personal property be left unattended in common areas of the
building, stairwells, building entrances, parking areas, sidewalks, or lawns or
elsewhere on the common elements."[7] As one judge declared in considering a

legal challenge to the powers of a particular neighborhood association, "although William Pitt, Earl of Chatham, may have declared, in a famous speech to Parliament, that a man's home is his castle, this is not necessarily true of condominiums" and other neighborhood associations.[8]

Many restrictions also go beyond property use. Many associations also maintain prohibitions or restrictions on unit rentals. Furthermore, collective controls may extend into various realms of social behavior, such as the playing of loud music or the hosting of late-night parties. Trigiani suggests that associations include a rule specifying that "all persons shall be properly attired when appearing in any common area of the Property including stairwells, community buildings, and any other public spaces."[9] Reflecting an apparent residual puritanism, a few associations have even regulated swimwear and public displays of affection. In 1991, a 51-year-old California woman received an official reprimand from her condominium association because she was seen "parking in [a] circular driveway . . . kissing and doing bad things for over one hour" with a local businessman; the association threatened a fine if there were repetitions.[10] In the 1970s, a Florida association banned the use of alcoholic beverages in the neighborhood clubhouse.

Some association rules are very specific. Many associations restrict pet ownership, sometimes based on animal size and weight.* Neighborhood associations commonly prohibit any home-based businesses, in some cases even personal businesses interior to a housing unit that generate little or no automobile traffic or any other external impacts. In some cases, neighborhood associations regulate the use of patio furniture, the hosting of outdoor barbeques, the frequency of toilet flushing, and the type of soap used in dishwashers. Associations often have rules prohibiting any salesmen or other solicitors from doing business in the neighborhood.

Green Valley is a master-planned community near Las Vegas, Nevada. As described by one observer, this private community controls the uses of neighborhood properties in all of the following ways:

> In Green Valley the restrictions are detailed and pervasive. . . . Clotheslines and Winnebagos are not permitted, for example; no fowl, reptile, fish, or insect may be raised; there are to be no exterior speakers, horns, whistles, or bells. No debris of any kind,

---

*In one instance, a neighborhood association limited dogs' weight to less than 30 pounds. When a resident had a dog of about this weight, the association conducted a weigh-in. This policy raised the obvious question—What if the dog weighs 29.5 pounds one day, and 30.5 pounds the next? It also raised the specter of dogs being deprived of food and drink in the period before the formal weigh-in, much as human boxers and wrestlers who compete in certain weight categories must often do. See David J. Kennedy, "Residential Associations as State Actors: Regulating the Impact of Gated Communities on Nonmembers," *Yale Law Journal* 105 (December 1995), 762 n. 8.

no open fires, no noise. Entries, signs, lights, mailboxes, sidewalks, rear yards, side yards, carports, sheds—the planners have had their say about each. . . . [They also regulate] the number of dogs and cats you can own . . . as well as the placement of garbage cans, barbecue pits, satellite dishes, and utility boxes. The color of your home, the number of stories, the materials used, its accents and trim. The interior of your garage, the way to park your truck, the plants in your yard, the angle of your flagpole, the size of your address numbers, the placement of mirrored glass balls and birdbaths, the grade of your lawn's slope, and the size of your FOR SALE sign should you decide you want to leave.[11]

Court Oversight

The rules of neighborhood associations thus routinely impose tight controls on matters of neighborhood aesthetics that have been traditionally considered beyond the purview of municipal zoning. A neighborhood association's private status, however, does not protect it from legal challenges. Unit owners, in fact, frequently take their associations to court. In the past the courts have been more likely to overturn a neighborhood restriction that affected only the interior portions of a unit—and thus seemingly had no direct impact on anyone other than the one property owner involved.* A neighborhood association in California, for example, lost in court when it sought to ban the installation of a TV satellite dish, even though that dish would have been placed in a way that it remained out of the view of any other neighborhood resident.[12]

In other cases, courts have ruled against association actions that were regarded as too intrusive. A court thus overturned a neighborhood rule that sought to ban the parking of a small noncommercial pickup truck in a driveway—although an ordinary car would have been allowed in the same place under association rules. The court reasoned that "cultural perceptions" change and that neighborhoods must also adjust; in recent years light trucks have shed a "pejorative connotation" and have instead for many people become fashionable—perhaps even the contemporary social "equivalent of a convertible in earlier years."[13] Hence, as this court decided, it was now unreasonable for the association to ban the parking of small pickup trucks in neighborhood driveways.

---

*Admittedly, some indirect "psychological" and thus broader effects on the whole neighborhood might be asserted, based solely on the common knowledge among neighborhood residents of the "offending" activity's very existence. Environmental economists have developed a substantial body of writings concerning the "existence value" of, say, an endangered species or a wilderness area. Even though I may be sure that I will never visit a wilderness area, I may place a considerable value on the creation of such an area. Perhaps neighborhoods can have "existence values" as well for the activities conducted within individual units.

Gerald Korngold, dean of the Case Western Reserve University law school, argues that, though there will be a few such cases that warrant outside intervention, the courts should nevertheless respect the autonomy of neighborhood associations in controlling their own land uses "in virtually all situations." Indeed, the restrictions of neighborhood associations "in almost every case" should not be subject to judicial second-guessing.[14] Yet as courts across the United States are increasingly asked to review such issues, challenges to neighborhood management practices have become a fast-growing area of the law.[15] Much as Korngold advocates, however, the courts have mostly deferred to the private autonomy of neighborhood associations.

One should give substantial respect, the courts seem to be saying, to the expressed preferences of the more than 50 million Americans who live in a neighborhood association with tight mutual controls. These people knew in advance what they were getting into (or had ample opportunity to know), and agreed to the neighborhood restrictions in their initial contract. Hence, except in rare circumstances, an association's decisionmaking and enforcement procedures should be allowed to operate according to the guiding rules of the founding documents—the "neighborhood constitution." Concern about being inundated with unit owner complaints has also probably influenced the courts' reluctance to enter into this area.

In a much-cited 1975 case in Florida, a court upheld the prohibition (noted above) on the use of alcoholic beverages within the clubhouse area of the Hidden Harbour Estate Association. In its ruling, the Florida Court of Appeals first described the routine workings of neighborhood associations:

> Inherent in the condominium concept is the principle that to promote the health, happiness, and peace of mind of the majority of the unit owners since they are living in such close proximity and using facilities in common, each unit owner must give up a certain degree of freedom of choice which he might otherwise enjoy in separate, privately owned property. Condominium unit owners comprise a little democratic sub-society of necessity more restrictive as it pertains to use of condominium property than may be existent outside the condominium organization. The Declaration of Condominium involved herein is replete with examples of the curtailment of individual rights usually associated with the private ownership of property. It provides, for example, that no sale may be effectuated without approval; no minors may be permanent residents; no pets are allowed.[16]

In upholding the restrictive actions of the Hidden Harbour association, the Florida court made the following statement—in language that would repeated by many other courts: "Certainly, the association is not at liberty to adopt arbitrary or capricious rules bearing no relationship to the health, happiness and enjoyment of life of the various unit owners. On the contrary, we believe the test is reasonableness. If a rule is reasonable, the association can adopt it; if not, it cannot."[17]

The Reasonableness Standard

What is "unreasonable," to be sure, is up for debate. The California Supreme Court later sought to give further illumination. In this case a unit owner, Natore Nahrstedt, owned three cats and therefore was in violation of a ban that had been imposed by the Lakeside Village Condominium Association.[18] According to the association rules, unit owners were not allowed to have pets. However, Mrs. Nahrstedt argued that, because her three cats were not allowed to go outside her unit, it was unreasonable that she should be forced to find a new home for them (or alternatively be forced to move out of the neighborhood herself). Her neighbors countered that she had known about the association rules all along, and had blatantly defied the express wishes of fellow unit owners. This cat lover lost in the first court to consider the case, won at an appeals level, but finally lost on further appeal to the California Supreme Court.

Using widely cited language, the California Supreme Court declared that "subordination of individual property rights to the collective judgment of the owners association together with restrictions on the use of real property comprise the chief attributes of owning property in a common interest development."[19] That is to say, the collective preferences of the unit owners, as clearly expressed in restrictive use covenants included in the founding documents of an association, must not be easily overthrown.* Following this California ruling, the common interpretation among state courts is that a restriction imposed by a neighborhood association should be legally sustained as "reasonable" if it can meet three tests. It must not "(1) violate a fundamental public policy, (2) bear no rational relationship to the protection, preservation, operation, or purpose of the affected land, or (3) create more harmful effects on homeowners' land use than benefits."[20] (This third test, it must be admitted, seems to invite considerable judicial intervention in association affairs, if carried out to the full letter of the court language. For the most part, it seems to have been interpreted narrowly.)

Although the courts have supported the enforcement of neighborhood association covenants in the great majority of cases, this area of the law is still evolving. In 1997, the supreme court of Washington State showed that the courts do sometimes intervene aggressively. In 1992 William and Carolyn Riss

---

*The California Supreme Court was also committed, as one legal commentary notes, to establish a "judicial barricade" to relieve the court system from the significant "problem of judicial, social, and financial burdens resulting from the detailed factual determinations necessary under the previous, fact-specific standard"—a situation involving potentially many thousands of individual cases. See "The Reasonable Pet: An Examination of the Enforcement of Restrictions in California Common Interest Developments after *Nahrstedt v. Lakeside Village Condominium Association, Inc.,*" *Santa Clara Law Review* 36, no. 3 (1996), 808–9.

purchased a home in the Mercia Heights area of Clyde Hill, Washington. The Risses later sought the approval of the Mercia Homeowners Association to tear town their existing home and to build a new one. The new home would have complied fully with the covenants as recorded by the original developer in the 1950s. The board of directors turned down the request and then, after an appeal from the Risses to the full membership, the association members also voted decisively against the request. The state supreme court, however, overturned the associations' actions. In ruling in favor of the Risses, the court found that the Mercia Homeowners Association had acted "without adequate investigation, . . . based on inaccurate information, and thus was unreasonable and arbitrary."[21] The Mercia homeowners were probably objecting most of all to the neighborhood disruptions resulting from demolishing an existing home and constructing a new one. However, that type of concern was not explicitly addressed in the association's covenants, and the Washington court therefore apparently felt free to interject its own judgment.

The courts often distinguish between land use restrictions that are contained in an association's founding documents and any subsequent rules that the association has adopted. Each new buyer of a unit in an association must agree formally to the neighborhood's basic covenants and other land use restrictions as a condition of purchase. New entrants thus voluntarily accept the internal rules of the game in choosing to move into a neighborhood. As Wayne Hyatt and Jo Anne Stubblefield write, the courts have generally given a "strong presumption of validity" to restrictions contained in the founding documents.[22] Indeed, the Florida Court of Appeals stated in 1981 that even though there may be "a certain degree of unreasonableness" with respect to the enforcement of the original covenants, the courts should nevertheless sustain the actions of an association.[23]

However, when the association board of directors (or a full vote of the membership) adopts a new rule, unanimous consent is not necessary. Lacking universal agreement, the courts have been less deferential. In such cases, "rational rules and restrictions that are rationally enforced—and that promote a legitimate goal—will generally be considered reasonable," but the courts accept a greater responsibility to scrutinize the actions of a neighborhood association to ensure their "reasonableness."[24]

The potential range of decisions that the governing officers of neighborhood associations are called upon to resolve can seem almost limitless. Most of these decisions, fortunately, do not end up in court. In a neighborhood association in Fairfax County (Virginia), for example, the 30 or so unit owners in the late 1990s were pondering a puzzling question.[25] The neighborhood streets had been privately maintained, and some of these streets were in need of significant capital improvements that required a special capital assessment of around $2,000 per unit owner. However, a few members of the association lived in housing units that fronted on a public road. They made little use of—and, in theory, could make no use at all of—the association's internal road network. These outside-facing owners would therefore derive little or no direct benefit from the street improvements. Should they nevertheless pay the full amount? Or perhaps should they be given a discount, or even complete relief from having to pay for the cost of the internal road improvements?

Another thorny issue this same northern Virginia association faced involved the question of placing Christmas lights on a part of the association's common area. Most of the unit owners were Christian, and most of them wanted to decorate with the lights during the holiday season—a project that would cost the association no more than a few hundred dollars. However, a few association members were Jewish and at least one of these members objected. Recognizing that the rights to the common areas amount to a form of "property ownership," the objector believed that it would be offensive to his religious beliefs for him to help pay to put Christmas lights on, in part at least, "his" property. The association had to consider whether this was a reasonable view or an unreasonable objection that would frustrate the will of most of the unit owners—people who were simply looking to celebrate in a few small ways the Christmas holiday season.

A difficult issue facing many neighborhood associations is the extent free speech is protected within their boundaries. Under the U.S. Constitution, the level of such protections typically differs according to the setting—public or private—and whether or not a "state actor" is involved. In a 1990s Pennsylvania court case, an association homeowner placed a "for sale" sign in his window. When the association demanded that the sign be removed (prior written permission for any signs was mandatory under association rules), the owner claimed that his constitutional rights of free speech under the First Amendment were being violated. A lower court agreed, but on appeal a higher court sustained the association's action, declaring that freedom of speech may have to give way to the rights of private property as reflected in existing covenants within a neighborhood association.[26]

Similarly, an association would very likely have the right to ban the placement of political signs for candidates in elections—and for other political causes—within a neighborhood. In most cases, by contrast, a municipal government could not enforce such a prohibition. One attorney explains the current state of the law with respect to these forms of free speech: "There is nothing constitutionally impermissible per se in a private agreement regarding [restrictions on] signs in a planned residential community."[27]

The Business Judgment Rule

Although some neighborhood associations are not incorporated, most have nonprofit corporation status. A board of directors' legal status and obligations

are thus often derived from the fact that its association operates as a corporation under the same general legal framework as a business corporation. As
attorney Kimberly Wind explains,

> An association is a nonprofit corporation under the laws of California. The associ-
> ation has an elected board of directors, who run the corporation. . . .
>   The board of directors, like a profit corporation, should rely on the expertise of
> others, when needed. The executive board members are "fiduciaries"—members who
> are subject to the insulations from liability provided for directors of [profit and non-
> profit] corporations by the state of California.[28]

The legal obligations of the officers and members of a private business corporation's board of directors are basically guided by the "business judgment
rule." Obviously, the practice of business is often a risky undertaking. Shareholders and employees may be bitterly disappointed when a risk turns bad. In
the passions of the moment, they may pursue legal actions against the corporation's top decisionmakers. Yet, the vitality of the American free enterprise
system depends on corporate leaders' freedom to incur risks. Indeed, many of
the risks end up generating large profits, even as others end up generating large
losses. The courts have thus generally refused to hold corporate leaders liable
for business failures except in cases of outright dishonesty or gross abuse of
authority. As long as corporate leaders act in "good faith" and do not blatantly
disregarded stockholder interests, the courts will not intervene.

In 1990 the New York Court of Appeals applied this standard to the actions
of a New York City cooperative's board of directors. The board had rejected a
unit owner's remodeling plan, and the occupant then sued the association. The
court refused to become involved, asserting that "the responsibility for business
judgments must rest with the corporate directors."[29] The California Supreme
Court took a similar position in 1999 when a condominium unit owner sued
the association's board over its policy for dealing with termites. The board had
ordered "spot treatment," while the unit owner argued that a broader fumiga-
tion of the whole property was required. The court argued, "We adopt today
for California courts a rule of judicial deference to community association
board decision-making that applies . . . when owners in common interest
developments seek to litigate ordinary maintenance decisions." As a general
matter, the courts should not second-guess boards of directors of neighborhood associations when they make "the detailed and peculiar economic decisions necessary in the maintenance of these developments."[30]

There are thus now two standards of judicial review for neighborhood associations in California. When it comes to the enforcement of covenants relating
to permissible uses of land and property, the "reasonableness" standard will
apply. However, when the board of directors is making "discretionary economic decisions," the business judgment rule applies.[31] To be sure, there are

likely to be further opinions in this area, both in California and in other states. These opinions will be an important part of the broader evolution in associations' legal status in the years to come.

Controls on Entry

Neighborhood associations may also want to maintain a desired neighborhood environment by limiting the age, sex, marital status, and other personal characteristics of prospective entrants. Given the long history of racial discrimination in the United States, this is a particularly sensitive and controversial area of neighborhood control over the shared environment.

Although private restrictive covenants to exclude racial minorities were once widespread in the United States, the U.S. Supreme Court in 1948 declared them unconstitutional in *Shelley v. Kraemer.*[32] However, an association's right to accept or reject new unit owners based on other personal characteristics is less clear cut. Discriminatory actions that are unconstitutional in a "public" setting may well be constitutional in a "private" setting. Even overt racial discrimination is legal in a host of "private" areas of life. Racial motives, for example, obviously—and legally—enter into many private decisions over marriage partners for whites and blacks alike (if race were not a factor, statistically, one would expect many more interracial marriages). Defining the exact settings where "public" values will prevail, in contrast to other settings where "private" values are given full freedom of expression, can be difficult. The courts at times have appeared to be as confused as the rest of society.

Some forms of social discrimination—such as excluding potential entrants based on wealth and income—are entirely legal. A person has to be able to afford the price of a home in a neighborhood association, and the amount of income required can even be measured rather precisely (savings and loan and other mortgage institutions use tables showing the incomes required for mortgage eligibility). Still other forms of discrimination are not constitutionally prohibited, but may currently be illegal under one statute or another. In these cases, the law could be changed, and the decision to make such a change is potentially an important public policy issue.

In general, a community's ability to assert strong social values may depend on its ability to exclude people who do not share its common values. As Michael Sarbanes and Kathleen Skullney comment, community maintenance is "filled with the related tension between cohesion and exclusion. The very self-definition which binds some people within a community is likely to exclude others."[33] One legal authority comments that "real communities are very selective about whom they include. . . . A Jewish community comprised of a mixture of Christians, Jews, and secular individuals is a contradiction.

An Italian-American community half comprised of Irish or Russians is impossible."[34]

Many neighborhood associations have acquired a special character without imposing any legal requirements. The association history often plays a key role. In 1989 the sports agent Mark McCormack bought a home in Isleworth, an exclusive association located in the lake district west of Orlando, Florida. Soon other prominent figures in American sports followed suit. Today, Tiger Woods, Ken Griffey Jr., Shaquille O'Neal, Grant Hill, Vince Carter, Orel Hershiser, and a number of other celebrities all live in Isleworth. It is not primarily the fancy homes or other qualities of the physical environment that have attracted these famous people; indeed, Isleworth has homes ranging from $800,000 to more than $10 million and "the smallish lots and strict building codes keep most houses looking modest by mansion standards." The leading attraction for the athletes is the presence of so many other celebrities. Isleworth residents have become accustomed to prominent athletes; they don't ask for autographs. Given the tight security provided, among "all places on Earth," the *Wall Street Journal* reports, this particular neighborhood association has acquired a strong community identity as "the favored spot of the jockistocracy."[35]

Since the 1960s, U.S. public policy has often emphasized individual rights over the rights of people to form an exclusive community. However, concern over the need to provide greater encouragement to the communal institutions in American life has been growing in recent years. This trend reflects in part some anxiety that the value structures of American society may be eroding; therefore, it may be necessary to give a higher priority to the role of strong communities in inculcating values—especially among the young. Though the legal acceptability of many exclusionary practices is being contested, the issue remains cloudy and, for the most part, remains to be resolved.[36]

Age-Group Communities

Thus far, the question of a neighborhood association's legal right to engage in discriminatory practices with respect to age has received the greatest attention.[37] Public policy has been caught between two powerful societal trends. Legislatures in general have been moving to include age as a prohibited category for discriminatory actions. On the other hand, the creation of neighborhood associations that limit residents to certain age groups has proven extremely popular; about 8 percent of associations in 1995 were age restricted.[38]

The *New York Times,* for example, recently reported that the appeal of private neighborhoods is growing as the baby boomer generation nears retirement age.* Neighborhood associations for senior citizens that feature many high-end luxuries (full-time "resorts" for retirement living, as some observers have called them) have been sprouting up across New Jersey and represent the fastest-growing segment of the housing market. It is true that some residents "complain about the rules and restrictions, set by elected association boards, which govern everything from landscaping to window treatments." Yet, as the *Times* reported, "for many, the appeal of such communities outweighs the drawbacks." Indeed, the demand has been so great that developers have been unable to keep up with it. The *Times* reported just such a case in 2001:

> Three weeks ago, when the development company K. Hovnanian opened a series of model homes at its Four Seasons at Upper Freehold, more than 300 hundred people showed up in one weekend.
> "People are just clamoring for this product," said Michael Villane, vice president for marketing and sales in K. Hovnanian's Northeast division, which has nine age-restricted communities under construction in New Jersey. "We just can't build them fast enough."[39]

From the 1960s to the late 1980s, many other neighborhood associations (not just for senior citizens) also limited residents to adults only; their founding documents typically prohibited families with children (individuals below a certain age) from living there.[†] Such actions were soon challenged in the courts as an unconstitutional or otherwise illegal form of discrimination. There is little doubt that if a municipal government in the public sector sought to limit residency based on age, this form of exclusion would be struck down in the courts. In cases involving neighborhood associations, however, the state courts generally upheld restrictions on the entry of families with children.

---

*An insightful description of life in senior citizen communities—the great majority governed by neighborhood associations—is provided by Frances Fitzgerald for Sun City, Florida. Such communities, she notes, represent a new "subculture of the aging," based on the fact that "older people" are now developing a greater sense of "group consciousness." It is also a product of new social phenomena such as "the twenty-five year increase in life expectancy, the expansion and growing length of retirement, [and] the migration of elderly people away from their children and hometowns." Overall, she says, "the present generation of people in their sixties and seventies may be the most privileged generation of elderly people in history." Until now, reflecting the harder realities of earlier times, "no society . . . has ever had whole villages—whole cities—composed exclusively of elderly people." It is a large and potentially momentous social experiment in American life. The final results are not yet in, but Fitzgerald reports that "measuring the attitudes of residents by 'life satisfaction' scales and other tests of their own devising, researchers . . . found that the inhabitants of retirement communities were generally satisfied with their communities." See Frances Fitzgerald, *Cities on a Hill: A Journey through Contemporary American Cultures* (New York: Simon and Schuster, 1987), 211, 210, 208, 212, 213.

†Although it was not restricted to neighborhood associations, a 1980 nationwide survey by the Department of Housing and Urban Development found that 25 percent of all U.S. rental units did not permit occupancy by children.

In 1978, for example, a California court of appeals upheld a neighborhood association's requirement that permanent occupants had to be at least 18 years old.[40] In a much-noted 1979 case, the Florida Supreme Court similarly upheld a restriction imposed by the White Egret neighborhood association denying occupancy to any family with children under age 12. The Florida court reasoned that:

> The urbanization of this country requiring substantial portions of our population to live closer together coupled with the desire for varying types of family units and recreational activities have brought about new concepts in living accommodations. There are residential units designed specifically for young adults, for families with young children, and for senior citizens. The desires and demands of each category are different. . . . The units designed principally for families are two- to four-bedroom units with recreational facilities geared for children, including playgrounds and small children's swimming pools. . . . We cannot ignore the fact that some housing complexes are designed for certain age groups. In our view, age restrictions are a reasonable means to identify and characterize the varying desires of our population. The law is now clear that a restriction on individual rights on the basis of age need not pass the "strict scrutiny" test, and therefore age is not a suspect classification. . . . We do recognize, however, that these age restrictions cannot be used to unreasonably or arbitrarily restrict certain classes of individuals from obtaining desirable housing. Whenever an age restriction is attacked on due process or equal protection grounds, we find the test is: (1) whether the restriction under the particular circumstances of the case is reasonable; and (2) whether it is discriminatory, arbitrary, or oppressive in its application.[41]

The court in essence found that a neighborhood should have substantial freedom to define its own social as well as physical environment. Moreover, the presence of children in a neighborhood could impose significant burdens on other residents. Neighborhood associations might legitimately decide to specialize—some providing suitable playground and other facilities for children, others choosing not to offer such items. Furthermore, the owners of a housing unit in a neighborhood association would not have any legal right to impose on other unit owners the costs of meeting their own children's needs. Internal redistribution of income to one favored class is not among the constitutional requirements that the courts should impose on a neighborhood association.

The 1988 Fair Housing Act Amendments

Across the entire United States, the wide range of legislative and judicial arenas in existence means that it is possible to lose in one and still prevail in another. After losing in California, Florida, and most state courts, the opponents of age-based housing restrictions finally prevailed in 1988 in the U.S. Congress. The enactment of the Fair Housing Act Amendments in that year significantly altered the legal environment for age discrimination by neighborhood associations (and other participants in the housing market). Congress declared any housing discrimination on the basis of "familial status" to be illegal under federal law.* ("Familial status" is defined by the presence of a child under 18 years of age who is living permanently as a member of the family.)

Neighborhoods for senior citizens, however, were given an exemption. As of the early 1990s, more than 25,000 condominiums nationwide had age restrictions designed to limit occupancy to senior citizens.[42] As specified in the 1988 law, the senior citizen exemption could be obtained in either of two ways. First, any association that limited all residents to age 62 and older could automatically qualify for senior citizen status. Second, a neighborhood association could also qualify if at least 80 percent of its units had at least one occupant 55 years or older, and if this association could further demonstrate that it was providing "significant facilities and services" intended for use by older people.

This second avenue of qualifying for senior citizen status, not surprisingly, soon produced widespread confusion and legal uncertainty.[43] Some neighborhoods already occupied mostly by senior citizens were forced to buy new equipment and other physical facilities in order to keep their senior citizen status. There were complaints that "the imposition of federally mandated requirements . . . forced some adult communities to have a nursing home feel."[44] The Department of Housing and Urban Development (HUD) compounded the problems by failing to clarify matters in regulation implementation, and then by treating many neighborhood associations in a legalistic, adversarial manner. HUD officials seemingly were determined to keep every loophole closed and thereby to ensure that no neighborhood association would illegally exclude children by falsely claiming status as a senior citizen community.

By 1995 Congress, forced to address widespread public anger and confusion, rescinded the requirement that adult communities provide facilities and services appropriate for senior citizens. The judiciary also heard the congressional message. Since the 1995 amendments, most neighborhood associations with 80 percent or more of their units occupied by at least one person 55 years or older have had little trouble in qualifying for senior citizen status. As a result, a large number of American households are in fact eligible to locate in a neighborhood association that excludes children. According to the 1989

---

*The seeming legal need to avoid even the slightest appearance of age discrimination was illustrated by recent advice coming from the Community Associations Institute to "drop the 'adults-only' swim hour and change it to the 'lap time/exercise hour' " that could be enjoyed by any association member. This step was necessary in order that the "specified swim hour could not be construed as discrimination against children," a situation that might provoke a lawsuit against the association. When Congress seeks to regulate the everyday life of all Americans, many unexpected consequences are likely to arise. See William S. Dunlevy, "Ask the Expert," *Common Ground* (May/June 2004), 61.

housing census, which reflects the shifting patterns of American demographics, 43 percent of the homes in the United States had at least one individual 55 years or older.[45]

The issue of age discrimination is not likely to go away for other reasons as well. It will often be possible to limit the presence of children indirectly. In the northern Virginia municipality of Falls Church, for example, the 2003 zoning approval of the Broadway condominium (with its 80 planned units) came with certain conditions. First, no more than eight children could live in the condominium. In an effort to avoid new educational expenses, the municipality required the developer to pay $15,000 per year for each child above this limit. Second, a census would be conducted each year for five years, and the developer could be required to pay up to $225,000 in total fines for the presence of "extra" children. Asked if this would be illegal discrimination, one local lawyer responded, "A developer is not required to put in child-friendly facilities." Moreover, the average price of a unit in the Broadway condominium is about $500,000, putting it out of the reach of most families that face the educational and other financial burdens of child rearing.[46]

In exercising their private property rights, neighborhood associations thus can engage in forms of social discrimination that a municipal government would not permit. To be sure, the precise extent of legally acceptable exclusions—which kinds of people can be kept out legally, and which forms of discrimination will be prohibited—are currently being worked out in the courts, legislative bodies, and other policymaking forums. Whether it would be possible to create a neighborhood association limited, say, to unmarried adults, gay people, or people who are deaf or blind remains legally in question.

Such issues may have to be confronted in the near future. As the *New York Times* reported in 2004, "Retirement communities are springing up that let you grow old in the company of people with similar backgrounds or mutual passions that go far deeper than a shared interest in golf." They range from "communities for gay men and lesbians to centers shaped for members of specific ethnic groups. Retired military officers have formed communities around the country."[47] The *Washington Post* found similarly in 2004 that developers were "building an archipelago of gay retirement communities across the Sun Belt."[48] The demand for new homes has been exceeding the supply in these gay neighborhood associations, creating long waiting lists and high prices—and high profits for developers clamoring to build more such developments. Carefree Cove is a gated community for gay men and lesbian women in the Blue Ridge Mountains of North Carolina. On discovering she could move to such a neighborhood association, one prospective resident exclaimed, "Oh, my God—there's my dream right there."[49] In reflecting on the appeal of living among people who share the same social preferences, one resident who had recently moved to a gay neighborhood association commented that "it's just wonderful to be able to take a walk and hold hands" in your own neighborhood.[50]

The trend toward specialized social environments for senior citizens reflects the fact that retirees are not tied to job locations. Enjoying longer life expectancies and active lifestyles following retirement, and released from the constraints of earning a living in a particular place, senior citizens are now free to join with others of similar tastes and interests in a common neighborhood environment. The future may see retirement neighborhoods created specifically for the most avid tennis players, bridge players, book readers, or Italian speakers.

For some people, choosing a living arrangement based on common consumptive motives may seem unworthy or trivial in a nation founded on puritan values of hard work (and in which its citizens on average still work more days per year than the citizens of other similarly rich nations). Where social segregation occurred in the past, it was often based on a shared need for housing close to a common job location—in the extreme case, an industry town. Indeed, Yale law professor Carol Rose suggests that part of the opposition to social segregation in neighborhood associations today may reflect "some sort of Puritanism going on—people are now sorting themselves on the basis of what they like to do, rather than what they have to do, their jobs," and this seems objectionable to at least some of our latter-day puritans.[51]

Some people assume that neighborhood association residents want conformity, but the *New York Times* finds otherwise in at least some cases. Reporting on a community in southern California, the *Times* reported, "Sunset Hall in Los Angeles bills itself as a 'home for free-thinking elders.' " Other examples identified by the *Times* include "a residence for artists in the works in Manhattan, the ElderSpirit Center . . . [a community] based on spiritual principles . . . in Abingdon, Virginia, and an assisted-living center in Gresham, Oregon, for retirees who are deaf or blind."[52] In a recently created northern Virginia neighborhood association, EcoVillage, "the idea is to live in harmony with Earth, and with one another. Residents have forged an uncommonly tight-knit neighborhood, with covenants designed to foster a sense of community, and promoted an equally remarkable devotion to protecting the environment, with homes and land use rules that take nature into consideration."[53]

Many associations center on shared religious beliefs. At the Martha Franks Baptist Retirement Center in South Carolina, one resident commented, "One can become more faithful here in church attendance because they make it so convenient." She added, "I feel like I need the support of Christian people," who are among her neighbors.[54] Eric Jacobsen, associate pastor at the First Presbyterian Church in Missoula, Montana, asserts that a successful "community also requires grace." Most neighborhoods will experience internal tensions, and the presence of a shared religious commitment may go far to defuse resident disagreements. As Jacobsen explains, "We also need forgiveness from our neighbors whom we will invariably offend in the course of living in close proximity to one another. And, as it is nearly impossible to offer grace until we have experienced grace, therefore, the theological promise that God provides grace freely is foundational to many communities." The building of a healthy social environment may require "some more visiting among neighbors" and this will be encouraged in those neighborhoods where "the church and the Christians in that community have a distinct and vital role to play."[55]

Another rapidly growing area of development involves the building of assisted-living communities for the advanced elderly, communities that provide on-site medical facilities and tailor their services to senior citizens who are in their 70s, 80s, and 90s—decades when uncertain health becomes a greater concern. If a unit owner's health deteriorates significantly, he or she can move into an intensive care facility located within the neighborhood association. Purchasing a unit in this type of neighborhood association becomes in effect a new form of private health insurance. To a degree many health care professionals do not yet seem to appreciate, these advanced-elderly communities are likely to become an important part of the nation's future health care system.

Although there seems to be little interest in enforcement, some of the new socially segregated neighborhood associations would seem to violate the Fair Housing Act's prohibitions against discrimination based on "race, color, national origin, religion, sex, handicap or familial status."[56] In cases involving racial discrimination, federal law is enforced, not only against explicit discriminatory actions, but also against informal "steering" practices designed to maintain racially homogeneous communities. Even if it is currently illegal, however, few Americans would likely object to the creation of an Irish, Chinese, or other neighborhood association based on national origin. The fact that enforcement is presently limited mainly to racial discrimination probably reflects a deep national ambivalence about the demands of strong community and the need to enforce existing laws against a wide range of discrimination.

The tendency may increasingly be—again, race excluded—to look the other way with respect to violations of the Fair Housing Act's precise language. It may also be possible to get around this legislation—for example, by requiring that a resident of a neighborhood association "speak" as opposed to "be" Norwegian (thus potentially avoiding the federal prohibition against discrimination based on national origin). Harvard political scientist Nancy Rosenblum asks whether a new neighborhood association "formed by orthodox Jews" should be permitted by the law to enforce the requirement "that males must wear yarmulkes in common areas on holy days." According to Rosenblum, "the consensus of commentators is that courts should enforce this covenant" as long as it really represents "the unanimous wishes of the original members."[57] If few non-Jews choose to join such an association, the result for all practical purposes will be the formation of a private neighborhood association limited to orthodox Jews.

Tastes in America are infinitely varied. While one community association might define its character by wearing yarmulkes on the Sabbath, other associations might have much different ideas. Reporting in the *Chicago Tribune*, Mary Umberger notes, "I've come across residential enclaves that appeal specifically to golfers, airplane owners, horse lovers, and even to Latvians." A neighborhood association she found near Las Vegas set a "new standard," however. In 1999, it included 177 custom homes and 350 condominiums on 550 acres, but—distinctively—the plans also included "more than a dozen shooting ranges." As Umberger noted, this new association was designed for a special group of unit owners, a community of "gun lovers."[58]

University of Virginia law professor Glen Robinson comments, "Conventional wisdom is that covenants based on such personal attributes as race, religion, or ethnicity are unenforceable, though aside from racial restrictions . . . there is remarkably little case law to support this assumption. There is equally little examination of why it should be so."[59] Such issues are likely to receive growing judicial attention; as law professor Stewart Sterk notes, "Community association law is in its infancy, or at best early adolescence."[60]

Conclusion

The United States is an individualistic society; Americans are known as a people who emphasize individual rights and freedoms. Marxism never had much appeal in this country. European democratic socialism was more successful— it won a few important converts, such as Eugene Debs and Norman Thomas— but was never able to challenge the established Republican and Democratic parties. Yet the rise of private neighborhood associations has shown a different side of the American character. The neighborhood association might be described as socialism, American style—privately established, voluntarily chosen individual by individual, and limited to a small geographic scale.

In most neighborhood associations, members must conform very closely to group rules and expectations. Nevertheless, Americans today are apparently demonstrating a wide desire for physical and social association with similar kinds of people in a closely shared immediate environment. At least at the neighborhood level, many Americans are seemingly willing to put up with tight collective controls over their own actions in order to gain similarly tight controls over their neighbors' actions. By contrast, if local governments in the public sector attempted to impose this type of discipline, strong criticisms and protests would likely result. In the context of private neighborhood associations, however, such tight controls have been accepted as a legitimate exercise of consumer sovereignty. In this circumstance, paradoxically, exercising the freedom of individual choice results in the future surrender of significant spheres of personal choice. Yet the right to make such a choice, however paradoxical, is itself an important part of the full set of individual rights enjoyed by all Americans.

NOTES

1. *Village of Belle Terre v. Boraas,* 416 U.S. 1 (1974).
2. William Cronon, "The Trouble with Wilderness; or, Getting Back to the Wrong Nature," in Cronon, ed., *Uncommon Ground: Rethinking the Human Place in Nature* (New York: Norton, 1995), 87, 88, 89–90. See also William Cronon, *Changes in the Land: Indians, Colonists and the Ecology of New England* (New York: Hill and Wang, 1983).
3. Garrett Hardin, "The Tragedy of the Commons," *Science* 162 (December 13, 1968).
4. James L. Winokur, "The Mixed Blessings of Promissory Servitudes: Toward Optimizing Economic Utility, Individual Liberty, and Personal Identity," *Wisconsin Law Review* 1989 (January/February 1989), 18.
5. Paula A. Franzese, "Common Interest Communities: Standards of Review and Review of Standards," *Washington University Journal of Law & Policy* 3 (2000), 674.
6. Susan Straight, "Wellington Clicks with New Residents," *Washington Post,* February 15, 2003, J2.
7. Lucia Anna Trigiani, "Sample Rules That Really Work," paper presented to the Community Leadership Forum, sponsored by the Community Associations Institute, Orlando, Florida, October 24–26, 2002.
8. Cited in Michael C. Kim, "Involuntary Sale: Banishing an Owner from the Condominium Community," *John Marshall Law Review* 31 (Winter 1998), 430.
9. Trigiani, "Sample Rules That Really Work."
10. Kenneth Budd, *Be Reasonable!: How Community Associations Can Enforce Rules without Antagonizing Residents, Going to Court, or Starting World War III* (Alexandria, VA: Community Associations Institute, 1998), 7.
11. David Guterson, "No Place Like Home," *Harper's* 287 (November 1992).
12. *Portola Hills Community Association v. James,* 4 Cal. App. 4th 289 (1992).
13. *Berrardo Villas Management Corp. Number Two v. Black,* 190 Cal. App. 3d 153 (1987).
14. Gerald Korngold, *Private Land Use Controls: Balancing Private Initiative and the Public Interest in the Homeowners Association Context* (Cambridge, MA: Lincoln Institute of Land Policy, 1995), 10, 9, 6, 5, 7.
15. See Katharine N. Rosenberry, "Home Businesses, Llamas, and Aluminum Siding: Trends in Covenant Enforcement," *John Marshall Law Review* 31 (Winter 1998), 487.
16. *Hidden Harbour Estates, Inc. v. Norman,* Court of Appeals of Florida, Fourth District, 309 So. 2d at 181–82 (1975).
17. Ibid., 182.
18. See "The Reasonable Pet: An Examination of the Enforcement of Restrictions in California Common Interest Developments after *Nahrstedt v. Lakeside Village Condominium Association, Inc.,*" *Santa Clara Law Review* 36, no. 3 (1996), 795.
19. *Nahrstedt v. Lakeside Village Condominium Association,* 878 P. 2d at 1282 (Cal. 1994).
20. See Budd, *Be Reasonable!,* 15.

21. Casey J. Little, "*Riss v. Angel:* Washington Remodels the Framework for Interpreting Restrictive Covenants," *Washington Law Review* 73 (April 1998), 435.

22. Wayne S. Hyatt and Jo Anne P. Stubblefield, "The Identity Crisis of Community Associations: In Search of The Appropriate Analogy," *Real Property, Probate & Trust Journal* 27 (Winter 1993), 691–92.

23. *Hidden Harbour Estates v. Basso,* 393 So. 2d at 640 (Fla. 1981). This case is discussed in Franzese, "Common Interest Communities," 685.

24. Budd, *Be Reasonable!,* 16.

25. Information related by a personal acquaintance living in the association.

26. *Midlake on Big Boulder Lake, Condominium Association v. Cappucio,* Superior Court of Pennsylvania, 673 A. 2d 340 (1996); see discussion of this case in Wayne S. Hyatt and Susan F. French, *Community Association Law* (Durham, NC: Carolina Academic Press, 1998), 228–29.

27. Quoted in Budd, *Be Reasonable!,* 63.

28. Kimberly J. Wind, "When an Association Needs an Attorney," *Condo Management Online* (1998), http://www.condomgmt.com/Articles/legal/010.html (accessed December 13, 2002).

29. *Levandusky v. One First Avenue Apartment Corporation,* 553 N.E. 2nd at 1322 (N.Y. 1990).

30. *Lamden v. La Jolla Shores Clubdominium Homeowners Association,* 980 P. 2d at 942, 954 (Cal. 1999).

31. Franzese, "Common Interest Communities," 680.

32. *Shelley v. Kraemer,* 334 U.S. 1 (1948).

33. Michael Sarbanes and Kathleen Skullney, "Taking Communities Seriously: Should Community Associations Have Standing in Maryland?" *Maryland Journal of Contemporary Legal Issues* 6 (Spring/Summer 1995), 296.

34. Glen O. Robinson, "Communities," *Virginia Law Review* 83 (March 1997), 299–300.

35. Sam Walker, "New Jock City," *Wall Street Journal,* February 28, 2003, W4.

36. Robinson, "Communities."

37. See Nicole Napolitano, "The Fair Housing Act Amendments and Age Restrictive Covenants in Condominiums and Cooperatives," *St. John's Law Review* 73 (Winter 1999).

38. Doreen Heisler and Warren Klein, *Inside Look at Community Association Homeownership—Facts, Perceptions* (Alexandria, VA: Community Associations Institute, 1996), 65.

39. Andrew Jacobs, "Still Working, Boomers 'Retire' to Resorts," *New York Times,* August 26, 2001, 1.

40. *Ritchey v. Villa Nueva Condominium Association,* 81 Cal. App. 3d 688 (1978).

41. *White Egret Condominium, Inc. v. Franklin,* Supreme Court of Florida, 379 So. 2d at 351 (1979).

42. Napolitano, "The Fair Housing Amendments Act and Age Restrictive Covenants in Condominiums and Cooperatives," 283.

43. Ibid., 280–85.

44. Laurence E. Kinsolving, "Age Restricted Communities," *Condo Management Online* (1998), http://www.condomgmt.com/Articles/legal/024.html (accessed December 13, 2002).

45. Ellen Hirsch de Haan, "Aging in Place—The Development of Naturally Occurring Retirement Communities," *CAI's Jou. nal of Community Association Law* 1, no. 1 (1998), 15.

46. See Peter Whoriskey, "No Children? No Problem!: Builder's Deal Aimed at Curbing Falls Church School Growth," *Washington Post* (May 25, 2003), A1.

47. Hilary Appelman, "All Your Neighbors Are Just Like You," *New York Times* (April 13, 2004), E1.

48. Lee Hockstader, "Gray and Gay?: These Communities Want You," *Washington Post* (May 31, 2004), A1

49. Appelman, "All Your Neighbors Are Just Like You."

50. Hockstader, "Gray and Gay."

51. Comments made at a conference on "Private Neighborhood Associations and Liberty," Montreal, Canada, June 3–6, 2004.

52. Appelman, "All Your Neighbors Are Just Like You," E1.

53. Jason Ukman, "New Standard of Living Blossoms at 'EcoVillage': Loudoun Subdivision's Residents Bond through Social, Environmental Pact," *Washington Post* (May 31, 2004), B1.

54. Appelman, "All Your Neighbors Are Just Like You," E1.

55. Eric O. Jacobsen, "Receiving Community: The Church and the Future of the New Urbanist Movement," *Journal of Markets and Morality* 6 (Spring 2003), 78–79.

56. 42 U.S.C. 3604 (Section 804).

57. Nancy L. Rosenblum, *Membership and Morals: The Personal Uses of Pluralism in America* (Princeton, NJ: Princeton University Press, 1998), 126.

58. Mary Umberger, "A Builder with a Target Audience: Gun Lovers," *Chicago Tribune* (May 15, 1999), New Homes 1.

59. Robinson, "Communities," 302.

60. Stewart E. Sterk, "Minority Protection in Residential Private Governments," *Boston University Law Review* 77 (April 1997), 307.

3
Neighborhood Association Governance

A home is not only a place in which to live but also one of the most important forms of individual financial investment—and increasingly American homes are located in neighborhood associations. At present, the value of U.S. housing in neighborhood associations exceeds $1.8 trillion, which is more than 15 percent of the value of all residential real estate (and 9 percent of the value of real estate of all kinds).[1] A single, large neighborhood association can easily include $500 million in total investment value among all the unit owners. Currently, unit-owner equity in U.S. neighborhood associations equals about one-third of the total value of all the shareholdings in U.S. business corporations.

As a result, the quality of neighborhood governance can significantly influence not only the quality of the surrounding environment but also the unit owners' financial well-being.[2] Even if residents plan to move away in the near future, the expected long-run quality of their neighborhood environment will still be important to them because it can significantly affect their home's selling price. Similarly, nonresident owners will have a strong financial incentive to demand high-quality neighborhood governance—not only because they can charge higher rents at present, but also because expert leadership increases the value of their investment.

One important area of neighborhood association decisionmaking, as described in chapter 2, is the regulation of land use through covenants and other association rules. Associations also have two other important responsibilities: providing neighborhood services and collecting monetary assessments to pay for these services. According to Sandra Rosen, a long-time advisor to neighborhood associations, "No community can run efficiently and successfully without some sort of orderly government. . . . A condominium association," like other neighborhood associations, "is created to fill the need for government" according to the provisions of the neighborhood constitution.[3]

Neighborhood "Public" Services

As part of maintaining an attractive neighborhood, most private neighborhood governments provide services. Nationally, 64 percent of neighborhood associations take care of garage collection; 54 percent clean up the streets; 53 percent assume the responsibility for street lighting; and 12 percent provide police patrols.[4] According to one survey, neighborhood associations with between 151 and 350 housing units offered the following popular amenities: a swimming pool (76 percent); a clubhouse (56 percent); tennis courts (45 percent); a playground (37 percent); a lake/pond (30 percent); a park area (29 percent); and a golf course (4 percent). (Among neighborhood associations with more than 500 housing units, 19 percent had golf courses.)[5] To pay for such services, the typical operating budget of a neighborhood association ranges from $100,000 to $400,000 per year. However, 5 percent of the neighborhood associations belonging to the Community Associations Institute had annual budgets in 1991 of more than $1.5 million.[6]

Neighborhood associations are responsible for the routine maintenance of the common areas. Numerous small details must be handled properly to maintain an attractive environment. One report, for example, described some of the mundane but important considerations necessary in maintaining the landscaping around a neighborhood swimming pool:

> One concern . . . in relationship to plantings around pools is tree roots, which can prove to be a very serious problem. Both ficus and eucalyptus trees, which are popular around swimming pools, have some of the most aggressive water-seeking tree roots. These aggressive roots can wreak havoc around a pool.
>
> Plantings around pools also raise homeowner concerns about bees and plant debris and how they can affect the enjoyment of the pool area. We all know that flowers attract bees and that flowers are also an important part of what makes a landscape appealing. Most homeowners, after some thought, would rather have the bees than a bland landscape with no flowers.[7]

Neighborhood associations are responsible for maintaining the common walls, building entrances, plumbing and electricity, and other parts of neighborhood properties exterior to the individual units. One association even provided maintenance for its unit owners' garage doors. So when 80 of the 300 doors malfunctioned, association management proposed replacing these 80 with an improved model; however, the association bylaws required that all garage doors be manufactured by the same company and otherwise uniform.

The highly contentious decision came down to fixing only the 80 broken doors or replacing all 300 doors with the improved model—a costly proposition that would have required an increased assessment.[8]

Another important function in many neighborhood associations is protecting residents' personal security. Due in part to the popularity of neighborhood associations, the total number of private security guards in the United States is now greater than the total number of police officers in the public sector.[9] Some neighborhood associations also provide such services as bus transportation, child care, nursery schools, health clinics, and a community newsletter. Fully 95 percent of association board members surveyed nationwide in 1990 believed their association's full membership regarded it as either an "excellent" or "good" provider of common services. Only 22 percent believed that a local public government could deliver some current association services more efficiently.[10] Indeed, past studies have suggested that, compared with service delivery by a private company, government provision of a service on average about doubles the cost.[11]

Neighborhood associations also benefit from a more homogeneous population, which allows for establishing clearer goals in service delivery. No matter how diverse preferences are within a municipal jurisdiction, one level of service is usually provided for all, leaving some groups or individuals disappointed. Because of their typically smaller size and tighter entrance controls, neighborhood associations can avoid this problem by attracting similar unit owners who demand about the same levels and qualities of services.*

Neighborhood associations may assume even more service responsibilities in the future. However, double taxation is currently inhibiting that process. Association unit owners pay not only for services that are delivered privately within their own association, but also for some of the same services delivered elsewhere in the municipality. Furthermore, though usually organized as nonprofit corporations, neighborhood associations are not tax-exempt and thus may be responsible for paying property taxes on the common elements (the unit owners pay property taxes on their own individual units directly to their municipality). An incorporated neighborhood association maintains nonprofit status because it does not distribute association income as dividends to unit owners or as payments to its officers.

Neighborhood associations also complain that property taxes and association assessments are treated differently with respect to federal (and some state) income taxes. For federal tax purposes, municipal property taxes are deductible,

---

*To be sure, as neighborhood associations mature over time, they may become more diverse in their populations. After 20 or 30 years, for example, some of the older residents whose children have grown up and moved away will still be living in the same place, creating a mixture of older and younger unit owners.

while private assessments paid to neighborhood associations are not. Therefore, neighborhood associations have a significant tax incentive to incorporate as a municipality. The fact that so many neighborhood associations have been created, despite the tax disadvantages, further testifies to the attractiveness of collective property ownership for home buyers.

Admittedly, double taxation and the less favorable tax treatment of assessments may well diminish and eventually disappear. As the number of neighborhood associations grows, unit owners' political clout will increase correspondingly. Some entrepreneurial politicians are likely to run for office on the slogan "Fair treatment for neighborhood associations," and the federal government and state legislatures are likely at some point to respond. Locally, some jurisdictions, such as Houston, Kansas City, and Montgomery County, Maryland, have already established rebate programs to partly compensate neighborhood associations for assuming public service burdens.[12] At the state level, New Jersey's Municipal Services Act (1991) requires local governments to reimburse neighborhood associations in part for the common services—such as garbage collection—they provide.

If the current tax differences are eliminated, however, neighborhood associations may come to be seen more and more as equivalent to public municipalities. If neighborhood associations then are seen legally as "state actors," their governance flexibility and operating freedom—currently derived from their perceived private status—could be curtailed or abolished. Neighborhood associations will have to carefully assess this risk in planning future political strategy.

Neighborhood "Taxes"

To cover the costs of common service delivery and other management activities, neighborhood associations levy financial assessments—"private taxes"—on their unit owners. In an average neighborhood association, assessments range from $100 to $300 per month, although some are much higher—in the thousands of dollars monthly for luxury condominiums and cooperatives. The total assessments collected by neighborhood associations across the United States now equal about $30 billion per year, while residential and business property taxes assessed by local governments total around $250 billion per year.

Unlike municipalities, neighborhood associations rarely base their assessments on the precise market value of the individual units. Instead, assessments are generally levied in the same proportions as voting rights are allocated. Many neighborhood associations assign one vote to each unit, so assessments are also equal among all the unit owners. Another common method of allocating voting rights and assessment burdens is by the proportion of square feet of each unit compared with all other units.

A main goal in designing a neighborhood association's constitution is to prevent any one subgroup within the association from "taxing" another group for its own purposes. Indeed, the effectiveness of the constitutional protections against internal redistribution could affect significantly the value of the housing units and the developer's profits. A wealthy home buyer will usually be unwilling to join a neighborhood association if there is any real prospect that his or her wealth will be tapped for the general benefit of other unit owners. Given the absence of redistributive purposes, a neighborhood association would be most unlikely to seek to impose an internal income tax on its unit owners.

The Neighborhood "Legislature"

Neighborhood associations, as noted previously, are usually organized under state law as nonprofit private corporations. As such, their governance features follow many of the standard arrangements of corporate governance found most widely in American business. The final authority for association actions rests with the board of directors (in other words, the board is the association's governing "legislature"). In turn, the board—frequently five to seven members—is directly elected by the unit owners (the neighborhood "stockholders"). According to one survey, 70 percent of unit owners voted in their association's most recent election—a proportion much higher than typically found in federal and state elections in the public sector.[13]

Subject to the provisions of the neighborhood constitution, including any limits that may be imposed therein on board actions, the board of directors sets the policies for covenant enforcement, the use of neighborhood common areas, the provision of neighborhood services, and the conduct of other neighborhood activities. Like the directors of a private business corporation, association board members legally have a "fiduciary duty" to the association. Board members, for example, must disclose any conflicts of interest arising from their roles on the board and their status as potential contractors with the association. Tonia Sellers and Jay Lazega note that "due to time or budgetary constraints, boards routinely prioritize. . . . This creates a potential conflict of interest in that board members could prioritize repairs affecting their homes ahead of others with a greater need for repair. Board members have a strict [legal] duty in these situations to exercise their judgment in the best interests of the association" as a whole.[14]

With an elected board of directors, a neighborhood association is thus not a direct democracy. For many issues, the neighborhood association might be described as a small representative democracy—a small private "republic."

However, most neighborhood boards submit some especially important questions to a full vote of all the unit owners. Under state law in Florida, if a condominium board has approved a budget requiring more than a 15 percent increase in spending, a petition signed by 10 percent of the unit owners can force a vote of the full membership to reconsider the budget. Therefore, a neighborhood association might in effect have two legislative bodies, the board of directors for many decisions, and the full membership of all unit owners for other decisions. In this respect, the association's governance system resembles town democracies in New England.

Board membership is voluntary; unlike business corporations, members are not paid. Yet, board members face difficult decisions, high demands on their time, possible legal risks, frequent complaints from other unit owners, and the occasional abusive critic. It is not surprising that, in many associations, recruiting new board members is difficult. Absent monetary compensation, board members must be attracted by other considerations, ranging from an altruistic concern to serve the neighborhood to petty desires for personal gain. Rosen comments that "the reasons for volunteering are as varied as the people who volunteer. Some who volunteer want to gain recognition, or accomplish something they feel is important. Others simply want to contribute to their community, while others seek to meet people and feel a part of a group activity."[15] Still others may simply be on a "power trip."

The smallest neighborhood associations may have no separate board of directors—the board in effect is the full set of unit owners. For example, the Brookwood Farm Homeowner Association in Maryland consists of 16 large homes located along a single street, with a large "natural" common area on both sides of the street where it intersects with a county road. According to association rules, nonfinancial matters must be approved by a full majority vote of all the unit owners and financial matters, such as the annual budget, by a two-thirds vote. When it proved impossible in many cases to find the necessary 11 members to attend meetings regarding financial decisions, the association in 2003 amended the constitution to allow voting by email. (In order to guarantee an honest count, each unit owner "cc's" his or her vote to all the other unit owners. The one unit owner without email still votes by paper ballot.)

Most neighborhood associations, however, are larger and elect board members for a term from one to three years. Terms longer than one year are usually staggered to maintain a continuity of membership. Most associations have constitutional provisions that allow unit owners to recall board members before their terms expire. Under Florida law, if 10 percent of condominium owners so petition, a recall election must be held with the results decided by a simple majority.

Board members generally organize themselves by choosing a chairperson—and subcommittee chairpersons—from among themselves. Otherwise, each member has an equal status; unit owners do not vote on separate offices (such as president, treasurer, or legal counsel). Board candidates historically have run as individuals without party labels. In the election, all nominated candidates run against each other and the winners are those candidates who receive the highest number of votes—up to the total number of board seats to be filled in that election. A unit owner may have one vote to cast, or may have a number of votes equal to the number of open board seats. Each unit owner can then distribute his or her votes among the candidates.

Most neighborhood associations do not require that a winning board member receive some minimum percentage of votes. Hence, if the field of candidates is large, the results may become less predictable and the chances of a fringe candidate winning election may be greater. In order to avoid this problem, various new alternative methods are now available that neighborhood associations might adopt for future elections (see chapter 15).

In a few associations, however, each board member needs at least 50 percent of the votes to win; this requirement can necessitate additional rounds of voting (or a voting procedure for the transfer of votes from initially lower-ranked candidates to higher-ranked candidates).[16] One voting system used by some associations (and by about 10 percent of U.S. business corporations) is called "cumulative voting," under which voters can assign multiple votes to the same candidate. Thus, if there are three open seats, and each voter has three votes, he or she can assign all three votes to the same individual (or can distribute the three votes among candidates in any other manner desired).

In most neighborhood associations, the elections are "at large"; all board members thus represent the full body of association unit owners. However, in some particularly large associations, the association may be divided into separate districts (like city wards). Each district might then have its own local board of directors to oversee the microinteractions among the housing units within this subneighborhood area. One district (or several combined) may also send a representative to an associationwide board of directors. For example, the private government of Reston, Virginia, comprises nine local subneighborhoods ("cluster associations"), each of which has its own governing board. These subneighborhoods together send four "district" representatives to the "Reston Association" board of directors, which also includes four "at large" members and one representative of Reston apartment owners.

If a unit has more than one legal owner, these owners must decide among themselves how to cast their single unit vote. Some associations require multiple owners to designate their official vote caster in writing. As is also the case with business corporations, unit owners can sign proxies so that their vote can be officially counted even when they are not physically present for an annual meeting or other election. Moreover, unlike public-sector practices, individuals who own more than one unit in a neighborhood association have multiple votes.

An association's board of directors generally operates by simple majority rule. It may decide, however, to submit an important issue to the full membership. Amendments to the neighborhood covenants, for example, generally require a supermajority vote of all the unit owners. Moreover, the required supermajority for amending a neighborhood constitution can vary with the type of amendment sought. In general, the more the amendment will alter the unit owners' original expectations, the higher the required supermajority.

There are typically subcommittees of the board of directors, such as the architectural review committee that in many associations handles covenants and other land use restrictions. Such a committee may have the authority to approve or reject specific applications from unit owners to modify their properties. An executive subcommittee of the board of directors may have the authority to take official action for the entire board. Other board subcommittees may simply have an advisory role. Any member of the neighborhood association may serve on such an advisory committee.

A neighborhood association is also subject to the jurisdiction of its municipal or other local public government. In a sense, then, the unit owners of a neighborhood association have two "local legislatures." They vote in neighborhood association elections as property owners and in municipal elections as residents of the public jurisdiction. Unit owners may be important political actors in the municipality even though many municipal decisions—such as the internal zoning of neighborhoods other than their own association—may not affect them very much. They may vote on local taxes that pay for municipal services of little benefit to their own neighborhood association. The existence of these dual legislatures can make the political workings of the municipality and the neighborhood association complex and uncertain.

The "Executive Branch"

As in the U.S. constitution, the role of the executive branch is established in a neighborhood constitution. The American constitution divides governing functions between the legislative, judicial, and executive branches and sets rules for their interactions. In other nations, the legislature may be the final governing authority and the leading executives are chosen directly from the legislature.* The board of directors of an American business corporation is more like a parliamentary regime, including some directors who are also executives. As in the

---

*Great Britain, for example, has no executive body independent of the legislature. Instead, the controlling party (or coalition of parties) in the Parliament chooses the Prime Minister and other cabinet members, most of whom are themselves also members of the legislature, and who then execute the laws.

business model, the neighborhood board of directors has final authority both in legislative and executive matters. Neighborhood associations have no president, mayor, or other top executive specifically elected to that office by the unit owners. Rather, the neighborhood officers are selected by the board of directors.

In about two-thirds of American business corporations at present, the chairperson of the corporation's board of directors has also been selected to be its chief executive officer (CEO). Most neighborhood associations follow a similar practice in which the top neighborhood executive is also the chairperson of the association's board of directors (he or she usually functions in both roles under the one title of neighborhood association "president"). Unless it is specifically stated in a neighborhood constitution, the president and other neighborhood association officers are not legally required to be members of the board of directors.

The president of a neighborhood association conducts board meetings, oversees the administration of association affairs, and has the authority to execute contracts and other documents. However, major decisions generally require the approval of the entire board. A neighborhood association president, for example, would typically need board approval in order to borrow any significant amounts of money in the association's name or to implement a plan for significant neighborhood improvements.

Given the association's governance structure, such tasks as assessment collection, parking enforcement, and covenant compliance checks are routinely handled in one of three ways. First, in some associations, board members or other unit owners may perform these tasks (this usually happens in the smallest associations). In other cases, the association may hire one or more employees to help carry out neighborhood functions. These employees report directly to the association's president and the board of directors. A third possibility is that the association may hire an outside professional manager or management firm.

According to the Community Associations Institute (CAI), about 50 percent of neighborhood associations hire a management company. The smaller associations, typically no more than 30 to 40 units, generally are run entirely by volunteers. CAI estimates that about 10 percent of associations operate on this basis. About 30 percent of neighborhood associations are managed by their own administrative staff of direct employees. (The remaining associations fall in intermediate categories.)[17]

CAI recommends that associations with more than 1,000 units or budgets of greater than $1 million have a full-time, on-site manager. At present about 7 percent of neighborhood associations have such "large scale association managers."[18] This person reports to the board of directors and is responsible for administering association affairs, which includes preparing a draft budget, hiring employees, negotiating contracts, and enforcing the covenants. Such managers of larger associations, according to CAI, should have "extensive business experience" and a university "educational background that includes public or recreational administration, or business administration, at the undergraduate or graduate level."[19]

There are also hybrid arrangements. The neighborhood association may rely for most functions on its own employees, but outsource some tasks to private contractors. Few neighborhood associations are large enough, for example, to employ their own crews to handle mechanical repair work. At the same time, some associations that hire management firms may directly employ their own pool lifeguards or security guards.

Outside Management Firms

If an outside management firm is hired, this selection (made by the association's "executive branch") is made as a business decision, not a political decision as in a municipal government. Private management firms are likely to bring greater professional expertise and past experience in association maintenance and upkeep. If a subsequent change is necessary, the act of selecting a new management firm is tantamount to dismissing the civil service of a municipal government, although considerably easier. In a 2000 CAI survey, 19 percent of the responding management companies had total budgets of more than $2 million, 14 percent had responsibility for more than 10,000 neighborhood association units, and the average CEO salary was $89,016.[20] Community association managers need a wide range of skills and may require formal study for this purpose. Under Florida law, the manager of a condominium with 50 or more units or an annual budget of greater than $100,000 must be licensed by the state's Department of Business and Professional Regulation and must pass a technical examination.[21]

Under the terms of a management contract, the manager from a private firm will have the delegated power to make some collective decisions for the neighborhood association. The manager might, for example, have the independent authority to hire and fire employees responsible for managing the association's golf course. The manager may choose outside subcontractors to clean the streets. He or she will have to have detailed working knowledge in many areas. For example, one landscape expert warns, "[It is important] to inspect the contractor's lawn equipment to ensure it is up to OSHA requirements. In addition, ask about how often the blades on the lawn mowers are sharpened. This will affect the way the turf appears after service. If the blades are sharp, the turf will appear well groomed; if the blades are not sharp, the turf will look like it has been 'hacked.' "[22]

An outside manager may also need to handle certain types of internal disagreements over acceptable land uses. Unfortunately, many associations obtain little professional assistance in interpreting and enforcing their covenants. But neutral outsiders can help to relieve tensions for neighbors who would otherwise be forced to pursue enforcement actions against other neighbors. Even in smaller neighborhood associations, one observer reports, the hiring of a professional manager to mediate among unit owners can "eliminate tension among owners"; not only that, "it increases the value of the units."[23] Where a management firm is hired, the top manager will normally have no personal connection with the neighborhood residents. Indeed, it is best that he or she not be a unit owner since, as one management expert says, the manager's job in dealing with complaining and sometimes unreasonable unit owners "is to shield the board [of directors] and to try to bring the situation under control."[24]

Early in the 20th century, the political theorists of the Progressive Era prescribed separating American government functions into distinct domains of "politics and administration."[25] At the "politics" level, the government's broad policy directions should be set, necessarily reflecting value choices. At the "administration" level, professional experts should implement these policies in a scientific and value-neutral fashion. In the following years, many small- and medium-sized municipalities in the United States adopted the "city manager" system of local government based on this concept. The local city council selected a professional to administer municipal affairs, subject to council oversight. Indeed, about half of all municipalities in the United States operate today under a city manager system of government.[26]

A city manager system can have a mayor, but many local municipalities operate without any elected executive officers. The city council, like the neighborhood association's board, is the only elected body and is the final authority in local government. Indeed, hiring an outside private management firm may come the closest to the original Progressive Era vision for a full separation of politics and administration in local government. In this respect, the rise of the private neighborhood association might even reflect the "progressive" tradition. As the President's Commission on Privatization pointed out in 1988, "Contracting out, for some, represents a revival in a new form of the old Progressive distinction between politics and administration, with the private contractor now taking the former place of the expert government administrator. . . . Just as the Progressives emphasized efficiency, the goal of contracting is to achieve maximum efficient service delivery for the price the government is willing to pay."[27]

The "Judicial Branch"

Neighborhood associations also need a way to accomplish basic judicial tasks—providing a process for appeal of neighborhood association decisions and enforcing the final decisions. Ultimately, as do other parts of American society, neighborhood associations may turn to federal and state courts. (The U.S. Supreme Court thus far has not heard a case that addressed a neighborhood association's legal authority.) Some unit owners in neighborhood associations, in fact, have already turned to state and other lower courts. Indeed, one report finds a "tidal wave of litigation" involving neighborhood associations.[28] Often the disputes erupt over management details; the unit owner is hoping to find a friendly court to overturn an association decision. Many unit owners say they want to protect their neighborhood association's autonomy until they end up on the losing side of a neighborhood dispute. Understandably, the courts are reluctant to override association boards of directors on small administrative details, so most legal challenges by unit owners have been unsuccessful.

Neighborhood associations do offer some internal appeal processes, however. A unit owner who receives a negative decision from an architectural review subcommittee can appeal to the full board of directors. If the board offers no help, the unit owner may in some cases be able to obtain a referendum vote among the association's full membership. Florida condominium lawyer R. Michael Kennedy notes that many existing condominiums have "complaint committees" that can "act as an unbiased buffer between the board and the unit owner." Although these "grievance committees" may not be specifically mentioned in the association's constitution, and thus lack a "substantial legal foundation" for enforcing their decisions, they have nevertheless been effective. The committee can use social pressure and its own powers of persuasion to make its decisions stick, and experience to date has shown that "quite often the committee's suggested resolution is adopted by all concerned."[29]

On the whole, however, the neighborhood association's "judicial branch" is still undeveloped. Informal methods of judicial action aside, most standard neighborhood constitutions written by real estate developers do not provide for an internal appeals process. Yet, given the long delays and high costs associated with going to court, neighborhood associations may want to create alternative private instruments for dispute resolution. Labor unions and employers have long used arbitration (both nonbinding and binding) to help settle disagreements. Some disputes between unit owners and neighborhood associations might similarly be assigned to outside arbitrators—groups perhaps comprised of architectural, land use design, or other urban professionals (see chapter 17).[30] Florida at present requires parties in a dispute to enter into nonbinding arbitration before taking their case to court.

A neighborhood judicial system's second basic function is to interpret, and penalize those who violate, the association's rules. Neighborhood associations often find it difficult to enforce their covenants, collect the assessments owed by unit owners, and generally enforce compliance with their rules. Unlike a municipality, these associations do not have the authority to jail someone who defies them; in order to obtain direct coercive methods, they must turn either to a state or local court or to the officers of their public government.

A particularly sensitive issue for neighborhood associations is the enforcement of rules about owning and handling unit owners' pets. Pet owners may become irate about and resist attempts to control their animals. One expert in neighborhood association law suggests that "man's best friend" may be "the association's worst enemy."[31] Another advisor to neighborhood associations reports that "the biggest problem with pet regulations [is that] they have no teeth." Even "fines do no good in most cases. It used to be that you could lien a property for fines. Now the only thing you can do is go through small-claims court."[32]

In many ways, the private government overseeing a neighborhood association is an alternative to a municipal government. It resolves matters that in a municipal context would be regarded as a local issue. Yet the distinction can also be overdrawn. One commentator described the interdependence of public and private authority with regard to enforcing pet rules:

> There are numerous advantages to taking your case to the local authorities, foremost among them swift resolution. Animal-control violations are like any other civil or criminal matters, after all, carrying with them the right to a speedy trial.
>
> Stronger sanctions are another plus. Municipal courts administer state and local statutes that have bite, and they can impose fines as well as jail sentences. Also, some states allow the impoundment of an offending animal, and, in the proper circumstances, the animal can be destroyed.
>
> On the negative side, when you opt for municipal involvement, you lose the promise of confidentiality given to complainants. Even more importantly, you bear an increased burden of proof, because municipal violations must be proved beyond a reasonable doubt, as opposed to the looser general standard of a preponderance of evidence used to enforce most covenants.[33]

Neighborhood associations also sometimes find it difficult to get unit owners to pay their assessments, and some associations end up facing major problems with some unit owners' long-term nonpayment. Existing sanctions may be too severe (outright repossession) or too mild (a lien paid when the unit is sold). Critics of neighborhood associations commonly complain about the arbitrary enforcement of draconian rules against those who have not paid their assessments. Many stories have circulated—no doubt true in some cases—about the "elderly widow" who, with little advance notice, was ousted from her home by a heartless neighborhood association.

Law professor James Winokur reports that neighborhood associations have had problems in collecting assessments in part because of the "extremely inefficient and often frustrating" methods available for handling delinquencies.[34] One problem is that associations typically have had a junior status among creditors. If a bankruptcy occurs, there is often nothing left for the neighborhood association once higher-ranking creditors have been paid.

This problem might be resolved, as Winokur suggests, by following the recommendations of the 1982 Uniform Common Interest Ownership Act, which includes upgrading neighborhood associations' creditor status. With these new and better methods, it should be possible to "substantially improve the financial strength of associations" and to reduce conflicts over nonpayment of assessments.[35]

Conclusion

Although it has a nonprofit status, the neighborhood association's basic governing structure generally follows the corporate model. The board of directors holds the final legal authority for the association's actions and acts as the unit owners' official representative. Board actions are subject to review by the unit owners themselves—and can be overturned by a direct vote of the full membership—and by outside governments and the American judicial system. In recent years, state governments have become increasingly involved in overseeing neighborhood association governance, in some areas setting out mandatory rules and procedures for association affairs.

A business model of governance is appropriate for many of the tasks inherent to a neighborhood association. However, the American corporate governance system itself is in flux today. The stockholders of major corporations, for example, have typically had less influence as "the owners" than they theoretically should have had. Boards of directors have often been captive to their corporations' top management. As a result, many business experts today are arguing for reform of corporate governance, for example, proposing new rules to prohibit a board chairperson from also being a corporation's chief executive officer.[36]

All this debate can be very important on the bottom line. A leading American student of corporate governance reports, "Institutional investors polled worldwide were willing to place, on average, a 25 percent premium on a company with good governance. The premium in the United States was 18 percent."[37] If the premium for good management is anywhere near as large in a neighborhood association, American unit owners will have many billions of dollars at stake in the quality of their neighborhood governance systems.

The association's governance system must function well to protect the quality of the neighborhood environment, deliver the neighborhood services, and undertake other neighborhood tasks. At present, the range of governance options considered in most neighborhood constitutions has been limited. Most developers and their lawyers pull boilerplate documents off the shelves. However, much as American business today is exploring new methods of corporate governance, there are also many options for changing neighborhood association governance (see part V).

NOTES

1. Clifford J. Treese, *Community Associations Factbook,* 1999 ed. (Alexandria, VA: Community Associations Institute, 1999), 19.

2. This point is emphasized with respect to local public governments in William A. Fischel, *The Homevoter Hypothesis: How Home Values Influence Local Government Taxation, School Finance, and Land-Use Policies* (Cambridge, MA: Harvard University Press, 2001).

3. Sandra F. Rosen, *Become an Effective Condo Board Member* (Lincoln, NE: iUniverse.com, Inc., 2000), 15.

4. *Community Associations Factbook,* 1999 ed., 13.

5. Clifford J. Treese, ed., *Community Associations Factbook,* 1993 ed., (Alexandria, VA: Community Associations Institute, 1993), 20.

6. Ibid., 22.

7. Robert Mayberry, "Relaxing By the Pool: Valuing Your Property's Amenities," *Condo Management Online* (1998), http://www.condomgmt.com/Articles/Pool/014.html (accessed December 13, 2002).

8. Jasmine Martirossian, *Decision Making in Communities: Why Groups of Smart People Sometimes Make Bad Decisions* (Alexandria, VA: Community Associations Institute, 2001), 36.

9. David J. Kennedy, "Residential Associations as State Actors: Regulating the Impact of Gated Communities on Nonmembers," *Yale Law Journal* 105 (December 1995), 766.

10. Cited in Robert Jay Dilger, *Neighborhood Politics: Residential Community Associations in American Governance* (New York: New York University Press, 1992), 90.

11. Dennis C. Mueller, *Constitutional Democracy* (New York: Oxford University Press, 1996), 258. See also Dilger, *Neighborhood Politics,* 89, which offers estimates that neighborhood associations are able to provide many public services at costs 30 to 60 percent below local governments in the public sector.

12. Dilger, *Neighborhood Politics,* 29.

13. Community Associations Institute, *National Survey of Community Association Homeowner Satisfaction,* Conducted by the Gallop Organization in March 1999 (Alexandria, VA: Community Associations Institute, June 23, 1999), 28.

14. Tonia C. Sellers and Jay S. Lazega, *Conflicts of Interest,* 3rd ed. (Alexandria, VA: Community Associations Institute, 2003), 5–6.

15. Rosen, *Become an Effective Condo Board Member,* 44.

16. P. Michael Nagle, *Guide to Annual Meetings, Special Meetings, and Elections,* 2nd ed., GAP Report No. 21 (Alexandria, VA: Community Associations Institute, 1997), 34.

17. Clifford J. Treese, *Introduction to Community Association Management, Governance and Services* (Alexandria, VA: Community Associations Institute, 2002), 5–6.

18. Ibid., 6.

19. Thomas Burgess, *Selecting an On-Site Manager,* 2nd ed. (Alexandria, VA: Community Associations Institute, 1996), 7.

20. Community Associations Institute, *Community Association Manager Compensation and Salary Survey* (Alexandria, VA: CAI Research Foundation, 2000), 6, 7, 16.

21. Peter M. Dunbar, *The Condominium Concept: A Practical Guide for Officers, Owners and Directors of Florida Condominiums,* 7th ed. (Tallahassee, FL: Aras Publishing, 2000), 39.

22. Steven T. Richart, "How Can I Select a Good Landscape Contractor for My Property?" *Condo Management Online* (2004), http://www.condomgmt.com/Articles/Landscaping/006.html (accessed December 6, 2004).

23. Ruth Ann Gould and Jeanne MacLellan, "Managing the Small Condominium," *Condo Management Online* (1998), http://www.condomgmt.com/Articles/manage/023.html (accessed December 13, 2002).

24. Ellen Dolan, "How to Grow the Best Manager," *Condo Management Online* (1998), http://www.condomgmt.com/Articles/manage/019.html (accessed December 13, 2002).

25. See Dwight Waldo, *The Administrative State: A Study of the Political Theory of American Public Administration* (New York: Holmes and Meier, 1984 [1948]).

26. International City/County Management Association, *The Municipal Year Book, 2001* (Washington, DC: International City/County Management Association), xii.

27. *Privatization: Toward More Effective Governance,* Report of the President's Commission on Privatization (Washington, DC, March 1988), 243–44.

28. Scott E. Mollen, "Alternative Dispute Resolution of Condominium and Cooperative Conflicts," *St. John's Law Review* 73 (Winter 1999), 81.

29. R. Michael Kennedy, "Enforcement of Covenants, Bylaws and Rules," *Condo Management Online* (1998), http://www.condomgmt.com/Articles/legal/022.html (accessed December 5, 2002).

30. Kenneth Budd, *Be Reasonable! How Community Associations Can Enforce Rules Without Antagonizing Residents, Going to Court, or Starting World War III* (Alexandria, VA: Community Associations Institute, 1998), 34–35.

31. Jordan I. Shifrin, *Guilt by Association: A Survival Guide for Homeowners, Board Members and Property Managers,* 2nd ed. (Lincoln, NE: Writers Club Press, 2001), 160.

32. Marge Imfeld, quoted in Julia E. Pheifer, "Beast Practices," *Common Ground—CAI's Magazine for Condominium and Homeowner Associations* (January/February 2001), 30.

33. Pheifer, "Beast Practices," 30.

34. James L. Winokur, "Meaner Lienor Community Associations: The 'Super Priority' Lien and Related Reforms under the Uniform Common Interest Ownership Act," *Wake Forest Law Review* 27, no. 2 (1992), 356, 357.

35. Ibid., 395, 394.

36. See, for example, Dana Hermanson, "21st Century Principles for U.S. Public Companies" (2002), statement provided by the Corporate Governance Center of Kennesaw State University, Kennesaw, Georgia, advising that "the roles of Board Chair and CEO should be separate."

37. B. Espen Eckbo, comments made at a roundtable on "Emerging Trends in Corporate Governance," *Corporate Board Member* (2001 Special Supplement), 6.

4

Other Constitutional Provisions

Writers of neighborhood association constitutions face many issues: How should the constitution be ratified initially? How can it be amended? Which neighborhood matters should be resolved in the constitution, and which left to unit owners to resolve later? Should the constitution formally establish a unit owners' "bill of rights"? If an issue of interpreting the constitution arises, how might it be resolved?

Since the U.S. constitution was first crafted (submitted to the 13 original states in 1787 and ratified by the last [Rhode Island] in 1790), many other nations have written constitutions and, in some cases, have written them multiple times. In fact, we are presently experiencing a period of unusual constitutional ferment in Europe and indeed all over the world. Although the U.S. constitution has not been significantly amended since 1919 (women's voting rights), several lesser amendments have been ratified, and state and local constitutions have continued to experience revision. In 2002, for example, the voters of San Francisco approved a basic change in their method for choosing their mayor, adopting a system of transferable voting in place of the more traditional methods.

The widest exercise in constitution writing in the United States today, however, is occurring at the neighborhood level. Since 1980, more than 150,000 neighborhood associations have been created in the United States, each with its own governance system set out in a constitution. Of course, many of these documents are very similar, often based on standard forms that real estate developers and their attorneys use. Yet, whether a neighborhood association chooses to or not, it is legally permitted to tailor its constitution to its own needs and preferences. Many of today's roughly 250,000 neighborhood associations may want to consider the desirability of significantly amending their constitutions in light of their governing experiences to date.

Speaking as both a current unit owner and advocate of reforms in neighborhood association governance, Joni Greenwalt finds that the original founding documents of many associations contain "too strict, outmoded, or too ridiculous rules," but that what "is written by man can be changed or completely thrown away by man (by woman too)." Thus, for many associations, the process of "changing, updating, and softening the covenants can be an extremely viable solution."[1] With specific regard to covenants, Greenwalt reports on the results of a volunteer panel's effort to revise its association's 20-year-old founding documents. Resident Michael Garard explained the revision process, noting that the original covenants "were okay for the time they were written, but things change over 20 years." He went on to explain:

> Because of our strong community support, we were able to use block captains and to coordinate several meetings with approximately 20 homeowners per meeting. All residents had a chance to voice their opinions.
> Some examples of the outdated ideas the original covenants contained included:
> —Garage doors must be closed.
> —No vans allowed
> —No satellite dishes
> —No in-home businesses
> We revised and softened the above, plus tried to give other items a more "black and white" definition.
> Out of homes, we had over 80% approval of the new covenants.[2]

The United States needed two tries to write the current U.S. constitution (replacing the Articles of Confederation). New York State's constitution requires a statewide referendum every 20 years on the issue of calling for a new constitutional convention.[3] Perhaps tomorrow's neighborhood associations will also explicitly mandate a process of constitutional review and potential change. Rather than simply copying standard language found in so many existing neighborhood constitutions, each neighborhood might think more grandly about the larger political issues of constitutional choice for its own future.

Ratifying the Neighborhood Constitution

In a neighborhood association, the initial decision to approve the constitution has been approved unanimously. As a condition of purchase, every buyer must agree to accept the association's governing rules—the land use covenants, the process for setting financial assessments, the neighborhood election procedures, and other constitutional provisions. Any subsequent purchasers must also meet the consent requirement. Although John Locke famously conceived of government as a voluntary compact formed among people previously living in a state of nature, the private neighborhood association is one of the few instances in the real world where all the governed have actually given their consent on the dotted line.

What purchasers have agreed to, to be sure, may not be as simple as it first appears. If every future contingency could be specified and if each prospective association member could read and understand the full constitutional document, then one could say that voluntary consent has been granted to all future association actions. In the real world, of course, advance knowledge is never perfect, people have limited time for reading, and most contracts allow for a wide range of future unspecified contingencies. The people who sign contracts implicitly assume that the other party's behavior will be "reasonable"—and if it is not, that a court will enforce such a behavioral standard, even without explicit language for every possible issue and outcome.

Homeowners are not always satisfied with court rulings, however. A California unit owner applied for permission to build a new perimeter fence on her property and a turret-style addition to her living and family rooms. Her association denied the request. In upholding this denial, the California court stated that neighborhood associations have "a broad authority to apply standards that are inherently subjective, and by their nature cannot be measured or qualified."[4] Although there may be no easy remedy, this subjectivity in making aesthetic judgments produces many neighborhood tensions and arouses considerable anxiety in some unit owners. One critic of neighborhood association powers maintains that "these mini governments, with the blessing of the courts, can reign supreme with the judicially conferred power to impose subjective, immeasurable, and unqualified standards."[5]

Another legal expert warns that, before moving in, prospective buyers should spend as much time studying a neighborhood association's "culture" as its legal documents.[6] A contract necessarily takes on a meaning within the context of a given society and set of behavioral expectations. In the case of a neighborhood association, the most relevant world will be that of the neighborhood itself. The buyer of a home in a neighborhood association is entering into a small society that may have many unstated rules. Some people will be good at "reading" these informal rules in advance, but others unfortunately will not.

Like the living constitution of the United States, a neighborhood constitution thus is less a precise formula that can determine exact future outcomes and more a set of rules and procedures by which neighborhood political institutions will function today and can change tomorrow. The most novel element new unit owners encounter is the high degree of collective controls placed on the use of their own property. When many people buy into a neighborhood association—and its constitution—they no doubt have an imperfect understanding of all the legal constraints that they are accepting. They may assume in particular that some of the normal American limitations on government interference with regard to private property use will continue to apply to their new neighborhood government.

Buyer ignorance can lead to trouble. In one survey of unit owners conducted by the Community Associations Institute, only 56 percent reported that they clearly understood the extent of the neighborhood land use restrictions before completing their unit purchase. Another 13 percent learned of the restrictions during the closing process, leaving another 31 percent who made this discovery "after moving in."[7] As James Winokur comments,

> Most prospective purchasers do not intelligently review the restrictions to which they subject themselves upon acceptance of a deed to land burdened by servitudes. The documentation typically makes long, boring reading for laypersons, who rarely retain counsel to review the documentation involved in home purchases. Even those who read the restrictions in advance may miscalculate their own future attitudes toward servitude restrictions, perhaps inaccurately expecting that friendly relations with neighbors will eliminate hostile disagreements between residents. Such optimistic expectations are often disappointed.[8]

Although some of the lack of communication is unavoidable, many real estate agents and neighborhood associations do a poor job of educating prospective buyers. Similarly, neighborhood documents often use obscure and confusing legal terms. Nevertheless significant uncertainties will remain, even if developers provide buyers with information in clearer language and with simpler examples, and if states adopt laws requiring real estate agents to disclose other additional details. Neighborhood association covenants, for example, may declare that future land use changes must be "consistent with" the neighborhood ambience. Such language is not likely to convey much information to the prospective purchaser. Similarly, the potential magnitude of future financial assessments will necessarily be left largely to the internal political processes of the association (although forms of "taxpayer rights" could be written into neighborhood constitutions).

In such respects, the act of ratifying a neighborhood constitution can be seen partly as a symbolic statement of joining a neighborhood community. The unit owner agrees to abide by the outcomes of community decisionmaking, both formal and informal. It is an agreement to accept the results as long as the neighborhood political process is conducted according to the prescribed rules of the neighborhood constitution. It will necessarily reflect to some extent an act of faith in the good will and common sense of fellow unit owners.

Transition to Unit Owner Control

The final approval of the initial neighborhood constitution may take several years, as more new purchasers move in. During this time, the neighborhood association must have a means of governance. This task normally falls to the developer, who will also have prepared the initial constitutional documents. Having made a large financial investment, the developer understandably is unwilling to turn over management control early in the project and risk home-owner interference with construction plans. For example, given the authority, the early unit owners might decide that they prefer more open space and many fewer housing units than shown in the development plans. As Amanda Hyatt comments, "the developer may fear that the unit owners will interfere with building and marketing efforts," acting to serve their own purposes in opposition to the developer's expectations for a more profitable project.[9]

It is generally accepted in the real estate industry that the developer of a neighborhood association must be legally protected from any such possibility. In almost all new associations, the founding documents specify that the developer will retain enough votes to control management until the latter stages of the project. In the most common arrangement, the developer in a new neighborhood association retains the majority of votes on the board of directors until 75 percent of the units are sold and occupied.[10] As a result, the neighborhood's early occupants are effectively disenfranchised, often for a year or more (and occasionally much longer, although state laws may limit the transitional period). A neighborhood association, then, begins its political life as a developer dictatorship and only gradually becomes a democracy of unit owners.

Even after the transition to unit owner control, the developer is generally protected from unit owners interfering with completion plans. By contrast, in a newly developing public municipality, each new resident receives full voting rights soon after arrival. In many real world cases, the newer residents have used their voting power to overturn the municipality's land development plans. As a result, large remaining vacant areas have been rezoned for much lower housing densities, or even for agricultural use, leaving farmers and other owners of undeveloped land exposed to large losses of their land value (see chapter 13).

Amending the Constitution

Some neighborhood associations are already facing the need to amend their constitutions. Many associations, for instance, are coming under pressure to relax existing limitations on home-based businesses, given the communications revolution in the American workplace and the growing popularity of part-time or even full-time work from home. In a 1995 survey by the Community Associations Institute, 28 percent of neighborhood associations had tried at least once to amend their covenants, conditions, and restrictions (CC&Rs), and 67 percent had obtained the required neighborhood vote to win approval.[11]

Such a constitutional amendment in a neighborhood association generally requires a vote of the full membership. The percentage required for amendment approval, however, may vary considerably from neighborhood to neighborhood and issue to issue. Although unanimous consent would in principle be desirable, in practice there are almost certain to be dissenters and holdouts, some of whom might be hoping to "sell" their vote at the end of the negotiation process. For practical reasons then, in most neighborhood associations, a constitutional amendment requires a vote considerably greater than 50 percent, but also well below unanimous consent.

The Pennsylvania Uniform Planned Community Act, as adopted in 1996, requires a two-thirds vote to approve most amendments. If the amendment entails a more radical departure from the initial neighborhood terms of agreement, then a higher percentage is likely to be necessary. Under the Pennsylvania legislation, four-fifths of the unit owners must approve the sale of any of the association's common property. Terminating the neighborhood association altogether similarly requires a four-fifths vote.[12]

Table 4.1 shows the distribution of required voting percentages for a typical change in the constitutional provisions of a neighborhood association, as found in a 1996 survey for the Community Associations Institute. In some neighborhood associations, the required vote for amending the constitution is calculated as a percentage of the total number of unit owners eligible to vote. In others, the required vote is calculated as a percentage of unit own-

Table 4.1. *Distribution of Voting Requirements to Amend a Neighborhood Constitution, 1996*

Required vote for approval of amendment (%)	Base includes all unit owners[a](%)	Base is unit owners actually voting[b] (%)
51	12	10
60	2	8
66	24	31
75	33	27
80	2	4
90	11	4
100	3	0
Other	13	16

Source: Doreen Heisler and Warren Klein, *Inside Look at Community Association Homeownership— Facts, Perceptions* (Alexandria, VA: Community Associations Institute, 1996), 32.

Notes: a. Associations in which the required vote for approval is a percentage of all units in the association.

b. Associations in which the required vote for approval is a percentage of voting units only.

ers who actually voted. As table 4.1 shows, the percentages of voters required to approve an amendment differ considerably from neighborhood to neighborhood. Among the neighborhood associations where the required percentage includes all unit owners, 12 percent of them require only a simple majority of 51 percent. The most common approval requirement (in 33 percent of such associations) is 75 percent. In 3 percent of these associations, full unanimity is required to approve a constitutional amendment. There is a similarly wide range of required voting percentages in cases where the calculation involves actual voters only. The most common requirement in such associations is a 66 percent affirmative vote to change the neighborhood constitution.

In *The Calculus of Consent* (1962), James Buchanan and Gordon Tullock explored the trade-offs in setting a voting requirement for collective action.[13] They noted that simple majority rule was the prevailing standard. However, in their view this rule was more a matter of convention than of any inherent desirability. Indeed, the required percentage for approval ideally should vary with the specific circumstances of each collective organization, as neighborhood associations have been doing. Buchanan and Tullock identified a basic trade-off involving two types of costs in collective decisionmaking. One type of cost is the negotiation and decisionmaking cost involved in reaching any minimum percentage to approve a collective decision. As the required vote approaches unanimity, the costs of decisionmaking will frequently become exorbitant. Another type of cost might be labeled the "losing-side" cost. Whenever individuals vote "no," and yet the action is approved, the individual welfare of each of the losing voters will decline at least to some extent. The great advantage of a rule of unanimity is that these losing-side costs equal zero—each and every voter will have to be no worse or hopefully better off.

By contrast, the negotiation and other transactions costs will tend to be minimal with a vote requirement of 51 percent. At the same time, the losing-side costs—now potentially as many as 49 percent of all voters—will be at a maximum. Thus, as losing-side costs go up, transaction costs go down, and vice versa. As Buchanan and Tullock showed more formally through a geometric exposition, there is an "optimal" required voting percentage (in most cases, more than 51 percent) that minimizes the total decisionmaking costs. Although few if any neighborhood associations go through such formal calculations, many have had to set their decision rules for collective action, and most have, as Buchanan and Tullock recommended, required a vote of more than 51 percent to approve a constitutional amendment. These associations have been implicitly applying the principles of "constitutional economics" on perhaps a wider scale than has ever been seen before.

Neighborhood Termination

The founding documents of many neighborhood associations say little or nothing about the possible termination of the association. After an earthquake in Los Angeles, however, some California neighborhoods experienced massive destruction and sensibly decided to go out of business, though legally there was no easy way to do it. More commonly, the possibility of neighborhood termination might arise as a result of radically altered economic and land use circumstances. In normal urban land development, neighborhoods might be stable for many years; however, most will one day face strong economic pressures compelling them to consider submitting their properties to an altogether new type of use. The construction of a new subway stop, for example, could double or triple the dollar value of land and property in the nearby area. Surrounding homes would stand in the way of more efficient land use, such as an office tower or large apartment complex. In that case, if the homes were in a neighborhood association, most unit owners might prefer to terminate the association, walking away with a large profit; the homes would then be demolished by the new buyer.

Each neighborhood association constitution should thus provide a way to end the life of the association. The Uniform Common Interest Ownership Act suggests that the founding documents provide for termination with approval by 80 percent of the unit owners.* Following such a vote, all the neighborhood properties might be sold as a single package to a land developer and the resulting proceeds distributed among the unit owners.[14] In much the same way, the shareholders in a business can also vote to abolish the corporation, selling its assets outright or accepting a takeover.

Some observers argue that an 80 percent approval requirement for termination might be too high. Columbia law professor Michael Heller argues that socially beneficial transitions in land uses are often blocked by association rules. In theory, this should not happen because "rational developers should prefer to offer value-maximizing governance rules that prevent people from blocking valuable adjustments."[15] A developer would not set the requirement at

---

*A requirement of 85 percent was adopted informally in one northern Virginia suburb of Washington, D.C. A neighborhood well placed for redevelopment into a new use was also isolated by the major highways along its boundaries. The land's commercial value was growing rapidly, so most of the homeowners announced their preference to sell their properties at a premium, a price several times their existing value as single-family homes. However, a few homeowners were strongly opposed to moving away from the neighborhood.

In this case, the Fairfax County government had to rezone the land to commercial use in order for a full neighborhood transition to occur. The county was aware that a large majority of property owners preferred to move. Therefore, the county informally announced that it would make the necessary zoning change when 85 percent of the neighborhood homeowners agreed to leave.

80 percent if unit owners preferred a lower figure, since not satisfying the unit owners would cost the developer money. However, economic theory has often ignored the transaction costs of doing business in the real world. Heller comments on actual practice:

> Because [unit] owners [in neighborhood associations] underestimate the likelihood of change and overestimate the ease of future negotiations, they do not demand, and developers therefore have little incentive to offer, change-supporting governance rules. Indeed, developers who offer more flexible governance mechanisms may scare off those potential buyers who predictably, but inaccurately, appraise their future needs. Instead, voting rules in condominiums or homeowner associations continue to give excessive veto power to minorities of unit owners. Because of holdouts and bargaining difficulties, CICs [common interest communities] may find themselves locked into low value uses.[16]

To be sure, the other side of the coin is the possibility that a unit owner would be forced to accept a neighborhood termination that he or she opposes. No matter the exact vote required for association termination, there are also the important issues of the voting procedure, the packaging of neighborhood properties for collective sale, and (in cases of single-package sales) the division of total profits from the sale (for example, in proportion to square feet, in proportion to individual property assessments, or in other ways). At present, few neighborhood associations include in their constitutions any detailed provisions for such radical forms of action.

A constitutional provision for terminating a neighborhood association might be regarded as a new system of private land assembly. Urban renewal was employed in the 1950s and 1960s to put together land parcels large enough for comprehensive redevelopment. However, participation in urban renewal was not necessarily voluntary; the government had the power to condemn properties in renewal areas. Furthermore, the government often gained the most monetarily when the land was resold because property owners received only fair market value for their properties at the time of condemnation. Indeed, by the 1970s, the ill will created among residents and property owners in renewal areas destined for government acquisition led to the program's demise.

A constitutional process for terminating a neighborhood association would offer a superior method of land assembly. It would not be entirely voluntary for every unit owner because some share—perhaps as many as 20 percent—of unit owners might vote against termination. However, the dissenting minority would at least be a small part of the total association membership. In most cases, all the unit owners would receive payments well above the market value of their properties as currently used, and the decision to end the neighborhood's life would be in the collective hands of the property owners themselves, rather than in the hands of distant municipal zoning authorities or other officials.

A Neighborhood Bill of Rights

The purchasers of units in a neighborhood association may want to have a certain set of basic rights that the association government cannot infringe upon. At present, for example, an association can limit the placement of political or "for sale" signs on neighborhood yards and properties. Many associations restrict the flying of the American flag, and limit a unit owner's rights to put up a basketball hoop or to install a swing set for children to use. Some associations have gone so far as to prevent neighborhood children from putting up a lemonade stand. A neighborhood bill of rights would deal with issues such as these.

According to James Winokur, many people today desire precise social controls over their neighbor's actions because of "heightened aesthetic sensibilities . . . to adjacent uses." Nevertheless, he also asserts that the desire for order in neighborhood environments can go too far, creating "aesthetically undifferentiated and culturally desolate" environments. Some unit owners may resent "straitjacket" restrictions that "invade aspects of home life previously left to personal choice."[17] The existence, real or potential, of such tight restrictions may surprise recent arrivals to neighborhood associations, especially those who have not done all their "homework" before entering.

Moreover, it may not be enough for a prospective buyer to find a neighborhood association where such rules do not now exist because that neighborhood's constitution could always be amended in the future. Some use restrictions may be within the discretion of the board of directors. Even if prospective buyers have confidence in the current neighborhood unit owners, the neighborhood character could always change. Later entrants might want more draconian rules and seek to alter the neighborhood constitution accordingly.

New unit owners might therefore want the neighborhood constitution to contain a formal bill of rights. The right to put up a political sign, for example, might be guaranteed. A bill of rights, however, would not provide absolute protection because of the possibility of constitutional amendments. Nevertheless, setting the voting requirement for amendment approval at a particularly high proportion—say 85 or 90 percent of the unit owners, or conceivably even 100 percent—would represent a formidable obstacle to any future loss of individual rights.

A neighborhood bill of rights would be regarded as an item of consumer choice. Some neighborhoods might choose fewer guarantees of individual rights and tighter restrictions on unit owners' actions. Neighborhoods like these might restrict the freedom to fly the American flag. Other neighborhoods might prefer fewer neighborhood controls. Either way, prospective purchasers of units in these neighborhoods might want assurances that matters will not change. As Susan French argues,

The contents of the constitution and bill of rights for any particular development should be tailored to the interests and fears of the group the developer intends to target. People who are interested in living in communities designed for special activities or interest groups will obviously be willing to give up more or different liberties than those who simply want good housing in a good neighborhood that will retain its value. Even within the group of those who are simply looking for housing, the degrees of liberty people are willing to give up to acquire various amenities will vary. However, certain fears are likely to appear with sufficient frequency that developers should consider addressing them in the constitutions for any community they create.[18]

Conceivably, the range of preferences in this regard may extend from the tightest of controls to almost no rules at all (other than those rules traditionally found in nuisance law that prohibit doing direct harm to another person). In fact, some libertarians have recently proposed that the greatest freedom-lovers in America should agree to move to one state where they would have sufficient political weight to protect themselves against more coercive measures. In a nationally publicized Internet vote to select this "free state," New Hampshire was the preferred state among libertarians, and Wyoming was the second most popular.[19] A few libertarians have already moved to New Hampshire with this purpose in mind. Developing a libertarian neighborhood association is a considerably more realistic target, however, than creating a libertarian state.

A Hierarchy of Rights

"Rights" therefore can be an item of consumer choice that varies according to the wishes of community members. Moreover, there are many levels of "community" in the United States—the neighborhood community, the state community, and the national community (and maybe even being part of a "world community"). The wider the geographic scope of the community—especially given the correspondingly increased difficulty in agreeing on common values—the less restrictive the set of basic rights should probably be.

Above neighborhood rights is another level of rights found in a given state's constitution. These rights may vary somewhat from state to state, depending on each state's constitutional language and the history of each state's judicial interpretations. (The rights of individual property owners, for example, have in recent decades been treated with considerably more respect in Virginia than in California.) Above the state level is the constitution of the United States, which trumps state constitutions in matters of core rights. Finally, some rights may be regarded as "basic human rights"—although the constitutional mechanisms for defining and enforcing these rights around the world are still rudimentary at best.

The "cumulative constitution" that applies to a given neighborhood association will incorporate all the higher levels of rights of the relevant jurisdictions in which the neighborhood is found. For any U.S. neighborhood, federal law and the U.S. constitution will prohibit any discriminatory actions based on race and some other categories. Within a given state, further guarantees of rights under the state constitution may apply, subject to federal rules. State courts, for example, originally ruled that neighborhood associations could discriminate on the basis of age—and thus exclude children—but federal legislation in 1988 made this illegal throughout the United States (except in senior citizen communities). The federal and state courts have yet to speak on many other types of potential discriminatory actions, but when they do, their verdicts will automatically apply throughout the relevant jurisdictions.

Evolving Rights

The precise status—or even the existence—of rights may change with the times within a given area. Before the advent of air travel, a property owner presumably owned everything up to and including the sky above him. Later, television altered the meaning of "freedom of speech" and of "public assembly"— which now must include the ability to hear the president's State of the Union address or to learn further news details, such as we did on the morning of September 11, 2001. Hence, the right to receive a television signal might now be regarded as a key element in maintaining two basic constitutional freedoms guaranteed to all Americans. Reflecting this changed circumstance, in 1996 the Congress enacted the Telecommunications Act, which prohibits any party— including a neighborhood association—from preventing a person from receiving a television signal through a satellite dish (as long as the dish is less than one meter wide, as most now are). According to Federal Communications Commission (FCC) regulations, if the dish is in public view, the association can require some form of camouflage provided it is not unreasonably costly or does not interfere with signal quality.[20]

Admittedly, technology has improved rapidly, satellite dishes are smaller, and the real need to ban them has vanished. Yet many neighborhood associations have cumbersome, time-consuming procedures for amending their constitutions. By 1996, most neighborhood associations were likely happy to have Congress abolish their old rules. By adopting such a rule nationwide, Congress saved many neighborhood associations a great deal of unnecessary time and money. Despite the dangers it creates, one of government's practical roles is to limit what might otherwise be exorbitant transaction costs in collective actions.

Evolving social trends may also change conceptions about basic individual rights. As increasing numbers of Americans live alone, or in small households without children, many of them live with pets. As individual social isolation increases, these contemporary pets can assume an importance as personal "companions" or "friends," roles that few dogs or cats had in the past. An elderly person, for example, may today be living alone thousands of miles from children and other relatives and may rely on a pet to provide needed daily interaction with some other animate being. Animal research is also suggesting that dogs and cats may have "thinking" powers closer to human reasoning than previously suspected. Hence, it is increasingly true that denying the right to have a pet is seriously infringing on individual rights.

California is often at the forefront of social change. Indeed, for better or worse, it has been illegal under California law since 2001 for a new neighborhood association to ban the possession of a pet. Older neighborhood associations with existing rules against pets were permitted to retain their rules. However, even older neighborhood associations that previously allowed pets are now prohibited from adopting new rules to exclude them. A pet is defined to include any domesticated bird, cat, dog, or aquatic animal kept within an aquarium.[21] As matters stand now in California, grandparents in a new senior citizen neighborhood association can be prohibited under state law from bringing their grandchildren to live with them (due to parental absence or death, for example), but the same association is not legally allowed to block the possession of a pet.*

When the U.S. Constitution was written in 1787, the main methods of transportation were walking, riding a horse, or riding in a carriage. Protection of person and property was the key element in maintaining the right to gather in assemblies and otherwise to move around. In an automotive age, however, the right to assemble may require a new legal definition. Under a basic "right of mobility," each physically able person perhaps must have a constitutional right to possess and drive a car. However many find a motorcycle cheaper and easier to park. Indeed, one state assemblyman in California recently introduced a bill (AB 1268) that would have overridden any neighborhood association

---

*It is interesting that events have been moving in an opposite direction with respect to cigarette smoking, another act, like the possession of a pet, that commonly imposes costs on nearby people. As smoking has been banned in airlines, restaurants, office buildings, and other places, the individual opportunity to smoke has been steadily circumscribed. Although the smoking ban has sometimes been justified for public health reasons, it is apparent that aesthetic and moral considerations are often paramount (some religions have long banned smoking on moral grounds, although they received little government support until recently). It is quite likely that a neighborhood association would be legally permitted—perhaps most probable of all in California—to prohibit smoking within its boundaries. The evolving contrasting attitudes toward the potential nuisance impacts of smoking and pets are no doubt reflective of evolving public sensibilities in American life, and perhaps might be studied as one good way of gaining further insight into such trends.

rule relating to the operation, parking, or storage of a motorcycle within association premises. Had this bill passed, the right to possess a motorcycle—like the right to have a pet under the recent law—would effectively have become part of the bill of rights in neighborhood associations throughout California.

Homeowner rights issues vary from state to state. In Florida, state law presently guarantees a condominium unit owner's right to install hurricane shutters. Responding to a state water crisis in Colorado, Representative Paul Weissmann recently introduced a bill prohibiting homeowner associations from installing water-intensive landscaping. Weissmann declared, "I, like you, hate to tell people what to do, but there are communities that require high-water lawns"; this situation was hindering state efforts to conserve scarce water.[22] In Arizona, a resident in the Arrowhead Ranch Homeowners Association complained about a neighbor giving piano lessons at home. Although the piano teacher had been giving lessons for 42 years, the association instructed her to stop, citing the association's rule against home businesses. In response, Scott Bundgaard, Arizona state senator, introduced a bill declaring that the teaching of music at home is not a commercial activity under Arizona law—and thus under state law falls outside the permissible scope of neighborhood association control. Bundgaard argued that home music teachers "don't make a lot of money. They are doing it out of the goodness of their hearts."[23]

Testifying in 2000 before the Homeowners Association Study Committee of the Arizona legislature, the director of the HOA Network (a group of disaffected unit owners) demanded a new "Homeowner's Declaration of Independence" from oppressive boards of directors. George Staropoli called on the state legislature to adopt a "homeowners bill of rights" that would be incorporated automatically into the founding documents of every neighborhood association and provide for "legal sanctions against the abuse of these rights by boards of directors."[24] Under the proposal, the state government would systematically consider the full range of possible individual rights and identify some for mandatory protection under association constitutions, leaving others to the discretion of each neighborhood.

It may seem odd to think of individual rights as matters of consumer choice. In a pluralist world, however, conceptions of rights differ. Travelers' rights depend on which nation they are visiting; the rights of Americans in China are at present substantially abridged. Within a country as large as the United States, the "national community" can reach a consensus only on certain core rights. Proposals to go beyond these basic rights throughout the nation would inevitably create many frictions and controversies and probably would not be enforceable in some places. Yet, smaller communities may easily agree on a wider range of basic local rights. To deny the legitimacy of "local rights" is to unnecessarily limit the constitutional protections of rights now and in the future.

Democracy versus Dictatorship

At the national or state level, most Americans—given a choice between a dictatorship and a democracy—would obviously choose democracy. However, both options have long existed at the residential neighborhood level. Many Americans have in effect chosen a dictatorship. They have chosen to rent apartments in large complexes owned by a single developer who is actually a benevolent dictator, responsible for honoring lease contracts, but otherwise given wide private discretion in managing the community land and housing. The renters in these communities have exercised yet another constitutional choice at the neighborhood level, opting in this case for a dictatorship over a democracy of unit owners.

A renter might have made this choice in part because democracy is not a cost-free exercise. Indeed, running a governing system democratically is time-consuming and cumbersome. Democracies require elections, membership meetings (which can take up large amounts of time), and democratic decisions (which may represent awkward compromises). In the commercial market for retail space, the unit occupants usually opt for a dictatorship. Although shopping centers have proliferated during much the same period as have neighborhood associations, they are seldom collectively owned by the occupants. Instead, the individual stores rent their properties from a shopping center's single owner, who also chooses the management.

In a neighborhood of renters, the owner/landlord's incentive to maximize the net economic return on the property works to protect the residents' as well as his own future interests. A neighborhood improvement that allows the owner to charge higher rents is privately profitable—a matter simply of good business practice, not of democratic government at work. A small and mostly unheralded body of literature seeks to make the case for a constitutional system of "neighborhood dictatorship" in private housing projects, as opposed to the current system offering a proliferation of democratic neighborhood associations.

In 1936, amid the New Deal and as many intellectuals were questioning America's capitalist system, Spencer Heath boldly predicted that over time "the proprietary department eventually will take on and exercise its full administrative functions over all the public services"—and thus replace the historic role of local public governments by providing basic services privately.[25] Private developers would provide services to neighborhood residents (including enforcement of land use restrictions), charge land rents, and keep the residual (or profit) as compensation. A visionary, Heath saw the commercial hotel as the appropriate model for the future legal status of residential housing projects across the United States. A hotel represented "an organized community with such services in common as policing, water, drainage, heat, light and power, communications and transportation, even educational and recreational facilities such as libraries, musical and literary entertainment, swimming pools, gardens and golf courses, with courteous services by the community officers and employees."[26] In the future, aggregations of hundreds of homes and other properties, as Heath presciently suggested more than half a century ago, would be widely organized and managed like private hotels.

Heath's grandson, Spencer Heath MacCallum, has taken up Heath's arguments.[27] Before almost any other social scientists were exploring the "social" character of housing ownership in the United States, MacCallum observed the many new, emerging collective forms of local property ownership—integrated shopping centers, industrial parks, professional and research centers, marinas, mobile home parks, medical centers, and many types of multifunctional building complexes. In these organizations, "all of the [old] functional requirements of municipalities" were being met on a private basis.[28] Indeed, as MacCallum argued, "There are no longer any political functions being performed at the municipal level and upward in our society that differ substantially from those that we can observe being performed on a smaller scale entirely within the context of normal property relations."[29]

In *The Art of Community* (1970), MacCallum carried these arguments further. In private ownerships, he contended, "The manner of the relationship of each toward others is specified in the terms of the individual contracts, the sum of which at any time is the social charter or constitution of the community."[30] A neighborhood's private constitution would set well-defined and hard-to-change rules for governing relations among people living within its boundaries. If private neighborhoods competed to attract residents, this competition would stimulate more efficient service delivery and reward a higher neighborhood quality. It would extend as well to the design of the most desirable set of constitutional rules—desirable from the point of view of home buyers—for neighborhood governance.

MacCallum's strong preference for neighborhood governance is the single proprietary owner who rents out housing units—the benevolent dictator motivated to serve his "citizenry" of renters by private profit. This model avoids the high transaction costs typically associated with democratic decisionmaking by a large group of owners. "Judging from the numbers of complaints and litigation, these neighborhood governments are often arbitrary, unresponsive, and dictatorial," says MacCallum today. The threat is that the "attractive features of the traditional American lifestyle, such as tolerance, neighborliness, and freedom to enjoy the use of one's property, are being lost" in the current stressful environments found in so many neighborhood associations.[31]

Comparing neighborhood associations and proprietary ownerships, MacCallum notes the large "behavioral differences resulting from two very different incentive structures." As all this works out, "the incentive structure in the one [proprietary communities] inclines it toward optimization of resident satisfactions whereas in the other [neighborhood associations] it does not. That is the premise of the land-lease community, which is in business to succeed in a competitive market environment."[32] Yet despite MacCallum, the great majority of housing purchasers in recent years have chosen the democratic over the dictatorial option, apparently preferring to manage their neighborhood affairs by democratic means no matter the stresses and strains.

Nevertheless, MacCallum raises an important question: Why is the neighborhood association widely preferred to the large apartment complex (including potentially "apartments" of single-family homes)? Put another way, why do shopping centers mostly rent space to commercial retail establishments, while the developers of large residential neighborhoods mostly sell off units to individual home buyers in neighborhood associations? MacCallum attributes this outcome partly to the tax advantages afforded to housing ownership in the United States. Homeowners implicitly rent the units to themselves; furthermore they pay no federal or state income taxes on this large imputed source of income (20 to 30 percent of total income for many people).[33] The tax advantages to the unit owners might in fact exceed in value the additional transaction costs associated with democratic decisionmaking.

Americans have in fact shown a strong preference for owning their homes since at least the late 19th century, well before federal income taxes existed.* Many rental properties in the United States also generate significant tax advantages for the owners. Further complicating the issue, the tax advantage of unit ownership can be preserved even if unit owners turn over most management responsibilities to an outside firm. This firm might enjoy much of the operating autonomy of a typical landlord (with the management contract subject to renewal every few years and bonuses given for a high level of performance).

Indeed, a leading American land developer, Charles Fraser, has recently proposed restructuring neighborhood covenants and restrictions "to encourage community associations to hire competent and experienced management companies" to bear the primary responsibility for administration. Fraser would like to see "the ownership of common properties . . . placed in a trust"

---

*In his definitive history of the American suburbs, Kenneth Jackson describes the case of Garden City on Long Island, an early American suburb from the 1870s. Garden City was unusual then (and now) in that the developer created it as a rental community. Although celebrated for its design innovations, the project proved to be a financial failure, partly because the rental feature was unpopular. As Jackson says, "The most enduring lesson of A. T. Stewart's planned suburb was negative; it demonstrated that affluent families would not support a rental market for expensive detached homes." Those who could afford to live in "a substantial home on a large plot would not be satisfied with anything less than full ownership." See Kenneth T. Jackson, *Crabgrass Frontier: The Suburbanization of the United States* (New York: Oxford University Press, 1985), 84, 86.

governed by a set of trustees who would "select a 'town hall' management company to contract to provide the services needed by the community in five- to ten-year terms." The management contract would automatically be renewed unless a majority of unit owners voted to select another company, although the contract could also be abrogated at any time with a vote of 65 percent of the unit owners.[34] Even now, if a neighborhood association wants a benevolent dictator, in this way it can make this choice without surrendering the longer-run prerogatives of housing ownership.

Neighborhood Transaction Costs

Many other factors affect the constitutional choice of a neighborhood form of ownership and governance. The issues mentioned here parallel questions traditionally raised in the field of industrial organization—Why do the markets in some industries evolve toward a large group of atomistic firms, while other markets are dominated by a few large business corporations? Following Oliver Williamson's pioneering 1970s research into the impact of transaction costs on business organization, a new school of institutional economics has addressed such issues.[35] Since most private contracts leave many contingencies unresolved, it may be difficult and costly to enforce these contracts in the future. Indeed, the success of the large business corporation may reflect much lower transaction costs, compared with numerous independent contractors pursuing the same set of economic activities through a complex web of external market transactions.[36] The problems of controlling "opportunism," for example, may not be as great in a large business where the employees all benefit together from a higher level of corporate profit. Partly because private contracts are inherently incomplete, a market in the real world differs greatly from the abstract world of economic theory where perfect information is assumed— and thus perfect equilibrium and costless transactions are assured.[37]

Such considerations will apply as well in determining the economic organization of the housing market.[38] The dangers of opportunistic behavior may be particularly great in housing because contractual commitments frequently extend over very long periods. Law professor Stewart Sterk comments that in a neighborhood "the range of opportunities for collective action is so great that express contracts cannot contemplate all of the circumstances that might lead a majority to act opportunistically."[39] Thus, a main purpose of a neighborhood association constitution will be to provide institutional barriers— including a system of neighborhood democracy capable of adapting to changing circumstances—that work to inhibit potentially opportunistic behavior.

In his classic analysis of the economic role of transaction costs, Ronald Coase observed that the design of social institutions, including the initial assignment of legal rights, could significantly affect bargaining, negotiation, and other transaction costs.[40] The "principle-agent" relationship, for example, may take one form in a commercial shopping center and another in a neighborhood association of individually owned homes. Many retail stores have time horizons of 5 years or less, while purchasers of homes and other residential units may plan to stay for 20 years or more. It may be much less costly for a store to move out of a failing shopping center with weak management than for a homeowner to leave a failing neighborhood association.

The subjectivity of residential esthetics makes it hard to specify contractual standards of neighborhood quality that can be enforced over a long time period. Patrick Randolph acknowledges that "the complexities of common interest ownership . . . are such that it would be impossible to address [fully in advance] each of the myriad issues that necessarily come within the jurisdiction of the association board."[41] As a result, residents may prefer to democratically control their own neighborhood environments through direct unit ownership. By contrast, the long-run contracting problems in business "neighborhoods," such as shopping centers, may be less severe, leading to organizational forms in which management control remains in the hands of a single owner.

Another factor affecting the optimal contractual arrangement between unit occupants and management is the risk of price changes in housing and other markets. A 30-year fixed mortgage shifts the risk of any future general inflation to the financial institution. Partly for this reason, few 30-year lease agreements— even with inflation adjustment mechanisms—are available in the rental market. Owners of rental property are simply unwilling to assume the risk of unpredictable shifts in prices or other unexpected events over such a long period (or they demand such a high-risk premium that renters are unwilling to pay it—preferring instead to "self-insure").

Democracy as a Consumer Good

Many people simply prefer democracy (with all its flaws) to a dictatorship— even the dictatorship of a benevolent proprietor motivated by profit to serve the unit occupants. The idea of joining together in political debate and decisionmaking in a neighborhood association may be in itself an attraction. Working jointly with others in a common task may foster a stronger sense of community. Although standard economic analysis treats individual welfare as a product exclusively of the levels of goods and services consumed, economists Bruno Frey and Alois Stutzer find that "people's happiness is influenced by the kind of political system they live in." This is partly a matter of achieving better political outcomes more closely aligned with the citizen's consumptive preferences in collective goods. However, it is also true that "people are likely to experience happiness not only from the actual outcomes" of the political process but also from the "procedural utility"—a sense of satisfaction in being a member of a democratic process and of participating in the group decisionmaking.[42]

A prominent lawyer in the field, Wayne Hyatt, comments that a neighborhood "association is a grass roots counterweight" to the rootlessness and isolation of big city life. It provides for "many who have never had it a sense of pride in a community and a great share of the responsibility for developing and maintaining that community."[43] Economist Fred Foldvary suggests that neighborhood associations are popular partly because of the "economic and cultural values of living in a democratically run community."[44] Furthermore, the very idea of property ownership (even when the bank lender may actually own the property for most of a working lifetime) may produce significant psychic benefits.

Economic models based strictly on self-interest seem to underestimate the influence of shared norms and collective enthusiasms in human behavior. As University of Chicago law professor Eric Posner comments, "Economic theories of cooperation predict less cooperation than actually exists."[45] A sense of commitment to a community is a valuable social asset that should be protected and conserved because it can avoid wider, clumsier government action and present strong barriers to rent-seeking activities. As Posner puts it,

> Most people do not take their disputes to lawyers and judges. Norms, rather than laws, provide the rules of conduct; friends, relatives, and coworkers, rather than juries, make findings of fact; shame and ostracism, rather than imprisonment or legal damages, punish the wrongdoer. Court is held not in a courthouse, but in homes, work places, and neighborhoods, among networks of kin, friends, and associates. In a sufficiently close-knit group, where norms are well defined and nonlegal sanctions are effective, the law has little impact on behavior.[46]

Conclusion

For better or for worse, a group of neighbors who share the ownership of a common environment will be thrown into many close interactions with one another. Like a family, the necessity of such a close relationship may create a strong sense of common identity and foster the pleasures of friendship and shared responsibilities. Alternatively, and also like some families, it may create severe internal tensions and strains. As some marriages end in divorce, some unit owners will feel so embittered that they will be compelled to move out of their neighborhood association.

In the real world, no group receives a guarantee that the development of a community of shared norms will be easy. A neighborhood association creates an opportunity to experience common activities and other aspects of group life, but offers no guarantees. The rise of the private neighborhood association thus does not mean that widespread neighborhood harmony will suddenly break out across the United States. Rather, the neighborhood association offers homeowners the freedom to try their hand in a new collective setting in American society. Their efforts will take place within the institutional framework of a founding constitutional document that sets the rules for their neighborhood association governance. Increasingly in the United States, the private form of government is taking the place of local government in the public sector.

NOTES

1. Joni Greenwalt, *Homeowner Associations: A Nightmare or a Dream Come True?* (Denver, CO: Cassie Publications, Inc., 2001), 50–51.

2. Ibid., 50.

3. Richard Briffault, "Local Government and the New York State Constitution," *Hofstra Law & Policy Symposium* 1 (1996), 79.

4. *Dolan-King v. Rancho Santa Fe Association,* 81 Cal. App. 4th at 976 (2000).

5. Sharon L. Bush, "Beware the Associations: How Homeowners' Associations Control You and Infringe Upon Your Inalienable Rights!!" *Western State University Law Review* 30 (Spring 2003), 17.

6. Jordan I. Shifrin, *Guilt by Association: A Survival Guide for Homeowners, Board Members, and Property Managers,* 2nd ed. (Lincoln, NE: Writers Club Press, 2001), 2.

7. Doreen Heisler and Warren Klein, *Inside Look at Community Association Homeownership: Facts, Perceptions* (Alexandria, VA: Community Associations Institute, 1996), 30.

8. James L. Winokur, "The Mixed Blessings of Promissory Servitudes: Toward Optimizing Economic Utility, Individual Liberty, and Personal Identity," *Wisconsin Law Review,* 1989 (January/February 1989), 59–60.

9. Amanda G. Hyatt, *Transition from Developer Control, 2nd ed.* (Alexandria, VA: Community Associations Institute, 1996), 5.

10. Ibid., 10–11.

11. Heisler and Klein, *Inside Look at Community Association Homeownership—Facts, Perceptions,* 28.

12. Michael L. Utz, "Common Interest Ownership in Pennsylvania: An Examination of Statutory Reform and Implications for Practitioners," *Duquesne University Law Review* 37 (Spring 1999), 484–85.

13. James M. Buchanan and Gordon Tullock, *The Calculus of Consent: Logical Foundations of Constitutional Democracy* (Ann Arbor: University of Michigan Press, 1962).

14. Katharine N. Rosenberry and Curtis G. Sproul, "A Comparison of California Common Interest Development Law and the Uniform Common Interest Ownership Act," *Santa Clara Law Review* 38 (1998), 1050–52.

15. Michael A. Heller, "The Boundaries of Private Property," *Yale Law Journal* 108 (April 1999), 1185.

16. Ibid.

17. Winokur, "The Mixed Blessings of Promissory Servitudes," 75, 4.

18. Susan F. French, "The Constitution of a Private Residential Government Should Include a Bill of Rights," *Wake Forest Law Review* 27, no. 2 (1992), 350.

19. Max Orhai, "A Revolution by Other Means," *Liberty* 18 (June 2004).

20. See Lara E. Howley, "Interpretation of the Over-the-Air Reception Devices Rule under the Declaratory Ruling Process," *CAI's Journal of Community Association Law* 1, no. 2 (1998).

21. Jan Hickenbottom, *Questions & Answers about Community Associations: A Collection of 'Condo Q & A' Columns As Published in the Los Angeles Times*, 2nd ed. (Irvine, CA: Miller Publishing Co., 2002), 432.

22. Quoted in Sandra Fish, "Republicans Reject Water Bill," *Boulder (CO) Daily Camera*, January 24, 2003.

23. Hal Mattern, "Bill Would Put Music Teacher Back to Work," *Arizona Republic*, June 16, 2000, B3.

24. George K. Staropoli, "Homeowners Declaration of Independence," statement prepared for presentation to the Homeowners Association Study Committee of the Arizona State Legislature, September 7, 2000.

25. Spencer Heath, "Outline of the Economic, Political, and Proprietary Departments of Society" (unpublished manuscript 1936), 65–66, cited in Fred Foldvary, *Public Goods and Private Communities: The Market Provision of Social Services* (Brookfield, VT: Edward Elgar, 1994), 88.

26. Spencer Heath, *Citadel, Market and Altar* (Baltimore, MD: Science of Society Foundation, 1957), 82, cited in Foldvary, *Public Goods and Private Communities*, 88.

27. Spencer Heath MacCallum, "The Social Nature of Ownership," *Modern Age* 9 (Winter 1964–65). See also Spencer Heath MacCallum, "Associated Individualism: A Victorian Dream of Freedom," *Reason* 4 (April 1972).

28. Ibid., 58.

29. MacCallum, "The Social Nature of Ownership," cited in Foldvary, *Public Goods and Private Communities*, 90.

30. Spencer Heath MacCallum, *The Art of Community* (Menlo Park, CA: Institute for Humane Studies, 1970), 5.

31. Spencer Heath MacCallum, "The Case for Land Lease versus Subdivision: Homeowners' Associations Reconsidered," in David T. Beito, Peter Gordon, and Alexander Tabarrok, eds., *The Voluntary City: Choice, Community, and Civil Society* (Ann Arbor: University of Michigan Press and the Independent Institute, 2002), 372.

32. Ibid., 381, 381–82.

33. See Henry Hansmann, "Condominium and Cooperative Housing: Transactional Efficiency, Tax Subsidies, and Tenure Choice," *Journal of Legal Studies* 20 (January 1991), 25, 39–40.

34. Charles Fraser, " 'Town Hall' Governance for Community Associations," in Bill Overton, ed., *Community First!: Emerging Visions Reshaping America's Condominium and Homeowner Associations* (Alexandria, VA: Community Associations Institute, 1999), 69–71.

35. Oliver E. Williamson, *Markets and Hierarchies: Analysis and Antitrust Implications* (New York: Free Press, 1975); and Oliver E. Williamson, *The Economic Institutions of Capitalism* (New York: Free Press, 1985).

36. Eirik G. Furubotn and Rudolf Richter, *Institutions and Economic Theory: The Contribution of the New Institutional Economics* (Ann Arbor: University of Michigan Press, 1997).

37. Joseph E. Stiglitz, *Whither Socialism?* (Cambridge, MA: MIT Press, 1994); also Joseph E. Stiglitz, *Economics* (New York: Norton, 1993).

38. Austin J. Jaffe, "On the Role of Transaction Costs and Property Rights in Housing Markets," *Housing Studies* 11 (July 1, 1996).

39. Stewart E. Sterk, "Minority Protection in Residential Private Governments," *Boston University Law Review* 77 (April 1997), 320.

40. See Ronald H. Coase, "The Nature of the Firm," *Economica* 4 (November 1937); and Ronald H. Coase, "The Problem of Social Cost," *Journal of Law and Economics* 3 (October 1960).

41. Patrick A. Randolph Jr., "Changing the Rules: Should Courts Limit the Power of Common Interest Communities to Alter Unit Owners' Privileges in the Face of Vested Expectations?" *Santa Clara Law Review* 38 (1998), 1084.

42. Bruno S. Frey and Alois Stutzer, *Happiness and Economics: How the Economy and Institutions Affect Human Well-Being* (Princeton, NJ: Princeton University Press, 2002), 133, 153.

43. Wayne S. Hyatt, "Condominium and Home Owner Associations: Formation and Development," *Emory Law Journal* 24 (Fall 1975), 1008.

44. Foldvary, *Public Goods and Private Communities,* 97.

45. Eric A. Posner, "The Regulation of Groups: The Influence of Legal and Nonlegal Sanctions on Collective Action," *University of Chicago Law Review* 63 (Winter 1996), 139 n. 12.

46. Ibid., 133.

5

Neighborhood
Democracy in Action

An estimated 1.25 million Americans serve on a neighborhood association's board of directors.[1] As a rapidly growing area of democratic practice in American life, neighborhood associations are putting to the test
longstanding ideas about the workings of local democracy. Some of the leading political theorists in our nation's history saw local democracy as a threat to
Americans' basic civil liberties and a poor method of governing. Others, however, saw it as virtually the salvation of the nation.

Madison versus Jefferson

In a democratic form of government, ultimate authority must rest with "the
people." Yet many of the framers of the American constitution were distrustful
of democracy; among their concerns was that democracy might yield a tyranny
of the majority. Having made heroic sacrifices to free themselves from English
rule, the founding fathers sought constitutional protections against any future
forms of oppression. One basic strategy for this was to create multiple sources
of power. Besides the three separate branches at the federal level, the constitution further divided power among the federal government and sovereign states.

In the public debates prior to constitutional ratification, James Madison
declared that the problem of "faction" was "the great object" of concern and
inquiry. It would be essential that "the majority, having such coexistent passion
or interest, must be rendered, by their number and local situation, unable to
concert and carry into effect schemes of oppression." There must be strong

protections because "neither moral nor religious motives can be relied on as an adequate control" over the "ruling passion or interest." Left on their own, the actions of a majority could endanger "both the public good and the rights of other citizens."[2]

Madison saw the new American government's divided structure as offering protection from such "passions" of the people. Madison was skeptical, however, when it came to smaller groups. For one thing, a single community might not have a wide enough range of interests to create a balance of powers. If community members sought to govern themselves through a direct democracy, the dangers would be greater still. As Madison wrote in *The Federalist Papers,*

> From the view of the subject it may be concluded that a pure democracy, by which I mean a society consisting of a small number of citizens, who assemble and administer the government in person, can admit of no cure for the mischiefs of faction. A common passion or interest will, in almost every case, be felt by a majority of the whole; a communication and concert results from the form of government itself; and there is nothing to check the inducements to sacrifice the weaker party or an obnoxious individual. Hence it is that such democracies have ever been spectacles of turbulence and contention; have ever been found incompatible with personal security or the rights of property; and have in general been as short in their lives as they have been violent in their deaths.[3]

If Madison's assessment is accurate, it augurs poorly for the prospects of neighborhood associations today. Indeed, there are many reports from current associations that fit the Madison diagnosis. Tempers flare; fierce disputes break out among the unit owners; and lone individuals are treated badly by the majority. One acrimonious dispute within a California association is a classic example:

> Even though the board now supported the need to raise monies, the past president did not accept their authority. He rose to insist there be someone other than a board member to monitor the large sums of monies that would be collected. The board agreed to this although several members were visibly and vocally upset at the implication they could not be trusted. The ex-president next proposed an end to secrecy and closed board meetings. The membership drifted out, tempers rose, and personal attacks were directed against both sides. With one board member screaming and others walking out of the room, the meeting ended. After the meeting, a board member began legal proceedings against the past president for slander.[4]

One observer of neighborhood associations finds that some boards act like a suburban "Gestapo." Dysfunctional boards of directors are under the control of little "Hitlers" who leave unit owners feeling "beaten down and bludgeoned."[5] In Nevada, state senator Mike Schneider was moved by such problems to seek greater state oversight of neighborhood associations, declaring, "We've seen some guys who turn into little Nazis when they get onto a board [of directors]."[6] In Florida, the director of the Fair Housing Center of the Greater Palm Beaches said in 2003 that his organization had received thousands of calls from "homeowners being run through the ringer by unscrupulous heads of associations."[7] The problem is aggravated by the self-selection mechanisms available to candidates for neighborhood office. People who "perceive no delight in exercising control over others" are often reluctant to run for a neighborhood board of directors.[8]

Yet as Winston Churchill famously declared, democracy—local or otherwise—may be the worst form of government, except for all the others. There are many reports of successful neighborhood governance as well. Among the founding fathers, Madison's views were countered by others of equal reputation. Thomas Jefferson had little confidence in any large government; for him the future well-being of the United States depended on a radical decentralization of authority. Indeed, the ideal political arrangement was a nation of small agrarian communities. Jefferson once wrote, "As Cato concluded every speech with the words, *Carthago delenda est,* so do I every opinion, with the injunction 'divide the counties into wards.' " Skeptical of central government, Jefferson sought "not to trust it all to one, but to divide it among the many, distributing to everyone exactly the functions he is competent to." His plan was to "dissolve [government] into the unity of society . . . [by] republicanism, decentralization, and specialization."[9]

Jefferson's vision is being realized today with the rise of neighborhood associations across the United States. Admittedly, there is not much farming going on in these places. However, a neighborhood association accomplishes the decentralization of governing authority to its fullest extent. The neighborhood association, as Jefferson sought, places the responsibility at the lowest possible governing level.

New England Democracy

A few decades later, Alexis de Tocqueville took a view closer to Jefferson's, finding that "the strength of free peoples resides in the local community." A leading example of the local community was the New England township. Tocqueville calculated that in 1830 the average township in Massachusetts had a population of 2,000 people. Speaking of New England direct democracy, Tocqueville commented, "In all that concerns themselves alone the townships remain independent bodies, and I do not think one could find a single inhabitant of New England who would recognize the right of the government of the state to control matters of purely municipal interest."[10]

In Europe it was rare to find such autonomy at the most local level, Tocqueville observed: "It often happens in Europe that governments themselves regret the absence of municipal spirit, for everyone agrees that municipal spirit is an important element in order and public tranquility, but they do not know how to produce it." Moreover, higher levels of government in Europe feared that multiple sources of authority might spread power too widely and expose "the state to risks of anarchy."[11] In New England, however, it was different; the governing role of a township was a key ingredient in developing the broader habits of democratic governance. Tocqueville observed,

> The New England township combines two advantages which, wherever they are found, keenly excite men's interest; they are independence and power. It acts, it is true, within a sphere beyond which it cannot pass, but within that domain its movements are free. This independence alone would give a real importance not warranted by size or population.
>
> The New Englander is attached to his township because it is strong and independent; he has an interest in it because he shares in its management; he loves it because he has no reason to complain of his lot; he invests his ambition and his future in it; in the restricted sphere within his scope, he learns to rule society; he gets to know those formalities without which freedom can advance only through revolutions, and becoming imbued with their spirit, develops a taste for order, understands the harmony of powers, and in the end accumulates clear practical ideas about the nature of his duties and the extent of his rights.[12]

In the New England democracy, all the citizens could (and many still can) vote on the selection of town leaders and on other key local decisions. Neighborhood associations, unlike most other modern democracies, also often practice democracy in this more direct form today. As Donald Stabile observes, the "advocates of CAs [community associations] often liken them to the New England town."[13] There is at least some empirical support in neighborhood associations for Tocqueville's positive view of small democracies. Examining data from California neighborhood associations, Tracy Gordon found recently that planned developments had higher rates of voter registration and turnout in public elections than did other California neighborhoods. The residents of planned developments are somewhat richer and do tend to vote somewhat more for Republican candidates than do residents in other California neighborhoods. Nevertheless, as Gordon concluded, "concerns about planned developments siphoning off the wealthiest Californians and their participation in public life are unwarranted"; many of these residents do actively contribute in wider arenas. Moreover, she found that California planned communities are "more heterogeneous than their image as exclusive luxury enclaves would suggest," and include many middle-income residents. This is one reason that "the contribution of planned developments to overall metropolitan area segregation in California is actually quite small"—accounting for only about 2 percent of overall segregation.[14]

The Free-Rider Problem

Leading political philosophers of the past are not the only authorities shedding useful light on the workings of neighborhood associations. In *The Logic of*

Collective Action, economist Mancur Olson in 1965 offered insights applicable to today's neighborhood associations.[15] Prior to Olson's analysis, social scientists typically assumed that group behavior is much like individual behavior. Olson stressed, however, that life in groups is much more complicated.

The actions of any one individual will have a small, sometimes even negligible, impact on the overall product of most group efforts. For all practical purposes, 3001 contributors to the United Way will have the same impact as 3000. Since his or her efforts make no practical difference for the outcome, the private incentive will therefore be to shirk individual contributions to the United Way. So unless individuals—"economically rational" individuals (those who pursue their self-interest)—actually enjoy the act of participation, they should never volunteer for any large group efforts.

If individuals never volunteer, Olson famously pointed out, it will be impossible to sustain the group. This can happen even when the total benefits to all the group members are much greater than the total costs. Unlike Adam Smith's free-market world, there is no invisible hand to ensure that self-interested individuals acting together collectively will best serve their own or society's interests. Indeed, free-rider incentives may frequently result in no collective action at all, even when doing so would be to everyone's great advantage.

Creating a government—with accompanying coercive powers—is one institutional response; potential free riders can be compelled to contribute. However, many private groups manage to survive without relying on the powers of a government. Olson in fact described a number of ways in which a private group might prosper. One approach would be to design group activities that provide benefits directly linked to individual participation in group affairs. Many "public interest" groups, for example, enlist members by publishing magazines. As long as the magazine is worth more than the dues, members will be attracted to join the group.

In a neighborhood association, one free-rider problem is overcome by the developer. The buyer of a unit is required as a condition of purchase to become a member of the neighborhood "group." Nevertheless, a significant free-rider problem will remain with respect to day-to-day governance.[16] According to Olson's analysis, most unit owners will likely seek to avoid serving on boards of directors and other neighborhood duties. They fear such involvement will probably cost them a great deal of time and effort and produce little overall effect on neighborhood quality.* Indeed, there is ample evidence to support this theory.

---

*Another element of the free-rider problem is the tendency for "rational ignorance" among each group member. Given the costs of information gathering, a "rational" group member will not take the trouble, leaving it to others. In neighborhood associations, this will means that most people can be expected to know little about the details of association governance—such as the budget, the exact land use restrictions, litigation that may be facing the association, etc.

Motivating unit owners to contribute to their associations is one of the biggest problems facing neighborhood associations. Stephen Barton and Carol Silverman report that in California condominiums "apathy and avoidance predominate." Unit owners often see association activities "as something to be endured and avoided rather than valued."[17] A national authority on neighborhood associations reports that "attendance at association meetings is often sparse, with a majority of members actually rarely attending."[18] Many presidents and other officers, the "old hands" report, are newcomers who do not know any better.

Many neighborhood observers attribute such wide apathy to an inadequate sense of civic responsibility or other moral failings on the part of association members and the lack of any real interest in association affairs. Some commentators further suggest that the lack of active participation strongly suggests that neighborhood associations are not serving their unit owners well. Yet the absence of a greater personal involvement might simply be "the logic of collective action." A group can serve its members well, yet they can still strongly resist close involvement. Indeed, given the strong free-rider incentives, perhaps the greater surprise is the extent to which many people do participate in neighborhood affairs with enthusiasm and energy.

Neighborhood Tensions

In some neighborhoods, the problem is not apathy but excessive involvement. There are almost as many complaints about "nosy" and "intrusive" neighbors as there are about the lack of participation in neighborhood affairs. Some observers, it seems, judge neighborhood associations by different standards of perfection. One person sees an excess of apathy, while another sees an excess of zeal. Whatever they do, some neighborhood associations can never seem to get it right.

Some neighborhood issues are difficult, and their outcomes are bound to offend some parties. Consider the case of the Preston Village Homeowner Association in North Carolina. One homeowner was accustomed to saving elderly dogs from shelters where they would have been euthanized. Given their advanced age, the dogs were not active or aggressive. Facing complaints, this homeowner argued that the covenants made no explicit reference to a total number of pets allowed. The association was in fact willing to allow this homeowner to keep up to three dogs at a time, but this concession did not satisfy the pet lover. In a spirit of charity, the association might have allowed more dogs, but doing so would have produced disruptions for other unit owners. No choice satisfied everyone.

As the Community Associations Institute (CAI) acknowledges, a major problem of living in a neighborhood association is "the adversarial nature that so often pervades the resident-board relationship."[19] Neighborhood associations must operate by written rules, even though it is often difficult to capture the nuances of neighborhood objectives in writing. The neighborhood covenants may specify, for example, that the construction of a new deck must be "unobtrusive." Just what does this mean in practice? This kind of decision is typically left to an architectural subcommittee of the board of directors. Committee decisions might differ from year to year, depending on the unit owners who serve on the committee. An owner might have a deck modification rejected one year, and approved the next. Accusations of favoritism, subjectivity, and partiality are common in neighborhood associations.

If rules are to have much force, a neighborhood association may feel that it is necessary to deny almost all exceptions. Otherwise the association may enter onto a "slippery slope," making some exceptions, then making further exceptions, and finally ending up with a rule that can no longer be enforced. Balancing strict enforcement with flexible judgment is bound to be difficult, and few neighborhoods at present seem to be handling this balancing act well. The literature is rife with complaints about lax enforcement on the one hand and foolishly rigid enforcement on the other. Showcasing an example of extreme rigidity, the *St. Petersburg Times* reported,

> Deed restrictions in Tampa Palms require removal of a treehouse, the only place where a boy with leukemia finds peace and solace. . . . To his parents . . . the treehouse is a symbol of hope, a reminder of the brief time doctors thought Brage had beaten cancer and he felt well enough to build it with his father. . . . Yet, the homeowners association that governs the Tampa Palms community has decided that the treehouse must come down: it violates deed restrictions. . . . [The association manager complained that] "your treehouse structure is in direct violation of the Covenants, Conditions and Restrictions for Tampa Palms."[20]

In the end, it required severe media pressure from outside to force the association to back down and allow the treehouse to remain.

Many neighborhood associations produce tensions by regulating seemingly minor practices. For example, some regulate the flying of the American flag, often limiting its display to official holidays. The lack of common sense demonstrated by many associations was vividly illustrated in the wake of the September 11 terrorist attacks. One association resident complained, "When the terrorists struck, . . . I immediately put my American flag out on my balcony. Within an hour, the board put a notice in my mailbox fining me $70 for flying my flag on a day that was not a 'recognized American holiday' and for not obtaining prior written permission from the board." With many other neighborhood associations behaving similarly, CAI—hoping to head off further bad publicity—promptly launched a new initiative, Operation Old Glory, proposing a six-month moratorium on association flag restrictions.[21]

In another case, a unit owner in Illinois was promoted by his company. As a result, the company gave him a pickup truck to use. Though the truck was in good condition, the homeowners association complained that the truck's door displayed the company logo and thus was a commercial vehicle excluded by neighborhood rules. The association also banned the overnight storage of tool-boxes in the truck bed. Facing continuing fines, the unit owner complained that his only available options were "to either sell his townhouse or quit his job."[22]

There will always be people pushing for extreme measures. In studying the evolving American suburbs, Joel Garreau found substantial discord within the many associations that he visited. In Sun City, a large private community of 46,000 residents near Phoenix, Arizona, Garreau heard unhappy people complaining of a "legally franchised, armed, unpaid private posse" that roamed the streets, verifying compliance with a host of association rules and regulations. Quite a few Sun City residents seemed to regard their private association's government as a new form of "big brother" with "powers far beyond those ever granted rulers in this country before."[23]

Life is not much better for board members who wield this authority. They are often confronted with irate unit owners. John Manougian, past president of CAI's Washington metropolitan chapter, reports, "In polling many managers, insurance agents, and attorneys around the country, it appears that aggressive [unit owner] behavior is a constant problem with many associations," including common attempts to "shout down board members" that occasionally escalate into "verbal and physical attacks." Manougian recommends that there will be some situations where it is even necessary to call in local police simply to maintain order and protect board members. He further recommends that boards "not sweep aggressive behavior" by unit owners "under the rug, but rather inform the community of such instances and keep them informed of potentially violent situations."[24]

In 1989 James Winokur stated his concern that "neighborhoods conducive to human flourishing" must be places where "each individual's identity can be based on personal control of a unique place in the residential environment." At that time, too many neighborhoods were substantially limiting this individual freedom, subordinating it to broader association controls. The result, as Winokur observed, was "severe frustration" and disenchantment among the unit owners in many neighborhood associations. "There is growing evidence," Winoker reported, "that homeowner acceptance of the restrictive servitude regimes substantially erodes over the years after decisions to purchase within such regimes are made." Unit owner unhappiness sometimes boils over into emotional outbursts. On the whole, as Winokur concluded, "the anticipated advantages of participatory democracy and 'public freedom' have not materialized sufficiently to offset the limitations on individual autonomy inherent" to the workings of neighborhood associations.[25]

As of 2002, law professor Paula Franzese saw little improvement. Life in neighborhood associations was "litigious, often acrimonious." Rather than promoting a sense of community harmony, "in actuality the predicates for successful community building are apt to be stifled, if not obliterated, by the sort of restrictiveness and attendant preoccupation with compliance that is inherent in the traditional CIC [Common Interest Community] model." Indeed, the "patterns of regimentation . . . do more to destroy community than to build it." Developers were suffering financially as well: "The term 'No HOA' ("No Homeowner Association") is starting to appear in real estate ads because, in the words of one realtor, 'for most people it is a real selling point.' "[26]

Maintaining Realistic Expectations

To be sure, joint living is never likely to be easy. Finding ways for several hundred people to agree is likely to be a significant challenge for any group—especially when the stakes are high, as in decisions that concern property ownership and use. Local zoning decisions are often charged with bitter emotion and controversy. On a smaller scale, most families encounter at least occasional nasty disputes. Perhaps neighborhood associations are being held to a higher standard because they are newer. Moreover, the promoters of neighborhood associations also often advertise them in glowing terms that may be impossible to live up to. Another factor may be a negative reaction to the very idea of a government that is "private." During the 20th century, many leading intellectuals sought to build a unified national—or even world—community in which narrow and selfish motives would be abolished and governments would serve the widest "public interest."

In the real world, there will always be disagreeable people. Ignorance, bias, prejudice, and other failings of human nature are bound to be present in many situations of collective action. As one experienced condominium manager explains it, "Every association has at least one unit owner who makes outrageous demands, is uncooperative or a nuisance to his or her neighbor, or is verbally abusive."[27] Despite the problems, Barton and Silverman also consider that it is important to maintain "a very realistic understanding of the difficulties of public life."[28] Perfect harmony is an impossible goal. In a 1999 Gallop survey, 70 percent of unit owners rated the rules and restrictions for their communities as either "extremely appropriate" or "very appropriate," while 2 percent found them "not appropriate at all" and 6 percent found them "somewhat inappropriate."[29]

Some protesting unit owners have little actual grounds for complaint. One couple on Marco Island in Florida painted their house a "bright pink" without prior approval of their association, as required. When the neighborhood sought to enforce its rules, the couple sued for $15 million in civil damages. In another case, a unit owner painted over an existing mural on a wall facing his swimming pool. Although the unit owner argued it was an "inside wall," the association said it was an "exterior wall" visible to others and that association approval was necessary. Whatever the actual truth of the matter was, the unit owner should have consulted the association in advance. Where unit owners have acted in violation of the covenants, they are often required to tear down newly built roofs, decks, and other structural alterations. Given the costs, inconvenience, and public embarrassment, it is hardly surprising that some unit owners react angrily.

In a Fort Myers, Florida, case, a unit owner parked his $40,000 pickup truck in his driveway. When the association protested, the unit owner complied with the rules and parked his truck in his garage. However, he then borrowed a friend's World War II British armored vehicle and parked it in his driveway instead. As this unit owner now argued, the association's rules did not specifically address the parking of armored vehicles. In this case, unlike many others, the parties did manage to keep their composure. The board did not take the bait, and the unit owner moved the armored vehicle a month later.[30]

Joe Adams, a local attorney and part-time newspaper columnist, observes that "by and large, the vast majority try to work out the problem before it comes to the point of friction." Many of the cases of serious dispute arise when individuals buy into a neighborhood association and then decide that the rules do not apply to them. As Adams says, "The media often paints it as the big bad association picking on individual rights, but you have to keep in mind, when people buy into a deed restriction community, they are buying into a contract with all their neighbors."[31]

Where people instead manage their small-scale interactions through local public governments, similar complaints are heard. A neighborhood association resembles a historic district in the comprehensive extent of its controls. In Alexandria, Virginia, a board of architectural review must issue a "certificate of appropriateness" for almost any exterior change in the Old Town historic district. The pettiness and arbitrariness of this review board, Clint Bolick observes, are the "stuff of local legend." Alexandria is a new "leviathan in the suburbs," with 74 local boards and review committees in this "hopelessly over-governed city."[32]

Living in a neighborhood association is not an obligation. Some people will find the burdens of collective private living greater than the gains and should avoid neighborhood associations. If they are in the minority, to be sure, the result could be a significant reduction in their range of housing choices. Neighborhood associations today predominate in many newly developing areas of the United States. The people with an antipathy to collective living should not expect that their preferences will necessarily win out over the majority.

Michael Utz finds that "one of the reasons for the success" of neighborhood associations is their contribution to a stronger "feeling of community or belonging." Although community is a "somewhat nebulous" concept, "there is, nevertheless, empirical support for this proposition."[33] In a 1995 poll, CAI found that 30 percent of unit owners "completely agree" with the statement that "community association homeownership is a satisfactory housing choice." Another 52 percent said that they "mostly agree." The proportions saying that they "mostly disagree" or "completely disagree" were 5 percent and 2 percent, respectively.[34] (Admittedly, people with strong negative feelings were under-represented because most will not be living in a neighborhood association.) Another study of gated communities found that these neighborhoods "provide a real sense of community. . . . When they gather in these developments, residents find they have a good deal in common, which forms a key basis for community."[35]

The horror stories get the press coverage. Yet there are many less publicized instances of associations that function well and board members who have enjoyed their experience. Erwin Baumann, president of the Blue Lagoon Community Association, commented on his 20 years as a board member: "Our community has been through most of the challenges that come down the road and survived them all." It helps to have a large dose of common sense. In one conflict a unit owner sought to plant shrubs, but they would have blocked another owner's view. Baumann pragmatically suggested "the planting of a combination of Hibiscus and Night Blooming Jasmine in a hedge row located on the lower one-third of several terraced embankments. This afforded the privacy at the lower levels where the growth was denser and didn't interfere with the views at the higher levels."[36]

A resident of the Lake Linganore Homeowners Association near Frederick, Maryland, John Ramboz is an avid hunter, often supplying his family meat requirements by killing deer. One day Ramboz was cutting up a carcass in his front yard. The neighbor across the street passed by, was offended, and reacted belligerently, demanding that the association board create a new rule against "rendering of wildlife." The board agreed to hold a public meeting in which unit owners spoke out largely supporting Ramboz. The board then voted four to one against any new restrictions.[37] Appearances sometimes to the contrary, not all association boards seek to maximize their cumulative power over the actions of unit owners.

Overall, there are as many strong defenders of neighborhood associations as there are critics. Political scientist Robert Dilger reports that many people "gladly transfer some of their property rights" to their neighborhood association "in exchange for the protection it provides against any eccentric or egregious behavior by their neighbors." Dilger thinks that many unit owners actually agree with Albert Riendeau, a resident of Leisure World in the Washington, D.C., suburbs: "We've got the greenest grass in the world. Great esprit de corps. We have a saying, 'If heaven is any nicer than this, it must be one hell of a place.' "[38] In Florida, as the *Financial Times* reported, the newer "gated communities are taking on the appearance of theme parks." At the Wycliffe development in South Florida, homes typically face a golf course or a lake—or both. At one recently developed community, homes are built on "man-made islands in man-made lakes." Salty Cohen, a retired businessman from New York State, believes this is all wonderful: "This is a structured suburbia," he comments. "I look at some of these places and say 'This is what God would have built if He could have gotten financing.' "[39]

On the Learning Curve

We are still at an early point in the history of neighborhood associations. If wide discontent with "oppressive" associations exists, then there are numerous means available for changing such practices.[40] Not every neighborhood association has a real need to control the precise placement of every sign or flower. Some associations may want to eliminate a range of restrictive authorities from their constitutions altogether.

Developers have tended to follow a monolithic model for their neighborhood constitutions. As they encounter wider complaints, however, developers may find it worthwhile to exercise greater creativity. Potential home buyers, for their part, may want to ask more probing questions concerning their future system of neighborhood governance. If buyers really desire fewer restrictions or different methods of covenant enforcement, then land developers and their attorneys will certainly respond to their preferences.[41]

Unit owners can also learn to adjust their behavior.[42] One unit owner reports that internal changes in his neighborhood produced a more harmonious working climate: "Meetings are now pleasant and productive. They used to be a war of words to see who could out-scream the other."[43] CAI is actively working to educate its membership.[44] In fact, one recent CAI report suggests that neighborhood associations should "search for ways to relax rigid rules and accommodate more flexible enforcement."[45] Although critical of many current associations, Franzese observes that "developers are (and should be) experimenting with new formats, if not altruistically, then opportunistically. Strife does not sell."[46] Southern Florida in 2003 witnessed a "growing movement to reform homeowner associations," reflecting many existing unit owners' great dissatisfaction with their own associations.[47]

Wayne Hyatt similarly suggests that past tensions can be diminished. Attempts to control every element of the neighborhood environment contributes to "excessive detail and non-discretionary responses to deviations from the predetermined norms" by boards of directors. Hyatt finds, however, that significant self-corrective actions are now under way in the real estate industry. Builders find that "highly regimented, non-community focused developments do not sell as well as those that are less restrictive." Neighborhood associations therefore are moving beyond the "pets, parking, children, and trash" syndrome of the past. Indeed, Hyatt finds a new trend in which neighborhood associations are becoming "involved in programs and activities that enliven and revitalize not only the common interest community itself but the greater public community."[48] Idealism aside, creating an attractive social as well as physical environment can be profitable.

Neighborhood "Social Capital"

The writings of Mancur Olson and others in the "public choice" school left some key issues unresolved.* Empirically, many more groups seem to survive—and even to thrive—than the public choice analysis would predict. The act of voting in elections, for example, is individually irrational from the perspective of self-interest alone. A person might spend considerable time and effort in the voting process, and yet there is virtually no chance that his or her vote will decide the result. (Public choice theorists have pointed out that the probability of being killed in a car crash on the way to the ballot box is often similar to the probability of deciding an election.)[49] Yet, tens of millions of Americans regularly vote. The acts of contributing to a charity, volunteering for public service, and participating in public life in a host of other ways are also difficult to reconcile with a wholly individualistic way of thinking. Outside the United States, Elinor Ostrom found that many tribal groups, villages, and other local communities had long histories of effective collective action, even when they lacked any formal mechanisms to control individual behavior through a system of property rights or government regulation.[50]

Some studies find surprisingly high levels of unit-owner participation in neighborhood associations, despite all the complaints about apathy and lack of involvement. A 1999 Gallop poll found that 39 percent of unit owners volunteer in some manner at least once a month. Fifteen percent of respondents reported going to every meeting of their neighborhood association, and 34 percent reported going to "most meetings;" only 20 percent reported going to none.[51] Many neighborhood property owners, it would seem, are choosing not to be free-riders, however inconsistent this behavior may be with economic models of the "rational" pursuit of self-interest.

---

*The public choice school of economics was founded in the 1960s to apply economic methods of analysis to political institutions. Political actors are assumed, like participants in the marketplace, to pursue their own self-interest. The public choice school then analyzes the consequences of such self-interested behavior for the workings of the political process.

Attempting to explain such empirical observations, several leading social scientists—including Ostrom, James Coleman, and Robert Putnam—argued in the 1990s that "social capital" is also a powerful influence on group actions.* Economists had long used the term "capital" to refer to industrial plants, office buildings, and other physical facilities. Then, following Gary Becker in the 1960s, they recognized that education and other forms of "human capital" also represent important forms of investment. It now seemed necessary to recognize a third form of capital that would incorporate such essentials as language, moral codes, religion, ethnic identity, and other elements of culture. The worldwide spread of the use of the English language in recent years, for example, is having major economic as well as social implications—it often saves greatly on transactions costs. A society with strong bonds of mutual trust and understanding will also have lower transaction costs among its members. Even a strong set of religious bonds can be "economically efficient"—whatever the "truth content" of the religion.

Thus far, there have been few attempts to study social capital's forms and development in neighborhood associations. Workers in the field, however, report that a "sense of community" can be important to achieving "resident participation in association affairs and compliance with the covenants."[52] Law professor Clayton Gillette suggests that a neighborhood with a strong sense of group identity may offer a superior alternative to legalistic enforcement of covenants. Whatever the details of its constitutional structure, a neighborhood with strong communal bonds may function well. Gillette thus argues that "attention must be paid to the 'social relations' within the [neighborhood] group in order to determine from an 'economic' or 'contractarian' perspective, the proper interaction between association practices and legal intervention."[53] As Gillette elaborates,

> Neighbors may evolve a set of mutually beneficial norms that govern their unique circumstances, even when these norms contravene positive law that applies to the broader society. Norms have the feature of being sustained by the approval or disapproval of those who share them. . . . Those who violate the norms will have difficulty avoiding punishment, since the only escape lies in departure from the relationship. . . .

---

*Based on statistical analyses he developed, Putnam found that different levels of social capital largely explained the divergent economic results in northern Italy and southern Italy. Throughout Italy, the presence or absence of civic commitment could go far to explain the level of "norms of generalized reciprocity and networks of civic engagement [that] encourage social trust and cooperation because they reduce incentives to defect, reduce uncertainty, and provide models for future cooperation." Startling as it was for some economic determinists to hear, Putnam found that it was initial trust that produced later economic success, not a healthy economy that produced a later climate of trust. As Putnam reported, in Italy "the contemporary [strong] correlation between civics and economics reflects primarily the impact of civics on economics, not the reverse." See Robert D. Putnam, *Making Democracy Work: Civic Traditions in Modern Italy* (Princeton, NJ: Princeton University Press, 1993), 155–57, 178.

The combination of vague [contractual] terms that can only roughly specify the nature of the relationship combined with extralegal enforcement mechanisms by those who can fill in the details of the relationship may create a situation in which legal (judicial) enforcement is inferior to reliance on the parties themselves to keep the common understanding together.[54]

However, and despite a large body of recent writings, social scientists have yet to explain in practice how a high level of social capital can be created. How does a "healthy," "efficient," or "economically productive" set of neighborhood common values—a neighborhood culture that holds transaction costs to a minimum—come into existence? A common language is a key element of social capital, but the sharing of a language among a group of people is seldom the result of any policy decision.

There are some practical ways neighborhoods can build social capital. A youth sports team organized to compete with other neighborhoods might help to inspire a sense of neighborhood "spirit." Enlisting unit owners to participate together in wider political processes—in cases where regional or citywide decisions might affect the whole neighborhood—is another potential way of bonding. A neighborhood newsletter or web site might help. Neighborhood parties and other social events could promote a common identity. Indeed, many practical devices could potentially increase social capital within neighborhood associations.

While industry leaders may not think of their efforts in terms of social science language, they are well aware of the practical need to encourage stronger bonds of community. An Arizona attorney in the field of neighborhood association law, Donald Dykeman suggests that a neighborhood's founding constitution should include explicit approval for the following association activities: "primary and adult education programs"; "recreation and social programs"; "cultural, arts, environmental, and wellness programs"; "community internet and intranet sites"; and "charter clubs and other volunteer organizations and activities."[55] A recent CAI report states that, besides the physical environment, the building of "community software" is a key to a successful neighborhood association.

> Communities need to create a sense of collegiality. Developers realize that this atmosphere is marketable, quite frankly, and are "willing and eager" to spend money on fostering community spirit. The strategies can include the development of good public spaces, the mixing of uses to create attractive and accessible retail and office space in a "town center" and the creation of a pedestrian friendly environment. These features often foster spontaneous interaction among residents. In addition, there needs to be a broader definition of community—one that includes stores, places of worship, schools, daycare and entertainment in addition to any area government by the community association. "Thoughtful design," when integrated with innovative technology and attention to the "community software" . . . is the equivalent of "rocket fuel" for real-estate values.[56]

Not all people, admittedly, want to bond with their neighbors. Some people will be put off by measures to foster neighborhood spirit. A study in California finds that "the overwhelming majority of residents chose to live in a common interest development because it had the best location and type of home they could afford, not because they wanted to be members of a mandatory homeowners association."[57] These homeowners were not motivated by any desire to participate in a shared lifestyle with other residents. Developers should also work to provide neighborhood constitutions that suit such individual tastes for greater personal autonomy. The creation of a neighborhood association does not mandate a specific system of governance; it instead offers a flexible framework that must first be filled in by the developer and later completed by the unit owners themselves.

Conclusion

The problems of private democracy at the neighborhood level have been so great that a few commentators even question whether neighborhood associations should have a future. Yet the difficulties experienced may be inherent to any local collective undertaking—public or private. It is not the "private" but the "collective" aspect of life in neighborhood associations that creates the greatest tensions. Anyone who thinks that "public" neighborhoods are any different may be suffering from utopian fantasies.

Most Americans in congested urban and suburban areas seem to want a significant degree of control over their neighbors' actions. They may complain bitterly about "dictatorial" neighborhood associations, but in the end they prefer a regulated to an unregulated surrounding environment. The minority of people who want to avoid close dealings with their neighbors may need to move to an older neighborhood without an association (although zoning will likely still be present). The majority who want collective controls but may be unhappy with their current neighborhood association may simply have to work more closely with their neighbors to improve its workings.

Political scientists are demonstrating new interest in American private associations of all kinds because they hope that association members will learn democratic habits that will benefit the wider political process and contribute to a higher overall level of social capital in American society.[58] Is such a development likely to be the result of interactions among unit owners in neighborhood associations? It is certainly true that many millions of Americans are obtaining experience in government processes at the most local of levels. Yet some commentators argue that, rather than improving their outlook, this experience brings out the worst in many people; conceivably, the supply of social capital across the nation could even suffer. On the other hand, dealing with offensive behavior is part of the art of politics. Having experienced the tensions of neighborhood democracy and survived—and perhaps even enjoyed the process—some unit owners may be encouraged to try their hand in a wider political arena.

Neighborhood associations are criticized because their members are encouraged to turn inward and ignore the wider problems of American society. Parents who send their children to private schools may similarly show less concern for the educational quality of the public schools. It seems doubtful, however, that unit owners will show any less interest in national politics than any other group. Indeed, because these residents have higher incomes on average, and the resources to become involved, they actually may show more democratic participation. It is quite possible, however, that in matters of state and city politics the residents of neighborhood associations will show the greatest concern for those public issues that particularly affect them.

Such behavior, to be sure, would not distinguish neighborhood association unit owners from most other groups in society. Concern for one's own interest is not a rare quality in American politics. Indeed, a greater problem may be that neighborhood associations in the future may become too successful. As Mancur Olson has emphasized, collective action is difficult and may often be frustrated altogether. Olson commented that large American businesses might have undue political influence because they have already overcome organizational obstacles for private business reasons. The same, however, will be true of private neighborhood associations. Neighborhood associations have had limited wider political involvement to date, but it would not be surprising if, at some point fairly soon, their broader political involvement and their particular effectiveness in that capacity relative to other less well organized groups raises new issues for political scientists to explore.

NOTES

1. Clifford J. Treese, *Community Associations Factbook, 1999 edition* (Alexandria, VA: Community Associations Institute, 1999), 9.

2. James Madison, Federalist Paper No. 10, in *The Federalist Papers* (New York: New American Library, 1961), 80–81.

3. Ibid., 81.

4. Carol J. Silverman and Stephen E. Barton, "Managing Interdependence: The Effects of Neighboring Style on Neighborhood Organization," in Barton and Silverman, eds., *Common Interest Communities: Private Governments and the Public Interest* (Berkeley: Institute of Government Studies Press, University of California, 1994), 180.

5. Joni Greenwalt, *Homeowner Associations: A Nightmare or a Dream Come True?* (Denver, CO: Cassie Publications, Inc., 2001), 92.

6. Ken Ward, "Homeowners' Association Law Takes on 'Little Nazis,'" *Las Vegas Business Press,* January 5, 1998, 12.

7. Vince Larkins, director of the Fair Housing Center of the Greater Palm Beaches, quoted in Tal Abbady, "Residents Get Help to Reform Associations," (South Florida) *Sun-Sentinel,* June 21, 2003.

8. Greenwalt, *Homeowner Associations,* 100.

9. See (quoting Jefferson) Georgette C. Poindexter, "Collective Individualism: Deconstructing the Legal City," *University of Pennsylvania Law Review* 145 (January 1997), 624–25.

10. Alexis de Tocqueville, *Democracy in America,* translation by George Lawrence (New York: Anchor Books, 1969), 62–63, 67.

11. Ibid., 68.

12. Ibid., 68, 70.

13. Donald R. Stabile, *Community Associations: The Emergence and Acceptance of a Quiet Innovation in Housing* (Westport, CO: Greenwood Press, 2000), 47.

14. Tracy M. Gordon, *Planned Developments in California: Private Communities and Public Life* (San Francisco, CA: Public Policy Institute of California, 2004), 41, ix, 32, 36–37.

15. Mancur Olson, *The Logic of Collective Action: Public Goods and the Theory of Groups* (Cambridge, MA: Harvard University Press, 1965).

16. See Carol Paul, *Revitalizing Apathetic Communities,* 3rd ed. (Alexandria, VA: Community Associations Institute, 1996).

17. Stephen E. Barton and Carol J. Silverman, "Public Life and Private Property in the Urban Community," in Barton and Silverman, eds., *Common Interest Communities,* 305, 306.

18. James L. Winokur, "The Mixed Blessings of Promissory Servitudes: Toward Optimizing Economic Utility, Individual Liberty, and Personal Identity," *Wisconsin Law Review,* 1989 (January/February 1989), 62.

19. Erin M. Fuller and Christopher Durso, eds. *A Sense of Place and Harmony: Outcomes from the Communities of Tomorrow Summit,* summary report of a conference of the Community Associations Institute and the American Institute of Architects, September 8–9, 1999, Arlington, VA (Alexandria, VA: Community Associations Institute Research Foundation, n.d.), 12.

20. Quoted in Paula A. Franzese, "Common Interest Communities: Standards of Review and Review of Standards," *Washington University Journal of Law and Policy* 3 (2000), 663–64.

21. *Common Ground,* the magazine of the Community Associations Institute (Alexandria, VA: Community Associations Institute, November/December 2001), 13, 49.

22. National Homeowner Association Registry, http://www.dcwindustries.com/hoas/il.htm (accessed January 15, 2003).

23. Joel Garreau, *Edge City: Life on the New Frontier* (New York: Anchor Books, 1988), 184–85.

24. John Manougian, "Effective Boards—Revisited," *Quorum,* the magazine of the Washington chapter of CAI (August 2004), 18.

25. Winokur, "The Mixed Blessings of Promissory Servitudes," 5, 29, 21, 62.

26. Paula A. Franzese, "Does It Take a Village?: Privatization, Patterns of Restrictiveness and the Demise of Community," *Villanova Law Review* 47, no. 3 (2002), 558, 560, 575.

27. Ellen Dolan, "How to Grow the Best Manager," *Condo Management Online,* http://www.condomgmt.com/Articles/manage/019.html (accessed December 13, 2002).

28. Barton and Silverman, "Public Life and Private Property in the Urban Community," 307.

29. *National Survey of Community Association Homeowner Satisfaction,* conducted by the Gallop Organization for the Community Associations Institute Research Foundation, March 1999 (Alexandria, VA: Community Associations Institute, 1999), 42.

30. Wendy Fullerton, "Weapons Include Lawsuits, Attorneys, Tanks," *Fort Myers (FL) News-Press,* April 7, 2002; and Wendy Fullerton, "Protester Removes Tank from Driveway," *Fort Myers (FL) News-Press,* May 9, 2002.

31. Quoted in Fullerton, "Weapons Include Lawsuits, Attorneys, Tanks."

32. See Clint Bolick, "Leviathan in the Suburbs," *Weekly Standard,* December 18, 1995, 25, 26; see also Clint Bolick, *Grassroots Tyranny: The Limits of Federalism* (Washington, DC: Cato Institute, 1993).

33. Michael L. Utz, "Common Interest Ownership in Pennsylvania: An Examination of Statutory Reform and Implications for Practitioners," *Duquesne Law Review* 37 (Spring 1999), 473.

34. Doreen Heisler and Warren Klein, *Inside Look at Community Association Homeownership—Facts, Perceptions* (Alexandria, VA: Community Associations Institute, 1996), 43.

35. Robert E. Lang and Karen A. Danielsen, "Gated Communities in America: Walling Out the World," *Housing Policy Debate* 8, no. 4 (1997), 873.

36. Bob Biederman, "Blue Lagoon Community Association Goes Through Management and Landscape Changes With Smiles All Around," *Condo Management Online,* http://www.condomgmt.com/Articles/Landscaping/014.html (accessed December 13, 2002).

37. Elizabeth Williamson, "Hunter Becomes the Target in Neighborhood Dispute," *Washington Post,* March 16, 2003, C5.

38. Robert Jay Dilger, *Neighborhood Politics: Residential Community Associations in American Governance* (New York: New York University Press, 1992), 11.

39. Gary Silverman, "Flocking to Florida: The World Chases Its Dreams on America's New Frontier," *Financial Times,* May 24, 2004, 11.

40. Bill Overton, ed., *Community First! Emerging Visions Reshaping America's Condominium and Homeowner Associations* (Alexandria, VA: Community Associations Institute, 1999).

41. See Lee Anne Fennell, "Contracting Communities," *University of Illinois Law Review* (2004), 829–898.

42. See Paul, *Revitalizing Apathetic Communities.*

43. Unnamed unit owner, quoted in Greenwalt, *Homeowner Associations,* 27.

44. See Kenneth Budd, *Be Reasonable: How Community Associations Can Enforce Rules Without Antagonizing Residents, Going to Court, or Starting World War III* (Alexandria, VA: Community Associations Institute, 1998).

45. Fuller and Durso, eds., *A Sense of Place and Harmony,* 4.

46. Franzese, "Does It Take a Village?" 589.

47. Abbady, "Residents Get Help to Reform Associations."

48. Wayne S. Hyatt, "Common Interest Communities: Evolution and Reinvention," *John Marshall Law Review* 31 (Winter 1998), 357, 359, 360.

49. Cecil E. Bohanon and T. Norman Van Cott, "Now More Than Ever, Your Vote Doesn't Matter," *The Independent Review* 6 (Spring 2002), 591.

50. See Elinor Ostrom, *Governing the Commons: The Evolution of Institutions for Collective Action* (New York: Cambridge University Press, 1990).

51. *National Survey of Community Association Homeowner Satisfaction,* 19, 28.

52. Mary Avgerinos, *Alternative Dispute Resolution & Consensus Building for Community Associations* (Alexandria, VA: Community Associations Institute, 1997), 5.

53. Clayton P. Gillette, "Courts, Covenants, and Communities," *University of Chicago Law Review* 61 (Fall 1994), 1416.

54. Ibid., 1414–15.

55. Model neighborhood association declaration presented by Donald E. Dykeman to the Governance Symposium on "Creating a Governance Model That Really Works," sponsored by the Community Associations Institute Research Foundation, Arlington, VA, October 31, 2003.

56. Fuller and Durso, eds., *A Sense of Place and Harmony,* 9.

57. Silverman and Barton, "Managing Interdependence," 171.

58. William A. Galston, *Liberal Purposes: Goods, Virtues, and Diversity in the Liberal State* (New York: Cambridge University Press, 1991).

PART II
From Public Zoning to Private Neighborhood Associations

For many American neighborhoods, the history of collective action to control land use did not begin with a neighborhood association. The protection of shared environments began instead with zoning. As Katia Brener writes, the Supreme Court and most state courts endorsed a view of "local government not as an agent of the state, but as an agent of local families." In the American suburbs, a main purpose of local government was to erect "a moat protecting home and family from crime, congestion, and the pollution of the outside world." This was to be accomplished by excluding "not only commercial uses, but also apartment houses, other multifamily dwellings, and publicly subsidized housing"—and in many cases zoning kept out even a single family home on a lot size of less than one or two acres. As a result, "as American suburbs flourished, local zoning enabled people to preserve the homogeneous character of their neighborhoods and to control who entered their communities."[1]

The spread of neighborhood zoning initially occurred in the Northeast and Midwest. In New Jersey, 13 percent of municipalities employed zoning in 1925; by 1971, 96 percent of New Jersey municipalities had zoning ordinances. In older parts of the United States, developed neighborhoods often preceded zoning. So the "privatization" of an existing neighborhood required government action. The transaction costs of assembling a new collective property right through private efforts alone would have been prohibitive. The practical solution therefore was to enact a public zoning ordinance that did not require the property owners' unanimous voluntary consent.

Further south and west in the United States, a much larger and different sort of land development took place in the second half of the 20th century. By then, private neighborhood associations were becoming a routine part of American life. In such areas, a private association could be created as part of a neighborhood's original plan. The land use controls that private neighborhood associations and public zoning exercise thus are distinguished more by the manner of their creation than by their subsequent regulatory contents. As urban historian Jon Teaford comments, in the last few decades of the 20th century, "miniature private governments were thus filling the role previously played by public governments" in providing "the defenses desired by suburbanites."[2]

In areas of the United States where neighborhood associations flourish, county government often also assumes greater importance as the leading instrument of local public government. In a newly evolving pattern of American local governance, private associations regulate the small-scale land interactions and provide "micro" services at the neighborhood level. County governments provide the "macro" services, such as arterial highways, water supply, and sewage collection and disposal. In Prince George's County in the Washington suburbs, almost all the municipalities were created before World War II, but from then on "homeowners associations and a more sophisticated county government took on some of the roles of municipal corporations"—this private and public mix becoming the operative new system of local government over most of the county.[3] In a few places such as Phoenix and Houston, the central city expanded through aggressive annexation to encompass a major part of the metropolitan area, and assumed many of the regionwide governance responsibilities.

In light of this history, the roots of the private neighborhood association can be traced to two sources. As we examined in part I, homeowners associations, condominiums, and cooperatives as forms of American housing ownership have grown. But equally important to the privatization of the American neighborhood has been the rise of zoning. Similar to the rights given to a private property owner in an association, zoning created the power to exclude others from the use of a common neighborhood environment.

The institutional evolution of both types of collective controls over neighborhood land use took place gradually, incrementally, and informally. This process is typical of the evolution of property rights over the centuries. New rights to land and property are seldom created from whole cloth. They usually emerge from common practice that may even be at odds with the accepted legal theories of the day. Legal fictions then arise to obscure the contradictions between the theory and the practice. As experience accumulates, the informal workings come to be better understood and the merits more fully appreciated.*

---

*In the case of agricultural land, the relevant time frames have often been particularly long. Robert Ellickson notes that the practical advantages of private ownership have meant that "the institution of private property in crops" around the world is "practically ubiquitous." Such land tenure systems were

At a still later stage, the legislature may codify the new property realities. Thus, in describing the evolution of the rights to land in England over many centuries, Sir Frederick Pollock once wrote that "the history of our land laws, it cannot be too often repeated, is a history of legal fictions and evasions, with which the Legislature vainly endeavored to keep pace until their results . . . were perforce acquiesced in as a settled part of the law itself."[4]

Indeed, for much of history, as Harvard historian Richard Pipes writes, "land was universally considered a resource that one could exploit exclusively but not own and sell."[5] So in the face of religious and other cultural opposition, the spread of modern ideas about transferable property at first had to take place in a disguised manner. Pollock describes the evolution of these ideas in Britain from the 13th century: "The system underwent a series of grave modifications. Grave as these were, however, the main lines of the feudal theory were always ostensibly preserved. And to this day [in the late 19th century], though the really characteristic incidents of the feudal tenures have disappeared or left only the faintest of traces, the scheme of our land laws can, as to its form, be described only as a modified feudalism."[*,6]

In the 19th century, the disposal of public lands in the western United States often began with illegal squatting. The federal government regarded the squatters as criminal lawbreakers, but was powerless to halt their advance on a distant frontier. After a few years, strong political pressures frequently resulted in new laws by which Congress retroactively confirmed the recent acts of squatter occupancy, granting a full legal title. The Homestead Act of 1862 did not create a new system of land settlement, but represented a final recognition that squatting was an unavoidable fact of life on the western frontier.

Zoning is now following in this same path. The real workings of zoning law have been submerged beneath layers of zoning legal fiction. As recently as 1998, two zoning authorities wrote of the "elaborate charades" that still characterize the processes of land use control in the United States.[7] At the neighborhood level, zoning has actually been functioning for many years as a private property right. The high priests of zoning, however, could not acknowledge this reality; it contradicted all that they had said for much of the 20th century about the progressive "public purposes" of zoning.

---

not the product of any government plan or social design. Rather, "the people on the ground who established this property rule did not do so deductively, but through trial and error over many millennia." See Robert C. Ellickson, "Property in Land," *Yale Law Journal* 102 (April 1993), 1399–1400.

*Remarkably enough, Scotland abolished the last vestiges of feudal land tenure only very recently. According to a 2002 report, "Scotland has kept feudal land laws for 800 years. The feudal system of land tenure, under which all land ultimately belonged to the monarch, at the top of a hierarchical pyramid, was formally abolished only two years ago, in a law establishing absolute ownership and finally abolishing feudal duties—the token fees paid to feudal superiors for land titles." See David White, "Scots Stake Their Claims in Land Shake-Up," *Financial Times*, March 5, 2002, 10.

The traditional forms of rational policy analysis—based on the idea of the existence of a real world of hard facts—apparently offer only a partial view. In the contemporary world, it would seem that the study of public policy must also incorporate "rhetorical" analysis as well, delving into the policy impacts of "sound bites," and other public use of language—along with the willingness of judges to accept such language as if it describes reality. Indeed, the use of elaborate legal fictions to justify and defend the workings of zoning is an important element of the history of American land use controls in the 20th century.

Part II will examine how the practice of zoning first gave rise to private neighborhoods on a widespread basis in the United States. Chapter 6 explains how zoning has been a de facto collective property right in suburban neighborhoods. Chapter 7 reviews the literature from a new zoning school that emerged in the 1970s to expose the yawning gap between zoning realities and zoning law. The writings of these "zoning heretics" received wide attention among students of zoning, though their policy recommendations had little direct impact on official zoning practices. Chapter 8 shows how municipal public zoning in the 1980s and 1990s nevertheless continued to evolve informally, gaining status as a private property right. In such ways, the privatization of zoning in the 20th century prefigured the rise of the private neighborhood association.

NOTES

1. Katia Brener, "Belle Terre and Single-Family Home Ordinances: Judicial Perceptions of Local Government and the Presumption of Validity," *New York University Law Review* 74 (May 1999), 464, 468, 466, 465.

2. Jon C. Teaford, *Post-Suburbia: Government and Politics in the Edge Cities* (Baltimore: Johns Hopkins University Press, 1997), 97–98.

3. Susan Saulny, "At the Most Basic Level, It's Poll Time; Cast of Many Appears on Ballots Throughout County's Diverse and Myriad Municipalities," *Washington Post,* April 28, 1999, M8.

4. Frederick Pollock, *The Land Laws* (London: Macmillan and Co., 1883), 62.

5. Richard Pipes, *Property and Freedom* (New York: Vintage Books, 1999), 89.

6. Pollock, *The Land Laws,* 51–52.

7. Michael M. Berger and Gideon Kanner, "The Need for Takings Law Reform: A View from the Trenches—A Response to Taking Stock of the Takings Debate," *Santa Clara Law Review* 38, no. 3 (1998), 856.

6

The Privatization of Zoning

The first modern zoning ordinance in the United States was established in 1916 to protect the merchants along New York City's Fifth Avenue. Within 10 years, more than 500 cities and towns had adopted zoning controls. The U.S. Department of Commerce encouraged even wider use with the 1924 publication of a Standard State Zoning Enabling Act.[1] Even during an era of conservative judicial views, the U.S. Supreme Court upheld zoning in its 1926 *Euclid* decision.[2] Zoning imposed large restrictions on the rights of property owners, but the Court in the end found grounds to approve zoning as a new way to protect private property. The Court also justified zoning as a progressive instrument of modern land use planning.

The Planning Rationale

The planning argument for zoning drew on trends in American intellectual life during the early 20th century. Defenders of zoning argued that it was a necessary instrument of the scientific management of land use. Hopes were high among many Progressive Era Americans that scientific knowledge could be applied to all areas of American society, greatly improving the efficiency of American business and government alike. In an urban setting, scientific management would require implementing comprehensive land use plans. Instead of the disorderly patterns of urban land development typical of the past, progressive theorists proposed that America's cities should be developed systematically according to a rational design. Land uses would be coordinated across

139

an entire metropolitan area, taking full account of the interrelated needs of residential and commercial uses. As a result, the built environment of the United States would not only be more productive economically, but it would have a higher visual quality.[3]

As comprehensive land use planning was being put into practice, a city staff of experts would study housing, transportation, job market, and other economic and social trends. The required amounts of land for various types of future uses would then be allocated among areas of the city—for example, for garden apartments in one district, homes on quarter-acre lots in another district, and homes on two-acre lots in yet another. Zoning laws, according to the received theory, would provide the legal instrument to enforce the comprehensive plan. Zoning would ensure that each new housing unit or other land use was located in the district for which it was intended, as scientifically—and thus objectively—determined "by planning experts."[4] According to Patricia Burgess, from the 1910s onwards, "as part of their efforts at professionalization, city planners had begun to emphasize the 'science,' rather than the 'art,' of city planning."[5]

It all sounded logical to leading urban thinkers of the time. So did ideas of Fabian socialists and other advocates of future scientific planning for whole societies. As the history of the 20th century shows, it was possible for large numbers of prominent intellectuals to be possessed of grand illusions. To be sure, the whole edifice of "scientific planning" in eastern Europe, the former Soviet Union, and elsewhere would collapse by the end of the century. In the United States, the goal of scientific management of American cities proved almost as utopian. The realities of American land use, as it turned out, had little to do with the results of American land use planning.

Scientific management of large jurisdictions assumed a predictability of economic events and a capacity for assembling economic information that actual planners would never achieve.[6] Although progressive theory said that politicians should concede the decisionmaking role to expert professionals in "scientific" matters, the politicians had other ideas. They were in fact on solid ground. Decisions about proper land use involve a society's basic values, issues that cannot be left to technicians to resolve.* In addition, with planning and zoning being undertaken at the municipal level, it was almost inevitable that localities would "decide their zoning policies in the interests of their own residents with little regard to their effect on outsiders" located throughout the rest of their metropolitan areas.[7]

---

*As Dennis Coyle has commented, "Beneath the arcane language and technicalities, disputes about property rights [to land] reveal fundamental clashes between opposing perspectives on the proper society." See Dennis J. Coyle, *Property Rights and the Constitution: Shaping Society through Land Use Regulation* (Albany: State University of New York Press, 1993), 18.

A Legal Necessity

The precise details of city planning and zoning were as much a product of the American legal mind as they were a product of formal planning theories. Early on, some professional planners knew that dividing a city into districts, with particular uses specified by law for each district, would not produce a livable city. Jane Jacobs would later emphasize such arguments in her writings. Vital neighborhoods often evolve in unpredictable and undirected ways; they can benefit from diverse mixtures of uses. Although zoning typically prohibited it, many people would have welcomed a convenience store or a small restaurant nearby within their neighborhood.

With its fixed areas prescribed for each type of land use, the American zoning system posed a large obstacle to any such creative mixing of uses. Zoning incorporated into the law an official expectation that the American landscape should be precisely segregated by housing type, and thus indirectly by social and economic type. A "zone," by definition, is a place where each land use fits the common prescription.

Nevertheless, and despite their social and economic failings, well-defined zones were essential to the theories of zoning lawyers. These lawyers were rightly concerned about the potential for abuse in the administration of the formidable government powers inherent to zoning. A favorable zoning ruling might be worth millions of dollars to a private land developer. The dangers of large private influences, and perhaps even corruption among local officials, were obvious. It was important, therefore, to ensure that zoning was insulated from ordinary politics. Zoning actions had to reflect the determinations of expert professionals and not the subjective judgments of ordinary city politicians. In 1968, a New York State court declared that, in the absence of a comprehensive plan, "there can be no rational allocation of land use" and that the plan "is the insurance that the public welfare is being served and that zoning does not become nothing more than just a Gallop poll."[8]

It was essential therefore to the very existence of zoning that professional planners have the independence to assign land uses in advance to clearly specified areas of land, all this according to objective—"expert"—criteria.* Any large

---

*Martha Lees comments that "while city planners probably would have used scientific methods regardless of how they felt these methods would affect judges' acceptance of zoning, their use of scientific methodology was motivated to some degree by their belief that it would command judicial respect." Judges were inclined to follow their own common sense in many areas, but were more likely to defer to any conclusions that could be defended as "scientific." The legal advocates for zoning powers could play to this judicial deference by arguing that scientific planning and zoning "was a complex matter that only experts with specialized knowledge could understand." Thus, one judge declared that

elements of discretion in such matters would endanger the basic integrity of the whole zoning system. As attorney Joel Kosman observes, the early creators of zoning showed great "judicial savvy" in their "understanding of the need to package zoning as a tool for achieving legitimate, laudable ends [that would be] acceptable to the courts."[9]

Planning Illusions

Events in the real world, however, would soon show the impracticality of the legal approach to planning and zoning.[10] The burden placed on land use "science" was much greater than planning professionals could sustain. By default, as events unfolded, land development occurred incrementally and opportunistically. A housing project (or commercial development) might be proposed for a particular site. The municipal government would then decide whether it wanted that particular development in that particular place at that particular time. In making such determinations, towns and cities found that they could not rely on existing land use plans.* Instead, new land use assessments were necessary, tailored specifically to the information needs of an individual decision. The relevant municipal studies were case-specific, focused on the particular land development proposal and its projected impacts on the city—economically, aesthetically, socially, and otherwise.

Approval of new land development thus was not an administrative action carried out to verify consistency with existing regulations. Rather, a city typically had to amend its zoning ordinance—a legislative act by the city council—on a case-by-case basis to grant approvals for individual projects. Overall, the process became a private business transaction between the city and the land developer. The two parties either made or did not make a deal, depending on the specific advantages to each party. A leading study of zoning practice comments that in mid-Manhattan during the 1960s, "almost every new building was constructed through a special permit, exception, text change, or variance. The process more resembled a Middle Eastern bazaar than the government of the world's most prestigious city."[11]

---

he was not qualified to review municipal zoning actions because he "was not versed in the 'sciences' of traffic congestion and sanitation." See Martha A. Lees, "Preserving Property Values? Preserving Proper Homes? Preserving Privilege?: The Pre-Euclid Debate over Zoning for Exclusively Private Residential Areas, 1916–1926," *University of Pittsburgh Law Review* 56 (Winter 1994), 399, 398, 400, 401.

*In the early years, there were often no plans to consult. Despite the necessity of the planning role in the official legal theories, the courts at first did not insist that a plan must be prepared prior to zoning. Indeed, in 1941 there were 10 times as many zoning ordinances in existence as comprehensive city plans. See Patricia Burgess, *Planning for the Private Interest: Land Use Controls and Residential Patterns in Columbus, Ohio, 1900–1970* (Columbus: Ohio State University Press, 1994), 73, 81.

The granting of zoning approvals worked in a similar fashion throughout America's developing suburbs. Although local governments were officially "public," their behavior in practice was much like that of a private owner of land rights. A municipality would typically zone large areas for very low densities. A developer wanting to build would have to apply for a zoning change for such areas. The municipality's willingness to grant the change would depend on the developers "offer"; legislating the necessary zoning change amounted to "signing the deal."

Throughout the United States, formal comprehensive plans often gathered dust on shelves. In 1968, the National Commission on Urban Problems— chaired by former Senator Paul Douglas of Illinois (who earlier had been a well-known professor of economics at the University of Chicago)—declared:

> It could hardly be clearer that formal plans are not furnishing a unifying basis for most local regulations and other needed development guidance measures. Many communities regulate without meaningful plans. Some of those that do have plans pay little attention to them in making regulatory decisions. Still others find that plans provide little guidance in answering many regulatory questions. In any event, the failure to formulate guiding policies precludes effective development guidance.[12]

A long-time leading practitioner of zoning law, Richard Babcock commented in 1966 that municipalities had been operating without any "principles by which the execution of zoning law is capable of being measured."[13] All in all, as law professor Dan Tarlock (another insightful observer of the zoning system) commented in 1972, there was "remarkably little consensus about why zoning is necessary"; the whole zoning system simply lacked any "satisfactory rationale" for its existence.[14] As Patricia Burgess would put it in 1994, in the decades after World War II zoning "essentially protected private property in the guise of regulating it," despite all the years of protestations by zoning lawyers and planners to the contrary.[15] The mainstream "progressive" defenders of zoning, however, were unwilling to acknowledge the contrary reality—zoning was functioning as a private property right.

The official law of zoning thus continued formally to require a comprehensive plan, however obviously fictional such plans were becoming. As a result, the professional practitioners of land use planning continued to churn them out. From the 1930s to the 1950s, Burgess comments, "planners continually reiterated the theoretical planning-zoning connection," even as they also "bewailed its absence in practice."[16] Christine Boyer observes that "the planning dialogue in pursuit of an order for the American city persisted over decades in spite of its obvious failures to implement its plans."[17] By the 1970s, some of the more conscientious and thoughtful planners had become thoroughly disenchanted.[18] Still, being a government planner was a well-paying job for many people. Many working planners were content to collect their pay-checks, acting out the myths of zoning legal theory.*

The Nuisance Rationale

The second official justification for zoning was that it provided a desirable reform of nuisance law. Zoning could be seen as an extension and improve-ment on the traditional law of nuisances; it provided advance notice of those uses acceptable in a particular district. Zoning thereby standardized the former ad hoc procedures in which individual judges issued nuisance determinations case by case. It provided needed investment security prior to a large financial commitment to a development project. The nuisance justification was also necessary to zoning because nuisance law was an accepted exercise of the state's police power, and municipal zoning would require state coercion in controlling the future use of land.

This justification was all, however, another large zoning fiction. In some instances zoning did actually regulate a genuine nuisance; it might be employed, for example, to exclude a factory giving off offensive smells from an area of single-family homes. Yet in most cases, as Martha Lees observes, zon-ing's legal defenders found it necessary "to shade the truth" because "businesses and apartments were not traditional nuisances."[19] A typical zoning ordinance might require lot sizes of one acre or larger. A home on a lot of three-quarters of an acre was excluded. This home posed no danger of a genuine "harm" according to any traditional understanding of nuisance law. The reality was that "city planning reports, judicial opinions, and legal briefs [are] documents that by their nature are intended to legitimate and sometimes obfuscate their creators' beliefs rather than to depict them truthfully."[20]

In practice, zoning's most important role was to maintain the existing char-acter of high-quality residential neighborhoods. A three-quarter acre lot was

---

*Much as has been argued above, Yale law professor Carol Rose notes that "to a very considerable degree, the emergence of plan jurisdiction is the work of the courts." Yet, misconceptions of legal the-orists led to a variety of evasions and misunderstandings. As Rose elaborated:

> Legal commentators have deplored local government's evasions of planning, and their unwilling-ness to deal with development proposals in the generalized way implicit in the idea of planning. But . . . these repeated local efforts to evade end-state planning . . . suggest that the plan/imple-menting ordinance model simply may not be compatible with the local land use decisionmaking process. This local process seems to move in the direction of more bargaining, more participation, and more personal knowledge and one-on-one contact. An effort to make local decisionmakers behave in a markedly different manner might well backfire, encouraging [more] false and evasive plans, and false and evasive escapes therefrom. See Carol M. Rose, "Planning and Dealing: Piecemeal Land Controls as a Problem of Local Legitimacy," *California Law Review* 71 (May 1983), 881.

undesirable in a neighborhood of one-acre lots because it was inconsistent with the "ambiance," the "prestigiousness," and the "quality." The rapid spread of low-density living from the 1920s, coinciding with the rise of the automobile as the principal means of local transportation, gave a powerful impetus to zoning. Well-off suburban neighborhoods in the automotive age were threatened by housing at higher densities. In an attractive low-density neighborhood, there was always a risk that some individual owner might want to build an apartment building at a high density (or sell to someone else for this purpose). Such an action might enrich this one owner in the neighborhood, even as it significantly reduced the surrounding environmental attractiveness for other residents. It was a classic circumstance of a "tragedy of the commons"; a neighborhood owner pursuing his own individual interest would threaten the well-being of the whole group of owners.

Zoning in effect blocked any such free riding in neighborhoods.* As the Supreme Court had declared in 1926, zoning legitimately blocked the "parasitical" behavior of an apartment seeking entry to an attractive neighborhood. In 1940, a prominent American planner Hugh Pomeroy stated that, in zoning, "the important thing is to provide protection for the character of the neighborhood. . . . Low density neighborhoods occupied by higher income families should not be faced with the danger of intrusion or encroachment by small lot developers that would destroy their character. The danger is always that the less intensive occupancy will be impaired by encroachment by more intensive occupancy."[21]

Zoning was a powerful instrument of income and class segregation.[22] Despite legal theories and other high-minded official explanations, the real

---

*In 1918, Robert Whitten already had clearly grasped the main purpose of zoning, explaining to a city-planning conference:

> As soon as the confidence of the home owner in the maintenance of the character of the neighborhood is broken down through the coming of the store or of the apartment, his civic pride and his economic interest in the permanent welfare of the section declines. As the home owner is replaced by the renting class, there is a further decline of civic interest and the neighborhood that once took a live and intelligent interest in all matters affecting its welfare becomes absolutely dead in so far as its civic and social life is concerned. Zoning is absolutely essential to preserve the morale of the neighborhood.

If an apartment house could undermine the quality of a neighborhood, the entry of a minority race could have the same effect. Both involved—in the language of economics—a negative "externality." As Whitten further commented:

> Often the growth or change of districts inhabited by members of a race considered inferior, like the Chinese or Negroes, or the desire of some of its members for betterment, brings them into contact with other peoples in the same block. . . . This invasion of the inferior produces more or less discomfort, or disorder, and has a distinct tendency to lower property values. See Robert Whitten, "The Zoning of Residence Sections," in *Proceedings of the National Conference on City Planning* (1918), quoted in Joel Kosman, "Toward an Inclusionary Jurisprudence: A Reconceptualization of Zoning," *Catholic University Law Review* 43 (Fall 1993), 82.

functions of zoning were widely understood by at least the 1960s. In 1968, the National Commission on Urban Problems stated:

> Zoning . . . very effectively keeps the poor and those with low incomes out of suburban areas by stipulating lot sizes way beyond their economic reach. Many suburbs prohibit or severely limit the construction of apartments, townhouses, or planned unit developments which could accommodate more people in less space at potential savings.[23]
>
> [Zoning] regulations still do their best job when they deal with the type of situation for which many of them were first intended; when the objective is to protect established character and when that established character is uniformly residential. It is in the "nice" neighborhoods, where the regulatory job is easiest, that regulations do their best job.[24]

The U.S. Supreme Court in 1974 would officially endorse this protective role for zoning in its *Belle Terre* decision—the first local zoning case heard by the Court since 1928. The Village of Belle Terre on Long Island limited housing to one-family dwellings and defined a family as containing no more than two unrelated individuals. Following this rule, Belle Terre had evicted six college students from a shared home. In upholding Belle Terre's action, Justice William Douglas declared for the Court that "a quiet place where yards are wide, people few, and motor vehicles restricted are legitimate guidelines in a land-use project addressed to family needs. . . . The police power . . . [may] lay out zones where family values, youth values, and the blessings of quiet seclusion and clean air make the area a sanctuary for people."[25]

As Katia Brener remarks, the Supreme Court blessed "a community's right to preserve the atmosphere of a neighborhood." Zoning now had the highest approval to promote a secure neighborhood environment of high quality in which "friendly relationships with neighbors" could be formed.[26] Or as Harvard law professor Gerald Frug states, the main purpose of zoning has been "the protection . . . of the private sphere of home and family, property, and community." Cities are commonly "envisioned, and regulated, like property owners. Both property owners and cities can be defined in terms of territory, organized to advance 'parochial interests,' and be understood as having a concrete self-interest to promote."[27]

A Collective Property Right

The legal power to exclude others is the defining feature of a private property right.* By providing a legal means of excluding unwanted uses, zoning thus

---

*Law professor Thomas Merrill declares that "the right to exclude others is a necessary and sufficient condition of identifying the existence of property. . . . The right to exclude is in this sense fundamental to the concept of property." See Thomas W. Merrill, "Property and the Right to Exclude," *Nebraska Law Review* 77 (1998), 731.

functions in the role of a property right.[28] That is to say, zoning in practice gives the neighborhood residents, acting through the local political process, a collective property right to their common neighborhood environment.[29] As critics of "exclusionary zoning" argued, zoning segregates suburban neighborhoods by economic status. Yet this is the normal consequence of property ownership. Poor people eat at McDonalds, while rich people eat at fancy French restaurants; the poor drive old Chevrolets, while the rich drive BMWs. With zoning, the distribution of neighborhood environmental quality has exhibited the same pattern as any other private consumption. In the face of zoning restrictions, a poor person can no more move into a rich neighborhood than drive off with a rich person's Porsche.

For most Americans, it has become obvious and inevitable that the rich live better than the poor—all part of a market system based on private property rights. As Georgette Poindexter observes, "Economic segregation does not challenge American society's value structure as does racial segregation."[30] In America, wide economic disparities are not a sufficient basis for government interference with the market system. Indeed, well-defended property rights are a fundamental requirement of an orderly, productive society. Socialists once decried the inequalities resulting from private property, but that debate has now faded into history.

Neighborhood zoning serves the same kind of social purpose as other private property rights. The zoning power to exclude sustains private incentive to build attractive neighborhoods in the first place—and then to maintain the neighborhoods at a high environmental quality. Without exclusionary powers—whether derived from zoning or some other means (such as the private rights of a neighborhood association)—there would be many fewer attractive neighborhoods built. A system of "neighborhood socialism" would not mean wide sharing of high-quality neighborhoods; it would mean instead an equality of less attractive environments—much as socialist economic systems of whole nations led to a greater equality of relative poverty.

An Exercise in Coercion

Although private neighborhood associations were only then coming into wide use, the National Commission on Urban Problems in 1968 recognized their similarity of function with zoning. The commission's report suggested in the following for existing neighborhoods:

> Another [reform] approach would be to create forms of land tenure which would recognize the interest of owners in what their neighbors do. Such tenure forms, which do not exist but which might resemble condominium tenure, might more effectively reconcile the conflicting interests of neighboring property owners than do conven-

tional regulations. The objective of such tenure would be to leave the small scale rela-tionships among neighbors for resolution entirely within the private sector, while public regulation would continue to apply to the neighborhood as a whole. In addi-tion to giving neighborhood residents greater control over minor land-use changes within their neighborhood, such tenure could include provision for cooperative maintenance of properties where owners desire such services.[31]

The commission did not follow up on this privatization proposal with any specific implementation plans. Most suburban neighborhoods continued to rely on traditional public zoning for protection. It would have been impossible in practice for most established neighborhoods to do otherwise. By contrast, in first implementing zoning, it had had the advantage that, as a form of govern-ment regulation, it could be imposed on an existing neighborhood by fiat. As Richard Briffault comments, "as a political rather than a private act, zoning required the approval of only a majority of residents, not the unanimous con-sent of all property owners."[32]

When a neighborhood was first zoned, government was in effect engaged in an act of internal property right redistribution. The imposition of zoning cancelled some individual rights of ownership; a neighborhood landowner was no longer free, for example, to construct low-cost housing for poorer peo-ple on his or her land. At the same time, zoning created new collective rights. Although the municipality "took" important individual rights, it thus also provided the constitutionally required "compensation" in the form of an own-ership share in other new rights within the neighborhood. Zoning in such circumstances in part derived its legitimacy from the fact that it was a "com-pensated taking."*

To be sure, there would inevitably be some objectors in most neighbor-hoods who did not feel they were adequately compensated. Under municipal zoning, any such minority of holdouts would have to accept the government action; the municipality had the legal authority—the courts almost always sus-tained it—to act according to the political wishes of the neighborhood major-ity. Stephen Barton and Carol Silverman observe that municipal zoning was needed by existing neighborhoods because it "could be passed by a majority

---

*As a libertarian, University of Chicago law professor Richard Epstein declares that "one proposi-tion that I'm reluctant to accept, but in the interest of candor must acknowledge, is that all government actions do not always have negative social consequences." Indeed, some government actions satisfy "the government's obligation to compensate for regulatory takings." For example, "if the government imposes like restrictions on you and your neighbor, such that you are benefited by the restriction on your neighbor and he is benefited by the restriction upon you, then both of you have at least received some of the constitutionally required compensation." Indeed, the great popularity of zoning suggests that in most cases the compensation was fully sufficient for the majority of neighborhood property owners. See Richard A. Epstein, "The Harms and Benefits of Nollan and Dolan," *Northern Illinois Uni-versity Law Review* 15 (Summer 1995), 489.

rather than requiring unanimous consent or prior creation by a developer," as is the case in a private neighborhood association.[33]

A Supermajority Decision Rule

From this perspective zoning was as much an innovation in the rules of collective choice as a land use device. It allowed basic changes in the structure of neighborhood property rights with less-than-unanimous consent. As James Buchanan and Gordon Tullock explored in *The Calculus of Consent,* a requirement of unanimous consent will preclude many collective actions. For most collective decisions, Buchanan and Tullock therefore recommended a vote of approval short of unanimity—if well above a simple majority. The exact voting majority required to impose zoning on a neighborhood—whether it be 66 percent, 75 percent, or 85 percent in favor of the new zoning—was never formally specified. There were too many zoning fictions standing in the way, and so there was never any official count of neighborhood ballots. Instead, it simply fell to the municipal political leaders to "divine" the true desires of the existing residents of a neighborhood.

There was nothing, admittedly, in American legal and political history to justify a coercive redistribution of property rights within an existing neighborhood. If zoning had been described explicitly from the first as a mandatory redistribution of property rights, it would very likely have been declared unconstitutional. The number of private neighborhood associations was still very small early in the 20th century; the courts would have been unlikely to approve the mandatory creation of new "neighborhood zoning associations" by supermajority vote in existing neighborhoods. At a minimum, courts would have insisted that state legislatures provide an explicit statutory basis for condemning some part of the bundle of individual rights in a neighborhood, while creating new collective rights as compensation.

However, it never happened that way. Zoning instead accomplished these functions almost surreptitiously, operating under a set of legal myths and fictions. It was one more episode in the long history of the indirect and spontaneous evolution of property rights outside the official pronouncements of the law.

Conclusion

In retrospect, however fictional, the nuisance law and planning justifications for zoning had important practical purposes. They provided the necessary camouflage, as it were, for a fundamental innovation in American land law more radical than the early advocates of zoning ever admitted—and perhaps than they even understood clearly themselves. By now, of course, zoning is long established. The system of collective property rights, as created by zoning, has been in existence in some areas for many decades.

Given this history, it would now be much less radical to acknowledge officially the actual workings of municipal zoning. An outright privatizing of zoning would merely recognize and ratify a long-standing, property-right regime existing in many neighborhoods. As one practical consequence, privatizing would bring the law of suburban land use into much closer conformance with the realities on the ground. Land use lawyers and judges would finally be relieved of pretending that the zoning emperor really does have clothes. As the exercise of a collective private property right, there would also be other significant advantages over the current administration of public zoning (see part IV).

NOTES

1. U.S. Department of Commerce, *A Standard State Zoning Enabling Act* (Washington, DC, 1924).

2. *Village of Euclid v. Ambler Realty Co.,* 272 U.S. 365 (1926).

3. See Advisory Committee on Zoning, U.S. Department of Commerce, *A City Planning Primer* (Washington, DC, 1928).

4. Charles M. Haar, "In Accordance with a Comprehensive Plan," *Harvard Law Review* 68 (May 1955), 1155.

5. Patricia Burgess, *Planning for the Private Interest: Land Use Controls and Residential Patterns in Columbus, Ohio, 1900–1970* (Columbus: Ohio State University Press, 1994), 71.

6. This is not to say that all city planning must fail. There is a long history of planning in the United States and some successes to report—typically when the infrastructure for a new city was being planned, and when the objective was less ambitious than the progressive-era aspirations to the "scientific management" of a whole city. See John W. Reps, *The Making of Urban America: A History of City Planning in the United States* (Princeton, NJ: Princeton University Press, 1965).

7. Jerry Frug, "Decentering Decentralization," *University of Chicago Law Review* 60 (Spring 1993), 280.

8. *Udell v. Haas,* 288 N.Y.S. 2d at 893–94 (1968), quoted in J. Gregory Richards, "Zoning for Direct Social Control," *Duke Law Journal,* 1982 (November 1982), 821.

9. Joel Kosman, "Toward an Inclusionary Jurisprudence: A Reconceptualization of Zoning," *Catholic University Law Review* 43 (Fall 1993), 62.

10. M. Christine Boyer, *Dreaming the Rational City: The Myth of American City Planning* (Cambridge, MA: MIT Press, 1983).

11. Richard F. Babcock and Wendy U. Larsen, *Special Districts: The Ultimate in Neighborhood Zoning* (Cambridge, MA: Lincoln Institute of Land Policy, 1990), 74.

12. National Commission on Urban Problems, *Building the American City: Report of the National Commission on Urban Problems* (New York: Praeger, 1969), 223.

13. Richard F. Babcock, *The Zoning Game: Municipal Practices and Policies* (Madison: University of Wisconsin Press, 1966), xv.

14. A. Dan Tarlock, "Toward a Revised Theory of Zoning," in F. S. Bangs, ed., *Land Use Controls Annual* (Chicago: American Society of Planning Officials, 1972), 144.

15. Burgess, *Planning for the Private Interest,* 70.

16. Ibid., 59.

17. Boyer, *Dreaming the Rational City,* ix.

18. See Marshall Kaplan, *Urban Planning in the 1960s: A Design for Irrelevancy* (New York: Praeger Publishers, 1973); and Alan A. Altshuler, *The City Planning Process: A Political Analysis* (Ithaca, NY: Cornell University Press, 1965).

19. Martha A. Lees, "Preserving Property Values? Preserving Proper Homes? Preserving Privilege?: The Pre-Euclid Debate over Zoning for Exclusively Private Residential Areas, 1916–1926," *University of Pittsburgh Law Review* 56 (Winter 1994), 402, 375.

20. Ibid., 370.

21. Hugh Pomeroy, "A Planning Manual for Zoning (Urban and Suburban)," report prepared for the American Society of Planning Officials, 1940.

22. See Michael N. Danielson, *The Politics of Exclusion* (New York: Columbia University Press, 1976); and Sidney Plotkin, *Keep Out: The Struggle for Land Use Control* (Berkeley: University of California Press, 1987).

23. National Commission on Urban Problems, *Building the American City,* 7.

24. Ibid., 219.

25. *Village of Belle Terre v. Boraas,* 416 U.S. at 9 (1974).

26. Katia Brener, "Belle Terre and Single-Family Home Ordinances: Judicial Perceptions of Local Government and the Presumption of Validity," *New York University Law Review* 74 (May 1999), 455, 456.

27. Frug, "Decentering Decentralization," 270.

28. Lee Anne Fennell, "Hard Bargains and Real Steals: Land Use Exactions Revisited," *Iowa Law Review* 86 (October 2000), 16–17.

29. See Robert H. Nelson, *Zoning and Property Rights: An Analysis of the American System of Land Use Regulation* (Cambridge, MA: MIT Press, 1977); also Robert H. Nelson, "A Property Right Theory of Zoning," *The Urban Lawyer* 11 (Fall 1979); Robert H. Nelson, "Zoning Myth and Practice—From Euclid into the Future," in Charles M. Haar and Jerold S. Kayden, eds., *Zoning and the American Dream: Promises Still to Keep* (Chicago: American Planning Association—Planners Press, l989); and Robert H. Nelson, "The Privatization of Local Government: From Zoning to RCAs," in U.S. Advisory Commission on Intergovernmental Relations, *Residential Community Associations: Private Governments in the Intergovernmental System?* (Washington, DC, May 1989).

30. Georgette C. Poindexter, "Collective Individualism: Deconstructing the Legal City," *University of Pennsylvania Law Review* 145 (January 1997), 647.

31. National Commission on Urban Problems, *Building the American City,* 248.

32. Richard Briffault, "Our Localism: Part II—Localism and Legal Theory," *Columbia Law Review* 90 (March 1990), 367.

33. Stephen E. Barton and Carol J. Silverman, "History and Structure of the Common Interest Community," in Barton and Silverman, eds., *Common Interest Communities: Private Governments and the Public Interest* (Berkeley: Institute of Governmental Studies Press, University of California, 1994), 9.

7

Zoning Heretics

As the zoning and other land laws have evolved under cover of various legal fictions, some critics have sought to reveal their weaknesses. Yet any wide acceptance of such critical views might have undermined the legitimacy of the existing property right regime. Such an outcome obviously could not be tolerated; widespread social confusion and economic inefficiency might result. If religious heretics once were burned at the stake for their "falsehoods," modern land rights "heretics" were simply ignored.

Richard Babcock took a dangerous step toward heresy by accurately depicting zoning practices in communities across the United States during the 1960s. His book, aptly titled *The Zoning Game*, demonstrated that there was little connection between received legal theories of zoning and actual zoning practices.[1] Babcock avoided condemnation as an outright heretic, however, by confessing his "sins," avoiding proposals for radical "cures," and recommending that the solution to zoning problems lay in a renewed commitment to the zoning system's original purpose—appropriate land use planning. According to Babcock, the true zoning "faith" had not failed, but had been mistakenly and unjustly applied.

It was instead the members of a new "property right" school who entered fully into the realm of zoning heresy. And while these critics have differed on specific points, they have all dismissed traditional nuisance and planning rationales, and viewed zoning in actuality as a redistribution of the property rights to land. They propose that better solutions for zoning ailments are to be found in an improved property right regime. If property rights are defined more suitably, the market for metropolitan land will work more competitively and efficiently—and in many cases more equitably as well—than the outcomes of our current planning and zoning system.

A "Coasian" Framework

Ronald Coase won the Nobel Prize in economics in 1991, partly for his 1960 article, "The Problem of Social Cost."[2] This article revived interest in the institution of private property rights, first among economists and then among legal scholars in the "law and economics" movement. Coase pointed out that many economic problems that we long thought needed a government solution could actually be resolved through private negotiations alone. A market "externality," for example, did not necessarily require government regulation. In other words, an individual negatively affected by the external impact of some action might pay directly to stop or modify it. Alternatively, if the individual already had the legal right to halt the offending activity, others might pay that individual sufficient compensation to continue the activity. The damaged party might prefer compensation to the traditional nuisance remedy—stopping the offensive action.

Coase argued that the economic importance of well-defined property rights lay in the possibility of reducing the level of transaction costs within the economy. Even if the ultimate result was the same, one arrangement of property rights might work much better to hold down transaction costs. Coase's 1960 article thus suggested a systematic reexamination of American property institutions to determine whether they indeed promoted efficient transactions. Coase's writings played an important role in setting the stage for what has come to be called "the new institutional economics," a field in which the workings of property rights are often prominent.[3]

In 1972, Guido Calabresi and Douglas Melamed applied such thinking to existing property and tort laws.[4] They proposed a unified theory that combined these traditionally separate areas of the law. As a rule, in situations where land use posed potentially negative impacts on a neighboring use (e.g., a factory emitting pollutants), the law had offered several possible ways of dealing with the problem. Under a standard "property rule," the user negatively impacted could seek an injunction to halt the offending activity. Under a "liability rule," as grounded in tort law, the activity would not be banned in advance, but its perpetrators would be required to pay compensation for any damages later caused. A third possibility would be to permit the activity to continue without making any compensatory payments at all, based on a determination that the damages caused fell short of a legal nuisance. A fourth option, though seldom applied, would allow the issuance of a cease-and-desist order against an offending activity, but the person seeking this order would have to compensate the losing party.[5]

Given any offensive land use, one of these four approaches had to be followed. Yet, choices were often made without any examination of all the alternatives. Indeed, existing laws often raised transaction costs unnecessarily. In some cases laws had arisen from long-past economic and social circumstances. It followed directly that an important new task should now be set before the legal profession: Legal and other researchers should systematically reassess the laws of property and liability. As Calabresi and Melamed proposed, the criteria of economic efficiency, impacts on income distribution, and "other justice reasons" should provide the basis for this reassessment.[6]

Neighborhood Zoning Rights

Since zoning dealt with the interdependency of neighborhood land uses, its practice was an obvious candidate for the application of the new Coasian thinking. Among the first scholars to accomplish this was law professor Dan Tarlock. In 1972, Tarlock argued that "contemporary zoning should be conceptualized as a system of joint [property] ownership between the public entity and the regulated private owner. It is a form of joint ownership in which the owner of the fee [title to the land] retains possession and the right to manage subject to a veto by a co-manager, the public entity."[7] Without government assistance, Tarlock observed, the high transaction costs of protecting neighborhood quality would make private action alone impossible. Once government stepped in, it would become in effect a "co-owner" of the neighborhood environment.

Zoning thus was a second-best solution. This practice could be justified because by itself "private collective action fails to provide sufficient quantities of a desired public good, in this case [neighborhood environmental] amenity levels."[8] However, Tarlock recognized a problem in municipalities' rigid approach to administering zoning. Since municipalities are not supposed to profit monetarily from the transfer of land rights to a new party, the explicit "sale" of zoning in the neighborhood would be seen as a form of municipal corruption.

To address this problem, and to improve the overall efficiency of the land system, Tarlock proposed that neighborhood users take "some sort of collective action to bind themselves to a bargain such as a voting procedure or the creation of a board to act for them."[9] With this collective organization—very much like a private neighborhood association—they could bargain for direct money payments with potential entrants into the neighborhood. Tarlock explained the benefits of his proposed arrangement:

> Under the existing zoning system subsequent users who wish to deviate from the surrounding land-use pattern must "buy" their way in through the political process. Majority approval from an appointed commission or elected local legislative body is required. The process, I have argued, is very costly and produces doubtful efficiency

gains. Arguably the costs of administering a zoning system would be decreased and efficiency gains more certain if entrants had to bargain directly with surrounding landowners. The function of the government would be to impose an initial covenant scheme and then let the market or a close proxy determine subsequent reallocations of land.[10]

In other words, neighborhood residents should collectively take possession of the rights to their neighborhood common areas, including the option to sell these newly private rights, and thus open the neighborhood to wider and easier entry of new uses. If the residents of a neighborhood wanted a convenience store or a small restaurant in their midst, they could sell the right of entry, perhaps compensating adjacent landowners with a portion of the proceeds. In its workings, a free market might be described as in some sense a system of legalized and institutionalized bribery—in other words, I am authorized to "bribe" (pay) you to do what I want. A government official could not be paid, but more and better systems of legalized bribery in the private marketplace for land, Tarlock was saying, might help free up access to metropolitan land and promote its more efficient use.

Shared Development Rights

Yet another zoning heretic, (now) Yale law professor Robert Ellickson, offered a similar argument in the 1970s. Nuisance law and zoning, Ellickson noted, ignored important neighborhood options that might promote higher-value land uses. In practice, if the courts found an activity sufficiently offensive, they would simply issue an injunction under nuisance law. A more efficient result, however, might be to allow the offensive use to continue, while the offender pays compensation to the damaged parties. Ellickson suggested that for some types of "unneighborly uses" that harmed others, a community "nuisance board" might set a fixed schedule of appropriate compensating payments (see also chapter 17).[11]

Ellickson in 1977 extended this line of analysis to the outer suburbs, where zoning often regulated large areas of undeveloped land (often farming land).[12] In a developing area, he argued, government could set a "normal" standard of zoning restriction. If the municipality wanted to impose tighter restrictions on a particular parcel of land—say, to preserve open space—it would be required to pay the landowner for the resulting loss of land value. In effect, the definition of a "normal" standard established a legal benchmark. Some development "sticks" in the overall land bundle of rights—the "sticks" up to the "normal" standard of development permission—would remain in the sole possession of the landowner. Ownership of the remaining land rights would be shared by the landowner and the municipality. Each party would have to agree before any new use could take place above the "normal" standard of land use intensity.

Ellickson's design for zoning reform would have been complex to administer, since "normal" development standards can be hard to define.* Nevertheless, whatever the practical problems, his underlying view of zoning was radically new. Like other zoning heretics, Ellickson saw zoning as a redistribution of the property rights to land, and identified the resulting system of land rights as the source of major inefficiencies in metropolitan land use. Indeed, Ellickson found the existing zoning system as a whole so flawed that he argued it "must be severely curtailed if not entirely replaced."[13]

Zoning Injustice

Another leading critic of zoning, law professor Bernard Siegan, in the 1970s attacked the equity as well as efficiency consequences of zoning. Siegan agreed that the traditional nuisance and planning justifications for zoning were diversionary tactics. In developing suburbs, zoning was being used to keep out lower- and moderate-income housing. Large areas of land remained vacant for long periods, awaiting a suitable high-income use. The net effect, Siegan argued, was to artificially inflate the available supply of luxury housing for the rich. Even an elementary supply-and-demand analysis could easily predict the consequence: the price of such housing would fall while the price of land for lower- and moderate-income housing (now artificially constrained by government action) would rise. Large areas of land in the developing suburbs were being preserved as open space in the guise of "rational" land use plans, even as imbalances in suburban land use were causing housing prices for most people to escalate.

Richard Briffault comments that "local zoning power" allows rich jurisdictions "to protect local social values and community character."[14] Given the negative consequences for others, Briffault agrees with Siegan that Amer-

---

*Carol Rose writes with respect to Ellickson's proposed regulatory scheme: "The prospect of differing norms . . . raises an important ambiguity. . . . Whose norms apply, anyway? Are the relevant norms supposed to be local? State? National?" These norms as seen from different jurisdictional perspectives might vary greatly, all part of the substantial "trickiness of defining norms" of land use. See Carol M. Rose, "Book Review of *Regulatory Takings* by William A. Fischel," *Yale Law Journal* 105 (January 1996), 1045, 1046. Indeed, in circumstances of significant land use transition (as in the outer suburbs), where future uses will appropriately differ significantly from the surrounding uses at present, it would require a comprehensive planning model to determine the levels of "normal" use in Ellickson's terms. In this respect, Ellickson's thinking would have required a turn back to the old planning solutions of which in other respects he was so critical.

ican zoning is "too often a recipe for the perpetuation of injustice."[15] Environmentally, as Siegan further argued, zoning is equally detrimental. When new housing is forced by zoning restrictions to locate further out in the suburbs, it leaves large areas of intervening open space. Indeed, zoning is perhaps the single leading cause of the "leapfrog" land use patterns in the United States today. According to two long-time critics, zoning is "environmentally counterproductive. It promotes sprawl, consumes agricultural land, requires a more widespread infrastructure, and [results in] greater energy consumption. Moreover, it lengthens commuting distances, adds to air pollution, and prevents efficient use of mass transportation."[16] Or as Dartmouth economist William Fischel declares, "The net result of [local government] growth controls . . . is urban sprawl."[17]

Zoning failures over the 20th century followed in the path of other failed progressive systems of regulation that repeatedly had been captured for private purposes. Under zoning, the land in undeveloped areas had been controlled for the benefit of privileged Americans. One disillusioned historian of the entire Progressive movement, Gabriel Kolko, was led to label its ostensible reform efforts as actually "the triumph of conservatism" in the United States, efforts that in reality advanced business and other wealthier class interests on a broad basis.[18] Whatever the standard American political rhetoric might be to the contrary, the zoning system simply provided another graphic example of a widespread political outcome of the Progressive Era.

Given such realities, as Siegan would write of zoning, there was no justification—in legal thought or in economic theory—for the coerced redistribution of property rights accomplished by zoning.[19] Zoning offered a classic spectacle of "rent seeking" in action—a process in which, once the government introduced a new instrument of power, an intense and wasteful competition followed to put this government authority to use for private purposes. Municipal zoning was also unnecessary. Siegan showed how in Houston—the only large city in the United States without zoning—neighborhood associations' private regulations fully protected their environmental quality.* The solution, Siegan argued, was straightforward. Like the other unhappy legacies of Progressive Era regulatory theories, zoning should be abolished—land use should be "deregulated"—throughout the United States.

---

*Houston voters have rejected zoning three times in referenda, most recently in 1993. The opposition came from both ends of the economic spectrum. Higher-income neighborhoods did not need zoning because they already had secure private protections through covenants enforced by neighborhood associations. Poorer neighborhoods opposed zoning because they preferred mixtures of residential and commercial uses in their own neighborhoods and saw zoning as a means of excluding them from other neighborhoods. In the 1993 referendum, 70 percent of lower-income voters in Houston opposed zoning. See Robert H. Nelson, "The Zoning Racket," Forbes, January 3, 1994.

An Incomplete Design

Yet Siegan's plan to deregulate American land use made little progress over the next 25 years, even as the Interstate Commerce Commission, the Civil Aeronautics Board, and other legacies of Progressive-Era theories were either abolished or substantially deregulated. Siegan was a better critic than designer, and abolishing zoning outright would have raised several basic problems for which he had no answers.

Even though private neighborhood associations were doing a better job than zoning, a free market offers no easy path to creating a new private association in an established neighborhood. With separate ownership of homes, the transaction costs would be prohibitive. Lacking the assurance of adequate private protections as a substitute for zoning, any proposal to abolish zoning would have been fiercely resisted by many of America's better-quality neighborhoods. Indeed, it would have been politically hopeless.

Siegan also did not distinguish clearly between two much different circumstances of zoning—(1) the zoning of developed neighborhoods and (2) the zoning of undeveloped land. Yet the second circumstance offered much more promise for zoning reform. In newly developing areas, farmers and other owners of undeveloped land lost much of their development rights when the zoning was first imposed. Unlike residents of developed neighborhoods, these landowners received no new collective rights in return. According to Pietro Nivola of the Brookings Institution, in such circumstances "the development rights [are] confiscated from property owners" without any compensation.[20]

Why, then, is an act of municipal zoning of undeveloped land not considered an unconstitutional "taking"—prohibited by the Fifth Amendment? For one thing, the farmer does retain some minimal value because of the land's use in farming. Moreover, the courts have long accepted the fiction that zoning of undeveloped land is socially beneficial as the means of implementing land use planning. Even though, as Yale law professor Carol Rose explains, "the quasi-judicial procedures in applying the plan become an elaborate charade—and so does the judicial review of those quasi-judicial decisions," this charade has been enough to keep the courts from intervening.[21]

The acquisition of undeveloped land rights admittedly may not be permanent. Indeed, much of suburban zoning would essentially equate to a total expropriation of all development rights were it not for the possibility of future rezoning. Nevertheless, a denial of most development rights for 10 or 15 years, given a normal rate of interest, may reduce land value by 50 percent or more. In fact, the Supreme Court has recognized that even temporary confiscations of property rights in some circumstances can be a real form of "taking."[22]

Europeans once found sufficient reasons to "take" the land of North America from its original Native American occupants (who supposedly were not "civilized" enough, would not properly develop the land in a maximally efficient way, or lacked formal systems of property rights based on the European model). As is often said, "might makes right" in matters of war and property rights (the two often go together). In the outer portions of U.S. metropolitan areas in the 20th century, the municipalities had the "might." Municipal authorities offered new reasons for confiscating the development rights to millions of acres of land.[23] Given the absence of any redeeming social purpose, as University of Illinois law professor Lee Anne Fennell comments, the "land use entitlement" exercised by municipalities was effectively "stolen, either from the landowner or from third parties. Preventing such theft by placing appropriate limits on land use regulation" is essential in the future.[24]

Yet it is now often impossible to redress the original injustice. The greatest problem with Siegan's proposed counterrevolution in zoning is the passage of time, particularly for undeveloped land areas. If zoning has occurred many years—or even many decades—earlier, the prospects of restoring development rights might be remote. Many of the original owners would have died in the intervening years; others might have sold the land. Aware of the tight zoning restrictions, the new purchasers would have paid a reduced price, reflecting the more limited set of development rights to the land. Indeed, the removal of zoning restrictions would potentially result in a large financial windfall to the present owners. Another potential complication arising from Siegan's proposal would be that many other people might have developed a large stake in the *current* zoned use of the property based on reasonable expectations. Therefore it is not always possible to redress an earlier land use—or other—injustice.*

Municipal Sale of Zoning

Historically, property rights have typically been redistributed through the exercise of force. A thousand years ago, the Normans conquered England and gave the land to their warriors. Under this approach—"legal realism," as opposed to a "natural law" concept of the "just" disposition of private property (which

---

*This issue received the attention of the U.S. Supreme Court in the 2001 *Palazzolo* case. The State of Rhode Island created a new Coastal Resources Council in 1971, and this council issued regulations tightly limiting development of "coastal wetlands"—including the property at issue in this case. Anthony Palazzolo acquired clear title to the property in 1978. The Rhode Island Supreme Court ruled that, because the regulations took effect before the 1978 possession of the property, Palazzolo could not file an inverse condemnation claim. The U.S. Supreme Court reversed this ruling, finding that a takings claim that would be valid for one owner survived the transfer of the property to a new owner—even though the new owner was fully aware of the restrictive regulatory regime into which he or she was buying. See *Palazzolo v. Rhode Island* 533 U.S. 606 (2001). This issue is also discussed in depth in Gregory M. Stein, "Who Gets the Takings Claim?: Changes in Land Use Law, Pre-Enactment Owners, and Post-Enactment Buyers," *Ohio State Law Journal* 61 (2000).

seeks to ground the law in ethical principles)—the past municipal confiscations of suburban development rights might now be treated as an accomplished fact. Perhaps municipalities today should simply be treated as
"suburban squatters"—allowed to keep the development rights that they took
in the past, like many other squatters in history. These municipalities, for
example, could then sell zoning changes to developers, depositing the revenues
in their municipal treasuries and perhaps reducing municipal taxes. The sale of
zoning would help to meet the urgent need for more suburban land for many
types of housing.[25] Given the incentives of the current zoning system, municipalities now often lock up development rights. Unable to sell them for a profit,
there is little municipal gain in transferring the rights to anyone else. Overall,
the American zoning system as it developed over the course of the 20th century
would have required the wide practice of municipal charity in order to make
sufficient land available for the full range of American housing needs.

The case for the sale of zoning was advanced in a series of articles, beginning
in 1978, by Dartmouth economist William Fischel, yet another of the zoning
heretics.[26] Fischel began his analysis with the observation that—shorn of its
"public interest" camouflage—zoning amounted to a coerced redistribution
of property rights that benefited some people and harmed others. Large-lot
zoning was typically sought by recent arrivals in newly developing areas—the
"door slammers," as some labeled them. In a newly developing community,
the political power would gradually shift from the older landowners to the
newcomers. Once the newcomers had a sufficient majority and could get organized, they would rezone the municipality for their own benefit.

As a result of this zoning, entire regions experienced shortages of land for
multifamily housing. By 1970, zoning in the New York area had closed off more
than 99 percent of northeastern New Jersey's developable land to multifamily
housing. In Bergen County, 27,000 acres of developable land was available for
single-family homes, but only a miniscule 131 acres was zoned for apartments.
By the early 1970s, 12 of the 16 counties in developing areas of New Jersey prohibited mobile homes—many poor families' best chance at home ownership—
altogether.[27] Minimum lot requirements of one acre or more covered 89 percent
of Fairfield County, Connecticut. The average size of a developable lot in
Westchester County, New York, rose from 0.3 acres in 1953 to 1.5 acres in 1968.[28]

When the land throughout a metropolitan area is zoned by its local governments, a certain amount of land is available cumulatively for one-quarter-acre
lots, a certain amount for one-acre lots, and so forth. Like other central plans,
however, the metropolitan rationing scheme is likely to misallocate supplies in
relation to demands. Under the American zoning system, which has favored
high-income housing, it is as though government regulators ordered Detroit
automakers to manufacture five times as many Lincolns and Cadillacs as Fords
and Chevrolets.

Fischel was less bothered by the social injustices of past zoning confiscations than the resulting economic inefficiency. Indeed, justice aside, there was
no great economic problem per se in confiscating development rights. However, the same zoning fictions that rationalized a municipal confiscation also
meant that the development rights were used inefficiently. Local governments
could not make a profit from a change in regulation; if a zoning change benefits a particular government official, it is an act of "corruption." Hence, the
zoning of undeveloped land had simply removed large amounts of development rights from the land market, quarantining these rights indefinitely.

A Marketable Commodity

Admittedly, more zoning was available for sale than could be officially
acknowledged. Dennis O'Harrow, executive director of the American Society
of Planning Officials, reported in 1965 that zoning had become a "marketable
commodity" in many parts of the United States. In a speech to the Society's
annual convention, he quoted a respected municipal planner: "You can buy
with money any kind of zoning you want in half the communities of the
United States." Another person described developers meeting for a drink who
"start comparing the prices they have to pay for zoning." In suggesting that it
would be better to stop speaking up in public about widespread zoning corruption, one developer commented, "We know where we stand now—$25,000
for a trailer park in this county. Why upset things by talking about it?"[29]

Observing the pervasive role of money in local zoning decisions, economist
Marion Clawson of Resources for the Future (Washington, D.C.) proposed in
1966 that it would be simpler and more efficient to dispense with zoning fictions and to have "open, competitive sale of zoning and zoning classifica-
tions."[30] By the 1970s, zoning sales were less likely to involve the outright
bribery of public officials. Instead, as Robert Ellickson described the process, a
community would "place owners of undeveloped land in a straightjacket, and
then . . . agree to free the owners at a price. . . . The rezonings [would be] con-
ditioned on developer donations of land, land improvements and money." In
a leading case, the zoning practices of Mount Laurel Township, New Jersey,
were subject to scrutiny by the state courts. As the facts were put before the
New Jersey courts, Mount Laurel had offered "a classic example of such sub-
urbanite profit-maximizing. Mount Laurel placed most of its undeveloped
land in holding zones and then sold development rights (via PUD approvals)
in return for substantial (and often illegal) developer contributions."[31]

The existence of black markets is often economically beneficial; without
them, the economy of the old Soviet Union, for example, would have suffered
greatly. Perhaps a "white market" in zoning changes was needed in the United

States. Indeed, in 1979, Fischel proposed that "any existing zoning restriction may be sold by the community." The payments "should be made to the general municipal treasury, to be dispersed as decided upon by community rules."[32] If municipalities could sell their zoning, wide areas of land would become newly available for housing development, much of it likely in the middle-income categories.

Zoning under Siege

By the mid-1980s, the suggestion to abolish zoning no longer qualified as serious heresy. In fact, the zoning heretics' views had entered the mainstream of legal scholarship. Influential articles were published in leading law journals with such titles as "Abolish Zoning," "California's Land Planning Requirements: The Case for Deregulation," "Deregulating Land Use: An Alternative Free Enterprise Development System," "Brandeis Brief for Decontrol of Land Use: A Plea for Constitutional Reform," and "Local Land Use Controls: An Idea Whose Time Has Passed."[33] In 1983, Douglas Porter of the Urban Land Institute commented, "Who likes zoning? Hardly anyone, if you listen to recent criticisms of zoning standards, zoning procedures, and the whole zoning concept. Bemoaning zoning seems to be a major sport these days."[34]

Jan Krasnowiecki, a leading zoning practitioner and professor at the University of Pennsylvania law school, summarized in 1980 the failings of zoning: Zoning was based on assumptions that were "utterly naive" and demonstrated an "obvious lack of realism." In seeking municipal adherence to zoning "myth," the courts had been engaged in "a wild goose chase." It was altogether unrealistic, for example, to expect that any municipality could plan comprehensively for new development years in advance. As zoning really worked in practice, "outside the urban core, no land was ever zoned for [intensive] uses in advance of development."[35]

In the real world of land development, Krasnowiecki observed, municipalities in newly developing areas simply "zone[d] all of their undeveloped land short of the level at which any significant development can occur."[36] Some described it as a system of "wait-and-see" zoning.[37] Any new housing project then required a specific act of rezoning by the municipal legislative body. Such an arrangement gave the municipality control over the precise timing of development at a given site, as well as time to research the developer's reputation and to review the design details for any planned development. Negotiations might continue until either a mutually acceptable land use proposal for the site emerged or one of the parties walked away. For example, in Somerset County, New Jersey, no land was zoned for multifamily housing in 1970, yet 22 percent of the building permits issued between 1960 and 1970 had been for multifamily housing—issued on a "spot" basis as communities had found particularly attractive projects that they were willing to accept.[38]

Zoning in the American suburbs, contrary to formal appearances, had already been privatized. When they occurred, zoning changes were in essence market transactions, the transfer of a property right from one party to another in exchange for adequate consideration. In light of all this, Krasnowiecki proposed, it was time to jettison the formal myths surrounding zoning. A complete rethinking of the zoning system was necessary.

The *Report of the President's Commission on Housing* (Bernard Siegan served as a member of the commission) in 1982 carried zoning critics' arguments from the law journals to the public policy arena. The President's Commission found that "excessive restrictions on housing production" had "driven up the price of housing generally," creating concern for "the plight of millions of Americans of average and lesser income" who could not afford homes or apartments. The commission estimated that inefficient and inequitable regulatory burdens were adding as much as 25 percent to the average price of an American home.[39]

In previous years, the many strong criticisms of zoning put forward by national commissions and expert study groups had been followed by calls for improved planning and greater involvement in land development approval by higher levels of metropolitan government. The President's Commission, however, reflected the new thinking about zoning, and recommended a detailed "program of land use deregulation," including significant loosening of zoning restrictions. Breaking with 60 years of conventional wisdom, the President's Commission proposed that "density of development should be left to the marketplace."[40]

The California Experiment

Facing heavy demands for land from a rapidly growing population, and possessing a strong ethic of environmental protection, California has presented a testing ground for the impacts of tight land use restrictions. Responding to a new political mood that questioned the social benefits of economic growth and development, California's courts beginning in the 1960s came down squarely in favor of strong local powers to limit housing densities. Among the 50 states, as one legal observer notes, California courts over the years have been "at one end of the spectrum."[41] Another legal authority comments that "developers rarely win major lawsuits" in California courts.[42] Indeed, California courts will sustain virtually everything local governments do to restrict land use.

By the late 1980s, more than 900 growth-control or growth-management measures had been adopted by California municipalities.[43] As one study found, housing in such California communities was selling at prices 17 to 38 percent higher than housing in communities without such controls.[44] From one perspective, the growth controls were working wonderfully—the higher quality of the local environment was demonstrated in part by the higher price of entry into the community. However, it also meant that a smaller percentage of Californians could afford to move into such communities. Among renters, a typical Californian paid half of his or her income for rent, compared with the national average of 28 percent. Despite a statewide economic recession, the average price of a single-family home in California reached $320,000 in 2002, and equaled $570,000 in Santa Clara County, the heart of Silicon Valley.

Even in the 1970s, as the enthusiasm for growth controls was taking hold, the price of California housing on average was well above the rest of the nation.[45] Adjusted for quality, one 1978 estimate showed that California housing was 57 percent more expensive. And with further tightening of land use controls in the 1980s, California housing was 79 percent more expensive than the national average and, by 1990, it had become 147 percent more expensive.[46] According to Fischel, the evidence strongly pointed to "an enormous and persistent divergence between California housing prices and those of the rest of the country that began in the early 1970s."[47] All in all, as one observer commented recently, California "has been America's poster child for municipal land use policies that create shortages of housing and higher-cost housing."[48]

As many Californians struggled to cope, they often had to live farther and farther away from their workplaces. Nationwide, the median commuting time among recent home buyers declined from 19.5 minutes in 1985 to 17.5 minutes in 1995. In California metropolitan areas, however, median commuting times increased significantly over the same period—from 20 minutes to 25 minutes. California's tight restrictions on local land use not only raised the cost of housing, but also added to traffic congestion and the dispersion of housing over ever-wider areas of land—in other words, suburban sprawl.

In 1991, yet another national study group, the Commission on Regulatory Barriers to Affordable Housing, warned that California represented only the extreme case; the entire United States faced a proliferation of "restrictive zoning and subdivision ordinances, counterproductive growth controls, and uncoordinated development approval and permit processing being used with special zeal in suburban and high-growth areas." As a result, "households seeking affordable housing" often found little or none available, contributing to "escalating land costs and housing prices in preferred locations where development pressures are greatest."[49] Over the course of the 1990s, as the commission had forewarned, the shortage of developable land in the suburbs continued to put pressure on housing markets. In 1996, for example, the average home mortgage payment in the United States was 33 percent of income, compared with 24 percent in 1976.[50]

Conclusion

Despite all the criticisms, zoning proved more resistant to change than the airline, trucking, banking, telecommunications, and other American industries that experienced significant deregulation in the late 20th century. Local regulatory powers still reigned supreme in the land market. Although the zoning heretics had a significant effect on the intellectual debate, they made little impact on actual land use practices.

If any significant changes in zoning were to occur, it appeared that such changes would have to be accomplished in the time-honored fashion of the land laws—gradually, incrementally and informally. Indeed, given the very high stakes for so many Americans, and the importance of respecting past expectations, it seems no radical surgery on zoning would be possible. Yet major new changes—consistent with the views of the zoning heretics—were brewing in the American suburbs with the rise of the private neighborhood association. The neighborhood association officially substituted private zoning controls for the de facto collective property rights that had arisen informally under "public" zoning. If the 20th century had witnessed the informal "privatization of zoning," the creation of private neighborhood associations at the end of the century was making all this official and legal.

NOTES

1. Richard F. Babcock, *The Zoning Game: Municipal Practices and Policies* (Madison: University of Wisconsin Press, 1966).

2. Ronald H. Coase, "The Problem of Social Cost," *Journal of Law and Economics* 3 (October 1960).

3. See Eirik G. Furubotn and Rudolf Richter, *Institutions and Economic Theory: The Contribution of the New Institutional Economics* (Ann Arbor: University of Michigan Press, 1997).

4. Guido Calabresi and A. Douglas Melamed, "Property Rules, Liability Rules, and Inalienability: One View of the Cathedral," *Harvard Law Review* 85 (April 1972).

5. Ibid., 1115–16.

6. Ibid., 1093.

7. A. Dan Tarlock, "Toward a Revised Theory of Zoning," in F. S. Bangs, ed., *Land Use Controls Annual* (Chicago: American Society of Planning Officials, 1972), 141.

8. Ibid., 145.

9. Ibid., 146.

10. Ibid., 147.

11. Robert C. Ellickson, "Alternatives to Zoning: Covenants, Nuisance Rules, and Fines as Land Use Controls," *University of Chicago Law Review* 40 (Summer 1973).

12. Robert C. Ellickson, "Suburban Growth Controls: An Economic and Legal Analysis," *Yale Law Journal* 86 (January 1977).

13. Ellickson, "Alternatives to Zoning," 781.

14. Richard Briffault, "Our Localism: Part I—The Structure of Local Government Law," *Columbia Law Review* 90 (January 1990), 58.

15. Richard Briffault, "Our Localism: Part II—Localism and Legal Theory," *Columbia Law Review* 90 (March 1990), 453.

16. Michael M. Berger and Gideon Kanner, "The Need for Takings Law Reform: A View From the Trenches—A Response to Taking Stock of the Takings Debate," *Santa Clara Law Review* 38, no. 3 (1998), 856.

17. William A. Fischel, "Zoning and Land Use Regulation," in Boudewijn Bouckaert and Gerrit De Geest, eds., *Encyclopedia of Law and Economics, Volume II* (Cheltenham, UK: Edward Elgar, 2000), 421.

18. Gabriel Kolko, *The Triumph of Conservatism: A Reinterpretation of American History, 1900–1916* (New York: Free Press, 1963).

19. Bernard H. Siegan, *Land Use Without Zoning* (Lexington, MA: Lexington Books, 1972); also Bernard H. Siegan, *Other People's Property* (Lexington, MA: Lexington Books, 1976).

20. Pietro S. Nivola, *Laws of the Landscape: How Policies Shape Cities in Europe and America* (Washington, DC: Brookings Institution Press, 1999), 61.

21. See Carol M. Rose, "Planning and Dealing: Piecemeal Land Controls as a Problem of Local Legitimacy," *California Law Review* 71 (May 1983), 880.

22. *First English Evangelical Lutheran Church of Glendale v. County of Los Angeles, California,* 482 U.S. 304 (1987).

23. See James V. DeLong, *Property Matters: How Property Rights Are Under Assault—And Why You Should Care* (New York: The Free Press, 1997).

24. Lee Anne Fennell, "Hard Bargains and Real Steals: Land Use Exactions Revisited," *Iowa Law Review* 86 (October 2000), 85. See also Lee Anne Fennell, "Beyond Exit and Voice: User Participation in the Production of Local Public Goods," *Texas Law Review* 80 (November 2001); and Lee Anne Fennell, "Homes Rule" (Book review of *The Homevoter Hypothesis* by William A. Fischel), *Yale Law Journal* 112 (December 2002).

25. Robert H. Nelson, "Marketable Zoning: A Cure for the Zoning System," *Land Use Law and Zoning Digest* 37, no. 11 (November 1985).

26. See William A. Fischel, *The Economics of Zoning Laws: A Property Rights Approach to American Land Use Controls* (Baltimore: Johns Hopkins University Press, 1985). See also William A. Fischel, "A Property Rights Approach to Municipal Zoning," *Land Economics* 54 (February 1978); William A. Fischel, "Equity and Efficiency Aspects of Zoning Reform," *Public Policy* 27 (Summer 1979); and William A. Fischel, "Zoning and Land Use Reform: A Property Rights Perspective," *Virginia Journal of Natural Resource Law* 1 (Spring 1980).

27. Lynne B. Sagalyn and George Sternlieb, *Zoning and Housing Costs: The Impact of Land-Use Controls on Housing Price* (New Brunswick, NJ: Center for Urban Policy Research, Rutgers University, 1972), 107.

28. Briffault, "Our Localism: Part I," 41.

29. Alfred Balk, "Invitation to Bribery," *Harper's,* October 1966, 18–19.

30. Marion Clawson, "Why Not Sell Zoning and Rezoning (Legally, That Is)?" *Cry California* (Winter 1966–67), 9.

31. Robert C. Ellickson, "The Role of Economics in the Teaching of Land-Use Law," *UCLA Journal of Environmental Law and Policy* 1 (Fall 1980), 7.

32. Fischel, "Equity and Efficiency Aspects of Zoning Reform," 322.

33. Jan Z. Krasnowiecki, "Abolish Zoning," *Syracuse Law Review* 31 (Summer 1980); George Lefcoe, "California's Land Planning Requirements: The Case for Deregulation," *Southern Califor-*

nia Law Review 54, no. 3 (1981); Douglas W. Kmiec, "Deregulating Land Use: Alternative Free Enterprise Development System," *University of Pennsylvania Law Review* 130 (November 1981); Mark S. Pulliam, "Brandeis Brief for Decontrol of Land Use: A Plea for Constitutional Reform," *Southwestern University Law Review* 13, no. 3 (1983); and Orlando E. Delogu, "Local Land Use Controls: An Idea Whose Time Has Passed," *Maine Law Review* 36, no. 2 (1984).

34. Douglas R. Porter, "On Bemoaning Zoning," *Urban Land,* March 1983, 34.

35. Krasnowiecki, "Abolish Zoning," 731, 745, 720, 733.

36. Ibid., 734.

37. National Commission on Urban Problems, *Building the American City: Report of the National Commission on Urban Problems* (New York: Praeger, 1969), 206.

38. Sagalyn and Sternlieb, *Zoning and Housing Costs,* 109.

39. *The Report of the President's Commission on Housing* (Washington, DC, 1982), 199, xxxiii.

40. Ibid., 199, xxxiv.

41. Richard Damstra, "Don't Fence Us Out: The Municipal Power to Ban Gated Communities and the Federal Takings Clause," *Valparaiso University Law Review* 35 (Summer 2001), 552.

42. Katia Brener, "Belle Terre and Single-Family Home Ordinances: Judicial Perceptions of Local Government and the Presumption of Validity," *New York University Law Review* 74 (May 1999), 474.

43. *"Not in My Backyard": Removing Barriers to Affordable Housing,* Report to President Bush and Secretary Kemp by the Advisory Commission on Regulatory Barriers to Affordable Housing (Washington, DC, 1991), 2-2.

44. William A. Fischel, *Regulatory Takings: Law, Economics and Politics* (Cambridge, MA: Harvard University Press, 1995), 223.

45. For an early strong criticism of the social and economic consequences of California land use control practices, see Bernard J. Frieden, *The Environmental Protection Hustle* (Cambridge, MA: MIT Press, 1979).

46. Fischel, *Regulatory Takings,* 233.

47. Ibid., 236.

48. Henry R. Richmond, "Sprawl and Its Enemies: Why the Enemies Are Losing," *Connecticut Law Review* 34 (Winter 2002), 574.

49. *"Not in My Backyard,"* 2-1.

50. Michael L. Utz, "Common Interest Ownership in Pennsylvania: An Examination of Statutory Reform and Implications for Practitioners," *Duquesne University Law Review* 37 (Spring 1999), 465 n.2.

8

More Zoning Fictions

What did all the scholarly attacks on zoning during the 1970s and 1980s mean? For the old zoning warrior, Richard Babcock, they were the lamentations of academics well removed from the real world. According to Babcock, despite the opinions of legal and economic scholars, "people love zoning" and therefore the institution of zoning was "alive and well . . . in every urban and suburban neighborhood"—and would be around for a long time to come.[1] No mainstream politician was suggesting that zoning be abolished, or even substantially deregulated. Zoning was shaping American suburbs according to popular demand—or at least the demands of the richest and most politically powerful citizens. For a public official to offer a frontal challenge would have been political suicide.

Yet zoning was not entirely immune from the privatization and deregulation trends of the times. Zoning in practice was increasingly taking on the character of a private property right, but this process was taking place outside the official formulations of the law. In fact, there has hardly been a time when the formal defenses of land laws have not rested on some significant fictions. As Richard Pipes writes in his history of private property, this area has experienced a longstanding "difficulty of distinguishing law from reality."[2] The judiciary has learned to look the other way when obvious discrepancies between legal theory and land practice arose. In many cases, judges seeking to enforce land laws precisely as written would have created a virtual Bolshevik revolution in local property rights.

Municipal "Exactions"

In his studies during the 1980s, Babcock discerned two basic trends in zoning practice: exactions and new regulatory mechanisms. The first trend involved municipalities' increasing insistence on direct payment for zoning changes. Babcock offered one example:

> Governments simply are not playing the game unless they demand exactions. In one of the last cases in which I was involved, a city asked the developer of a particular project to build a $750,000 swimming pool—on the other side of town from the project! What did the developer do? After figuring out the cost of litigation, the time it would take, and the interest on the construction loan he was paying the bank, he agreed to build the swimming pool—even though it had nothing to do with his development.[3]

In Washington, D.C., the Department of Housing and Community Development wanted its payments in cash, which is more fungible and thus more valuable to a municipality. In 1987, for example, the Hadid Development Company proposed construction of a large office building near the D.C. Convention Center. In exchange for permission to develop, Hadid offered to donate $1.4 million to a general-purpose, low-income housing fund. As the *Washington Post* reported, "The zoning commission sent the entire Hadid case to the housing agency to determine if the cash offer was appropriate."[4] The District government then countered with a demand for $4.6 million for the housing fund. The District had already approved a price of $1.5 million in exchange for four more floors on a new office building and it would eventually reach a similar "cash-for-zoning" deal with Haddad.[5] In many other places as well, "localities . . . now condition zoning approvals for office buildings on the developers' agreement to subsidize low- and moderate-income housing."[6]

Across the United States, one comprehensive study of "regulation for revenues" found that the 1970s and 1980s had witnessed "a virtual revolution" in the extent of impact fees and other exactions on new development. By 1991, according to one estimate, the average impact fee charged for new housing in the United States was $7,691 per single-family housing unit.[7] In a study of 100 municipalities in California and other rapidly growing areas—where exactions were most common—the average amounts totaled more than $12,000 per housing unit. Commenting on the lack of ground rules, Alan Altshuler and Jose Gomez-Ibanez noted, "Most exactions are negotiated, and judicial oversight is rare."[8]

In the absence of any formula, municipalities would ask for "voluntary" contributions, but few developers considered these payments voluntary. Indeed, as Altshuler and Gomez-Ibanez observed, "Most local officials . . . perceive developers as reaping windfall profits from booms they did nothing to create and have few compunctions about asking, on behalf of their constituents, for all they can get." Local officials understood that "when negotiating exactions, [they] must avoid the appearance of 'selling' development permissions, because that is illegal." This merely resulted in another zoning fiction, however, whose rituals were reenacted for judges and other outsiders. In fact, as Altshuler and Gomez-Ibanez remarked, "Many local officials believe . . . that selling the privilege of developing in their community is entirely legitimate, if 'to sell' means to seek the best possible financial outcome for one's clients (or, in this case, constituents)."[9]

Exactions thus became common in metropolitan municipalities across the country. Babcock observed that "bargaining for zoning—the let's make a deal mentality . . . became the common denominator of zoning in the 1980s. . . . Cynical observers suggested that the system of bargains and exactions was little more than 'zoning for sale.' "[10] According to Jerold Kayden, "Faced with intensifying social needs and fiscal constraints, more and more cities 'mint' money through their zoning codes to finance a wide array of public amenities."[11] The situation was much the same in the 1990s. Montgomery County, Maryland (a large suburb of Washington, D.C.), collected $1.2 million in buyouts, giving relief from only one small section of its zoning requirements for development approval over the period of 1989 to 2003. By 2000 in the Phoenix area, most communities were collecting large exactions; the Village of North Gateway, for example, was collecting residential impact fees of $9,471 per new single-family home.[12] Some of this charge covered municipal infrastructure costs, but another major part amounted to the local price of the development permit. William Fischel reported in 2000, "On the whole, [municipal] sales of development rights are ubiquitous."[13]

California again represented an extreme case. By 2002 in the San Francisco Bay area, impact fees and other development exactions exceeded $30,000 per housing unit, amounting to more than 15 percent of the cost of producing such housing. In many other states as well, large-lot and other exclusionary zoning practices had transferred valuable development rights from landowners to municipal governments. It should have come as no surprise that the municipalities would eventually want to sell their development rights for cash—or developer "contributions." No sensible property owner would have done otherwise. In matters of local zoning, as Michael Berger and Gideon Kanner observed in 1998, it had become a "dealmaking process" that operated "more like a bazaar" than the "vaunted 'rule of law.' "[14]

Hence the free-market critics of zoning were perhaps losing the battle but winning the war. The 1970s recommendations of zoning heretics such as Tarlock, Ellickson, and Fischel were in fact being followed in significant part. Zoning was being regarded more and more in practice as a form of marketable private right. Regulatory permissions for land and housing were routinely sold by cities and towns for cash payments.* Indeed the rising levels of municipal exactions of the 1980s and 1990s were a substantial improvement over zoning "sales" in earlier years. In the old days, corrupt local officials had simply pocketed many of the proceeds of zoning sales for their personal benefit. The money from zoning sales was now more often being paid above board and could be put to use for wider municipal benefit.†

Marketable zoning was also having the salutary effect of making new land areas of the suburbs available for housing. According to Arthur Nelson, "A main reason developers do not object more to paying impact fees is that they see the fees as essential for overcoming political obstacles to approval of their projects."[15] New York University law professor Vicki Been also explains that if a local government does not accept "the payment of exactions, it may prevent development that would be socially beneficial."[16] Indeed, the ability to sell zoning may have been necessary to the very survival of the entire zoning system. In the absence of any form of payment, suburban local governments might well have refused the great majority of development proposals. With rapidly growing demands for housing that could not be satisfied in any other fashion, the zoning system would have been a pressure cooker with no release valve. Eventually, zoning constraints would have to give—one way or another.

---

*Such practices could be found in other countries as well. In São Paulo, Brazil, the leftist mayor in 2004 announced a plan to sell marketable securities called "Sepacs" which would enable a builder to exceed the existing height and bulk limits in the zoning. As one observer commented, "The city is doing rezoning for payment and by having a secondary market, the city creates a way for the rezoning to be used by the highest bidders—the people who value the space most." Highly in debt and desperate for any source of funds, São Paulo was abandoning any pretense and officially selling one of its most valuable financial assets—the zoning rights to develop land at higher densities in the city. See Terry Wade, "Mayor Tries to Pull Cash Out of the Air," *Wall Street Journal,* April 28, 2004, A14B.

†A study of "incentive zoning" in New York City described how for many years the city has "granted floor area bonuses and other valuable regulatory concessions to office and residential developers who would agree to provide plazas, arcades, atriums, and other outdoor and indoor spaces at their buildings." Over the years, New York had approved 16 million square feet of bonus additions to the existing zoning, involving 320 commercial, residential, and institutional buildings. The price paid by developers for these zoning concessions was 88 arcades, 57 residential plazas, 32 urban plazas, 15 covered pedestrian spaces, 12 sidewalk widenings, and still other additions to available public space—all in all a total of 3,584,034 square feet. However, according to a study by Jerold Kayden, much of this space that had been made available by developers provided limited public benefits. Such findings suggest that New York City would have been better off to obtain a direct cash payment from developers for its zoning approval of extra development space. In other words, it would have been better to sell the zoning directly—another example of the truism that market transactions are likely to be more efficient than barter transactions. See Jerold S. Kayden, "Using and Misusing Zoning Law to Design Cities: An Empirical Study of New York City's Privately Owned Public Spaces (Part 1)," *Land Use Law & Zoning Digest* 53 (February 2001), 3–5.

The Folly of *Nollan* and *Dolan*

The courts, to be sure, muddied the water. If confronted with the clear evidence that zoning was as a practical matter being sold, they were offended by the apparent "ethical" lapse. They found it difficult to approve the treatment of zoning as a marketable commodity, even though zoning sales generated large social benefits and kept the zoning system alive. Indeed, the U.S. Supreme Court issued rulings in two cases that, applied literally and widely, could well have significantly limited the future sale of zoning rights. Had the lower courts extensively followed these rulings, the most likely outcome would have been a substantial further curtailment of housing supplies for ordinary Americans. Fortunately, the lower courts showed greater sense.

The first of these Supreme Court decisions was *Nollan v. California Coastal Commission* in 1987.[17] The Nollans, the owners of a small bungalow on a Pacific Ocean beachfront lot, had sought the approval of the California Coastal Commission to tear down their bungalow and build a new three-bedroom home. As a condition for granting this permit, the commission had required the Nollans to dedicate an access easement allowing the public to walk along the beach in the front of their lot. In ruling that this action was unconstitutional, the Supreme Court declared that the Coastal Commission had failed to demonstrate a "nexus" between the regulatory action and the condition imposed. Lacking such a connection, the Coastal Commission could not "sell" the zoning in the manner proposed.

Whether the Court realized it or not, the *Nollan* ruling threatened to consign coastal development rights to a permanent status outside the market system. While some zoning sales might still be possible, the *Nollan* ruling effectively declared as public policy frequent social waste in the use of America's land resources.* Land development rights, the Supreme Court seemed to be saying, can only be made easily available as an act of public generosity. As Lee Anne Fennell comments, the *Nollan* decision placed many "land use regulations . . . in an odd sort of limbo: they need not be lifted at all, but if they are to be lifted, they must be lifted for free."[18] Altruism, however, is not always the most powerful motive in human affairs. In many circumstances the *Nollan* reasoning would support maintaining the land use status quo indefinitely.

---

*Ironically, it was the dissenters in *Nollan,* such as Justice William Brennan, who were doing the most to uphold a free market in land. Describing Brennan's reasoning, Richard Epstein writes, "[Brennan] extols the virtues of freedom of contract by saying to the extent that you [the Nollans] wish to get this permit you have to surrender something in exchange. . . . If the transaction leaves both sides better off, who should possibly wish to upset it?" See Richard A. Epstein, "The Harms and Benefits of Nollan and Dolan," *Northern Illinois University Law Review* 15 (Summer 1995), 482.

Widespread application of the *Nollan* decision to the entire California coast-line, for example, would have prevented many development projects there—fewer new resorts, fewer new restaurants to serve tourists, fewer new homes along the coast, etc. It would have further aggravated what some observers already saw as "an unprecedented low-income housing crisis caused by the barriers erected through suburban zoning ordinances."[19] Although written by Justice Antonin Scalia and supported by other conservative justices, the *Nollan* decision, according to Vicki Been, was a "departure from the ideology of the free market." She wonders why the market forces that work so well in other areas of society "suddenly just won't do when the government makes an offer to a developer" to sell its zoning or other land use controls for a suitable payment.[20]

The *Dolan v. City of Tigard* case in 1994 involved similar circumstances and reached a similar Supreme Court outcome.[21] Florence Dolan, the owner of a plumbing and electric supply store, sought municipal approval to double the size of her store, which would have included paving a 39-space parking lot. In response, the City of Tigard (Oregon) required as a condition of approval that Dolan dedicate the portion of the property adjacent to a nearby creek as open space for the town's future public use (most likely a pedestrian/bicycle pathway). The circumstances thus were similar to *Nollan*. The Court in this instance found that a nexus existed, but ruled that it failed to meet a further requirement of "rough proportionality" between the regulatory requirement and the condition imposed for approval. Once again, the practical effect of the Court's opinion, if widely followed, would be to keep many development rights off the market.

Admittedly, aspects of the *Nollan* and *Dolan* decisions reflected the newer thinking put forth by the zoning heretics (see chapter 7). The Supreme Court showed a healthy skepticism toward the official rationales for zoning and other land-use regulations. Furthermore, the Court deemed that the California Coastal Commission and the City of Tigard were treating their zoning decisions as saleable items. However, the Court itself failed to recognize the fundamental character of the problem. The sales of zoning were a mere symptom of basic problems with the whole zoning system itself. Without a broader solution, attacking the symptoms would simply make the problem worse.

According to Fennell, the *Nollan* and *Dolan* decisions made many conservative critics of zoning feel good because the decisions offered a "symbolically significant response to a government power that is perceived as unbounded and deeply threatening." Yet for these zoning critics, the decisions were also short-sighted. Considered more dispassionately, the *Nollan* and *Dolan* decisions were a "logically incoherent" outcome that in practice were likely to achieve "the worst of both worlds." *Nollan* and *Dolan* left "landowners exposed to excessive land use regulation while constricting their ability to bargain for regulatory adjustments." The legal limits the Supreme Court imposed on bargaining could be "expected to block a large category of mutually beneficial land use transactions." Fennell commented on their effects on the use of the metropolitan land resources of the United States: "It is plain that the *Nollan* and *Dolan* limits actually shortchange landowners and can lead to very inefficient results."[22]

Revolutionaries sometimes argue that the old must first be totally destroyed before the new can assert itself. If the Supreme Court had been seeking to destroy the old zoning system, it might have found—however inadvertently—a powerful enough legal bomb. As the least likely of revolutionaries, however, most lower courts continued to ignore *Nollan* and *Dolan* and to allow the necessary zoning deals to be cut.[23] So a real market in zoning development rights survived and prospered.

Fictions of Historic Significance

The second important trend that Richard Babcock observed in looking back on the 1980s was the spreading adoption of innovative regulatory mechanisms, typically established in special districts smaller than a whole municipality and in areas often of neighborhood size. The first "historic district"—tightly limiting changes in properties in order to preserve the historic character of the area—was created in 1931 in Charleston, South Carolina. The legal basis for historic districts was further advanced by a 1954 Supreme Court decision, *Berman v. Parker,* which upheld the government's power to condemn land for urban renewal and generally offered an expansive interpretation of the full scope of government powers. The Supreme Court declared that "the concept of the public welfare is broad and inclusive" and the police powers of government can be employed for purposes that are "spiritual as well as physical, aesthetic as well as monetary."[24]

Extended to the area of land use regulation, the Court language thus helped to relieve lingering doubts that tight government controls over "aesthetic" matters would pass legal muster. By 1981, the number of historic districts in the United States reached almost 2,000, and many more would follow. With a more comprehensive reach than an ordinary zoning district, a historic district typically can prohibit almost any action deemed incompatible with the historical character of the neighborhood, including the paint color used on homes, the construction of decks or other additions, and even minor physical alterations to structures—encompassing the full scope of "detailed regulation of changes in the exterior features of buildings."[25] In short, a historic district's regulatory powers closely resemble the land use controls exercised by a private neighborhood association.

Yet to obtain such comprehensive controls, a neighborhood must be able to qualify as "historic." The subjectivity of this term provided options for neighborhoods seeking greater regulatory authority. Urban residents often sought historic status, as one commentator notes, "as a substitute for zoning or as a corrective for what they regard[ed] as zoning's failures."[26] A former chairperson of the New York City Landmarks Preservation Commission commented, "It is becoming increasingly apparent that there is a growing tendency to use [historic] designation for purposes outside the jurisdiction of the [historic district] law." Many neighborhoods sought historic status principally "to stop demolition, to prevent development and change, [and] to prevent a high-rise with change in use, bulk, scale, etc."[27]

Historic districts have often been created at the request of neighborhood homeowners. In one California city, more than half of the property owners are required to agree formally to their area's inclusion in a historic district. In Kensington, Maryland (near Washington, D.C.), residents sought classification as a historic district because doing so would "preserve the character of the town, . . . [keeping it] an intact Victorian suburb rather than part of the continuous sprawl" typical of the rest of the Washington area.[28]

The formation of a historic district is often particularly attractive to older urban neighborhoods where the standard zoning based on density controls does not work well. Housing for the poor can be built there at the same densities as housing for the rich. As David Fein comments, many historic districts have been created to serve "the same function in cities that exclusionary zoning serves in the suburbs." The establishment of a historic district has provided regulatory authority enabling "wealthier residents in effect to preclude minorities and the poor from living in designated [historic] neighborhoods."[29] Such regulation occurs on a neighborhood-by-neighborhood basis, unlike the city-wide administration of general zoning law.

Benefits for historic districts typically extend beyond the physical environment. Carol Rose comments that "modern historic preservation law is communitarian in both the substantive and procedural senses." In fact, "a major public purpose underlying modern preservation law is the fostering of community cohesion. . . . Preservation law encourages a physical environment that supports community; it also provides procedures that can themselves organize a community, both by focusing the members' attention on aspects of the physical environment that can make them feel at home and by defining a smaller community's contribution to a larger."[30]

Numerous studies have found that historic districts can indeed improve neighborhood quality. One study reports that "historic preservation activity in urban historic districts has contributed significantly to the revitalization of those districts and [has] encouraged a return-to-the-city movement."[31] Concrete evidence of such improvements appears in the increase in property values often experienced after historic designation. In the Strand Historic District in Galveston, Texas, property values rose by 85 percent in the first three years after the formal historic designation. Individual historic districts in Washington, D.C., San Francisco, Atlanta, Boston, Cincinnati, and Brooklyn have also seen property values rise following their designations.[32]

A historic district's regulatory powers resemble closely those of a private neighborhood association. It is true that in most established neighborhoods in big cities, it is impossible to create a new neighborhood association. However, the assignment of historic status makes it possible to create the practical equivalent of a neighborhood association within a city—at least with regard to regulatory procedures. Because public powers are employed, it is not necessary to have unanimous consent from the residents of the district. Many residents of big city neighborhoods apparently want the kinds of comprehensive regulation characteristic of neighborhood associations and are willing to take whatever steps are necessary to achieve it.

Other Neighborhood Governance

In New York City, other "special districts" (besides historic districts) have been created over the past 30 years—districts described by Richard Babcock and Wendy Larsen as "the ultimate in neighborhood zoning."[33] The first such special district was established in Times Square in 1967. To obtain zoning approval, the City of New York required the builders of new hotels and office space in the "Times Square Special District" to include a new Broadway theatre. The district was formed therefore to negotiate the precise benefits to the area—in effect, the price of the zoning change—that the private developer would have to provide.

New York City today has more than 35 special districts, including the Midtown, South Street Seaport, Madison Avenue, Clinton, and Yorkville-East 86th Street districts. Each has somewhat different land use controls and goals.[34] The Clinton Special District is unusual in that it sought to promote affordable housing by raising regulatory obstacles to neighborhood gentrification. The Fifth Avenue Special District sought to keep new banks and airline offices out and to encourage residential uses above commercial space, thus maintaining the area's traditional shopping character. Babcock and Larsen comment that, like most zoning, the special districts in New York have worked best where the goal was "to stop economic change," not to stimulate it for some broader neighborhood purpose.[35] A government can stop development easily enough, but the precise location and timing of new development is largely outside its control, and finding private partners who share particular government objectives has generally proven difficult.

Richard Briffault comments that special districts differ from conventional zoning in that they "impose rules tailored to the concerns of particular neighborhoods. This difference is often reflected in the very titles of the special districts, which typically refer not to the type of use permitted but to the popular name of the district."[36] As Briffault further explains,

> Special district zoning, in effect, creates miniature, district specific zoning ordinances for particular neighborhoods. Although special zoning districts are created by city governments and do not entail district-level political or administrative structures, in practice neighborhood-level associations of residents or businesses play an important role in the initial decision to enact a special zoning district. Similarly, neighborhood groups, by lobbying and voicing their complaints to city agencies, are taking a leading role in enforcing district rules. Thus, the special zoning districts provide a form of sublocal regulation, sublocal initiation, and sublocal implementation of district-specific land use rules.[37]

Indeed, special districts sound very much like inner-city, private neighborhood associations, created well after the fact of neighborhood development, and thus requiring public action.

Selling Whole Neighborhoods

While zoning serves existing suburban neighborhoods well by excluding most other land uses, some neighborhoods will still face problems from time to time. Consider a suburban residential neighborhood located near a major new transportation facility, such as a new highway interchange or a new subway stop. Powerful economic pressures will arise at such locations, pushing for a basic change in the character of neighborhood land use. A developer, for example, might want to build a large shopping center near the highway interchange.

If the economic pressure is great enough, an existing residential neighborhood likely will eventually give way to the shopping center—or some other high-intensity use. However, the transition under existing zoning laws will be slow and messy, creating inequities among the neighborhood residents, and stresses and strains for all concerned. Speculators are likely first to move into the neighborhood to buy up some of the properties, the neighborhood might then deteriorate, some other owners will feel pressured to sell, and so on. In the end, the largest gains in land value may go to the speculators. Many of the original homeowners will not be around when the final package of rights has been assembled and the land can be put to its highest-value use.

In the 1980s the residents of a few suburban neighborhoods facing this kind of problem sought a radically new approach. They proposed organizing the homeowners in a new private association in order to sell the entire set of neighborhood properties jointly as one package. If they could succeed, the neighborhood owners might be able to capture most of the increase in land value for themselves and control more precisely the timing of the transition, avoiding the typical lengthy and stressful period characterized by mixed ownership and property deterioration resulting from purchases by speculators.

Even with the potential for such large gains, however, forming a new private association for this purpose was bound to be difficult, given the need for unanimous (or near unanimous) voluntary participation by the homeowners. Yet despite the obstacles, several neighborhoods in the Atlanta and Washington, D.C., suburbs managed to organize themselves in this fashion.[38] In Atlanta, 118 homeowners in the Kingsborough-Spring Mill subdivision formed a single corporation by voluntary agreement to negotiate the sale of all the neighborhood homes for a total price of $25 million. Under the neighborhood-sharing rule, each homeowner received approximately double or triple the existing value of his or her property as a residence. Payment was contingent upon a zoning change that the neighborhood residents, in concert with the land developer, would request from the city. As Harvard law professor Charles Haar later commented on the practical effect of such neighborhood efforts in Atlanta: "We have finally reached the point where zoning is a form of private property right." In this Atlanta neighborhood, the association had found a practical way "to sell its zoning as a right of ownership" for the whole neighborhood.[39]

In Arlington, Virginia, a suburb of Washington, D.C., the 24 residents of the Courtlands neighborhood—located near a new subway stop—signed a contract in 1988 to sell their homes as a single package to the Moyarta Corporation, doubling their existing home values.[40] Other neighborhoods in Atlanta and in Northern Virginia made similar efforts, and at least one additional Virginia neighborhood of more than 30 homes received about three times the total existing value of the homes.[41] Yet, most neighborhood attempts of this kind have failed.* Heroic commitments of time and effort on the part of some energetic neighborhood entrepreneurs were necessary. There were often major problems with holdouts, who either demanded higher payments or refused to sell altogether.

Many private neighborhood associations in the future might face circumstances similar to those in the Atlanta and Northern Virginia neighborhoods. However, no new neighborhood organization will be needed. As a form of private property, a neighborhood association can resolve such issues under its existing procedures for collective decisionmaking. Following the provisions of the neighborhood constitution, the association can hold a vote on whether to terminate its existence. If the neighborhood units are worth two or three times

---

*Some neighborhoods have continued to try, however. A recent, rare successful effort occurred in Fairfax County, Virginia, near the Vienna metro stop. Owners of 70 homes covering 40 acres banded together in 2004 to sell the homes collectively to an apartment developer for $760,000 or more per unit, compared with current home values of $400,000 in single-family use. See Peter Whoriskey, "N. Va. Neighbors Hoping to Raze, Rebuild, Profit," *Washington Post,* September 20, 2004, A1.

more in a brand-new use, then it may well be possible to achieve the necessary high supermajority support for termination.

Property as a Civil Right

As long ago as 1953, Harvard law professor Charles Haar criticized the New Jersey Supreme Court for tolerating exclusionary zoning to keep out the poor. Haar declared that "the New Jersey court substituted shibboleths for reasoning and used liberal shibboleths to attain an illiberal result—a decision which can only still further distort the problems arising from the complex relationship of city and country."[42] Nevertheless, few states heeded Haar's call for the judiciary to intervene and prevent suburban municipalities from adopting "illiberal" zoning measures.

By the 1980s, the U.S. Supreme Court was exhibiting more skepticism about municipal zoning justifications. The Court would no longer ignore entirely the confiscations of development rights under zoning and other land use regulations. It was also moving, as Dan Tarlock stated in 1984, to address the problem of "the intellectual bankruptcy of the judicial doctrines used by the courts" to resolve "takings" cases. The failures of previous court efforts in this area meant that, in practice, there was "no law of what constitutes [a] taking."[43] Michael Berger and Gideon Kanner were more blunt: "All commentators concede," they reported, "that judge-made substantive takings law is incoherent."[44] It rested on still more fictions of the land laws. When individual judges made sound decisions—as they often did—these decisions might be described as merely "applied common sense" that required little in the way of formal legal training or other special knowledge.

The process of reexamining the fundamentals of takings law began for the Supreme Court in 1980 with *Agins v. City of Tiburon.*[45] The Court again upheld a local regulatory action, but suggested that in the future it might no longer completely defer to the local legislature, enunciating several standards that would have to be met for a local land use regulation to be legally sustained. The Court then in 1987 affirmed and further clarified these standards in *Keystone Bituminous Coal Association v. DeBenedictus.*[46] While perhaps overstating the matter, Bernard Siegan describes the Court blessing given for the "Agins formula" as "a major event in takings-clause jurisprudence." The 1981 and 1987 cases in combination established three standards for determining the legal validity of a local land use regulation: (1) it must serve a "legitimate state interest," (2) it must "substantially advance" this interest, and (3) it must not deny altogether any "economically viable use" of the land.[47]

Another indication of changing times came in a 1981 Supreme Court dissent in *San Diego Gas and Electric Company v. San Diego,* authored by Justice

William Brennan. Brennan had long been famous on the Court for defending the freedoms of speech, religion, assembly, and other civil rights. By the 1980s, he was beginning to extend his civil rights concerns to individual property owners as well, acknowledging that property owners could also be abused by the overzealous application of government powers.[48] Given the circumstances of the case, the traditional judicial approach would have been to refuse to become involved in such a legal challenge. In the *San Diego* case, the city had designated land for open space, but voters had rejected its purchase in a referendum. Arguing that city regulations were still blocking development, the landowner sought monetary compensation for the loss of property value. Although the Supreme Court did not accept this argument, Justice Brennan issued a strong dissent: "Police power regulations such as zoning ordinances and other land use restrictions can destroy the use and enjoyment of property in order to promote the public good just as effectively as formal condemnation or physical invasion of property." As a result, a government regulation could also serve as "a *de facto* exercise of the power of eminent domain, where the effects completely deprive the owner of all or most of his interest in the property," thereby necessitating public compensation.[49]

Brennan emphasized his newfound interest in "property liberties" by declaring that, even if the City of San Diego now agreed to drop any objection to development, it would still owe compensation for the long delay in resolving the issue. The City's "invalidation unaccompanied by payment of damages would hardly compensate the landowner for any economic loss suffered during the time his property was taken." Indeed, as Brennan now argued, the fact that "a 'regulatory taking' may be temporary, by virtue of the government's power to rescind or amend the regulation, does not make it any less of a constitutional 'taking.'" Hence, Brennan argued further, any "temporary reversible 'taking' should be analyzed according to the same constitutional framework applied to permanent irreversible 'takings.'"[50]

This general constitutional prohibition on takings, as Brennan saw the matter, was "designed to bar the government from forcing some individuals to bear burdens which, in all fairness, should be borne by the public as a whole."[51] That is to say, when a government action has a general public benefit, as Brennan was now suggesting, it should not be able to impose all the costs on one or a few property owners and thus relieve the general public of any burden of payment. This was simply a matter of basic social fairness and equity.[52]

There was also a strong case in terms of economic efficiency: if the government could provide public benefits to most people "for free" (by imposing the costs on a select few property owners), politicians might vote for many wasteful projects from a wider public perspective. A large majority might be tempted to oppress a small minority too politically weak to resist. Therefore, as Brennan argued in *San Diego Gas and Electric,* the judiciary, acting under the takings clause of the constitution, should intervene to ensure that "one person is [not] asked to assume more than a fair share of the public burden." Instead, by requiring "the payment of just compensation," the purpose would be "to redistribute that economic cost from the individual to the public at large," thus appropriately acting to require political leaders to consider the full costs of their actions and to weigh these costs against the benefits. The takings clause, as one might say, is a main constitutional protection against a potential "tyranny of the majority."[53]

Justice Brennan was an unlikely ally of the 1970s zoning heretics. Yet he was acknowledging that, for any given site, there are many land use rights, and the zoning's practical effect is to transfer some of these rights from one party to another. Brennan was further acknowledging that a municipal confiscation of some part of these rights is equivalent to a taking for constitutional purposes. Notwithstanding the judicial deference to local zoning authority over the previous half-century, it was time to recognize that a governmental regulatory power over land and property could also infringe on important individual rights.

Brennan, to be sure, was also a realist. He did not say so, but his focus on temporary takings in *San Diego Gas and Electric* perhaps reflected an understanding that a temporary taking might offer a better target than a permanent taking—the latter having occurred perhaps as long as 40 or 50 years earlier. The victimized party was likely to still be around—indeed, likely bringing the case—and determining the economic impact on the damaged landowner was easier. The Supreme Court might have failed in some of its duties in the past, but the zoning injustices did not have to go on indefinitely.

A New Court Majority

Brennan's dissent in *San Diego Gas and Electric* became the majority view in 1987 in the Court's *First English Evangelical Lutheran Church of Glendale v. County of Los Angeles, California,* decision.[54] The First English Evangelical Lutheran Church owned a retreat/recreation center for handicapped children (Lutherglen) that was destroyed in a 1978 flood. Declaring the area a floodplain, the County of Los Angeles thereafter prohibited any redevelopment of the 21 acres of land and its properties. Alleging an act of "inverse condemnation," the owners of Lutherglen sought from the County financial compensation for losing their land's use. In response, the County argued that the owners' only recourse was to seek relief in further court actions. A trial judge agreed with the County that any application of inverse condemnation law was premature. If the County should later lose this case, it could avoid any payment of compensation simply by dropping the regulation. In other words, a municipality could prevent land development for 10 years, then find in the end that its regulation was illegal, abandon the regulation, and suffer no ill consequences.

Chief Justice William Rehnquist, joined by Justice Brennan and four other justices, overruled the California courts. The Supreme Court declared that the U.S. Constitution required "compensation for that period" during which the land could not be used, even if the taking should turn out to be temporary.[55] Hence, the owners of Lutherglen could proceed with their current suit for monetary damages. As Chief Justice Rehnquist wrote for the majority:

> We realize that . . . our present holding will undoubtedly lessen to some extent the freedom and flexibility of land-use planners and governing bodies of municipal corporations when enacting land-use regulations. But such consequences necessarily flow from any decision upholding a claim of constitutional right; many of the provisions of the Constitution are designed to limit the flexibility and freedom of governmental authorities and the Just Compensation Clause of the Fifth Amendment is one of them. As Justice Holmes aptly noted more than 50 years ago, "a strong desire to improve the public condition is not enough to warrant achieving the desire by a shorter cut than the constitutional way of paying for the change."[56]

Justices Rehnquist and Brennan represented an unusual alliance, but they were in fact both saying much the same thing. If a government wanted to regulate land for a wider public purpose, it should not expect a small number of landowners to bear the main economic burden. Compensation would have to be paid, or the regulation would be invalid. In the case of zoning newly imposed on an existing neighborhood, the necessary compensation took the form of new collective property rights in place of the individual rights that had been "taken" from the neighborhood property owners by government action. In the case of zoning newly imposed on undeveloped land, however, there was no compensation offered or paid. An application of the Brennan-Rehnquist line of reasoning, therefore, would have yielded a clear conclusion: much of the zoning regulation of undeveloped land in the outer suburbs was a governmental taking that required either the payment of compensation or the rescinding of the zoning regulation.

Such a conclusion, to be sure, would have been a political bombshell, upsetting longstanding zoning practices across the United States. It would have immersed the courts in the management of large areas of undeveloped suburban land. Although there was a growing legal literature advocating the outright abolition of zoning, the lower courts had done little to pave the way for such a radical redirection of American land use practices. Moreover, few of the legal analysts had made the necessary clear distinction between the arguably constitutionally permissible zoning of existing neighborhoods and the much less constitutionally permissible zoning of undeveloped land. Not surprisingly, therefore, and however directly applicable the logic of the Rehnquist-Brennan reasoning, the Supreme Court did not follow up in this sensitive area of American land use practice in the developing suburbs.

It did, however, take some small further steps in the years to come. The Court finally acted in 1992's *Lucas v. South Carolina Coastal Council* to directly overturn a government land use regulation on takings grounds.[57] In 1986, David Lucas had bought two lots for $975,000 along the South Carolina coastline and proposed to develop the lots in the same manner as his immediate neighbors had. When the State of South Carolina, acting under a new coastal zone management program, refused to allow this (or any other) development, Lucas sued. Joined by four other members of the court, Justice Scalia found that a 100 percent deprivation of property value, as Lucas had experienced, could not be justified unless the regulation at issue provided protection from a genuine nuisance offense.*

The Lucas case was widely read as another Supreme Court step to put new—if still rather modest—constraints on local government's power to regulate landowners. In an earlier (1982) case in New York City, the U.S. Supreme Court had ruled that the government could not require a building owner to make physical space available to a cable TV operator.[58] There were now at least three circumstances in which the Supreme Court had had declared an illegal taking: (1) a temporary confiscation of rights, (2) a 100 percent loss of property value due to a regulation; and (3) a direct physical invasion of property. In a mild form, the zoning heresies of the 1970s and 1980s were even showing up in the Supreme Court's chambers.

These new judicial attitudes nevertheless affected only a small portion of American land use regulation. Takings law was clarified in a few special circumstances, but on the whole it remained as confused as ever.† As demonstrated in its

---

*After losing in the U.S. Supreme Court, the State of South Carolina had to pay David Lucas for the value of his lands. Rather than keeping its newly acquired lands, South Carolina soon turned around and sold them for $785,000 for development purposes. A private preservationist, according to press reports, had offered $315,000 for one of the lots. As William Fischel comments, when the State of South Carolina had to put its own money on the table—as opposed to taking a "free" regulatory action—it "was unwilling to forgo $77,500 to preserve one of the lots whose previous value of $600,000 to the owner it had denied was a compensable loss." As this case illustrated, a more rigorous enforcement of the Constitution's takings clause would require governments to undertake essential balancing of benefits and costs on a wider basis. See William A. Fischel, *Regulatory Takings: Law, Economics, and Politics* (Cambridge, MA: Harvard University Press, 1995), 61.

†The Supreme Court also limited the likely scope of any "temporary takings" claims in a 2003 decision involving land use restrictions around Lake Tahoe. However, the Court declined to hold that this was a compensable restriction of landowner rights. Instead, the Court held that it was a reasonable delay in the normal process of land use regulation. Once again, the Supreme Court had added to the wide confusion surrounding takings law. No one could say what would be a "reasonable" or an "unreasonable" delay in the workings of land use regulation. It would seemingly fall to the courts to make such determinations on a case-by-case basis, but the courts would never have the resources to make such decisions for the many thousands of individual circumstances where takings issues might arise. In practical effect, therefore, the result of the Court's various actions in this area was that there was no principled law of temporary takings. It was all ad hoc. See *Tahoe-Sierra Preservation Council, Inc. v. Tahoe Regional Planning Agency*, 535 U.S. 302 (2002).

misguided *Nollan* and *Dolan* decisions, the Supreme Court was unable to penetrate more fully the fictions that surround zoning. *Nollan* and *Dolan* might have made sense if the Court had been prepared to overturn the widespread takings of undeveloped land in rapidly growing suburban areas. Short of this step, however, it would frequently be necessary to pay local governments to accommodate new land development.

Land Socialism, American Style

When a government zones undeveloped land in the outer suburbs, one might say that such actions "nationalize" the part of the development rights—typically a large part—that are taken. In the former socialist countries of Eastern Europe and elsewhere, economic systems—based on government ownership of the means of production—were notoriously inefficient, and most were eventually abandoned by the end of the 20th century. Today, America's land system—particularly in newly developing suburban areas—exhibits many of the same economic failings, and especially a large mismatch between government allocations of land supplies and the actual demands of land users.

Also as in the Eastern European nations of the past that had nationalized much of their economies, the pressures of supply and demand produce "black markets." When the government does "provide" some new land that is in short supply—such as land for low- and moderate-income housing—there are long lines of "buyers" hoping to obtain the available "supplies." Certain private groups—generally the well-off—learn how to exploit the government system of economic controls. All in all, when a government owns and manages the use of an important natural or other productive resource, historical experience shows that the use of this resource is likely to be very inefficient.

Two economists from Harvard and the University of Pennsylvania recently attempted to estimate the cost of these inefficiencies. The numbers turn out to be extraordinarily large. Edward Glaeser and Joseph Gyourko first observe that vacant land in a newly developing area of a metropolitan region is valuable in two ways.[59] A given lot has an "average value" (total value divided by square feet) and a "marginal value" (the value of one more square foot added to the lot). In an efficient land market, the two forms of land value will necessarily converge.

For example, assume that people are willing to pay $1 per square foot for additional yard space (the "marginal value" of more land). An acre of land containing 43,560 square feet will sell for $43,560 at this price of land. However, assume that a lot of 22,000 square feet will sell for $30,000 in total, equal to an average value of $1.36 per square foot. This circumstance cannot persist in an unregulated market. A lot owner with the 43,560 square feet will divide the lot in half, and have two lots with a higher combined property value (almost $60,000). Indeed, similar calculations will demonstrate that any profit-maximizing landowner will keep subdividing until the point at which the average land value equals the marginal value.*

Of course, most metropolitan areas exercise tight zoning and other restrictions on land subdivision. As a result, the gap between the average land value and the marginal land value may remain large. Indeed, as Glaeser and Gyourko point out, the size of this gap is a good measure of the efficiency—or inefficiency—of land use in a particular metropolitan area. Analyzing actual land markets across the United States, Glaeser and Gyourko found that consumers were generally willing to pay $1 to $2 per square foot for additional land for consumptive purposes (for the enjoyment of a larger lot size). However, when they calculated average land values based on buyers' willingness to pay for an entire lot, the numbers were dramatically higher. For example, in Chicago in recent years, the price of a lot averaged $15 per square foot; in Boston—$13; in Seattle—$19; in San Diego—$26; and in San Francisco (the highest)—$64.[60]

In San Francisco, the same quarter-acre, worth perhaps $30,000 as additional space for an existing lot, would be worth perhaps $600,000 as a brand new lot. Zoning, however, prevented landowners there from creating a new lot; instead, they had to provide a much larger lot to only one buyer. In many metropolitan areas, a typical owner could increase the total value of his or her undeveloped land by four or five times or even more if government regulations did not prevent its subdivision into multiple smaller parcels. The resulting land inefficiencies in a high-demand metropolitan area could be in the many billions of dollars for that area alone. Glaeser and Gyourko describe their findings: "Empirically, we found that the hedonic estimates produce [marginal] land values that often are about one-tenth of the [average] values calculated. . . . We believe that the dramatic difference between the two sets of estimates is our best evidence of the critical role that zoning plays in creating high housing costs."[61]

Glaeser and Gyourko note that the traditional explanation for high land costs in many U.S. metropolitan areas "is that they have genuine shortages of

---

*Geometrically, this situation can be shown as follows in figure 8.1. The average value of a lot is shown by the heavy line, beginning at point A. A property owner will maximize the value of his or her parcel of land by selling lots of size AB—the lot size at which the marginal value of an additional square foot of lot space is precisely equal to the average value per square foot of the lot. A government zoning requirement, however, may require the lot owner to sell a much larger lot, equal say to a size of AC. As the figure shows, the average value per square foot of a lot of size AC will be much reduced from the average value of a lot of size AB, a burden of economic inefficiency borne by both the landowner and society at large. At a point such as AC, moreover, the marginal value of additional lot space is much below the average value of the lot space, providing a good measure of the degree of economic inefficiency imposed by the government regulation.

Figure 8.1. *Optimum Lot Size for Landowners*

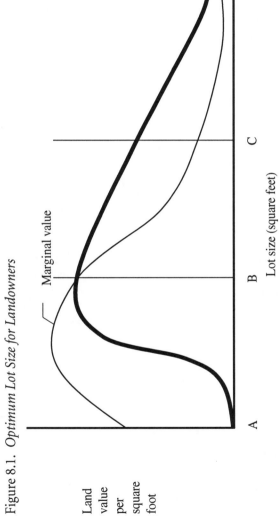

Marginal value

Land value per square foot

Lot size (square feet)

A   B   C

land on which to build." Their research demonstrates, however, that "homes are expensive in these areas because government artificially restricts development, in effect imposing a high 'zoning tax.' "[62] If American society wants to reduce housing costs, Glaeser and Gyourko recommend, "building small numbers of subsidized housing units is likely to have a trivial impact on average housing prices (given any reasonable demand elasticity), even if well-targeted toward deserving poor households. However, reducing the implied zoning tax on new construction could well have a massive impact on housing prices" for middle-income groups.[63] Nationwide, the inefficiencies caused by uneconomic local zoning controls on the use of undeveloped land were in all likelihood costing the nation hundreds of billions of dollars in lost long-run land value. This expense was not buying any wider environmental benefits; to the contrary, local zoning was the leading cause of the sprawling pattern of land development characteristic of the American suburbs.

That is to say, the American system in which local suburban governments take possession of the key development rights to land is about as efficient—and as environmentally constructive—as the government ownership of the old steel mills, shipyards, and coal mines in the formerly socialist Poland and East Germany. Yet, among the day-to-day practitioners, the zoning heretics in the United States have been no more heeded than were the dissident economists in Eastern Europe. Until finally vindicated by the "revolution of 1989," these economists sought without much success to persuade their fellow citizens about the follies of the old systems. Perhaps one day there will be a similar zoning revolution in the United States. This revolution, admittedly, is most likely to occur slowly and unnoticed, and will then be discovered as an accomplished fact by some future generation of land use scholars.

Conclusion

The evolution of zoning has taken place not only on the ground, but in the fictions used to hide its real workings. By the 1970s, the attacks on "exclusionary zoning" were having their effect. In the egalitarian spirit of American life of that period, few people wanted to advocate government policies that worked to keep out minorities and the poor from wealthier suburban areas. Rather than change land use practices, however, it was easier to alter the rhetoric. Indeed, the old zoning exclusions metamorphosed into "growth controls," "agricultural land preservation," "maintenance of green space," and, most broadly, "environmental protection" of farmlands and any remaining open forests and fields in the outer American suburbs.

By the 1990s, however, the 1970s and 1980s imagery was itself becoming suspect. New camouflage thus would be necessary. No one can object in principle to "smart growth," but in practice the applications of smart growth in the American suburbs have differed little from the old exclusionary practices. Indeed, as long as suburban local governments are permitted to possess significant land development rights, they will frequently exercise these rights in ways that impose large costs on the rest of society—however much they may seek to disguise such actions through land law fictions.

Just as experiments in government ownership of core productive resources have ended in many other nations around the world, so should America's experiment in government ownership of most rights to use of undeveloped suburban land. Rather than a top-down solution, the answers to zoning excesses may have to be found in a radically new direction: the genuine empowerment of local neighborhoods and landowners to act privately and collectively under a more appropriate system of collective property rights for the ownership of suburban land. This approach might extend the principles and legal status of the neighborhood association to encourage the establishment of new forms of private neighborhood associations that would be suitable for collective ownership of undeveloped land (see chapter 13).

NOTES

1. Richard Babcock, "The Outlook for Zoning," *Urban Land,* November 1984, 34.

2. Richard Pipes, *Property and Freedom* (New York: Vintage Books, 1999), 65.

3. Babcock, "The Outlook for Zoning," 34.

4. Tom Precious, "D.C. Seeks to Raise Hadid 'Linkage' Fee," *Washington Post,* November 14, 1987, E1.

5. Tom Precious, "D.C. Zoning Board Approves Second 'Linkage' Project," *Washington Post,* November 21, 1987, E1.

6. Jerry Frug, "Decentering Decentralization," *University of Chicago Law Review* 60 (Spring 1993), 327.

7. Timothy J. Choppin, "Breaking the Exclusionary Land Use Regulation Barrier: Policies to Promote Affordable Housing in the Suburbs," *Georgetown Law Journal* 82 (July 1994), 2052.

8. Alan A. Altshuler and Jose A. Gomez-Ibanez, *Regulation for Revenue: The Political Economy of Land Use Exactions* (Washington, DC: Brookings Institution and the Lincoln Institute of Land Policy, 1993), 39, 54.

9. Ibid., 54, 56.

10. Richard F. Babcock and Wendy U. Larsen, *Special Districts: The Ultimate in Neighborhood Zoning* (Cambridge, MA: Lincoln Institute of Land Policy, 1990), 1–2.

11. Jerold S. Kayden, "Zoning for Dollars: New Rules for an Old Game? Comments on the Municipal Art Society and Nollan Cases," *Washington University Journal of Urban and Contemporary Law* 39 (Spring 1991), 3.

12. Carol E. Heim, "Leapfrogging, Urban Sprawl, and Growth Management: Phoenix, 1950–2000," *American Journal of Economics and Sociology* 60 (January 2001), 261.

13. William A. Fischel, "Zoning and Land Use Regulation," in Boudewijn Bouckaert and Gerrit De Geest, eds., *Encyclopedia of Law and Economics, Volume II* (Cheltenham, UK: Edward Elgar, 2000), 413.

14. Michael M. Berger and Gideon Kanner, "The Need for Takings Law Reform: A View From the Trenches—A Response to Taking Stock of the Takings Debate," *Santa Clara Law Review* 38, no. 3 (1998), 880.

15. Arthur C. Nelson, "Development Impact Fees—Introduction," *Journal of the American Planning Association* 54 (Winter 1988), 4.

16. Vicki Been, " 'Exit' as a Constraint on Land Use Exactions: Rethinking the Unconstitutional Conditions Doctrine," *Columbia Law Review* 91 (April 1991), 488.

17. *Nollan v. California Coastal Commission,* 483 U.S. 825 (1987).

18. Lee Anne Fennell, "Hard Bargains and Real Steals: Land Use Exactions Revisited," *Iowa Law Review* 86 (October 2000), 52.

19. Joel Kosman, "Toward an Inclusionary Jurisprudence: A Reconceptualization of Zoning," *Catholic University Law Review* 43 (Fall 1993), 60–61.

20. Been, " 'Exit' as a Constraint on Land Use Exactions," 545.

21. *Dolan v. City of Tigard,* 114 S. Ct. 2309 (1994).

22. Fennell, "Hard Bargains and Real Steals," 4–5, 27.

23. Legal scholars soon also suggested the constitutional merits of interpreting Nollan narrowly. See "Municipal Development Exactions, The Rational Nexus Test, and the Federal Constitution," *Harvard Law Review* 102 (March 1989).

24. *Berman v. Parker,* 348 U.S. at 33 (1954).

25. Carol M. Rose, "Preservation and Community: New Directions in the Law of Historic Preservation," *Stanford Law Review* 33 (February 1981), 507.

26. David B. Fein, "Historic Districts: Preserving City Neighborhoods for the Privileged," *New York University Law Review* 60 (April 1985), 89.

27. Quoted in ibid., 90.

28. Richard Fausset, "Historic Designation—A Bureaucratic Boon?" *Chevy Chase (MD) Gazette,* August 20, 1997, A12.

29. Fein, "Historic Districts," 89, 92.

30. Rose, "Preservation and Community," 533–34.

31. Advisory Council on Historic Preservation, *The Contribution of Historic Preservation to Urban Revitalization* (1979), quoted in Fein, "Historic Districts," 83.

32. Fein, "Historic Districts," 86.

33. Babcock and Larsen, *Special Districts.*

34. See Richard Briffault, "The Rise of Sublocal Structures in Urban Governance," *Minnesota Law Review* 82 (December 1997), 514–17.

35. Babcock and Larsen, *Special Districts,* 46, 57, 71.

36. Briffault, "The Rise of Sublocal Structures in Urban Governance," 515.

37. Ibid., 517.

38. Robert Guenther, "Atlanta Neighborhoods Unite To Sell Homes to Developers," *Wall Street Journal,* May 23, 1984, 33.

39. Quoted in "Lake Hearn: The Great Debate," *Atlanta Constitution,* June 20, 1985, Dekalb Supplement, 6A, col. 4.

40. Evelyn Hsu, "Courtlands Residents Savor Sale of A Decade: Years of Effort End in United, $20 Million Deal with Developer," *Washington Post,* February 4, 1988, C1.

41. Wendy Swallow, "Homeowners Sell Land as a Group: More Than 30 Sign $7.5 Million Deal," *Washington Post,* October 20, 1984, E1.

42. Charles M. Haar, "Zoning for Minimum Standards: The Wayne Township Case," *Harvard Law Review* 66 (April 1953), 1063.

43. A. Dan Tarlock, "Regulatory Takings," *Chicago-Kent Law Review* 60 (1984), 28.

44. Berger and Kanner, "The Need for Takings Law Reform," 838.

45. *City of Tiburon v. Agins,* 447 U.S. 255 (1980).

46. *Keystone Bituminous Coal Association v. DeBenedictus,* 480 U.S. 470 (1987).

47. Bernard H. Siegan, *Property and Freedom: The Constitution, the Courts, and Land-Use Regulation* (New Brunswick, NJ: Transaction Publishers, 1997), 115, 114.

48. Legal scholars were also showing a new concern that right to private property might be an important element of the package of civil rights. See Margaret Jane Radin, "Property and Personhood," *Stanford Law Review* 34 (May 1982).

49. *San Diego Gas and Electric Company v. City of San Diego* 450 U.S. at 652–53 (1981).

50. Ibid., at 655, 657.

51. Ibid., at 656.

52. See Steven Eagle, *Regulatory Takings* (Charlottesville, VA: Michie Law Publishers, 1996).

53. *San Diego Gas and Electric Company,* at 656.

54. *First English Evangelical Lutheran Church of Glendale v. County of Los Angeles, California* 482 U.S. 304 (1987).

55. Ibid., at 307.

56. Ibid., at 321–22.

57. *David H. Lucas v. South Carolina Coastal Council* 505 U.S. 1003 (1992).

58. *Loretto v. Teleprompter Manhattan CATV Corp.,* 458 U.S. 419 (1982).

59. Edward Glaeser and Joseph Gyourko, "The Impact of Building Restrictions on Housing Affordability," paper written for a conference on "Policies to Promote Housing Affordability," organized by the Federal Reserve Bank of New York, February 2002. The results of their research are summarized in Edward Glaeser and Joseph Gyourko, "Zoning's Steep Price," *Regulation* 25 (Fall 2002).

60. Glaeser and Gyourko, "Zoning's Steep Price," 28.

61. Ibid.

62. Edward Glaeser and Joseph Gyourko, "The Steep Price of Zoning," *The Taubman Center Report* (Cambridge, MA: Center for State and Local Government, John F. Kennedy School of Government, Harvard University, 2003), 2.

63. Glaeser and Gyourko, "Zoning's Steep Price," 30.

PART III
Neighborhoods in Political and Economic Thought

The classics of modern political and economic thought have had little to say about neighborhoods. However, what they have said is generally negative. A world of free markets—including free trade across the entire earth—is a world in which real neighborhood autonomy can have little place. The comprehensive designs of central planners would also be frustrated in a world of many neighborhoods, each with significant governing powers. The height of localism in Western civilization was the medieval era; indeed, neighborhood autonomy is sometimes said to have a "feudal" quality to it. Romantic imagery of the Knights of the Roundtable might be good for the movies, but in modern times, there is seemingly little to be learned from medieval social organization.

The nation and the individual instead have been the building blocks from which modern political and economic thought has been developed. The United States was created—as the Declaration of Independence famously stated in 1776—to advance each and every individual's inalienable right to life, liberty, and the pursuit of happiness. In 1787, the U.S. Constitution gathered together a loose affiliation of states to form a single, unified nation. Individuals, states, and the nation were important political actors, but the founding political documents of the United States had little or nothing to say about neighborhoods. No important political leader in America has since sought to rally the electorate around a cause of neighborhood identity and independent authority. To assert a right of "free association" at the neighborhood level is to speak a civic language unfamiliar to most Americans.

A greater role for neighborhoods in American life would require a reversal of the trend toward consolidation into larger units that was a defining feature

195

of the modern age. For example, in the second half of the 19th century, the nation-states of Germany and Italy were formed by uniting formerly independent cities and regions. At the end of that century, the modern City of New York was created by combining five independent boroughs into a single political unit. And General Motors was created early in the 20th century through the consolidation of Buick, Oldsmobile, Cadillac, and other car manufacturers and suppliers.

The advance of scientific knowledge in the 20th century took place on a worldwide scale; the community of research physicists whose scientific discoveries transformed the century operated across national boundaries. The reach of world trade has since steadily expanded in the modern era; Wal-Mart stores today are filled with goods from China and Southeast Asia. A worldwide community of musicians and philosophers has come into existence. Leading sports competitions, such as the Olympics, soccer's World Cup, the British Open, and others attract competitors and spectators from around the world. While each person of necessity must physically live in some neighborhood, most people's desires for a powerful sense of community in the 20th century were directed to larger arenas—to the city, the state, the nation, and even, for some, the world.

The astonishing technological developments of the modern age also undermined the importance of neighborhoods. Improvements in transportation meant that people could live in one place and work in another. With modern methods of communication, people could listen to radio and watch television programs that might have originated hundreds and even thousands of miles away. The Internet facilitated easy communication across the entire earth. The increasing productivity of modern agriculture, combined with improvements in transportation in developed nations, meant that most food was no longer produced near the neighborhood in which it was consumed.

The greatest wars of the 20th century—World War I, World War II, and the Cold War—were fought among powerful nation-states that combined large economic resources within one political jurisdiction. The effective prosecution of war turned citizens' attentions away from local attachments and toward a common membership in a single community large enough to wage war effectively—the nation-state. Neighborhood concerns seemed to border on the trivial. Modern trends seemingly meant, in short, that neighborhoods no longer performed essential functions. Even if neighborhoods could still offer a sense of local community, they increasingly faced competition from many other forms of human association that transcended neighborhood boundaries.

The second half of the 20th century may have marked a turning point in this trend, however. In the first half of the century, many prominent intellectuals were Marxists or socialists who advocated the creation of a world society according to their particular vision. Later on, however, a newer generation of intellectuals—the new "radicals" and "revolutionaries" disillusioned with large agglomerations of military and economic power—began advocating the merits of decentralized institutions in society. Smaller might actually be better.[1] The current rise of neighborhoods is one sign that the core values of the modern age are being challenged and that perhaps we may really be entering into a "postmodern" era.

Indeed, the 1990s witnessed signs that subdividing society into smaller units might be a hallmark of the coming century. Secession was in the air.[2] In 1991, the former Soviet Union broke up into a host of independent nations, as did the former Czechoslovakia and the former Yugoslavia not long after. Northern Italy threatened to secede from southern Italy, Scotland from England, and Quebec from Canada. In New York City, the citizens of Staten Island voted in 1990 to take initial steps toward a "divorce" from the city after the U.S. Supreme Court found that the city's Board of Estimates did not meet the constitutional requirement for one person/one vote—and Staten Island thus was suffering a significant loss in political influence within the city.[3] On the West Coast, many residents of the San Fernando Valley (with a population of 1.2 million) were suggesting the previously unthinkable—secession from the City of Los Angeles.

Commenting on the possibility that Los Angeles might actually break apart, the state librarian of California, historian Kevin Starr, declared that ideas such as "creative destruction" were becoming newly important. In great contrast to the centralizing impetus in so much of modern political and economic thought, Starr was seeing the rise of whole new ways of thinking about the future of American cities: "Modernism, after all—and Los Angeles was at the time the most modern of modern U.S. cities—preferred large, generalized, almost abstract organizations of corporate and/or governmental power." In actuality,

> Los Angeles was able to handle its postwar growth through an exercise of civic intervention based upon economies of scale. The bigger and more unified a governmental entity, the more efficient it seemed. Into the 1960s, one Los Angeles government saw itself serving one Los Angeles people, who, in turn, perceived themselves as one homogeneous group . . . living in one place with a more or less standardized lifestyle.
>
> Today, large entities, whether public or private, arouse immediate suspicion, if not outright hostility. Our postmodernist sensibility prizes the non-standardized, the local. Far from embodying one sensibility, the Los Angeles of today embodies multiple states of consciousness, in which each Los Angeleno assembles a civic identity out of factors of race, class, ethnicity, religion, language—and neighborhood. Everyone is demanding an intensification of local value and context.[4]

Near the end of the century, David Brooks skillfully analyzed the cultural attitudes of the people who had come to power in American society after the 1960s and felt torn between their desire to be "bohemian" and their contradictory desire to be economically successful and otherwise "bourgeois." The attempt to reconcile these conflicting motives produced a somewhat schizophrenic "Bobo" ("bourgeois/bohemian") lifestyle. Brooks agreed with Starr: "We no longer feel we are living in an age of consolidation; on the contrary, deconsolidation seems to be the order of the day." So today, Bobo leadership in American society believes the highest forms of "political action" are conducted on "the local level, where communication can be face to face and where debate tends to be less ideological. When confronted with thorny national problems like poverty and education, Bobos tend to favor devolution, decentralizing power to the lowest level possible. This way each person or community can discover its own pragmatic solution without having to engage in seemingly futile debates over first principles." Bobos, for example, "value . . . the small intermediating institutions that make up a neighborhood and town."[5]

There is still a tension experienced with the egalitarian values and associated desire for a single community encompassing rich and poor that are also strong among Bobos. For Robert Reich, the rise of private neighborhood associations represents the "secession of the successful" from the lives of their fellow American citizens.[6] A private status does in fact convey many of the attributes of sovereignty, including wide discretion to control neighborhood entry and to set rules and regulations for the conduct of internal affairs. When such qualities of privateness are extended to territorial areas, the result might even be described as the functional equivalent of a tiny nation-state. A metropolitan region composed largely of neighborhood associations also in some ways actually exhibits a "feudal" character. Urban planners Edward Blakely and Mary Gail Snyder describe the rise of gated communities as "this new fortress settlement pattern" based on the protections of "gates, walls, and security guards." These new walled enclaves in America's urban areas threaten to "separate our communities, block social contact, and weaken the social contract."[7]

Thus, American intellectuals' views about the private neighborhood association have mostly been negative. A postmodern philosophy might indeed be taking hold, but most political scientists and other urban students have not connected this new way of thinking to the rise of the private neighborhood association. For them, private neighborhoods have been a divisive presence—a new turn away from the old idea of an all-inclusive American community. Without strong national bonds, they believe, such neighborhoods represent new obstacles to national progress. If the 20th century witnessed a steady growth of federal power in the name of "progressive" ideals, these intellectuals now deem the rise of many autonomous private neighborhoods to be "anti-progressive." This ongoing privatization of the neighborhood environment would impede the federal government's ability to plan and orchestrate the economic development of the nation in the greatest overall public interest.

Yet, some past trends in American intellectual life have proved favorable to neighborhoods. Alexis de Tocqueville spoke glowingly as long ago as the 1840s about the importance of private associations in American life. More recently, following the Vietnam War, the Watergate scandal, and other disturbing events that served to reduce public confidence in the national government, a neighborhood movement emerged in the United States in the late 1960s and 1970s. A neighborhood, it was suggested, should become more than a zip code; neighborhoods perhaps should take on actual governing responsibilities. They might well perform the neighborhood-level functions of government much better than the failing bureaucracies found in so many big-city governments across the United States.

In the 1980s and 1990s, a "communitarian" movement lamented the atomization of American life and the decline of civic commitment in the nation. It reflected a concern that perhaps the common bonds might no longer be strong enough to sustain a single community of all Americans organized around a core set of national values. Communitarians proposed a larger role for social clubs, churches, charitable organizations, labor unions, and a host of other "mediating institutions" between the individual and the state—and they often included the neighborhood prominently in this list. Even if stronger shared values among Americans might frequently differ significantly from one neighborhood to another, it could at least be argued that some strongly held values were better than few values at all—a newly urgent danger, as it now increasingly appeared to many observers of American life.

In these senses, the rise of the private neighborhood association might itself be characterized as a leading postmodern development in American society. Reflecting the declining usefulness of the traditional distinction between public and private, the neighborhood association is neither truly one or the other, emphasizing rather the small over the large, and the local over the national. Its rise reflects a new skepticism that technological advance and national economic progress must be given their full leeway; it accepts a basic pluralism of social values as at least a long-run, if perhaps not permanent, American state of affairs. In the modern age, economic forces displaced many people from their traditional ties to local community. In a postmodern world, perhaps these ties will have to be rediscovered and reasserted in new ways—and the local neighborhood could be a focal point for any such social revival.

Few people connected with the rise of the private neighborhood association, to be sure, have regarded its emergence in such grand terms. Indeed, the establishment of more than 200,000 neighborhood associations across the United States has been largely a grassroots movement led by the real estate industry and assisted by real estate attorneys, a few government civil servants in the housing agencies, and other men and women involved in the ordinary affairs of life. It has been a social revolution with the most mundane of origins. Its purpose has been straightforward—to provide housing at a reasonable cost and in an attractive neighborhood setting for many millions of Americans, while making a profit for the private entrepreneurs.

Whatever the mundane origins, the longer-run future of neighborhood associations in the United States will not be resolved as an issue of land development and housing policy alone. The place of neighborhood associations in American society has become too important to be left to the real estate industry to determine by itself. As political and economic theorists begin to take more seriously the place of neighborhood associations in American life, their opinions are likely to have a growing influence. Their political and economic ideas will have to work out an appropriate role for private neighborhood associations in broader American institutions of governance. Some such commentators may wish to limit sharply associations' future role, while others may hope to expand it significantly.

If the rapid rise of neighborhood associations of the past 40 years is to continue, neighborhood associations must be integrated into broader thinking about American political and economic affairs. We will need a more widely accepted theoretical explanation and justification for the association's extensive political and economic autonomy.

Part III will examine briefly such issues and outline some future possibilities for a new political and economic approach to thinking about private neighborhood associations' place in American life. As chapter 9 will review briefly, the neighborhood's place in Western society steadily eroded from the medieval era to the modern age. Chapter 10 offers evidence of a new, more favorable outlook on neighborhoods that may be emerging as neighborhood governments since the 1960s have come to be seen as potentially important contributors to the political structures of American society. Chapter 11 speculates on the possibility that local government will come increasingly to be seen as a private function, part of an emerging postmodern political philosophy of greater acceptance of pluralism in American society.

NOTES

1. E. F. Schumacher, *Small Is Beautiful: Economics as if People Mattered* (New York: Harper & Row, 1973).

2. David Gordon, ed., *Secession, State & Liberty* (New Brunswick, NJ: Transaction Publishers, 1998).

3. Richard Briffault, "Voting Rights, Home Rule, and Metropolitan Governance: The Secession of Staten Island as a Case Study in the Dilemmas of Local Self-Determination," *Columbia Law Review* 92 (May 1992).

4. Kevin Starr, "To Stem Secessionism, Adopt a Borough System," *Los Angeles Times,* January 7, 2001, M1.

5. David Brooks, *Bobos in Paradise: The New Upper Class and How They Got There* (New York: Simon and Schuster, 2000), 264–65, 267.

6. Robert Reich, "Secession of the Successful," *New York Times Magazine,* January 20, 1991.

7. Edward J. Blakely and Mary Gail Snyder, *Fortress America: Gated Communities in the United States* (Washington, DC: Brookings Institution and the Lincoln Institute of Land Policy, 1997), 175, 177.

9

Neighborhoods versus the Modern World

Ⅰn terms of the geography of social and economic relationships, medieval society was a world of "neighborhoods." The trade in goods and services among manors, monasteries, towns, and other units of medieval society was by present-day standards remarkably little. Each locality was mainly self-sufficient in the essential provisions of food, shelter, and clothing. The vertical elements in medieval society existed largely in the lines of authority within the Roman Catholic Church, and feudal relationships were based on military ties between the king and his vassals. The boundaries of nation-states that are so prominent today counted for little in the political geography of medieval Europe.

During the long transition from the medieval to the modern age, all this changed—partly as a result of the Protestant Reformation. In the new national governments of Europe, the king was now often an all-powerful leader of both the church and the state. Although medieval Europe was built upon a political structure of one continent with one church—and many thousands of "neighborhoods"—a greater diversity of powerful nations evolved, often based partly on a Protestant state religion. Protestantism created a tension that survives to this day, emphasizing in its core theological precepts the individual's religious autonomy, and yet tending to undermine the separation of church and state that previously had acted to protect the individual from state power.

In the 17th century, Thomas Hobbes, a leading defender of the powerful state, offered a new secularized version of Reformation theology. Martin Luther had taught that a good Christian should submit to his ruler. Original sin had gravely affected the actions and thoughts of all men and women; therefore, a rule by the strong was necessary, Luther and many other Protestants thought—and Hobbes would reiterate in newly secular terms—simply to curb the spread of unruly impulses in a sinful and depraved world.

John Locke's political theories highlighted another side to Protestantism, however. In England, the Puritans fought zealously to protect their own religious freedoms from state interference, even beheading a king. Like other Calvinists, the Puritans conceived of their own church society as a covenant among freely consenting individuals—believers who also had entered into a covenant with God. Locke secularized this Puritan conception, proposing that government should be understood as a social contract formed among rational individuals in a state of nature—a contract that could be broken with sufficient cause.[1]

The Protestant Reformation thus contributed to a newly emerging vision of Western society that assigned central roles to the state and to the individual. Adam Smith drew upon these ideas in articulating his world of self-interest, as expressed in the marketplace, operating within a framework of contract and other law maintained by national governments (the wealth of "nations" was the defining goal for his ideal economic order). On the European continent, the role envisioned for the state would be still larger, partly because the state was conceived as the bearer of linguistic, ethnic, and other important traditions. Throughout Europe, the intermediate institutions of society lost out. Eventually, there would be little place for such medieval relics as dukedoms, manors, or guilds. When neighborhoods became identifiable units in modern cities, their positions as important political jurisdictions fell into much the same category— outmoded throwbacks to "feudalism." Scott Gordon notes that, although Holland had earlier granted substantial local political autonomy to its towns, in the 19th century it "followed the rest of Europe in subordinating local authorities to the national government."[2]

Municipal Corporations

Urban historian Jon Teaford observes that according to the "ancient model," the local municipality was a "commercial community."[3] The municipal governments of old routinely regulated the prices of goods, membership in guilds, the quality of products sold, and other aspects of business conducted within their boundaries. Local government leaders were drawn from the participants in commercial affairs. Medieval towns first existed legally in the same category and with the same political autonomy as business corporations. As Gordon notes, in England "royal charters" were granted to newly "incorporated boroughs, [charters] which usually contained specific promises by the king not to interfere in local affairs."[4] Later, one of the most famous cases in the history of English law involved the legal significance of the City of London's corporate status. As

Joseph Viteritti comments, the legal autonomy "went hand in hand with the town's economic strength and independence. The mercantile class considered local autonomy to be a property right that was synonymous with liberty itself."[5]

Indeed, for many centuries, municipal corporations were organized under the same general laws of incorporation as private business corporations. In some cases, it was possible for a single corporate entity to have the roles both of territorial governance and of private profit-making. The Hudson's Bay Company thus played an important part in the early governance of the North American continent, as did the East India Company during almost 100 years of British private rule over India.

For hundreds of years, the corporate legal status of a municipality—often no bigger than a neighborhood—thus limited attempts by higher levels of government to infringe on local prerogatives. As Harvard law professor Gerald Frug comments, in England "the towns remained economic corporations whose franchises provided protection against control by the king." These towns were able to retain "much of their autonomy and power" until the modern era. In the colonial United States as well, "there was no legal distinction . . . between cities (municipal corporations) and business corporations. All corporations had the same rights, and all of them were subject to the same protections against national and state control."[6] It was not until the 19th century that a clear legal distinction arose between municipal and business corporations.

The rise of the nation-state, Frug observes, "was understood as simultaneously advancing both state and individual interests." It was part of a spread of public philosophies that "undermined the vitality of all groups that had held an intermediate position between what we now think of as the sphere of the individual and that of the state."[7] But by the end of the 19th century, state laws routinely provided for the incorporation of large business organizations that would shape America's industrial future.[8] As they operated under state law, these business corporations had an independence from state interference in their affairs similar to the autonomy once granted by kings to municipal corporations. This freedom no longer existed, however, for municipal governments.

An Obstacle to "Progress"

By the middle of the 19th century, the economic potential of modern industry to end age-old struggles for food, shelter, and clothing was coming into clearer view. Railroad construction was achieving drastic reductions in transportation costs across the American continent, making it possible for many manufacturing firms to serve a national market for the first time. The miraculous properties of electricity soon led to telephones, radios, washing machines, movies, refrigerators, and a host of new inventions to ease the chores of daily life. The

evidence was everywhere that a new age of unprecedented economic abun-
dance was arriving. Many ordinary people in the 20th century would in fact
enjoy transportation, food, communications, and health care of better quality
than that enjoyed by kings and queens only a few centuries earlier.

This vast growth of material productivity held out the prospect that past
conflicts over resources might be tamed or even abolished. Many leading intellectuals believed a great improvement in the human condition lay in store.
Indeed for many people, new secular religions, based on ideas of salvation
through economic progress here on earth, displaced hopes for a salvation in
the hereafter.[9] Historical winners—the triumphant class of Marxism, the successful businessmen of social Darwinism, and still others—were blessed by
new modern gods whose worldly truths were revealed by the "scientific" laws
of economics. None of these secular religions, however, had much to say about
neighborhoods. None assigned any important role to local governments in the
historical "march of progress" to a new heaven on earth.

By contrast, the private business corporation was an essential element in
American economic progress. Even Karl Marx taught that capitalism was a
marvelous triumph of human ingenuity that was solving the problem of material scarcity in the world and was thus an indispensable stage in economic
history on the way to the predestined triumph of the proletariat. From Adam
Smith to Herbert Spencer, the leading economic theorists of the English-
speaking world preached that the operating independence of the private business corporation must be protected. If every large business, for example, had to
submit to varying regulatory and other demands put forth by numerous state
and local authorities across the United States, economic confusion if not chaos
would result. Protecting a corporation's "private" status would limit the government's ability to intervene in business affairs, allowing the corporation to
play its necessary role in the advance of economic progress.*

Attitudes toward municipal corporations, however, were much different.
Any large degree of operating autonomy would more likely impede the
nation's economic progress. If American businesses needed wide freedom of
operation, American municipalities instead needed to be tightly limited in
their independent exercise of political authority. An owner of private property

---

*John Micklethwait and Adrian Wooldridge have recently traced the spread of the "revolutionary
idea" of the modern business corporation. In England, the businesses of that nation were "set free by
'the Act of 1862,' " providing for the first time for a routine process of incorporation. Assessing the
enormous impact, Micklethwait and Wooldridge comment, "The foremost contribution of the company to society has been through economic progress." The evidence of the past 150 years has shown that
"both government and companies have generally prospered most when the line between them has been
fairly thick." See John Micklethwait and Adrian Wooldridge, *The Company: A Short History of a Revolutionary Idea* (New York: Random House, 2003), xiv, 191.

today has a wide scope of legal autonomy; he or she can exclude others and can use the property as desired. To put the municipal corporation in the same legal category as a private business corporation would have been to grant virtual sovereign status to the municipal jurisdictions of the United States. The cost to the nation in terms of a loss of business efficiency might have been very large indeed.

The municipality's legal status thus was shifting throughout the 19th century from "private" to "public."[10] As the future legal status of the U.S. municipal corporation was being finally resolved, the Civil War had recently been fought to preserve the Union against Southern states' secession efforts. Any elements of genuine sovereignty among such small territorial units as municipalities (or neighborhoods) might be seen as another form of "secession" from the national community. Sovereign (or private—there was not so much difference in practice) municipalities would stand in the way of "modern" and "progressive" trends, a rebuke to the ideals of Abraham Lincoln and a triumph for the heirs to Jefferson Davis.*

In short, as American municipal law evolved in the second half of the 19th century, American municipalities had to be tightly subordinated in the law to higher levels of government.[11] According to "Dillon's rule"—formulated by Iowa judge John Dillon in the 1870s—the municipality's legal status would be reconceived to make it a creature of state government. Under this emerging legal concept, a state government could now abolish any municipality, redraw its boundaries, alter its taxing authority, and assign or withdraw public service responsibilities, all at the state's total discretion. In 1907, the U.S. Supreme Court in *Hunter v. City of Pittsburgh* went so far as to declare that:

> The State . . . at its pleasure may modify or withdraw all [city] powers, may take without compensation [city] property, hold it itself, or vest it in other agencies, expand or contract the territorial area, unite the whole or a part of it with another municipality, repeal the charter and destroy the corporation. All this may be done, conditionally or unconditionally, with or without the consent of the citizens, or even against their protest. In all these respects the State is supreme, and its legislative body, conforming its action to the state constitution, may do as it will [with respect to towns and cities], unrestrained by any provision of the Constitution of the United States.[12]

---

*Municipalities in practice had also assumed the responsibilities for the provision of more and more governmental services. As Hendrik Hartog explains, New York City "became a public entity during the quarter century that followed the American Revolution" in terms of its functions, if not its precise legal status. It was increasingly engaged in the provision of "public goods for public consumption" in response to the demands of the local political society for greater collective services. It was difficult, however, for judges to square the increasing governmental role of New York City with its quasi-private status as a municipal corporation. The legal solution was to redefine the municipality as a public entity. See Hendrik Hartog, *Public Property and Private Power: The Corporation of the City of New York in American Law, 1730–1870* (Chapel Hill: University of North Carolina Press, 1983), 6, 8.

One of the most important applications of this state power was annexation policy. In 1888, a large annexation of outlying areas enabled Baltimore to double its size. In 1889, Chicago added 133 square miles, including Hyde Park and Kenwood and most of what is now the far South Side. At that time, 225,000 people lived in this area newly added to Chicago; within 30 years there would be one million. Such annexations were common in American cities and might be approved by state legislatures against the wishes of residents in the areas being added to the city. As urban historian Kenneth Jackson comments, "The predominant view of the 19th century was the doctrine of forcible annexation. No small territory could be allowed to retard the development of the metropolitan community." In the utilitarian spirit of Jeremy Bentham, "The most important consideration" for a state legislature in reviewing a proposed annexation "was simply the greatest good for the greatest number" in the whole metropolitan area—not only the current residents, but also the prospective residents, whose arrival would bring additional economic prosperity to the area.[13]

Annexation thus helped to shape the organization of American metropolitan government in the second half of the 19th century. State legislatures felt free to ignore the demands of local groups and existing governments in redrawing urban boundaries. Taming the legal autonomy of small municipalities, in short, was a key part of the modern project in the 19th century. If a conflict between the "values of association" in a small geographic area and the values of individual business "property rights" had to be resolved, then business rights would necessarily trump the rights of group association at the local level.[14] In an age when economic progress was virtually the national religion of the United States, nothing less than the future salvation of the nation—and perhaps, in the long run, the world—might be at stake.

Formally at least, the legal status of municipalities is little changed today. As Richard Briffault comments, "Under both federal and state constitutional law, local governments have no rights against their states." Unlike a private person or corporation, "localities may not assert the contracts clause, the equal protection clause or the privileges and immunities clause against their state governments. Nor do the residents of local governments have any inherent right to local self-government: local residents may not assert a constitutional claim to belong to a particular government or to have any local government at all."[15] Under the laws of New York State, for example, municipalities are—with a few exceptions—not allowed to own the stock or bonds of a private corporation. The state government of New York imposes "obligations on local governments" in contracting and employment practices "that have no analogue to the obligations that the state imposes on private firms." Local taxation is comprehensively regulated by the state; thus, another of "the striking features of New York's intergovernmental relations is the relative lack of local autonomy with respect to fiscal matters." State government often uses unfunded mandates to "commandeer local governments to state ends and [to] divert local resources from local control to state-determined programs."[16]

All in all, Briffault finds, local governments formally have "next to no protection" legally from state control over their affairs. Their only protection is that afforded by their own political skills and power in the state legislative and executive arenas—which can of course be very large, as the history of zoning in the 20th century shows.* Briffault thus recommends revising the New York State constitution to newly "protect the structural integrity of local governments, broadly defined to include employment, contracting, and other 'housing-keeping' aspects of local performance of local government functions."[17]

The municipality's weak formal standing in American law stands in considerable contrast to the protections the Constitution affords for private property. Under the Constitution, for example, the federal government or a state government cannot "take" private property without compensation. These higher levels of government are constitutionally required to observe due process, equal protection, and other procedural requirements in their dealings with private parties. However, local municipalities are not afforded such protections. If we should seek in the future to empower municipalities, or neighborhoods, then establishing a newly private legal status for such small governments would be one way of accomplishing this goal.

Scientific Management of America

In the 19th century, any substantial degree of legal autonomy for neighborhoods would have created an unacceptable barrier to free-market enterprise. As the century came to a close, however, the Progressive movement sought greater public control over the operation of the private market. This did not mean, however, a turn back to neighborhoods. To the contrary, American Progressivism introduced perhaps a greater centralizing impetus to government. The Progressive movement was dedicated to the scientific management of American society as a whole. It was in the name of progressive ideas that Washington, D.C., grew in the 20th century from a sleepy southern town to the nation's administrative headquarters.

---

*"Home rule" laws do provide some legal autonomy for localities, but these laws themselves could be changed or amended at any time by the state legislature. As a result, the governing rules and regulations of any municipality could be wiped out with one stroke of the pen of the state legislature. See Michael Monroe Kellogg Sebree, "One Century of Constitutional Home Rule: A Progress Report?" *Washington Law Review* 64 (January 1989); and Stephen Cianca, "Home Rule in Ohio Counties: Legal and Constitutional Perspectives," *Dayton Law Review* 19 (Winter 1994).

With the benefit of increased scientific knowledge, progressives were confident that coordinated government planning could guide the nation. According
to progressives, the marketplace operated under a wasteful process in which
many companies went bankrupt, consumers rejected product designs, and other
numerous failures took place in what was essentially a trial-and-error economic
system. In the business world itself, the large corporation was replacing the atomistic marketplace of old. As business corporations introduced new systems of
internal planning and management, progressives now argued that government
administration should also benefit from the same professional methods. They
believed that American government at all levels must reject the patronage-
ridden, backward political machines of the 19th century and embrace new, sleek
administrative systems based on the technical skills of experts.

Eliza Lee further describes these aspirations typical of progressive thinkers.
The ideas of scientific management involved not only the application of scientific methods to government administration but represented a full-fledged
political theory in their own right, offering a particular view of the proper relationship among the different parts of American government. Progressives
believed that the political and the technical elements of government should be
delegated to different domains. Lee explains, "Scientific management redefines
what had hitherto been political problems as management problems, the solution of which is governed by the logic of science." Progressive advocates of scientific management thus sought "the establishment of science as the institution of governance and the centralization of power in the hands of scientists"
and others who would know best how to apply expert methods. This was possible in progressive thinking because the processes of public management were
regarded as "objective, universal, natural, altogether devoid of historical and
cultural contexts, and dictated only by scientific laws."[18]

The ideas of scientific management thus aimed to transcend politicians' former preoccupations with raw power, as had characterized most of history. While
such ideas may have already seemed utopian by the second half of the 20th century, they had earlier seemed to be ordinary common sense to many millions of
progressive true believers in the United States. A revolution in material prosperity was occurring, and a similar revolution—or so it seemed—would take place
in governmental realms. This kind of thinking was an American version—
though more democratic, and less antagonistic toward private business—of the
European socialism capturing popular imaginations across the Atlantic at about
the same time.

In urban affairs, as Christine Boyer observes, Progressivism sought "to transform the style of city administration into more consolidated and centralized
structures that were more conducive to expert opinion and rational decision
making."[19] Similarly, as Kenneth Jackson writes, the progressives believed that "a
large [city] organization was more efficient than a small one and that substantial

economies would accrue from the consolidation of municipal governments"—
as illustrated by the formation of New York City in 1898. Small local jurisdictions, by contrast, almost inevitably suffered with inefficient management; "large
cities, on the other hand, could be run by highly paid experts." In an era when
"the cry for efficiency" trumped almost any other social value, the progressive
reformers enthusiastically advocated "the notion that 'bigger is better' " in American cities.[20] Law professor Edward Zelinsky recently characterized the progressive plan for urban America as a "vision of large-scale, managerial government
run efficiently and benignly by city planners and other urban experts under the
aegis of civic and business elites"—in this manner achieving "local governance
without local politics" and without the inevitable corruptions of the public interest resulting from the application of crass political considerations and other elements of local politics gone awry.[21]

Progressives also believed that a bigger city would boost an area's "social
capital." As Jackson comments, "Not only would a city gain additional residents by expanding its borders, but the fact of growth often inspired citizens
with renewed confidence in a community's future and spurred them to greater
efforts in civic development."[22] Progressivism was aptly called the "gospel of
efficiency," and signs of economic growth and efficiency stirred the faithful to
march forth with even greater efforts and enthusiasm. The "NIMBY" ("not in
my backyard") thinking that became typical of the late 20th century was much
discouraged in such an environment; in progressive terms, such resistance to
change—in neighborhoods or elsewhere—would have been seen as privately
selfish and antisocial. To take a NIMBY position might have identified a citizen
as almost a social malefactor.

Backward Neighborhoods

Progressivism in American political thought did not augur well for neighborhoods and other local institutions of government. A local neighborhood, like
a small firm, could never afford the best and the brightest of the professions.
The comprehensive planning of American land use required a vision and an
ability to coordinate on a geographic scale wider than the boundaries of any
individual neighborhood. Many progressives would try to consolidate land use
responsibilities at the county, the regional, the full metropolitan, or even at the
national level of government. Any significant political autonomy for neighborhoods, or municipalities, was likely to impede the efficient urban use of
American land. Frug thus writes,

> To ensure its fully "public" nature, government had to be organized so that it could
> attract to power those in the community best able to govern. Class legislation in favor
> of either the rich or the poor had to be avoided—neither a government of private

greed nor one of mass ignorance could be tolerated. Instead, it was the role of the best people to assume responsibility by recognizing and fulfilling their communal obligations. . . . Cities presented problems that seemed almost "inherent" in their nature. By merging the public and private spheres, [the] cities [of old] had extravagantly invested in private businesses, performing functions "better left to private enterprise."

The [new progressive] answer seemed to lie in state control of cities and in judicial supervision of that control. State control, though political, was purely public, and the "best fitted" could more likely be attracted to its government.[23]

The progressives thus sought to undermine the powers of Tammany Hall and other political machines whose supporters were often living in ethnic neighborhoods of recent origin. In Chicago, the many neighborhoods offered "a Cook's tour of the world's cultures." In these places, the "working-class saloons often were centers of neighborhood politics." One Chicago district of 120,000 working-class residents reportedly had 500 saloons. In New Orleans, another district contained "some of the finest brothels" in the nation.[24] Such urban neighborhoods, however, were offensive to the era's progressive "reform" agenda, which attacked the "moral corruption" centered in the cities and their "wayward" neighborhoods. The Progressive Era campaign against alcohol eventually led to the 1919 adoption of the Eighteenth Amendment to the U.S. Constitution, which prohibited the sale of alcoholic beverages throughout the nation and served as yet another example of both the powerful centralizing impetus and the prevailing moralism central to the American progressive mentality.

As progressive reformers campaigned to clean up the nation's urban neighborhoods, practical "scientific management" thus often had less to do with science and more to do with asserting the middle-class virtues of the day.[25] Under the banner of the scientific claims to value-neutral expertise, old-fashioned Christian values could be newly imposed as "modern," "efficient," and "professional."[26] The diverse mixtures characteristic of ethnic city neighborhoods also clashed with the progressive conviction that all Americans should be bound together tightly in a single national community—a "melting pot" of shared higher values that amounted to a modern church of the nation-state. Members of the "social gospel movement," as it had emerged in the Protestant churches of America in the late 19th century, were often among urban reform's leading advocates. Social gospelers transposed their Christian aspirations for a heaven in the hereafter to a new commitment to a perfect world right here on earth. Urban historian Jon Teaford comments,

The goal of these concerned individuals was to create a city free of poverty, prostitution, alcohol, ignorance, corruption, congestion, and ugliness—a homogenized community cleansed of wrong that would share a vision of the good life. During the early years of this century, righting the urban wrongs became a passion of these earnest reformers.

In New York City, Chicago and San Francisco, the problems of irresponsible wealth and devastating poverty were juxtaposed in such glaring contrast, and the ethnic, cultural and moral divisions were so sharply drawn, that reform-minded people felt compelled to take action. Rapid urbanization and unprecedented industrialization had produced a city of ill-fitting parts, but many who enjoyed the comfort, security, and self-confidence associated with middle- or upper-class status believed that they could refashion the city, creating a better, less divided urban community. Their efforts resulted in that series of projects, programs, and policies known as urban progressivism.[27]

Science versus Democracy

In 1896, 79 percent of Americans who were eligible to vote went to the polls in national elections. By 1924, voter participation rates nationally had plummeted to 49 percent (roughly today's level).[28] In short, while representing a period of great ferment in the design of American governance institutions, the Progressive Era nevertheless witnessed the nation's sharpest decline in democratic participation in political processes in its history.* Paradoxically, progressive reformers were at this time advancing a host of political institutions designed to promote popular democracy. For example, progressive political innovations included the direct election of U.S. senators, the primary election as a method of nominating party candidates for elective office, voter recalls, popular referenda and initiatives, and finally (in 1919), universal suffrage for women.

Historians such as Robert Wiebe trace the loss of the democratic habit—the increasing alienation of "the People" from American political processes—to the very content of the progressive plan for American government.[29] Indeed, viewing government as an exercise in scientific management was bound to pose a conflict with democratic political traditions. With professional experts making decisions, the ordinary citizen seemingly became a mere bystander. Voting became merely an exercise in ratifying the authority of experts who made the key decisions.

In studying the history of city planning during the Progressive Era, Christine Boyer thus finds that "expanding the role of the technical expert within municipal administrations meant concomitantly producing a depoliticized public, shut off from understanding the technical and organizational necessities of an

---

*To be sure, part of the explanation for the sharply declining voter participation early in the 20th century was the disenfranchisement of blacks in the South, taking hold from the adoption of Jim Crow policies in the 1890s (occurring at the same time, and not altogether coincidentally, with the rise of state power in the Progressive Era). The arrival of large numbers of European immigrants and then the granting of women's suffrage in 1919 created large new blocks of voters unaccustomed to going to the polls and perhaps less inclined to vote for this reason.

urban society." The progressive goal of "increasing administrative expertise meant decreasing public opinion." This created a powerful tension with the traditions of American democracy because "the centralization and consolidation of decision-making power in the expert hands of a few aligned itself in direct opposition to the American expectation of popular control and direction."[30]

According to one possible interpretation, the professed enthusiasm of Progressive Era intellectuals for both scientific management and popular democracy might have been a form of compensation for the virtual certainty of a less-than-democratic result. Perhaps some progressives found it difficult to face the full political implications of truly scientific management of society—the empowerment of an elite, the opposite of government by "the people." Yet it would have been impossible to explicitly reject popular government, given the strength of the American commitment to "democracy." Such acts of internal denial are familiar in human history, although they have often produced confused theories and policies—a verdict of intellectual confusion later rendered with respect to many of the progressive designs for American government.*

The basic problem is that the practice of science can never be a democratic process. In the scientific method, proposed new theories are sorted and evaluated by rigorous empirical testing according to the strict canons of scientific truth. The merits of a scientific theory, then, should never be decided by popular vote. If the administration of government and other social matters are to become "scientific," wide areas of government activity will necessarily fall outside any legitimate scope for ordinary democratic politics. For example, the opinions of MIT professors will necessarily count for much more in the halls of future government than will the opinions of ordinary voters—or any neighborhood political leaders. Moreover, progressives believed that wider and wider areas of government would come under the methods of scientific management as the levels of scientific understanding advanced in more and more areas. There are only a few hundred Nobel Prize winners in the world at any given time—which is about the same as the number of chief executive officers (CEOs) of major business corporations—and the two groups have perhaps had about equal cumulative influence on society's future directions.

---

*The historian Samuel Hays finds that there was a basic tension at the heart of President Theodore Roosevelt's thinking; Roosevelt was the most prominent advocate of the progressive cause in that era. His "emphasis on applied science and his conception of the good society as the classless agrarian society were contradictory trends of thought. The one, a faith which looked to the future, accepted wholeheartedly the basic elements of the new technology. The other, essentially backward looking, longed for the simple agrarian arcadia which, if it ever existed, could never be revived." Roosevelt, Hays says, was never able to resolve this contradiction in his thought. See Samuel P. Hays, *Conservation and the Gospel of Efficiency: The Progressive Conservation Movement, 1890–1920* (Cambridge, MA: Harvard University Press), 268–69.

Wiebe thus comments that, although there were some leading American progressives who "pictured the experts supplementing electoral democracy," a number of the most influential, such as Walter Lippmann, "pictured them substituting for it." For the new professional classes who came to power to put progressive ideas into practice, the "ideal-type citizen subsisted on a regimen of facts, scientifically digested" and impersonally verified and applied by nationally qualified experts. The result of such thinking, as Wiebe says, was "a crisis in democracy [along with] a crisis in citizenship."[31] Ordinary people were no longer the masters of their government but had become instead objects to be manipulated according to its "scientific designs." If ordinary citizens had a political role to play, it was in ensuring by voting and other actions that the legitimate experts were not overwhelmed and defeated by the illegitimate—"evil"—forces of traditional interest-group or even outright corrupt "politics."

One Nation, One Church

The political aims of the Progressive movement were blessed with all the power of a secular religion.[32] Despite the movement's ostensibly scientific grounding, progressives took up their cause with a religious energy. Indeed, as we mentioned earlier, historians have labeled the progressive credo as "the gospel of efficiency."[33] The 18th and 19th centuries had witnessed great awakenings of religious enthusiasm in American society. In the Progressive Era, as historian Samuel Haber writes, the new "efficiency craze" was in its essence a modern form of mass religious movement, "a secular Great Awakening."[34] Advocates believed that implementing their plan for American government was doing God's work in the world. Gifford Pinchot, a leading progressive and the founder in 1905 of the U.S. Forest Service, declared that the ultimate object of his work was "to help in bringing the Kingdom of God on earth."[35] In the urban realm, Boyer comments, "planning was not simply a disciplined technique of city building; above all else it was a social consciousness."[36]

American society, one might say, became a kind of national church with an official catechism of economic progress based on the application of scientific planning and management. The Progressive Era marked a national turning point when secular ideas displaced Christianity as the most powerful religious force in America. In this era, Harvard University turned from educating ministers to producing a new kind of clergy—the scientists, economists, businessmen, and other professionals of the nation. A leading American student of the progressive method of public administration, Dwight Waldo would later look back in wonder on the enthusiasms characteristic of the era. As he remarked in 1948, "Every era has a few words that epitomize its world-view and that are fixed points by which all else can be measured. In the Middle Ages they were such words as faith, grace and God; in the eighteenth century they were such words as reason, nature, and rights; during the past 50 years in America they have been such words as cause, reaction, scientific, expert, progress—and efficient."[37]

As the United States took on the character of one overarching church of economic progress, William Schambra finds that Americans increasingly thought of themselves as part of a single "great national community."[38] It was a shared community in which ethnic and class rivalries—the group identities that had characterized the multiple publics of the 19th century—should be put aside. The old fierce antagonisms of "Protestant" and "Catholic" must—and would—recede, reflecting Christian theology's declining importance to progressive Americans. The old American diversity of cultures, religions, and other forms of private association needed in fact to give way to a new set of modern and "enlightened" national values. The progressive church of America was to be a universal church, as Christianity has always aspired to be a universal religion. Instead of Rome, the headquarters of this national church would be in Washington, D.C., a unique political jurisdiction, like the Vatican, within the nation-state. Schambra explains that, for progressives,

> The decentralized, self-governing, civically vital way of [19th century] life within America's "island communities" . . . was doomed. . . . Irresistible forces of modernity were beginning to sweep away the boundaries that historically had contained and preserved our island communities. Modern means of transportation and communication—the railroad, telegraph, telephone, and high-speed press—had breached the small town's borders. . . . Technology had given rise to vast corporate giants whose operations reached far beyond the jurisdiction of any single state or city. Great cities had sprung up, populated by aggregates of isolated, disconnected individuals, rather than by tightly knit neighbors.
>
> In short, the forces of modernity had precipitated a crisis of community and civil society in America: the small town and its civic virtues had been shattered. . . . Although it was pointless, in the Progressives' view, to try to preserve or restore the civic and moral ethos of the small town (that had been the failed Populist response), it was now possible to move to a new and higher form of community: the great, national community.[39]

There could be little place in this vision for any autonomous neighborhoods. Any real empowering of American neighborhoods would impede the central planning and administrative efficiency necessary to the rational perfection of American society. The reference point for economic success would, of course, be the nation as a whole. If strong neighborhood powers were a threat to the efficient workings of free markets in the 19th century, they equally represented obstacles to the progressive political aspirations for an efficient American society in the 20th century. Indeed, the thrust of progressive reforms for many decades was the consolidation of governing authority, above all at the national level but also in larger cities, larger school districts, and other larger units of government that could more efficiently encompass wider areas within their scope of administrative authority. The neighborhood, by contrast, was a relic of the past.

Chastened Progressives

American historians commonly regard 1920 as the year marking the end of the Progressive Era. If an ever-increasing degree of affluence had been expected to yield an ever-growing harmony among men and women, the useless slaughter of 8 million young men on the battlefields of Europe suggested that some essential element in the human condition must have been overlooked. World War I severely challenged the progressive conviction of a coming heaven on earth based on the rapid advance of scientific and material progress. Over the next 30 years, more terrible events would follow, culminating in a second and still more destructive war covering much of the world. In fact, some of the worst offenses against ordinary human decency occurred in Germany, paradoxically the leading scientific nation in the world up to that point, and possessed of a high material standard of living as well.

Although the American philosopher John Dewey was born in 1860, his most influential writings came late in life, many in the period from 1920 to 1940. Dewey was concerned that the enormous material progress made during the modern age had failed to bring about a corresponding moral improvement. Instead, during the first half of the 20th century, Western culture had witnessed the wide ethical "confusion that accompanies transition from an old order to a new one." Many people had been plunged into "an economic regime so novel that there was no adequate preparation for it . . . [a system that] dislocated the established relations of persons with one another."[40]

Without significant progress on the ethical front, the success of progressives' hopes for continuing economic and other wider social improvement were cast into doubt. For example, the professional classes, given their wide scope of authority in managing American government, had to behave according to high ethical standards. If they did not, their growing power in society might be exercised at the expense of other ordinary Americans. By the time Dewey's *Freedom and Culture* was published, the world was witnessing the disturbing spectacle of Nazi persecution of the Jews, a practice grounded in obnoxious racial theories. As Dewey sought to deal with such unsettling events, he wrote that Germany seemed to be acting in search of a primitive "racial and social union" that reflected an unresolved modern "yearning for emotional fusion." Hence, the many indications of a prevailing "disturbance of the moral side" of life meant that addressing the "moral nature of the social problem" was at least as important as concentrating on its scientific and economic aspects.[41]

One major solution, as Dewey would suggest in his writings, was very much at odds with the trends of the times. Dewey had come to think that the large size of many modern institutions significantly contributed to society's grave ethical problems. As he wrote in 1939, "Individuals can find the security and protection that are prerequisites for freedom only in association with others"—that is to say, a healthy "individuality demands [close] association to develop and sustain it."[42] Strong bonds of association were more likely to be found in local interactions— such as those occurring in neighborhoods—than in the functioning of such modern behemoths as large nation-states or multinational business corporations. Dewey warned,

> Evils which are uncritically and indiscriminately laid at the door of industrialism and democracy might, with greater intelligence, be referred to the dislocation and unsettlement of local communities. Vital and thorough attachments are bred only in the intimacy of an intercourse which is of necessity restricted in range. . . . Democracy must begin at home and its home is the neighborly community.[43]

In short, balancing the scientific and economic exigencies of modern life against the society's need for moral nourishment would require a new commitment to protect and advance social institutions on a smaller geographic scale. If Dewey thought that no real solution had thus far been found in America, he remained in the end an optimist. America was a blessed nation that had within it the necessary resources to make it not only an economic and military giant, but also "a New World in a human sense."[44] Neighborhoods, surprisingly enough, might have a vital role to play in this new world order as it would be taking shape in the United States.

Conclusion

Spectacular successes in understanding the physical world, which took place during the modern age of physics and other natural sciences, created the hope of a similar set of successes in understanding the workings of the social world. Progressives believed that there would be discovered a universally correct "economic science" of goods and services production and distribution, and also a generally valid "psychological science" of the workings of the human mind. If the perfection of human knowledge could be achieved in both the physical and social worlds, then the religious quarrels that had so often pitted one group against another would increasingly become a thing of the past. It was economic scarcity coupled with widespread ignorance and superstition that had often set one society against another in the "dark ages" preceding the 18th century era of modern "enlightenment."

A world possessing universal scientific truths about nature and society would also boast one correct system everywhere on earth. A small locality, such as a neighborhood, might have drawn its previous identity from the presence of particular knowledge, distinct values, varying ethnicities, multiple religious sects, and many other—as they could now be seen in light of modern understanding—vestiges of an earlier time. While the neighborhood may have been a central institution of medieval society, modernists were determined to banish such remaining elements of medieval backwardness. A fundamental transformation in the human condition had occurred. According to progressives, government and the modern institutions of society must be revised accordingly, reflecting the accelerated accumulation of economic, political, administrative, and other universal scientific knowledge.

By the end of the 20th century, however, these modern certainties were appearing more and more as the "biases" or "prejudices" of yet another period in history, a period convinced of its own unique access to religious—if now secular religious—truth. Other ages had also known with certainty that one or another god had specially chosen them as the special instrument for saving the world. Although the natural sciences had (astonishingly enough) met modern expectations in the realm of physical nature, corresponding results fell far short in the study of human affairs. The social sciences were marked by grand claims and in many (probably most) cases, a poverty of results to match these claims.

Expectations that "one truth"—one progressive scientific religion, really— would emerge on earth to encompass all aspects of life, including the moral, faded. Indeed, old-fashioned religion was making a comeback. Fundamentalism in various forms was capturing increasing numbers of young minds. There was a growing acceptance that a condition of basic pluralism—in matters of politics, economics, and psychology, as well as religion—might be a long-lasting (perhaps even permanent) human condition. A diversity of acceptable forms of social organization seemingly would follow. The rise of this new pluralism, characteristic of a "postmodern" mentality, augured particularly well for the neighborhood's role as a leading institution of American society. Few if any leaders of the American real estate industry saw themselves at the leading edge in putting postmodern thought into practice, but their actions in building many tens of thousands of private neighborhood associations across the United States were actually doing a great deal to advance this outcome.

NOTES

1. See Robert H. Nelson, *Reaching for Heaven on Earth: The Theological Meaning of Economics* (Lanham, MD: Rowman & Littlefield, 1991), Ch. 3.

2. Scott Gordon, *Controlling the State: Constitutionalism from Ancient Athens to Today* (Cambridge, MA: Harvard University Press, 1999), 197.

3. Jon C. Teaford, *The Municipal Revolution in America: Origins of Modern Urban Government, 1650–1825* (Chicago: University of Chicago Press, 1975), 113. See also Ernest S. Griffith,

History of American City Government: The Colonial Period (New York: Oxford University Press, 1938).

4. Gordon, *Controlling the State,* 230.

5. Joseph P. Viteritti, "Municipal Home Rule and the Conditions of Justifiable Secession," *Fordham Urban Law Journal* 23 (Fall 1995), 7.

6. Gerald E. Frug, *City Making, Building Communities Without Building Walls* (Princeton, NJ: Princeton University Press, 1999), 32–33, 5.

7. Ibid., 32, 31.

8. Joan C. Williams, "The Invention of the Municipal Corporation: A Case Study in Legal Change," *American University Law Review* 34 (Winter 1985). See also Joan C. Williams, "The Constitutional Vulnerability of American Local Government: The Politics of City Status in American Law," *Wisconsin Law Review,* no. 1 (1986).

9. Nelson, *Reaching for Heaven on Earth;* also Robert H. Nelson, *Economics as Religion: From Samuelson to Chicago and Beyond* (University Park: Pennsylvania State University Press, 2001).

10. Hendrik Hartog, *Public Property and Private Power: The Corporation of the City of New York in American Law, 1730–1870* (Chapel Hill: University of North Carolina Press, 1983).

11. Charles R. Adrian and Ernest S. Griffith, *A History of American City Government: The Formation of Traditions, 1775–1870* (New York: Praeger Publishers, 1976); and Ernest S. Griffith, *A History of American City Government: The Conspicuous Failure, 1870–1900* (New York: Praeger Publishers, 1974).

12. *Hunter v. City of Pittsburgh,* 207 U.S. at 178–79 (1907).

13. Kenneth T. Jackson, *Crabgrass Frontier: The Suburbanization of the United States* (New York: Oxford University Press, 1985), 142–43, 147.

14. Frug, *City Making,* 44.

15. Richard Briffault, "Our Localism: Part I—The Structure of Local Government Law," *Columbia Law Review* 90 (January 1990), 7.

16. Richard Briffault, "Local Government and the New York State Constitution," *Hofstra Law & Policy Symposium* 1 (1996), 91, 101, 101–2, 105.

17. Ibid., 99, 101.

18. Eliza Wing-yee Lee, "Political Science, Public Administration, and the Rise of the American Administrative State," *Public Administration Review* 55 (November/December 1995), 543.

19. M. Christine Boyer, *Dreaming the Rational City: The Myth of American City Planning* (Cambridge, MA: MIT Press, 1983), 126–27.

20. Jackson, *Crabgrass Frontier,* 144, 145, 144.

21. Edward A. Zelinsky, "Metropolitanism, Progressivism, and Race," *Columbia Law Review* 98 (April 1998), 670–71, 667.

22. Jackson, *Crabgrass Frontier,* 144.

23. Frug, *City Making,* 46–47.

24. Jon C. Teaford, *The Twentieth-Century American City: Problem, Promise, and Reality* (Baltimore, MD: Johns Hopkins University Press, 1986), 24, 29, 29.

25. Paul Boyer, *Urban Masses and Moral Order in America, 1820–1920* (Cambridge, MA: Harvard University Press, 1978).

26. See Nelson, *Reaching for Heaven on Earth,* and Nelson, *Economics as Religion.*

27. Teaford, *The Twentieth-Century American City,* 30–31.

28. Frances Fox Piven and Richard A. Cloward, *Why Americans Don't Vote* (New York: Pantheon Books, 1988), 54.

29. Robert H. Wiebe, *Self-Rule: A Cultural History of American Democracy* (Chicago: University of Chicago Press, 1995), 172.

30. Boyer, *Dreaming the Rational City,* 127.

31. Wiebe, *Self-Rule,* 175, 176.

32. See Robert William Fogel, *The Fourth Great Awakening and the Future of Egalitarianism* (Chicago: University of Chicago Press, 2000), 121.

33. Samuel P. Hays, *Conservation and the Gospel of Efficiency: The Progressive Conservation Movement, 1890–1920* (Cambridge, MA: Harvard University Press, 1959).

34. Samuel Haber, *Efficiency and Uplift: Scientific Management in the Progressive Era, 1890–1920* (Chicago: University of Chicago Press, 1964), ix.

35. Gifford Pinchot, *The Fight for Conservation* (1910; Seattle: University of Washington Press, 1967), 95.

36. Boyer, *Dreaming the Rational City,* 134.

37. Dwight Waldo, *The Administrative State: A Study of the Political Theory of American Public Administration* (1948; New York: Holmes and Meier, 1984), 19.

38. William A. Schambra, "Is There Civic Life Beyond the Great National Community?," in Robert K. Fullinwider, ed., *Civil Society, Democracy, and Civic Renewal* (Lanham, MD: Rowman & Littlefield, 1999), 97.

39. Ibid., 98.

40. John Dewey, *Freedom and Culture* (New York: G. P. Putnam's Sons, 1939), 162–63.

41. Ibid., 37, 168, 172.

42. Ibid., 166.

43. John Dewey, *The Public and Its Problems* (1927), quoted in Dewey, *Freedom and Culture,* 160.

44. Dewey, *Freedom and Culture,* 174.

10

A Private Neighborhood Movement

The aftermath of World War II saw the height of public confidence in the U.S. federal government. The nation had mobilized its resources and skillfully conducted a war on a worldwide scale. The victories over Germany and Japan were decisive steps in the United States' rise to its position of world leadership, a key moment in defining "the American century." When future historians look back, perhaps they will identify the two epochal accomplishments of the 20th century as the development of the atom bomb and the successful transport of human beings to and from the moon, organized and paid for by the U.S. national government.

Theologically, the atom bomb and the moon landing were symbols of humankind's unique emerging capacity to manipulate and control the forces of nature. Before the modern age, only God had such awesome powers—either to destroy the world or to rise into the heavens. Within the space of a mere few generations, human beings had become the first creatures on earth ever to be able to "play God." The progressives had hoped—indeed, confidently expected—that such astonishing new human powers would soon lead to a new heaven on earth. John Maynard Keynes had once even predicted that achieving this would take only about 100 more years of rapid economic growth. It would be the millennium reached by human action as economic progress would soon "lead us out of the tunnel of economic necessity into daylight."[1]

In this respect, the history of the 20th century ultimately proved to be a great disappointment. Progressive hopes for the scientific and economic perfection of the world have not been realized in the United States or any other nation. True, the satisfaction of most basic material needs has in fact been achieved as prophesied by progressive thinkers—at least in the more economically advanced nations. However, despite earlier high hopes, this accomplishment has not meant the end of lying, stealing, cheating, and other human "sins." Economic progress, it seems, may be a necessary condition for the arrival of heaven on earth, but it is not enough.

Social scientists have generally paid little attention to theology in studying the formation of American public policy. Yet, theology (broadly understood) had a significant impact on urban and other policy arenas in the second half of the 20th century. Indeed, a number of factors contributed to the waning of the progressive design for American government. However, a loss of faith in the "gospel of efficiency," the American denomination of a worldwide "religion of progress," ranks high on the list.[2]

Back to Pluralist Politics

In the United States, the fading of the progressive vision also resulted partly from more practical failures in government policy and management. By the 1950s and 1960s, a new generation of political scientists—including David Truman, Robert Dahl, Charles Lindblom, Grant McConnell, and Norton Long—were making their reputations by demonstrating the large gap between progressive political prescriptions and the realities of U.S. government. One problem was the very concept of the "public interest," supposedly transcending the narrower private purposes of businesses, unions, farmers, real estate developers, and other "special interests" in American society. Reflecting the new thinking as it was taking shape in the 1950s, Truman explained in *The Governmental Process* that it was a myth to think that American government was capable of defining a set of common goals for the whole nation and then pursuing them efficiently and expertly.[3]

The processes in American government were instead a never-ending struggle for political power and influence among a wide range of contending groups—an opinion expressed even by James Madison, but often forgotten in the burst of progressive optimism prevalent in the early part of the 20th century. Leading political scientists such as Truman were now increasingly asserting that in the real world of government, when someone spoke of "the public interest," it should frequently be understood as a rhetorical cover that was designed to camouflage a private aim. Truman thus explained in 1951 that the "assertion of an inclusive 'national' or 'public interest' is an effective device in many . . . situations. . . . In themselves, these claims are part of the data of politics. However, they do not describe any actual or possible political situation within a complex modern nation."[4]

There was a growing recognition that the progressive design for government was failing in other respects as well. Herbert Simon (later to win a Nobel Prize in economics) complained as early as 1946 that the research results achieved to that point within the field of public administration were turning out—despite several decades of intense effort—to be much less impressive than the progressive theorists had promised.[5] Charles Lindblom famously stated in 1959 that the two governmental functions of broad goal-setting and detailed administration were inextricably interwoven in a process of "muddling through."[6] Government typically proceeded incrementally; history was important because what happened today would normally be only a small change from what had happened yesterday.

This meant, among other things, that any aspirations for comprehensive social and economic planning were likely to be utopian. Indeed, the attempt to set out society's broad goals was likely to yield only vague generalities. Efforts to formulate substantive goals easily provoked strong political disagreements and controversies. Politicians and other men and women of practical affairs typically avoided such processes, which produced small returns to society and high potential costs to them.

The crisis of progressive thought in the 1960s and 1970s was felt in many areas of public policy. In the area of urban land use, the workings of public zoning in practice illustrated a common outcome of progressive aspirations.[7] Narrow interests in local governments had captured zoning for their own benefit. Instead of planned and coordinated urban land patterns on a metropolitan scale, a new fragmentation erupted. "Exclusionary zoning" was being used across the United States to keep the poor out of the suburbs.* Rather than practicing the "scientific management" of metropolitan land use, public planning and zoning officials were defending something closer to a "feudal" or "private" pattern of suburban land development. As one informed observer wrote, zoning had not turned out to be an instrument of regional land use coordination, but had empowered new "local lords of the manor" throughout the American suburbs. Indeed, "the ideal suburban village was a walled preserve, protected by zoning ordinances and municipal status from the threatening forces of the world."[8]

---

*In addition, it was not only with zoning that governments applied their "progressive" instruments to keep the poor bottled up in the city. The public housing program, created in 1937, concentrated the poor in large housing projects in inner cities. Until the late 1940s, FHA administrators viewed the presence of African Americans so negatively that Charles Abrams, a leading student of American housing policy, has written that in those years FHA had "adopted a racial policy that could well have been culled from the Nuremberg laws." Viewing federal urban policies in their totality, Kenneth Jackson comments: "The basic direction of federal policies toward housing has been the concentration of the poor in the central city and the dispersal of the affluent to the suburbs." See Kenneth T. Jackson, *Crabgrass Frontier: The Suburbanization of the United States* (New York: Oxford University Press, 1985), 214 (quoting from Abrams), 230.

A leading political scientist of the 1950s and 1960s, Robert Wood took a traditional scientific management approach. Pointing to the balkanization of responsibilities among as many as 1400 local governments in the New York metropolitan region, he lamented the resulting fragmentation of governmental responsibility and inability to plan comprehensively. As Wood argued, "The individual strategies of individual municipalities are condemned to frustration because of the sheer number of their neighbors."[9] Wood was representative of many urban reformers in the old progressive mold who "had long deplored the fragmentation of suburbia into a multitude of separate municipalities, townships, and special districts. Accounts of suburban government and politics used such terms as *crazy quilt* and such damning phrases as *overlapping jurisdiction* and *wasteful duplication*. The governmental institutions of the metropolitan fringe were political perversions, violating textbook formulas of good government."[10] By 1990, Chicago was surrounded by 261 suburban municipalities, Cleveland by 237, and Detroit by 268, each an independent political jurisdiction that planned and zoned largely in its own private interest.[11]

Another urban student of the old progressive school, Harvard law professor Charles Haar declared that in metropolitan areas there was a basic "need for a revamping of the distribution of responsibilities and powers within metropolitan areas to allow for unitary response at appropriate levels of scale to problems that are inherently indivisible." If land use problems could not be addressed through a more "unified approach," the preconditions would be altogether lacking "to make solutions even possible" to fundamental issues that required metropolitan coordination. However, Haar realized by 1972 that trends were running against him. Metropolitan-level government had never been popular in the United States, even in the years during which the public demonstrated much greater willingness to defer to expert authority. As Haar acknowledged, "For many years the balance has been on the side of technical skills: the use of neutral 'experts,' the emergence of the 'technocracy' as a controlling force in both public and private sectors of the economy, [and] the attempted exclusion of 'political' considerations from local decision making." However, such opinions were increasingly "coming under attack."[12]

For one thing, Haar admitted, contrary to progressive assertions about experts' value-neutrality, there had often been "implicit, but nonetheless, distinct" value assumptions in the "scientific" formulations. The relentless pursuit of efficiency—a core value in the progressive gospel—reflected in itself a powerful value judgment; there must always be some losers in the "march of progress." Even the act of assigning jurisdictional responsibility for governmental functions, typically said to be an expert determination based on objective administrative criteria, Haar had to concede, was "frequently a de facto resolution of substantive [policy] questions" guided by important social values.[13] Planners and other professionals had sought to assert a decisionmaking authority for the metropolitan future that was based, as another law professor put it more recently, on the "sham neutrality of technical expertise."[14]

One of the largest obstacles to the progressive urban vision was large cities' growing inability to annex their surrounding suburbs. Progressive advocates of scientific management had long favored the creation of large city governments through the frequent addition of newly developing areas. In Milwaukee, for example, heirs to the progressive tradition sought "a city with unfixed boundaries and greater powers of annexation" that would be able to achieve "a central structure of metropolitan government," fulfilling the requirements for comprehensive planning and land use controls throughout the region.[15] The Wisconsin Supreme Court generally upheld Milwaukee's annexation powers in the first half of the 20th century, but reversed this position in a key 1951 decision. The state legislature in 1955 then clearly established local citizens' power to block the annexation of their area by granting them the right to incorporate as a new municipality if their community contained at least 5,000 people.

Once this law was enacted, Nathan Zolick reports, "Milwaukee's bid for territorial expansion dwindled into nonexistence." By 1966, it was clear to Milwaukee that there would be no further growth of its land area and for the foreseeable future "its boundary was fixed." Even in Wisconsin—where the progressive movement had taken root and had perhaps more influence than in any other state—the courts and the state legislature by the mid-20th century were embarked on "a clear policy shift from pro-city to pro-suburb." Between 1900 and 1950, several of the mayors of Milwaukee had been members of the socialist party; their efforts to annex territory reflected a political philosophy of "city collectivism." By the 1950s, however, a new political philosophy of "suburban localism" was triumphing throughout the state of Wisconsin.[16]

Rather than social—or metropolitan—solidarity, the suburbs of Milwaukee and many other American cities had effectively declared their individual rights to advance their residents' self-interests. The residents had come together as a group by virtue of living in the same geographic area, but otherwise their municipal motives were similar to those of a private business corporation—or a private neighborhood association today. The privatization of local government and its exercise of zoning powers were already well advanced in American life by the 1950s and 1960s.

A Crisis of Legitimacy

Another leading political scientist, Theodore Lowi, would famously declare in the late 1960s that the pursuit of private motives had become widely acceptable in every arena of American government. The economist John Kenneth Galbraith, for example, had previously written favorably of an American system grounded in the routine political interactions of "countervailing powers," including prominently private businesses and private unions.[17] Lowi christened such new political ideas as "interest-group liberalism;" its rise had given a new political legitimacy to the pursuit of private interests in government— essentially, laissez-faire economics transferred to political domains.[18] Such thinking had extended as well to international arenas, where the economist Gunnar Myrdal commented approvingly in 1960 that "in the fully realized welfare state" of Sweden, "resource allocation would be accomplished through a process of bargaining among the leading social interests."[19] If government could not agree in advance on its ends, and if no principled scientific method existed for resolving the claims of contending parties in the political process, no other real option existed. The alternative to accepting the private pursuit of group interests in government would be civil strife in society, an obviously unacceptable outcome.

However, the best that interest-group liberalism could offer might be described as a new political philosophy opposed to all other political philosophies—an "ideology of anti-ideology." Such a vague formulation could hardly provide a compelling basis for governmental activism on the vast scale required by the modern welfare and regulatory state. Hence, if the numerous governing institutions grounded in the American progressive gospel of the early 20th century were to be sustained, some new set of higher aspirations would have to be formulated to govern these institutions. Lacking such a higher purpose, American government would not work; it might be preferable simply to abolish large parts of it, retaining only the core functions, such as national defense and the operation of the treasury. The 1970s and 1980s did in fact see the rise of a strong libertarian element in American political thought, an element that advocated a solution very much along these lines.

The problems were most severe at the federal level, the part of the government most removed from the citizenry and that had grown especially rapidly under the banner of progressive ideas.* Government at a neighborhood level, by contrast, was less affected; the very concept of "interest-group liberalism" had less meaning here. A neighborhood's political process consisted of the personal interactions—admittedly not always harmonious—of friends and neighbors.

---

*The American system of public lands was largely established in the Progressive Era and reflected closely the precepts of progressive political thinking. By the 1990s, however, there was agreement among a wide range of observers that the management of the public lands—the 30 percent of the United States set aside for continued ownership and management by the federal government—was broken and indeed had become dysfunctional in many respects. It was a graphic illustration of wider problems of governance at the federal level. See Robert H. Nelson, *Public Lands and Private Rights: The Failure of Scientific Management* (Lanham, MD: Rowman & Littlefield, 1995); and Robert H. Nelson, *A Burning Issue: A Case for Abolishing the U.S. Forest Service* (Lanham, MD: Rowman & Littlefield, 2000).

Small groups of people at the neighborhood level were more likely to be homo-geneous, posing less of a problem for reconciling issues. Each person, more-over, could seek a neighborhood in which fellow residents held a similar set of values and preferences for public services and environmental amenities, thus diminishing the likelihood of future conflict.

In general, as the size of the government decreased and as the level of gov-ernment became more local, its failings as a pluralist system of politics proved less severe. Direct contacts among neighbors revealed the bad local actors soon enough, leading to informal social sanctions. Fast talkers and others skilled in rhetorical manipulations might have found the national media and the national political scene well suited to their talents; their clever maneuvers would more quickly be ferreted out, however, in the daily interactions of a group of close neighbors.

If neighborhoods had the ability to restrict entry of outsiders, they could act on their own to ensure the presence of a group of people with homogeneous preferences in public services, tax rates, and other elements of neighborhood choice. There would be less possibility of internal division, less need for the very arts of politics that are traditionally designed to satisfactorily resolve a complex set of conflicting objectives. James Madison had argued that the prob-lems of "faction" would be most severe at the local level, but he had neglected to consider the potential for eliminating local disagreements by clustering together in small groups of like-minded citizens.

Not in My Neighborhood Backyard

As long as progressivism held sway in American life, some leading urban plan-ners, such as Robert Moses in New York City, were able to succeed in many of their grand designs.[20] They could sustain the political support to build far-reaching urban transportation networks including bridges and highways, con-struct housing projects displacing whole neighborhoods, and take other steps that might require the relocation of hundreds, or even thousands, of people. It was all considered a necessary part of the price of progress; most Americans accepted that they had a "civic duty" to make way for such change. By the mid-1960s, however, such large-scale displacement of whole groups of people—including whole neighborhoods—was increasingly contested. The advocates of neighborhood stability vigorously challenged the claims that the wholesale elimination of an established neighborhood might be within a government agency's legitimate powers. Such evacuations became all the more questionable when they involved mostly poor neighborhoods.

In the 1960s, a new generation of citizen activists emerged to lead political campaigns defending neighborhood autonomy. These neighborhood advocates deployed innovative arguments in developing legal challenges, engaged in street theatre, offered graphic images to attract media, and used other novel methods of political activism. Increasingly in the 1960s and 1970s, grassroots advocates for neighborhood causes prevailed. The urban renewal program was gradually halted. A number of roads that had been planned for the national interstate highway system to go through downtown areas of New York City, Washington, D.C., and other major cities were cancelled.

Once challenged, the alleged "scientific" qualities of urban plans often dissolved in the light of close scrutiny. These land use plans tended to reflect strongly the political values of the planners themselves (and their political patrons). Urban planners, for example, showed a strong disposition toward land use arrangements that were "orderly," and were likely to be put off by arrangements that appeared "messy." For neighborhood advocates, it was usually easy to debunk the planners' "expert" claims of "value-neutral" land use. In the past, these plans had survived only because ordinary citizens had been intimidated by the "expert" authority asserted by the modern "priesthoods" of economics, engineering, and forestry, among others.

In an era of interest-group liberalism, the residents of a particular neighborhood might appear as yet another interest group. Like other interest groups, these residents could now be expected to fight for their own cause, even if it negatively affected other groups in society. In a political world of interest-group liberalism, there was less need to show restraint in fighting for any causes, including those of the neighborhood. All over American society, other self-interested parties were fighting in the political process for their own private gains. Why should a neighborhood "group" of homeowners or apartment renters be any different?

Many of the most enthusiastic grassroots defenders of neighborhood causes were people who, a decade or two earlier, might well have been committing their energies to European socialist or American progressive causes. Perhaps not fully recognizing the magnitude of the shift, they were now often effectively advocating a "privatization" of American political life. Both the free market and American politics could be seen as arenas where the results would—and should, since there was no other practical possibility—be determined by a competition among private interests.

In the early 1940s, Woodie Guthrie sang folk ballads celebrating the construction of the Grand Coulee Dam in Washington State, seen in those days as part of a grand social engineering effort for power, irrigation, and other heroic public goals in the Pacific Northwest. However, in the 1960s and 1970s, such grand engineering of regional outcomes was increasingly labeled "bureaucratic," "coercive," "technocratic," and other opprobrious terms. For more and more observers, scientific management of American society was neither feasible nor desirable. The old democratic and participatory sides of progressivism, the concerns that John Dewey had elevated in his political philosophy earlier in the century, were advancing to the fore in American political thought. As Joseph Viteritti puts it, "the 'community revolution' that encompassed urban areas during the nineteen sixties and seventies was a reaction to big city government. Community activists sought to bring decision making down to the neighborhood so that government could become more responsive and operate on a human level"—a reaction to their experience with "large impersonal bureaucratic municipalities."[21]

These social trends were manifested as well in the rise of the environmental movement, symbolized by the first Earth Day in 1970. Power plants, dams, ski resorts, timber harvests, oil wells, and all manner of development projects were being blocked all over the United States. These projects had often been conceived and planned by experts trained in progressive ways of thinking. However, instead of "socialist solidarity" in the name of national scientific and economic progress, the vanguard of American social activism could now be found in the "not-in-my-backyard" (or "NIMBY") phenomenon. Prominent American intellectuals were proclaiming the merits of local autonomy, including a substantial degree of individual and neighborhood independence from federal, state, city, or other higher levels of government.

The "Privatization" of the Neighborhood

In the 1960s, as core progressive values came under question, neighborhood residents increasingly saw their collective interaction with the outside world as a private transaction. Absent adequate financial or other forms of compensation designed to bring about voluntary compliance, city political leaders found that they could no longer impose large burdens on individual neighborhoods. Negotiations with neighborhoods increasingly took on the character of a business deal; an agreement had to be reached, and a method of payment (often informal) to the neighborhood had to be worked out. Neighborhood residents were effectively "selling" their willingness to bear future costs of social adjustment; they were no longer willing to offer this service for free out of some commitment to a higher cause.

Neighborhood residents were not alone. Within the family, divorce rates soared as the parties to a marriage increasingly regarded it as a private contract for the individual benefit of each partner. One report on marriage trends at the end of the 20th century described the shifting marital agreements as the "privatization of family law," much as the relationship between neighborhoods and the broader society increasingly was being privatized.[22] In other areas as well—abortion, gay rights, drug use, euthanasia—advocates for individual choice were winning a new freedom from old social conventions. Individual rights were widely emphasized at the expense of collective obligations to society. As the results of 1998 polling for the *Washington Post* described,

[Over the past 30 years], trust in government has . . . declined radically. In 1968, 61 per-cent said they trusted the government in Washington to do the right thing most or all the time; in 1998, only 33 percent felt that way.

Pollster Dan Yankelovich wrote that "the transformation of values from the mid-'60s to the late-'70s confronts us with one of the sharpest discontinuities in our cultural history." In that period's "radical extension of individualism . . . from the political domain to personal lifestyle," he notes, the concepts of duty, social conformity, respectability and sexual morality were devalued, in favor of [individual] expressiveness and pleasure seeking.[23]

It was part of a new libertarian trend in American society that was deriving impetus from both sides of the political spectrum. In more and more areas, a government measure imposing costs on an individual (or on a neighborhood) could no longer be adequately justified by a claim of national purpose and expertise. It all went together—loss of confidence in national expertise, a decline in social trust, a greater focus on individual self-expression, and a new resistance to central authority.

A core principle of a libertarian political philosophy—voluntary agreement as a fundamental organizing principle in society—was thus increasingly being accepted across wide areas of American life. Libertarian tendencies of thought (to be distinguished from the dogmatism of the official Libertarian Party), along with environmentalism, had become the cutting edge of American political and economic thinking. Whatever their other significant differences, libertarianism and environmentalism both adopted as their starting point the failure of the old progressive designs for the scientific management of American society.[24] Both groups lacked confidence in the expert skills of the national government to plan and implement the future of American life. If science in the past had made large claims to understand the world, and to be able to predict future events with certainty and precision, both environmentalists and libertarians now found their own reasons to doubt these claims.

Advocating the Neighborhood Cause

While the neighborhood movement in the 1960s was mostly a populist affair led by local political activists, a more formal body of writings in defense of neighborhood government was emerging by the 1970s.[25] In 1975's *Neighborhood Power: The New Localism*, David Morris and Karl Hess (a well-known advocate of libertarian causes) commented, "Throughout the twentieth century the scale of social organization has been moving away from and not toward the scale of neighborhoods." More and more people were living at a "huge, dehumanized scale in social organization, economic organization, and in the organization of resources and technology."[26] In today's large nation-states comprised of many millions of people, Morris and Hess argued, most people found active political involvement to be impossible; they were being overwhelmed by the sheer scale of national institutions and as a result becoming passive "residents" of the nation rather than active "citizens" in a genuine democratic political process.

Many critics of large government advocated the free market as an alternative. As Morris and Hess saw matters, however, the market could also squash the individual in its relentless pursuit of economic growth and efficiency. The market was yet another product of the modern mentality—pursuing the broadest social goals, typically justified in abstract, grandiose ways. Free market and governmental central planning were actually very much alike in their dedication to an efficient economic system of far-reaching scope; their real disagreement centered on the best ways of achieving much the same universal goals. In either a world of free markets or of large governments, the security of the individual—or the neighborhood—must be subordinated to the higher demands of economic progress.

By their very nature, however, as Morris and Hess argued, people "enjoy living with, being with, working with, loving with, arguing with, and creating with and for other people." These healthy impulses, nevertheless, were being stifled in American society by the reality that "every part of the official structure, both corporate and political, encourages a concept of people as highly competitive, as wanting to be isolated, and as believing that their only hope for survival is to get what they can without reference to other people."[27] While the lone individual had long been the starting point for political and economic theory, Morris and Hess newly emphasized the importance of an active community life in promoting individual happiness.

An ongoing revival of social institutions at a neighborhood scale, Morris and Hess argued, could thus be grounds for hope in the future. Prior to the modern era of industrial progress, the neighborhood had been "the way people [had] lived historically throughout the world." It had been the natural manner of human existence for millennia. Reviving neighborhoods would raise the possibility that "human activity could be brought back together so that work, play, love, life, politics, science, and art could be a shared experience by people sharing a space, sharing agreements as to how to live together, and mutually aiding one another to enjoy the fullest, ripest existence as human beings in a humane setting."[28] This language admittedly sounds rather utopian, but the directions of utopian thought have often held important clues to future events in the real world.

Neighborhood Consciousness-Raising

The neighborhood movement brought together an unusual coalition from both ends of the American political spectrum. Another prominent advocate of neighborhood empowerment, Harry Boyte, came from a background in social activism for the poor. In *The Backyard Revolution,* Boyte contended in 1980 that the processes of "community renewal" in American life "had to begin within the neighborhoods themselves." Neighborhood power was an implicit rebuke to organizations willing to sacrifice ordinary people to the needs of technocratic efficiency—organizations such as banks, military contractors, large builders, oil companies, and federal agencies. Big businesses wanted to be free to relocate employees wherever and whenever it was useful; implicitly, the message was that loyalty to the firm should transcend loyalty of the residents to any shared geographic space. However, by the late 1970s, Boyte was seeing the ongoing rise of a "neighborhood consciousness" that was yielding a "new sense of pride and dignity" for neighborhood communities.[29]

Indeed, according to Boyte, 20 million people were members of one or another neighborhood group in the 1970s, and at least several million engaged during that decade in some form of neighborhood activism—from protesting against a proposed road to demanding better services from city hall. Boyte sought a reorganization of municipal functions, seeking "changes in city charters and governance laws" that would accomplish a "decentralization of functions like planning and zoning" to the level of the neighborhood.[30] This transformation would require basic changes in American governmental organization, oriented toward a newly decentralized structure of governing authority:

> The political traditions of left and right, which criticize either big business or big government, tend to be myopic about how their hopes are undermined by the megastructures they favor. . . . No further substantive democratic advance of any sort is likely to be achieved without a major shift in emphasis, away from big government or big business as the protector of democracy, toward the concept of the citizen power over both public and economic activity.
>
> The neighborhood movement across the country has made the demand for decentralization of decision making a central theme.[31]

Significant interest in neighborhood government by the mid-1970s spawned the National Association of Neighborhoods. The association's director declared, "The country's not going to be saved by experts and bureaucracies. It's going to be saved by some moral vision and some moral hope coming from the grassroots and the neighborhoods."[32] At its 1976 national convention, the association presented its "Neighborhood Bill of Responsibilities and Rights," which advocated the following philosophy:

> The ideal of neighborhood government rests upon the belief that people can and should govern themselves democratically and justly. The essence of a democratic government is that people are responsible collectively to make choices which directly affect their lives together. The neighborhood is a political unit which makes this possible, since the smallness of the neighborhood enables all residents to deliberate, decide and act together for the common good.

> In the past neighborhoods and their citizens have been denied the opportunity for exercising their political rights and assuming their responsibilities. Consequently justice has not been achieved. In order to overcome this past failure, we assert that all governments and private institutions must recognize [the new rights of neighborhoods].[33]

The National Commission on Neighborhoods

In the late 1970s, the Democratic Congress and Democratic President Jimmy Carter worked together to establish a National Commission on Neighborhoods. The commission issued a report in 1979 advocating a revival of the neighborhood as a key governing institution in American life. In the commission's opinion, if legal barriers and other obstacles were removed, newly revitalized neighborhoods could accomplish great things: "Neighborhoods are human in scale, and they are immediate in people's experience. Since their scale is manageable, they nurture confidence and a sense of control over the environment. . . . The neighborhood is a place where one's physical surroundings become a focus for community and a sense of belonging."[34]

The federal sponsorship of the Neighborhood Commission did not prevent it from sharply criticizing the national government's current workings. In expressing its opposition to the existing centralization of many areas of government planning and management, the commission saw federal agencies as frequently distant from the American people. Federal and state administrators were more often concerned with their own prerogatives than serving the people who were supposed to benefit from federal programs. To be sure, the most extreme examples existed outside the United States. Many socialist governments in Eastern Europe, Africa, and elsewhere oppressed their citizens; sometimes a small governing class could be found looting the national treasury and otherwise using their powers for private gain.[35] Fortunately, corruption and abuse had never reached these levels in the United States; nonetheless, the commission reported,

> Middle income, working, and poor neighborhoods alike experience the frustration of government that does too little, costs too much, and denies meaningful influence to the vast majority. Power has been more centralized; people have become more alienated. More Americans live together, yet live alone. Increasingly government deals with Americans as clients, not citizens; as sources of revenue, but not of authority.[36]

The Neighborhood Commission proposed a series of measures to encourage a diversity of neighborhoods that could serve as testing grounds for land use and other innovations. Given the necessary authority and flexibility, new governing institutions at the neighborhood level could tailor their operations to the specific needs of each geographic place. It would all work to promote more responsive and democratic institutions of governance:

The diversity of neighborhood groups, which may seem to be a weakness, in fact is an important strength. They can respond flexibly, with different organizational structures, across a range of issues from sanitation services to discriminatory insurance rates. Community development organizations and advocacy groups are best suited to certain tasks; neighborhood government can deal better with problems such as juvenile crime with which larger social institutions deal badly, if at all.[37]

Big city police departments in the 1970s were in many cases sending white patrolmen into black neighborhoods where they often functioned more like an invading army. Alienated from the citizens, the police failed to protect these neighborhoods from crime. Neighborhood drug bazaars often functioned with minimal interference. The schools in many urban neighborhoods, run by central-city school systems with large administrative staffs, often verged on the dysfunctional. Even basic tasks, such as fixing potholes and plowing snowfall from clogged streets, were very poorly executed.

The suburbs, by contrast, were governed at a much smaller scale, often a neighborhood scale. A small suburban municipality might have 1,000 residents or fewer. Suburban schools in many instances provided a first-class system of education that in some of the wealthier localities was comparable with that found in the best private schools. With sufficient income levels to pay for high-quality schools and environments, the upper middle class flocked to these privileged suburban enclaves characterized by decentralized, neighborhood-level governance. Once there, residents employed zoning and other land use regulations— de facto collective private property rights—to protect their neighborhood prerogatives.

Over much of the United States, it seemed, the central cities were managed by large bureaucracies championing the old progressive ideals of scientific management in the public interest. Meanwhile, the better-off members of society lived in small suburban enclaves that were effectively private neighborhoods. The large cities often served their residents very poorly; the private suburban neighborhoods often served their residents very well. The neighborhood movement, as one might say, now sought to extend the suburban model of decentralized governance into the big city as well.

The Neighborhood as a "Mediating Structure"

In a revival of themes that Dewey explored earlier in the century, the 1970s and 1980s witnessed a growing belief that America's value-generating and defending institutions were in crisis. The 1960s had spawned a rebellion against traditional social authority. The old social values were no longer holding across wide areas of American life. Such concerns in part led Peter Berger and Richard Neuhaus in 1977 to make an argument for a new emphasis in American society on "mediating structures." A mediating structure—a church, labor union, sports club, Boy Scout troop, or other group of people organized to participate in a common cause—was typically private and frequently nonprofit. Berger and Neuhaus included "the neighborhood . . . as a key mediating structure in the reordering of our national life."[38]

For much of the 20th century, many such mediating institutions had fared poorly. In the 19th century, care for the poor, for example, had been a church responsibility, but in the 20th century this task was assumed by the welfare state.[39] Large state university systems provided an education that earlier would have been obtained at a private college. The family historically had supported the elderly, but in the 20th century the federal government began providing Social Security—and in the 1960s public assistance for the elderly was extended to include medical care.

American progressive theorists had not denied the importance of community. However, they sought to focus American loyalties onto the national community. Berger and Neuhaus argued, however, that the bonds of national community were not strong enough. National patriotism could serve well enough to hold all Americans together in time of war or other national crisis; however, a state of war hopefully would remain the exception in American life. Absent a war, or some other "moral equivalent of war," the American nation was simply too large and diverse to function as the one main value-sustaining institution of 280 million people. Waves of immigration from places such as India and Vietnam added further to America's religious and cultural diversity.

In the face of the new American pluralism, as it seemed to communitarians such as Berger and Neuhaus, important value-generating and defending institutions increasingly would have to be found at an intermediate level between the individual and the state. At this level, people were held together more by the routines of daily life. Neighborhood-level community offered a more reliable and less dangerous bonding agent than the fierce nationalism that had justified so many government applications of power over the course of the 20th century.

If an individual was too aggressive in the neighborhood, the censure of neighborhood opinion could be directed against him or her. Informal sanctions were an important part of neighborhood life. By contrast, in a community as large as the nation-state, censure would have to be achieved through legal system formalities. This might often be clumsy, perhaps involving an excessive penalty that could be permanently damaging, or in other cases an insufficient sanction that would make little difference in offenders' future behavior. It had all been a great mistake, as Berger and Neuhaus believed, to assume that there was "a unitary national community rather than a national community composed of thousands of communities," many of them of neighborhood size.[40] If there were a wider range of local institutions with real governing powers, people could sort themselves out in their choice of neighborhoods and other mediating institutions according to their individual values and needs.

Neighborhoods need not all be alike; indeed, diversity should reign. Civil libertarians, for example, should be prepared to tolerate tight limitations on the availability of pornographic materials in some neighborhoods, as long as the restraints accurately reflect the local residents' desires. The adoption of such strict censorship, however, would be unreasonable for the political community of the whole nation—and perhaps even for a whole state or big city jurisdiction.

Yet, because of past attempts to set one common standard everywhere in the nation, as Berger and Neuhaus contended, many local jurisdictions across the United States were being "denied the right to determine democratically the character of the community in which they live." As a rule, a local community should instead be able to choose on its own to allow, or not to allow, various forms of behavior; no single national judgment should apply. In short, the United States should be "an exercise in pluralism, as the *unum* within which myriad *plures* are sustained."[41] And neighborhoods might have a large future role to play in this new world of "diversity in homogeneity."

Many other writers would argue the critical importance of organizations outside of government in the 1980s and 1990s.[42] Political theorists increasingly looked to such organizations in civil society to solve problems that previously would have been assigned to the public sector. The neighborhood might have an especially important role here.[43] The Urban Institute in Washington, D.C., thus reported in 1997 that "it is at the local level that some of the boldest changes to the concept of the public sector as we know it are being discussed and implemented." There now exists a "wider consensus that money alone is inadequate without strong civic institutions within poor communities." What is needed are strong "partnerships across existing neighborhood institutions and between institutions and residents. Residents then take the lead role in designing and implementing strategies for community improvement."[44] In 1998, the National Commission on Civic Renewal issued a warning: "Our character-forming institutions are enfeebled," and concerned citizens needed to take steps to bolster key "institutions such as families, neighborhoods, schools, faith communities, local governments and political movements." The commission recommended, "Neighborhoods are places where citizens learn the importance of what they have in common and of what they can accomplish when they act in concert. Every neighborhood should assume responsibility for matters of significant local concern, emphasizing areas where neighbors can do meaningful civic work together."[45]

A Private Neighborhood Movement

The intellectuals who advocated neighborhood empowerment in the last decades of the 20th century mostly had in mind neighborhood governments in the public sector. By the end of the century, however, not much actual decentralization of public governing authority to the neighborhood level had occurred. Too many interests had too much stake in the existing organizational forms of American public government.

Instead, as often happens in history, new forces had to be exerted in new and unexpected ways. There was in fact a powerful neighborhood movement in the last part of the 20th century. However, to the surprise of earlier neighborhood advocates, it turned out to be mainly a private neighborhood movement. As this book described in part I, the transformation in local government, housing, and property rights over the last few decades of the 20th century was based on the rise of the private neighborhood association, which combined the government's collective functions with the property owner's traditional private autonomy.

To be sure, this revolution was not advocated by leading American political scientists, economists, or other intellectuals. The private neighborhood association arose simply as a practical way devised by the real estate industry to solve the problem of providing housing and common services within an attractive shared environment. It was adopted one neighborhood at a time across the United States as land developers searched for better ways to manage the individual projects they were putting up for sale.

Nevertheless, despite these mundane origins, the rise of the private neighborhood association did more to decentralize the structures of American governance than any other political development of the 20th century. To be sure, neighborhood associations have not diminished the extent of regulatory control over individual property. A private neighborhood is something of a paradox. A product of the free market, it also represents—much like a private business corporation—a turn away from the individual actor's autonomy in the marketplace. Indeed, private neighborhoods have probably enhanced substantially the total extent of collective authority in American life. This outcome, ironically, has been the result of millions of individual voluntary decisions made privately in the American land and housing market.

Conclusion

Many American suburbanites still rely on public zoning for their neighborhood's private protections. Reflecting the "progressive" origins of zoning, they continue to insist that elaborate land use plans be written, following the original scripts for scientific management in the public interest. Such Americans thus advocate old-fashioned progressive values as a matter of public form, even as the substance of their own personal existence at the local suburban level has become deeply private.

Given the great popularity of the suburbs' private character, one might suggest that a similar "privatization" should be extended into the big cities of America. Perhaps there should be a sharp devolution of political power to the neighborhood level. After all, the basic governing structures of most U.S. big cities have changed little for at least 50 years. Even as the suburbs have experimented widely in newly private forms of governance, it has been impossible to engage in a similar experimentation within the boundaries of the larger cities themselves.

The leading victims of this urban paralysis have been the poor, who by and large have been served poorly by their big-city governments. Perhaps it is time to grant inner-city residents the same governing privileges. Perhaps poorer neighborhoods in the inner cities as well should be privatized—officially or at a minimum in a de facto way—granting the residents there the same prerogatives that have long been enjoyed by their wealthier counterparts in the suburbs. Admittedly, this may require some stepping away from many of these suburbanites' traditional formulations of their "progressive" values. They may have to discover greater merits in "private" actions in society. It may then become politically feasible to extend the rise of the private neighborhood association from the suburbs into the inner city as well (see chapter 14).

NOTES

1. John Maynard Keynes, "Economic Possibilities for Our Grandchildren," in Keynes, *Essays in Persuasion* (1930; New York: W. W. Norton, 1963), 372.

2. Robert H. Nelson, *Economics as Religion: From Samuelson to Chicago and Beyond* (University Park: Pennsylvania State University Press, 2001).

3. David B. Truman, *The Governmental Process: Political Interests and Public Opinion* (New York: Alfred A. Knopf, 1951).

4. Ibid., 50–51.

5. Herbert Simon, "The Proverbs of Administration," *Public Administration Review* (Winter 1946).

6. Charles E. Lindblom, "The Science of 'Muddling Through,' " *Public Administration Review* 19 (Spring 1959). See also Norton Long, "Power and Administration," *Public Administration Review* 9 (Autumn 1949); and Norton E. Long, "Public Policy and Administration: The Goals of Rationality and Responsibility," *Public Administration Review* 14 (Winter 1954).

7. Edward C. Banfield, *The Unheavenly City: The Nature and Future of Our Urban Crisis* (Boston: Little, Brown, 1968); also Edward C. Banfield and James Q. Wilson, *City Politics* (Cambridge, MA: Harvard University Press, 1963).

8. Jon C. Teaford, *Post-Suburbia: Government and Politics in the Edge Cities* (Baltimore: Johns Hopkins University Press, 1997), 16, 27.

9. Robert C. Wood, "The Political Economy of the Future," in Benjamin Chinitz, ed., *City and Suburb: The Economics of Metropolitan Growth* (Englewood Cliffs, NJ: Prentice-Hall, 1964), 153. This chapter is excerpted from Robert C. Wood, *1400 Governments: The Political Economy of the New York Metropolitan Region* (Cambridge, MA: Harvard University Press, 1961).

10. Teaford, *Post-Suburbia*, 2–3.

11. Henry R. Richmond, "Sprawl and Its Enemies: Why the Enemies Are Losing," *Connecticut Law Review* 34 (Winter 2002), 555.

12. Charles M. Haar, "Introduction: Metropolitanization and Public Services," in *Metropolitanization and Public Services* (Washington, DC: Resources for the Future, 1972), 4–5.

13. Ibid., 5.

14. Richard Thompson Ford, "Beyond Borders: A Partial Response to Richard Briffault," *Stanford Law Review* 48 (May 1996), 1184.

15. Nathan J. Zolik, "Suburbs, Separatism, and Segregation: The Story of Milwaukee's Boundary Through the Lens of Annexation Law," *Wisconsin Law Review* 2001 (No. 2, 2001), 522.

16. Ibid., 507, 519, 517, 523.

17. John Kenneth Galbraith, *American Capitalism: The Concept of Countervailing Power* (Boston: Houghton Mifflin, 1952).

18. Theodore J. Lowi, *The End of Liberalism: Ideology, Policy, and the Crisis of Public Authority* (New York: W. W. Norton, 1969), 46.

19. Gunnar Myrdal, *Beyond the Welfare State: Economic Planning and Its International Implications* (New Haven, CT: Yale University Press, 1960), 96.

20. See Robert A. Caro, *The Power Broker: Robert Moses and the Fall of New York* (New York: Vintage Books, 1975).

21. Joseph P. Viteritti, "Municipal Home Rule and the Conditions of Justifiable Secession," *Fordham Urban Law Journal* 23 (Fall 1995), 23.

22. Elizabeth S. Scott and Robert E. Scott, "A Contract Theory of Marriage," in F. H. Buckley, ed., *The Fall and Rise of Freedom of Contract* (Durham, NC: Duke University Press, 1999), 203.

23. David S. Broder and Richard Morin, "Struggle Over New Standards," *Washington Post,* December 27, 1998, A1.

24. See Robert H. Nelson, "Is 'Libertarian Environmentalist' an Oxymoron? The Crisis of Progressive Faith and the Environmental and Libertarian Search for a New Guiding Vision," in John A. Baden and Donald Snow, eds., *The Next West: Public Lands, Community and Economy in the American West* (Washington, DC: Island Press, 1997).

25. See Milton Kotler, *Neighborhood Government: The Local Foundations of Political Life* (New York: Bobbs-Merrill, 1969); Douglas Yates, *Neighborhood Democracy: The Politics and Impacts of Decentralization* (Lexington, MA: Lexington Books, 1973); George Frederickson, ed., *Neighborhood Control in the 1970s: Politics, Administration, and Citizen Participation* (New York: Chandler Publishing Co., 1973); and Curt Lamb, *Political Power in Poor Neighborhoods* (New York: John Wiley, 1975).

26. David Morris and Karl Hess, *Neighborhood Power: The New Localism* (Boston: Beacon Press, 1975), 3, 5.

27. Ibid., 12.

28. Ibid., 11, 13.

29. Harry C. Boyte, *The Backyard Revolution: Understanding the New Citizen Movement* (Philadelphia: Temple University Press, 1980), 68, 69.

30. Ibid., 70.

31. Ibid., 189–90.

32. Statement of Milton Kotler, quoted in Boyte, *The Backyard Revolution,* 69.

33. Quoted in Boyte, *The Backyard Revolution,* 69–70.

34. National Commission on Neighborhoods, *People, Building Neighborhoods: Final Report to the President and the Congress of the United States* (Washington, DC: Government Printing Office, March 19, 1979), 276.

35. Jean-Francois Bayart, Stephen Ellis, and Beatrice Hibou, *The Criminalization of the State in Africa* (Bloomington: Indiana University Press, 1999).

36. National Commission on Neighborhoods, *People, Building Neighborhoods*, 7.

37. Ibid., 9.

38. Peter L. Berger and Richard John Neuhaus, *To Empower People: The Role of Mediating Structures in Public Policy* (Washington, DC: American Enterprise Institute, 1977), 8.

39. David T. Beito, *From Mutual Aid to the Welfare State: Fraternal Societies and Social Services, 1890–1970* (Chapel Hill: University of North Carolina Press, 2000).

40. Berger and Neuhaus, *To Empower People*, 11.

41. Ibid., 11–12, 13.

42. E. J. Dionne Jr., ed., *Community Works: The Revival of Civil Society in America* (Washington, DC: Brookings Institution Press, 1998); Robert Wuthnow, *Sharing the Journey: Support Groups and Americans' New Quest for Community* (New York: Free Press, 1994); Robert D. Putnam, *Bowling Alone: The Collapse and Revival of American Community* (New York: Simon and Schuster, 2000); Carmen Sirianni and Lewis Friedland, *Civic Innovation in America: Community Empowerment, Public Policy, and the Movement for Civic Renewal* (Berkeley: University of California Press, 2001); and Archon Fung and Erik OlinWright, eds., *Deepening Democracy: Institutional Innovations in Empowered Participatory Democracy* (New York: Verso, 2003).

43. Jeffrey M. Berry, Kent E. Portney, and Ken Thomson, *The Rebirth of Urban Democracy* (Washington, DC: Brookings Institution, 1993).

44. G. Thomas Kingsley and James O. Gibson, *Civil Society, the Public Sector, and Poor Communities*, Urban Institute Series on "The Future of the Public Sector," No. 12 (Washington, DC: The Urban Institute, August 1997), 1, 2.

45. National Commission on Civic Renewal, *A Nation of Spectators: How Civic Disengagement Weakens America and What We Can Do About It, Final Report* (College Park, MD: Institute for Philosophy and Public Policy, School of Public Policy, University of Maryland, 1998), 5, 8, 13.

11

Local Governments in a Postmodern World

We are entering into a "postmodern" age. The modern age, according to the standard account, began in the Enlightenment. With the rise of science, human beings gained new confidence in their ability to solve the most ancient problems of human existence. Economic progress would end poverty and bring on a much more rational and peaceful world. As modern enlightenment spread across the earth, the hatreds and bigotries based on ignorance of the past would give way to a world community of harmony and shared values.

Our postmodern age now questions such assumptions. Scientific powers developed to control physical nature now seem a double-edged sword, capable of greatly harming our environment, for example. Perhaps economic progress will not abolish wars and other age-old conflicts after all; the modern faith that these conflicts were rooted in remediable material scarcities and other economic factors may have been misplaced. If the scientific method is applicable mainly to the understanding of physical nature, there may not be a convergence of basic beliefs about the best forms of society. Indeed, the world may face a long-run future of pluralism. Citizens in a postmodern age may express a new willingness to sacrifice economic efficiency for a stronger sense of immediate community.

Such trends may augur well for social institutions—such as neighborhoods— that once played a larger role in western society. Yet, even if neighborhoods do become more autonomous, they will of course still necessarily exist within some much broader political and economic framework set by governments at higher levels. It is impossible to imagine any future world of autarky, so the real issues are how more independent neighborhoods might relate to the higher orders of governing authority. Such issues raise fundamental questions of political philosophy that of course do not lend themselves to any easy answers. Nevertheless, this chapter will attempt to explore the possible future place of local governments in a postmodern political order.

The principal conclusion will be that these governments are likely to continue and extend the 20th-century trends discussed in previous chapters toward a greater privatization of the constitutional understanding of local government. This trend is nothing new; it is a return to the concepts of local independence that characterized premodern periods in the West before the rise of the nation-state.

The Frug-Ellickson Exchange

Reflecting views similar to those expressed by the 1970s neighborhood movement, Gerald Frug argued in 1980 for "a genuine transfer of power to the decentralized units"—the regions, cities, and neighborhoods—of American society. The objective would be to create a new "ability of a group of people, working together, to control actively the basic social decisions that affect their lives." This would be no small task, however, because "real decentralization requires rethinking and, ultimately, restructuring American society itself," including an end to "the current powerlessness" of America's cities and neighborhoods.[1]

Frug advocated, as one element, "recognizing the rights of the city as an exercise of freedom of association." This process would involve the revival of a mostly premodern model in which cities were seen as the legal equivalent of business corporations and "there was no difference between a corporation's property rights and its rights of group self-government." If this older concept were revived, the city could be "an association promoted by a powerful sense of community and an identification with the defense of property." Regrettably, cities today have "lost the elements of association and economic strength that had formerly enabled them to play an important part in the development of Western society."[2]

Business corporations and local governments represent alternative forms of close association among a group of people. The municipal corporation rests on territorial group association, while the business corporation is based on individuals coming together for the purpose of producing goods and services. Yet, as Peter Drucker has observed, the modern business corporation, "in addition to being an economic tool, is a political and social body; its social function as a community is as important as its economic function as an efficient producer."[3] Indeed, Frug suggests that the business corporation's private status over the past century has given it a large and unfair advantage in meeting many Americans' needs for community. To equalize the competition, he proposes that municipal corporations should have many of the same powers that business corporations currently have. Municipalities should be free, for example, to operate their own local banks, credit unions, insurance companies, and retail food outlets, among other traditional private enterprise roles. More broadly, municipalities should have a brand-new degree of governing autonomy; they should have greater freedom from outside governmental meddling in their affairs, as business corporations do at present. In short, and although Frug himself might not go along with this particular characterization (however much it accords with his views), the municipality should have a newly "private" status in American society.

Cities, neighborhoods, and other smaller territorial units should be given stronger powers because geographic forms of association represent an especially promising ground for reintroducing elements of community that were lost in society's headlong rush to modernization. Drucker acknowledges a "lack of dignity and fulfillment which is so obviously the major problem of industrial society," a society that is today based so heavily on one particular form of group association, the private business corporation.[4] Unlike a business corporation, however, as Frug explains,

> A territorial association . . . can readily include every individual in the geographic area, thereby presenting the greatest opportunity for widespread participation in its decisions. Because of this inclusiveness, it can further a broad range of possibilities for human association. It can also further stable expectations, since once formed, it cannot simply pack up its economic assets and leave town.[5]

Given such a position, it is surprising that Frug did not look to the rise of the private neighborhood association as a promising step in his plan. Indeed, current neighborhood associations have much of the autonomy and freedom of action Frug was advocating for his postmodern municipalities. In comparison, reconstituting the public municipality as Frug was suggesting would require a minor revolution in legal views. Many Supreme Court decisions would have to be overturned and other important laws rewritten by legislatures. It would be much simpler and easier to build on the private neighborhood association's existing legal status. Most neighborhood associations are already established legally as nonprofit private corporations. If neighborhood associations increasingly adopt the political role of public municipalities, it might be possible to achieve a small political revolution in the role of American local government without drastically changing the U.S. constitutional order.

Although Frug did not make this argument (and still seems to be no fan of neighborhood associations), Robert Ellickson shortly thereafter proposed just such a course of neighborhood empowerment. Ellickson observed that "the private homeowners association . . . is the obvious private alternative" to enhance the autonomy and defend vigorously the rights of small localities, much as Frug was proposing. Ellickson also suggested jettisoning some of the main legal distinctions between local governments in the public sector and private neighborhood associations, including overruling "*Avery* (and related decisions) to eliminate the current federal constitutional requirement that local elections be conducted on a one-resident/one-vote basis." Municipalities in the public sector, like existing neighborhood associations, would then be able to adopt "some system that weighted votes by acreage or property value."[6]

Local Government as Private Property

Relegating a large part of U.S. local government to a private status would reflect the fact that much of the function of local government is "business-like." The U.S. federal government commits most of its direct expenditures to two functions—national defense and the internal redistribution of income. In other areas, and whatever the Constitution might say to the contrary, state governments in many respects evolved in the 20th century to become the federal government's administrative apparatus, controlled by significant federal funding and requirements.[7] Local governments, however, engaged in a much different set of activities—picking up the garbage, policing the streets, and running the schools—activities that could be and often still are provided privately in other circumstances.

Richard Briffault argues that a suburban municipality not only often functions privately like a "firm," but also generally has a mission "to defend the private sphere surrounding home and family."[8] Indeed, as described earlier, "public" zoning often becomes the practical equivalent of a collective private property right for defending the shared environment of a group of neighborhood property owners. In 2001, economist William Fischel similarly argued that local "city governance is more like that of business corporations than it is like state government." When they interact with land developers and other parties, municipalities effectively engage in deal-making involving "voluntary exchange [that] makes municipalities better off in the same way that it makes individuals and consensual organizations better off" in ordinary private transactions in the marketplace.[9]

"Dell" Governments

The American computer manufacturer Dell, Inc., bears little relationship to such industrial giants as AT&T, General Motors, and General Electric, companies that dominated the U.S. economy for much of the 20th century. Dell sells directly to customers, cutting out the traditional role of the retailer. Its computer components are made by outside firms, leaving Dell employees to complete only the final assembly, which is conducted on a "just-in-time" basis to minimize holding inventory. The most important roles for Dell employees are designing, selling, and servicing the computers and organizing production and distribution. Dell is not alone; many other U.S. firms created in the past decade or two operate in a similar "virtual" fashion.

Local government in a postmodern world might follow in Dell's path. The main tasks of local government might be conceptual and coordinating—establishing the "values" and "meaning" of a particular "community." Local governments in the public sector would leave issues of neighborhood scale to private neighborhood associations, which in turn might outsource most service provision requirements to private companies. Local governments—probably considerably larger than most current municipalities—would mediate between neighborhoods, as needed. Where local government became involved in direct service provision, it would most likely involve collective services relating to arterial highways, water systems, sewer systems, and other such services that require coordination across wide geographic areas and involve major economies of scale.

At the national level, the federal government currently supervises the money supply, fights wars, sends people into space, funds basic scientific research, and undertakes other tasks that differ greatly in character from neighborhood services and may be inherently governmental. At the neighborhood level, however, there is little about the local service role that requires any direct involvement of a government in the public sector. Neighborhood associations have already demonstrated that even basic governance tasks at this micro level can be undertaken privately. An advisor to neighborhood associations comments that an association is "both a community and a business to meet the expectations of the members" and appropriately functions privately in both these capacities.[10] All in all, there may be in the postmodern era a radical privatization of many local government functions, both in concept and in execution.

Reducing Transaction Costs

In the 20th century, zoning was a "public" responsibility because it was too difficult in older, established neighborhoods to create a new private association with the powers to regulate land use. Unlike a private system of land use control, the establishment of public zoning required no unanimous prior consent. Other collective functions beyond land use regulation, however, pose similar start-up issues. The solution in these cases as well has been found in local public governments.

In their laws for municipal incorporation, states set out specific requirements for creating new municipalities. Under a typical state law, residents vote on the issue of an area proposed for incorporation. Thus, in most cases, there must in practice be substantial political agreement, though unanimous agreement is not required. A "public" entity has the authority to compel holdouts, free riders, and other potential objectors to become "citizens" of a new local government. In a "private" setting, by contrast, even a tiny minority possesses veto power over the creation of a new, private territorial entity within common boundaries.

The institution of local government, in short, can be seen as an innovation in voting rules. For an ordinary good or service, the decision to purchase, or not to purchase, can be made one individual at a time. I may decide to buy a new television of a particular brand; you may decide to buy another brand. Most of the time, my action does not make any difference to you. For certain goods with a common territorial aspect, however, either everyone receives the good or service within a common geographic area, or no one receives it. Whenever new private contractual arrangements are desired among such a group, the transaction costs of a purely private solution—necessarily based on a unanimous vote—have been prohibitive.

Because of the greater opportunity for coercion in the "public" form of collective geographic contracting, society enforces different ground rules, designed to protect any minority in a "local government contract" from exploitation. When some people are forced by the state to enter into a contract, there should be stronger safeguards against majority abuse. One protection is the freedom to exit the local area; however, the costs of exiting can be high. Society therefore offers special protections for local government "customers," which are greater than those offered to the customers of an ordinary business corporation (who have all joined voluntarily in the sense that they all individually bought its products). Local governments, as "state actors," have to meet stricter legal requirements. A mandatory neighborhood association, by contrast, is more like a business corporation in which both the stockholders and the customers participate voluntarily—there is no exercise of coercion involved. Everyone in a neighborhood association has consented in advance (as an initial condition of home purchase); the association therefore is not treated as a state actor, even though it assumes real governmental powers.

Neighborhood "Mergers" and "Divestitures"

As a "customer," the unit owner in a neighborhood association not only receives services, but also acts as an "investor." Indeed, the unit owner's home often constitutes a significant portion of his or her total financial assets. In an ordinary business corporation, each investor joins by purchasing shares. Later changes in the organization's "citizenship" are accomplished by buying and selling the stock. One corporation thus can take over the physical assets of another corporation by buying out most of its stockholders. Mergers and acquisitions, along with divestitures, are a routine part of life in the American business world. All these ownership changes entail moderate transaction costs. Stockholders who disapprove of the way a corporation is being managed can "exit" the organization simply by selling their shares on Wall Street.

The territorial aspect of a neighborhood "corporation," however, again greatly complicates any such processes of entry and exit, either individually or collectively. In the latter case, "merging" or "divesting" neighborhoods at present is very cumbersome. In a private neighborhood association, a split of one group from the association would require a large supermajority vote and perhaps unanimous consent. In the public sector, such a separation would amount to an act of secession from a municipality. Indeed, there are provisions for secession—or "detachment" from the municipal corporation—in the laws of most states. However, few detachments have occurred over the years, due in part to the high transaction costs associated with state approval of a secession/detachment from an existing municipality.[11]

In principle, the "industrial organization" of the "business" of local government, like other industrial sectors, could be determined by a process of competition in the marketplace. Indeed, some students of urban affairs argue that a key to improved delivery of local public services rests in much greater flexibility among municipal boundaries. It should be easier to assemble new governments covering larger areas and responsibilities from building blocks of smaller units, or perhaps instead to divest smaller units from existing larger ones. An important area of law in the future may be the appropriate provision of voting rules and other procedures for the approval of boundary changes and other structural adjustments to local government.

Ronald Oakerson in the mid-1980s directed a study of the structures of local governance across the United States for the U.S. Advisory Commission on Intergovernmental Relations (ACIR). The ACIR report concluded that much wider opportunity for experimentation in local service delivery is needed. As Oakerson puts it, "Of central importance is the authority to create, modify, and dissolve [local service] provision units. The structure of the provision side—including the variety of provision units—depends on who can exercise this authority and under what conditions."[12] In this way, a Darwinian process of natural selection among local governments of many sizes and types could shape what one might call the "local government industry"—one important sector of the overall private economy.

Oakerson also argues that neighborhood-level institutions of local government are missing in the schemes of American government. He continues, "What is essential is that small-scale communities have the capability to organize themselves to act collectively with respect to common problems. This requires that locally defined communities be able to self-govern, exercising the powers of government within a limited sphere—limited in terms of both territory and the scope of authority." Many goods and services can best be "provided on a 'neighborhood' scale." At present, however, the governance structures of metropolitan areas "tend to preclude or inhibit the development of smaller, nested provision units—neighborhood governments—within [wider city] boundaries."[13] As a result, neighborhood forms of governance are simply left out of the evolutionary competition to determine a future metropolitan organization of local governments in the public sector.

Oakerson said little about the radical political changes necessary to ease the formation of new local governments and to simplify the processes of boundary adjustment.* Moreover, although Oakerson clearly recognized the growing importance of private neighborhood associations, he did not necessarily advocate them as the main preferred instrument of improved neighborhood governance. Yet, a big advantage attached to the neighborhood association is the greater ease of integration, owing to its private status, into the workings of a market economy—potentially allowing, for example, the buying and selling of entry permission for new land uses within the neighborhood as a matter of the sale of a private right. Properly written, an association's constitution can allow for the routine expansion, contraction, termination, or other modification of the association and its boundaries, as a private business act and as economic circumstances change, and with a flexibility that would be more difficult to achieve in the public sector.

It would be helpful, for example, if more neighborhood constitutions provided for private "divestitures" of appropriate association subunits (for "private secessions"), assuming a contiguous subgroup within a given private neighborhood association desires to leave. There is no legal reason why this could not be done more easily, as compared with existing municipal corporations that are bound by laws governing subunit departures ("public secessions"). Furthermore, these private constitutions should stipulate a well-defined process for

---

*California and about ten other states have thus far taken some steps in this direction by creating official oversight mechanisms to review modifications in the structure of local government. In California, the Cortese-Knox Local Government Reorganization Act was enacted in 1985 to consolidate previous authorities and to provide for a "Local Agency Formation Commission" (LAFCO) in each county. Each county LAFCO is authorized to review, and to approve or disapprove, changes in the structure of local government—including annexations, municipal incorporations, secessions, reorganizations, and any other changes in the boundaries of local government within that county. The modification of a governmental structure should broadly serve, among other criteria, the promotion of "planned, well-ordered, efficient urban development patterns," including open space and the discouraging of urban sprawl. See Brian P. Janiskee, "The Problem of Local Government in California," *Nexus, A Journal of Opinion* 6 (Spring 2001).

appropriate private neighborhood "acquisitions" of new areas. While few neighborhood associations may have thus far considered such matters of private secession or enlargement, these adjustments could in concept be accomplished without great legal stresses and strains within a private legal framework.

Vertical and Horizontal Integration

If it is opened up in this manner, the evolutionary workings of a market process can be expected to yield new units of local governance, not only at the neighborhood level but also of many sizes and shapes. In the ordinary business world, large corporations have typically won out over small firms in the market. These large business corporations are in effect small "planned economies" based internally on central planning and management (although perhaps making use of internal market-like incentives). Since Oliver Williamson's pioneering work in the 1970s, a "new institutional economics" has shed greater light on the economic forces that can yield more or less vertical and horizontal integration within an industry.[14]

A metropolitan system of governance faces similar economic issues of transactions costs and economies of scale, issues that will influence future organizational structures. A larger unit of local government might be able to deliver services such as water and sewer at less cost. A big city may have access to various forms of specialized professional knowledge. A large city, however, might be at a significant disadvantage in other respects. It might be difficult to create a system of positive incentives that will serve to motivate a large-city bureaucracy. Large city size will involve a greater diversity of citizens and thus greater discrepancies between individual service demands and the common levels of services typically provided citywide. Demonstrating resistance to a further expansion of city boundaries, a mayor of Chicago once declared, "The ideal city is compact. With its area fully occupied, the care of all branches of administration can be applied to all sections expeditiously and well." In response to any proposals "to increase this territory" of Chicago, the appropriate response should be "instant and emphatic discouragement."[15]

A very small neighborhood also may not be ideal. The time investments required for full democratic participation and other transaction costs associated with neighborhood governance might be too large for each homeowner. Economies of scale in service delivery may be impossible to achieve. A neighborhood should, therefore, be large enough to offer a self-contained physical environment of high quality. In general, however, there will be trade-offs between various benefits and costs associated with larger and smaller neighborhoods.[16]

Given a host of such factors, Oakerson argues, the best way to resolve these trade-offs may be through an evolutionary process driven by competition among governmental forms within an overall framework of metropolitan governance:

> There is no fully objective way of determining an appropriate set of provision units apart from the expressed preferences of local citizens for public goods and services. The ease with which a single provision unit can satisfy individual preferences decreases with the preference heterogeneity of the community. By the same token, the ability to satisfy diverse preferences increases with an increase in the number of provision units in a local public economy—at least up to some point. The creation of provision units is constrained by the expected transaction costs of organizing and operating an additional unit. Transaction costs include the costs of citizen participation. The choice is between greater preference satisfaction, obtained by creating an additional provision unit, and lower transaction costs. Citizens face a trade-off that only they can decide.[17]

A Private Tiebout World

The economist Charles Tiebout famously suggested many years ago that competition among units of local government could result in the delivery of public services roughly as efficiently as a market solution.[18] Local taxes would function as prices; each person would choose a local community in which the common level of public services corresponded to his or her service demands at the given local "tax price." If there were enough communities (i.e., economies of scale were not large in relation to total population), and moving among communities was possible at low enough costs, each person would be able to cluster with others of similar economic means and preferences.[19] Indeed, in a hypothetical world of economic analysis in which there were no transaction costs at all (an assumption typical of economic modeling at the time Tiebout was writing in the 1950s), each person would in theory enter a community with an optimal level of public services and pay a property tax precisely equal to his or her share of the costs of these services. In the overall local government equilibrium, there would be a perfect match of service supplies with service demands, corresponding collectively to the perfect equilibrium long depicted in the standard abstract economic model of competitive markets for individually purchased goods and services.

The assumptions required to achieve a perfect Tiebout world are heroic, to say the least. However, it may be possible in practice to realize a very rough approximation. Even this possibility, however, is likely to depend on the creation of much wider flexibility in local governmental forms and boundaries than exists at present.[20] Such flexibility could reduce significantly the dynamic burdens—the transaction costs—of metropolitan adjustments. Rather than having to physically move to a new area (at high cost), for example, a group of people already living in a neighborhood might be free to secede to form their own new unit of local government and thus obtain the levels of collective services that they want at this scale and without exorbitant transaction costs.

If there were more room for such trial and error in the reorganization of local government, then we would not need to attempt to prescribe an ideal size or arrangement for such governments. In the absence of such flexibility, a system of metropolitan governance is like a private industry in which the sizes and boundaries of business firms already have largely been fixed by some outside decisionmaker. In such circumstances, it should not be surprising that the system of metropolitan governance tends toward much less efficient forms, as compared with the competitive workings of the ordinary private business world. The standard processes of evolutionary change that drive market efficiency in business are simply absent in a metropolitan system comprising units of governance whose boundaries and other features in practice are almost permanently fixed by municipal incorporations and other actions to set governing forms long ago.

Other large obstacles also obstruct the trial-and-error movement toward a higher quality of local governance. Even where technically feasible and efficient, units of local government are often prevented from selling their services to other local governments or to the private sector. As Briffault comments, "Localities actually lack the authority to provide extra local services and require a special legislative grant of power before they are permitted to project their services across the local boundary line."[21] Local governments in general are supposed to avoid direct entry into private markets so as to avoid the appearance of offering "unfair" competition to ordinary private businesses.

Functional Overlapping Competing Jurisdictions (FOCJs)

Bruno Frey, a Swiss economist, notes that local government historically has held a territorial monopoly over collective service provision within its geographic boundaries. However, as Frey argues, this outcome is neither necessary nor desirable. Unitary governments may once have been suited to the collective tasks of the rural village. However, modern communications and other developments have greatly reduced the transaction costs associated with divesting functions from unitary local government to a diverse range of local forms of service providers.

Frey thus suggests that many current tasks carried out by local government should instead be performed by "Functional Overlapping Competing Jurisdictions"—or "FOCJs."[22] A FOCJ, unlike a traditional local government, would be more specialized by function and could overlap with the territory of another FOCJ. Thus, two FOCJs could often find themselves in competition with one another. Consumers would choose among competing FOCJs much in the same way that they now choose between Wal-Mart and Home

Depot. However, a FOCJ would differ from an ordinary business because it would employ a collective form of purchasing activity; the purchasers would own the business and FOCJ management would be overseen by a democratic process of purchaser/owner decisionmaking. Resembling private clubs but extending beyond golf and tennis to include a wide range of local collective services, Frey argues that FOCJs would be genuinely "governmental," partly because they would have "enforcement power" and could "levy taxes."[23]

Frey finds a worldwide proliferation today in the forms of governance. For example, at the global level, the International Olympic Committee might be regarded as a form of "government" that is limited to one particular function—conducting the Olympic Games every four years. Locally, Washington Area Girls Soccer (WAGS), a private, nonprofit organization, oversees advanced soccer competitions for girls 10 to 18 years of age, crossing many jurisdictional boundaries throughout the Washington, D.C., region. Elsewhere, a similar local soccer league might be organized and coordinated by a large city's public recreation department. In another domain—education—the "school choice" movement has adopted an FOCJ stance—the establishment of overlapping jurisdictions for public service providers. Charter schools and private school vouchers go farther still, in the first case allowing schools to operate with considerable independence from traditional education rules and regulations, and in the second providing for the direct private operation of some schools with at least partial public funding.

The evolution of the long-distance telephone industry over the past 20 years shows another transition from a single geographic monopolistic arrangement to systems of competing and overlapping telephone companies (although AT&T, which held the monopoly, was private, it operated under tight government oversight). The case of the telephone industry illustrates how technological innovation can alter the desirable organizational forms of public service delivery. Yet, the first new competitor in long-distance telephone service, MCI, had to struggle long and hard in the courts before it was permitted even to complete with AT&T. Locally, the telephone system continued as a monopoly into the 1990s. The emergence of cell telephones has further encouraged today's proliferation of more competitive local telephone services.

Already partially realized, Frey's vision of functionally oriented forms of "local government" that overlap and compete with one another could expand into the territories of other public monopolies. A turn toward FOCJs could hold out the prospect of whole new forms of more "business-like" local governance. Moreover, although Frey puts FOCJs in the category of "public" government, there would seem to be little about them that would prevent their functioning as private entities altogether. The rise of the private neighborhood association has shown that even many tasks previously considered exclusively public and governmental can in fact be carried out privately.

Two Views of FOCJs

Commenting on Frey's vision, economist Jurgen Eichberger finds much to praise, but offers two criticisms. First, some aspects of government involve defining the rules of the game, and may require an exclusive territorial jurisdiction. As Eichberger suggests, "A legal system, jurisdiction, regulation, and enforcement of rules require a territorial government. Though one may envisage each club organizing its own protective force, this appears utterly inefficient"—seemingly a turn back to an original state of nature as once portrayed by John Locke. Second, Eichberger questions each FOCJ's need for "direct election of management by members." Frey proposes that FOCJ "constitutions" should "encourage members . . . to participate actively in the management of FOCJ affairs," but Eichberger suggests that we need not automatically presume "the general superiority of [a] participatory membership rule. . . . [and] that the appropriate form of FOCJs will vary with their functions."[24]

In a second view, Wolfgang Kerber finds that "the concept of FOCJ shows convincingly that many tasks traditionally fulfilled by local jurisdictions with territorial monopoly powers can also be provided by other types of jurisdictions (e.g., functional ones)." Yet, an "underlying legal order" would still be needed to provide, among other things, "a set of metarules that ensure that a system of FOCJs is really able to enhance the welfare of the citizens." Yet, Kerber thinks that in the future a competitive process may be put to work in the development of many parts of the legal order as well; it may be possible for "individuals or firms [to] have the right to choose between legal rules or whole legal orders. This will lead to competition among legal rules or legal orders, a phenomenon that can already be observed. If firms do business on an international level, they have the right to choose which kind of contract law they want to use, e.g., German, British, or U.S. law."[25]

Kerber considers Frey's work to be an important contribution to the rethinking of local government's role and function. With "the FOCJ concept," Frey points to the "reality [that] we do not have 'the' government but a multitude of governments."[26] This raises a basic federalism issue as to the "proper scope of government" at all levels:

> Already in traditional federalism theory, different tasks are assigned to the governments of the jurisdictions on different federal levels. It is the optimal number of federal levels, the optimum size of these territorially defined jurisdictions on each level, and the vertical assignment of tasks to the different levels that make up the question of the proper scopes of governments. If we take into account the potential establishment of functional jurisdictions according to the FOCJ concept, additional types of governments emerge, implying new kinds of "proper scopes." Consequently, the question of the proper scope of government is being transformed into the question of the proper structure of the entire system of territorially and nonterritorially

defined jurisdictions, including the proper assignments of tasks and competences to these various jurisdictions. . . . Their determination is an additional task for the underlying competitive order.[27]

Conclusion

Local governments in the United States provide many services that have a private, business-like character. To take advantage of economies of scale while acting to minimize transaction costs, local government's optimum size thus might best be determined by a trial-and-error process of competition. Different institutional forms at the local level of government could compete with one another. Rather than developing a central administrative plan for a system of local governance, the nature and tasks of local government in a postmodern world might then be determined in a "local government private market." Under such a new regime, a much greater flexibility involving boundary adjustments and other basic changes among the units of local government would be necessary. It would bring the local government system much closer to the assumptions made by Tiebout in portraying an efficient system of local government service delivery. Similar considerations would apply with respect to other elements of the local government package, such as the provision of a high-quality environment corresponding to the desires of resident homeowners.

If any such reconception of local government is to take place in the United States, it will likely have to be accompanied by reassigning local government's standing from its traditional "public" status in the law to a private status. Currently, public sector laws are more rigid with regard to the range of local governmental forms permitted and the processes for altering these forms. A private concept of local government could instead facilitate a routine flow of "mergers," "breakups," "divestitures," and other competitive organizational rearrangements. Following in the path of industrial organization studies of American business, such issues might form the core subject matter of a new field of scholarly research—the "industrial organization" of government at the local level, based on study of the outcomes of competitive interactions among private "local government corporations."

Speculating more boldly, a fundamental change in property rights in the 21st century might be the total privatization of American local government.[28] Postmodern local government activities would fall under a brand-new legal category—the exercise of a collective private property right in the manner of a private club. Before the modern era, business corporations and municipal corporations were chartered under the same state laws of incorporation and enjoyed a similar independence from higher state oversight. In the future, the workings of local government may turn back to these older legal models, and local governments may once again be private governments operating in a manner similar to private business corporations. Indeed, surprising as it may seem, the rise of the private neighborhood association since the 1960s has already anticipated key elements of a new, postmodern local government model of this kind.

NOTES

1. Gerald E. Frug, "The City as a Legal Concept," *Harvard Law Review* 93 (April 1980), 1070, 1122, 1060.

2. Ibid., 1106, 1107, 1119, 1119–20.

3. Peter F. Drucker, *Concept of the Corporation* (1946; Boston: Beacon Press, 1960), 140.

4. Ibid., 151.

5. Frug, "The City as a Legal Concept," 1145.

6. Robert C. Ellickson, "Cities and Homeowners Associations," *University of Pennsylvania Law Review* 130 (June 1982), 1519, 1558, 1560–61.

7. Christopher K. Leman and Robert H. Nelson, "The Rise of Managerial Federalism: An Assessment of Benefits and Costs," *Environmental Law* 12 (Summer 1982).

8. Richard Briffault, "Our Localism: Part II—Localism and Legal Theory," *Columbia Law Review* 90 (March 1990), 382.

9. William A. Fischel, *The Homevoter Hypothesis: How Home Values Influence Local Government Taxation, School Finance, and Land-Use Policies* (Cambridge, MA: Harvard University Press, 2001), 23, 182.

10. Robert T. Dennistoun, *The Role of the Association President,* 3rd ed. (Alexandria, VA: Community Associations Institute, 1999), 5.

11. The workings of metropolitan government, and the procedures for structural change, are described in Advisory Commission on Intergovernmental Relations, *Metropolitan America: Challenge to Federalism* (1966; New York: Arno Press, 1978).

12. Ronald J. Oakerson, *Governing Local Public Economies: Creating the Civic Metropolis* (Institute for Contemporary Studies, Oakland, CA: ICS Press, 1999), 81. This is a revised edition of Oakerson's original 1987 report done for the Advisory Commission on Intergovernmental Relations.

13. Ibid., 127, 85, 86.

14. See Oliver E. Williamson, *Markets and Hierarchies: Analysis and Antitrust Implications* (New York: Free Press, 1975); and Oliver E. Williamson, *The Economic Institutions of Capitalism: Firms, Markets, Rational Contracting* (New York: Free Press, 1985). See also Eirik G. Furubotn and Rudolf Richter, *Institutions and Economic Theory: The Contribution of the New Institutional Economics* (Ann Arbor: University of Michigan Press, 1997).

15. Comment in 1902 of Chicago Mayor Carter H. Harrison, quoted in Kenneth T. Jackson, *Crabgrass Frontier: The Suburbanization of the United States* (New York: Oxford University Press, 1985), 150.

16. Albert Breton, *Competitive Governments: An Economic Theory of Politics and Public Finance* (New York: Cambridge University Press, 1996).

17. Oakerson, *Governing Local Public Economies,* 115.

18. Charles M. Tiebout, "A Pure Theory of Local Expenditures," *Journal of Political Economy* 64 (October 1956).

19. Wallace E. Oates, *Fiscal Federalism* (New York: Harcourt Brace Jovanovich, 1972).

20. Dean Stansel, "Interjurisdictional Competition and Local Economic Performance: A Cross-Sectional Examination of U.S. Metropolitan Areas," Department of Economics Working Paper (Fairfax, VA: George Mason University, March 2002).

21. Richard Briffault, "The Local Government Boundary Problem in Metropolitan Areas," *Stanford Law Review* 48 (May 1996), 1130.

22. Bruno S. Frey, "A Utopia? Government Without Territorial Monopoly," *Journal of Theoretical and Institutional Economics* 157 (March 2001), 167.

23. Ibid., 168.

24. Jurgen Eichberger, "Comment" on Frey, *Journal of Institutional and Theoretical Economics* 157 (March 2001), 178.

25. Wolfgang Kerber, "Comment" on Frey, *Journal of Institutional and Theoretical Economics* 157 (March 2001), 181, 180, 181, 183.

26. Ibid., 184.

27. Ibid.

28. See Robert H. Nelson, "Local Government as Private Property: Towards the Post-Modern Municipality," in Harvey M. Jacobs, ed., *Private Property in the 21st Century: The Future of an American Ideal* (Northampton, MA: Edward Elgar with the Lincoln Institute of Land Policy, 2004).

PART IV
A Policy Proposal:
New Neighborhood
Associations for
Old Neighborhoods

The creation of a private neighborhood association is now effectively limited to new areas of land development. Yet, most metropolitan areas include many neighborhoods that were built up before the rise of the private neighborhood association. These neighborhoods now typically protect their environmental quality through public zoning. If they could do it all over again, however, many of them might choose the legal instrument of a private neighborhood association; they would establish their own private government and private regulatory controls to protect their surrounding environmental quality. As a private entity, a neighborhood association might also provide common services more efficiently and more closely tailored to neighborhood homeowners' specific desires.

In part IV, I therefore propose that state governments enact new legislation to provide for the creation of new private neighborhood associations in older neighborhoods of existing homes.[1] The owners in an established neighborhood of homes and other properties could vote to accept or reject the creation of such an association. In order to be approved, the affirmative vote would have to be well above a simple majority, but less than complete unanimity. If the vote were successful, the minority of property owners who voted against the proposal would nevertheless be required to join the association and would become subject to its private regulations.

This procedure would offer a third way in which a neighborhood might deal with the high transaction costs of organizing collective actions to protect its environmental quality. As described in previous chapters, current private neighborhood associations establish their constitutions in advance of development and then obtain unanimous consent by requiring all home buyers to agree to their terms. Zoning solves the collective action problem by using government's coercive powers. The initial imposition of zoning resembles an exercise in eminent domain; government for practical purposes condemns certain individual rights of property owners in the neighborhood and then provides compensation in the form of new collective rights that are assigned to all the owners. If some particular neighborhood individuals are inevitably opposed to this zoning transfer of rights, their losses are regarded by the broader society as an acceptable price to pay for the collective gains in neighborhood environmental protection.

The proposal made in part IV would provide for the creation of a new private neighborhood association in place of existing zoning and also with less than unanimous consent. This approach can be defended within a utilitarian framework of thought—as a system of private neighborhood controls that will work better than municipal zoning in protecting environmental quality in neighborhoods. Even if the "disutility" of the use of government coercion is factored into the equation, the social benefits may exceed the overall costs. If the margin of difference is large, there are ample precedents for government actions where collective benefits exceed collective costs—even when the exercise of state power is necessary to override the objections of a losing minority of voters. The very institution of government can be seen as an institutional response to the impossibility (in most circumstances) of organizing collective action in a group of any significant size by unanimous consent.

Although it involves applying government coercion, the proposal outlined here may nevertheless be defended as a step forward in the overall freedoms of Americans.[2] Individual liberty is never absolute. Although it is often portrayed in the writings of libertarian theorists, there has never been a society in which the infringements on personal freedom were limited to preventing direct harms to one individual resulting from others' actions. The very use of income taxation, for example, amounts to the "taking" by the state of a certain portion of each person's earnings. Even in a private neighborhood association, it is impossible to write a contract that specifies all future contingencies. Many unit owners thus find that their freedoms are limited in ways that they did not fully anticipate or understand in advance. In short, there will always be real world trade-offs of one form of freedom for another.

Substituting private neighborhood associations for municipal zoning, I suggest, would advance neighborhoods' rights to act outside of wider government control. Instead of being subject to municipal decisionmaking, neighbors themselves would collectively take the actions required to protect their own neighborhood environment. If the paint color of each home is to be regulated, then the neighborhood itself would decide the permissible colors. The domain of private property—and the reach of "takings," due process, and other constitutional protections of private property—would be extended to encompass private neighborhood actions in this sphere. As a form of private property, a neighborhood association would enjoy many other rights not available at present to a public municipality. These might include the right to sell entry rights to a commercial facility, or the right to conduct the private sale of an entire set of neighborhood properties in one package. In general, the freedom of neighborhood unit owners to organize their own affairs according to their own desires and wishes would be much enhanced by granting them official private status as a neighborhood association.

It would also provide a wider range of choice for new residents in search of a neighborhood physical and social environment corresponding to their own individual preferences. The ability to join with others in shaping a common neighborhood environment is itself an important individual right. It is a part of the individual liberties associated with "freedom of association." Thus, greater neighborhood autonomy, even when it involves tight restrictions on individual behavior within most neighborhoods, still advances the freedom of Americans in this other dimension of their rights.

This is not to say that the utilitarian or libertarian issues mentioned above will be fully resolved in the pages to follow. The merits of the proposal in part IV are not likely to be decided by an "expert" study or plan for a metropolitan system of local governance, public or private. The final resolution should be carried out empirically and through the old-fashioned democratic process. No established neighborhood should be required to adopt a private system of land use controls in place of its current zoning. Creating a new private neighborhood association in an established neighborhood would require an affirmative vote by a large supermajority of unit owners.

Under this proposal, state legislatures would have to enact legislation to provide for the creation of new neighborhood associations in older established neighborhoods. One important consideration for state legislators might be the character of the resulting infringements on individual freedoms. It is one thing to regulate the exterior paint color of homes, yet quite another to demand that each neighborhood resident profess allegiance to Allah. A state legislature might be more concerned about limiting the reach of private neighborhood governance that is being established after the fact in an old neighborhood. Brand-new neighborhood associations in newly developing areas are created by unanimous consent. Such associations might be free to regulate internal religious speech, for example, in ways that would not be permissible where a neighborhood association is retroactively created in an old neighborhood—and where not everyone has agreed to the neighborhood religious rules in advance.

State legislators might also want to consider the cost of exiting the neighborhood. An owner who objects strongly enough must always have the option of selling and leaving a neighborhood association. Many other housing choices may be readily available in a large metropolitan area, but in a rural area those who pick up stakes may have many fewer options. In such circumstances, state law should perhaps require some degree of compensation for the costs of moving out of a neighborhood. A newly formed neighborhood association in an established neighborhood, for example, might have to pay the moving costs for any property owners who may choose the exit option within one year, or perhaps guarantee a certain minimum purchase price for the properties of any residents moving out of the neighborhood during that period.

If state governments were to adopt the proposal developed here, and if many older established neighborhoods chose to adopt a system of internal private regulation, such a move would represent a large step toward the outright abolition of public zoning.[3] With immediate neighborhood environments tightly protected through new private controls, it might also become politically feasible to challenge the zoning system's particularly harmful features as they have become evident in newly developing areas. As part of a broader deregulation of public zoning, any additional actions by local governments to zone new areas of undeveloped land in the outer suburbs would also be prohibited.

The full abolition of zoning would be a fitting end for yet another failed experiment in the scientific management of American society—a goal sought originally by the political theorists of the Progressive Era and implemented over the course of the 20th century. Public-sector zoning would join the Civil Aeronautics Board, the Interstate Commerce Commission, and other regulatory institutions created in the name of high progressive ideals that have been either substantially deregulated or abolished outright in the past few decades. During the 20th century, many people were convinced that the world had become a rational place, and applying scientific methods to solve social problems would result in drastically more effective government plans and actions. Entire American professions, such as public administration and urban planning, were built on such core assumptions.

The history of the 20th century, however, as zoning well illustrated, showed that much of this was a conceit of the modern age. The coercive powers of governments were frequently captured for private benefit. Government actions led in many cases to results much different from the original intentions. In the area of land use laws, the ancient pattern of evolution was little altered. The practice of zoning moved in radically new directions without much formal acknowledgment in the legal profession. A host of zoning legal fictions camouflaged the private realities of zoning practice.

Today may be the time to dispense with zoning myths and fictions and to align our official laws with the realities on the ground. If nothing else, this process would result in greater intellectual honesty—and potentially, assuming an accurate diagnosis helps in finding a cure, in improved public policies. In established neighborhoods, zoning would be officially recognized for what it became long ago in practice—a collective private property right to the shared neighborhood environment. A new private institution, the neighborhood association, would accomplish this result directly, replacing the long-standing administration of public zoning for private purposes.

Chapter 12 proposes a specific set of legal and administrative procedures for the creation of a new neighborhood association in place of zoning in older established neighborhoods. Chapter 13 examines the useful role that new private associations of farmers and other owners of undeveloped land—organized legally as one particular form of private neighborhood association—might play in controlling the land development process in rapidly growing areas on the outer suburban fringe. Chapter 14 describes how the creation of new private neighborhood associations in many older inner-city areas might offer large benefits to the residents there and to the city as a whole.

NOTES

1. An earlier version of this proposal was presented in Robert H. Nelson, "Privatizing the Neighborhood: A Proposal to Replace Zoning with Private Collective Property Rights to Existing Neighborhoods," *George Mason Law Review* 7 (Summer 1999). A revised version was reprinted as Robert H. Nelson, "Privatizing the Neighborhood: A Proposal to Replace Zoning with Private Collective Property Rights to Existing Neighborhoods," in David T. Beito, Peter Gordon, and Alexander Tabarrok, eds., *The Voluntary City: Choice, Community, and Civil Society* (Ann Arbor: University of Michigan Press, 2002). See also Robert H. Nelson, "Zoning by Private Contract," in F. H. Buckley, ed., *The Fall and Rise of Freedom of Contract* (Durham, NC: Duke University Press, 1999); Robert H. Nelson, "The Rise of the Private Neighborhood Association: A Constitutional Revolution in Local Government," in Dick Netzer, ed., *The Property Tax, Land Use and Land Use Regulation* (Northampton, MA: Edward Elgar with the Lincoln Institute of Land Policy, 2003); and Robert H. Nelson, "Local Government as Private Property: Towards the Post-Modern Municipality," in Harvey M. Jacobs, ed., *Private Property in the 21st Century: The Future of an American Ideal* (Northampton, MA: Edward Elgar with the Lincoln Institute of Land Policy, 2004).

2. For criticism of the proposal of part IV in terms of its infringement on individual liberty and the private property rights of a losing minority, see Steven J. Eagle, "Privatizing Urban Land Use Regulation: The Problem of Consent," *George Mason Law Review* 7 (Summer 1999); and Steven J. Eagle, "Devolutionary Proposals and Contractarian Principles," in F. H. Buckley, ed., *The Fall and Rise of Freedom of Contract* (Durham, NC: Duke University Press, 1999).

3. See also Robert H. Nelson, *Zoning and Property Rights: An Analysis of the American System of Land Use Regulation* (Cambridge, MA: MIT Press, 1977), chs. 8, 9. I first proposed the substitution of private collective rights for zoning in this book, and then developed this idea further in other writings about zoning in the late 1970s, 1980s, and 1990s. See Robert H. Nelson, "A Private Property Right Theory of Zoning," *The Urban Lawyer* 11 (Fall 1979); Robert H. Nelson, "Making Zoning a Collective Private Property Right," *Planning* 47 (January 1981); Robert H. Nelson, "The Privatization of Local Government: From Zoning to RCAs," in U.S. Advisory Commission on Intergovernmental Relations, *Residential Community Associations: Private Governments in the Intergovernmental System?* (Washington, D.C., May 1989); and Robert H. Nelson, "Privatize Inner-City Neighborhoods," *The American Enterprise* 7 (November/December 1996).

12

Creating Private Governments in Older Established Neighborhoods

I n the newly developing parts of the United States, a large and growing share of housing development involves private neighborhood associations. The popularity of these associations suggests that many older established neighborhoods might also wish to have the same legal form of collective ownership. However, as discussed earlier, even if most of the residents of an older neighborhood wished to create their own new association, the transaction costs of assembling unanimous consent would generally be prohibitive. As Michael Sarbanes and Kathleen Skullney comment, at present "a deed-based remedy to quality of life issues obviously bypasses older communities, whose deeds were created before this technique was widespread. Even if it made legal sense, the amending of every deed would be a daunting logistical task."[1]

Hence, state governments should provide a new legal mechanism by which an older established neighborhood could act to create its own association. Under this plan, a new private neighborhood association could be created without unanimous consent. Neighborhood property owners would be authorized to vote—with some high supermajority required for approval—to ratify a private constitution for a new neighborhood association. The result would be the creation of a "Neighborhood Association in an Established Neighborhood"—or "NASSEN."

Robert Ellickson observes that, in most times and places, property rights have been in a constant state of evolution. A system of rights appropriate to the technology and other circumstances of today may not work nearly as well 50 years from now. One problem is that property rights may become "excessively decomposed," making it hard to aggregate rights into functional economic units. In

265

general, "when a group is stymied by large-number coordination problems, it is possible that a state or other higher authority may usefully intervene to facilitate" a new property-right solution.[2] From this perspective, creating NASSENs offers a specific new solution to an older general problem.

A Six-Step Process

For the purposes of discussion, the following six-step process represents an approval procedure for creating a NASSEN, recognizing that many variations in the specific details are possible.

1. **A Petition Request**—A group of individual property owners in an older established neighborhood petition the state to form a private neighborhood association. The petition describes the boundaries of the proposed neighborhood association and the instruments of collective private governance intended for it. The petition states the services the association expects to perform and offers an estimate of the required monthly assessments. The petitioning owners must include cumulatively more than 40 percent of the neighborhood property owners, representing at least 60 percent of the total value of existing neighborhood properties.

2. **State Review**—The state then certifies that the proposed area of private neighborhood government meets certain standards of reasonableness, including the presence of a contiguous area; boundaries of a regular shape; an appropriate relationship to major streets, streams, valleys and other geographic features; and other relevant considerations. The state also verifies that the proposed private constitution meets state standards for neighborhood associations.

3. **Municipal-Neighborhood Negotiations**—If the application meets state requirements, a neighborhood committee is formed to negotiate a service transfer agreement with the municipal (or other local) government with jurisdiction over the neighborhood. The agreement specifies the future possible transfer of ownership of municipal streets, parks, swimming pools, tennis courts, and other existing municipal lands and facilities located within the proposed private neighborhood association, possibly including some compensation to the municipality. It specifies the future private assumption of garbage collection, snow removal, policing, fire protection, and other services—to the degree that the private neighborhood government assumes responsibility for such common services. The transfer agreement also specifies future tax arrangements, including any property or other tax credits that the neighborhood association might receive in compensation for assuming existing municipal service burdens. Other matters of importance to the municipality and to the

proposed neighborhood association are also addressed. As needed, the state government serves as an overseer and mediator in this negotiation process.

4. **A Neighborhood Vote**—Once state certification of the neighborhood proposal to create a NASSEN is received, and a municipal transfer agreement has been negotiated, a neighborhood election is called for a future date. The election should occur no less than one year after the certification process is completed and a full description of the neighborhood proposal is available to all interested parties, including the founding documents for the neighborhood association, the municipal transfer agreement, estimates of assessment burdens, a comprehensive appraisal of the values of individual neighborhood properties, and other relevant information. During the one-year waiting period, the state oversees a process to inform property owners and other residents of the neighborhood of the details of the proposal and to facilitate public discussion and debate.

5. **Required Percentages of Voter Approval**—In the actual election, approval of the creation of a NASSEN requires (1) an affirmative vote by 70 percent or more of the individual unit owners in the neighborhood and (2) that these affirmative voters must cumulatively represent 80 percent or more of the total value of neighborhood property. If these conditions are met, all property owners in the neighborhood are required to join the neighborhood association and are subject to the full terms and conditions laid out in the neighborhood association founding documents (the "declaration," or as it would amount to in practice, the neighborhood "constitution").

6. **A New Private Right**—Following the establishment of a NASSEN, the municipal government transfers the legal responsibility for regulating land use in the neighborhood to the unit owners in the neighborhood association, acting through their instruments of collective decision-making. The municipal zoning authority within the boundaries of the neighborhood association is abolished—except where such zoning regulates significant adverse impacts of one NASSEN on properties that are located outside its boundaries. (The activities within a neighborhood association are not permitted to create a nuisance for other neighborhoods outside the association.)

Why Municipal Zoning Is No Longer Necessary or Desirable

Many of the functions of private neighborhood associations are already being served by municipal zoning. Why, then, go to the trouble of devising a new property right institution? While public zoning and a private system of regulatory protection do in fact overlap in many respects, a NASSEN has a number of advantages over the traditional zoning system. These include:

- **More Complete Control**—Except in a historic or other special district, municipal zoning does not provide for fine control over the details of neighborhood architecture, placement of trees and shrubbery, yard maintenance, and other matters that can have a significant impact on the environmental quality of a neighborhood. As Gerald Korngold comments, neighborhood associations "can modify covenants more quickly and cheaply than public government can amend zoning, resulting in lowered transaction costs and efficiencies for the community. Moreover, governing boards of homeowners associations can develop an extensive regulatory scheme and system of rules, providing for a more controlled—and desirable from the owner's perspective—living environment."[3]
- **Neighborhood Self-Determination**—The municipal administration of public zoning typically allows many people who are not neighborhood residents to participate in neighborhood decisionmaking. In a big city, participants may even be members of a distant city council. Yet, there is no need for broader municipal involvement in the fine details of neighborhood architectural control. Indeed, under today's public zoning laws, the potential involvement of municipal outsiders—and of the courts, which feel freer to involve themselves in public zoning matters—leaves neighborhoods exposed to regulatory actions they do not want. Law professor Clayton Gillette thus notes that neighborhood associations make possible "private zoning by those who, for instance, consider living next to an ostentatious house or a multistory dwelling to be an undesirable externality. Individuals who wish to opt out of public lawmaking because they find it too imprecise or—with respect to nuisances—underinclusive, may also desire to opt out of public enforcement mechanisms for fear that those arbiters (courts) would bring to any dispute the perceptions created in litigation borne of the very public law principles that the residents are attempting to elude."[4]
- **Private Sales of Rights**—Because zoning is regarded as a form of public regulation, the direct sale of zoning would be an act of "bribery" or "corruption." Even when the revenues from the sale of zoning are deposited in the public treasury, rather than individual private pockets, courts remain legally skeptical. However, if the admission of a new land use into a neighborhood were regarded as the ordinary exercise of a private property right—as would be the case in a NASSEN—neighborhoods would be free to sell entry rights (say for a new convenience store). They could also sell rights to make broader changes in land use within the neighborhood, or even sell the whole set of neighborhood properties in a single package for comprehensive redevelopment in an altogether new type of land use.

- **Better Provision of Common Services**—A NASSEN can also more effectively and efficiently provide neighborhood common services. Private provision of common services might particularly benefit many urban neighborhoods in big cities now receiving these services from distant public bureaucracies. One testimony to such potential improvements is offered by Linda Morrison, a former top official in the Philadelphia government who was charged with implementing the "competitive contracting program" there in the early 1990s. By contracting out a limited number of "targeted services" to the private sector, as Morrison recently reported, "hundreds of millions were saved on these few targeted services. . . . The savings ranged from 28 percent for the city's warehouse operation to 53 percent for the Philadelphia Nursing Home to 46 percent for turf maintenance in parks. In every case, service was improved."[5] Yet, opposition from unions and other interests to Philadelphia's privatization program soon mounted, and the initiative ground to a halt within three years, leaving the old system of inefficient public delivery of most city services in place.
- **Neighborhood Social Capital**—The creation of a neighborhood association can establish and sustain a strong spirit of community and sense of identity within a neighborhood. As a smaller and more cohesive governing unit, a private neighborhood can help to stimulate residents to be more involved in public affairs, creating "social capital" within the neighborhood itself and perhaps even greater democratic involvement in the metropolitan region or, indeed, the nation. As Jason Mazzone reports, "A large body of research in the social sciences demonstrates that the ability of high social capital groups to choose their own members, free from any compulsion, is often a vital condition for the cohesiveness, and effectiveness, of the groups, as well as for the commitment of members to a group and their trust in each other." Conversely, an action that works "to undermine the association's social capital" is also likely to diminish "the association's contribution to popular sovereignty."[6]
- **Local Constitutional Experimentation**—Because a NASSEN would have wider flexibility in its constitutional design, competition in the private marketplace would extend to the constitutional arrangements for neighborhood governance. Not only states and cities, but now local neighborhoods as well could be the "laboratories of democracy." Private neighborhoods could more easily merge, or perhaps break apart, than those neighborhoods subject to current municipal annexation and deannexation procedures. Market forces in the real estate industry would determine the degree of horizontal and vertical integration in the governing institutions of a metropolitan area, much as market forces now determine the structure of an ordinary American industry. Although wider governments would set the overall institutional framework of property

rights, there would be no need for detailed "state planning" of the precise boundaries and administrative structures of metropolitan governance.

- **Real Decentralization**—As described in previous chapters, major decentralization of existing governing powers to the neighborhood level has many advocates. However, there is no possibility that neighborhoods of today will become small autarkies. There will be no return to feudalism. A neighborhood must fit within a broader social and economic framework and be accountable to it. If the neighborhood is a "political" creation— i.e., a small local government—it will be accountable to higher orders of political authority. If it receives its funding from federal, state, or big-city governments, its actions will in the end be determined there. The alternative is to be accountable to the market, which also imposes a higher-order discipline (and a market is of course ultimately also a political choice, but in a different sense). The market is capable of coordinating activities from Asia to Africa to Latin America. If a private neighborhood association can pass the market test—that is, the unit owners can pay for the land and housing, and cover the costs of their services—it will be as close to real decentralization of neighborhood authority as will ever be feasible in our closely interlinked world.

"Unitization" Precedents

There are precedents in other areas of the law for the state to assist a group of property owners in pooling their assets for collective management. Such an assembly process takes place in the oil and gas industries, for example, under the legal procedures for "unitization" of oil and gas holdings. Consider a case in which a single oil pool is discovered beneath the land parcels of many individual owners. If each owner were to develop the oil individually, the result could be a potential "tragedy of the commons," where each owner quickly drills a well to drain off as much of the total oil pool ahead of other landowners as possible. In the resulting rush to drill, oil reserves would be depleted at an excessive rate and other significant economic losses would result. Unitization of the oil pool allows for collective management to maximize the total value of the oil pool to all the property owners.

One might argue that private markets will solve the oil and gas problem. The landowners collectively will benefit by joining together in a cooperative manner under a single management plan. However, the transaction costs of assembling the various owners are likely to be prohibitive. Holdouts are likely to frustrate the assembly process, especially if misinformed about the relative contribution of their own property to the total value of the oil pool. Recognizing such problems, every oil state except Texas (where there is statewide regulation of individual oil well production) provides a legal mechanism by which an oil pool can be unitized with less than unanimous consent of the rights owners.

These state laws vary in a number of details, such as the percentage of owners required to approve a unitization. In Oklahoma, the voting requirement for a compulsory unitization is 63 percent. The vote of each individual owner is weighted by his or her relative share of the total acreage above the pool. One study finds that there was less than unanimous consent in more than half the cases of successful unitizations in Oklahoma.[7]

The institutional problems of groundwater management are much the same as those associated with an underground pool of oil. In many areas with little or no control over groundwater use, water supplies have rapidly depleted. Some states are therefore turning to regulatory systems rather than private unitization to control groundwater use.[8] Arizona, for example, requires state permits within areas of special groundwater concern (Active Management Areas).[9] The development of formal unitization laws for groundwater has been slow, relative to oil, partly reflecting water's lower value and the resulting smaller incentives to bear the costs of devising new institutional mechanisms.[10]

Another precedent for the NASSEN proposal here exists in labor law. It is difficult to obtain the voluntary agreement of 100 percent of a business or industry work force to support a single bargaining agent. However, if a subgroup of workers negotiates a better wage rate, all the workers benefit. To address this free-rider problem, Congress enacted the Wagner Act in 1935 to provide that, if a simple majority of workers vote to join a union, the union by law becomes the sole collective bargaining agent, and individual workers must accept the bargaining outcome. This labor union "unitization" law, which created a system of government-supervised union elections, provided a charter that helped establish the current role of labor unions in American industrial relations. A new "Wagner Act" for private neighborhood associations—but with a supermajority requirement for approval—could have a similarly large impact on the future workings of urban land development in the United States.

The Tragedy of the "Anticommons"

The familiar "tragedy of the commons" involves a large number of individuals who possess equal access to a resource, thus leading to overexploitation of open rangelands and many other commons. In several recent articles, Columbia University law professor Michael Heller has described a "tragedy of the anticommons."[11] In this situation, a large number of individuals have the rights to a resource, but these rights may be useless individually when each holder possesses a veto on the coordinated use of the rights. The tragedy then is not the overexploitation but the underexploitation of the common resource. To use the resource, many individual rights would have to be assembled—but the cost would be prohibitive. Heller offers the example of a new technological innovation that requires the accumulation of many patents held by diverse private parties. The usual holdout and other transaction costs may easily frustrate the assembly of the full set of patent rights and thus prevent the development or use of an important new technology. As Heller explains,

> The danger with fragmentation is that it may operate as a one-way ratchet: Because of high transaction costs, strategic behaviors, and cognitive biases, people may find it easier to divide property than to recombine it. If too many people gain rights to use or exclude, then bargaining among owners may break down. With too many owners of property fragments, resources become prone to waste either through overuse in a commons or through underuse in an anticommons.[12]

Traditionally, one solution to this problem has been to limit the division of property rights in the first place. Historically, primogeniture laws had this purpose, preventing equal property division among siblings. The "rule against perpetuities" also limited the ability of current owners to divide the future property rights in order to control permanently the actions of later owners.[13] If individual rights are nevertheless so divided that they become useless, then the reassembly process might reasonably be undertaken even without compensating the owners of the rights. As Heller explains, "When resources are so fragmented that internal governance mechanisms predictably fail and multiple owners cannot productively manage the resource with respect to the external world, then the ownership fragments are no longer usefully protected as private property"—and it may no longer be appropriate to apply the constitutional protection against "takings" of these fragments.

In other cases, the separate rights might be worth much more grouped together as part of the development of a common unit, though each right still has some value individually. In such cases, a government plan for consolidating rights will necessarily include compensating the individual rights holders. In many cases, that compensation might well consist of an individual ownership share in the future common property. In effect, government's role will be to employ its powers to transform the management of the resource from a decision rule of unanimity to a voting rule of less than unanimity. Whatever the specific institutional mechanism, as Heller observes, there is a long tradition in "the private law of property [that] routinely develops anti-fragmentation mechanisms that prevent, and sometimes abolish, valuable [individual] privately-held interests" for the social purpose of promoting a more valuable coordinated use of the newly combined land and property holdings.[14]

The anticommons issues raised by Heller bear directly on the NASSEN possibility. The circumstance of an older, established neighborhood in current diverse ownership represents an anticommons in Heller's language. In an inner-city area, for example, a given neighborhood may be run down at present, but have a high location value. If the full neighborhood properties could be assembled in one collective unit for joint management, the development value of the consolidated neighborhood properties might greatly exceed the sum of the individual properties in their current uses.

In seeking collective management, it will be essential to devise a fair and reasonable formula of compensation for current users. In a NASSEN, as proposed in this chapter, new individual rights in the resulting common property would be granted, meeting the compensation requirement in this way. The urban renewal programs of the 1950s and 1960s took a less satisfactory approach that failed to provide adequate compensation to affected property owners and this assembly process was soon discredited. Other nations, however, have been more imaginative in this regard and have provided legal mechanisms for pooling land areas and granting new rights in the newly combined properties to the old owners.[15] The United States perhaps should now follow suit.

Related Neighborhood Proposals

Other writers, including Baltimore lawyer George Liebmann, have offered similar proposals to the creation of NASSENs. In 1993, Liebmann advocated a substantial "devolution of power to community and block associations."[16] Such associations, he suggested, could assume a greater role in providing service functions, such as day care, traffic regulation, zoning adjustments, schooling, and law enforcement in neighborhoods. Liebmann proposed that state governments enact new legislation authorizing the formation of community associations in existing neighborhoods. To establish such associations, he recommended that at a minimum of two-thirds of the neighborhood residents in a given neighborhood sign a petition giving their approval.[17] Government review and verification of such petitions would result in mandatory association membership for all residents of such neighborhoods.

According to Liebmann's proposal, new community associations would possess the legal authority to provide many services in the neighborhood. They would have a greater flexibility than municipal zoning allows in administering controls over new land uses. Liebmann suggested that his proposed local associations would have the authority to:

1. Operate or permit the operation of family day care centers.
2. Operate or permit the operation of convenience store or stores, of not more than 1,000 square feet in area, whose signage is not visible from a public road.
3. Permit the creation of accessory apartments where a principal residence continues to be owner-occupied.
4. Cooperatively acquire building materials and services for the benefit of its members.

5. Partially close roads and streets, impose right of way regulations, and enhance safety barriers, except where local government finds that the closure, regulation, or obstruction interferes with a street necessary to through traffic.
6. Petition local government for imposition of a juvenile curfew on association property.
7. Contract with local government to assume responsibility for street paving, trash collection, street lighting, snow removal, and other services.
8. Acquire from local government contiguous or nearby public lands.
9. Petition local government for realignment of election precinct and voting district boundaries to conform to association boundaries.
10. Maintain an unarmed security force and appropriate communications facilities.
11. Issue newsletters, which may contain paid advertising.
12. Operate a credit union, to the extent otherwise permissible under state or federal law.[18]

In Liebmann's view, a neighborhood government with such responsibilities and with a wider flexibility in its administration would promote a happier blend of activities traditionally divided artificially into public and private realms.

In 2001, another proponent of new methods of urban governance, Randal O'Toole, offered a neighborhood privatization plan that he labeled "the American Dream Alternative."[19] O'Toole argued that many recent "smart-growth" proposals in metropolitan areas would not work as expected and might well entail undesirable social consequences. He suggested instead that new property rights institutions would be a better—a truly "smarter"—approach to urban reform.

In older, established neighborhoods, O'Toole proposed substituting an initial endowment of private collective rights in place of the current zoning; in essence, recommending that a newly created neighborhood association—some kind of NASSEN—take over the existing zoning controls. Since the regulatory regime would change little, a vote of 60 percent would be high enough to approve a new neighborhood association in such neighborhoods. Any subsequent tightening of the regulatory regime beyond the existing zoning would then require a neighborhood constitutional amendment—probably ratified by a higher vote of 66 or 75 percent in a typical neighborhood association.

With such a new private governance system in place in an older neighborhood, a normal market process could control entry into the neighborhood. O'Toole offers the following example:

> Suppose a city has a surplus of areas with single-family homes and a shortage of apartments. Developers could approach neighborhood associations and offer to pay money or provide services in exchange for building apartments in the neighborhoods. No doubt the developers would also provide assurance that the apartments

did not reduce property values. Some associations would accept, others would not. In this way, a city could evolve in response to changing conditions on a more voluntary basis than used by current planning and zoning.[20]

O'Toole sees this plan as a way to "completely replace zoning." By turning over land use controls to their private neighborhood association, property owners would be protected from wider municipal "imposition of developments that the neighborhood does not want." Admittedly, existing zoning has protected many neighborhoods well enough. When the time for major land use change has come, however, municipal zoning almost everywhere has lacked the flexibility to accommodate brand-new uses without great stresses and strains. A private neighborhood government, in contrast, would provide for more "orderly neighborhood transitions." When a neighborhood has to make way for a new use, the neighborhood association could sell the development rights and the residents would not feel "that their land had been devalued" by an incompatible use and yet they had received no "compensation," monetary or otherwise.[21]

Finally, O'Toole proposes that a significant part of existing federal and state funds for acquiring land for open spaces could be turned over to his proposed private neighborhood associations. They could make more effective use of these funds for open space, for instance, creating new parks and improving existing parks within neighborhoods. Several neighborhoods might join together to purchase land outside of their own boundaries to form perhaps a regional private park. Such actions might supplement the efforts of current organizations, such as the Nature Conservancy, that seek to protect valuable ecosystems and biodiversity through private land acquisitions.[22]

Conclusion

From its inception almost 90 years ago, zoning has rarely been an effective tool of public planning, and has seldom been successfully used to guide new land development. In contrast, zoning has been very useful in protecting the environmental quality of older, established neighborhoods. In such circumstances, it has functioned like a private property right held collectively by the neighborhood residents. As Gerald Frug observes, in the past few decades, "every level of American government has adopted policies that reduce the amount of public space in metropolitan areas." With great "power and pervasiveness," both the government and the private sector have shown "support for the privatized version of the metropolitan type of individual" who seeks to withdraw "into family life, condominiums, office complexes, and shopping malls, as well as into the cars that allow people to travel in seclusion from one of these private places to another."[23] The demand to sustain the exclusionary powers of small governments in the suburbs has been politically and judicially irresistible, whether in public or (more recently) in private governments. Perhaps the time has come to set the record straight and base future actions explicitly on what the American public has clearly shown it prefers—the privatization of the American suburbs.

The fictional quality of so much of our public policy discussion about zoning has come at a cost. Although public zoning has served constructive purposes in older, established neighborhoods, it has also imposed large and unnecessary costs on American society in newly developing areas. These costs have been widely recognized among leading students of zoning for many years, but their proposals for zoning reform have encountered public and legislative indifference. Responding to the continuing hold of the progressive ambition to publicly plan land use, zoning's leading critics have time and time again proposed that municipal zoning actions should be overseen by higher levels of government. Time and again, however, these proposals for wider metropolitan governance have been rejected in state and local democratic processes throughout the United States.

When Margaret Thatcher sought to reform public housing in the United Kingdom, she did not propose new and better government administration of public housing projects. She proposed instead to give the housing to the people who had long been living in it—and who already "owned" it in practice, if not in the law. This idea was a large shift in thinking at the time, but the formal transfer of housing ownership proved so popular that the Labor Party never seriously challenged it. This chapter's proposal also views zoning at the neighborhood level as a collective, private property right already owned by neighborhood residents. Under a new policy of truth in zoning, zoning advocates would stop pretending that zoning is a form of "public" regulation. Instead, the long-standing private property realities of zoning would be newly ratified in the law.

In the past, zoning too often has been characterized in blanket terms. All zoning is good, or all zoning is bad. That zoning functions in good and bad ways according to the specific circumstances in which it is being applied has been insufficiently recognized. As this chapter proposes, the socially "good" side of zoning—the protection of established neighborhoods' environmental quality—could be made even better through a new, formal recognition created by a law establishing a NASSEN's collective private property rights. Inner-city neighborhoods' resulting ability to gain greater control over their environments in this manner would stimulate additional investment and other improvements in their quality of life. By means of improved property right institutions, the residents of many poor neighborhoods would be able to do more to improve their own lives, rather than having to look to outside agencies for assistance.

The socially "bad" side of zoning—the regulation of undeveloped land on the outer suburban fringes, which serves to ration the availability of metropolitan land in economically wasteful and otherwise irrational ways—might then simply be abolished. In place of the zoning of undeveloped land, new private associations of undeveloped landowners—landowner NASSENs—could assume the responsibility for guiding the land development process and regulating the "micro" interactions among nearby parcels of undeveloped land on the suburban fringe. All the old solutions have failed; there is little to lose in trying new property right approaches that would be radically different in the inner cities and outer suburbs.

NOTES

1. Michael Sarbanes and Kathleen Skullney, "Taking Communities Seriously: Should Community Associations Have Standing in Maryland?" *Maryland Journal of Contemporary Legal Issues* 6 (Spring/Summer 1995), 305.

2. Robert C. Ellickson, "Property in Land," *Yale Law Journal* 102 (April 1993), 1392.

3. Gerald Korngold, "The Emergence of Private Land Use Controls in Large-Scale Subdivisions: The Companion Story to *Village of Euclid v. Ambler Realty Co.*," *Case Western Reserve Law Review* 51 (Summer 2001), 642.

4. Clayton P. Gillette, "Courts, Covenants, and Communities," *University of Chicago Law Review* 61 (Fall 1994), 1401–2.

5. Linda Morrison, "Confessions of a City Budget Cutter," *Philadelphia Daily News,* March 6, 2002. See also Geoffrey F. Segal, ed., *Annual Privatization Report 2004* (Santa Monica, CA: Reason Foundation, 2004); and similar reports from the Reason Foundation in earlier years.

6. Jason Mazzone, "Freedom's Associations," *Washington Law Review* 77 (July 2002), 762.

7. Gary D. Libecap and Steven N. Wiggins, "The Influence of Private Contractual Failure on Regulation: The Case of Oil Field Unitization," *Journal of Political Economy* 93 (August 1985), 701, 706.

8. Kevin L. Patrick and Kelly E. Archer, "A Comparison of State Groundwater Laws," *Tulsa Law Journal* 30 (Fall 1994); and Stephanie E. Hayes Lusk, "Texas Groundwater: Reconciling the Rule of Capture with Environmental and Community Demands," *St. Mary's Law Journal* 30 (1998).

9. Desmond D. Connall Jr., "A History of the Arizona Groundwater Management Act," 1982 *Arizona State Law Journal* 313 (1982).

10. Terry L. Anderson and P. J. Hill, "The Evolution of Property Rights: A Study of the American West," *Journal of Law and Economics* 18 (April 1975).

11. Michael A. Heller, "The Tragedy of the Anticommons: Property in the Transition from Marx to Markets," *Harvard Law Review* 111 (January 1998); and Michael A. Heller, "The Boundaries of Private Property," *Yale Law Journal* 108 (April 1999).

12. Heller, "The Boundaries of Private Property," 1165–66.

13. Angela M. Vallario, "Death by a Thousand Cuts: The Rule Against Perpetuities," *Journal of Legislation* 25 (1999).

14. Ibid., 1217.

15. See William A. Doebele, *Land Readjustment: A Different Approach to Financing Urbanization* (Lexington, MA: Lexington Books, 1982).

16. George W. Liebmann, "Devolution of Power to Community and Block Associations," *The Urban Lawyer* 25 (Spring 1993). See also George W. Liebmann, *The Little Platoons: Sub-Local Governments in Modern History* (Westport, CT: Praeger, 1995).

17. Liebmann, "Devolution of Power to Community and Block Associations," 382–83.

18. Ibid., 381–82.

19. Randal O'Toole, *The Vanishing Automobile and Other Urban Myths: How Smart Growth Will Harm American Cities* (Bandon, OR: The Thoreau Institute, 2001), 486–90.

20. Ibid., 488.

21. Ibid., 489.

22. Ibid.

23. Jerry Frug, "The Geography of Community," *Stanford Law Review* 48 (May 1996), 1076.

13

Landowner Associations for Developing Areas

The architects of the planning and zoning system in the 1920s and 1930s believed that comprehensive land use planning should be undertaken at a full metropolitan or regional scale. They thought it would be difficult for many small municipalities, each planning according to its own needs and each with its own planning staff, to write plans that met the broader housing and other land use needs of their metropolitan area. Yet, planning and zoning turned out to be a local function. Despite the strong advocacy of many urban experts, only a few limited experiments have been carried out in the United States—Portland, Oregon, and Minneapolis are the best known—with wider planning and zoning on a metropolitan scale.[1]

The potentially negative consequences of municipal zoning were recognized early on. Patricia Burgess reports, "Planners pointed to the ramifications of zoning without [wider] planning in 1935. The amount of land zoned for various uses did not match communities' needs" for different uses of land. Zoning in practice was not guiding new development, but was serving to "preserve an outdated status quo." By the 1950s, it was apparent to many observers that "in application . . . zoning often operated without planning and consequently exacerbated the very conditions it had been created to cure."[2]

The problems associated with planning and zoning at the local level are no less today. Cumulatively, too much undeveloped land in metropolitan areas is set aside for high-quality housing. When demand for this use falters, the land sits idle. It may be set aside officially for environmental purposes that may or may not be commensurate with its high land-development value—and that often result instead in the development of some other, more distant, places.

Meanwhile, the needs for lower-and moderate-income housing are redirected to the older housing stock in the inner city and to still more remote fringes of the metropolitan area. Indeed, the exclusionary effects of large-lot and other zoning restrictions have been probably the single greatest cause of excessive suburban sprawl.

Over the past quarter-century, the New York metropolitan area added 5 percent in population while it was expanding by 61 percent in developed land area. According to Richard Briffault, this scenario exemplifies a " 'leapfrog' pattern of development, in which local land use regulation drives households and firms to move to less restrictive outlying areas." In these more distant places, "land prices tend to be lower and 'the political climate, at least initially, is more favorable to development.' "[3] All in all, the system of planning and zoning by many individual municipalities has encouraged inefficient use of metropolitan land, a bias in favor of higher-income purchasers of housing, and a widely dispersed pattern of suburban land development that is environmentally harmful and requires unnecessarily large infrastructure costs to serve.[4]

In 1977, the secretary of housing and urban development organized a task force to address the problem of "sharply escalating housing costs." In its report, the task force noted that a study of seven metropolitan areas found that land costs rose 20 to 30 percent per year between 1970 and 1974. The task force found three "major reasons" for the rapidly rising land costs: (1) "constraints on the supply of developable land" resulting principally from "restrictions on the use of land through zoning and related controls"; (2) "high site development costs" that were often "caused by higher governmental standards and fees"; and (3) "procedural delays" resulting from "the proliferation of governmental regulations affecting land development."[5] The HUD task force found that government regulations, most of them imposed by the suburban local governments in rapidly developing areas, were generating large financial burdens for new purchasers of housing across the United States.

In response to similar diagnoses, many urban students have proposed to substitute wider state and metropolitan authority for the current local planning and zoning responsibility.[6] The HUD task force report, for example, recommended development of federal standards "identifying land-use controls having cost-increasing and exclusionary effects" harmful to metropolitan housing markets.[7] HUD would enforce guidelines for local zoning by withholding federal funds from offending local governments. More recently, the former director for community development in the Clinton White House, Sheryll Cashin, proposed "regional land use planning, regional tax-base sharing, regional affordable housing development, and regional governance" as the best means to "put our nation on a course toward more fairness, opportunity, and . . . civic engagement" in its use of metropolitan land.[8]

However, as noted, such proposals—made by a host of expert study groups and individual commentators over the past 70 years—have only slightly

affected the practice of land use regulation on the ground.[9] Such analyses usually implicitly take as given the premises of the progressive scientific management design for "rational" planning and zoning. Formally, of course, most
Americans also accept these premises, but, just as people often disguise their
true intentions (even to themselves) with "rationalizations," the broader society is capable of a similar behavior—which in the area of land use often takes
the form of the zoning fictions examined in previous chapters. By now, it
should be clear that most Americans have no real intention of giving up the
local land use autonomy typical of the current metropolitan governance system. Despite all the official public rhetoric to the contrary, the democratic
process has spoken—most Americans regard a suburban municipality or other
small local government as similar to a private entity. Zoning has been popular
in the United States, not because it has imposed comprehensive government
controls over wider land use, but because it has protected private property in
established neighborhoods.

Yet, the nation's land use "rationalizations"—for example, treating suburban
local government officially and formally as a "public" body, while in reality it has
been functioning in a "private" capacity—have had their costs. Government's
willful refusal to acknowledge the actual workings of the American zoning system has hindered a sound diagnosis of its problems, and thus made it more difficult to design practical solutions with much chance of success. Thus, few
urban analysts have considered that a better answer to excessively dispersed suburban land patterns and other metropolitan land problems might be found in
an altogether different approach—the creation of new types of private property
rights to metropolitan land in undeveloped areas. Rather than a greater centralization of control over land use, it might be better to empower owners of
undeveloped land to resolve their own problems directly and privately among
themselves.

If state NASSEN legislation (as proposed in chapter 12) were adopted, it
would allow for the creation of private neighborhood associations for existing
farmers and other owners of undeveloped land as well. Such new private associations could help many undeveloped-land owners to plan coordinated land
development over considerably larger areas than normally occurs with individual outer-suburban ownership of undeveloped land. Such legislation would
recognize that wider—and more profitable—planning of urban land in America requires above all a new mechanism of land assembly to put together larger
development units in which "the externalities can be internalized." A NASSEN
of undeveloped-land owners would provide just such an assembly process,
operating privately and subject to voluntary (or at least supermajority) consent
of the directly involved landowners. Within these privately assembled blocks of
land on the outer metropolitan fringes, market incentives would act to ensure
that the land use was planned more carefully and with a more efficient and
equitable result than occurs at present.

The Zoning Politics of Suburban Sprawl

To understand better the political dynamics that have produced existing waste-ful patterns of metropolitan land use in America, and how the NASSEN proposal might work, consider a hypothetical suburban municipality on the fringes of a metropolitan area, a place where the land is now used mainly for farming. Assume that, due to the metropolitan area's overall growth, new housing devel-opment is imminent, land speculators are showing a growing interest, and the price of land is beginning to rise. At some point, the rising land prices will become attractive enough that some of the farmers will decide to sell to housing developers. Their fellow farmers are not likely to employ local zoning to block such development, partly because many of these same farmers will also expect to sell their own land at some point in the future. Hence, the municipality will probably allow the new development, granting the necessary zoning approval for new home projects on, say, one or one-half acre lots. Such rezonings are likely to occur piecemeal as developers propose new subdivisions and as the farmers and the municipality respond to some of the proposals favorably.

At some point, however, as growth proceeds in this fashion, the incoming residents of the recently built housing, living at much higher densities, will outnumber the farmers. At some further point, the newcomers will become organized enough to gain political control within the municipality, including the power to make zoning decisions. At that point, a brand new dynamic in municipal politics will come into play. According to Melvyn Durchslag, "Today's [restrictive] environmental zoning ordinances . . . reflect the desire of those who dominate the political process, resident homeowners."[10] Unlike the original farmers, the newer residents will often be motivated to limit tightly any further housing development—typifying the so-called "doorslammer" phenomenon. In this way, these residents can limit future traffic increases, pre-serve open space, and maintain for their own future enjoyment the community's other environmental amenities. Furthermore, limiting future development sig-nificantly boosts the capital value of the residents' own housing, as reduced supplies of available developable land give it greater scarcity value.

If the courts, such as those in California and many other states, allow the more recent entrants into a municipality to exclude almost any prospective development, and if they are indifferent to the fair treatment of the farmers, then new residents may simply refuse to make almost any further land available for new housing. If many local governments behave in this way, they will effec-tively remove a significant portion of metropolitan land from availability for future housing development.[11] Formally, a municipality may announce that it stands ready to accommodate some especially high-quality (and low-density) housing projects, but in practice the demand for such housing will not be likely to materialize.

The result will be an excess supply of metropolitan land available for high-quality housing projects, and a shortage of land for housing projects designed for ordinary middle-income groups—including municipal civil servants such as teachers and firefighters. This situation is like an agricultural rationing system in which the government might grant allotments of 20 million acres to be planted in turnips, and 3 million acres for potatoes—leaving potatoes in very scarce supply indeed, while most of the turnip acreage goes unused. However, the people who especially like turnips admittedly will be happy; the price of turnips will be very low. Or as William Fischel puts it, "Communities do not have to do anything approximating benefit-cost analysis before imposing land use regulation. This leads to overregulation and residential densities that are too low" over significant parts of the American suburbs.[12]

While the example above was hypothetical, and the typical circumstances in the real world involve many more players and more complex motives, the same basic scenario has been played out many times in outer metropolitan communities across the United States. Timothy Choppin describes the situation:

> The ability of the groups affected by development regulations to influence the political process varies greatly. The interests of current residents [of a developing suburb] are clear and direct, and overcome the costs of concerted action. In contrast, the groups that are likely to oppose the [restrictive suburban] regulation—potential residents and members of the development industry—lack those political advantages. Developers have interests at stake that overcome the costs of concerted action, but their numbers are small and they may have divided loyalties. . . .
>
> Potential [future] residents also have several disadvantages: the high cost of collective action in challenging the regulation, little or no ability to vote in the regulating jurisdiction, limited legal standing for judicial action, and prior legal precedent that generally supports a municipality's authority to enact such regulations.
>
> Furthermore, political forces cannot effectively promote action on the state level to break these barriers. First, the diffuse nature of the interests that might support a loosening of the housing market makes political action unlikely. Moreover, prospective homeowners have not identified the land development regulations as the cause of the problem of affordability, a necessary step to forming a political coalition on the state level. Prospective residents have no political influence over the exclusionary practices of a municipality.[13]

The American zoning system in developing areas thus works mainly to the benefit of better-off Americans and to the detriment of lower- and moderate-income Americans—a main reason, no doubt, why it has been so difficult politically to change. As two zoning authorities commented recently, municipal practices in the zoning of undeveloped land across the United States have created "a massive wealth transfer . . . to homeowners" who arrive early in newly developing areas and who tend to come mostly from the higher-income categories.[14] Other existing homeowners closer to the center of the city also benefit, as metropolitan housing prices in general rise to reflect overall supply and demand conditions.

Loudoun County, Virginia

Loudoun County, a northern Virginia suburb of Washington, D.C., is a recent example of such political dynamics. Loudoun County's population grew from 86,129 in 1990 to 169,599 in 2000, making it one of the fastest-growing counties in the United States. New residents purchasing new homes were mostly upper-middle class; the average household income rose from $72,433 in 1990 to $97,987 in 2000. The average housing unit in 2000 sold for more than $250,000—and single-family homes in 2000 averaged $346,205. Most of the new development occurred in eastern Loudoun County, the area closest to Washington, D.C., and therefore most convenient for commuters.[15]

By 2001, many Loudoun County residents concluded that further growth would add to traffic, raise tax burdens, and in other ways threaten the amenities that had attracted them to the area in the first place. A new board of supervisors voted to impose tight restrictions on development in the remaining western parts of the county, an area covering fully two-thirds of the county's total area. All of this land was to be set aside as a new "rural preservation zone" in which housing development would be limited to one home per 20 acres (and in some areas as little as one home per 50 acres). In the eastern parts of the county, where large numbers of newcomers had located during the 1990s, zoning typically had allowed up to four homes per acre.

Not surprisingly, many developers, farmers, and other owners of existing undeveloped land in the new rural zones objected strenuously. They complained that the board of supervisors was adopting "snob zoning"; "This is America, the land of opportunity," they protested; "anybody who wants to buy a home should be able to buy a home."[16] The *Washington Post* elaborated:

> The debate . . . has proved to be a volatile blend of hypocrisy, idealism, political sales-manship and, at times, pure nastiness. It's not just the vitriol at county meetings, where real estate interests are denounced as landscape rapists and environmentalists cast as frog-kissing Stalinists. "It's like the Civil War," said Middleburg real estate broker John Weidlein. "It's brother against brother, Loudouner against Loudouner."[17]

Loudoun is not the only local government in the Washington, D.C., metropolitan region that employs tightly restrictive strategies of land use control.* Prince William County, also in northern Virginia, set aside a "rural crescent" of

---

*Developers, however, were not without resources and poured large funds into the 2003 Loudoun County election campaign for the county council. A slate of council members more favorable to development was elected. In Virginia, it was possible to make an ideological appeal to the defense of private property rights, and there is a deeper tradition of skepticism with respect to government regulation, as compared with many other parts of the country. Other special local factors also played a role. As of this writing, it is not clear how far the new Loudoun County council will go in reversing the previously approved land use restrictions.

80,000 acres. On the Maryland side of the Potomac River, Montgomery County placed 90,000 acres in an agricultural reserve. For these three counties alone, more than 500 square miles of land—enough to house at least 600,000 people at normal suburban densities—was removed from the total available supply of land for new development. Following a 2003 *Washington Post* survey of 14 counties in the greater Washington metropolitan region, the investigators found that fully half of the developable land in these counties—3,300 square miles out of 6,000 square miles in the region—was set aside for minimum lot sizes of three acres or higher per home. As a result, as the *Post* reported, "land consumption is outpacing population growth" by factors of two or three.[18]

Tight limits on available land supplies throughout the Washington metropolitan area do not mean that the flow of new jobs and population into the region has ceased. So as the Washington region continues to grow rapidly, new development is being redirected in many cases to still more distant areas, such as West Virginia and Pennsylvania. This growth is also contributing to the gentrification of older neighborhoods in Washington, D.C. The *Post* found that "while the limits on rural building are supposed to be saving farmland, forests and meadows, a regional view of development patterns indicates that many of these anti-sprawl measures have accelerated the consumption of woods and fields and pushed developers outward in their search for home sites." Indeed, the net result is to "extend sprawl" still further and at a more rapid pace, "creating enclaves of [large lot] estates in 'rural' preserves"—what some critics now label as "Gucci sprawl."[19]

Local restrictions in the Washington metropolitan area have helped to "push real estate prices out of the reach of many," further aggravating the "well-documented housing shortage in the region."[20] Such restrictions have also produced additional traffic throughout the region as workers must live in more remote locations and then drive long distances to get to their jobs closer to Washington. Indeed, the Washington area now has some of the highest housing prices in the nation and some of the worst traffic. According to one 2001 study of comparable housing across the United States, a home costing $190,000 in Charlotte, North Carolina, or $260,000 in Atlanta, Georgia, would cost $331,000 in Montgomery County, Maryland.[21] Prices in the Washington region have risen most rapidly in the past decade, reflecting the impact of many years of increasingly restrictive land use controls throughout the region in combination with the absence of new roads and other infrastructure that could open up more new areas for housing development.

The Message of Mt. Laurel

When the American judicial system changes the basic constitutional rules of the game, it may be because a "political failure" necessitates a strong judicial response. Racial segregation in the South, for example, would not have lasted long if blacks had been free to vote, but without voting rights they could not change the system democratically. Judicial intervention in the 1960s to correct the malapportionment of many state legislative bodies in the United States involved a similar political catch-22. The legislatures badly needed to be reapportioned, but the malapportionment itself prevented the corrective actions necessary to a more legitimate democratic process.

Do the current suburban abuses of zoning authority represent a similar political failure? If they could get in, the potential residents of a newly developing municipality on the outer suburban fringe would benefit from access to greater housing opportunities there. However, residence outside the municipality's boundaries prevents such individuals from voting and thereby gaining access to the community. If they could somehow move into the municipality, they would no doubt strongly support actions making land available for their own occupancy. Of course, this is now impossible—the catch-22 of municipal land use politics—and large numbers of prospective residents continue to be excluded by current zoning policies.

There might thus be a strong case here for judicial intervention. An activist judicial posture, however, is not without its own potential pitfalls. If a judicial land use solution were now sought in the nation's developing outer suburbs, the courts could risk ending up as the effective planners and zoners of last resort for a large amount of land in metropolitan America—probably an impossible burden on the legal system. Perhaps for this reason, very few state courts have attempted to frontally challenge zoning abuses in newly developing areas. The best-known effort involved two New Jersey Supreme Court decisions in 1975 and 1983 pertaining to the township of Mt. Laurel, a rapidly developing community in the southern part of the state and an outer suburb of Philadelphia.[22] As matters turned out, the results were not encouraging for other state judicial systems.

Seeking to insulate itself from further growth pressures, and like many other American municipalities in similar circumstances, Mt. Laurel provided almost no land for multifamily housing and zoned much of its acreage for continued agricultural use. Recognizing that Mt. Laurel was not alone in its restrictive policies, the New Jersey court sought to fashion a statewide solution that would expand the availability of land for lower- and middle-income housing. Indeed, it required Mr. Laurel—along with other developing suburban municipalities throughout New Jersey—to make land newly available for lower-and moderate-income housing. Jurisdictional compliance with the court requirements was to be verified by a statewide system for allocating fair shares of such housing among growing communities.

The New Jersey Supreme Court's efforts encountered fierce resistance from virtually the entire political establishment in the state. The governor and the state legislature both worked actively to undermine the court. In the end, the Mt. Laurel rulings had little impact, failing to make available any significant amounts of "more affordable housing for the poor" or in "ameliorating the racial residential segregation in New Jersey."[23] Even in a judicial system sometimes accused of having "imperial" tendencies, the burden to plan and zone the future of metropolitan land use may be a larger responsibility than American courts can handle. Admittedly, federal courts were once able to overcome wholesale southern white defiance of mandated racial integration; however, much less consensus exists today in the broader society as to the need for opening up the suburbs. It is unlikely that federal troops, once called upon to overcome recalcitrant southern leadership in Little Rock, Arkansas, would be used for this purpose.

Nonjudicial Options

Given the absence of an effective judicial response, other commentators have optimistically proposed that state governments—possessing a broader perspective than local governments and greater administrative resources than the courts—should curb the political abuses associated with suburban regulation of undeveloped land.[24] One such advocate, Henry Richmond, finds that the "broad, judicially unreviewable and politically unaccountable grants of zoning authority" to local governments have been harmful to statewide interests.[25] A few efforts to establish wider state oversight have in fact been made. A "snob zoning law" in Massachusetts authorizes a state body to override local zoning in certain circumstances where such zoning is preventing needed housing. However, the Massachusetts law has had limited effect.[26] Most other states have not even tried to address the problem. The beneficiaries of current zoning practices are politically powerful and well connected at the state level; those suffering as a result of suburban restrictions are more likely to be diffused and poorly organized. Many have little technical understanding of the dynamics of metropolitan land and housing markets and the consequences for themselves. Indeed, states such as Oregon and Vermont that have assumed greater statewide responsibility for land use controls have been more likely to tighten existing land use restrictions than to open wider areas for housing development.*

---

*Where state oversight of local land use has actually increased significantly, the leading justification for the greater state role has been the need for stronger environmental protections—not the need to open up the suburbs to provide more housing for the less privileged. See, for example, Fred Bosselman and David Callies, *The Quiet Revolution in Land Use Control,* prepared for the U.S. Council on Environmental Quality (Washington, DC: Government Printing Office, 1971).

As discussed in chapter 7, some leading "zoning heretics" have proposed allowing municipalities in developing areas of the outer suburbs to sell their zoning. If put into practice, this strategy would very likely be effective in opening up more land for middle-income housing. Offered enough money, most municipalities would probably be willing to sell a considerable portion of their development rights (change the zoning), thereby granting entry to a wider variety of housing. The process of land development would be newly driven by a market process of supply and demand. On the supply side, municipalities would offer development rights for sale; on the demand side, private builders would bid against one another to purchase these development rights from municipalities. There might even be a formal auction in some municipalities. Some outer suburban municipalities might end up with so much revenue from the sale of land development rights that they could significantly reduce their local property taxes.

The main problem with this strategy is not economic; it is legal (and some would say ethical). In allowing municipalities to sell changes in zoning (upfront sales of zoning, rather than the customary very high "municipal exaction fees" or other current disguised forms of zoning sale), the courts would have to approve a radical legal reconception of zoning—and indeed of local government as a whole, casting it explicitly in a newly private role. However, as discussed in chapter 8, the Supreme Court in its *Nollan* (1987) and *Dolan* (1994) decisions went in the opposite direction. Applied broadly, the Court's reasoning might limit or even prevent altogether many of the informal zoning transactions that now already occur on such a widespread basis.

Neighborhood Associations of Farmers

One promising strategy for addressing the problem of local zoning in developing suburban areas has not been explored thus far. It would provide for the creation of private neighborhood associations of farmers and other owners of undeveloped land, thus giving control over the development process to "farmer NASSENs." Most new development in outer suburban areas is already taking place in private neighborhood associations. However, these neighborhood associations are created by land developers who usually must assemble the necessary land parcels by buying them individually from farmers and other owners of undeveloped land.

As proposed here, the novel element would be that the farmers and other original landowners themselves would organize their own neighborhood association in advance of land development. With a superior method of land assembly, the resulting blocks of consolidated land might also often be somewhat larger than current development projects. To see how this proposal might open up more land for development, consider the same hypothetical municipality (described earlier) on the developing fringe of a metropolitan area. The critical difference would now be that, instead of a suburban municipality regulating land use, the farmers who own the undeveloped land would have formed a private neighborhood association—perhaps coinciding with the municipal boundaries—to hold and manage their land development rights collectively. Since zoning would now be superfluous in the presence of a private system of regulation, the municipality would give up its zoning authority within this area (or at least take a permissive view of new development).

Consider now the normal operating procedure for land developers who have assembled a large tract of land and are building a new housing project as a private neighborhood association. The collective management of the neighborhood properties will ultimately be turned over to the incoming unit owners. In the process of developing a large private project, however, it is generally understood that a potential conflict of interest exists between the land developer and the incoming purchasers of housing units. It is accepted throughout the real estate industry, and by government overseers, that the land developer needs protection from the unit owners' premature political takeover of project management.

Thus, almost universally, the constitutional rules for voting in new neighborhood associations (as written by the developer) provide that the developer will retain the voting control until the later stages of project completion—typically until 75 percent of the neighborhood units have been sold and occupied. As Amanda Hyatt comments, the rules of neighborhood associations generally provide for "an extended *process of transition,* during which the [incoming new] owners are gradually involved in the association's operations and decisions."[27] Model language for a neighborhood association constitution, as suggested by one attorney in the field, would include a developer's "reasonable right to develop," and explicitly state: "No [subsequent] rule by the association or executive board shall unreasonably impede the declarant's right to develop in accordance with the plat and this declaration."[28]

In the interim, the developer may shift control over certain day-to-day elements of neighborhood management to the unit owners. However, the developer retains voting control over the full plan for land use in the project. Hence, if the farmers/landowners in the hypothetical example above establish a standard set of private arrangements for a neighborhood association, then they would have transitional voting rules to protect themselves from a premature political takeover by newly arriving residents.

Seen in this light, the problem with municipal zoning in the outer suburbs rests in the transitional voting rules of current public municipalities in these areas. Automatic full enfranchisement of recently arrived homeowners leads to the cancellation of existing land development plans and then to systematic misallocation in the use of local land. If such voting rules could be modified to prevent incoming residents from assuming premature political control—say by preventing the new residents from changing the zoning until the development of the public municipality is at least 75 percent complete—then the current zoning problem in these areas would be much reduced. However, given past Supreme Court rulings requiring a democratic process of one person/one vote, this practical solution is at present legally precluded.

If the farmers join together in a neighborhood association to manage all their lands collectively, however, there would not be any current legal barrier to such a private voting rule. Instead, the original unit owners in the NASSEN (the farmers and other owners of undeveloped land) would collectively act like a single developer in the normal process of building a housing project.* The farmer NASSEN would retain voting control over new uses of undeveloped land until the plan for development was nearing 75 percent completion (or some other appropriate threshold). In short, unlike the current system of municipal zoning, the incoming purchasers of housing in the private neighborhood association would not be able to exercise a growing political muscle to unreasonably restrict new land development. They could not declare a sudden new aesthetic appreciation for open space or agricultural land preservation and then employ local regulatory powers to satisfy this new taste for vacant land at no cost to themselves.

Remember that a local government would still be present and still possess zoning powers that could be employed to block the farmers' development plans for their NASSEN. However, such local government interference with a private contractual agreement, previously accepted by all the incoming residents of a neighborhood association, would be legally more vulnerable than current municipal zoning actions. The recent arrivals in the locality would have to explain to a court why they now proposed to change the basic property right structure for their development project, an assignment of rights to which they had recently agreed formally in writing.

---

*During the stages of neighborhood development, as particular parcels of undeveloped land are sold off, there would be a variety of possible ways of sharing among land owner/members of the NASSEN. One option would assign the full sale price of a land parcel to the original party who had contributed that parcel to the neighborhood assemblage of land rights. The neighborhood association in this case would have only a planning and oversight role in the process of land sales, preparing some form of land development plan and setting certain guidelines before a parcel could be sold.

At the opposite end of the spectrum, and probably more feasible, all the contributing farmers and other owners of undeveloped land might pool all their holdings to be managed and sold as a single unit by their common association. Each participating owner of undeveloped land in the NASSEN would receive an appropriate ownership share (like a share of stock in a corporation) in the combined holdings, based on his or her initial contribution of land. The NASSEN would then distribute any land sale revenues as they accrued, not according to the original owner of the particular parcel being sold, but according to the relative ownership interests of each shareholder in the neighborhood association.

NASSENs versus Large Local Governments

In a smaller political jurisdiction, typical of many suburbs in the Northeast and Midwest, a NASSEN of farmers might coincide closely with the existing boundaries of a local suburban government. The farmers would have to be sure to establish their neighborhood association before any significant housing development commenced. Initially, they would control the local political process and thus could create such a private neighborhood association before many potential "doorslammers" had arrived.

However, for very large jurisdictions like Loudoun County, the farmers might already have lost political control in their own area. Loudoun County, for example, would probably refuse to accept the creation of any new NASSENs to control the land development process in currently undeveloped areas. If Loudoun County had already zoned the land for agricultural use, the best a NASSEN could do would be to give the farmers a more effective political instrument for expressing their collective demands to the county government.

Thus, in some large suburban jurisdictions like Loudoun County, a zoning reform strategy based on the creation of NASSENs would still require the intervention of some outside body—either a state agency or a court. This body would have to require the county or other large local jurisdiction to authorize a NASSEN, even when the local government might be opposed to it.* Loudoun County's zoning authority would be limited to neighborhoods that were already more densely developed—and zoning might also be superfluous there because of the presence of still other private neighborhood associations with the power to control internal land use.†

If a local government sought to block the formation of a NASSEN composed of the owners of undeveloped land, then the courts might declare this

---

*For the larger neighborhood associations—say those of more than 500 housing units—the process of approving the building of a new neighborhood project might be transferred altogether to the state level of government, reflecting a significant statewide interest in such a large project. In the 1970s, the American Law Institute (ALI) proposed that state governments assume a wider role in the regulation of land use. Municipalities should continue to have the primary role, as the ALI proposed, but states should assume greater responsibilities for "areas of critical concern" (often with environmental assets) and for individual housing and other "projects of regional impact." See American Law Institute, *A Model Land Development Code* (Philadelphia, PA: American Law Institute, 1976).

†A less radical reform with much the same purpose would be to revise state laws of municipal incorporation. The state might set new standards for incorporating a municipality without the approval of the wider local government. If the standards were met, for example, a local government such as Loudoun County would have no authority to block the municipal incorporation. A "right of local municipal incorporation" would offer many of the same social and economic benefits as a new "right to form a neighborhood association," including private neighborhoods' legal ability to substitute their own land use regulations for public zoning.

action to be an unconstitutional taking of private property. Courts have been reluctant to take such bold action to limit local regulation in the past, partly because they feared the consequences if suburban land were developed one small parcel at a time. In a NASSEN, however, the microlevel interactions among nearby individual properties would be encompassed within its wider boundaries, providing close and privately based land coordination across the whole neighborhood area.

A Boost to Planning

This proposal, if adopted, might significantly increase the total amount of land use planning in the outer suburbs. However, such planning would occur as private planning by land developers for new neighborhood associations. The privately prepared plans would comprehensively account for the small-scale interdependencies among all the properties within the neighborhood association boundaries, acting to maximize the total value of all NASSEN land. If some land parcel were designated for a park or for tennis courts as part of the profit calculations of a private developer, the one farmer-owner of that parcel would still have an ownership share in the wider association, and would benefit equally with other unit owners from a plan to maximize the total value of all association land.

The authorization by state legislatures of farmer NASSENs, as proposed in this chapter, would offer a new means for assembling many separate land parcels under one collective ownership. A NASSEN would need a large supermajority, but would not require complete unanimity among its owners of undeveloped land, thus reducing the transactions costs of land assembly. A developer who reached an agreement with a NASSEN of farmers would be able to implement a full, neighborhood land use design according to his or her integrated vision of a desirable landscape.

Where land has already been assembled under existing procedures, and where it has been possible to obtain regulatory approval, private planners are increasingly offering bolder neighborhood designs.* One private planner of

---

*Attempting to distinguish their new neighborhoods from competing projects on the market, developers are increasingly planning their projects to offer a "vision" or "theme." This is now being seen in newly developing areas of northern Virginia, as reported by the *Washington Post:*

> To harmonize with the traditional masonry architecture of . . . Roseland Estates, . . . [the private development planner] fashioned a brick entrance monument with a pavilion, plus brick piers and wooden fencing. The designs, he said, are based on historic structures at Colonial Williamsburg and Mount Vernon.

new neighborhood projects comments, "We think about space in the same way that a movie is made." The architectural concepts of the "new urbanism" are making their way into the building of more private neighborhoods. As reported in the *Washington Post,* one sees increasingly that "architectural treatments of newer subdivisions are influenced by the popularity of denser, pedestrian-oriented neotraditional developments such as Kentlands and Fallsgrove in Montgomery County [Maryland]."[29] With state legislation to authorize NASSENs, such forms of comprehensive neighborhood development would be easier to achieve. However, no specific design for a neighborhood would be mandated as a matter of law (as may occur under zoning); each neighborhood design would either pass or fail the practical test of the marketplace.

Land Market Efficiency

If developers have much greater opportunity to plan larger projects to sell in the market, then the types and prices of housing available in the suburbs will expand significantly. Some developers will build neighborhoods of mansions on five-acre lots for the very rich, while others will build modest homes on quarter-acre lots for the lower middle class. As one commentator has observed, because a private developer is "economically motivated," he will act to ensure that the value of the neighborhood land is maximized by building at a suitable intensity of use, thus avoiding the "problems of suburban isolationism."[30]

"We're seeing more correlation between the style of the entrance monument and the homes in newer developments . . . They now hang together as a cohesive unit." [Neighborhood planner Mark] Leahy said this coordinated image helps to distinguish adjacent, competing developments from one another and attract buyers.

The image [in yet another private development] is "agrarian" and meant to differentiate the development from an adjacent subdivision "where the styles of architecture are much more disparate," he said.

In other communities, signs and landscaping play up the natural features that are already part of the site. At the entrance to River Creek, a 615-acre golf course community of 700 homes outside Leesburg [Virginia], a waterfall spills over artificial boulders into a creek. The theatrical design was created . . . to recall the stone bluffs of the Potomac River, which borders the development. It is part of a package meant to create the impression that you're in nature, not a subdivision, according to Silver Spring developer Marc Montgomery.

Open spaces—golf courses, parks, and village greens—play a critical role in establishing a theme [in many new neighborhoods]. "Fifteen years ago, we would have hidden parks from view off cul-de-sacs. Now we integrate them into the entrances, road system and community so residents can enjoy them." For Brambleton, a 2,000-acre new town in Loudoun County, [the planner Peter] Crowley designed a quarter-mile long park that leads from a waterfall at the entrance to the town center. See Deborah K. Dietsch, "Staging a Grand Entrance: More Developers Are Building Elaborate Gateways, Adding Other Landscape Features, to Lure Buyers," *Washington Post,* March 8, 2003, F1.

The efficiency and other benefits of a free-market system are widely under-stood for most types of private goods and services. It is less well understood that within a suitable framework of property rights, a market system can provide similar benefits in the development of metropolitan land.[31] For example, land that has a particularly desirable location—for example, near a newly opened sub-way stop—will command an usually high price. Only a developer who plans to build high-density housing will be able to pay this price. The result will be eco-nomically efficient—a higher density of development at a particularly desirable location for housing. Left to the workings of the private market, and without zoning restrictions to artificially support their choice, those who want to live on a spacious lot with an acre or two of land will find it too expensive unless they are prepared to move far from the city (or are exceptionally rich).[32]

To be sure, land speculators sometimes hold undeveloped land in hopes of selling for higher prices in future years. Contrary to much popular opinion, private speculation of this kind can serve an important economic purpose by promoting the proper timing of land development. Land speculation might be described as "private conservation" that prevents a land resource from being developed prematurely in a lower-value use. It would be economically waste-ful, for instance, to develop a well-located lot today with a single-family home when this lot will be more economically suitable for an apartment building in a few years. A land speculator, buying the land and holding it for its maximum future value, prevents that from happening.

The strong negative connotations of "suburban sprawl" reflect a lack of public understanding of the land-development process.[33] Efficient land devel-opment will inevitably involve significant "leapfrogging" of one kind of devel-opment past another. In maximizing the total value of all metropolitan land, it will always be efficient to retain significant areas of vacant land inside existing areas of development. There is a social problem only when there is too much leapfrogging, or too much vacant land being kept out of development. In the past, the leading explanation for too much vacant land has been misguided regulation of local land use.

However, defining precisely how much is "too much" is difficult in practice. Indeed, this question is central to any future design for areawide metropolitan land use. The old land use plans from the 1930s to the 1960s typically assigned a specific use to every parcel of land in a political jurisdiction. They did not set aside temporary holding zones—agricultural or otherwise—and in general ignored almost entirely the critical questions of the precise future timing of land uses. The failure of so many past public planners to adequately account for the dynamic factors in metropolitan land development is one reason their formal land use plans were so widely ignored.

Even if a more sophisticated economic understanding of metropolitan land markets now emerges, there is little likelihood that the required technical plan-ning calculations can be made.[34] Indeed, central planning calculations for metropolitan land would be almost as complicated and as difficult to make as the central planning calculations for a full national economy. To be meaningful, a metropolitan land use plan must be not only a plan for land, but also a comprehensive economic development plan for the metropolitan area. However, some U.S. cities boast economies as large as (or larger than) entire nations in other parts of the world. The past failures of national economic planning do not bode well for the future central planning of metropolitan land use. In the end, comprehensive planning at a full metropolitan scale is not really an option in a free society like the United States.[35]

Zoning is politically popular because it can successfully block new land development in established neighborhoods, but almost nowhere has zoning been successful in positively coordinating development in new areas. In the end, metropolitan land development has been in the past and will continue to be driven by private market pressures. If necessary, and if otherwise frustrated in seeking access to land, developers will even eventually find ways to "buy" zoning in order to make things happen. Zoning thus may have an impact on the land development process, but mainly in haphazardly permitting some development here and denying it there, and generally raising costs.

Still, in the longer run, supply and demand will drive the metropolitan land result. No one can have imagined that tight restrictive zoning might somehow have blocked the development of Manhattan for two centuries. However, land use regulations can have a significant impact on the transitional burdens of getting from here to there. Indeed, the unnecessary costs of land adjustment are no small matter; as the "new institutional economics" of recent years has emphasized (see the writings of Ronald Coase, Oliver Williamson, and others in this economic school), a basic comparison of alternative economic systems must focus on the relative magnitudes of transaction costs.[36] Many economic systems will eventually arrive at a given final equilibrium state, but some will take much longer and face much greater social stresses and strains.

As Coase also suggested, it is possible to reduce transaction costs and to generally improve the transitional workings of a private market with a better institutional framework of property rights.[37] State legislation providing for the creation of NASSENs, available to landowners in outer developing suburban areas, holds the promise of such an institutional improvement.[38]

Conclusion

The problems of zoning restrictions in newly developing areas of the outer suburbs have thus far proven intractable for the American political system. While the solutions will not be easy under any circumstances, the problem's basic nature thus far has not been widely understood. Undue zoning restrictions result from the assignment of voting rights in America's local governments.

Recent newcomers in the outer suburbs are permitted to vote to alter long-standing development plans for their benefit, even as the resulting cancellation of existing plans (or development intentions) imposes large burdens on landowners, developers, and the rest of society.

Current voting rules in municipalities can be compared with a business corporation operating under a voting rule of one shareowner/one vote. In such a corporation, 51 percent of the individuals holding any shares of stock at all would be able to control the corporation. In theory, a 51 percent majority might consist of a group of owners holding a single share apiece. A "tyranny of the corporate majority" of small stockholders could even vote for corporate policies to transfer the business assets to themselves for their own benefit. The minority of individual owners of large numbers of shares would in effect be required to subsidize the more numerous small shareholders who would possess voting control of the corporation.

Obviously, no American business corporation would ever think of operating in such a fashion. However, small property owners in local suburban governments—also overseeing business-like functions of land development—have been encouraged to engage in similarly promiscuous transfers of local land and other property assets to themselves. When the small landowners become numerous enough, they can simply vote to appropriate the land development rights of the large landowners in the locality through new land use regulations. The owners of the much larger and more valuable parcels of land can thus be required under the political rules of U.S. local governments to subsidize the many owners of small amounts of land.

In the long run, local government, as suggested in part III, might better have a private legal status. Indeed, the rise of private neighborhood associations across the United States in recent decades has been showing the way. If the legal option were now made available, the establishment of private NASSENs would extend the instruments of private government to groups of farmers and other owners of undeveloped land in outer suburban areas. Such an option would facilitate comprehensive land use planning, increase land market efficiency, improve the environment, and promote greater social equity in the use of metropolitan land across the United States. It would be a "win-win" situation all around—except for a limited number of current suburban residents who would lose their present ability to confiscate the nearby development rights.

The small local governments in the suburbs have in effect been empowered to act with the autonomy of a private body under American law. They have not been held significantly accountable to any higher political authority. Yet, the world is too interdependent and complex to permit the creation of new "semi-feudal" enclaves that are free to act from local motives alone. The original architects of planning and zoning who wanted regional authority were correct. However, they simply assumed that the higher coordination had to be governmental and political. The alternative is to subject the local suburban government to the discipline of the market. The land market is capable of providing the necessary regional coordination of land uses—in fact, the workings of supply and demand may provide more effective and efficient coordination than any group of metropolitan planners or politicians could. In order to put the small suburban government in the market, it will be necessary to assign it a private status and allow it to legally operate like a private actor in the market and in American life. That may be the only truly acceptable path to real decentralization of neighborhood governing authority in the United States.

NOTES

1. See Anthony Downs, *Opening Up the Suburbs: An Urban Strategy for America* (New Haven, CT: Yale University Press, 1973); Anthony Downs, *New Visions for Metropolitan America* (Washington, DC: The Brookings Institution and the Lincoln Institute of Land Policy, 1994); and Frank J. Popper, *The Politics of Land-Use Reform* (Madison: University of Wisconsin Press, 1981).

2. Patricia Burgess, *Planning for the Private Interest: Land Use Controls and Residential Patterns in Columbus, Ohio, 1900–1970* (Columbus: Ohio State University Press, 1994), 100–101.

3. Richard Briffault, "The Local Government Boundary Problem in Metropolitan Areas," *Stanford Law Review* 48 (May 1996), 1135.

4. See Marion Clawson, *Suburban Land Conversion in the United States: An Economic and Governmental Process* (Baltimore, MD: Johns Hopkins Press for Resources for the Future, 1971); also Charles M. Haar, "A Federal Role in Metropolitanism," in Lowdon Wingo, ed., *Reform of Metropolitan Governments* (Washington, DC: Resources for the Future, 1972).

5. William J. White, chairman, U.S. Department of Housing and Urban Development, *Final Report of the Task Force on Housing Costs,* (Washington, DC: U.S. Department of Housing and Urban Development, May 1978), 13.

6. John W. Reps, "Public Land, Urban Development Policy, and the American Planning Tradition," in Marion Clawson, ed., *Modernizing Urban Land Policy* (Baltimore, MD: Johns Hopkins University Press for Resources for the Future, 1973); William K. Reilly, ed., *The Use of Land: A Citizen's Policy Guide to Urban Growth,* A Task Force Report Sponsored by the Rockefeller Brothers Fund (New York: Thomas Y. Crowell, 1973); and American Law Institute, *A Model Land Development Code* (Philadelphia, PA: American Law Institute, 1976). See also Katharine L. Bradbury, Anthony Downs, and Kenneth A. Small, *Urban Decline and the Future of American Cities* (Washington, DC: The Brookings Institution, 1982).

7. HUD, *Final Report of the Task Force on Housing Costs,* 20.

8. Sheryll D. Cashin, "Privatized Communities and the 'Secession of the Successful': Democracy and Fairness Beyond the Gate," *Fordham Urban Law Journal* 28 (June 2001), 1691–92.

9. John Kincaid, "Regulatory Regionalism in Metropolitan Areas: Voter Resistance and Reform Persistence," *Pace Law Review* 13 (Fall 1993).

10. Melvyn R. Durchslag, "*Village of Euclid v. Ambler Realty Co.,* Seventy-Five Years Later: This Is Not Your Father's Zoning Ordinance," *Case Western Reserve Law Review* 51 (Summer 2001), 647.

11. Sidney Plotkin, *Keep Out: The Struggle for Land Use Control* (Berkeley: University of California Press, 1987).

12. William A. Fischel, *The Economics of Zoning Laws: A Property Rights Approach to American Land Use Controls* (Baltimore, MD: Johns Hopkins University Press, 1985), 65.

13. Timothy J. Choppin, "Breaking the Exclusionary Land Use Regulation Barrier: Policies to Promote Affordable Housing in the Suburbs," *Georgetown Law Journal* 82 (July 1994), 2056.

14. Michael M. Berger and Gideon Kanner, "The Need for Takings Law Reform: A View from the Trenches—A Response to Taking Stock of the Takings Debate," *Santa Clara Law Review* 38, no. 3 (1998), 878.

15. See Michael Laris and Peter Whoriskey, "Loudoun's Ambitious Search for Perfection," *Washington Post,* July 22, 2001, A1; and Peter Whoriskey and Michael Laris, "Loudoun, Farming Serves as a Potent Symbol," *Washington Post,* July 23, 2001, A1.

16. Laris and Whoriskey, "Loudoun's Ambitious Search for Perfection," A15.

17. Ibid., A14.

18. Peter Whoriskey, "Density Limits Only Add to Sprawl: Large Lots Eat Up Area Countryside," *Washington Post,* March 9, 2003. See also a three-part front-page series in the *Washington Post* on August 8, 9, and 10, 2004—Peter Whoriskey, "Space for Employers, Not for Homes"; Peter Whoriskey, "Washington's Road to Outward Growth"; and Peter Whoriskey, "Planners' Brains vs. Public's Brawn." See also National Center for Smart Growth Research and Education, University of Maryland, *Smart Growth, Housing Markets, and Development Trends in the Baltimore-Washington Corridor* (November 2003).

19. Whoriskey, "Density Limits Only Add to Sprawl."

20. Ibid.

21. The data were provided by the Coldwell Banker real estate company for a prototypical home of 2,200 square feet. See "Check Out How Home Prices across USA Compare," *USA Today,* July 30, 2001, 6B.

22. *Southern Burlington County NAACP v. Township of Mt. Laurel,* 336 A.2d 713 (N.J. 1975); and *Southern Burlington County NAACP v. Township of Mt. Laurel,* 456 A.2d 390 (N.J. 1983). See David L. Kirp, John P. Dwyer, and Larry A. Rosenthal, *Our Town: Race, Housing and the Soul of Suburbia* (New Brunswick, NJ: Rutgers University Press, 1995).

23. Bernard K. Ham, "Exclusionary Zoning and Racial Segregation: A Reconsideration of the Mount. Laurel Doctrine," *Seton Hall Constitutional Law Journal* 7 (Winter 1997), 580–81.

24. Reilly, ed., *The Use of Land;* American Law Institute, *A Model Land Development Code;* John M. DeGrove, *Planning and Growth Management in the States: The New Frontier for Land Policy* (Cambridge, MA: Lincoln Institute of Land Policy, 1992); Downs, *New Visions for Metropolitan America,* Ch. 9; and Douglas R. Porter, *Managing Growth in America's Communities* (Washington, DC: Island Press, 1997).

25. Henry R. Richmond, "Sprawl and Its Enemies: Why the Enemies Are Losing," *Connecticut Law Review* 34 (Winter 2002), 554.

26. Paul K. Stockman, "Anti-Snob Zoning in Massachusetts: Assessing One Attempt at Opening the Suburbs to Affordable Housing," *Virginia Law Review* 78 (March 1992).

27. Amanda G. Hyatt, *Transition from Developer Control,* 2nd ed. (Alexandria, VA: Community Associations Institute, 1996), 5.

28. Model neighborhood association declaration presented by Donald E. Dykeman to the Governance Symposium on "Creating a Governance Model That Really Works," sponsored by the Community Associations Institute Research Foundation, Arlington, VA, October 31, 2003.

29. Deborah K. Dietsch, "Staging a Grand Entrance: More Developers Are Building Elaborate Gateways, Adding Other Landscape Features, to Lure Buyers," *Washington Post,* March 8, 2003, F1.

30. Uriel Reichman, "Residential Private Governments: An Introductory Survey," *University of Chicago Law Review* 43 (Winter 1976), 303.

31. Peter Gordon and Harry W. Richardson, "The Sprawl Debate: Let Markets Plan," *Publius* 31 (Fall 2001); and Peter Gordon and Harry W. Richardson, "Defending Suburban Sprawl," *The Public Interest* (Spring 2000).

32. Harry W. Richardson, *Urban Economics* (Middlesex, England: Penguin Books, 1971).

33. Robert Bruegmann, "Urban Density and Sprawl: An Historical Perspective," in Randall G. Holcombe and Samuel R. Staley, eds., *Smarter Growth: Market-Based Strategies for Land-Use Planning in the 21st Century* (Westport, CT: Greenwood Press, 2001); and Samuel R. Staley, "Markets, Smart Growth, and the Limits of Policy," in Holcombe and Staley, *Smarter Growth*. See also Edward L. Glaeser and Matthew E. Hahn, "Sprawl and Urban Growth," Discussion Paper No. 2004 (Cambridge, MA: Harvard Institute of Economic Research, May 2003).

34. Benjamin Chinitz, "City and Suburb," in Benjamin Chinitz, ed., *City and Suburb: The Economics of Metropolitan Growth* (Englewood Cliffs, NJ: Prentice-Hall, 1964).

35. Adrian T. Moore and Tom Rose, *Regulatory Reform at the Local Level: Regulating for Competition, Opportunity, and Prosperity* (Los Angeles: Reason Foundation, February 1998).

36. See Eirik G. Furubotn and Rudolf Richter, *Institutions and Economic Theory: The Rise of the New Institutional Economics* (Ann Arbor: University of Michigan Press, 1997).

37. For a wide range of institutional proposals, see David T. Beito, Peter Gordon, and Alexander Tabarrok, *The Voluntary City: Choice, Community, and Civil Society* (Ann Arbor: University of Michigan Press, 2002).

38. William A. Fischel, "Voting, Risk Aversion, and the NIMBY Syndrome: A Comment on Robert Nelson's 'Privatizing the Neighborhood,' " *George Mason Law Review* 7 (Summer 1999). Additional comments are provided in William A. Fischel, "Dealing with the NIMBY Problem," in F. H. Buckley, ed., *The Fall and Rise of Freedom of Contract* (Durham, NC: Duke University Press, 1999).

14

Neighborhood Associations for Inner-City Areas

The Peruvian economist Hernando de Soto argues that many nominally poor people around the world have considerably more wealth than it might seem. In many cities in developing nations, large areas are occupied by people who live in housing that they do not formally own. They typically moved into these areas as squatters and may have lived there for many years. These residents and their neighbors have often made significant physical improvements, sometimes creating attractive housing in a nice setting. People living in these areas are not likely to be evicted, but without formal ownership they cannot make full use of their "property."

They cannot, for example, use their housing assets as collateral for loans or be certain that they will be able to reap the benefits of new investments in their homes over the long term. Even if they have a good opportunity, they cannot easily move to another area of the city because selling their home may be difficult. De Soto estimates that around the world today there may be as much as $9 trillion worth of such informal "property" that is not fully accessible in a monetary way to its de facto "owners."[1] If these owners' rights were legally recognized, their personal wealth would be greatly increased and they would be able to do much more to improve their situation.*

---

*For example, in Kenya in 2003, "a group of Nairobi slum dwellers banded together and asked the city council to give them the land they had been squatting on illegally. In return, they promised to build proper houses, schools, and community centers without any government money." After the Kenyan government went along with the proposal, the secretary of the newly formed housing association, Peter Chege, recounted the process: "We went to the [city] council and said, 'We know this land belongs to

For many lower- and moderate-income groups in older U.S. cities, the story is similar. Neighborhoods in these cities often occupy valuable locations near downtown areas, but the property owners there lack the necessary property rights to capture the full locational benefits. For example, the site value of neighborhoods in New York City's Harlem is potentially very high. In the nearby Upper East and Upper West sides of Manhattan, small lots are worth millions of dollars. Capturing the location values of Harlem real estate, however, would require gaining collective control over the neighborhood externalities that have left the areas facing problems of crime, drug dealing, gang violence, and other social maladies. As in De Soto's analysis, changes in property right rules may be a key step to allowing residents to capture the full benefits of their valuable location.

If they could gain neighborhood control—say, by creating a NASSEN as described in chapter 12—the owners of housing in Harlem neighborhoods and in many other inner-city areas across the United States might well experience a large increase in their individual wealth. In some cases, neighborhood redevelopment might consist of the improvement of existing properties. In other instances—probably less common—the whole neighborhood might be demolished and rebuilt. The property owners in the neighborhood association could vote to approve a wholesale neighborhood buyout (ratification would require a high supermajority). Everyone would then have to move out by a given date, and would be compensated by a payment that in some cases might be two or three times the existing value of neighborhood properties in their current uses.

Terrence Farris argues that the infill development of inner urban sites is a key to better land use outcomes. However, there are major economic obstacles. In a typical suburban area, developable land might cost $0.25 to $4.00 per square foot; in the urban core, however, the costs of acquisition, relocation, demolition, environmental clearance, and site preparation under current rules and procedures might push that cost to $15 per square foot. In order to justify such costs, projects should be large enough to realize economies of scale and to revive a full neighborhood environment. Otherwise, inner-city "development is inhibited by negative externalities from remaining residents and structures." However, as Farris says, "assembling an area large enough to encourage investment and eliminate negative neighborhood spillover effects is a major barrier";

---

you, but we have lived here for 30 years and if you help us, we will make it a clean environment with good security.' " Such efforts are generally being promoted around the world by Slum Dwellers International, an Indian group that "encourages people living in slums to find their own solutions to housing problems." As a precursor to its efforts in Nairobi, Slum Dwellers International in the 1990s "helped slum residents in Bombay to claim the land they were squatting on and turn it into a proper residential estate with running water and electricity." See Meera Selva, "Kenyans Buy into Slum Plan," *Christian Science Monitor,* May 26, 2004.

by contrast, "assembly of outlying, vacant, suburban land is easier, with fewer transaction costs and risk of failure."[2]

Given holdout and other problems, Farris believes that the use of eminent domain power may be the only way to assemble large enough development sites within the city. Yet he finds little interest in this approach among public officials today, which is partly a reflection of lingering bad memories from the old urban renewal program. Another alternative would be the creation of a new private neighborhood association like that proposed in chapter 12. A supermajority of property owners within a given neighborhood would first have to vote in favor of an urban NASSEN that would control land use within the neighborhood boundaries. If a proposal arose later to convert the whole private neighborhood to a brand new use, then a second supermajority vote of property owners would also be required in order to terminate the NASSEN in exchange for a large financial buyout.

Because the neighborhood property owners would themselves have to approve these actions, the whole process of land assembly, and possibly future land conversion, would have greater legitimacy. If private NASSENs could be created in older city areas, then sites that are now in a distressed condition and offer little prospect of improvement anytime soon might experience widespread redevelopment. This process would extend further a current American trend that Richard Briffault describes as the "rise of sublocal structures in urban governance." Although these new sublocal governance structures are mostly public at present, they often display an essentially private character—representing a new turn toward a greater "place of private interests in urban governance."[3]

Part of the reason that municipal services in older cities are so poor is that, according to Briffault, "cities are likely to be more diverse, in terms of race, class, and land uses than suburban local governments. There is, therefore, likely to be much greater heterogeneity of preferences concerning local tax, service, and regulatory policies." However, big cities are seldom able to accommodate this diversity because they apply common policies and provide similar service levels over their full jurisdictions. A possible solution (much like a NASSEN) "might be to break up larger cities into smaller cities, by encouraging individual neighborhoods to secede or dissolving the big cities outright. Secessions and dissolutions, however, have been rare. Alternatively, cities could be restructured to provide for the decentralization of significant service, tax or regulatory responsibilities to neighborhoods or other discrete communities within cities."[4] Or, as Ronald Oakerson proposes, "The development of neighborhood governments in large cities would not only create new provision units but would also create potential contractors for direct services that continue to be provided by city governments. This could lead to more differentiated service sectors within large central cities," to the large benefit of the residents there.[5]

Saving the Inner City Privately

Poverty and other problems plaguing many U.S. inner-city neighborhoods have largely resisted the efforts of a whole generation of American urban reformers.[6] Broadly speaking, these reformers have pursued a two-pronged strategy. First, they have tried to improve conditions in inner-city neighborhoods by providing better public services. Second, they have sought to create greater opportunities for inner-city residents to move elsewhere. Reformers have hoped that if these residents could move out of their deteriorated city neighborhoods, then they would be able to share in the superior environmental quality characteristic of the suburbs. This latter effort has involved a long and sustained attack on "exclusionary" zoning and other regulatory devices that suburban municipalities have used to keep the poor bottled up in America's inner cities.

Both elements of this strategy, however, have largely failed.[7] The poor have not been granted entry into the suburbs and, as Pietro Nivola reports, big-city bureaucracies have continued to deliver "unsatisfactory public services, from ghastly schools to mediocre police departments."[8] Providing an institutional framework of property rights enabling inner-city residents to help themselves might well have done more good. Indeed, Anthony Downs argues that an especially promising option for aiding "declining big cities" is to build upon "the resources intrinsic to concentrated-poverty areas, such as their central locations, the untapped energies and talents of their residents, and the possible collective results of community efforts." Such a "community development approach" does not challenge the political prerogatives of other powerful vested interests as much as other approaches to central-city revitalization do. It does not require changing a longtime culture of inadequate service delivery. As a result, Downs rates it as "the most likely to occur" of any of the revitalization options that are presently available to poorer areas in American cities.[9]

Yet, the prospects for internal revitalization in such neighborhoods are not independent of the institutional arrangements there. As long ago as 1936, a St. Louis regional planning report noted that "the older residential districts which are depreciating in value and in character constitute one of the most serious problems in this region. . . . [Yet], even if [individual] owners wished to build new homes within them, it would be inadvisable because of the present character of the districts."[10] In other words, a solution to the problems of deteriorated urban neighborhoods should be collective in character. Individual efforts would be less effective because of the surrounding environment of urban decay and deterioration. It would be particularly important to obtain a greater collective control over crime within the neighborhood. As Downs notes, "Fear of crime is . . . probably the biggest obstacle to attracting middle-class households back into declining cities or retaining those that are there now."[11]

I propose that state legislatures should therefore create the necessary legal mechanism to allow property owners in an inner-city neighborhood to create their own NASSEN. Such a new private neighborhood association would have the authority to provide its own security patrols, garbage collection, street cleaning, snow removal, recreational facilities, and other collective services (perhaps with financial assistance from general revenues of the city, along with technical assistance as needed). New neighborhood associations in older cities could maintain aesthetic controls over changes in use and other alterations in neighborhood properties, much as neighborhood associations in the suburbs now do. This practice might include a requirement, for example, that all neighborhood property owners keep their yards clear of any trash or other debris. If a house needed painting or a lawn needed mowing, the neighborhood would have the authority to have it done and to bill the property owner.

The epitome of private suburban autonomy is a gated community. A private neighborhood in the inner city might derive even more benefit from such security. The inner-city neighborhood might want to close off streets, build fences, and otherwise establish a protected zone of peace and quiet for the residents. Tight control over entry into the neighborhood would result in less crime, drug use, and other urban problems. When the New York City Public Library wanted to clean up neighboring Bryant Park, it found that the most effective strategy was to build a fence. The library's former head, Vartan Gregorian, commented in an interview, "One way to clear away the drug dealers was to put a fence around the library [and the park]. This was the best $80,000 we ever spent."[12]

With the New York library's success in mind, consider how the opportunity to create a private neighborhood association might work in an existing urban neighborhood—perhaps on a high hill overlooking the entire city. At present, this area may have high crime rates and otherwise deteriorated living conditions that largely foreclose middle- and upper-income occupancy. If a NASSEN could be formed for this neighborhood, controlling entry over at least several contiguous blocks to protect a high-quality environment there, then new residents might soon pour in. The current property owners would initially experience a large increase in housing values and some might invest their new equity in further improvements. A "virtuous circle" might arise in place of the old "vicious circle" that has led to urban decay in so many areas.

Over time, some of the neighborhood's property owners might decide to relocate to other locations in the city with less stunning views and fewer locational advantages, but with less expensive housing. These property owners would be compensated for leaving their old neighborhood by a large capital gain from the sale of their housing unit. Alternatively, other property owners might chose to forego their windfall in order to retain the present and future benefits of living in a higher-quality neighborhood environment. Either way, the original property owners in the neighborhood would be significantly better off.

Fair Treatment for Renters

Renters living in these neighborhoods, however, might be losers. They might have to move out or pay higher rents. Lacking ownership rights in property, they would not financially benefit from leaving a neighborhood where the property values had risen sharply. It is, however, possible to accommodate renters' interests as well. Indeed, the political viability of inner-city NASSENs will depend on achieving a "win-win" outcome for all residents, including the renters in the neighborhood.

A solution in this case would be to recognize renters' "rights" in addition to the rights of neighborhood property owners. As a condition for establishing a NASSEN, the law governing this process might require that all renters be allowed to remain where they are for a certain period of time and without rent increases (beyond inflation). A similar practice occurs today when rental buildings are converted to condominiums. Resident renters are typically given the right to remain in their building after the conversion and also often receive an option to purchase their own rental unit at a significantly discounted price.

There are many alternative ways to give renters a share in a new NASSEN's bundle of rights. There should probably be a relationship between the amount of time a renter has lived in the neighborhood and the extent of the renter rights granted. One option would give each renter the right to stay in his or her existing unit at a rent-controlled price for the same number of years that he or she has lived in that unit (or perhaps in any building in the neighborhood). A renter in residence for 20 years would thus be given a right to 20 additional years in the same housing facility; a renter of 1 year would be given a right to 1 additional year.

If given such rights, many of these renters might end up selling their rights to investors, preferring cash in the short run to a longer-run higher level of neighborhood amenities. Like the neighborhood's property owners, renters might make different choices, some choosing to stay and others choosing to cash out their gain immediately. Some renters might bargain with land developers for a new unit in a rebuilt neighborhood in exchange for agreeing to move out during the transitional period of neighborhood reconstruction.

The St. Louis Experiment

One American city has conducted a limited experiment in neighborhood privatization. In 1867, St. Louis's first "private street," Benton Place, went on the market.[13] Subsequently, and with the strong encouragement of prominent architect Julius Pitzman, many other private streets were formed. Associations of property owners responsible for maintenance and other improvements managed the streets. As recently as the 1950s, the residents along sections of two public streets, Pershing and Westminster Avenues, petitioned the city and won approval to privatize their portions of the streets. As of 1986, there were more than 400 private streets in the St. Louis area, the majority of them located in St. Louis County (outside the city limits).

A 1989 study of these private streets, undertaken for the U.S. Advisory Commission on Intergovernmental Relations (ACIR), reported that "one of the major services provided by subdivisions that control their own streets is access restriction. Throughout much of University City and Clayton, streets that would otherwise provide access to subdivisions from city streets are chained off or barricaded." Such private streets also "accommodate diversity in [service] preferences among neighborhoods." Some neighborhoods exceed the municipal standards for street lighting, while others do not think the greater illumination is worth the expense. Overall, based on the experience of the St. Louis private streets, the ACIR study concluded that the private collective ownership of streets "offer[s] a number of advantages that their members value highly."[14]

Another study of these streets by community planner Oscar Newman found that, in the opinion of the residents themselves, "the physical closure of streets and their legal association together act to create social cohesion, stability and security."[15] Newman summarizes his findings concerning the St. Louis experiment in street privatization:

> For many students of the dilemma of American cities, the decline of St. Louis, Missouri, has come to epitomize the impotence of federal, state, and local resources in coping with the consequences of large-scale population change. Yet buried within those very areas of St. Louis which have been experiencing the most rapid turnover of population are a series of streets where residents have adopted a program to stabilize their communities, to deter crime, and to guarantee the necessities of a middle-class lifestyle. These residents have been able to create and maintain for themselves what their city was no longer able to provide: low crime rates, stable property values, and a sense of community. Even though the areas surrounding them are experiencing significant socio-economic change, high crime rates, physical deterioration, and abandonment, these streets are still characterized by middle-class ownership—both black and white. The distinguishing characteristic of these streets is that they have been deeded back from the city to the residents and are now legally owned and maintained by the residents themselves.[16]

Fencing Off Public Housing

In order to put together the full rights to sustain a more desirable neighborhood environment, most areas in America's inner cities would have to assemble a number of individually owned properties. However, there are some consolidated ownerships of full neighborhood size. A whole neighborhood under one ownership can often be found, for example, in a public housing project. Because the ownership rights are already assembled, it is possible now to fence off such neighborhoods. Indeed, that is precisely what several public housing projects in the United States are already doing.

In Richmond, Virginia, the local public housing authority in 1997 acted to exclude nonresidents from entering the Whitcomb Court project.[17] However, the legality of this action was challenged in court by Kevin Hicks, who received a summons (he was a frequent offender) in 1999 for trespassing in Whitcomb Court. In denying entry to Hicks, the Virginia Supreme Court explained that the housing authority was acting "in its capacity as [the new] owner of the private streets" within the project area. The Richmond Police Department received a clear directive: "Serve notice . . . to any person who is found on [Whitcomb Court] property when such person is not a resident, employee, or such person cannot demonstrate a legitimate business or social purpose for being on the premises."[18]

As the Virginia Supreme Court explained the housing authority's purpose, closing off the streets was designed to "eradicate illegal drug activity in Whitcomb Court, which was described as an 'open-air drug market.' " Even so, in its 2002 decision, the Virginia court overturned the housing authority's actions pertaining to Hicks, ruling that the authority was infringing on his constitutional rights of free speech.[19] On appeal to the U.S. Supreme Court, however, the Virginia court was overruled in June 2003.[20] The Supreme Court ruled that, since Hicks was not involved in an exercise of speech, he could not bring a constitutional claim on these grounds. Moreover, as Justice Ruth Bader Ginsburg observed in oral arguments before the Court, the actions of the Richmond housing authority were the practical equivalent of creating a "gated community" at Whitcomb Court. Justice Ginsburg commented further, "You're saying the public housing authority can't create for people in the projects a gated community. People who live outside can have it, but poor people can't have it."[21]

The public housing authority in Knoxville, Tennessee, also took over the streets and instituted similarly tight trespass rules. In Tampa, Florida, and El Paso, Texas, public housing authorities have asserted control over unauthorized entry into certain facilities, although they have not taken legal possession of streets. Reviewing these efforts, Peter Flanagan finds a "demonstrated success of [the new] trespass policies in reducing crime . . . within public housing developments." Similar to a NASSEN, Flanagan suggests that this model might be extended to other inner-city neighborhoods outside public housing projects. The process would require "the conveyance of public streets and sidewalks of logically and well-defined areas to neighborhood property owners. Whether they be public housing authorities or private associations, such thoroughfare conveyances promise the most circumspect eradication of drug crime, and crime in general, in those most severely distressed areas." Such a tactic would provide a new "means to enable preexisting and distressed communities to reap the advantages long enjoyed by newer and often suburban developments."[22]

Historic Districts

Historic districts offer another legally available means for establishing tighter environmental controls in inner-city neighborhoods. Nominally, these districts are established to protect "historic character." Their more important function, however, is often to promote neighborhood revitalization in decaying areas of the city. As Carol Rose explains, "Another motive that leads cities to designate historic districts is attracting taxpaying businesses and middle-class residents to the city. . . . Cities hope that historic district designation of a decaying residential or commercial area will call attention to the underlying quality of the structures of the area" and will provide a new investment security. Given their attractive locations, many inner-city neighborhoods can be just as attractive to developers as the outer suburbs if they can assert the same tight control over their immediate environment. Thus, as Rose observes, "historic district self-government" can help to "alleviate the power imbalance of older neighborhoods against newer areas" in the developing suburbs.[23]

The regulatory controls in historic districts go well beyond ordinary zoning. Indeed, they resemble closely the land use controls in private, suburban neighborhood associations. An historic district might be described as an inner-city neighborhood association minus the authority to provide services and to levy neighborhood taxes (these authorities remain at the city level). Some neighborhoods have won "historic" status even when such status was largely untrue. Many other neighborhoods, however, lack the rhetorical and imaginative skills for the necessary "fiction writing." With the legal authority to create a NASSEN, urban neighborhoods would not need to make any formal claims for "historic" status in order to establish comprehensive neighborhood regulations.

Improvements in environmental quality and increases in property values in city neighborhoods are often described as a process of "gentrification." Indeed, improvements in historic districts have occasionally been so great that they have acquired "overtones of snobbery and special interest." One critic declares that "it wasn't *black* history that the preservationists had in mind." Improvements in neighborhood quality may be so great that "the low income residents of old neighborhoods may be forced out by steeply rising rents." As a result, "poor black families might be displaced as middle class whites move into spruced-up 'historic' neighborhoods."[24]

Complaints about the gentrification of historic and other urban neighborhoods—where the rich move in and the poor move out—partly reflect the existing shortage of desirable city neighborhoods as a whole. Given the past obstacles to neighborhood renewal in older cities, there are still many more existing neighborhoods that could be significantly improved with regard to their environmental quality. An improved set of neighborhood property right institutions in inner cities—including the legal authority to create NASSENs— might produce many more attractive urban neighborhoods. Even if the rents in one neighborhood became too high to allow many people to remain, it would typically be possible for these residents to find other attractive neighborhoods with more reasonable rents.

Business Improvement Districts (BIDs)

Like zoning in 1916, the "business improvement district" (BID) represents yet another of New York City's land use innovations. BIDs were authorized by state and local legislation there in the early 1980s. The 14th Street–Union Square District (established in 1984) was the first BID in New York. A BID consists of an association mostly of business property owners who have banded together to improve their surrounding neighborhood environment.[25] There are now more than 40 BIDs in New York City alone.

To create a BID, an application must be filed with the New York City government—typically by an organization of businessmen in the area—and the City must give its approval. In New York, formal votes by local property owners are not necessary, but the creation of a BID can be blocked by an opposing petition from 51 percent of the owners in the area.[26] BIDs are authorized to assess neighborhood property owners for fees to pay for improvements. In 1994, the Grand Central District, for example, collected a fee of 11.5 cents per square foot from businesses in the neighborhood (admittedly a small amount compared with citywide property taxes of $8 to $12 per square foot). BID revenues have been used to install better street lighting, clean up litter, add more trash cans, put up clearer signs, and hire private security guards.

After becoming popular in New York City, BIDs spread rapidly to other parts of the country. By the late 1990s, there were more than 1,000 BIDs in the United States. A 1999 survey found 73 BIDs in California, 54 in Wisconsin, and 32 in North Carolina. Sixty percent had been created since 1990 and 28 percent since 1995. The average size of a BID was 20 blocks, though they ranged from a single block to 300 blocks. The BIDs were managed by governing boards consisting of an average of 16 members. The median annual budget of a BID was $200,000, although budgets ranged from $8,000 to $15 million.[27]

Outside of New York City, establishing a BID typically requires an affirmative vote by the area's property owners. This vote often takes the form of a petition submitted to the city government. The required vote for BID approval has ranged from 51 to 70 percent of those eligible to vote. BIDs are given credit for improving urban conditions where they have been created. In a 1999 survey of the impacts of BIDs, Jerry Mitchell found that

> BIDs have definitely become an integral part of the service delivery system of municipalities across the country. They are engaged with a diverse set of programs and projects, and even though the evidence is limited, they seem to be doing very well. It is obvious when walking around these districts that most of them are more visually appealing. No longer plagued by trash and grime, garish facades, deteriorating sidewalks, rundown parks, and nefarious individuals, there is a sense that the commercial centers of small, medium and large size communities have come back to life.[28]

BIDs represent a further evolution of city governance toward neighborhood empowerment similar to that of private neighborhood associations.[29] A BID in an older city performs some of the same service functions as a private, suburban neighborhood association. Indeed, a BID that happened to coincide with the boundaries of an historic district would for practical purposes almost be a private neighborhood association. This "super-BID" would regulate the fine details of neighborhood architecture and land use and would also have the authority to levy assessments to pay for common services.

Residential Improvement Districts

The favorable results of BIDs have led to similar proposals for rejuvenating residential areas in older cities. Perhaps there should be new laws providing for "residential improvement districts." Indeed, Robert Ellickson proposes a plan for "new institutions for old neighborhoods" of typically a few city blocks—to be called "Block Improvement Districts," or "BLIDs." According to Ellickson, the basic concept would be "to enable the retrofitting of the residential community association—an institution commonly found in new housing developments—to a previously subdivided block." Since this process would require state governments to create a new legal authority, the "legislative drafters could pattern these statutes after the ones that many states have enacted during the past decade to authorize the establishment of mandatory-membership Business Improvement Districts (BIDs)."[30]

Currently, Ellickson explains, efforts to improve many residential inner-city areas face the normal problems of collective action, including the free-rider problem. One property owner's decision "to paint facades or trim shrubbery" also creates significant external benefits for other nearby property owners. However, if BLIDs can provide a way to surmount the collective action problems, they may facilitate the transformation of run-down neighborhoods into bright, attractive environments. For this purpose, it will be necessary to go beyond "voluntary coordination" to create instead new neighborhood institutions that have "coercive powers."[31]

As in a private neighborhood association in the suburbs (and a BID), the voting rights in BLIDs would be assigned to the property owners. Ellickson proposes that the formation of a BLID should begin with a petition sent to the city authorities. The proposed BLID might have to meet a minimum size requirement (for example, two acres of land) perhaps involving at least 10 different ownerships. To win approval for a new BLID, two-thirds of the owners in the area might have to vote in its favor. Ellickson also suggests that all current residents (including renters) should also have to vote to approve the action. The BLID should have the authority to levy taxes (or impose assessments) within the neighborhood. There should also be provision for terminating a BLID that works poorly or has outlived its usefulness.

Ellickson recognizes that any such proposal—in essence, his own version of a NASSEN—is likely to be seen as a privatization of the inner city, potentially extending the workings of the "private suburb" into further areas of American life. Yet, as he concludes, the rapid spread of private neighborhood associations in the suburbs actually demonstrates "the merits of enabling the stakeholders in inner-city neighborhoods to mimic—at the block level—the micro-institutions commonly found in the suburbs." It would be precisely the "poor people living in inner cities [who] would benefit" the most from BLIDs in inner-city areas.[32] Such an institution would give poor residents the institutional means and the incentives to take command of their own surroundings and to improve significantly the quality of their existing neighborhood environments. They would no longer have to rely on well meaning but often-ineffective outsiders or out-of-touch bureaucrats at city hall to try to do the job.*

Conclusion

The governance systems of older American cities were shaped by the Progressive Era's scientific management philosophy, which assigned neighborhoods only a small role in their own administration. When by the mid-20th century the progressive schemes seemed to be failing, the newly developing suburbs opted for decentralized and privatized governance. Given the bureaucratic and ideological inertia typical of the older city, however, following a similar course

---

*As charter schools represent a partial and less politically controversial step than an outright grant of vouchers to attend private schools, urban activist Robert Scott suggests the creation of "charter neighborhoods" within the city of Los Angeles. A charter neighborhood would take over from the wider city many elements of existing neighborhood governance and service delivery. Like a charter school, it would be free of many current regulations and other burdensome central requirements. See Robert L. Scott, "Community-Based Governance," in *Rightsizing Local & Regional Government,* summary of the proceedings of a symposium at Universal City, California, February 5, 2001.

there proved impossible, and older cities were left to cope with a lack of institutional imagination and creativity in their leadership.

Enough is enough. The time has come to give a fair chance to older city neighborhoods as well. These neighborhoods should be able to create their own private associations—their NASSENs—to match the rapid spread of private neighborhood associations throughout the developing suburbs. If neighborhood associations are good enough for the rich, it is likely that they will be good enough for the poor as well.

It is hypocritical for suburbanites living in effectively private suburbs to suggest that there is something socially divisive or otherwise ethically wrong in the privatization of city neighborhoods. If the ideological straightjackets can be overcome, a legal regime might now be set in place to allow for the creation of private neighborhood associations throughout older city areas. Urban NASSENs may offer the best hope of solving the inner-city problems that previously have so often defeated the best intentions of urban reformers.

NOTES

1. Hernando de Soto, *The Mystery of Capital: Why Capitalism Triumphs in the West and Fails Everywhere Else* (New York: Basic Books, 2000), 35.

2. J. Terrence Farris, "The Barriers to Using Urban Infill Development to Achieve Smart Growth," *Housing Policy Debate* 12, no. 1 (2001), 9, 11, 13.

3. Richard Briffault, "The Rise of Sublocal Structures in Urban Governance," *Minnesota Law Review* 82 (December 1997), 508.

4. Ibid., 506–7.

5. Ronald J. Oakerson, *Governing Local Public Economies: Creating the Civic Metropolis* (Oakland, CA: ICS Press, 1999), 75.

6. See *A Decent Home: The Report of the President's Committee on Urban Housing*, Edgar F. Kaiser, Chairman (Washington, DC, 1968); Ira Michael Heyman, "Legal Assaults on Municipal Land Use Regulation," in Marion Clawson, ed., *Modernizing Urban Land Policy* (Baltimore: Johns Hopkins University Press for Resources for the Future, 1973); Daniel Wm. Fessler, "Casting the Courts in a Land Use Reform Effort: A Starring Role or a Supporting Part," in Clawson, ed., *Modernizing Urban Land Policy;* and Lawrence Gene Sager, "Tight Little Islands: Exclusionary Zoning, Equal Protection and the Indigent," *Stanford Law Review* 21 (April 1969).

7. Jon C. Teaford, *The Rough Road to Renaissance: Urban Revitalization in America, 1940–1985* (Baltimore: Johns Hopkins University Press, 1990); and Douglas S. Massey and Nancy A. Denton, *American Apartheid: Segregation and the Making of the Underclass* (Cambridge, MA: Harvard University Press, 1993).

8. Pietro S. Nivola, *Laws of the Landscape: How Policies Shape Cities in Europe and America* (Washington, DC: Brookings Institution Press, 1999), 79.

9. Anthony Downs, "The Challenge of Our Declining Big Cities," *Housing Policy Debate* 8, no. 2 (1997), 401, 404.

10. National Resources Committee, *Regional Planning, Part II—St. Louis Region* (Washington, DC, 1936), quoted in Kenneth T. Jackson, *Crabgrass Frontier: The Suburbanization of the United States* (New York: Oxford University Press, 1985), 201.

11. Downs, "The Challenge of Our Declining Big Cities," 390.

12. Claudia Dreifus, "It Is Better to Give Than to Receive," interview with Vartan Gregorian, *New York Times Magazine,* December 14, 1997, 52.

13. David T. Beito and Bruce Smith, "The Formation of Urban Infrastructure Through Nongovernmental Planning: The Private Places of St. Louis, 1869–1920," *Journal of Urban History* 16 (May 1990), 265; also David T. Beito and Bruce Smith, *Owning the "Commanding Heights:" Historical Perspectives on Private Streets* (Chicago: Public Works Historical Society, December 1989); Ronald J. Oakerson, "Private Street Associations in St. Louis County: Subdivisions as Service Providers," in U.S. Advisory Commission on Intergovernmental Relations, *Residential Community Associations: Private Governments in the Intergovernmental System?* (Washington, DC: May 1989).

14. Oakerson, "Private Street Associations in St. Louis County," 58, 60.

15. Oscar Newman, *Community of Interest* (New York: Doubleday, 1980), 126.

16. Ibid., 124.

17. Charles Lane, "High Court to Review Anti-Drug Policy: Rules Intended to Strictly Control Visitors to Richmond Public Housing Project," *Washington Post,* January 25, 2003, A8.

18. *Commonwealth of Virginia v. Kevin Lamont Hicks,* 264 Va. at 52 (June 2002).

19. Ibid., at 51.

20. *Virginia v. Hicks,* 539 U.S. 113 (2003).

21. Quoted in Charles Lane, "High Court Debates Trespassing Issue," *Washington Post,* May 1, 2003, A2.

22. Peter M. Flanagan, "Trespass-Zoning: Ensuring Neighborhoods a Safer Future by Excluding Those with a Criminal Past," *Notre Dame Law Review* 79 (December 2003), 375, 387, 386.

23. Carol M. Rose, "Preservation and Community: New Directions in the Law of Historic Preservation," *Stanford Law Review* 33 (February 1981), 512, 524.

24. Ibid., 478.

25. Richard Briffault, "A Government for Our Time?: Business Improvement Districts and Urban Governance," *Columbia Law Review* 99 (March 1999).

26. Douglas Martin, "Districts to Improve Business Proliferate," *New York Times,* March 25, 1994, B3.

27. Jerry Mitchell, *Business Improvement Districts and Innovative Service Delivery* (Arlington, VA: PricewaterhouseCoopers Endowment for the Business of Government, November 1999).

28. Ibid., 27.

29. See Mark S. Davies, "Business Improvement Districts," *Washington University Journal of Urban and Contemporary Law* 52 (1997).

30. Robert C. Ellickson, "New Institutions for Old Neighborhoods," *Duke Law Journal* 48 (October 1998), 77–78.

31. Ibid., 79.

32. Ibid., 109.

PART V
Writing a Neighborhood Constitution

A constitution's purpose is to set the ground rules for governance.[1] The U.S. Constitution established the House of Representatives, the Senate, the Supreme Court, and the presidency, among other political institutions, as the foundation of American government. Since the original document was written in 1787, 27 constitutional amendments have been ratified. The world today is witnessing a period of unusual constitutional ferment. Eastern European nations have had to write new constitutions in the wake of the collapse of the old Soviet empire, and the European Union is today writing the first European-wide constitution. The government of Kenya has been writing a new constitution, and many other postcolonial African nations are still searching for effective institutions of governance.

Yet, the rise of the private neighborhood association has resulted in far and away the largest number of new constitutions in recent years—more than 200,000 constitutions during the past three decades in the United States alone. For the most part, however, this area of constitutional activity has not attracted the attention of public choice or other leading constitutional scholars. The writing of neighborhood constitutions has been left mainly to real estate lawyers and their developer clients, who typically use boilerplate documents. According to one observer, "With no previous experience available to understand what the pros and cons would be to live in a community controlled by covenants, DABs [Declarations, Articles of Incorporation, and Bylaws] were born in approximately the 1960s. Operating within the bureaucratic framework created by VA and FHA, the legal profession created the collection of standard, boilerplate, 'canned' rules." So despite decades of obvious problems with this approach, "developers and attorneys still use wording from the original off-the-rack rules."[2]

Admittedly, there have been a few broader efforts—mostly within the legal profession—to rethink the basic provisions of neighborhood constitutions. In 1982, the National Conference of Commissioners on Uniform State Laws released model state legislation as the Uniform Common Interest Ownership Act; a revised version was issued in 1994.[3] This model legislation clarified state responsibilities relating to neighborhood associations and suggested various provisions, such as the required voting percentages for amending an association's constitution. Yet, for the most part, this effort simply fine-tuned the existing model.

In 2000, after a decade of discussions and drafting, the American Law Institute released its *Restatement of the Law Third, Property (Servitudes).*[4] This document offers guidance for rewriting state laws relating to the use of covenants, easements, and other restrictions that run with the land. Since the use of covenants to establish a private neighborhood association overburdened the traditional law of servitudes, it was necessary to clarify the means by which a covenant regime in a neighborhood association could be applied and ended. The *Restatement* addressed this and other legal issues, but remained on the whole a "cleaning-up" operation that did not address the possibility of fundamental innovations in neighborhood governance.

Thus, many important constitutional issues and options for neighborhood associations have never been seriously explored, and there is wide opportunity today for applying new ideas in writing neighborhood constitutions.[5] Even for established neighborhoods that already have a constitution, a "neighborhood constitutional convention" might be convened to consider changes in neighborhood governance. Thomas Jefferson argued that each new generation of Americans should have the right to create its own institutions of government, and suggested a rewriting of the U.S. Constitution at least every 20 years. Today, new neighborhood constitutions might provide for a periodic review of their neighborhood's governance structure, perhaps every 15 to 20 years. Since most neighborhood association constitutions already include procedures for adopting individual amendments as the need arises, rewriting might also occur in piecemeal fashion, as an alternative to a full-scale constitutional reconsideration.

Law professor Paula Franzese argues that neighborhood associations can have a beneficial future role, but at present are falling well short of their potential: "Most common interest communities put the cart before the horse, relying on elaborately prepackaged mandates to impose 'community,' rather than facilitating the development of a genuine social fabric. . . . 'We need a change in the way we draft documents.' " As a result, "the challenge for all of us as academics, practitioners, empiricists, CIC developers, planners, leaders and residents is not to lament the withering state of community, but to help guide its restoration."[6] Therefore, Franzese continues,

> Community associations must be redefined so that their central agenda is cast in terms of the very conscious resolve to rebuild . . . social bonds. Careful, deliberate and sustained attention must be given to the arduous task of finding ways to guide community engagement so that in time a strong social fabric will become the principal determinant of compatible, harmonious land use and behavior that is respectful of the rights of others.[7]

Some unit owners in current neighborhood associations also see a need for improved constitutional regimes. According to one disgruntled unit owner, "There is something about people that getting them together into these associations just brings out the worst in them." His own association has been plagued by "big disagreements . . . about driving speeds, whether dogs have to be on leashes at all times, what colors garage doors have to be painted, whether satellite dishes destroy the aesthetics of the units, etc." This owner believes that the poorly drawn rules of the association encourage such problems: "I don't think that most people care what color drapes their neighbors have, but once you form a condo, busybodies who enjoy telling others what to do seem to take over. Most rational people would rather stay at home with a good book while these despots with hard butts who enjoy sitting in meetings seek out control." All is not lost, however, because "this all seems to be a problem of a lack of a good contract. Surely there is money to be made in coming up with some kind of 'condominium constitution' which limits these despots to the type of control that is suitable."[8]

Franzese suggests including a less comprehensive set of rules in an association's founding documents—rules that would represent only a "skeletal frame"; unit owners would then later fill in the missing elements "on an as-needed basis."[9] Wayne Hyatt similarly suggests that the initial association constitution should "contain only a limited number, perhaps a severely limited number, of prohibitions and restrictions, including only those restrictions that the developer believes to be vital to the overall community development plan." Hyatt would then gradually rewrite the rules through "a method for permitting changes and for the adoption, modification, or abrogation of regulations" of the association. The neighborhood constitution thus should "create and institutionalize rule-making as a dynamic rather than a static process."[10] This would allow the constitutional provisions of each neighborhood association to be tailored more specifically to the concerns and objectives of the unit owners who actually end up living in the neighborhood.

However, a deferral of key constitutional decisions in such situations would require simplifying the process of amending the neighborhood constitution. Franzese thus proposes a "liberalizing [of] the amendment process," such as adopting lower supermajority requirements in order to leave "more room for change as the community takes form." This approach would admittedly place a burden on the unit owners, who would "have to accept their power and become engaged in the life of their developments, willing to accept the duties as well as the rewards of participation, collaboration and compromise."[11]

There are also good arguments, to be sure, for firmly fixing a neighborhood constitution's character in advance of the unit owners moving in. If the terms of the agreement are not well known, it may be more difficult for prospective owners to decide whether to buy a home in a neighborhood association. Few people go to work for a business corporation without knowing their starting salary, job responsibilities, and work location. Similarly, many people may want a well-defined set of neighborhood rules and procedures that are difficult to change. A compromise of some sort is perhaps desirable—and it need not be precisely the same compromise from neighborhood to neighborhood. If the constitution is too difficult to amend, it may leave the unit owners unable to revise a governing arrangement that they later find unsatisfactory. If the constitution is too easy to amend, many unit owners may find that their initial expectations at the time of purchase are not being fulfilled.

The rise of the private neighborhood association has created opportunities for a host of governmental innovations at the neighborhood level. Owing to their private status, neighborhood associations have wider legal flexibility in this regard than local governments in the public sector. In fact, the spread of neighborhood associations might be described as the emergence of a "pro-choice" movement in American neighborhood government.

Part V will explore alternatives for constitutional design in neighborhood associations, drawing in part on recent political science literature, including writings in the new field of constitutional economics.[12] These chapters provide a menu of possible constitutional options for neighborhood associations—both for initial document drafters and for existing unit owners who may be interested in rewriting their current constitution. Chapter 15 will explore constitutional options with respect to the neighborhood "legislature"—at present, the association's board of directors. Chapter 16 will review constitutional options from the perspective of the neighborhood "executive branch," while chapter 17 will look at the neighborhood "judicial branch."

NOTES

1. Scott Gordon, *Controlling the State: Constitutionalism from Ancient Athens to Today* (Cambridge, MA: Harvard University Press, 1999).

2. Joni Greenwalt, *Homeowner Associations: A Nightmare or a Dream Come True?* (Denver, CO: Cassie Publications Inc., 2001), 37.

3. National Conference of Commissioners on Uniform State Laws, *Uniform Common Interest Ownership Act (1994)*, (Chicago, IL: National Conference of Commissioners on Uniform State Laws, 1994).

4. *Restatement of the Law Third, Property (Servitudes)*, Susan F. French, reporter (St. Paul, MN: American Law Institute, 2000). See Susan F. French, "Tradition and Innovation in the New Restatement of Servitudes, A Report from Midpoint," *Connecticut Law Review* 27 (Fall 1994).

5. Robert D. Cooter, *The Strategic Constitution* (Princeton, NJ: Princeton University Press, 2000).

6. Paula A. Franzese, "Does It Take a Village?: Privatization, Patterns of Restrictiveness and the Demise of Community," *Villanova Law Review* 47, no. 3 (2002), 590, 592.

7. Ibid., 593.

8. E-mail discussion list on the subject of "Some Practical Experience with Homeowners' Associations," November 13, 2002. The name of the author of the quoted e-mail is withheld since this is a private list.

9. Franzese, "Does It Take a Village?" 591.

10. Wayne S. Hyatt, "Putting the Community Back in Community Associations: An Action Plan," in Bill Overton, ed., *Community First! Emerging Visions Reshaping America's Condominium and Homeowner Associations* (Alexandria, VA: Community Associations Institute, 1999), 104.

11. Franzese, "Does It Take a Village?" 592.

12. There is now even a journal, *Constitutional Political Economy,* devoted to investigations in this field. James Buchanan has written widely in this area. See, for example, James M. Buchanan, *The Logical Foundations of Constitutional Liberty* (Indianapolis: Liberty Fund, 1999). Another useful source is Dennis C. Mueller, *Constitutional Democracy* (New York: Oxford University Press, 1996).

15

The Neighborhood Legislature

Charles Fraser, founding chief executive officer of Hilton Head's Sea Pines Plantation, believes that a crisis of governance now exists in America's neighborhood associations. Even though these associations are democratic in theory, this prominent land developer has found that there is often in practice "control by the arbitrary few." Indeed, this problem "has been inflicted on most U.S. master-planned communities." Part of the difficulty rests with neighborhood associations' founding constitutions because the attorneys writing them have given "too little thought to the need to restrain abuses of power."[1]

The practice of democracy in neighborhood associations can be time consuming. Younger residents working to advance their careers or raising children may have little time to participate in neighborhood association governance. By contrast, retired people often have large amounts of time available and may even be looking for new activities. As a result, Fraser finds, the practice of democracy in neighborhood associations frequently results in "control over the young by the old." In some neighborhood associations, the board of directors exhibits "a virtually unchecked focus on the self-interests of the male resident aged 70 and older." It can be a problem for neighborhood associations of mixed age groups because "all sociological studies of differences among age groups . . . show sharp differences in the life interests of people 35 years old" when compared with those who are much older. In particular, there may be an especially large clash "between the interests of 35-year-old mothers and those of childless or empty-nester 70-year-old males."[2]

Among American land developers, Fraser is a free thinker. As a solution to the problem of the frequent "autocracy" in neighborhood associations, Fraser proposes a system of "proportional representation" under which "condominium and community boards . . . divide board membership into 50 percent women and 50 percent men, and then divide each half among three age groups: over age 70, ages 55 to 70, and under age 55."[3] Admittedly, this degree of specificity raises a number of concerns; what if, for example, there are few unit owners ages 55 to 70, but they still receive a one-third representation on the board of directors? Fraser's proposal nevertheless underscores the possibility of rethinking democratic governance structures in many neighborhood associations.

Indeed, Fraser is not the only person with such ideas. Wayne Hyatt also suggests that associations may want to explore a system of proportional representation as an alternative to the current "majoritarian win-lose exercise." For board member elections in most associations at present, each unit owner is eligible to vote and casts either a single vote or a specified number of votes that corresponds to the number of open seats on the board of directors. The highest total vote getters become board members. Under such a system, a majority of unit owners can consistently vote for the same types of candidates and policies, leaving a minority feeling unrepresented. Indeed, too many neighborhood boards, Hyatt says, "are dominated by members of a similar age, housing type, or a particular interest—e.g., golfers—and others are shut out," perpetuating "a negative governmental environment that feeds on itself."[4]

As it happens, concerns such as those expressed by Fraser and Hyatt are not limited to the democratic workings of private neighborhood associations. Other nations use the proportional systems of representation Fraser and Hyatt suggest in order to obtain a wider range of viewpoints in their legislatures. In fact, political scientists in recent years have broadly critiqued the public structures of American democracy. Existing systems for electing American legislatures do have the great advantage of familiarity—and thus the social legitimacy stemming from a long history of practice. However, analysts of the election systems most widely employed in the United States—the winning candidate is simply the one who receives the largest number of votes among all the candidates—typically conclude that these systems are primitive instruments of collective choice.* Many voting theorists argue that the usual

---

*The precise method used for conducting an election can make a big difference to the final result. Alexander Tabarrok and Lee Spector provocatively speculate that "[Stephen] Douglas, not Lincoln, would have won the election of 1860 under many voting systems other than plurality rule." For example, if Lincoln and Douglas had been the only candidates (there were actually four candidates who had significant popular support), "Douglas would have won." Indeed, Tabarrok and Spector find that "under some voting systems, it is quite possible that the compromise candidate John Bell might have won the election." It seems that, if a different election system had been employed for choosing American presidents, the U.S. Civil War might not have happened—for better or worse. See Alexander Tabarrok and Lee Spector, "Would the Borda Count Have Avoided the Civil War?" *Journal of Theoretical Politics* 11, no. 2 (1999), 262.

American system of "plurality voting is one of the worst of all possible choices."[5] Although most American elections are based on plurality voting, one such researcher, Alexander Tabarrok, argues that "almost anything looks good compared to it."[6]

In 1997, the newly elected government of Tony Blair established an independent commission to review the United Kingdom's perhaps antiquated voting methods. The commission report noted that following World War II, India was virtually the only nation in the world that had adopted the traditional English and American system of plurality voting.[7] Indeed, the commission recommended that a new method of voting—"the Alternate Vote," involving the transfer of votes from least preferred candidates to higher-ranked candidates (as indicated by second and third choices on the ballot), until one candidate has an absolute majority—should "be implemented throughout the United Kingdom" for those members of Parliament (the large majority) representing individual districts.[8] And in a 1995 survey article, Jonathan Levin and Barry Nalebuff reviewed 16 election alternatives, ranging from simple majority rule to much more complicated voting systems.[9] The systems most commonly employed in U.S. elections therefore represent only a few among a large number of voting possibilities.[10] (Readers interested in a more complete discussion can consult a large body of political science literature.[11])

Besides voting rules, another method of assuring minority representation in a neighborhood association is by the creation of election districts.[12] Even if the unit owners in a particular district represent only a small part of the total association, they may still be able to elect their own district representative to the board of directors. If a group of townhouses, for example, are located in an association of mostly single-family homes, these townhouses might be designated as one election district.

Besides the election method, many other constitutional issues arise in considering an ideal neighborhood "legislature." Consider first several national and corporate examples. In the United States, the Congress is constitutionally the most powerful branch of government. In Great Britain, by contrast, the House of Commons can precipitate a new election through a no-confidence vote, but mostly ratifies decisions made by the Prime Minister and other cabinet ministers—a system in which, some argue, "the winning party is dictator" but only for the period until the next election.[13] In business, the members of a corporate board of directors—the corporate "legislature"—are elected by the full body of qualified stockholders, the relevant "political jurisdiction" in this case. Unlike the U.S. Congress or the British House of Commons, corporate board members are all elected "at large," though they may be nominated to represent certain of the corporation's "constituencies" (particularly individual owners of large amounts of stock, bankers, and, in more recent years, women, racial minorities, and "public-interest" groups).

Neighborhood associations generally find it easier to assemble the unit owners for full neighborhood meetings, thus reducing the burdens of direct democracy. The policy and management issues facing a neighborhood association will typically be less technically complex than those facing federal and state legislatures and corporate boards. Another difference is that the "principal-agent" problem should be less severe in neighborhood associations.* The design of a neighborhood legislature may benefit from new constitutional approaches that reflect the particular voting transaction cost and other circumstances typical of neighborhood associations. This chapter will describe some of the options.

Private Neighborhood Federalism?

Students of government have long studied the ideal size for a local governance unit. They found, for example, that African tribes historically were often made up of self-governing clans that typically did not exceed a few hundred individuals. These clans were about the same size as the ancient Grecian "deme"—a "small territorially based association, which formed the basic political unit of the Athenian polity." Indeed, as Michael Sarbanes and Kathleen Skullney observe, the deme "shared many characteristics" with the contemporary neighborhood association.[14]

Modern sociologists suggest that the ideally sized social unit will permit a member to know most of the other members personally. A desirable size for an election district thus might be a few hundred people—or a hundred or so households. If the entire neighborhood association is about this size, then separate districts will not be needed. However, what about larger associations that often have a thousand or more unit owners?

Depending on geographic features, street routes, densities, and other circumstances, it may be desirable to divide a larger neighborhood association into smaller, "subneighborhood" groups of, say, 50 to 150 unit owners each. Each subneighborhood would then elect one or more members to the higher-

---

*In the language of economics, the voters can be considered the "principals" and the elected members of the legislature are the "agents"—who are supposed to serve the principals' interests. One can say that the "principal-agent" problem is smaller in a neighborhood association, as compared with many other political jurisdictions. Alternatively, one might say that the "asymmetry" of information between the voters and their elected representatives is less severe in a neighborhood association. It is easy enough for unit owners to see whether the grass has been regularly mown in a common area. The lesser degree of principal-agent problems and information asymmetries may significantly affect the "industrial organization"—the typical size and the internal organizational structure—of neighborhood associations. See David E. M. Sappington, "Incentives in Principal-Agent Relationships," *Journal of Economic Perspectives* (Spring 1991).

level association board. Within each subneighborhood, the unit owners might have their own "mini" governing association with its own board of directors. This most local of elected bodies would handle the most "micro" issues, such as the enforcement of covenant restrictions on land within the subneighborhood area. Although it would raise the transaction costs of democratic decision-making within the overall neighborhood association, such a constitutional system of "private neighborhood federalism" might have significant overall political advantages.

One concern, however, would be that association board members who represent a particular district might show greater commitment to the interests of that district. This narrow focus might prompt each board member to become particularly well informed about his or her district, but prove a liability when the neighborhood association must consider issues affecting all unit owners together. As the number of board members increases, the collective choice problems of free-rider behavior and "rational ignorance" on the part of individual members of the neighborhood legislature would also increase.*

If each member of a neighborhood legislature represents a particular district, then these members might also spend much of their time seeking to redirect spending to their own part of the neighborhood (more playgrounds, for example, for a neighborhood area with more children). As legislators compete with one another to "bring home the bacon," they might raise taxes and governmental services above levels that the unit owners desire. Constitution writers of new neighborhood associations may want to establish special barriers to logrolling and other such narrow coalition building practices, such as requiring a supermajority to approve any neighborhood budget increase above the inflation rate. This requirement may be especially important if a neighborhood association adopts a private federal structure of governance.

Proportional Representation

Aside from such practical disadvantages typical of a neighborhood federal structure, another consideration is that many minorities within a neighborhood association will not be clustered geographically. If the goal is to ensure a

---

*"Rational ignorance" is a term used by economists who treat political knowledge as a form of private investment. Given the costs of acquiring it, the individual private return to greater knowledge of political matters will often be negative. Hence, if a person behaves in a narrowing self-interested way (the standard economic assumption), he or she will rationally choose not to make the investment—to remain "rationally ignorant" with respect to a large number of political issues. Continuing in this economic way of understanding political behavior, only "political junkies" and other individuals who actually enjoy the study of politics as a form of private consumption will rationally choose to have detailed knowledge of many political issues.

wide range of views represented on the board, districting then will not work and some other election system will have to be found. Standard plurality voting may not achieve this goal because it often favors a dominant majority. Its wide use in the United States—including almost all current neighborhood associations—is mostly a product of American history and political tradition.[15] When the U.S. Constitution was written in 1787, few other electoral methods were available for consideration.

Under the plurality voting method currently used by most neighborhood associations, the manner of assigning votes is crucial to the electoral outcome. In some associations unit owners cast only one vote. If there are several open seats on the board of directors, then this procedure will increase the likelihood that minority viewpoints will be represented because members of each neighborhood group will tend to cast their single vote for the candidate who most closely reflects their views. If group A represents 75 percent of the unit owners, and if most members of group A cast their vote for the same attractive candidate, then there will be room for a candidate from group B with 25 percent of the votes to win second place, and thus a board seat as well. If members of group A divide their vote among several attractive candidates, to be sure, they may dominate the entire election result, and the candidate of group B may not be elected at all.

Moreover, the members of group A may feel that they should also be guaranteed a say about all the candidates elected to the board, including any second and third place winners. Thus, the most common electoral procedure in neighborhood associations is to assign a number of votes to each unit owner equal to the number of open seats. Under this election method, however, group A is likely to control the full election results, leaving the 25 percent of the unit owners in group B in many cases without any board representation at all.

In order to find better answers to such concerns, the writers of future neighborhood association constitutions may want to consider entirely new alternatives to traditional plurality voting methods typical of the United States. Election systems based on proportional representation, for example, are explicitly designed to elect a governing group that represents a wider range of voter opinion. Developed in the mid-19th century, and then adopted for many European parliamentary elections by the end of that century, proportional representation is now widely employed around the world.* In comparing "majoritarian" and proportional election systems, political scientist Bingham Powell concludes that the clear advantage lies with the latter "as instruments of democracy."[16]

---

*In the later 20th century, admittedly, the trend was toward greater use of mixtures of individual electoral districts and proportional representation in selecting legislatures. As in the Diet of Japan, many national legislatures today combine election of one group of members by proportional representation with the direct election of another—often-larger—group of members from specific electoral districts.

Under a system of proportional representation, a party prepares a list of potential legislators and ranks them. At the election, each party earns a total number of legislative slots in proportion to the total number of votes cast for that party. Given the absence of parties in neighborhood associations, proportional representation has generally been dismissed as impossible. However, at least in theory, it is possible to have a system of proportional representation involving only individual candidates without party labels.[17] In such a system, as in plurality voting, the candidates who receive the most votes win. However, instead of being assigned an equal vote, each elected member of the legislature receives voting power in proportion to the total number of votes he or she received. Thus, if candidates Jones and Smith were both elected to the board of directors of a neighborhood association, but Jones received twice as many votes as Smith, then Jones would also have twice as many votes on the board. With modern computers, such systems of weighted voting by individual representatives, based on the election results, have become a practical possibility even in large legislative bodies.

If employed in a neighborhood association, such a system might encourage a wider number of unit owners to offer themselves—or be nominated by other members of the association—as candidates for board membership. In the 19th century, the noted British economist John Stuart Mill endorsed such a voting system for national elections:

> Of all modes in which a national representation can possibly be constituted, this one affords the best security for the intellectual qualifications desirable in the representatives. At present, by universal admission, it is becoming more and more difficult for anyone who has only talents and character to gain admission into the House of Commons. . . . [Under the new system] those who did not like the local candidates, or who could not succeed in carrying the local candidate they preferred, would have the power to fill up their voting papers by a selection from all the persons of national reputation. . . . In no other way which it seems possible to suggest would Parliament be so certain of containing the very *elite* of the country.[18]

Today, the people most likely to win in a single nationwide vote for individuals to become members of Congress might be former movie stars and ex-professional athletes. At a neighborhood level, however, Mill's cadre of civic-minded and accomplished people might still be elected, and assume prominent decisionmaking roles on a neighborhood association's board of directors.

Political Parties

Originally, candidates for city councils in American municipalities usually ran without party labels. Gradually, however, more and more candidates began to declare a party identification. In neighborhood associations, the development of a party system is possible as associations become larger and assume wider local governing responsibilities. A party label serves to reduce information costs, indicating how a candidate for office might vote. Moreover, once a candidate has run under a party label, he or she may feel a stronger obligation to cast votes consistent with the party's general governing philosophy; in some cases, violators of this practice have experienced actual party sanctions.

In a neighborhood association election, the parties would not necessarily be Republicans and Democrats. One party might be the "Low Budget Party," and another might be the "High Budget Party." Alternatively, covenant enforcement might be the issue, and members of the "Flexible Enforcement Party" might battle against the "Rigid Enforcement Party" for control of the board of directors. If the neighborhood faced the fundamental choice of whether or not to terminate the association, the "Take the Money and Run Party" might contest with the "Preserve the Neighborhood Party."

Parties might also be formed within a neighborhood association around the personalities of charismatic individuals. Thus, there might be a "James Brown" party, with Mr. Brown at its head and a "party list" of his associates— following in this regard the British model in Parliamentary elections. Candidates from the "James Brown Party" might compete against the "Harold Washington Party," the "Elizabeth Berry Party," and potentially others. By knowing the party heads' positions on neighborhood issues, neighborhood unit owners could more easily bring about basic changes in neighborhood policies.

Introducing the party system to neighborhoods would make it feasible to adopt a standard proportional system of election. Rather than adopting the Fraser proposal, which assigns fixed numbers of board seats by age group, for example, the neighborhood association board might include members to represent the views of one party consisting of unit owners with children, and another party of 70-year-old unit owners, even though one or both of these groups might be a minority within the overall membership of unit owners. Under an electoral system of proportional representation, each group would have members on the board of directors in proportion to the total number of votes received by that "party/group."

Transferable Voting Systems

Some of the constitutional advantages of proportional representation can be gained in other ways. One such option is the "transferable voting system." Under this system, each unit owner orders his or her preferences on the ballot among all the candidates seeking election to the board of directors. To win election, a candidate must receive a minimum number of votes (e.g., the total number of unit owner votes divided by the number of board members to be elected). Once a candidate receives this total number of votes, his or her remaining additional votes are transferred to other candidates for the board. After all the transferred votes have been counted, and further winning candidates determined in a second round, the process is be repeated until the target number of board members has been reached.

Other methods of transferring second place and other lower-ranking votes can be employed. Depending on the exact procedures, each election system is likely to produce a somewhat different result. An approach sometimes called the "instant runoff" method transfers votes among candidates by first eliminating the candidate with the lowest total number of votes (counting only first choices of voters up to this point). The second-place choices of those voters who voted for the losing candidate are now counted instead. (Ballots of voters without second preferences are then discarded.) The process is repeated, continuing to eliminate the lowest ranking of the remaining candidates. Eventually, one candidate must have more than 50 percent of the votes and is declared the winner. If more than one seat is to be filled, the election process is concluded when the number of candidates still in the running is equal to the total number of new board members needed.

Such election methods involving transferable votes are used in various parts of the world. Among nations, Australia has long been particularly bold in experimenting with novel methods of holding elections; for more than 80 years, the Australian government has used a system of the "single-transferrable-vote" to select members of both the House of Representatives and the Senate. The Republic of Ireland, Malta, and Northern Ireland also elect representatives to the European Parliament via the single-transferable-vote system.[19] In 2002, San Francisco's city government adopted a variant of the instant runoff system for its elections for mayor, district attorney, and sheriff.

Multiple Election Rounds

In many jurisdictions, candidates must receive an absolute majority of votes to be elected to office. If the top candidate does not receive 50 percent of the votes, then the top two candidates compete against each other in a runoff election. This method is particularly desirable in situations where there are many candidates for one position. Otherwise, when a large number of mainstream candidates divide the votes among themselves, the highest vote-getter may actually be a fringe candidate with, say, only 20 percent of the vote. The disadvantage to multiple rounds of elections is the burden of actually conducting several elections. However, the fact that many neighborhood associations are compact and contain a smaller number of voters may work to keep the transaction costs of multiple election rounds to a minimum.* The multiple elections might well be held sequentially at the same neighborhood meeting.

Aside from potentially high transactions costs, political theory suggests that the results of multiple rounds of voting will normally be preferable to elections involving only a single trip to the ballot box. The additional rounds will allow the voters to change their voting preferences in light of the first and other earlier rounds of results. Where more than one person is being elected to the board, for example, the knowledge that one person is already elected might significantly change voter preferences for the next elected board member. It might become a higher priority for voters to elect someone who can work with—or stand up to—the person already elected to the board.

Election by Lottery

The lottery method has its roots in history. In ancient Athens, the Council of Five Hundred ran the city. The members of this council were selected each year by lottery from citizens over age 30 and in good standing in the community. Fifteenth-century Florence—the "Athens" of the Renaissance—also used a random method for selecting its representatives. As constitutional scholar Dennis Mueller reports, random selection "appears to have made all citizens feel that they were a part of the government, and that their interests were represented. It also appears to have led representatives to identify with the common interests of Florence."[20]

Mandatory service on boards of directors, as selected by lottery, might be one good way of surmounting the free-rider problem common to many neighborhood associations. At present, members of many neighborhood associations complain that too many "busybodies," power-hungry individuals, and other poorly qualified people end up on neighborhood boards. A lottery among unit owners might significantly increase the numbers of shy and quiet people—many well qualified for board service—who are chosen. Mandatory service, like current jury duty, would support the idea that each unit owner owes something to the neighborhood community. Indeed, one legal authority has suggested making "membership and participation on an association committee mandatory, as is payment of assessments."[21] Once a person had served,

---

*In the Internet age, an entire neighborhood association might be wired for the purpose of (among others) holding elections. The casting of ballots could then be done electronically from individual homes (or from anywhere via password-accessible Internet sites), and the results tabulated instantaneously.

he or she would be exempt from a further neighborhood "draft" for at least a certain number of years.*

If a lottery method is used to select an association's board of directors, a larger board size would help to ensure that its composition represents a full range of neighborhood opinion. If a board has only five members selected by lottery, three of them—a board majority—might randomly end up representing views well outside the mainstream of neighborhood opinion. A neighborhood board of directors selected by lottery thus should probably have at least 15 or so members.

Some prospective buyers, of course, might want to avoid any neighborhood where they could be drafted to neighborhood service. Whether or not to buy a home in a neighborhood association using a lottery election system could thus become yet another element in consumer housing choice.

Outside Board Members

The property owned in a neighborhood association is a major financial asset for most unit owners, as well as a place of residence. And in managing their financial assets, many people look to professional experts for help. The stockholders of a business corporation, for example, want some board members to have accounting, finance, personnel, administrative, legal, and other appropriate expertise. In a 2001 survey, the typical board of directors of a business corporation had nine "outside" directors and two "inside" directors (generally officers of the corporation).[22]

Given unit owners' high financial investments in neighborhood associations, choosing at least some outside board members may also be desirable. Managing a neighborhood association may involve complicated real estate, legal, environmental, civil engineering, and other issues, subjects about which board members may not have adequate knowledge. Assuming there is no adversarial relationship, a representative of the original developer might be included even after the unit owners have assumed management control. Having a well-respected architect as a member of the board might also be desirable. An outside attorney or a structural engineer could also offer valuable counsel.

---

*In present-day America, the system for selecting jury members for criminal trials has some of the elements of a lottery. Toward the end of the Vietnam War, the draft for military service in the United States adopted a lottery system of choosing new inductees into the Army. As in the military draft and jury selection, those people "drafted" for service on a neighborhood association board by lottery might be able to plead hardship or some other disability.

It will generally be necessary to pay outside directors.* The average member of a board of directors in an American business corporation receives $41,000 (and serves 156 hours) per year.[23] According to Hyatt, "the eventual possibility that there will be professional board members [on neighborhood association boards] is a real one." Indeed, "professionalism and compensation are both possible in the future board operation" of neighborhood associations.[24] Law professor Robert Natelson argues that internal directors might be paid something as well. The absence of compensation means that "many of those who do assume that responsibility [of board service] are precisely those least appropriate for the job,"—people who are looking "to expand their network of contacts" or for whom "the dominating motive is desire for power." Hence, even though "it is unlikely that any payment scheme will fully compensate directors for their time and effort, prohibitions of any compensation seem indefensible."[25]

The Term of Office

Choosing appropriate terms of office for board members is an important issue. A shorter period gives association unit owners a frequent opportunity to review and vote on board members' performance. A shorter period might also make it easier to attract candidates who, in the absence of compensation, would prefer a shorter time commitment. Many boards have had terms as short as one year. A longer tenure, however, provides more opportunity for mastering complex issues, allows greater continuity in board decisionmaking, and reduces the amount of time spent in campaigning and conducting elections.

Another issue is whether to set term limits. Putting a time limit on board membership—say two or three terms—would ensure a regular infusion of fresh ideas and impetus and reduce the risk that a small clique might dominate board affairs for many years. In ancient Athens, top officials served for one year and were barred from a second term. As a result, many Athenians acquired practical experience in the real workings of government. Ancient Rome also prescribed one-year terms for consuls, praetors, and other top officials selected by the Assembly.[26] The disadvantage of such short terms is that neighborhood board members who have provided exemplary service are not utilized to their best advantage.

Neighborhood constitutions espousing shorter terms would allow for the easy removal of poor performers from the board. At present, association con-

---

*The compensation need not be a cash payment. Board members could, for example, be given either a partial or a complete rebate on the payment of neighborhood association dues. Non-pecuniary forms of compensation might include catered dinners at board meetings, or preferential access in certain association amenities (e.g., the golf course).

stitutions often provide for recall elections. Such elections may be held when, for example, 33 percent of the unit owners sign a petition requesting a recall, and require a 66 percent vote to remove a board member. In some cases of severe board malfeasance, the possibility exists that all the members might be recalled at once.

Voting Rules in the Neighborhood Legislature

Studies of voting systems for collective choice within any given group date at least as far back as 1785 and Condorcet's "Essay of the Application of Mathematics to the Theory of Decision Making." Condorcet pointed out that a vote with three alternatives might reveal that choice A is preferred over choice B, choice B over choice C, and choice C over choice A. It is not possible then to say that A, B, or C is the single preferred result. If a vote is actually held, the final outcome will depend somewhat arbitrarily on the order in which the voting is held.* If no ordering rule is imposed, then there could be no outcome at all, as each result could simply be overturned in the next round of voting—a situation described in voting literature as the technical problem of "cycling."[27] Such theoretical results have also been extended beyond simple voting circumstances to more complicated and numerous possible choices.[28]

Most existing legislatures in the public sector operate today according to a principle of simple majority rule—50 percent of the votes, plus one, wins approval. However, if a false negative is seen as less costly than a false positive (for example, convicting an innocent man in a jury trial), then majority rule may not be optimal. In the U.S. Congress, for example, supermajorities are constitutionally required to approve some actions—for example, House and Senate overrides of a presidential veto, Senate approval of foreign treaties, or Senate conviction of a president who has been impeached by the House. In recent years, there has evolved an informal requirement of 60 percent (the proportion required to defeat a filibuster) to win Senate approval of many controversial issues.

Indeed, this recent Senate development is consistent with the views of many voting theorists. As discussed in chapter 4, James Buchanan and Gordon Tullock argued in 1962 that simple majority rule is an arbitrary criterion that can leave too many people worse off (potentially 49 percent can be "losers").[29] In a (hypothetical) world where political participation involved no costs, the "opti-

---

*In 1951, Kenneth Arrow published his "impossibility theorem," demonstrating once again that voting choices may inevitably involve somewhat arbitrary outcomes. Arrow's work stimulated a large body of research and writing on voting systems. See Kenneth J. Arrow, *Social Choice and Individual Values* (1951; New Haven, CT: Yale University Press, 1972).

mal" voting rule would be unanimous consent (the political equivalent of "Pareto optimality" in economic analyses). However, in the real world, unanimous consent involves impossibly large transaction costs—meetings could go on endlessly. Hence, a trade-off must be established. Elinor Ostrom reports that, based on case studies of collective decisionmaking in many societies around the world, the best results are likely to be achieved where "participants use collective-choice rules that fall between the extremes of unanimity or [a simple majority] . . . and, thus, avoid high transaction or high deprivation costs."[30] A neighborhood association might similarly require a favorable board vote of, say, 60 percent to adopt any new policy.

Incentives for Voting

Voting incentives vary around the world. Australia and some other countries legally require people to vote.[31] While not necessarily making voting compulsory, neighborhood associations might at least provide greater individual incentives for participation in association elections. For example, the Sky Bryce Association, located in a resort area in western Virginia, devised an innovative financial incentive to encourage voting. The association membership is dominated by second homes (771 units), although it is home to a significant number of permanent residents (160 units). More than 1,500 lots are still vacant. According to the governing documents, the owners of these undeveloped lots and the owners of existing homes have equal voting rights. Yet it has been difficult to persuade many of the eligible unit owners, especially nonresidents, to participate in association elections.

In 2000, this problem threatened the association's ability to amend its founding declaration—an amendment that was not in itself controversial. A successful vote of approval required not only a high percentage in favor of the amendment, but also a minimum total number of votes among all the unit owners. To address this problem, the Sky Bryce Association turned each ballot cast into a lottery ticket. The first voting unit owner's name drawn from a hat received $300, the second $200, and the third $100. With this financial encouragement, the total number of votes cast then proved sufficient to meet the minimum and pass the amendment.

There could be other prizes for voting. Compared with public municipalities, neighborhood associations have greater constitutional leeway to adopt innovative democratic practices. It is doubtful that any municipality today could offer its citizenry financial incentives to vote. Nevertheless, there are grounds in political theory for this practice; political machines in big cities once rewarded people with jobs and other perks for showing up at the polls. Without some counter to the free-rider problem, it can be argued that an election result will be systematically biased toward voters who are particularly motivated by emotional or ideological concerns. Other people may be more narrowly "rational," calculating that the economic cost of voting exceeds the economic return. One can argue that an election system should not work to exclude the "economic voters," leaving only the "ideological voters" to decide the outcome. It may make good sense for a society to pay people to vote (or to fine them if they fail to vote).

Legislative Functions

A neighborhood association's constitution should establish the "division of powers" among the association's legislative, executive, and judicial branches. Like a parliamentary regime, these domains need not be separated as strictly as the three branches of the U.S. federal government. In a neighborhood association, two bodies can potentially act in a legislative capacity—the board of directors and the body of unit owners. The constitution of a neighborhood association might explicitly spell out which (if any) types of legislative decisions should be made by a full vote of all unit owners and when and how to hold this vote.

Alternatively, the constitution might specify a discretionary procedure for putting an issue before all the unit owners. The board of directors might have the authority to call a neighborhood referendum on an issue. A neighborhood referendum might also be held if a required percentage—say 25 percent—of the unit owners submit a petition requesting this action. Legislative responsibilities in a neighborhood association—to be handled either by the board or the full membership—would include in most cases at least the following functions:

1. Approving the neighborhood association budget.
2. Giving the final say on actions relating to the neighborhood enforcement of covenants (and issuing of any covenant waivers).
3. Setting policies for the common areas.
4. Determining the neighborhood legal strategy in cases that involve the association as a defendant or plaintiff.
5. Selecting outside management firms and consultants to be hired by the association.
6. Setting personnel policies for association employees.
7. Establishing rules for neighborhood streets and parking areas, including speed limits, entrance gates, and other access controls.
8. Deciding the manner of representation of the neighborhood association in hearings, meetings, and other public fora outside the neighborhood.

For the Purposes of Discussion

The numerous options presented in this chapter raise complex political issues. Some of the elements of a constitutional package appropriate for a neighborhood association "legislature" are proposed below. The selection of one option may rule out certain other incompatible options. For the purposes of this discussion, assume that a typical neighborhood association comprises about 200 unit owners—a common size around the United States.

The board of directors—Each board member would be elected based on a neighborhood-wide vote. Candidates for the board of directors would not have to be unit owners. The election would held be electronically.[32] (Alternative arrangements would be made for any unit owner without a computer.) Electronic voting would make it feasible to hold multiple rounds at little cost. A winning candidate would have to obtain a vote of 50 percent of those voting. If no candidate received 50 percent of the vote initially, another round of voting would be held, minus the lowest vote getter, who would be removed from the ballot (and minus any other candidates who received less than 5 percent of the total vote). This process would continue until one candidate received more than 50 percent of the votes. If more than one new board member were required, then new rounds of voting would continue in the same manner until the board seats were filled.

Voting rules of the board—"Garden variety" actions of the board of directors would require a simple majority of 50 percent plus one. "Important" actions—such as assessment increases, new-rule making, and decisions to go to court—would require a 60 percent vote.

Unit owner referenda—Constitutional amendments within a neighborhood association would be approved by a vote of all unit owners with a supermajority of 66 percent. Proposed amendments or other policy issues could be put to the vote of all unit owners by board action or on submission of a petition containing names of 25 percent of the unit owners. A recall of a board member could be put before the unit owners in the same manner—and also requiring 66 percent for final approval.

Operation of the board—The board of directors would have 9 members (larger than most current boards) who would each serve for three years. The full board would meet a minimum of four times per year (less than the current average; most boards probably meet too often). The board would form various subcommittees to perform specific duties in the interim, and to make binding decisions in areas assigned to subcommittee responsibility—although there would be a process for appeal to the full board. The subcommittees would meet according to a schedule each determines. At the option of the full board, additional members of a subcommittee could be added from outside the board.

Board compensation—Each board member who is a unit owner would be compensated by relief from payment of association assessments. Outside directors would receive compensation of $5,000 per year (plus free use of golf clubs, tennis courts, and other neighborhood recreation facilities).

NOTES

1. Charles E. Fraser, "Condo Commandos: An Abuse of Power," in Adrienne Schmitz and Lloyd W. Bookout, eds., *Trends and Innovations in Master-Planned Communities* (Washington, DC: Urban Land Institute, 1998), 46.

2. Ibid.

3. Ibid.

4. Wayne S. Hyatt, "Putting the Community Back in Community Associations: An Action Plan," in Bill Overton, ed., *Community First! Emerging Visions Reshaping America's Condominium and Homeowner Associations* (Alexandria, VA: Community Associations Institute, 1999), 111.

5. Erica Klarreich, "Election Selection: Are We Using the Worst Voting Procedure?" *Science News* 162 (November 2, 2002). http://www.sciencenews.org/articles/20021102/bob8.asp.

6. Quoted in Klarreich, "Election Selection," 1.

7. *The Report of the Independent Commission on the Voting System,* Presented to Parliament by the Secretary of State for the Home Department by Command of Her Majesty, London, UK (October 1998), paragraph no. 76.

8. Ibid., Chapter 9, recommendation 3.

9. Jonathan Levin and Barry Nalebuff, "An Introduction to Vote-Counting Schemes," *Journal of Economic Perspectives* 9 (Winter 1995).

10. See Robert D. Cooter, *The Strategic Constitution* (Princeton, NJ: Princeton University Press, 2000).

11. Dennis C. Mueller, ed., *Perspectives on Public Choice: A Handbook* (New York: Cambridge University Press, 1997); and Kenneth A. Shepsle and Mark S. Bonchek, *Analyzing Politics: Rationality, Behavior, and Institutions* (New York: Norton, 1997).

12. Douglas W. Rae, "Using District Magnitude to Regulate Political Party Competition," *Journal of Economic Perspectives* 9 (Winter 1995).

13. Dennis C. Mueller, *Constitutional Democracy* (New York: Oxford University Press, 1996), 274.

14. Michael Sarbanes and Kathleen Skullney, "Taking Communities Seriously: Should Community Associations Have Standing in Maryland?" *Maryland Journal of Contemporary Legal Issues* 6 (Spring/Summer 1995), 292.

15. See G. Bingham Powell Jr., *Elections as Instruments of Democracy: Majoritarian and Proportional Visions* (New Haven, CT: Yale University Press, 2000).

16. Ibid., 254.

17. Mueller, *Constitutional Democracy,* 101–4.

18. John Stuart Mill, quoted in Mueller, *Constitutional Democracy,* 127.

19. Mueller, *Constitutional Democracy,* 135.

20. Ibid., 316.

21. David C. Drewes, "Putting the 'Community' Back in Common Interest Communities: A Proposal for Participation-Enhancing Procedural Review," *Columbia Law Review* 101 (March 2001), 340.

22. Korn/Ferry International, *28th Annual Board of Directors Study* (New York, NY: Korn/Ferry International, 2001), 12.

23. Ibid., 17, 19.

24. Wayne S. Hyatt, "The Evolution in Community Governance," in Schmitz and Bookout, eds, *Trends and Innovations in Master-Planned Communities,* 46.

25. Robert G. Natelson, *Law of Property Owners Associations* (Boston: Little, Brown and Co., 1989), 106.

26. Scott Gordon, *Controlling the State: Constitutionalism from Ancient Athens to Today* (Cambridge, MA: Harvard University Press, 1999), 73, 100–103.

27. Cooter, *The Strategic Constitution,* 37–40.

28. Peyton Young, "Optimal Voting Rules," *Journal of Economic Perspectives* 9 (Winter 1995), 55. See also H. Peyton Young, "Group Choice and Individual Judgments," in Mueller, ed., *Perspectives on Public Choice.*

29. James M. Buchanan and Gordon Tullock, *The Calculus of Consent: Logical Foundations of Constitutional Democracy* (Ann Arbor: University of Michigan Press, 1962); see also Gordon Tullock, *The Vote Motive: An Essay in the Economics of Politics, with Applications to the British Economy* (London: The Institute of Economic Affairs, 1976).

30. Elinor Ostrom, "Private and Common Property Rights," in Boudewijn Bouckaert and Gerrit De Geest, eds., *Encyclopedia of Law and Economics, Volume II* (Cheltenham, UK: Edward Elgar, 2000), 347.

31. *Report of the Independent Commission on the Voting System,* paragraph no. 74.

32. See Bill Mason, "I-Voting: Moving Associations Into the Brave New World," *Quorum,* the magazine of the Community Associations Institute, Washington Chapter (September 2001), 10.

16

The Neighborhood
Executive Office

The Chesapeake Bay, the largest estuary in North America, is home to 3,600 plant and animal species. Sixteen million people live in the area. Over the course of the 20th century, fish, oyster, and other populations suffered from growing pollution, including runoff from urban land development. During the 1980s, therefore, conservationists commenced heroic efforts to clean up the Bay's waters. As part of an evolving strategy to control runoff's harmful effects, developers are now often required to build ponds and small lakes in their communities to hold and filter rainwater. These bodies of water may also enhance the value of lakeshore and other nearby properties.[1] However, once all the housing units are sold, the developer leaves, turning over management responsibility to the new neighborhood association. Management tasks in these communities range from periodic dredging of the water bodies to the monitoring of stream flows—all in compliance with tight federal and state water-quality rules.

Environmentalists advocating Chesapeake Bay cleanup, however, find the critical management role of neighborhood associations troublesome. George Maurer of the Chesapeake Bay Foundation comments, "The problem with these [water] facilities is one of maintenance. Many are managed by homeowner associations, which are made up of mostly average citizens who don't have any expertise in storm-water management"—and who have often performed poorly in overseeing a sophisticated system of rainwater runoff controls.[2]

Such concerns about neighborhood associations' management abilities are widespread. In most cases, to be sure, the unit owners themselves experience most of the negative consequences. For example, one unit owner described how his neighborhood association sent "two burly men" on ten minutes' notice to investigate a building water leak that had been reported by another unit owner. The two plumbers "pushed their way into the bathroom and—fully ignoring [the owner]—started discussing how they would dismantle the sink and drill underneath it to reach the (yet unidentified) leak." Rendered momentarily speechless, the unit owner finally summoned her courage, there ensued a "screaming match [and the plumbers] left." This particular unit owner would later write a doctoral dissertation on neighborhood associations and a report for the Community Associations Institute offering many more examples of "bad decisions . . . made by community associations or by the professionals serving them."[3]

Charles Fraser reports that "during the last 30 years, a number of large community associations have lapsed into mismanagement. This situation has damaged the reputation of common-interest development in general."[4] Fraser offers a history of what might be labeled the "bad management syndrome":

> At first, the developers and their lawyers operated under the naïve assumption that the association boards established by the covenants would pick wise and capable nominating committee members. These nominating committees, in turn, would select competent candidates as directors, choosing directors from all age groups and familial-status categories.
>
> This did not always happen. Some boards represented the interests of only one category of homeowners. Board members rarely had any experience in the management of many functions established in the typical CC&Rs, such as landscaping, snow removal, garbage collection, swimming pool management, clubhouse operations, golf course maintenance, playground maintenance and so forth.
>
> Board meetings grew long and divisive. Busy and happy members of the community began to shun board meetings. Proposed new board members declined to serve. Some large-scale planned communities developed a reputation for poor management. Recognizing the problem, some large associations hired full-time managers to take over operations. These professional management companies grew and offered their services to multiple community associations. Unfortunately, the operational freedom of some of these management companies was limited by vague or restrictive language in the deed covenants. As a result, mismanagement lived on.[5]

Poor management is, as Fraser suggests, a principal source of internal frictions in many neighborhood associations. Complaints about dictatorial boards of directors, arbitrary judgments concerning acceptable property modifications, insider favoritism, and so on have spawned a minor industry of citizen protest groups. In Arizona, one such organization is the Citizens Against Private Government HOAs [Homeowners Associations]. One of its publications states that "while members may vote for board members as if they were electing councilmen or legislators, the HOA is not a real democratic institution." After buying into a homeowners association, many owners find that they have "surrendered their civil rights without any information that this was indeed what they had agreed to." According to this group, this lack of rights protection reflects in part the fact that "the HOA lacks a separation of powers doctrine as found in every level of American government," reflecting the fact that a neighborhood association typically "is governed according to and subject to corporation law and not municipality or city/town laws."[6]

A Nonprofit Corporation

As described in previous chapters, neighborhood associations are in fact usually organized as nonprofit corporations and follow standard corporate methods of governance. An elected board has the final authority for the conduct of neighborhood affairs. The board is directly elected by association unit owners and—subject to any limits specified in the neighborhood constitution—sets the policies for enforcing covenants, using common areas, providing neighborhood services, and conducting other areas of association activity.[7] Also following a corporate model, the neighborhood association board selects a president, secretary, and treasurer as the association's executive officers. The officers in practice are also generally board members, although this is not legally required. The president has the authority to act in the name of the association, which includes committing funds, hiring employees, and conducting other official actions.

Chapter 15 examined various options for selecting and operating the neighborhood association "legislature"—the board of directors. This chapter explores options with respect to the neighborhood association's "executive branch"—the individuals responsible for routine administration. Besides the president and other officers, executive personnel include any employees who may be directly hired by the association and any professional management personnel contracted to serve the neighborhood.

Some of the current tensions within neighborhood associations, as real estate lawyer Scott Mollen reports, reflect many unit owners' sense that "ownership and operational decisions are being made by individuals who may have no professional real estate expertise or experience." Neighborhood decisions may require technical knowledge that few if any members of the board have. As compared with decisions made by an outside organization with professional qualifications, unit owners "are often less willing to accept and respect decisions by the board" of fellow unit owners.[8] Keeping an association board of directors separate from direct operational responsibilities thus may be a key to improving the internal workings of many associations.[9] A wider separation of legislative and executive powers, in short, may become important to neighborhood associations, just as it has been in many other government and business jurisdictions.

Fraser similarly argues for a redefinition of the relationship between association boards of directors and administrators. In the future, he argues, neighborhood associations should make greater efforts "to hire competent and experienced management companies." Neighborhood associations should be willing to sign long-term contracts that assign much of their administrative responsibility to an outside firm. Fraser labels this approach as " 'town hall' management" by an experienced, "semi-independent" private company entering into perhaps a 5-to-10-year contract with the neighborhood association.[10] The long tenure would help to ensure frank communications and independence of judgment.

The Business Model

In the traditional business corporation, the legislative and executive functions are formally separated. The board of directors picks the chief executive officer (CEO) and perhaps approves a few other top executive officers. Beyond that, the business's executive team normally has wide decisionmaking authority.[11] The top executives develop the strategic business plan, prepare the budget, sign the loans, and make other fundamental business decisions. The board of directors may review some of these decisions, but a formal board vote of approval is seldom required. As one expert in corporate governance puts it, "the main job of the director is to hire, fire, and set compensation" for the CEO.[12] This job definition reflects the fact that, as another corporate authority states, the CEO "will have much more information than the other board members. Unless the board has lost faith in that individual, . . . it will trust this more informed person" to run the corporation.[13]

The separation of legislative and executive functions does not mean that the executives of a business corporation are precluded from serving on its board of directors. Corporate governance in this respect differs from the U.S. federal model and is more like a parliamentary political regime. A corporation's CEO is generally a member of the board of directors as well and indeed is frequently its chairperson (according to one survey, this is the case in 75 percent of American business corporations).[14] A leading business organization, the Business Roundtable, recently reaffirmed its support for this traditional model of corporate governance, declaring that "most American corporations are well served by a structure in which the CEO also serves as chairman of the board."[15]

However, some people understandably believe that a board of directors will find it difficult to evaluate a CEO's performance if that CEO sits as the board's chairperson. Still, as the Business Roundtable states, the traditional "governance model followed by most public corporations in the United States has historically been one of individual, rather than group, leadership."[16] It reflected a common view in American business that "good corporate governance has never created a great company—great leaders, great CEOs have done so."[17] In short, the board of directors may play a critical role in finding such a leader in the first place, but it should then step aside and let this person manage the organization.

In legal theory, a corporation is a democracy of the owners—the stockholders (who correspond to the unit owners of a neighborhood association). However, in the American business world, this is not necessarily the reality. Indeed, there has traditionally been, as one observer puts it, "a chasm that . . . separate[d] ownership from control in corporate America."[18] Except for members of the founding family or other exceptionally large stockholders, a corporation's formal owners—the stockholders—typically exert little influence on the selection of the directors or other corporate decisions. When a director resigns, the other directors generally choose his or her successor. The CEO—a constitutional dictator, in effect—often controls this process as well. The board of directors takes charge only in moments of crisis—if the corporation is in danger of bankruptcy, or if some other major problem has arisen.[19]

A powerful executive and a weak legislature have served many American business corporations well. Whatever the large failings of many specific businesses may be, American business overall is widely seen as a world model of efficiency and innovation. Perhaps private neighborhood associations should move closer to the business model in their manner of governance.

Neighborhoods and Businesses

In general, the instrument of governance chosen will partly depend on the management issues faced. These issues will differ at least somewhat between the business world and the world of neighborhood associations. A business has the great advantage of a clearly defined objective that can be expressed in a quantitative form—the maximization of business profit and shareholder gains, as reflected in part in the current stock price. True, a neighborhood association also has an important quantifiable financial goal—to maximize the investment value of the homes in the neighborhood. However, most of the unit owners will also live in their investments, and will be seeking the highest quality of current neighborhood environment as well.

To a considerable extent, the pursuit of the one objective will coincide with the pursuit of the other.[20] However, the short-run objective of maximizing a neighborhood's current environmental quality may sometimes conflict with the longer-run objective of maximizing future property values. The resources available to the association will have to be divided to some extent between the two goals, and the quality of the neighborhood environment will be more difficult to measure quantitatively and precisely than property (or stock) value.

Businesses and neighborhood associations also differ in that unit owners are better able to monitor the executive team's performance. The people living in a neighborhood association can observe the outcomes of association management activities day-to-day, just as corporate shareholders can follow fluctuations in the stock market. However, current stock prices are an uncertain barometer of future stock prices, and few stockholders have any significant degree of personal interaction with their corporation's top management or can in other ways directly assess the types and levels of skills corporate management possesses.[21] Moreover, the decisionmaking responsibilities may be more technically complex for the top leaders of a business than they are for a neighborhood association's management team. The leading executives of many major American business corporations must follow global economic (and political) developments, project trends in consumer buying habits, and monitor business competitors in diverse markets.

The scope of responsibility of the neighborhood association is more limited and better defined. It may be less important to have a leadership team made up of highly skilled professionals. That said, parking and pet decisions may stir fierce emotions in the neighborhood, so an effective neighborhood association leader may require especially high skills in diplomacy. Indeed, the job of neighborhood management may be more "political," while the job of business management may be more "economic." In their own ways, they may each require high levels of skill.[22]

Historically, then, unit owners have had greater democratic involvement in day-to-day affairs of their neighborhood associations than have the stockholders of most business corporations. But are neighborhood associations suffering from an excess of democracy? Some may not want a neighborhood CEO who is a virtual dictator, but may still want to borrow more heavily from the corporate business governance model. If so, the association's board might turn over greater management responsibility to a strong executive. In turn, the board might spend less time on managing routine operations and more time on setting basic neighborhood policies that the executive would implement. Like a business, the board of directors of a neighborhood association might focus more on selecting the best executive leadership for the neighborhood.

Of course, top business executives work on a full-time basis and are well paid for their services. On the other hand, the officers of most neighborhood associations today are typically part-time volunteers. If neighborhoods embrace this new shift toward the business model, then the typical size of a neighborhood association might also be affected. Neighborhoods governed by constitutions mandating full-time professional managers might find it necessary to pay these employees, say, $100,000 per year. So even for a neighborhood association comprising 1,000 units, each owner would be assessed $1,000 per year, or $83 per month, to cover this expense. Such expense might be a bargain, however, if it resulted in higher unit values and significantly improved neighborhood management.

Depending on the degree of executive independence and authority sought, standard neighborhood constitutions of the past might have to be rewritten. It might also be necessary in many cases to change state laws that currently prescribe many of the governance features specific to the basic neighborhood association.

Should There Be a Neighborhood "Mayor"?

Neighborhood associations in search of a more powerful executive have two options to consider. The top executive could be appointed by the neighborhood board of directors in the same way the president of a business corporation is selected. Alternatively, the top executive—basically, a neighborhood "mayor"—could be elected by the unit owners themselves.

If the job of chief executive of a neighborhood association is merely "technical" and "administrative," there would seem to be little need for an elected mayor. Like a business hiring a new CEO, a neighborhood association might simply hire a qualified professional to perform in the executive role. If a neighborhood is large enough to need a full-time manager, then this top neighborhood executive—chosen partly for professional skills and experience in association management—could work on-site in the neighborhood and report directly to the board. The traditional position of neighborhood "president," filled by a selected board member, might even be abolished so as not to create a confusion of authority with the top professional manager. There would instead simply be, as in the business world, an association "chairman of the board" and a non-elected "neighborhood CEO."

Public municipalities have also tried hiring their top executives. In the 1920s, Cleveland, Kansas City, Cincinnati, and a few other large American cities experimented with the hiring of professional city managers in place of elected mayors.[23] However, these cities soon abandoned these experiments (except for Cincinnati, which made the change much later), recognizing the impracticality of trying to separate policy from administration. This happened because, in large cities at least, hired professionals generally have neither the political skills nor the political legitimacy to run city governments. Large cities have diverse interests and constituencies; the job of the mayor often includes assembling a working coalition in order to solve citywide problems. The task is inherently "political" as well as administrative. A professional administrator's formal training and special expertise might not be much help in such politically charged aspects of city government.

Even in smaller jurisdictions, and contrary to the thinking prominent in the Progressive Era, few now argue that it is possible to separate the "political" from the "administrative" tasks of governance. As one legal authority states, local governments "have become too complex for a structure of government that attempts to separate policy from administration. Inevitably, an appointed manager makes policy decisions." Hence, city manager government "increases conflict and the potential for political gridlock. Experience shows that the council expects the manager to 'get things done.' But when the manager tries to take initiative or make policy decisions, he risks offending the council and getting fired." Yet, managers who are cautious are "blamed for 'not getting things done' " and they may lose their jobs. Thus Stephen Cianca concludes, "The executive role of government is too important to subordinate to a legislative body" in American public government.[24] Although his arguments address issues in the public sector, they also raise relevant concerns for the future writers of neighborhood association constitutions to consider.

Indeed, having an executive with some significant degree of independence from the legislature is a time-honored goal in traditional American systems of governance, systems in which the nation's president, state governors, and big-city mayors all serve at the pleasure of the voters. Unlike a corporate CEO, or the prime minister in a parliamentary regime, they cannot be fired at the will of the legislature. A powerful executive can thus stand as a check against legislative excesses, even as the legislature can counteract any threats of abuse of executive powers. Given the many past complaints about dictatorial board behavior in neighborhood associations—"gestapo"-type actions by directors and so forth—greater formal separation of executive and legislative powers within neighborhood associations might be a good idea here as well.

Under such a model, a neighborhood "mayor"—taking on the role of the association president—would be chosen by a direct vote of the unit owners. (He or she might still be called the "president.") Grounds for this mayor's "impeachment and conviction" would be limited, and impeachment would require a high supermajority vote (probably of the unit owners themselves). An elected president of a neighborhood association might have wide powers and substantial autonomy from the board of directors. This chief neighborhood executive could, for example, have veto authority over board actions, subject to a supermajority override by the board. He or she might have the independent authority to hire a management team or a professional management firm. The neighborhood president might administer the neighborhood covenants, oversee the maintenance decisions for the common areas, and develop the neighborhood budget, though in most cases these actions would be subject to board approval. The term of office for an elected neighborhood association president might run from two to four years.

The case for selecting a neighborhood president by vote becomes stronger as the size of the neighborhood becomes larger.* Yet, even some smaller neighborhood associations might want to elect their own chief executive officer, legitimating his or her stature and power within the neighborhood—an important advantage in resolving internal disputes and representing the neighborhood in outside arenas.

Admittedly, if large numbers of neighborhood associations were to start electing their own presidents, the courts might be more inclined to treat the neighborhood associations legally as "state actors," much like local public governments. In practice, of course, neighborhood associations have long straddled the line between a "public" governmental and a "private" business status. Thus, electing a president should not in itself be a decisive factor in resolving the future legal status of neighborhood associations.

The Manner of Executive Election

If a neighborhood association constitution dictates the election of the neighborhood president, the issue becomes how to do it.[25] One option would allow any unit owner to run for association president. Then, if no candidate received more than 50 percent (or perhaps 40 percent) of the votes, the top two candidates might compete in a runoff election. The second place finisher might be designated as the association's vice president (until 1804, in fact, this was the constitutional arrangement for selecting U.S. vice presidents). The vice president would then fill the position if the elected association president could no longer serve.

This type of election poses a problem, however, in that vote splintering may allow fringe candidates in a crowded field to prevail in the initial round. In the French presidential election in 2002, for example, the final choice was widely expected to be either Jacques Chirac (the sitting president of France and leader of the Gaullist Party) or Lionel Jospin (prime minister and leader of the Socialist Party). However, there were 16 candidates, and a fringe right wing candidate, Jean-Marie le Pen, unexpectedly drew more votes than Jospin to win second place. Chirac then won overwhelmingly and the result was to deny French voters any real choice in the final election.

---

*Among U.S. municipalities, 44 percent of those that boast a population larger than 2,500 have a mayor-council form of government. Among municipalities with more than 500,000 people, 78 percent have a mayor-council form of government. See International City/County Management Association, *The Municipal Year Book, 2001* (Washington, DC: International City/County Management Association, 2001), xii.

The American national political system solved this problem two centuries ago by creating a system of political parties that did most of the initial sorting among a large number of potential candidates. Until the 1960s, such winnowing took place mostly at national party conventions that chose a single party nominee. However, the old convention procedure has since been largely replaced by a system based on state primary elections. In the end, the electorate makes a choice already limited in practice to only the Republican and Democratic party nominees.

As discussed in chapter 15, it is possible that some kind of party system, also potentially including candidate selection, could also emerge within some neighborhood associations—though probably not along Republican and Democratic lines. Another option would be to create a neighborhood nominating committee to identify two or three "approved" candidates for each open seat (other unit owners would still be free to run, although without any committee blessing). The committee might consist of association board members or be a board subcommittee. Alternatively, the nominating committee might be a group of unit owners altogether separate from the board members. The nominating committee, whether board appointed or elected, might be formed (by constitutional provision) to represent each geographic area of the neighborhood, to achieve gender and age balance, and perhaps to include at least one lawyer and real estate professional.

If the board of directors were to choose the independent nominating committee, the principle of separation of powers would be violated. If an election were held, and any unit owners were free to seek election to the nominating committee, then the top 15 vote-getters, for example, might form the nominating committee. A fairly large nominating committee would assure representation of a broad range of legitimate neighborhood opinion. The main objection to this proposal would be the added voting and candidate recruitment burden it would place on associations already facing problems in this area.

Other options for directly electing a neighborhood association president can be drawn from a menu of alternative voting systems similar to those discussed in chapter 15 (election of board members). The writers of neighborhood association constitutions may want to examine the merits of the various transferable voting arrangements that require voters to rank more than one candidate, and then establish a procedure whereby the votes of losing candidates are transferred to higher-ranked candidates. Under many of these procedures, for example, the majority of votes for Ralph Nader in 2000 probably would have been transferred later to Al Gore (he would have been listed as the second choice on the ballots of these voters), Gore would have won Florida's electoral votes, and he would have become the president of the United States.

Should There Be a Neighborhood "City Manager"?

If the writers of a new neighborhood constitution decide against the option of electing the neighborhood president, they could consider a "city-manager" form of government.* The association's board would select the top executive for the neighborhood on its own authority—much as corporate business boards now choose their CEOs. The neighborhood manager may have a contract of several years—providing security of tenure—although the city council would always be able to dismiss this person on performance grounds (if it is willing to bear the expense of buying out the remaining years of the contract).

An association's professional manager perhaps could be a unit owner. However, in most cases, selecting a manager from outside the neighborhood association is preferable so that he or she is partly insulated from the passions and pressures of unit owners or board members. In the case of a small association, there might not be enough work to occupy a neighborhood manager on a full-time basis, so a part-time manager might be appointed. The same person might also manage several other neighborhood associations—spending, say, Monday with one association, Tuesday with another, and so forth.

The city-manager form of local government was devised in the United States during the Progressive Era as part of the broader progressive conviction that there should be a strict "dichotomy" of politics and administration.[26] The Federal Reserve Bank still functions formally according to this model where top professional leadership is significantly insulated from routine political interference. The U.S. president cannot fire the members of the Federal Reserve Board; ordinary board members are expected to have expert knowledge in economics and banking matters and are appointed to terms of 14 years; and the Fed chairman is appointed by the president for a fixed, four-year term.

Similar ideas, as noted above, were applied in the Progressive Era to city governance.[27] The city council would make the basic value choices and be responsible for the "political" functions. After that, it would be up to a professional city manager to carry out the council's policies. Alfred Willoughby, an advocate of the city-manager system of government, explained the concept: "In the face of overwhelming evidence to the contrary, there still are many well intentioned people who feel that democracy demands the popular election of long lists of public officials and that any citizen who can get himself elected is automatically qualified to manage the public's business." This does not, however, take into account the fact that "government, especially local government, is simply a group of services" that are provided in response to the collective demands of the public. Their delivery requires "business

---

*For the record, some cities have both elected mayors and professional city managers.

rather than political management" skills, and, in cities, "the highest standards have been set, in general, by communities which have adopted the council-manager form of government."[28]

According to Willoughby, this form of local governance is best because "it obtains efficiency by concentrating administration in a single officer, the manager. . . . Thus there can be no avoidance of responsibility either by the people's representatives for determination of policy or by the administrative appointee for actual administration [of the policy]."[29] Although the progressive political philosophy of "scientific management" is widely challenged today, and while it seems unrealistic that politics and administration can be clearly separated, there are still many professional city managers in the United States, and they are still responsible for administering more than half of all the local governments in smaller- and middle-sized jurisdictions.

Organizations need a leader. During World War II, Dwight Eisenhower was the designated commander-in-chief of all Allied forces on the Western front. Football teams have their head coaches. The Chicago Cubs tried in the early 1960s to function without a manager, but this radical experiment lasted only two years. Otherwise, all major league baseball teams have had one manager responsible for setting the batting order and choosing the pitchers for each game. Business corporations almost always have a single CEO. Neighborhood associations might also benefit from placing the administrative responsibilities for neighborhood governance on one person—a person who might be chosen by the board of directors as the "neighborhood president" or "neighborhood CEO." Unlike current neighborhood presidents, this person would not typically be a sitting member of the board of directors (although he or she might well join the board after being selected as CEO) and would be chosen for his or her professional qualifications.

An alternative version of this approach would be to hire a professional management firm. With, say, a three- or four-year contract, the firm could make one of its own employees the top executive officer for the neighborhood association. This person could be reassigned at the discretion of the management firm (as a result, for example, of extensive complaints from unit owners). The management firm would also be responsible for hiring the day-to-day workforce within the association. Such a firm as a whole would thus be held accountable for the overall results in neighborhood administration. The firm's on-site employees would be the private equivalent of a public municipality's professional civil servants.

The use of a professional management firm might be said to offer the fullest possible separation of politics and administration—a new strategy for reviving the old progressive concept. Given today's rapid spread of neighborhood associations, association management could be an important new area of American business growth. The Community Associations Institute, located in

Alexandria, Virginia, at present offers many instructional programs in neighborhood association management. Given the new importance of private systems of local governance, universities might enter the field as well, offering a variety of courses in this subject area.

The Powers of the Executive

Whether the association chief executive is appointed or elected, a neighborhood constitution should carefully identify the powers assigned to that office. In the U.S. federal system, the president is substantially insulated from congressional interference in the conduct of governmental administrative tasks. Neighborhood associations might also find it desirable to create a powerful office for their chief executives. These powers might include any or all of the following:

1. To hire and fire (subject to contractual terms) the members of the neighborhood executive team.
2. To administer and enforce the rules of the neighborhood for the use of common areas, as these rules have been established by the board of directors.
3. To enforce the covenants that specify permissible uses and modifications of individual neighborhood properties.
4. To develop a proposed budget for the neighborhood association, to be reviewed and approved by the board of directors.
5. To commit neighborhood funds for various purposes, in accordance with the budget approved by the board of directors.
6. To contract with outside firms and consultants for various purposes, subject to approval of the board of directors in cases where these contracts exceed a certain dollar threshold.
7. To bring legal actions and otherwise to organize the neighborhood representation in court.
8. To organize and supervise the conduct of elections and referenda within the neighborhood, according to the rules set out by the neighborhood constitution and by the board of directors.
9. To veto certain types of actions by the board of directors, as prescribed in the association's constitution, subject to the possibility of an override by a supermajority vote of the board.
10. To perform other executive functions as may be prescribed by the constitution or the board of directors.

If a neighborhood association president has veto powers over board actions, this authority could apply to any board action, or it might be limited by the neighborhood constitution to certain areas of board decisionmaking. For example, the neighborhood president might be able to veto board actions only with respect to the neighborhood budget. However, given the frequent controversies with respect to covenant enforcement, there might be a strong case for presidential veto authority in this area as well.

An alternative constitutional design would put any override decision in the hands of the unit owners. If a president vetoed a board action, then the constitution might automatically require a referendum vote of all unit owners. Until then, the board's action would not take effect—unless, say, three-quarters of the board voted for it to take effect immediately. An alternative to a veto power would be to give the neighborhood association president the independent authority to submit certain neighborhood issues to a full vote of the unit owners. Board actions would take effect immediately, but if the president objected, he or she would have the authority to call a vote of all unit owners.

If an association constitution grants substantial powers to the association president, then some might fear that the president would end up becoming a small "dictator." Hence, the writers of a neighborhood constitution might also want to consider options to protect the association (similar to the checks on executive powers in the U.S. federal constitution) against any abuses of presidential authority.

The president of a neighborhood association, for example, might have the authority under the neighborhood constitution to issue "variances" from the association's covenants—much as local public governments at present can issue zoning variances. Given the potentially controversial nature of such actions, the board of directors might have the authority to override a presidentially granted variance with a simple majority vote. This override authority might be extended to other areas where there is special administrative concern over the actions of a neighborhood president.

Converging Trends

Several trends are today stimulating a rethinking of the traditional manner of corporate governance in the business world. More than 50 percent of all U.S. stocks are now held by mutual funds, pension funds, and other large institutional investors. These large shareholders have the capacity—and are increasingly exercising it—to participate in corporate governance in ways that small shareholders never could. The Enron scandal and others like it have also called elements of the traditional business governance model into question.[30] Hence, there are new appeals for a clearer separation of powers within the business corporation.

One student of corporate governance now states without qualification that "the roles of Board Chair and CEO should be separate."[31] In a 2003 report, the Commission on Public Trust and Private Enterprise, organized by the Conference Board, recommended steps to achieve "an appropriate balance between the powers of the CEO and those of the independent directors." This may well involve "separating the offices of Chairman of the Board and CEO, with those two roles being performed by separate individuals."[32] As is being suggested, a corporate board of directors should function like more a traditional legislature in American politics, and the top officers more like a traditional executive branch.

In most American businesses (as in some neighborhood associations), the board in effect becomes a self-perpetuating institution because the current members nominate the future members. Although the stockholders could, in theory, reject the board nominees, this seldom happens. Another democratic reform proposed by the Conference Board requires that "shareholders, particularly long-term shareholders . . . act more like responsible owners of the corporation." New steps would be taken "to recognize the legitimate interests of shareowners in the nominees presented for election as directors" and to participate more meaningfully in the selection of future board members.[33]

As compared with neighborhood associations, business corporations have had a much longer and larger role in American history. Yet, leading corporate strategists are today raising the prospect of basic changes in the governance structure of the American business corporation. A similar boldness of thought could help upgrade and energize governance within private neighborhood associations across the United States. As in the business world, the governance choices of neighborhood associations need not be the same. Indeed, a healthy experimentation with different neighborhood governing forms through a trial-and-error process is to be desired. In the end, it would not be surprising to see some greater convergence of the business corporation and the neighborhood association governance models.

A Proposal for Neighborhood Leadership

For the purposes of discussion, I propose that a neighborhood association constitution should provide for the direct election by the unit owners of the association's chief executive officer. This person—the "president" of the association—would administer routine neighborhood affairs and serve a term of three years. The president could be—and perhaps frequently will be—a unit owner, though this need not be a requirement. The president's salary might be in the range of $75,000 per year ($125,000 per year for neighborhood associations with more than 1,000 units).

At least two candidates for association president, and no more than four, would be chosen by a neighborhood nominating committee. Any unit owner would be eligible to run in a neighborhood-wide election for the office of nominating committee member. The top twelve vote-getters would form the nominating committee. In the actual presidential election—to be conducted electronically—the winning candidate would have to receive a minimum of 50 percent of the votes. If no candidate received 50 percent, the candidate with the least votes (along with any other candidates receiving less than 10 percent) would be eliminated, and a runoff election among the two (or more) remaining candidates would be held, continuing in this way until some candidate received more than 50 percent of the votes.

The president of the neighborhood association would be removable by means of a recall election. To hold a recall, 30 percent of the unit owners would be required to submit a petition requesting such a vote. To remove the president, 66 percent of the unit owners would have to vote for removal. The board of directors would have the independent authority to remove the president for any reason on the vote of 80 percent of the board. If convicted in a court of law of any criminal activity or other serious offense, the association president would automatically be discharged from office.

The president would have the authority to enforce neighborhood rules and to form and supervise the neighborhood executive team, according to the board's general policies and instructions. In larger associations, the president would be expected to hire—or contract out to—competent professionals to deliver neighborhood services and perform other tasks. The neighborhood president would have the power to veto most board decisions. The board of directors would have the authority to override this veto with a vote of 60 percent of the board members.

Given the contentious character of the politics within many neighborhood associations, it is desirable to have greater separation of legislative and executive functions. As neighborhood associations assume greater responsibilities for local service delivery, it is also desirable to increase the technical and administrative skills of the neighborhood executive branch. The model of neighborhood governance suggested here aims to balance these considerations.

NOTES

1. Daniela Deane, "Treasured Lakes: Area's Man-Made Water Spots, Crucial to Bay Ecology, Command Top Dollar," *Washington Post*, August 23, 2003, F1.

2. Quoted in Deane, "Treasured Lakes."

3. Jasmine Martirossian, *Decision Making in Communities: Why Groups of Smart People Sometimes Make Bad Decisions* (Alexandria, VA: Community Associations Press, 2001), viii, ix.

4. Charles Fraser, " 'Town Hall' Governance for Community Associations," in Bill Overton, ed., *Community First! Emerging Visions Reshaping America's Condominium and Homeowner Associations* (Alexandria, VA: Community Associations Institute, 1999), 66.

5. Ibid., 67–68.

6. Citizens for Constitutional Local Government (formerly Citizens Against Private Government HOAs), http://pvtgov.org/pvtgov/ (accessed January 15, 2003). See also George K. Staropoli, ed., *Buyers Guide to Living in a Community Association* (Scottsdale, AZ: Citizens Against Private Government HOAs, Inc., 2001).

7. Wayne S. Hyatt and Susan F. French, *Community Association Law* (Durham, NC: Carolina Academic Press, 1998), 278–89.

8. Scott E. Mollen, "Alternative Dispute Resolution of Condominium and Cooperative Conflicts," *St. John's Law Review* 73 (Winter 1999), 80–81.

9. See Community Associations Institute, *Governance, Resident Involvement and Conflict Resolution,* Best Practices Report no. 2 (Alexandria, VA: Community Associations Institute, 2001), 4.

10. Fraser, " 'Town Hall' Governance for Community Associations," 69–70.

11. American Law Institute, *Principles of Corporate Governance: Analysis and Recommendations* (St. Paul, MN: American Law Institute Publishers, 1994).

12. B. Espen Eckbo, remarks quoted in "Emerging Trends in Corporate Governance," *Corporate Board Member—2001 Special Supplement,* 10.

13. William T. Allen, remarks quoted in "Emerging Trends in Corporate Governance," 8.

14. Stuart L. Gillan, Jay C. Hartzell, and Laura T. Starks, "Industries, Investment Opportunities, and Corporate Governance Structures," Working Paper Series 2002-003 (Newark, DE: Center for Corporate Governance, University of Delaware, November 2002), 10.

15. The Business Roundtable, *Principles of Corporate Governance* (Washington, DC: The Business Roundtable, May 2002), 11.

16. Ibid., 6.

17. Dissenting opinion of Commissioner John H. Biggs, The Conference Board Commission on Public Trust and Private Enterprise, *Findings and Recommendations, Part 2: Corporate Governance, Part 3, Audit and Accounting* (New York: The Conference Board, January 9, 2003), 28.

18. Patrick S. McGurn, remarks quoted in "Emerging Trends in Corporate Governance," 23.

19. Michael Bradley, Cindy A. Schipani, Anant K. Sundaram, and James P. Walsh, "The Purposes and Accountability of the Corporation in Contemporary Society: Corporate Governance at a Crossroads," *Law and Contemporary Problems* 62 (Summer 1999).

20. See also William A. Fischel, *The Homevoter Hypothesis: How Home Values Influence Local Government Taxation, School Finance, and Land-Use Policies* (Cambridge, MA: Harvard University Press, 2001).

21. See Lucian Arye Bebchuk, Jesse M. Fried, and David I. Walker, "Managerial Power and Rent Extraction in the Design of Executive Compensation," *University of Chicago Law Review* 69 (Summer 2002).

22. Kenneth Budd, *Be Reasonable! How Community Associations Can Enforce Rules Without Antagonizing Residents, Going to Court, or Starting World War III* (Alexandria, VA: Community Associations Institute, 1998).

23. Jon C. Teaford, *The Twentieth-Century American City: Problem, Promise, and Reality* (Baltimore: Johns Hopkins University Press, 1986), 50–56.

24. Stephen Cianca, "Home Rule in Ohio Counties: Legal and Constitutional Perspectives," *Dayton Law Review* 19 (Winter 1994), 542.

25. Kenneth A. Shepsle and Mark S. Bonchek, *Analyzing Politics: Rationality, Behavior and Institutions* (New York: Norton, 1997).

26. Jay M. Shafritz and E. W. Russell, *Introducing Public Administration* (New York: Longman, 1997), 109.

27. Ernest S. Griffith, *A History of American City Management: The Progressive Years and Their Aftermath, 1900–1920* (New York: Praeger, 1974).

28. Alfred Willoughby, "Management vs. Dictatorship," *National Municipal Review* (October 1942), reprinted in Charles M. Kneier and Guy Fox, *Readings in Municipal Government and Administration* (New York: Rinehart & Company, 1953), 293–94.

29. Ibid., 294–95.

30. Stuart L. Gillan and John D. Martin, "Financial Engineering, Corporate Governance, and the Collapse of Enron," Working Paper Series 2002-001 (Newark, DE: Center for Corporate Governance, University of Delaware, 2002).

31. Dana Hermanson, "21st Century Governance Principles for U.S. Public Companies," (October 2002), at *Corporate Board Member,* Resource Center, http://www.boardmember.com/ (accessed February 7, 2003).

32. The Conference Board Commission on Public Trust and Private Enterprise, *Findings and Recommendations, Part 2,* 21.

33. Ibid., 15, 16.

17

The Neighborhood
Judicial Branch

Scott Mollen, a real estate lawyer in New York, has seen it all. In the relationships among the unit owners living in New York condominiums and cooperatives, disputes often "erupt into diatribes of emotionally charged words which exponentially expand and intensify the conflict. The printable vocabulary of occupancy conflicts often includes words like 'livid,' 'vicious,' 'revenge,' 'fraud,' 'arrogant,' 'pompous,' 'power crazy,' 'breach of fiduciary duty,' 'self-dealing,' 'favoritism,' 'insensitive,' 'litigious,' 'stupid,' and 'troublemaker.' " Indeed, lawyers practicing in the field of collective ownership of housing commonly "believe that after relationships involving love and/or sex, the next most passionate relationship in our society is that of . . . condominium unit owner/condominium board of directors and cooperative shareholder/co-op board." Although the New York disagreements observed by Mollen often have arisen within a single building, he recognizes that the spread of such conflicts within neighborhood associations has been "national in scope."[1] In one nationwide survey, fully 41 percent of U.S. neighborhood associations had been involved in at least one lawsuit with a unit owner.[2]

The frequency with which unit owners go to court has resulted in an expenditure of "enormous resources, public and private." However, Mollen believes, "the judicial system is ill suited to resolve occupancy conflicts." It is also often a waste of time and money for unit owners who bring the suits because boards of directors generally prevail; there have been "relatively few decisions" in New York City in which a unit owner won a case.* There is a good reason for this; the

---

*According to a study for the Community Associations Institute, prospects for unit owners nationwide may be somewhat more promising. Neighborhood associations won 82 percent of the time in

courts understand that "a presumption of validity is essential to the orderly operation and fiscal soundness of the common interest developments. Associations could not function properly if decisions could be 'Monday morning quarterbacked' by each individual unit owner."[3]

Yet, even while litigation is ineffective for unit owners most of the time, Mollen finds that this widespread practice "reinforces and accelerates confrontation and feelings of animosity between parties who have been embroiled in personal disputes well before the conflicts have reached the litigation stage." Disputes may involve minor matters, such as water leaks or repairs, but unit owners become even more "angry when they are compelled to write checks for thousands of dollars to their counsel to pursue redress through the legal system." Moreover, boards of directors fear "that compromise would unleash a torrent of additional challenges by other occupants." As a result, "hostility may spiral even higher" and become like an "infectious disease" that spreads throughout a neighborhood association "as factions evolve."[4]

In one extreme case described in a report for the Community Associations Institute, a California homeowner and a neighborhood association became embroiled in a conflict involving a $750 fence. By the end of the litigation process, the association's legal fees had exceeded $60,000, and the homeowner had spent more than $40,000.[5] The dispute obviously had ceased to be about a fence and had become a simple contest of wills between intransigent parties that happened to be fought in a courtroom.

In light of such problems, which arise in too many neighborhood associations, this chapter addresses the constitutional provisions for the neighborhood "judicial" branch. This is probably the least developed side of neighborhood governance at present. Yet unit owners' perception that they have access to a reasonable process for appeal and final dispute resolution may serve as an alternative to continuing personal conflict, disagreement, and emotional outbursts. Wayne Hyatt argues that it will be important in the future to develop improved "procedures for owner involvement and owner appeals" relating to matters of covenant enforcement and other areas of association activity.[6]

The undeveloped character of the judicial branch in neighborhood associations reflects in part the corporate legal model for these associations. It has been assumed that disputes in neighborhood associations should be resolved in the traditional framework of contract law. However, the relationship among the unit owners in a neighborhood association is not that of a typical private

those lawsuits with unit owners that went to court. However, in 28 percent of all legal disputes between associations and unit owners, the insurance carrier for the association either settled with the unit owner prior to actual litigation, or the association paid to avoid a court fight. See Doreen Heisler and Warren Klein, *Inside Look at Community Association Homeownership—Facts, Perceptions* (Alexandria, VA: Community Associations Institute, 1996), 34.

contract. Instead, it resembles more closely the workings of a government. An association's controlling document is more like a political constitution than a private contract. It is a private constitution, however, and therefore new legal approaches to resolving neighborhood disagreements may be necessary. A formal law dealing with private constitutions does not presently exist in the American legal system, although it is being informally developed in the workings of neighborhood association (and some other areas of) law.

Marriage and neighborhood associations share some similar characteristics. The institution of marriage is a long-term contract where the parties are expected to resolve most of their disagreements among themselves. If they have to go to court, this is in itself a sign that the marriage is already failing. Similarly, there is a strong case for making it difficult to go outside a neighborhood association to resolve unit-owner disputes. The unit owners should be under pressure to find their own answers and resolutions. Hence, it might be desirable to establish a "judicial branch" within the neighborhood association to consider appeals of specific decisions that have been made by the association's legislative and executive branches.

An internal system of appeal could take many forms. A private "judge" could be appointed to hear appeals and to resolve other "judicial" issues—perhaps a particularly well-respected unit owner or a nonresident with real estate expertise. Small "juries" of unit owners could be convened to hear appeals. And though such a practice violates the strict concept of a separation of powers, the association's board of directors could serve as a special avenue of appeal. A neighborhood might enter into a contract with an outside arbitration firm—perhaps authorized to render a binding decision—in some cases where the parties cannot otherwise agree.[7]

A Formal Process for Covenant Enforcement

The most contentious matter facing neighborhood associations is the enforcement of covenants relating to neighborhood land uses.[8] In order to minimize such tensions, neighborhood covenant enforcement should be perceived as fair and equitable. It is desirable to have a well-defined process for the handling of proposals for structural modifications in neighborhood properties. This process should not impose large burdens of paperwork. Nevertheless, it should be formal enough that it establishes some form of written record—if perhaps very brief. These records should be maintained by the neighborhood association and should be readily available for review by other unit owners—and prospective unit owners as well who may find them informative.

Applications for "significant" modifications of unit-owner properties should also be submitted in writing. Other unit owners would be given adequate notice of the proposed change, and an opportunity to comment. Without requiring great detail, the application should contain a short statement of the proposed structural changes. Any proposal rejection should at least include a brief written statement substantiating the rejection. If others in the neighborhood have previously raised objections, and yet the proposed change is approved, a brief statement as to the grounds for approval should be offered.

At present, many neighborhood associations place the initial responsibility for the interpretation and enforcement of covenants with a board subcommittee—typically the "architectural review" subcommittee. This approach has several disadvantages. Frequent turnover in board membership may result in frequent changes in the membership of the architectural review subcommittee, which can then lead to inconsistent decisions from one year to the next. Furthermore, committee members (unit owners) are not likely to have much expertise in design issues. Consciously or unconsciously, they may favor—or, almost as much of a problem, appear to favor—friends and others within their own network of neighborhood acquaintances.

Hence, it may be desirable to put the initial review of proposed structural modifications in the hands of a professional. A large neighborhood association might assign one association employee with suitable qualifications to this task. In a smaller association, an outside architectural consultant might be hired. An alternative to hiring an outside professional would be to choose a well-respected unit owner to serve on a voluntary basis. He or she might have a long-term appointment, say for five years, with the goal of developing expertise and maintaining consistency in covenant enforcement. This person would not simply issue "yes" or "no" decisions; there could be a negotiation process in which mitigating actions and other changes might be discussed to make a proposal acceptable to the neighborhood association membership.

Covenant Appeals

The enforcement of covenants is likely to have greater legitimacy among unit owners if the association offers a reasonable and inexpensive avenue of appeal. Rather than acting as the decisionmaker of first resort, perhaps the board's architectural subcommittee could serve as this appeal body. In considering an appeal, the subcommittee would meet with the unit owner filing the appeal and hear his or her objections to the initial neighborhood decision. The person filing the appeal would also be expected to present a brief statement outlining the grounds for appeal. The architectural committee would also meet (perhaps separately) with the association employee, outside consultant, or other person responsible for making the initial decision. Whatever the outcome, the architectural committee would prepare a brief written statement explaining the appeal's resolution. In order to dissuade unit owners from filing frivolous appeals, associations might charge a modest appeal fee—say $100. If a unit owner wins an appeal, this fee might then be rebated. Unit owners are more likely to accept the outcome of an appeal if they can see that it is consistent with previous decisions made by the neighborhood association. In addition, those responsible for covenant enforcement will be more careful to treat each unit owner fairly and equitably if they know that their decisions will be formally recorded and can be compared with previous, similar enforcement actions. Written records will also allow current and future unit owners to understand in advance what is acceptable under association policies before even considering any structural changes in their properties.

The total volume of appeals existing in a given neighborhood association will give prospective purchasers an indication of the quality of neighborhood governance and the harmony or disharmony within the association. A common complaint today is that new purchasers of association units have little information about the rules that will be applied to them. Perhaps each new purchaser should be given a formal opportunity to read a summary of recent appeals and dispute resolutions before finalizing his or her purchase.

As an alternative to an architectural review subcommittee, a neighborhood association might consider establishing a "jury" system. As in other judicial arenas, a jury would consist of fellow citizens (unit owners). The jury might be picked at random. A disaffected unit owner could ask for a short neighborhood "trial" by a group of unit owners—say five other, randomly selected owners. Jury deliberations and voting records might be kept secret, with only the final result announced publicly. Perhaps the greatest disadvantage of this approach is the large amount of time potentially required of unit owners.*

A much different approach would be for the neighborhood association to hire an outside arbitration service to hear appeals. If this approach were widely adopted, new businesses specializing in arbitration services for neighborhood associations might spring up. If a unit owner filed an appeal, the owner might

---

*When ancient Athens was at its peak of influence and power, courts and juries played a large role in the practice of direct democracy and took up large amounts of citizen time. Scott Gordon reports that "the courts played a role in the Athenian system that goes well beyond their function in a modern state." Issues could be brought before the courts that went well beyond the traditional legal disputes, including matters of "political import" and of "constraining the power of the Athenian bureaucracy." There were no professional lawyers or prosecutors, leaving individual citizens to bring charges and to play the central roles throughout the process. The rules of court operation were informal, as "no distinction was made between matters of fact and matters of law, and the presiding officer did not instruct the jury as to its responsibilities." It seems that each case was disposed of by the jury in a single day or less. Decisions were made by simple majority vote of the jury members. See Scott Gordon, *Controlling the State: Constitutionalism from Ancient Athens to Today* (Cambridge, MA: Harvard University Press, 1999), 70–72.

have to pay for the cost of the arbitration service. If he or she won the case, the money might then be returned and the neighborhood association would be required to pay.

No matter which approach is adopted for the first round of appeal, association constitutions could also provide for a second appeal to a higher level. The appeal body at this level, for example, might consist of the association's entire board of directors. In order to prevent the board from being inundated with appeals, a significant barrier—perhaps a much higher filing fee (say $1,000)—could be put in place. The board could also require more extensive written documentation. Finally, like the U.S. Supreme Court, the board might have broad discretion to reject the consideration of any specific appeals.

Lacking resolution inside the neighborhood process, a unit owner always has the option to go to the U.S. court system. In the federal courts, a unit owner might allege an unconstitutional infringement, for example, of his or her civil rights. At state and municipal levels, a unit owner might allege that the constitution of the neighborhood association has been misinterpreted. To be sure, the U.S. judicial system should resist any temptation to become the final arbiter of the many routine decisions that arise in neighborhood covenant enforcement.

Collecting the Dues

For two years, 83-year-old Wenonah Blevins had failed to pay the Champions Community Improvement Association, located outside Houston, Texas, the $815 in assessments she owed. With penalties and legal fees, her debt had increased to $3,756. Frustrated with the delays, the association board evicted Ms. Blevins and auctioned off her house for $5,000. Her neighbors were understandably outraged, and Ms. Blevins filed suit. In the end, the sale was cancelled, and Ms. Blevins recovered her home and won a $300,000 damage settlement. The purchaser of her home at the auction—a property estimated to be worth around $150,000—also received a $95,000 payment of compensation from the association.[9] Responding to the public outcry over miscarriages such as this, the Texas legislature in 2001 provided strong new protections for unit owners, such as requiring associations to give advance notification and giving unit owners the ability to pay off their debts and recover their properties within 180 days of a foreclosure sale. Although Ms. Blevins's case was extreme, similar horror stories have been heard across the United States.[10]

Such events illustrate two basic problems in neighborhood association law. First, parties to neighborhood disputes frequently let their anger and emotions affect their rational judgment. Second, equally as important and yet more easily resolved, the institutional and legal framework in which such disputes must be resolved is flawed. For example, an association's board of directors is understandably frustrated when a unit owner refuses to pay assessments for months. Fines may not work because the unit owner may simply ignore them. Under current law, a lien can be placed on the property, but the actual money may not be recovered until years later when the property is sold and the lien paid off. If there are other creditors at that point, the association's lien may be assigned junior status and therefore never be paid.

Thus, establishing a wider range of enforcement methods would be helpful to neighborhood associations. Some of these methods may already be legally available, but many neighborhood boards may be unaware of them. Other options might have to be written into future neighborhood constitutions. Still others might require new state and local laws. Some of the possible ways of collecting overdue neighborhood association assessments include the following, in increasing order of severity:[11]

1. **Publicize members' names**—The association might prominently identify in the association newsletter and on the association web site any unit owner who has not paid his or her assessments for, say, two months, including the amount of delinquency. Public embarrassment can be a powerful motivating factor.

2. **Curtail association privileges**—If the unit owner has not paid assessments for, say, three months, curtailments of privileges within the association might begin. Voting privileges might first be revoked. The rights to use the tennis courts, swimming pool, and other common property might then be rescinded. In the next stage, parking privileges might be reduced or even eliminated. Access to the association's common cable system conceivably could be disconnected. If specified in advance in the association's constitution, such measures in most jurisdictions would probably be legal at present (and some associations are already doing some of these things).

3. **Brand the guilty party**—If a unit owner has not paid assessments for five months, for example, a large sign could be placed on the front lawn, describing the failure to pay the assessments and the amount of the delinquency.

4. **Sell off individual items of personal property**—The sale of a whole housing unit is a draconian measure that should be undertaken only as a very last resort. The sale of individual items of personal property might be sufficient to pay off the delinquency. For example, if a unit owner has two cars, the association might have the legal authority to sell one of the cars. For smaller debts, the association might have the authority to sell televisions, music systems, freezers, lawn furniture, and so forth.

5. **The last resort**—If all else has failed, and the assessments have not been paid for, say, 18 months, and the amount owed is more than $2,500, the neighborhood association should have the authority to evict the owner and to sell the unit. However, a concerted effort should be made to obtain the full market value of the unit (including engaging the services of a real estate agent). The neighborhood association would then retain only the amount of the delinquent assessments, plus enough to cover association costs. Any remaining sale proceeds should be turned back to the unit owner.

Delinquent unit owners should be fully notified in advance of the association taking any of the above actions, allowing the resident a reasonable amount of time to make the necessary payments and avoid the penalty. If swimming pool privileges are to be revoked, for example, the unit owner should be officially informed at least two weeks in advance. If a unit is actually to be sold off, the unit owner should be given at least three months' advance notice and ample opportunity to come up with the necessary money.

Private Arbitration

Chief Justice Warren Burger once stated that "for some disputes, trials will be the only means, but for many claims, trials by adversarial contest must in time go the way of the ancient trial by battle and blood." For many kinds of conflicts, our legal system "is too costly, too painful, too destructive, too inefficient for a truly civilized people."[12] According to Derek Bok, former dean of the Harvard Law School, "Most people find their legal rights severely compromised by the cost of legal services, the baffling complications of existing rules and procedures, and the long and frustrating delays involved in bringing proceedings to a conclusion."[13] Better means are surely available for resolving many of the disputes among unit owners and between unit owners and their associations that currently find their way into the U.S. judicial system.

One increasingly popular option for conflict resolution is private arbitration—either binding or nonbinding. There are many ways of handling the actual process of arbitration. As one authority writes,

> [The parties] have enormous latitude in designing the arbitration process. Parties may enter into agreements specifying procedural and substantive standards to be used in the arbitration process. Agreements will typically provide that the arbitrator shall be selected either by the parties, by a dispute resolution organization such as the American Arbitration Association, or by a combination thereof. Some agreements call for arbitrators to be selected by a court. Agreements may also specify the qualifications of the arbitrator. Arbitration procedures permit presentation of witnesses

and documents, cross-examination, and arguments to arbitrators. However, arbitration typically embodies procedural rules which are less formal than the procedural rules used in litigation.[14]

Another form of alternative dispute resolution (ADR) is the use of mediation services. Mediation differs from arbitration in that the mediator renders no decision. The parties involved may pledge to work with a mediator whenever they cannot resolve a dispute among themselves. The mediator may propose compromises that might not otherwise be apparent to the parties. The very fact that a resolution is proposed by a mediator can serve to make it more legitimate and acceptable in the minds of one or both of the involved parties. In general, a mediator can often bring a body of specialized knowledge that can help to identify the actual areas of disagreement. Mediators may be able to introduce important new information or point to the outcomes of similar past disputes. The American Arbitration Association reports a success rate of 75 to 90 percent in cases it mediates.

Nathan DeDino argues that neighborhood associations "should consider the inclusion of clauses requiring ADR as a first means of resolution" of disputes among neighborhoods, and that "community centers" should be employed for this purpose.[15] Some jurisdictions now require neighborhood association constitutions to provide for binding arbitration or mediation.[16] The State of Florida requires unit owners to enter into nonbinding arbitration prior to initiating any formal court action. The state's Division of Florida Land Sales, Condominiums and Mobile Homes retains full-time attorneys to serve in this arbitration capacity. If an arbitrator's nonbinding decision is not appealed within 30 days to a court, then it becomes binding. Moreover, the arbitration result is admissible in court and, if upheld, the losing party can be required to pay all legal fees for all the parties involved. Thus, while it is technically "nonbinding" arbitration, the arbitrator's decision has real teeth.

New Jersey requires that disputing parties in neighborhood associations enter into some form of alternative dispute resolution before entering formal litigation. Mollen finds that such mechanisms are still "embryonic" in neighborhood associations but thinks that "the potential benefits to be derived . . . are monumental."[17] Beth Grimm, a San Francisco lawyer specializing in homeowner association law, comments similarly that alternative private methods of dispute resolution, although they do not always work, on the whole are "less confrontational, less demanding, and more satisfying than litigation." The litigation route frequently involves "monstrous costs" that appear even more unreasonable in light of the small stakes in many unit owner disputes. She recommends in many cases binding arbitration, which "saves the public more money and grief than can be easily quantified."[18] If neighborhood association law in some ways resembles family law, then there is already ample precedent and experience with the use of alternative methods of dispute resolution within families (of course, these methods do not always work, nor will they always work in neighborhood associations).

Interpreting the Neighborhood Constitution

A different kind of neighborhood disagreement involves issues of interpreting the association's constitution. For example, the required supermajority vote might vary with the category of constitutional amendment proposed. Members could disagree as to the exact category in which a particular proposed amendment falls, and thus the supermajority necessary to pass the amendment. There might be issues relating to protecting unit owners' basic rights, as these rights may be specified in the constitution's "bill of rights." At present, if a unit owner disagrees with the neighborhood board of directors, his or her only avenue of appeal is the U.S. legal system.

A 2002 Florida Supreme Court decision illustrated the types of basic issues that may arise.[19] Changes in the voting interests or in any other basic property rights within a neighborhood association generally require unanimous consent. Other amendments to the neighborhood constitution can be made with smaller supermajorities—66 percent, for example, under Florida law in cases where a neighborhood association constitution does not specifically provide for an amendment procedure. In the Florida case, Woodside Village, a 288-unit condominium, decided in 1997 with the required two-thirds supermajority to amend its original constitution (dating to 1979), tightly restricting the leasing of units. Some purchasers had bought their units for the express purpose of leasing them, however, and argued that their core property interests had been violated. Therefore, as they argued, any such decision required unanimous consent.

A lower court agreed, but the Florida Supreme Court ruled that Woodside Village was within its rights to impose significant new leasing restrictions by a supermajority. The court reasoned that association living involves the subordination of individual rights to collective interests and that the purchasers of units for the purpose of leasing had known of the possibility of an amendment to change the leasing rules, and had voluntarily chosen to bear this risk. In a related Florida leasing case that reached a different outcome, a neighborhood association provided in its constitution that a tightening of leasing rules would require unanimous consent. Unable to obtain unanimity, the association decided by a supermajority vote to amend the constitutional rule itself, thus allowing a leasing change with less than unanimity. The association then changed the leasing rule in this manner. In this case, a Florida State arbitrator ruled that the association had employed a subterfuge to undermine the explicit original intent of its own constitution, thus violating the neighborhood rights of those owners who wanted to lease their units.[20]

If some neighborhood associations in the future have an elected president, then disagreements of constitutional interpretation might also arise between the board of directors and the president. The president might claim that the neighborhood association constitution authorizes certain executive actions without approval by the board. In light of this possibility, it might be desirable to have an internal judicial route, short of going to the courts, for resolving such disagreements. Neither the association's executive office nor its legislative branch would be suitable for resolving such an issue because each would be a party to the disagreement. Under one alternative, a private means of constitutional review could be established within the neighborhood itself. Under a second alternative, the task of constitutional adjudication might be assigned to a private body outside the neighborhood.

There might not be enough issues of constitutional scope to justify creating a full-time neighborhood "supreme court." However, it might be workable to have a part-time group of neighborhood volunteers who would meet as needed. When an issue of internal constitutional scope arose, this neighborhood committee would be convened. In the normal course of events, such a review committee might meet perhaps once or twice a year. Selecting the members of the neighborhood "supreme court" might be accomplished by popular vote. However, the complications inherent in various voting schemes, as described in chapter 15, might argue for a different method of selection. Similar to the procedures prescribed in the U.S. constitution for appointing Supreme Court justices, the president of the neighborhood association perhaps could propose members for board approval.

Nevertheless, it might be that, given the infrequency of constitutional issues in most neighborhood associations, the transaction costs to maintain this court would be too high. Moreover, a small neighborhood association might not have enough qualified unit owners. An alternative solution, therefore, would be for neighborhoods to work together on a private basis to create a wider constitutional review committee. A neighborhood might contract with such a private constitutional court for a fixed period—say five years—that would bind the neighborhood to go to this court for any issues of basic constitutional interpretation.

A State Court for Neighborhood Associations

Rather than establishing private courts, another way neighborhood associations could resolve internal disputes would be through the creation of a special branch of the state judiciary for neighborhood association affairs. As suggested earlier, the relationships among unit owners can resemble interactions within a family. Modern family life has generated such a large volume of litigation involving special legal considerations that many states have created special courts for family affairs. Similar considerations might apply to neighborhood associations (or to all forms of housing legal issues). Even though such a court would be in the public sector, each neighborhood association might still be charged a fee for using the court's services. The state legislature could designate criteria for state court review, seeking to exclude the day-to-day covenant, assessment, and other routine disagreements that arise in the normal course of association life.

A statewide special court for neighborhood associations would develop an expertise that should improve the quality of its decisions; it would develop a body of precedent and in general would have greater legitimacy as a fair and equitable means of resolving constitutional and other neighborhood legal issues of broad scope. The advantages offered by this option would depend in part on the number of neighborhood constitutional cases likely to arise, and the technical complexity of these cases.

Thus far, a few states have taken tentative steps in this direction. New York State has long operated a housing court and, in 1997, the New York State Court of Appeals created a pilot program to assign cases involving neighborhood associations to designated housing court judges.[21] No state has yet created a special state court, analogous to a family court, exclusively dedicated to neighborhood associations.

Paying for Nonconforming Uses

For many years, the U.S. airline industry faced a problem that seemed to defy any easy resolution. If an airline accepted reservations for the exact number of seats available on a flight, some people would not show up—and the seats went empty. Airlines thus estimated the likely number of "no-shows" and over-booked their flights. However, when a person with a reservation was denied a seat, as happened from time to time, this person was understandably angry with the airline.

In the 1980s, the airlines finally found a solution. Whenever an overbooking occurred, the company offered compensation—cash or free airline tickets—to people willing to give up their seats. If it did not have enough volunteers, the airline raised its offer. The people who volunteered were happy, and there were no longer people with reservations and no seat. It took the airlines decades to discover this simple solution. Aside from a lack of imagination in pricing policy, another obstacle was the general resistance of many people to the idea of making and accepting cash payments in social situations. Even today, if I offered to pay you $20 to take your place at the front of a movie line, you would more likely become offended than accept my $20 (even if you would, in fact, prefer the $20). Virtually every society has rejected the use of money payments to resolve certain social interactions (laws against prostitution being among the most ancient), and the range of such social prohibitions may be quite wide.

In the Middle Ages, even the sale of land was often considered socially unacceptable, though this attitude changed greatly over the centuries. Thus, what is saleable and not saleable in a given society can change radically over time. Indeed, Robert Ellickson proposed in a 1973 article that, like the airline solution to overbooking, market payments should be used to resolve some of the most contentious of local land use disputes.[22] If I want to build a new deck, and my neighbors object, I should be allowed simply to buy their permission to build my deck.

Ellickson's radical idea—an application of the work of Nobel Prize–winning economist Ronald Coase—is an important option that should at least be considered by the writers of future neighborhood constitutions.[23] Courts are often required to decide between Party A and Party B when the best choice would be half to Party A and half to party B. Bringing money to the table may facilitate more "half and half" deals. With such a compromise available, the need to go to court in the first place may often be averted.

Let us say, for example, that I want to plant a tree that, when autumn comes, will drop some large leaves in my neighbor's yard. Recognizing his likely objections, association rules might prohibit the planting of such leafy trees. If I simply ask the neighbor for permission, he or she is also likely to say no. However, if I offer this neighbor $300 for permission to plant my favorite kind of tree, he or she might very well say yes—assuming that he or she accepts the social legitimacy of such a cash offer in the first place (which, admittedly, most neighbors at present would not). As part of the deal, I might also agree to alter the tree's location in order to reduce the number of leaves likely to fall into the neighbor's yard.

Under current rules of neighborhood associations, I may be angry that I cannot plant the tree. I may feel that I never intended to surrender so much of my individual freedom as a private property owner. Very unhappy with the neighborhood association restrictions, I may go ahead, claiming that the tree is permitted under one or another interpretation of the association rules. The injured neighbor may then object, and demand that the neighborhood association cut down the tree. Yet another nasty brawl between unit owners may erupt, perhaps with both parties ending up in court, and with the neighborhood association in the middle.

At present, most association rules do not allow for exceptions that would accommodate particularly strong individual preferences.[24] A neighborhood rule prohibiting the planting of a leafy tree may not concern 98 percent of the unit owners. However, 2 percent of the unit owners may just love these types of trees. Other people may have other special preferences that lie outside the neighborhood norm. A few unit owners may have children who would just love to be able to swim in an above-ground pool. Another unit owner may prefer pink as a house color.

The rules of neighborhood associations are explicitly designed to prevent the satisfaction of such nonconforming preferences. If the neighborhood majority objects, the unit owner with the unconventional tastes must simply go along. In his 1973 article, however, Ellickson suggested that there are better ways of addressing such conflicting interests and desires. Two types of costs should be considered—the cost of an offensive land use, the "nuisance" cost, and another cost, the "prevention" cost. If the cost of the denial exceeds the negative impacts on others, then it is socially inefficient to prevent an offensive use of the land. Hence, the law (or a neighborhood association constitution) should provide for variances for nonconforming uses, although the user might have to compensate the injured party for the special variance. An owner's level of willingness to make a monetary payment for special permission would further serve as a test of the real intensity of his or her feelings.

Ellickson specifically proposed the creation of a "nuisance board" that would have the authority to approve nonconforming uses. A standard category of nonconforming use might require a fixed payment—for example, the neighborhood nuisance board might establish a charge of $250 per neighbor in order for the unit owner mentioned above to plant the leafy tree. This money—the damage payment—would then be turned over to the injured neighbor(s) as compensation for extra leaves on their property.[25]

Ellickson recognized, however, that the adjoining neighbors who were burdened by the tree might also happen in some cases to have very strong feelings. Most people might be happy enough to accept $250 as compensation. However, Ellickson proposed giving the potentially injured party the final say. The damaged neighbor could purchase a "compensated injunction," fixed by the nuisance board, to prevent the planting of the leafy tree. If an injured neighbor refused the $250 payment as compensation, he or she would be required to pay the leafy tree lover—who would now become the "damaged" party—a payment of, say, $100. As Ellickson stated, his overall scheme required the injured party "to choose between collecting damages and purchasing the termination of the nuisance."[26]

Ellickson offered several specific examples of how his new system of paying for nonconforming uses would work. The construction, for example, of a property owner's shed or other storehouse near a "side or rear lot line will generally affect the property values of only one of his neighbors, and never more than three or four, assuming the usual configuration of urban lots."[27] According to Ellickson,

> The Nuisance Board would promulgate general rules establishing threshold distances for unneighborly side yard construction. . . . If a landowner were violating the threshold, the adjacent neighbor would be entitled to choose between collecting damages . . .

and purchasing injunctive relief against the side yard incursion. In negotiating a resolution of the conflict, the parties would find targets for settlement in prior decisions of the Board and in any schedule of damages the Board might issue. Settlements or judgments would be recorded in order to bind transferees of the current owners.[28]

In another Ellickson example, a new convenience store might be seeking to locate in a residential neighborhood of the Santa Monica Mountains in Los Angeles. The convenience store might be a significant benefit to the whole mountain neighborhood; the residents there might now be driving 10 minutes on winding roads to buy a soda or a quart of milk. However, a few neighborhood residents, especially those immediately adjoining the store, might be negatively affected by increased traffic and noise. Under current nuisance law, their objections would typically prevail, and today many existing neighborhoods have no convenience store within their area. To deal with such circumstances, Ellickson proposed the following:

> The [Nuisance] Board would probably classify groceries as an unneighborly land use. Nevertheless, . . . it is unlikely that more than a score or so of the grocery's neighbors could prove substantial harm from its operation. If the parties could not reach a private settlement, the uncompensated neighbors could take their case to the Nuisance Board either to collect damages or to purchase the closing of the grocery. This approach would be much more likely than the present [zoning and nuisance law] system to assure the optimal number of groceries, as well as uses like multi-family dwellings, in the [Santa Monica] Mountains.[29]

At present, many neighborhood associations suffer from excessive rigidity in the application of their rules. The rules may work reasonably well to resolve most issues, but there is a need for a practical way to grant greater exceptions. If the exceptions are granted on the basis of "worthiness," "hardship," or some other subjective criteria, the result is likely to be endless argument within the neighborhood. Unit owners seeking nonconforming uses will plead their cases in emotional terms—if they don't get their way, "their happiness will be destroyed." If they are rejected, they may feel that they have been singled out for discriminatory treatment. Much ill will is bound to be created. For this reason, neighborhood associations have been reluctant to grant exceptions to their rules, even when the case for an exception may be strong. They worry that they will be entering onto a "slippery slope." The Ellickson proposal, however, may offer a practical way to get around these problems. A unit owner either pays for a variance, or he doesn't; there is not a lot to argue about.

A Proposal for Neighborhood Conflict Resolution

For discussion purposes, I propose that the neighborhood association's executive branch make the initial decisions on enforcement of covenants and other rules. If the association is large enough, this task should be assigned to a suitably qualified employee. Smaller associations should hire an outside architectural or other consultant. If a unit owner wants to appeal the executive-level decision, the appeal should be handled by the board's architectural review subcommittee. In most cases, this decision will be final. At its discretion, the full board might accept a few special cases for review, involving unusually large and important changes in the neighborhood, or other rare circumstances.

Unless constitutional civil rights or some other wider legal principles are at issue, the federal and state courts should refuse to consider the great majority of appeals stemming from actions within private neighborhood associations. Otherwise, these courts might well be overwhelmed with appeals from unit owners. Given the aesthetic and other subjective judgments at issue in many neighborhood disagreements, there is little basis for the courts to routinely overturn established decisionmaking processes within a neighborhood association.

This rule of nonintervention should not, however, foreclose outside court review of matters concerning basic issues of interpreting the neighborhood constitution. Here, the first step should be to adjudicate such cases in the state courts. If the volume of cases is low, the existing state courts (and occasionally a federal court) will not be overburdened. If the number of cases should turn out to be large, a special state court should be created for broader legal questions and other especially significant cases involving neighborhood associations.

Some associations may want to experiment with issuing variances for nonconforming uses on a wider basis. Ellickson's proposal that such variances should depend on monetary payment is worth experimenting with. If current state laws are likely to block this approach, then states should make the necessary modifications in neighborhood association law in order to at least permit experimentation in this area.

NOTES

1. Scott E. Mollen, "Alternative Dispute Resolution of Condominium and Cooperative Conflicts," *St. John's Law Review* 73 (Winter 1999), 75, 77.

2. Doreen Heisler and Warren Klein, *Inside Look at Community Association Homeownership: Facts, Perceptions* (Alexandria, VA: Community Associations Institute, 1996), 34.

3. Mollen, "Alternative Dispute Resolution of Condominium and Cooperative Conflicts," 76, 86, 85.

4. Ibid., 88.

5. Mary Avgerinos, *Alternative Dispute Resolution & Consensus Building for Community Associations,* GAP Report No. 26 (Alexandria, VA: Community Associations Institute, 1997), 17.

6. Wayne S. Hyatt, "Putting the Community Back in Community Associations: An Action Plan," in Bill Overton, ed., *Community First! Emerging Visions Reshaping America's Condominium and Homeowner Associations* (Alexandria, VA: Community Associations Institute, 1999), 104.

7. Avgerinos, *Alternative Dispute Resolution & Consensus Building for Community Associations.*

8. See Byron R. Hanke and Thomas S. Kenny, *Architectural Control: Design Review,* 4th ed. (Alexandria, VA: Community Associations Institute, 1998).

9. Alan Bernstein, "Evicted Widow Home for Holidays," *Houston Chronicle,* December 22, 2001.

10. Motoko Rich, "Homeowner Boards Blur Line of Just Who Rules Roost," *New York Times,* July 27, 2003, 1.

11. See also Thomas J. Hindman and Loura K. Sanchez, *Assessment Collection: Legal Remedies,* 3rd ed. (Alexandria, VA: Community Associations Institute, 2000).

12. Warren E. Burger, "Annual Message on the Administration of Justice," speech to Mid-Year Meeting of the American Bar Association, *United States Law Week* 52 (February 28, 1984), 2471.

13. Derek Bok, "Law and Its Discontents: A Critical Look at Our Legal System," *The Record* (publication of the Association of the Bar of the City of New York) 38 (1983), 12–13.

14. Mollen, "Alternative Dispute Resolution of Condominium and Cooperative Conflicts," 92–93.

15. Nathan K. DeDino, "When Fences Aren't Enough: The Use of Alternative Dispute Resolution to Resolve Disputes Between Neighbors," *Ohio State Journal on Dispute Resolution* 18, no. 3 (2003), 913.

16. See Community Associations Institute, *Governance, Resident Involvement and Conflict Resolution,* Best Practices Report No. 2 (Alexandria, VA: Community Associations Institute, 2001).

17. Mollen, "Alternative Dispute Resolution of Condominium and Cooperative Conflicts," 99.

18. Beth A. Grimm, "What's So Funny About Peace, Love, and Understanding?" *Common Ground* (March/April 2002), 16, 18.

19. *Woodside Village Condominium Association Inc. v. Jahren,* 806 So. 2d 452 (Fla. 2002).

20. See Gary A. Poliakoff and Karl M. Scheuerman, "The Woodside Covenants," *Florida Bar Journal* 77 (May 2003).

21. Jay Romano, "Co-op Cases Are Getting Own Court," *New York Times,* October 26, 1997, Section 11, 3.

22. Robert C. Ellickson, "Alternatives to Zoning: Covenants, Nuisance Rules, and Fines as Land Use Controls," *University of Chicago Law Review* 40 (Summer 1973).

23. See also Amos B. Elberg, "Remedies for Common Interest Development Rule Violations," *Columbia Law Review* 101 (December 2001).

24. Part of the inspiration for this approach is owed to the opportunity to read drafts of Lee Anne Fennell, "Contracting Communities," *University of Illinois Law Review* (2004), 829.

25. Ellickson, "Alternatives to Zoning," 762–63.

26. Ibid., 738, 780.

27. Ibid., 765.

28. Ibid., 765–66.

29. Ibid., 767–68.

PART VI
Neighborhood Associations in American Life

G iven the many important consequences for American society associated with the rise of the private neighborhood association, various legal challenges are bound to arise. In the next decade or two, some will likely reach the U.S. Supreme Court. The authority of neighborhood associations to discriminate in admitting new entrants, for example, is almost certain to be challenged. At present, not much in this respect is clear.[1] In 1948, the Supreme Court declared discrimination on the basis of race in the enforcement of neighborhood covenants to be unconstitutional. But what about discrimination on other bases?

In the Fair Housing Act, Congress declared that religious discrimination is illegal in the sale and rental of housing, but this leaves many questions unanswered. Whatever lawmakers might want to do, the Constitution would clearly override congressional designs to control the acceptable terms of membership in a church. A church, however, might assert the religious necessity for members to live together in a common geographic area. In that case, prohibiting a faith-based neighborhood association—a "territorial church"—from applying religious tests for owning a unit might be unconstitutional.

Federal law also prohibits housing discrimination on the basis of sex. But some women's colleges in the United States do discriminate on the basis of sex. These colleges sometimes house many female students in common areas about the size of many neighborhood associations. What if a neighborhood association limited entry to women and decided to provide educational services as well? Even assuming the current legal prohibition on sexual discrimination is properly applied, what is the public policy justification for preventing men or women from joining together to live in exclusive private communities of the same sex? For centuries, monks and nuns did the same as part of the pursuit of the highest spiritual experiences of the Roman Catholic religion. What if a neighborhood association asserted a similar prerogative, based on a deeply held conviction that interaction between the sexes inevitably provokes strong emotions that divert people from pursuing the highest truths?

Current law also prohibits housing discrimination based on ethnic origin. What is the national interest to justify a federal law to prohibit a group of Irishmen from joining together in their own exclusive neighborhood? Even if the laws are not repealed, they might simply not be enforced. The process of changing the laws in the United States has often involved a long process in which the law is at first not enforced rigorously, is then increasingly ignored, and finally the legislature acts to confirm an accomplished fact. The national 55-mile-per-hour speed limit, enacted in the 1970s, was effectively defunct well before Congress finally took it off the books in the 1990s. As in this case, when a law is not enforced, it is often because a large number of Americans do not find a sufficient offense to justify applying government sanctions.

Neighborhood associations might not officially engage in discrimination based on religion, sex, ethnicity, or other categories prohibited by federal law. However, they might informally encourage segregation according to prohibited categories and largely succeed on this basis. When the informal practices of real estate agents and others in the housing market have resulted in segregation by racial group, federal prosecutors have sought to apply the laws against discrimination. However, if there is little public concern for other forms of discrimination—resulting in religious, sexual, ethnic, and other unofficial segregation of housing patterns—prosecutors might simply look the other way. An important question is thus posed: whatever the current law says, should there be public concern about forms of housing exclusion other than those based on racial discrimination? Should groups wishing to maintain a strong community character have an ability to exclude nonconforming individuals? Does American law hope to ban the existence of such groups—at least when formed on a territorial basis—and, if so, why?

For much of American history, wide discretionary control over entry to a private housing project has been considered a basic right of private ownership. After the constitutional upheavals of the 1930s, however, the Supreme Court offered few protections for the legal autonomy of private property. In the 1980s, however, the Court moved modestly to rediscover the civil rights of private property owners. Given the complexities and constraints imposed by the last 50 years of Supreme Court decisions, policy in this area has understandably seemed confused and hesitant. The legal status of the private neighborhood association may be a leading American testing ground for the social role of private property in the 21st century.

Another key area of constitutional and policy debate is likely to be the permissible methods of neighborhood governance. Some observers have questioned the constitutionality of assigning voting rights in neighborhood associations based on the ownership of property. The Supreme Court will likely be asked to decide whether one person/one vote should also apply to the democratic workings of neighborhood associations. Such a challenge would question the validity of the corporate business model for neighborhood associations. No one has seriously argued that democratic voting in business corporations should be based on one stockholder/one vote. If the business model is rejected for neighborhood associations, what other body of legal thought and precedent might be substituted?

Today, neighborhood associations can be seen as partial secessions from municipalities. In the future, neighborhood associations may expand the range of services they deliver. This will be possible only if they receive property tax rebates (in whole or in part) from municipalities. If neighborhood services expand significantly and net tax payments to the public sector diminish, the creation of a private neighborhood association will come close to a full act of secession from a municipality.

Since the Civil War, the idea of secession has had strong negative connotations in America. Yet, there may be important practical gains from a secession option at the level of local government. Peter Kurrild-Klitgaard, for one, argues that "a constitutional right to wholly or partly 'exit' a political community, or specific institutions within that political community . . . may be the institutional guarantee against suboptimal collective decisions" in the public provision of local services. Among the possible forms of "secession," he includes the exit of "a neighborhood relative to a town."[2] If the local government structures in the United States become more flexible, thus allowing room for local jurisdictional boundaries to change more easily, and for innovating new governmental forms, a local right of free secession might encourage a trial and error process of political experimentation.

Part VI will take up, in a preliminary way (a full exploration would extend well beyond the scope of this book), the future role of private neighborhood associations in American life. Chapter 18 examines the social implications of permitting wider discrimination by neighborhood associations in admitting unit owners. Chapter 19 examines the future legal constraints on assigning voting rights in neighborhood associations. And chapter 20 considers the merits of easing the process of neighborhood secession from local governments in the public sector.

NOTES

1. See Glen O. Robinson, "Communities," *Virginia Law Review* 83 (March 1997), 297–307.

2. Peter Kurrild-Klitgaard, "Opting-Out: The Constitutional Economics of Exit," *American Journal of Economics and Sociology* 61 (January 2002), 124, 145.

18

Freedom of
Neighborhood Association

Paul Miller, a sociologist at the University of Montana, states that the rise of private neighborhood associations "fits into the more general process in the nation of increasing separation by race and class." Rather than helping to solve the problems of society, many people today are instead seeking to move away from these problems. According to Miller, "those who can purchase their separation increasingly do." Furthermore, Miller argues, "It's not a healthy thing for a community to have a gated, defensive structure, and it goes against the concept of a sustainable community, in which people share spaces and a common identity and are attuned to the needs of each other." According to one individual facing exclusion from a neighborhood association, "It makes you wonder what's wrong with you that you might be scary to others."[1]

The term "discrimination" has a strong negative connotation in American life. One person's discriminatory action is seen as limiting another person's individual freedom. Yet, the ability to discriminate is also necessary to another basic individual right—the "freedom of association." Although this right is not among those explicitly spelled out in the U.S. Constitution, the Supreme Court has increasingly recognized it in recent years.[2] As a federal district court stated in 2000, "The right to freedom of association . . . arises as a necessary concomitant to the Bill of Rights' protection of individual liberty."[3] Thus, a right of group association is capable in principle of constitutionally overriding other individual rights. For example, in 2000, the Supreme Court upheld the right of the Boy Scouts of America as a private organization to discharge a gay Eagle Scout, despite many existing laws against public discrimination based on sexual orientation.[4]

The courts are not alone in their thinking. Support for group rights of association is also coming from prominent American intellectuals. Former Princeton University philosopher Amy Gutmann (now president of the University of Pennsylvania) writes, "The term 'freedom of association' does not appear in the United States Constitution. . . . Yet freedom of association . . . is surely an essential part of individual freedom." There is no escaping the fact, moreover, that "the freedom to associate necessarily entails the freedom to exclude, and therefore limits our freedom of entry." Gutmann continues, "If I can enter any association of my choice, then you have no freedom not to associate with me. A requirement of open membership would undermine" any true freedom to shape strong communal groups in the United States.[5]

Reviving American Communities

Reflecting concerns for an eroding value structure in American life, and perhaps partly in reaction to the powerful new individualism that stemmed from the 1960s and 1970s, the goal to promote a stronger community life in American society became widespread among leading intellectuals in the 1990s.[6] While such thinking was not yet reflected in existing law, many such writers were suggesting that the freedom of association—and necessarily then, the right to discriminate—should be newly affirmed and given greater protections. Nancy Rosenblum (now chair of Harvard University's government department) argued in 1998 that a common lack of deep rootedness in a community—"the vicious effects of pluralism"—was a major problem in contemporary life. The development of stronger local bonds, however, could offer a "compensatory dynamic."* A person should "feel at home," and even a derived sense of "feeling superior" was not necessarily a bad thing and often worked, for instance, to enhance "self-respect." Rosenblum argued, "It is easy to see why expansive freedom of association—'the full and diverse internal life of the many communities of interests equal liberty allows'—is desirable."[7]

Yet, proponents argued, no one community would be suitable for everyone, and certainly no one should be required to join or remain in a particular com-

---

*The roots of such communitarian thinking can be traced at least back to the 1980s. As Charles Taylor commented in 1985, "Our identity is always partly defined in conversation with others or through the common understanding which underlies the practices of our society." Another leader of communitarian thought, Michael Sandel, remarked in 1982, "To say that the members of a society are bound by a sense of community is not simply to say that a great many of them profess communitarian sentiments and pursue communitarian aims, but rather that they conceive their identity—the subject and not just the object of their feelings and aspirations—as defined to some extent by the community of which they are a part." See Charles Taylor, *Philosophy and the Human Sciences* (New York: Cambridge University Press, 1985), 209 and Michael J. Sandel, *Liberalism and the Limits of Justice* (New York: Cambridge University Press, 1982), 150.

munity. There should be numerous forms of association and people should be free to exercise individual choice.[8] According to Rosenblum, a society like this requires "the most extensive pluralism combined with chances to exploit it, where men and women can enter and exit groups freely, where new associations are spontaneously formed and where shifting involvements is commonplace." Each community should be open to new members, but no one has the right to enter each small community. Indeed, "gatekeeping is a principal part of association. Members themselves or the group's leaders must be able to determine the association's character, which includes enforcing restrictive criteria for entry and acting on particular notions of desert."[9]

Following such principles in the housing area, admittedly, might necessitate the repeal of the Fair Housing Act (except in so far as its prohibitions address racial discrimination). Americans faced, as one urban authority writes, a "great paradox of a plural society"—a deep tension between their belief both in a strong community and in a world without discrimination.[10] Increasingly, and reversing the trends of earlier decades, the balance for many prominent American commentators shifted toward the community side of the equation.

Even in the area of race, where virtually no one was suggesting that past discrimination had been acceptable, such a tension could raise troublesome concerns. In celebrating the 50 years since *Brown v. Board of Education* in 1954, many observers lamented the slow progress in black educational achievement, even as there had been substantially greater (if still far from complete) racial integration of American schools. The original Brown case had involved Topeka, Kansas, and the black principal of Topeka High School, Clardy Vinson, declared, "We have achieved integration, but in the process we have lost a sense of community and social support. In the old days, blacks students had a built-in support system. They were in constant contact with people they could identify with—teachers, parents, pastors—who were working together to help them succeed." Vinson believed that the continuing "achievement gap" in poor black student performance was at least partly "the result of this support system not being in place."[11] One of the original petitioners in the 1954 Brown case, Joseph A. DeLaine, similarly told a *Washington Post* reporter that he had received "a better education" in the old segregated schools, reflecting the commitment of the black teaching staff, who were closely linked to the local community.[12]

No one was arguing that Brown was wrongly decided. It was necessary to take this and other steps in the civil rights movement to end the dark stain of official racism found even in the original Constitution. However, the bonds within the black community had in some important ways been eroded, resulting in disadvantages for blacks in education and elsewhere. Indeed, now that racial integration is the law of the land, the precise extent of school and housing integration has become less important for many blacks. Some black Americans now argue that their own black communities are superior to "soulless" suburban white neighborhoods. These and other commentators have expressed a new skepticism with respect to the benefits of "racial 'integration' as it is commonly conceived." They argue that "statistical integration means relinquishing political solidarity and cultural distinctiveness for the dubious privilege of entering the hostile environment of the white suburb."[13]

There were even new nostalgic remembrances of an earlier America in which "much association building . . . in the late nineteenth and early twentieth century arose from ethnic antagonisms and proceeded in furrows worn by religion" and other significant differences among Americans. In the process, as Harvard's Theda Skocpol writes, "Even when mobilization and countermobilization occurred between mutually exclusive groups, . . . civic lessons could be learned from voluntary participation" in a myriad of local groups. The fact of the matter was that "quests for moral influence and political power were always the rule, not the exception, in American civic life; and conflict and competition . . . the mother's milk of American democracy." In our "recently reorganized civic life," however, "too many valuable aspects of the old civic America are not being reproduced or reinvented in the new public world run largely by professional trustees and memberless organizations" with little active involvement of ordinary members.[14] Skocpol is among the growing number of American social scientists now concerned for the loss of close community experience throughout the nation. Americans in the past, as she has pointed out, could enjoy the camaraderie found in the local Rotary Club, the Kiwanis Club, the American Legion, and many other such organizations; now, however, most of these forms of local association are in decline.

Free Association as an Individual Right

While new communitarians find that the right of free association is necessary to a more vital community life in American society, others defend free association as an important individual right in itself. Thus, the right of free speech may require the defense of the individual right of free association. An oppressive government might deny its citizens the full freedoms of speech, religion, assembly, and other constitutionally protected rights simply by putting tight limits on citizens' capacity to band together for expressive purposes. The right of assembly may have to extend, therefore, to residential living arrangements as well as citizens gathering together in a town square to listen to a speech. Indeed, Jason Mazzone argues that there are historical grounds for finding a freedom of association in the original understanding of the American constitution:

> My bottom line is this: Freedom of association merits constitutional protection because association is a critical means of popular sovereignty. Associating is a way for citizens to exercise political influence, get things done, and keep government in check. This

idea, which underlies freedom of petition and assembly, informed early historical perspectives on associations. It also provides a useful basis for understanding the proper scope of freedom of association today.[15]

Richard Epstein, a libertarian theorist at the University of Chicago law school, would in fact guarantee virtually all rights of free association in private settings. Speaking in the context of servitudes and other private deed restrictions placed on the use of land, Epstein argues that private property in most respects should establish a protected domain in which "individuals may establish both the means and the ends for themselves, to pursue as they see fit." Unless there is some "very strong reason," society should defer to property owners' preferences, recognizing that many "eccentric" outcomes could result.[16] Indeed, the institution of private property may be vital to society precisely because it protects unconventional and minority views against the powerful tides of social conformism and majority opinion.*

Epstein agrees that free association is necessary to free speech and other individual liberties. The Supreme Court has indeed protected even odious forms of speech, such as protest marches carried out by American neo-Nazis. Epstein goes so far as to argue that freedom of association should be similarly unconstrained in private domains; it should be "flatly unconstitutional for the United States to force any private organization to adopt a color-blind or sex-blind policy in hiring or admission to membership. One university can go all-out for affirmative action; an all-girls school can hire only female teachers; a religious school can admit only co-religionists."[17] Applied to private neighborhood associations, Epstein's reasoning might make it legal for an association to welcome new black unit owners, but only up to a fixed quota of, say, 25 percent (a figure that might be regarded as a "tipping point" where white flight from the neighborhood association could become a problem).

Neighborhood Diversity in Homogeneity

Unlike most of the above writers, James Winokur is skeptical of freedom of association. He argues that American society must protect the individual right to be

---

*Critics often attack gated communities for being socially isolating and divisive. However, a gated community might also protect residents from wider oppression. An example of this was seen in Shanghai, China, where gated communities are common. Chinese authorities had attempted to clamp down on new cultural forces raging through Chinese society, and part of their strategy included the censorship of television. However, as the *Washington Post* recently reported, "Sky Wang and her friends saw the soap opera soon after it took off in Taiwan. Some of their rich friends in Shanghai saw it via illegal satellite TV dishes that can pick up Taiwanese television in their homes, located in gated communities generally beyond the purview of Chinese police." See John Pomfret, "Band Hits Sour Note in China: Groups Appeal Shows Rift between Culture, Party," *Washington Post,* June 10, 2002, A01.

"peculiarly one's self," based on "the notion of property as protecting personal identity, and home as a favored context for individual flourishing." In a neighborhood association, it may therefore be necessary to sacrifice the ability to control the "details of adjacent uses" because of the "central importance of home to an individual's sense of self, and to the shaping of that individual's unique history and future by the expression of his or her own distinctive personality."[18] Hence, as Winokur argues, higher levels of government would be justified in imposing tight new limits on neighborhood associations' ability to define their own social and physical environments. He contends that federal constitutional protections of freedom of speech, assembly, press, worship, and other individual rights should override the current powers of neighborhood associations. In essence, Winokur proposes that the neighborhood association should be considered equivalent to a local public government and thus constitutionally considered a "state actor."

In a neighborhood association, however, the ability to be "peculiarly one's self" may require the presence of a group of people who share a similar vision of "self." Some parents may find the social values taught in national television programs offensive. Yet, even if they ban television watching by their own children at home, their children may simply go next door. Contrary to their professed objectives, it seems that the advocates of internal "diversity" within neighborhood associations are actually seeking to impose a wider conformity within American life. They may believe that core social values are threatened by the prospect of nonconforming social environments. They may fear, for example, that religious "zealots" will attempt to "propagandize" their children in "false teachings" such as creationism or other literal interpretations of the Bible.

One way to limit any such unfortunate outcomes would be to mandate internal "diversity"—that the neighborhood is legally required to admit all kinds of persons. A powerful community identity, however, requires the presence of people who share a commitment to common values. A government rule, for example, that requires a nudist camp to admit all kinds of people, including people who are committed to wearing clothes in public, for all practical purposes eliminates the possibility of nudists joining together to satisfy their own private wishes.

Hence, rather than defending essential individual rights of expression, Mark Rosen finds that "imposing assimilation . . . violates rather than vindicates the first principle of justice." Social fairness may demand the expansion of "the set of reasonable comprehensive doctrines that can flourish" locally, including in neighborhood associations.[19] In contrast to Winokur's concerns about neighborhood limits on individual expression, Rosenblum argues that "if the ideal of democratic localism is small size and homogeneity along one or another dimension, economic development and the interests of home and family, then RCAs [residential community associations] come closer to fulfilling it today than most local communities."[20] The urban sociologist David Popenoe argues that most people once lived in small "urban villages" and such places should again be "encouraged to function and grow."[21]

Some critics of local autonomy are more explicit about their desire to promote the common values of a wider community. Sheryll Cashin believes that "the localist vision is undermining the value of citizen participation." She wants people to think of themselves not as residents of a neighborhood, but as "citizens of the metropolis." The goal in shaping the institutions of metropolitan governance should be to "enable citizens to develop a [metropolitan] regional identity or a notion of a collective regional interest." Under the current American commitment to neighborhoods and other smaller localities, however, "it is particularly difficult for the citizens of an atomized polity to recognize, much less pursue, a mutual destiny with persons outside their local political jurisdiction."[22] To be sure, the prospect of developing a strong sense of metropolitan shared identity is an open question. Most Americans today identify strongly with their nation, to some extent with their state and local governments, perhaps more with their neighborhood association if they live in one, and rather less with any "community" of their full metropolitan region.

Church and State

Freedom of association is perhaps most important in matters of religion.[23] A religion may seek to limit participation in some official activities to "true believers," and this may require exclusion from certain areas of common church land and property. Some churches, for example, operate summer retreats where a declared commitment to the faith is expected among those attending. Some private colleges require faculty members to make formal declarations of religious belief. In the future, religious bodies may similarly want to create neighborhood associations in which the members are of a particular faith.*

---

*The Reverend Jerry Falwell is seeking to build a new neighborhood association for fellow Christians in southwest Virginia. According to one report,

> Mr. Falwell thinks often about what will remain when he's gone. If he gets his way in federal court this summer, the conservative pastor will leave his most visible legacy twinkling below: a master-planned community where members of his flock can live from "birth to antiquity."
>
> "You'll never have to leave this place," Mr. Falwell says. "You can come in at age 2, in our early learning center . . . age 5 into our kindergarten, age 6 through 18 in our elementary and high school. And then on to Liberty University for four years."
>
> When Mr. Falwell's followers turn 55, they would be eligible to move into nearby Liberty Village, a 1,135-unit retirement center with its own markets, putting green, chapel, and associate pastor from Mr. Falwell's church. The retirement condos, which cost $80,000 to $300,000, are under construction just outside Lynchburg. See Chris Kahn, "Falwell Has Hopes of Christian Hamlet," *Washington Times,* June 16, 2002, A9.

Yet, the courts at present might well rule against any attempt to restrict residency in a neighborhood association to a particular religion—an association limited, say, to Methodists or Seventh-Day Adventists. To date, only one obscure court case involving the Theosophical Society in America has addressed this issue.* In 1983, a California court invalidated an attempt to limit residents in a retirement community to members of this Society. The court did not recognize the Society explicitly as religious, but nevertheless invalidated its covenant as a violation of state law against deed restrictions based on race, ethnicity, sex, or religion.[24] Similar federal provisions prohibiting discrimination in housing are contained in the Fair Housing Act.

However, laws such as these raise constitutional issues.[25] According to University of Chicago law professor Cass Sunstein, "Under a democratic constitution, people do have freedom to associate, and this right carries with it a general right of exclusion—a right to create deliberating enclaves of like-minded people. If, for example, the state forced a small group of deliberating people to admit people who fundamentally disagreed with them, the Constitution would be violated." As Sunstein notes, this right of association has been particularly important for Americans with respect to religion: "If the state required a religious group to employ people who did not share the group's religious conviction, there would be a clear constitutional problem."[26] He does not mention a religious neighborhood association, but a similar reasoning would seem to apply.

Law professor Thomas Berg argues that the courts' current treatment of religion may actually amount to a form of discrimination in favor of modern secular values. As Berg puts it, "As government grows, separationist efforts to shelter it from religious influence and to bar it from doing anything that aids religion are bound to push religion into a smaller and smaller corner of public life, violating both religious liberty and the equal status of religion with other ideas."[27] This issue has come before the U.S. Supreme Court in a limited way with respect to use of public school facilities by religious groups. In a 2001 decision involving a school in New York State, the Court directed that schools must make their facil-

---

*Although it did not involve a neighborhood association, another court case addressed similar issues with regard to the incorporated village of Kiryas Joel in upstate New York. The village was populated almost entirely by Satmar Jews who had moved there from Brooklyn. The Jewish residents had their own private school, but sought public support for the burdens of educating children who were included in federally mandated "special education" programs. Initially, they had sent their children to special education programs outside the village, but the children's strange appearance and unconventional behavior did not easily fit within the majority school culture. The New York State legislature in 1989 therefore enacted legislation to recognize Kiryas Joel as a separate school district that could provide special education limited to Kiryas Joel children. In 1994, however, the U.S. Supreme Court declared this arrangement to be an unconstitutional infringement on the separation of church and state. See Abner S. Greene, "Kiryas Joel and Two Mistakes about Equality," *Columbia Law Review* 96 (January 1996); and Martha L. Minow, "The Constitution and the Sub-Group Question," *Indiana Law Journal* 71 (Winter 1995).

ities available to religious groups if they are willing to do the same for nonreligious groups.[28] To do otherwise would be discriminating overtly against religion. If many forms of nonreligious discrimination by a neighborhood association are legal at present, might a similar reasoning apply to protect a neighborhood association's ability to discriminate on a religious basis? Reflecting the legal uncertainties, University of Virginia law professor Glen Robinson finds that the constitutional law of separation of church and state at present is "notoriously confused."[29]

When they eventually address such issues more closely with respect to neighborhood associations, the courts may accept the arguments of legal authorities such as Clayton Gillette, who asserts that it may be important to avoid a situation where "civil liberties are viewed as the enemy of communal values and law itself is pitted against the power of people to shape their own lives" through religion and other strong belief systems.[30] Another authority on neighborhood association law, Katharine Rosenberry, argues that "attempts to apply constitutional analysis in common-interest developments" will face major difficulties if such efforts are directed to neighborhood actions with respect to "voting rights, discrimination, inverse condemnation, or freedom of speech and religion." She finds that "common-interest developments are consensual in nature and constitutional principles which have evolved in response to actions of state and local governments are not necessarily applicable in the common-interest setting" (such as a private neighborhood association). Indeed, Rosenberry argues, whenever possible, courts "should refuse to apply the body of constitutional law to documents governing common-interest developments"—even if private associations admittedly "have many of the trappings of government."[31]

A neighborhood's small geographic size means that there can be a wide range of choices in neighborhood types across a full metropolitan region. As Gerald Korngold explains, "If a person does not want to be so restricted, then he can simply choose not to buy in the community."[32] The situation is much different in a large nation-state; exit would be very expensive and difficult for most U.S. citizens. Strong protections against overbearing government may thus be necessary at a national level, even as much tighter restrictions at a neighborhood level do not raise similar fundamental objections. Indeed, a wide range of neighborhood associations might be allowed to flower in all their religious and other diversity.

A freedom of private association might or might not mean greater neighborhood homogeneity; the result depends on millions of individual acts of housing choice. Many people privately prefer racially and otherwise diverse neighborhoods. Even during a period in which much of the new housing in the United States is being built in private neighborhood associations, a recent Urban Institute study finds that "more neighborhoods in metropolitan America are shared by blacks and whites today than a decade ago." From 1980 to 2000, the percentage of neighborhoods that were almost exclusively white (less than 5 percent black population) declined from 65 percent to 47 percent (in the 69 large metropolitan areas under study), part of a broader "major trend toward neighborhood integration."[33] Little of this racial progress has been achieved by means of changes in metropolitan zoning or other housing policies. Many people today simply prefer—or at a minimum have no objection to—integrated neighborhoods, as long as such integration poses no threat to the neighborhood's established character.

Despite considerable opinion to the contrary, it is even possible that the rise of private neighborhood associations will encourage the greater integration of neighbors with diverse backgrounds; the rules of the association will significantly reduce the risks of the unknown in accepting new neighbors. If a concern is that "unfamiliar" or "different" people will not mow their lawns, will litter the streets, or will otherwise not keep up the neighborhood, then the neighborhood association has the means to address the problem. If Americans can come together in diverse communities mostly through peaceful and voluntary acts of individuals, including entering and exiting neighborhood associations, then this process is likely to provoke less resistance and in the end be more successful than government action in this area.

Costs of Heterogeneity

The advantages of a competitive system of common service delivery by many local jurisdictions—a "Tiebout system"—were previously noted in chapter 11. In general, the transaction costs of meeting the Tiebout requirements for efficiency in public service delivery would be less in a world where many neighborhood associations are homogeneously populated. Pietro Nivola describes the advantages of a greater tailoring of public services to the specific demands of the citizens in each governing jurisdiction:

> Disparities among jurisdictions commonly reflect not only differential tax bases but varying local tastes for public goods. Inasmuch as unitary governmental institutions help equalize the quality of services within metropolitan areas by effectively sharing revenues on an area-wide basis, these arrangements may level local inequalities, thus promising a distributional adjustment, if not an efficiency gain. But inasmuch as equalization reduces the ability of communities and neighborhoods to choose their own preferred baskets of services, the process interferes with the exercise of consumer sovereignty. The logic of such interference is questionable.[34]

The economic advantages of a Tiebout world of public service delivery constitute a subset of the general set of practical advantages flowing from neighborhood homogeneity. The more homogeneous a neighborhood is, the simpler the workings of the political process will be. Consider a hypothetical neighborhood association of perfect homogeneity, where unit owners display identical social as well as economic characteristics. Under this (admittedly heroic) simplifying assumption, association members completely agree on the character of neighborhood environment desired and the common services to be provided. As long as the association requires that each unit owner be treated equally in matters of services and assessments, the political process tends to be irrelevant. There can even be a single neighborhood dictator because this person makes the same choices as anyone else. There is be no need to waste time and money on a neighborhood legislature; legislative decisions replicate the preferences already shared by all the unit owners. The transaction costs of democratic politics are held to a minimum.

University of Chicago law professor Eric Posner comments that two of the key "indicia of solidarity" within a given group are the "homogeneity of the members' interests" and the "homogeneity of the members' backgrounds."[35] Group solidarity has some specific advantages:

> When members of a solidary group transact, norms and nonlegal sanctions generally resolve disputes. When contingencies arise, norms allocate risks and specify means of resolution. Norms also prohibit bad faith and opportunism. The importance of maintaining a good reputation and of avoiding ostracism deters improper behavior. Accordingly, insiders can dispense with expensive formalities—lawyers, bonds, even writings—and with the unreliable courts.[36]

In contrast, a political jurisdiction's wide diversity, law professor Marshall Tracht observes, raises "the possibility that a majority will impose policies that benefit themselves at the expense of a minority." In order to protect themselves, purchasers of units in diverse neighborhoods will demand political protections, such as a high-supermajority voting requirement for approval of changes in a neighborhood constitution. More diverse neighborhoods will exhibit a greater likelihood of "deadweight losses as parties engage in rent-seeking and in defensive strategies to protect themselves against rent-seeking" by other unit owners.* Indeed, as Tracht notes, "this problem will be further exacerbated where [housing] units are heterogeneous, causing unit owners' interests to differ in accordance with their types of unit." In general, any government requirements of "mandated diversity" will result in "higher decision making costs and reduced flexibility" within private neighborhood associations. By contrast, "condominiums with more homogeneous units . . . are relatively immune to redistribution

---

*"Rent-seeking" is a term economists use to describe the pursuit of private interest in the public sector, such as the manipulation of government rules and other actions for individual benefit. For example, rather than produce a better product at a lower price, a rent-seeking firm may find that it can maximize its private profits by persuading the legislature to give it an exclusive monopoly franchise, or to adopt some other rule that discriminates in its favor relative to other firms.

because unit owners' interests are similar," and thus these neighborhood associations are more likely to be able to "reduce the costs of decision making."[37]

It is ironic that many of the same people who are most critical of discriminatory practices in granting neighborhood entry are also among the strongest critics of the "divisive" internal workings of neighborhood associations.* One might suggest that such people are trying to square a circle. Promoting neighborhood diversity promotes neighborhood conflict. According to Robert Natelson, existing research on neighborhood associations shows that "community heterogeneity, which many scholars see as a positive value, is in fact associated with severe association [operating] problems, including rule violations, assessment delinquencies, and low morale."[38]

Income Redistribution

Still, even if homogeneous neighborhoods are more economically efficient, they may be less equitable. Diversity potentially offers two main benefits: (1) it promotes a fairer distribution of income in American society as whole, and (2) it encourages greater integration of mixed populations within neighborhoods as a social end in itself. "Exclusionary" zoning practices (and now private neighborhoods), however, have long been criticized for promoting economic segregation in American society. In one view, the spread of neighborhood associations has contributed to a " 'two-tiered' society," one that violates basic American ideals of social equality.[39] Joel Garreau in *Edge City* portrays neighborhood associations as representing "governments by the wealthy, for the wealthy."[40] The richest neighborhood associations may, in fact, have Olympic-sized swimming pools, large areas of open space for hiking trails, a Robert Trent Jones golf course, and other luxury amenities.

---

*Evan McKenzie, for example, suggests that the promoters of neighborhood associations are making utopian claims—that the neighborhood association is a new form of urban "privatopia." McKenzie accurately describes the fierce internal disagreements in many associations, suggesting that neighborhood associations pose a stark choice between "conformity and conflict." Yet, McKenzie also thinks that neighborhood associations should be more diverse. He labels the rise of neighborhood associations as "privatization for the few," which threatens to "develop an attenuated sense of loyalty and commitment to the [wider] public communities" in which the neighborhood associations are located. Even the current degree of homogeneity of neighborhood associations, he argues, promotes divisions of "homeowners versus renters, suburbs against the cities, and the differences in race, class, and age that are associated with home ownership and residence." McKenzie acknowledges at a few points that perhaps a successful society could be constituted of a diversity of small communities, each of these communities in itself homogeneous. However, he also says that the rise of the private neighborhood association is such a great threat to the basic values of the nation that American society might even be justified in "resisting the construction of new" neighborhood associations in the future. See Evan McKenzie, *Privatopia: Homeowner Associations and the Rise of Residential Private Government* (New Haven, CT: Yale University Press, 1994), 19, 186, 187, 197.

The fact that the rich live better than the poor, to be sure, is not exactly news. Wealthy people travel to Switzerland for their winter ski vacations; poor people go ice-skating on a local pond. The rich eat filet mignon; the poor eat hamburger. It is much the same for the distribution of neighborhood environmental amenities. Why, then, should neighborhood amenities be distributed more equally when the great majority of private goods and services are distributed unequally in American life?

In response, one might argue that the unequal distribution of income in the United States should be opposed everywhere, and neighborhood associations perhaps offer a new and promising battleground in waging this old war. Even if the battle has been lost in other places, the private neighborhood association is relatively new in American society, and may offer more room for political and legal maneuvering in an attempt to shift overall American social outcomes in an egalitarian direction.

Arthur Okun, a leading American economist and former chairman of the Council of Economic Advisers in the Lyndon Johnson administration, once famously described the issue of economic efficiency versus economic equality as the "big tradeoff." According to Okun, an efficient economic system depends on "the prizes in the marketplace [which] provide the incentives for work effort and productive contribution. In their absence, society would thrash about for alternative incentives—some unreliable, like altruism; some perilous, like collective loyalty; some intolerable, like coercion or oppression."[41] Reflecting such considerations, American governments have many income redistribution and other programs to address the real concerns for social inequality, but few of them seek to promote increasing the direct sharing of a private good or service.

Some people historically have sought to abolish private property rights altogether as a way of promoting social equality, but Okun warned that in doing so, "the living standards of the lowly would fall along with those of the mighty." Indeed, if rich people were required to share high-quality neighborhoods with the poor, most developers would abandon efforts to build the most attractive neighborhoods in the first place. The result would be the same if rich people were all required to share their Mercedes Benz automobiles with the poor; this policy would not advance social equality as much as it would result in the production of very few Mercedes. In short, if neighborhood associations became a main instrument in the pursuit of social equality, the result in practice would be a deterioration in the environmental quality of American urban and suburban landscapes.

Luxury Goods

Yet, perhaps the neighborhood environment has a special character that makes it much more important to social equality than a typical private good. Good personal health, for example, has an especially large influence on an individual's ability to live well. While many of its citizens are still uninsured, the United States has still moved a long way in recognizing all citizens' general social "right" to good health care. Perhaps neighborhood environmental quality should be put in the same category. Sheryll Cashin suggests that the desire for "socioeconomic homogeneity"—thus allowing the rich to live in better neighborhoods than the poor—may be as ethically suspect in American life as is the desire for racial homogeneity.[42]

However, in ranking the social importance of consumable items, the quality of one's surrounding neighborhood environment may not rate especially high. Indeed, neighborhood environmental quality may rank above computer games, blue jeans, mountain bikes, and some of the other numerous products popular in our endlessly creative consumer society. And for a person living in a neighborhood beset by crime and other social maladies, the quality of the environment is likely to be an especially important determinant of well-being. However, for most people, the availability of good food, clothing, and a warm place to sleep may rank well above their surrounding neighborhood environment. As history seems to show, environmental quality is for most people a luxury good—and this probably includes the surrounding neighborhood environment as well.

Instead of providing more of specific items of consumption, such as housing, Okun argued that the United States should address income inequality by adopting a general safety net, and by providing job training. Okun commented, "I personally would not be greatly exercised about unequal prizes won in the marketplace if they merely determined who could buy beachfront condominiums."[43] It was important to set priorities in public spending, and at least some forms of housing prerogatives of the well off would not rank at the top of the list of items sought by lower income groups.

Better and Worse Ways to Redistribute Income

Despite such arguments, there remain many advocates for "inclusionary zoning" and other government programs requiring high-quality neighborhoods to include housing units for lower- and moderate-income owners. In effect, a part of the municipal "price" charged for approving the construction of a unit in a high-income neighborhood would be the provision of another less expensive housing unit. The zoning would be "sold," so to speak, and the municipal "revenue" from zoning sales would be directed for a select purpose—special access to cheaper housing units in a higher-quality neighborhood.

However, practically speaking, if American society is prepared to make such redistributive efforts on behalf of lower- and moderate-income people, some might well prefer to have the money instead of the opportunity to live in a neighborhood with the rich. The rich and poor may live together peacefully enough, but they are less likely to have a common basis for neighborhood community. People of much different economic means may not be able to join together in a discussion about the pleasures of recent European travel, or dining experiences at the best restaurants in New York.

Economists have long argued that the most effective redistributive policies involve direct monetary transfers to the poor—such as the earned income tax credit in existing federal law. Indirect redistribution through in-kind transfers is less efficient. For example, in an extreme case, let us say that the government decided to help out poor people by giving them free radios. Among those who qualified, some would probably be deaf. Obviously, these individuals would prefer the money and would want to sell their radios (assuming this is allowed) for whatever price they could get. These individuals would have been better served if they had received financial aid directly from the government.

Redistribution through in-kind transfers also often ends up creating its own inequities. Some poor people at the head of the list might get into an attractive suburban neighborhood, but inevitably there would not be enough room for many other people with lower and moderate incomes. Political influence and favoritism might come into play in determining the selection of the actual winning applicants. Income redistribution through direct income transfers better serves equity by giving equal amounts to each eligible person.

Diversity as the End in Itself

Having said all this, it may simply be desirable—social equality aside—to foster diverse neighborhood populations. In the education of children, for example, it may be beneficial that the children of richer parents should mix with the children of poorer parents. Children of Daughters of the American Revolution perhaps should have to become friends with children of recent immigrants. And what is true for the children is also true for the parents, though accomplishing this may perhaps be more difficult because of parents' busy work schedules.

Some people thus argue that a neighborhood with a wider mixture of people will simply be a more enjoyable place to live. Paula Franzese declares, "Eclectic housing styles and mixed uses are outward looking and fortify stocks of bridging (meaning inclusive) social capital. Diversity is an important aim. To this end, some new common interest communities are embracing 'diversity in uses, population, demographics, architectural character, and architectural style' to render developments more affordable and more heterogeneous"—and more profitable.[44] Diversity thus is becoming a selling point for some new developments. In simply responding to the demands of the market, increasing numbers of neighborhood associations may contain unit owners from many different origins. Such a goal may admittedly require changing zoning laws that now often block the mixing of housing types, but developers succeed financially by responding to their customers' desires.*

The issue for public policy is much different—whether diversity should be required as a matter of law when developers would not otherwise provide it. One justification for legislation in this area might be that buyers of units in neighborhood associations do not know what is good for them, and they will come to appreciate neighborhood diversity once they have experienced it. The government regulates private-school curricula and other features, for instance, partly because it considers that at least some parents are not capable of judging school quality in their children's best interests.

Alternatively, one might argue that there are "social externalities" in the existence of diverse neighborhoods. Left to their own devices, the purchasers of housing units may choose to live in a neighborhood association with a homogeneous population. However, learning to live with others who act and think differently may improve the character of the American people—including the workings of democracy. The benefits in this regard are likely to be especially large for the poor. By mixing populations in neighborhoods, people with "better" social values will teach others with "poorer" social values how to think and behave.

This argument, however, gives away the store. It is not diversity that is being sought, but in fact a homogeneity of American behavior. The purpose of "diversity" in neighborhood associations is to ensure that the neighborhood functions effectively in maintaining a single system of American core values, and that the neighborhood plays its part in assimilating any outsiders as rapidly as possible. Such a view reflects a long-standing, melting-pot view evident in American political life. As U.S. Senator George Edmunds stated at the end of the 19th century, "Fundamental to successful republicanism [is] homogeneous unity of the whole body of the citizens of a State." A policy of allowing the segregation of "men of special religious or special political or social ideas exclusively in one place" would undermine the strong common bonds among all Americans that would be essential to the future political success of the nation.[45]

---

*This is one of the goals of the architectural school of "the new urbanism." The neighborhood association of Kentlands in Montgomery County, Maryland—a poster child for the new urbanism—includes housing for a range of income groups. The builders of Kentlands contend that homeowners in fact prefer such diversity in their communities and have often been prevented by zoning and other restrictions from satisfying their real preferences. If properly designed and managed, and if government permits it, housing and population diversity, in short, will make money—in Kentlands, and many other places. See Andres Duany, Elizabeth Plater-Zyberk, and Jeff Speck, Suburban Nation: The Rise of Sprawl and the Decline of the American Dream (New York: Farrar, Straus and Giroux, 2000).

Many advocates of diversity in neighborhood associations do in fact seem to think that a stronger set of distinct neighborhood identities will endanger the single national community of all Americans. The questions posed for public policy discussion may thus be: Should the United States seek to require a common value system of "America," or should a diversity of neighborhoods reflect a wider range of values that might include groups of religious fanatics, ethnic zealots, racial bigots, libertarian misfits, and others from a far-ranging assortment of the ideas and personalities that make up the population of the United States? Do we need to "cure" these people of their false values and other illusions, or should we welcome—or at least tolerate—them in all their differences?*

For the Purposes of Discussion

Most Americans are patriotic; many have been willing to die defending their country. Large numbers of Americans do believe that the United States is a model for the world. Yet, one of the reasons for its greatness has always been its stand in defending individual liberty. If the United States is to possess a strong sense of a single national community, its common values must be sustained by free and voluntary choice. It would be a violation of the core principles of American liberty—the principles that have made America so attractive to so many people from around the world—to compel obedience to a single national standard of common belief.

When the best basis for promoting and sustaining group values is a small geographic area, the freedom of association then necessarily extends to the right to control membership in a neighborhood. This right should include the free ability to restrict entry into a private neighborhood according to age, sex, ethnicity, religious belief, and a host of other categories. In order to guarantee this right, fair housing laws would have to be rewritten, since housing discrimination in some of these main categories is now illegal. Major metropolitan areas can host

---

*Even groups of radical libertarians, for example, who might have a deep distrust of all authority, can be accommodated in a world of private neighborhood associations. They can simply create their own libertarian neighborhoods that have few if any collective restrictions—other than the standard libertarian rule of not doing any direct harm to others. Members of such libertarian neighborhoods might have the freedom to park mobile homes in their front yards; to hang laundry out to dry on the deck; to play their music at all hours of the night; to allow and patronize a liquor store on a corner lot; to operate a car repair facility in a home garage; to own a pit bull; to build apartments at sites in the neighborhood; and to allow any number of other possibilities for neighborhood land uses. The fact that most existing neighborhoods at present have tight controls on individual land uses in their boundaries does not mean that there is anything intrinsic to the institution of a neighborhood association that requires such controls. The central significance of a private status is the wider freedom of choice—including the freedom to reject almost all zoning or any other land use controls—that it allows.

potentially dozens or even hundreds of private neighborhood associations. So if a person does not like the common values of a given neighborhood association, he or she is free not to purchase a home there and is free to go elsewhere. In considering prospective home locations, homebuyers can rely on a written neighborhood constitution to provide assurances that existing neighborhood values and policies will be sustained.

Those who argue for a social goal of diversity within all neighborhood associations would in other respects be imposing a new conformity. If all neighborhoods have a great mixture of people, then the tendency will be toward a convergence of American neighborhoods towards the average of the nation. The neighborhoods of the nation will not be more diverse but more similar. Real freedom of association, and true diversity in American neighborhoods, will require that each neighborhood group be free to decide its own character—and thus to limit those who can live there. Hence, the special case of race aside, the right of a neighborhood association to discriminate among potential new unit owners should be protected as a basic matter of defending the right of freedom of association under the U.S. Constitution.

NOTES

1. Quoted in Florence Williams, "Behind the Gate," *High Country News,* November 11, 2002.

2. Jason Mazzone, "Freedom's Associations," *Washington Law Review* 77 (July 2002), 644.

3. *Johnson v. City of Cincinnati,* 119 F. Supp. 2d at 741 (2000).

4. *Boy Scouts of America v. Dale,* 530 U.S. 640 (2000).

5. Amy Gutmann, "Freedom of Association: An Introductory Essay," in Amy Gutmann, ed., *Freedom of Association* (Princeton, NJ: Princeton University Press, 1998), 17, 11.

6. Brian O'Connell, *Civil Society: The Underpinnings of American Democracy* (Hanover, NH: University Press of New England, 1999); Carmen Sirianni and Lewis Friedland, *Civic Innovation in America: Community Empowerment, Public Policy, and the Movement for Civic Renewal* (Berkeley: University of California Press, 2001); and Archon Fung and Erik Olin Wright, eds., *Deepening Democracy: Institutional Innovations in Empowered Participatory Governance* (New York: Verso, 2003).

7. Nancy L. Rosenblum, *Membership & Morals: The Personal Uses of Pluralism in America* (Princeton, NJ: Princeton University Press, 1998), 63, 64.

8. Mark E. Warren, *Democracy and Association* (Princeton, NJ: Princeton University Press, 2001).

9. Rosenblum, *Membership & Morals,* 63–64.

10. Joseph P. Viteritti, "Municipal Home Rule and the Conditions of Justifiable Secession," *Fordham Urban Law Journal* 23 (Fall 1995), 36.

11. Quoted in Michael Dobbs, "Progress Made in City's Schools, but More to Go," *Washington Post,* May 13, 2004, A1.

12. Michael Dobbs, "Schools and Lives That Are Still Separate," *Washington Post,* May 17, 2004, A1.

13. Richard Thompson Ford, "Beyond Borders: A Partial Response to Richard Briffault," *Stanford Law Review* 48 (May 1996), 1185.

14. Theda Skocpol, *Diminished Democracy: From Membership to Management in American Civic Life* (Norman: University of Oklahoma Press, 2003), 114, 115, 223, 222.

15. Jason Mazzone, "Freedom's Associations," 712.

16. Richard A. Epstein, "Notice and Freedom of Contract in the Law of Servitudes" *Southern California Law Review* 55 (September 1982), 1359. See also Richard A. Epstein, "Covenants and Constitutions," *Cornell Law Review* 73 (July 1988).

17. Richard A. Epstein, "Free Association: The Incoherence of Antidiscrimination Laws," *National Review,* October 9, 2000, 40. See also Richard A. Epstein, *Forbidden Grounds: The Case Against Employment Discrimination Laws* (Cambridge, MA: Harvard University Press, 1992).

18. James L. Winokur, "The Mixed Blessings of Promissory Servitudes: Toward Optimizing Economic Utility, Individual Liberty, and Personal Identity," *Wisconsin Law Review,* 1989 (January/February 1989), 75, 74.

19. Mark D. Rosen, "The Outer Limits of Community Self-Governance in Residential Associations, Municipalities, and Indian Country: A Liberal Theory," *Virginia Law Review* 84 (September 1998), 1143, 1125.

20. Nancy L. Rosenblum, "Democratic Education at Home: Residential Community Associations and 'Our Localism,' " *The Good Society* 7, no. 2 (Spring 1997), 14.

21. David Popenoe, *Private Pleasure: Public Plight: American Metropolitan Community Life in Comparative Perspective* (New Brunswick, NJ: Transaction Books, 1985), 149.

22. Sheryll D. Cashin, "Localism, Self-Interest, and the Tyranny of the Favored Quarter: Addressing the Barriers to New Regionalism," *Georgetown Law Journal* 88 (July 2000), 2043, 2044, 2021, 2020.

23. Kent Greenawalt, "Freedom of Association and Religious Association," in Amy Gutmann, ed., *Freedom of Association* (Princeton, NJ: Princeton University Press, 1998).

24. *Taormina Theosophical Community Inc. v. Silver,* 190 Cal. Rptr. 38 (California Court of Appeal, 1983).

25. Nancy L. Rosenblum, ed., *Obligations of Citizenship and Demands of Faith: Religious Accommodation in Pluralist Democracies* (Princeton, NJ: Princeton University Press, 2000).

26. Cass R. Sunstein, *Designing Democracy: What Constitutions Do* (New York: Oxford University Press, 2001), 215.

27. Thomas C. Berg, "Slouching Towards Secularism: A Comment on *Kiryas Joel School District v. Grumet,*" *Emory Law Journal* 44 (Spring 1995), 442.

28. *Good News Club v. Milford Central School,* 533 U.S. 98 (2001).

29. Glen O. Robinson, "Communities," *Virginia Law Review* 83 (March 1997), 310.

30. Clayton P. Gillette, "Courts, Covenants, and Communities," *University of Chicago Law Review* 61 (Fall 1994), 1432.

31. Katharine Rosenberry, "The Application of the Federal and State Constitutions to Condominiums, Cooperatives and Planned Developments," *Real Property, Probate and Trust Journal* (1984), 29, 30–31, 2.

32. Gerald Korngold, *Private Land Use Controls: Balancing Private Initiative and the Public Interest in the Homeowners Association Context* (Cambridge, MA: Lincoln Institute of Land Policy, 1995), 7.

33. Lynette Rawlings, Laura Harris, and Margery Austin Turner, with Sandra Padilla, "Race and Residence: Prospects for Stable Neighborhood Integration," *Neighborhood Change in Urban America,* Brief 3 (Washington, DC: The Urban Institute, March 2004), 2, 3.

34. See Pietro S. Nivola, *Laws of the Landscape: How Policies Shape Cities in Europe and America* (Washington, DC: Brookings Institution Press, 1999), 64.

35. Eric A. Posner, "The Regulation of Groups: The Influence of Legal and Nonlegal Sanctions on Collective Action," *University of Chicago Law Review* 63 (Winter 1996), 158.

36. Ibid., 155.

37. Marshall E. Tracht, "Co-Ownership and Condominium," in Boudewijn Bouckaert and Gerrit De Geest, eds., *Encyclopedia of Law and Economics, Volume II: Civil Law and Economics* (Cheltenham, UK: Edward Elgar, 2000), 80, 81.

38. Robert G. Natelson, "Consent, Coercion, and 'Reasonableness' in Private Law: The Special Case of the Property Owners Association," *Ohio State Law Journal* 51 (Winter 1990), 74.

39. Stephen E. Barton and Carol J. Silverman, "Common Interest Communities: Private Government and the Public Interest Revisited," in Barton and Silverman, eds., *Common Interest Communities: Private Governments and the Public Interest* (Berkeley: Institute of Governmental Studies Press, University of California, 1994), 32.

40. Quoting approvingly Harvard law professor Gerald Frug, cited in Joel Garreau, *Edge City: Life on the New Frontier* (New York: Doubleday, 1991), 201.

41. Arthur M. Okun, *Equality and Efficiency: The Big Tradeoff* (Washington, DC: Brookings Institution, 1975), 119.

42. Cashin, "Localism, Self-Interest, and the Tyranny of the Favored Quarter," 2046.

43. Okun, *Equality and Efficiency,* 120, 119, 118.

44. Paula A. Franzese, "Does It Take a Village? Privatization, Patterns of Restrictiveness and the Demise of Community," *Villanova Law Review* 47, no. 3 (2002), 592.

45. Quoted in Rosen, "The Outer Limits of Community Self-Governance in Residential Associations, Municipalities, and Indian Country," 1055.

19
A Democracy of Property Owners

The value of Americans' homes represents about 30 percent of their total financial wealth.[1] Entering a neighborhood association thus represents an important investment decision as well as the choice of a place to live. In advising on the responsibilities of an association's board of directors, Jan Hickenbottom maintains that the overall "goals of the board should be to preserve, maintain, and enhance the association's property in such a way that each owner's investment is protected. The association must be operated as a business, even though it is, legally, a nonprofit entity. Prudent business management practices should always prevail."[2]

In this aspect, buying into a neighborhood association is like buying the shares of a business corporation. From an investment standpoint, a shareholder and a unit owner have much in common—they both want to achieve a high rate of total return on their investment. A professional in the field of neighborhood association management reports that "association board members and managers are responsible for carrying out business that protects literally millions of dollars of real estate. Daily problems arise that range in magnitude and importance, but all require sound business judgment to resolve."[3]

The world of American business has been less than fully democratic, but over the long run, stockholders have earned around 7 percent per year on their investments in real terms—keeping them happy much of the time. Nevertheless, many commentators suggest that neighborhood associations should be held to the democratic requirement—one person/one vote—that the Supreme Court applies to local public municipalities. Yale political scientist Robert Dahl comments that "we have come to assume that democracy must guarantee virtually every adult citizen the right to vote."[4] A neighborhood association, it is currently argued by critics of existing voting rules, is in reality a form of local government. Its "private" status should not be allowed to shelter it from the normal American democratic requirements.

A neighborhood association, however, is a form of private government, like a business corporation, and thus perhaps should have wider constitutional freedom to conduct its affairs in its own way. Individuals entering neighborhood associations have voluntarily accepted the existing neighborhood form of governance; they have in fact signed on the dotted line to this effect. If private homebuyers want a democracy of individuals, then developers will respond to these market demands and neighborhood associations will have different voting rules. Neighborhood association governments as they exist now thus represent an exercise of consumer choice—and may derive a large degree of social legitimacy from this very fact alone.

Overturning *Avery* Privately

Although such viewpoints are commonly held by advocates for neighborhood associations, and have considerable merit, this chapter will examine a broader argument. Private governments are not the only systems that perhaps should be able to depart from the one person/one vote requirement. As Robert Ellickson has suggested, a case can be made that small municipalities at least should be given a similar constitutional freedom, and whether they exercise the freedom or not would be their decision.[5] In other words, the Supreme Court's 1968 *Avery v. Midland County* decision—applying the one person/one vote requirement to local public governments—may have been a mistake.[6] Even if *Avery* is let stand now with respect to public municipalities, extending the one person/one vote standard to private governments in neighborhood associations might compound the original mistake.

As explained in the Introduction, the distinction between "private" neighborhood associations and "public" municipalities is artificial. Indeed, as I have argued in previous chapters, the small suburban municipality is effectively a private institution in American society. As William Fischel commented recently, like the management of private neighborhood associations, local "city governance is more like that of business corporations than it is like state government." When they go to the polls, municipal voters are primarily concerned with electing people who know how to undertake municipal "activities that enhance property values."[7] Given the large investment in their homes, property owners may be even more concerned with the quality of neighborhood management than they are with the skills of the Wall Street broker overseeing their stock portfolios.* It might thus be argued that the constitutional standards applied to the governance of business corporations could just as well be applied to local governments—public and private alike. In the long run, as examined in chapter 11, local public governments in the United States—at least the types found in most suburban areas—might be reconceived as more appropriately a private-sector institution in which the governance laws and models are drawn from existing business practices.

According to Scott Makar and Michael Buckner, "Local governments are not the local equivalent of the United States Congress or a state" level of government.[8] The option of individual exit, for example, is much easier for a local resident. Municipalities face greater competition from other municipalities for new residents. Jurisdictional competition at the state level, by contrast, requires that a person be willing to move to another state, and at the national level, to move to another nation (assuming a person can even gain entry). Local governments are thus subject to a significant degree of market discipline that does not exist for state and national governments.

The rise of the private neighborhood association therefore might be seen as an opportunity for the Supreme Court to correct past errors. By drawing a legal distinction between "private" neighborhood associations and "public" municipalities, the Supreme Court can allow the governance structures of private neighborhood associations to flourish in all their private diversity. For constitutional purposes, the neighborhood association would then be regarded as the geographic equivalent of a private business corporation. Admittedly, the Supreme Court might be required to perpetuate a somewhat artificial distinction between "public" and "private." However, as one legal commentary notes, there already exists great "confusion, universally acknowledged, in the judicial

---

*Fischel in fact argues that homeowners as investors will be especially risk averse because of the greater difficulty of diversifying their investment in their one residential property, as compared with a portfolio of many stocks. This may go far to explain the behavior of homeowners as voters in municipal elections. As Fischel writes,

> I submit that local governments can be better understood if we examine them with the same economic lens with which business corporations are studied. The crucial difference is that the principal "shareholders" of most municipal corporations, homeowners, cannot diversify their assets like the shareholders of most business corporations do. Having all their assets in one location makes homeowners painfully attentive to the affairs of their municipalities. They are not content to sit back like diversified shareholders of business corporations and let the market take care of corporate affairs. Local politics is thus driven by real-estate economics.

See William A. Fischel, *The Homevoter Hypothesis: How Home Values Influence Local Government Taxation, School Finance, and Land-Use Policies* (Cambridge, MA: Harvard University Press, 2001), 19.

attempts to define what is governmental and what is proprietary."⁹ As seen in previous chapters, moreover, an artificial distinction between public and private would hardly be the first significant legal fiction in the United States regarding local government.

A Constitutional Law Critique

The idea that applying the one person/one vote requirement to local government is a mistake is not new. Indeed, this position was argued soon after the *Avery* decision by one of the most distinguished American authorities on constitutional law, Alexander Bickel of the Yale Law School.* Bickel found the Court actions regrettable on two grounds: (1) the Court should not in principle engage in such broad social policymaking, and (2) the Court's requirement of one person/one vote specifically was a policy mistake, especially when applied to local government institutions.

Bickel argued that a political philosophy of "broadly-conceived egalitarianism," not a legal opinion, drove the U.S. Supreme Court decisions "decreeing equal apportionment on a one-man, one-vote basis." In this and other decisions, the Warren Court sought "the enlargement of the dominion of law and the centralization in national institutions of the law-giving function." Bickel was critical of the "enveloping conception of the law as the sole system of ordering" social arrangements, including the political organization of American government. Indeed, he predicted that "there are other developments . . . which do seriously threaten the very survival of the one-man, one-vote rule. These developments are more evident on the local than on the state level, in school districts, in home-rule cities, and in counties."¹⁰ Bickel probably was not thinking of private neighborhood associations at this point, but their rise over the next 30 years would also uphold his argument.

Bickel found the arguments of the Supreme Court dissenters in *Avery* more persuasive than the majority opinion. In the conduct of local affairs, the impact of government actions on individuals might vary greatly, and it might be reasonable that these different impacts should be reflected in different voting powers. For example, the parents of school children have the greatest stake in the educational systems provided by local government, and might therefore be given a larger role in school board selection.† Indeed, Bickel considered the school

---

*Bickel presented this opinion in his 1969 Oliver Wendell Holmes Lectures to the Harvard Law School.

†In a later illustration of Bickel's concerns, the Chicago School Reform Act provided for the creation of a system of local school councils to oversee grammar and high schools throughout the City of Chicago. Each local school council was to have ten members, six of them selected by vote of the parents,

board cases among those in which "the difficulties created by the one-man, one-vote rule are most acute."[11] Approving of the Supreme Court dissent in *Avery*, Bickel wrote,

> The Court, said Justice Fortas, had failed to take into account "a complex of values and factors, and not merely the arithmetic simplicity of one equals one." It had failed to recognize that the interests of all citizens in an elected body are not necessarily the same, and that governing bodies might have only slight and remote impact on some of their constituents, as for example inhabitants of home rule cities, and a vast and direct impact on others. It had neglected to consider that much effective power is exercised by single executives elected by the entire constituency; that the power of such executives countervails that of malapportioned bodies with whom they are teamed; and that mathematical apportionment may result in representing one interest only, for example that of city dwellers, while entirely depriving other interests of power and even of a voice in their government.[12]

Bickel traced the underlying cause of the Warren Court's failures in this case—and in other leading examples of judicial policymaking—to its "confident reliance on the intuitive judicial capacity to identify the course of progress." The Warren Court was using the force of law to command national policies in an American progressive tradition that reflected an "act of faith." However, as Bickel commented, for Holmes, Brandeis, Frankfurter, and other older "progressive realists, the Constitution was not a catechism, and the judges were not priests reciting it." The 1960s Supreme Court, by contrast, had offered "a recital of selected historical slogans," among them its "one-man, one-vote simplicities." The true progressive ethos, however, was not religious, but was scientific thinking applied to the facts. If the Supreme Court had been more faithful to this progressive ideal, Bickel argued, it would have shown "a more faithful adherence to the method of analytical reason."[13] Instead, it was embracing a less attractive side of progressivism, the moralistic pieties that in the Progressive Era had often become a secular Great Awakening devoted to saving the world through economic progress.

Carried to the fullest extent, the logic of the Supreme Court decisions requiring one person/one vote implied the necessity of a single metropolitan government. Over full metropolitan areas, the very structure of local government was a clear violation of the principle that each vote should be equal to every other vote. By refusing annexation and otherwise asserting local autonomy, many suburban votes counted for much more in the governance of metropolitan affairs than did

---

two selected from the local community, and two from the schoolteachers. However, the Illinois Supreme Court in 1990 struck down this arrangement as giving the parents of school children a greater voting representation than the non-parent residents in the same area of the school—and thus it was constitutionally impermissible under the one person/one vote standard. See Richard Briffault, "Who Rules at Home? One Person/One Vote and Local Governments," *University of Chicago Law Review* 60 (Spring 1993), 372.

the votes of many central-city residents. An alternative might have been a political compromise creating a metropolitan system of government in which suburbanites and other political minorities within the region would have been assigned disproportionate voting power as a protective device—similar to the protections given to small states in the U.S. Senate. However, according to the dictates of the Supreme Court, any such political compromise was unconstitutional; as a result, metropolitan areas throughout the Northeast and Midwest often were carved into hundreds of autonomous political jurisdictions. One person/one vote was flagrantly ignored in the metropolitan political system.

Then, when asked to require metropolitanwide coordination, the Supreme Court soon abandoned the courage of its former progressive faith. In 1973's *San Antonio School District v. Rodriguez,* the Court refused to find a constitutional requirement to equalize school funding among jurisdictions with greatly varying economic resources—potentially, a large step in ending suburban economic segregation.[14] Then, in Detroit in 1974, the Court in *Milliken v. Bradley* refused to order school busing from the central city to the suburbs—which would have been the only practical way to achieve real racial integration on a full metropolitan scale and would have opened the way for many minority parents to send their children to mostly white suburban schools.[15] In the same year, as discussed in previous chapters, the Court enthusiastically endorsed the private use of zoning in its *Belle Terre v. Boraas* decision.[16] Thus, in these two years, the Supreme Court offered a ringing judicial endorsement of the privatization of the American suburbs, judgments very much at odds with the direction of the *Avery* decision only a few years earlier. This trend was another confirmation of Bickel's view that the Supreme Court cannot anticipate the full consequences of its decisions and is unlikely to be successful in imposing its will on a large and complex society.

Indeed, the Supreme Court may too often achieve the opposite of its intentions. Its *Avery* ruling created strong incentives for the political fragmentation of the suburbs, establishing a good method in practice of getting around the one person/one vote principle at a full metropolitan scale, and ending up encouraging further racial segregation in schools. It turned out that true school integration required housing integration, and that process simply exceeded either the Court's willingness or capacity to act. Having already overreached once, as Bickel's line of argument suggested, it might be a mistake to apply the one person/one vote principle in other areas, such as the governance of private neighborhood associations (a subject Bickel did not specifically address himself).

Property Qualifications in Colonial America

The assignment of voting rights in neighborhood associations based on property ownership is not a new development in democratic practice. Indeed, for most of the Colonial Era in America, citizens had to own property in order to vote. This practice reflected a commercial perspective on the role of colonial government. The original American colonies were often created as part of a land grant by the king, or as part of some other commercial enterprise. As one observer describes the origins of suffrage in the United States,

> In the very earliest times, the right to vote in a province or colony was claimed in very much the same way that one would claim a right to vote as a stockholder in a corporation. The early colonies were of the nature of business corporations and the analogy in voting right is not surprising. Hence the landed-property qualification was the one outstanding and universal requirement throughout the colonies, for real property was considered to be a block of stock, as it were, in the corporation and entitled the holder to a vote. . . . The underlying idea was that a man's property entitled him to vote—not his character, his nationality, beliefs, or residence, but his property.[17]

Property qualifications for voting persisted through the War of Independence. Until the American Revolution, Massachusetts residents had to have an income of 40 shillings per year, or other property with a value of at least 40 pounds, in order to vote. In Maryland, voters had to own 50 acres of land or possess personal property with a value of at least 40 pounds.[18] In the 18th century, American cities were commonly managed as a form of private activity, based explicitly on property concepts.[19] City government was often overseen by a board of directors chosen from the commercial sectors. Urban historian Jon Teaford observes that in "the 18th century, each of America's [municipal] corporations granted the right of political participation not only to freemen [involved in commerce] but also to those representatives of landed interests, the freeholders." Reflecting the prevailing commercial mind-set, the city of Albany required "that a man residing in one ward and working in another should vote and stand for office from the ward where he practiced his trade or occupation and not where he lived. Commerce, not residence, defined membership in the commercial community" as it operated in 18th-century municipal jurisdictions.[20]

In that historical period, ideas about the basic nature of government were greatly influenced by the thinking of John Locke. According to Locke, individuals in "a state of nature" have natural rights to property that come into existence when they apply work to create something of value. Locke argued that the institution of government is created to secure the rights to property. In his political philosophy, a government thus represents a social arrangement to defend property rights. It followed logically enough from the Lockean view that a "Civil Society or State is a number of proprietors of land within certain limits, united by a compact or mutual agreement, for making laws and appointing persons to execute these laws for their common benefit."[21]

These views were slow to change, even after the American Revolution. In Virginia, voters as late as 1829 were required to own freehold land—either 25 acres with at least a 12-foot-by-12-foot house, or 50 acres of undeveloped land.[22] State constitutions and city charters were not rewritten in almost all jurisdictions to eliminate property qualifications for voting until the middle of the 19th century, and many factors contributed to this transformation. Primarily, the political ideals of the American Revolution were difficult to square with tight restrictions on the voting franchise. If all Americans were equal, and government was legitimate because it expressed the voice of "the people," then it was difficult to explain why some people should vote and others should not (although, of course, Southern blacks had no right to vote until the second half of the 19th century, and women did not gain this right until the first quarter of the 20th century).

Yet, the belief remained strong that all voters should be genuinely independent in their thinking and voting. If one person was economically subordinate to another, as many argued, the subordinate would inevitably take his voting cues from the superior. Hence, it would be necessary to deny voting rights to those people who lacked their own independence as gained through property ownership. Even well after the American Revolution, as Robert Steinfeld reports, "most Americans . . . continued to believe that only property ownership conferred genuine independence on a man."[23] According to Steinfeld,

> The debate over suffrage . . . was relatively simple. Those who sought to maintain property qualifications appealed to the traditional view that property ownership was necessary for personal independence, and hence a prerequisite for political participation. Those who wished to replace formal property owning qualifications with taxpaying qualifications or manhood suffrage appealed to the proposition "that all men are by nature equally free and independent and have certain inherent rights."[24]

In cities, another factor that contributed to changes in voting laws was the changing understanding of the government's purpose. Leaders in the early 19th century increasingly saw the municipality as an agent for serving the welfare of the local populace. Local governments went well beyond the Lockean burden to protect property; they also delivered services, regulated activities that could cause disease, built roads, created public parks, and otherwise sought to improve the lives of individual residents. As the purpose of local government was no longer seen in strictly commercial and property terms, the qualifications for voting in local elections reasonably shifted from property ownership to simple residency.

Since the middle of the 19th century then, the right to vote in American federal, state, and municipal elections has almost always been assigned to individuals by virtue of their residence in the political jurisdiction. Since all people are equal in their right to pursue their own happiness and well-being, it follows that they should have equal voting rights. Yet, universal suffrage has always been an awkward fit for many local government functions. Public corporations, for example, are created by governments for public purposes, but do not select their leadership democratically. The members of many planning boards, regional councils, and other local public bodies that play important roles in the local political process also are not elected and do not follow a rule of one person/ one vote.

Even though the *Avery* decision prevents local governments of general purpose from adopting voting rules based on property ownership, it has been possible for some "limited-purpose" local governments to follow the business model more closely. A local irrigation district, for example, may nominally be a "public" institution, but many jurisdictions currently limit voting rights to the recipients of irrigation water—and the courts have upheld these arrangements. At other times, however, the courts have demanded strict legal conformance with the one person/one vote requirement, even in the case of districts with narrower purposes. The lack of legal clarity in this area, as Columbia law professor Richard Briffault writes, has left the "jurisprudence of local voting" with a very "uncertain theoretical foundation."[25] The legal issues raised with respect to the voting status of the private neighborhood association merely add to an existing confusion in this area:

> Cities and states have sought to create and expand local organizational forms, such as the public authority, the public benefit corporation, the public-private partnership, or the special-service district, that shift economic development decisionmaking away from popularly elected bodies to entities that are independent of direct popular control and look to the business community as their principal constituency. . . . Many of these local government structures tend to shift decisions regarding economic development outside the realm of one person/one vote.
>
> Local governance and local policymaking are complex mixtures of allocational, redistributive, and economic development activities. The proprietary model both confirms the place of business-oriented concepts in the design and function of local governments and signals that federal constitutional law concerning the right to vote may not be able to provide a basis for challenging the state and local structures intended to strengthen the institutional role of business and limit direct popular control over local government decisions.[26]

The Perils of Majoritarianism

The American constitutional scheme both embraces popular democracy and manifests a fear of its consequences. Among other reasons, the Supreme Court was created to insulate important parts of government from the democratic passions of the moment. This has been a continuing theme in many writings about the American political process. Reflecting his own ambivalence, for example, Tocqueville had feared that the spread of American democracy—combined with a powerful egalitarianism he also saw in American life—might prove in the long run to be its own undoing. Tocqueville warned, "Equality prompts men to indulge propensities very dangerous to freedom, and the legislator should always keep his eye on them." The results were not foreordained, however. For future nations, the specific character of their political institutions would determine "whether equality is to lead to servitude or freedom, knowledge or barbarism, prosperity or wretchedness."[27]

The rise of democratic habits, a strong commitment to equality, and spreading suffrage were all present in the United States by the mid-19th century. There were also dangers in these developments. Tocqueville explained: Nations "where lawmaking falls exclusively to the lot of the poor cannot hope for much economy in public expenditure; expenses will always be considerable, either because taxes cannot touch those who vote for them or because they are assessed in a way to prevent that." Tocqueville cited as inevitable the fact that "universal suffrage really does hand the government of society over to the poor" and others who benefit the most from its actions.[28] In a democracy, it will generally be the case that one or another numerical majority will face a temptation to tax or otherwise coerce a minority to its own advantage. As political theorists have long argued, it may therefore be necessary to have supermajority voting requirements, a division of powers, a constitutional bill of rights, and potentially other institutional protections of minorities—including among these possibilities a voting franchise based in part on ownership of property.

In the second half of the 20th century, the concerns of earlier analysts about the workings of the American democratic processes would be revisited in the writings of the "public choice" school of economics.[29] As James Gwartney and Richard Wagner state, "In an earlier era, constitutional limitations effectively constrained fiscal discrimination—that is, policies which were designed to benefit various subgroups of the population at the expense of their fellow citizens." However, the trends of modern government in the 20th century had worked to undermine the older limits on government. Through formal and informal processes of constitutional revision, "the United States . . . gradually moved from a limited constitutional government with enumerated powers to a government with virtually unconstrained authority to tax, spend and regulate." The result was the widespread use of American government "as an instrument to bestow fiscal favors on some while discriminating against others" in what has become "an unconstrained majoritarian political process."[30]

Considerable public choice literature has focused on the tendency of majoritarian government toward excessive taxing and spending. In 1959, for example, Gordon Tullock analyzed how this result follows from a system of decisionmaking by majority rule.[31] Each legislator, acting rationally to maximize the chance of being reelected, seeks to join voting coalitions providing projects of benefit to his or her district. If the coalition happens to fall short of the simple majority needed, it can always entice a few new members by offering an especially attractive project for their home district.

Since the taxes to pay for the approved projects come from the entire political jurisdiction, but the benefits are realized by only a portion of the whole political body, each favored group always receives an element of subsidy. For example, the additional federal taxes contributed by Wyoming residents are today only a tiny share of additional federal costs for any projects in Wyoming. As Tullock explained, in the normal course of events, legislators consider the tax contributions from those outside the coalition "as a free gift" (any additional federal money spent in Wyoming is, for all practical purposes, free to Wyoming residents). The results of voters simply following their private incentives is many "gold-plated" projects—in Wyoming and elsewhere—involving high costs relative to the beneficiaries' actual willingness to pay for these projects. In the case of a road-building coalition, Tullock explained that "each road would [therefore] be maintained at a level considerably higher and at greater expense than is rational from the standpoint" even of the people living along the road, particularly in terms of their actual marginal benefits relative to the marginal construction costs of a road of higher quality.[32]

Other potential coalitions might compete for swing voters in the legislature in the same way. They can win a simple majority for their own favored projects—and again, the spending and taxing incentives would result in gold-plated projects. The net result under democratic decisionmaking by majority rule is an inexorable upward trend of spending and taxing. In the end, most road construction—and most other governmental activity that benefits particular voters—results from one or another of the many coalitions of this kind, and thus, even though "each individual [voter] behaves rationally, . . . the outcome is irrational"—too much is spent on roads and other pet constituency projects. As Tullock explained, this outcome is not a result of ignorance, moral weaknesses, or any other individual failings on the part of the American voters, but simply illustrates the fact that "the system of [simple] majority voting is not by any means an optimal method of allocating resources."[33]

If one group can form a "tyranny of the majority," so can another group. Coalitions tend to be unstable and floating. The competition for political advantage in a world of simple majority decisionmaking produces a significant element of government waste and misallocation. Only some kind of political "disarmament treaty" that limits such tendencies can prevent a bloated government from providing more services than their actual benefits and costs can justify.* In 1957, the economist Anthony Downs had already argued that it was appropriate to think of a democracy as a political exchange system in which the participants are engaged in "selling policies for votes instead of products for money." In such a political system, "imperfect knowledge makes the governing party susceptible to bribery" in the form of campaign contributions and other payoffs. Moreover, voter ignorance is bound to be a normal state of affairs because "it is irrational" for an individual to commit large amounts of time and effort in order to be well informed for voting.[34] Indeed, many people will regard politics as

---

*State governments, for example, are typically required to maintain a balanced budget.

a burden; political involvement will only be justified in narrow economic terms when it leads to special favors for the participants.

Public choice scholar and Nobel Prize–winning economist James Buchanan concluded that basic constitutional revision is the only solution to the problems of majoritarian democracy.[35] Such a revision might need to include significant changes in legislative voting rules (for example, supermajority voting), constitutional limits on federal spending (relative to taxes), a revival of state sovereignty versus the federal government, and other fundamental changes in the U.S. political structure.[36] If private neighborhood associations want to avoid excessive internal redistribution as well, the writers of their constitutions might want to examine these and other potential barriers. The skill of constitution writers in this regard might even significantly affect a private development project's future profitability because new unit owners will want assurances that their resources will not be confiscated to benefit unduly others in the neighborhood (who may have a majority vote). The assignment of voting rights is likely to be a key neighborhood constitutional protection against undue internal redistribution.

The End of Private Property?

The desirable basis for voting rights in democratic politics has not been prominent in the public choice school's research agenda. However, the methods of public choice analysis—based on the assumption that individuals act to pursue their own interests in politics as well as in the marketplace—can be applied to this issue. In economics, it is often helpful to explore an abstract model based on a few heroic assumptions. In this instance, imagine a world of local governments operating according to some simplified democratic rules: (1) Voting rights in a local government jurisdiction are assigned on the basis of residency and (2) the political jurisdiction has the full freedom to regulate the use of property within its boundaries—without judicial or any other outside constraints.

Let us also assume that renters are in the political majority in a given locality. If they act to maximize their own private interests, they will vote to control tenancy and rent levels. If the renters have a short-run perspective, they will vote to minimize rents absolutely. In concept, they might even exercise their dominance of the local political process to set the rents at zero. However, in the longer run, it will be wiser for them to provide for building maintenance. Hence, rents in the longer run will equal the marginal cost of maintaining the building (leaving out any return on the sunk costs of the initial investment in the building). There may not be any new buildings constructed in the future, or many new entrants into the community, but this need not be a large concern for existing renters.

This outcome in fact is similar to the system of rent control for many older buildings in Manhattan. Such buildings effectively are "owned" by the government of the City of New York—or, more realistically, the buildings have become the "property" of the existing renters for whom the city government serves as a "trustee." The building "owner" is simply a management agent who may (or may not) be allowed a modest return on his or her investment. In practice, the older buildings today sometimes do take on greater value, but only to the extent that landlords have some hope that they can somehow escape rent controls.

Consider now another hypothetical local government that consists entirely of two groups. One group comprises 100 farmers, and each farm occupies an area of 250 acres; the second group comprises 500 recent homeowners on lots of one acre each. As explored in chapter 13, the home owners will be motivated to vote for zoning that gives them full control over the use of the farm land—perhaps to maintain it as open space. As a consequence of such political dynamics, the farmers will effectively no longer own their land. The 500 recent homeowners—acting through the instrument of the local government—will effectively share in the ownership of the land (or at least in the ownership of all the meaningful rights to develop the land).

Many other examples of a similar character could in concept be developed. In each case, the exercise of voting rights would permit a municipal voting majority to command the use of local property for its group benefit. Such a scenario is similar to a private business corporation allocating voting rights equally to each stockholder, independent of the number of shares owned. So if 50 wealthy individuals owned all the shares in a business corporation, then it would take just 51 new share holders, each buying one share of stock, to obtain collective control of corporate decisions. With voting based on individual "residency" as a participating shareholder, the holders of a very small number of total shares could in theory direct the full use of corporate assets for any legally allowable purpose that would benefit them. Of course, no business corporation operates this way, and no one has argued seriously for such an assignment of shareholder voting rights in the corporate world.

These hypothetical scenarios are, admittedly, extreme, and in practice there are constitutional and other limitations on the outright "taking" of private property by local governments in the United States. Nevertheless, the American system of allocating voting rights in local governments according to residency, rather than property, has led to widespread partial confiscations of property. Much of the economic damage caused by zoning exclusions in newly developing suburban areas is best understood, as analyzed previously, as a failure in the assignment of voting rights. Newcomers—the doorslammers—soon gain control of the use of much of the property within the municipality. However, the legal fictions that allow them to assert control over development rights do not as easily allow for the municipal sale of these rights, therefore effectively removing many land rights from the market altogether for considerable periods.

The concern over the potential infringements of majoritarian public governments on property owners is hardly new. As James Ely comments, delegates to the American constitutional convention in 1787 "viewed popular government as a potential threat to property rights." They included in the Constitution a number of provisions, including the takings clause of the Fifth Amendment, which "were designed to rectify the abuses [of property rights] that characterized the evolutionary era" and sought in this manner to restrict "the power of the new national government with respect to property and economic activity."[37] If the Supreme Court and other American courts today have in practice largely written these provisions out of the Constitution, then it may be time to reconsider—at least in the arena of local government at a small scale—this legal thinking.

Diverse Political Models

The public choice perspective on politics is often labeled as "cynical"—that individuals act in the governmental arena only according to their own private interests. Some might argue this modern political analysis falls in the tradition of Machiavelli. Most political theorists, however, have assumed otherwise—implicitly, if not explicitly. In the traditional utilitarian understanding, for example, the government's purpose is to maximize the people's total welfare ("the total utility"). Voting choices are not determined by voters' parochial interests but represent an effort to find the best available political leadership in the interests of the highest total social welfare.

Many Americans would go further and suggest that politics should ultimately serve higher purposes than the maximization of total utility. A political community should have a vision and its members should be willing to make significant sacrifices in the service of its ideals. For example, the original Puritans saw their Massachusetts colony as a "city on a hill" that would provide a beacon for all mankind. In their minds, God had blessed their efforts as a part of His grand design for the world. If a political body is analogous to a church, then members of society are the faithful of the church. Historically, protestant church leaders have often been democratically elected. The leaders of Roman Catholic churches have been selected through the internal processes of church decisionmaking. Yet another example of this decisionmaking approach can be found in the democratic methods of the business corporation. The neighborhood association, therefore, is only the newest addition to the already diverse ranks of American political systems.

Neighborhood Political Choice

In the contemporary world of neighborhood associations, no modern John Locke, Thomas Jefferson, James Madison, J. P. Morgan, or other political visionary has yet emerged to provide an appropriate political philosophy of neighborhoods. Indeed, the argument of this book has been that the institution of the neighborhood association offers a wide flexibility to implement a range of political visions. Some neighborhood associations may be seen as a social contract for the simple purpose of maximizing the neighborhood's total property value. Other associations may seek to maximize the unit owners' welfare, giving a high weight to the neighborhood's environmental quality. Still other neighborhood associations may advance a set of common social values in a small geographic area—the neighborhood association with a religious mission, organized in the manner of a church. Other neighborhoods may blend these and still other missions. Different voting schemes might be chosen according to an association's political vision. The voting arrangements of a political jurisdiction cannot be separated from the political philosophy that guides the jurisdiction's governance. (When voting rights in America have been altered, the change has been considered so fundamental as to require a constitutional amendment.)

A neighborhood association of Mormons, for example, might consult the Mormon Church elders to learn the best means of selecting their neighborhood leadership. A group of American Indians forming a neighborhood association might look to traditional tribal practices. A neighborhood association of Protestant Congregationalists would presumably elect its own leadership democratically, reflecting long-standing congregational practice.

Until now, the great majority of neighborhood associations have assigned voting rights according to how much property each member owns—suggesting, at least, an implicit corporate and business "political philosophy." Unit owners in such a neighborhood association will select a leadership skilled in maximizing property values and maintaining a high-quality neighborhood setting (the two are closely linked). Rather than for a strong commitment to any one set of religious or other social values, such local leaders will be chosen for their administrative knowledge in practical neighborhood affairs and for their political abilities in interpersonal communication and neighborhood diplomacy.

In short, no single neighborhood political model is uniformly required across the American landscape. A wide set of political possibilities, and ample opportunity for experimentation, should extend to the voting rights in neighborhood associations. The range of neighborhood constitutions may some day be as great as the diversity in other areas of investment decisionmaking and consumer choice. Some business corporations rely more heavily on bonds and others on stocks (of varied voting rights) to finance their investments. If the U.S. Supreme Court were to apply the one person/one vote standard to neighborhood associations, it would eliminate much of the opportunity for association political experimentation.

The Case of the U.S. Senate

Discussions about democracy today often assume implicitly that there is an accepted common understanding of proper democratic practice. Robert Dahl, however, states that 25 centuries of democratic debate and practice in the western world "have not, it seems, produced agreement on some of the most fundamental questions about democracy."[38] A good illustration of the diversity of democratic practice is the constitutional status of the U.S. Senate. The American constitutional scheme includes a variety of protections against an unconstrained majoritarianism, including a bicameral national legislature that further divides the powers of the state. Indeed, the Senate is organized politically somewhat like a private neighborhood association. Voting rights in the Senate are assigned to each "unit" (each of the 50 states) without regard to the number of "occupants" (state residents).

In a neighborhood association, one home might have four or five adults and only one unit owner vote, but this is admittedly much less extreme than California, with more than 50 times the population of Wyoming and yet the same number of Senators. As a result of the Senate's distribution of voting rights, it is theoretically possible for the 51 Senators from the 26 least populated states (who represent only 18 percent of the U.S. population) to block a Senate action.

Moreover, for many controversial issues it now takes 60 percent (enough to override a filibuster) to get a bill through the Senate. Instead of 18 percent of the U.S. population, it now requires as few as 11 percent (from the 21 least populated states) to assemble 41 Senate votes. As this new supermajority voting requirement shows, Americans in recent years seem to think that democratic protections for minorities may be even more important than in the past. This shift to a 60-percent voting requirement in the Senate has occurred by informal agreement between the Republican and Democratic party leadership, and without a constitutional amendment. (This further illustrates that informal practices in American politics and administration are often more important than the laws on the books.)

Some might argue that the Senate is an antiquated institution, and its voting rules should be changed, even though this would require a constitutional amendment. Yet, despite some complaints, there has not been much public debate or criticism of the Senate's constitutional status. Americans accept that voting representation by geographic unit, independent of population, makes considerable democratic sense. The lack of criticism also suggests that American democratic attitudes are more nuanced than high school civics (or some Supreme Court rulings) suggest. The Electoral College, another American political institution that violates ordinary democratic principles (witness the 2000 presidential election result), has also withstood challenges to its constitutional status without great difficulty. Perhaps the private neighborhood association, like the private business corporation, the Senate, and the Electoral College, should be viewed in light of a long-standing American understanding that democracy in practice is rather complicated.

Indeed, a valid democracy can take many forms and shapes, and must be tailored to reflect specific political and social concerns and objectives. There is no need for a one-size-fits-all solution to private neighborhood associations in the United States. The private status of the neighborhood association may thus be a fortunate opportunity to engage in wider political experimentation in the methods—including the voting methods—of local governments in the United States.

Economic versus Political Communities

Criticisms of democratic practices in neighborhood associations tend to focus on the denial of full voting privileges to renters and multiple residents of the same unit. However, many people able to vote in private neighborhood associations are denied the right to vote in a public municipality: millions of American immigrants who are not yet U.S. citizens—and some who have no intention of ever becoming citizens—can vote as unit owners but not as municipal residents. The same applies (with less chance of acquiring citizenship) to additional millions of illegal immigrants. For example, a Frenchman who lives in Paris and owns a condominium in Colorado can vote there for his association's board of directors. A foreign diplomat living in the suburbs of Washington, D.C., can vote in a private neighborhood election. Millions of Americans spend half the year at one property and the other half at a different property, but they are almost always required to choose one place of residency and one voting place. As property owners in two neighborhood associations, however, they could have simultaneous votes in a summer neighborhood in Ohio and a winter neighborhood in Florida.

Basing voting rights on one place of official residency, and on U.S. citizenship, requires each person to choose a "political community" where their ultimate loyalty lies. People today, however, are often members of multiple communities in different locations. They sometimes live in different countries and may want to participate in the collective decisions of each country, even when they do not become citizens. Economic relationships, in short, are multiple and worldwide in character, whereas national "citizenship" suggests exclusion and limitations on individual identity. In a commercial concept of voting rights, the same individual can vote in many economic communities all over the world. This approach recognizes that many people today regard themselves as "citizens of the world" as much as they do of one nation. In light of this, they may also want to vote in many small jurisdictions around the world where they have strong connections, as shown in the ownership of property.

Ordinary Neighborhood Associations

While American neighborhood associations should be free to pursue a political philosophy and voting system of their choice, it nevertheless seems likely that many will have similar goals. Unit owners will look to make good financial investments and to have attractive homes and surrounding environments for themselves and their families. Unlike federal and state governments, most unit owners will not see their neighborhood association as an instrument of internal income redistribution or as a means to benefit wider groups with special claims for collective assistance.

Hence, the constitutional designers of most neighborhood associations will probably seek to prevent the formation of internal coalitions that could dominate the democratic process for the benefit of one group. Few unit owners will be attracted to a majoritarian version of neighborhood redistributive politics. Hence, under the marketplace's competitive pressures, these constitution writers are likely to build in strong political barriers to any compulsory, internal redistribution of neighborhood income. As previous chapters have examined, supermajority voting requirements are common for this purpose. Robert Ellickson has suggested that some neighborhood associations may want to include in their private constitutions a prohibition on the uncompensated "taking" of unit owner property—analogous to the takings provision in the U.S. Constitution.[39]

Few if any neighborhoods base their association assessments on unit owners' personal income or wealth. In order to "tax" unit owners' incomes, a change in the neighborhood constitution would be required—much as the U.S. Constitution had to be amended in 1913 to permit an income tax, opening the way for the full development of the American welfare state of the 20th century. If unit owners seek to preclude any such "neighborhood welfare state," they might favor strong constitutional provisions that prohibit any future shift to neighborhood assessments based on income.

Admittedly, the economic segregation that characterizes most neighborhood associations diminishes the risk of compulsory internal redistribution. When people of similar economic means cluster together in a common neighborhood association, there is less incentive for any majority of unit owners to seek a more progressive collection of unit owner assessments, or more egalitarian levels of common service spending. For this reason, the small municipality in the public sector, even though it nominally follows the principle of one person/one vote, may also resist designs for redistributing local wealth and income. Under most zoning laws, it is necessary to own a minimum amount of property to live in a municipality. That is, a "public" municipality may not have a formal property qualification for voting in local elections, but it frequently has a de facto property qualification that is almost as stringent and effective.

As in other respects, the difference between a neighborhood association and a local municipality thus appears to be greater than it is. Whether it is a "private" neighborhood association or a small "public" municipality in the American suburbs, no simple majority of people with incomes below the average will be able to tax the resources of richer people for their benefit. If the goal is redistribution, American political philosophy prefers to accomplish it at the federal and state levels of government.

Paradoxically, it is even possible that the one person/one vote requirement in public municipalities has increased economic segregation in these jurisdictions, as compared with unit owners of private neighborhood associations. In a neighborhood association, the constitution can be written to make internal redistribution by a simple majority very difficult. A rich unit owner is thus protected against the neighborhood taxing his or her private wealth for a "greater public benefit," even if many unit owners with lower incomes might gain from redistribution. The voting rules and other governance arrangements of a public municipality, however, offer weaker protections against internal redistribution. In order to make sure that suburban municipalities do not engage in local redistribution, a stricter segregation of municipal residents by wealth and income is necessary. Indeed, as enforced by zoning, this has resulted across many American suburbs.

For the Purposes of Discussion

Neighborhood associations should have wide flexibility in assigning voting rights. The eligibility for voting will reflect the broader political philosophy on which any given neighborhood association is founded. This basic outlook need not be the same everywhere. In a typical neighborhood association, the model of the private business corporation is likely to reflect most closely unit owners' goals. The right to vote in such a neighborhood association will then be based on the ownership of property.

If the rental value of a housing unit declines, the unit's capital value declines as well. Thus, even unit owners who do not live in the neighborhood have a strong financial incentive to select the most effective neighborhood management to ensure that their property's value is well served by the managers. If a neighborhood wants to encourage a stronger sense of membership in the community among renters, it should be able to give renters the right to vote, as some neighborhood associations have already done.

The best solution therefore may be to maintain the legal status quo. The unit owners in a current neighborhood association entered into that association with an expectation that the constitutional provisions applicable to a "private" status would continue to apply. The homeowners buying into a municipality had their own set of different constitutional expectations based on *Avery* and a "public" status. The two legal systems might simply coexist and evolve on their own courses. Given the different histories that stretch back several decades, there would be large "transaction" and "disequilibrium" costs associated with upsetting the legal order in either area.

Rather than a single outcome based on a court's legal reasoning, the resolution of some basic legal questions concerning neighborhood associations may follow a more Darwinian path. If the law accepts a more evolutionary view, a contest among legal systems could be waged. Such a struggle, between the legal forms of the "private" neighborhood association and the "public" municipality, could then be fought in the future. American homebuyers, not courts, would decide future governmental forms within their own neighborhoods.

I submit that local governments can be better understood if we examine them with the same economic lens with which business corporations are studied. The crucial difference is that the principal "shareholders" of most municipal corporations, homeowners, cannot diversify their assets like the shareholders of most business corporations do. Having all their assets in one location makes homeowners painfully attentive to the affairs of their municipalities. They are not content to sit back like diversified shareholders of business corporations and let the market take care of corporate affairs. Local politics is thus driven by real-estate economics.

NOTES

1. Special Supplement on "A Survey of Property," *The Economist*, May 31, 2003.

2. Jan Hickenbottom, *Questions & Answers About Community Associations: A Collection of "Condo Q & A" Columns, as published in the Los Angeles Times*, 2nd ed. (Irvine, CA: Miller Publishing Co., 2002), 27.

3. Mary Avgerinos, *Alternative Dispute Resolution and Consensus Building for Community Associations* (Alexandria, VA: Community Associations Institute, 1997), 27.

4. Robert A. Dahl, *On Democracy* (New Haven, CT: Yale University Press, 1998), 3.

5. Robert C. Ellickson, "Cities and Homeowners Associations," *University of Pennsylvania Law Review* 130 (June 1982).

6. *Avery v. Midland County,* 390 U.S. 474 (1968).

7. William A. Fischel, *The Homevoter Hypothesis: How Home Values Influence Local Government Taxation, School Finance, and Land-Use Policies* (Cambridge, MA: Harvard University Press, 2001), 23, 187. For a discussion of Fischel's book, see also Lee Anne Fennell, "Homes Rule," *Yale Law Journal* 112 (December 2002).

8. Scott D. Makar and Michael L. Buckner, "Son of Synder: Municipal Annexations and Quasi-Judicial Proceedings," *Florida Coastal Law Journal* 1 (Spring/Summer 1999), 155–56.

9. Daniel R. Mandelker, Dawn Clark Netsch, Peter W. Salsich Jr., and Judith Welch Wegner, *State and Local Government in a Federal System,* 3rd ed. (Charlottesville, VA: Michie, 1989), 455.

10. Alexander M. Bickel, *The Supreme Court and the Idea of Progress* (1970; New Haven, CT: Yale University Press, 1978), 103, 107, 165–66.

11. Ibid., 169.

12. Ibid., 167–68.

13. Ibid., 173–74, 19, 174, 173.

14. *San Antonio Independent School District v. Rodriguez,* 411 U.S. 1 (1973).

15. *Milliken v. Bradley,* 418 U.S. 717 (1974).

16. *Village of Belle Terre v. Boraas,* 416 U.S. 1 (1974).

17. Kirk Harold Porter, *A History of Suffrage in the United States* (Chicago: University of Chicago Press, 1918), 2–3.

18. Ibid., 9–10.

19. Ernest S. Griffith, *History of American City Government: The Colonial Period* (New York: Oxford University Press, 1938).

20. Jon C. Teaford, *The Municipal Revolution in America: Origins of Modern Urban Government, 1650–1825* (Chicago: University of Chicago Press, 1975), 30.

21. C. Williamson, *American Suffrage: From Property to Democracy,* quoted in Robert J. Steinfeld, "Property and Suffrage in the Early American Republic," *Stanford Law Review* 41 (January 1989), 341–42.

22. Steinfeld, "Property and Suffrage in the Early American Republic," 355.

23. Ibid., 352.

24. Ibid., 352–53.

25. Richard Briffault, "Who Rules At Home? One Person/One Vote and Local Governments," *University of Chicago Law Review* 60 (Spring 1993), 397.

26. Ibid., 384.

27. Alexis de Tocqueville, *Democracy in America,* J. P. Mayer, ed. (Garden City, NY: Doubleday, 1969), 698, 705.

28. Ibid., 210.

29. See Dennis C. Mueller, ed., *Perspectives on Public Choice: A Handbook* (New York: Cambridge University Press, 1997); and James M. Buchanan, *The Demand and Supply of Public Goods: Volume 5 of the Collective Works of James M. Buchanan* (Indianapolis, IN: Liberty Fund, 1999).

30. James D. Gwartney and Richard E. Wagner, "Public Choice and the Conduct of Representative Government," in James D. Gwartney and Richard E. Wagner, eds., *Public Choice and Constitutional Economics* (Greenwich, CT: JAI Press, 1988), 17.

31. Gordon Tullock, "Problems of Majority Voting," *Journal of Political Economy* 67 (December 1959). See also Gordon Tullock, *The Vote Motive* (London: Institute of Economic Affairs, 1976).

32. Tullock, "Problems of Majority Voting," 575.

33. Ibid., 575, 579.

34. Anthony Downs, "An Economic Theory of Political Action in a Democracy," *Journal of Political Economy* 65 (April 1957), 137, 141, 147.

35. James M. Buchanan, "The Constitution of Economic Policy," *American Economic Review* 77 (June 1987). See also James M. Buchanan, *The Limits of Liberty: Between Anarchy and Leviathan* (Chicago: University of Chicago Press, 1975).

36. See James M. Buchanan, *The Logical Foundations of Constitutional Liberty: Volume 1 of the Collected Works of James M. Buchanan* (Indianapolis, IN: Liberty Fund, 1999); and James M. Buchanan, *Choice, Contract, and Constitutions: Volume 16 of the Collected Works of James M. Buchanan* (Indianapolis, IN: Liberty Fund, 2001).

37. James W. Ely Jr., *The Guardian of Every Other Right: A Constitutional History of Property Rights,* 2nd ed. (New York: Oxford University Press, 1998), 42, 43.

38. Dahl, *On Democracy,* 3.

39. Ellickson, "Cities and Homeowners Associations," 1580.

Neighborhood Secession

The great northeastern snowfall of February 2003 dumped 24 inches in my yard in Chevy Chase, Maryland. After the snow finally stopped falling, the streets were impassable and an out-of-town guest could not leave for two days. At one point, he asked if I could call my local government to see about plowing the streets. As I explained, my local government represents a Montgomery County population of about 900,000. Individual phone calls do not get much personal attention.

Several days of waiting anxiously for the snow to be plowed prompted new discussions in my neighborhood. The State of Maryland and Montgomery County rebate taxes and provide other funds to local municipalities within their jurisdictions. Part of this money is available for the municipal provision of certain public service functions—including snow removal—that would substitute for the state or county provision. My neighbors are now holding public meetings and wondering whether they should formally incorporate as a community of about 2,000 residents, which would result in a new Maryland municipality of "Rollingwood." We could then hire our own private contractor for snow removal and provide our own neighborhood services such as garbage collection, street cleaning, or extra police patrols (Montgomery County would still have the principal policing responsibility). Several nearby neighborhoods in Chevy Chase have already done this and report wide citizen satisfaction with the results.

In order to incorporate under state law, 25 percent of the neighborhood residents would have to present a petition to Montgomery County. The county government—by action of the county leadership (there would be no vote of county residents)—would then have to agree to the proposed municipal incorporation.

If the county agreed, a vote would subsequently be held in my neighborhood area, requiring a simple majority of 51 percent of those voting to create a new municipality.

My neighborhood's schools are funded and run by the county, and there is little interest in changing that arrangement; the local public schools are now some of the best in the nation, partly because of intense parental involvement. However, in 2003, the Maryland legislature enacted a bill to promote charter schools. The movement for charter schools has progressed in many states but has been held back in Maryland by the education establishment. Nevertheless, Governor Robert Ehrlich is more enthusiastic. If the quality of county schools were to decline, my neighborhood might try to establish its own charter school, and a board of directors could be formed within the neighborhood.[1] Montgomery County would rebate an amount to the neighborhood school corresponding roughly to the average of per pupil spending in the county. If this were to happen, the Rollingwood neighborhood would not only be removing its own snow but also providing its own education.

These steps might be described as a partial secession of my neighborhood from Montgomery County. If the steps were carried far enough—if the neighborhood provided almost all local services, received rebates on most county taxes, and collected additional tax revenues—the result would come close to an act of full local secession. Legally, my neighborhood would remain part of Montgomery County but for practical purposes it would be an autonomous local political jurisdiction.

As an older area of the county, municipal incorporation would be the only way at present to obtain such neighborhood self-government. However, if the State of Maryland adopted chapter 12's proposal to allow for the creation of new "neighborhood associations in established neighborhoods" (NASSENs), my neighbors and I would also have the option of forming a new private neighborhood association. In more rural parts of the county, almost all new development projects of any size already involve creating a neighborhood association. The scarcity of incorporated municipalities in these parts of the county reflects a shift of governing responsibility in matters of immediate neighborhood concern from the public to the private sector. The evidence in Montgomery County suggests that, where a small municipality and a private neighborhood association are alternative governmental forms, many people now prefer the private regime.

Neighborhood associations' ability to secede from local government is controversial, and a wider authority would be even more contentious. Since the Civil War, talk of "secession" has evoked negative images in American life. Some people suggest that neighborhood secessionary motives would divide the metropolitan and state "union" unduly. Rather than encourage a wider diversity of autonomous local communities, perhaps a more powerful set of common bonds is required to solve regional land use and other problems. It may be important to encourage Americans to join in collective action rather than to divide the citizenry into additional competing jurisdictions. In short, the ability of neighborhoods to withdraw from existing local governments—to secede—is a key question in addressing the future of neighborhood associations in America.

Exit or Voice

Seceding falls within the category of "exit," as Harvard economist Albert Hirschman describes in 1970 in *Exit, Voice, and Loyalty.*[2] Hirschman notes that a person unhappy with his or her current circumstance faces two basic options. One possibility is to work to improve things under existing arrangements—the "voice" option. The other is to leave in search of a better alternative— the "exit" option. Hirschman offered an analysis of the benefits and costs of each. This thinking can be applied to neighborhoods in which service delivery and other local government actions fail to meet residents' needs and expectations.

As Hirschman explained, a first response might be to complain about the local government's performance. If changes then produce satisfactory performance, the residents will have resolved their problem through "voice." However, governments often do not hear the complaints of their citizens or are simply unable to respond for one reason or another. Nevertheless, the "exit" option likely involves considerable costs, especially when it might mean selling a home and moving to another location. When confronted with the high costs of moving, most homeowners are likely to first raise the volume of their complaints. They may also hope that the passage of time will solve the problem—a new set of local officials, for example, may be elected. As Hirschman explained,

> The decision not to exit in the face of a clearly better buy (or organization) could also be taken by customers (or members) who expect the complaints and protests of others, combined with their own faithfulness, to be successful. Others may not care to switch . . . when they feel that they would soon want to switch back, because of the costs that may be involved. Finally there are those who stay . . . out of "loyalty," that is, in a less rational, though far from wholly irrational, fashion. Many of these "loyalists" will actively participate in actions designed to change . . . policies and practices, but some may simply refuse to exit, . . . confident that things will soon get better.[3]

The individual calculations in deciding whether or not to stay put can be complex. In the market for an ordinary good or service, exit is easy and likely occurs after one or two unsatisfactory purchasing experiences. The consumer can easily switch to another company's product. In the case of a local government, however, there is a "public good" aspect to exit. For example, assume that all the current residents agree on the inadequacy of local performance. If complaints do not improve things, it may be necessary to send a stronger "signal" by someone actually leaving. However, it may not be necessary for everyone, or even a majority, to leave. In that case, the exiters will bear the costs of moving but the residents who remain will receive significant benefits in improved service provision at little cost to themselves—they will be free riders. That is to say, the supply of exiters may be considerably less than socially optimal unless some mechanism can be devised to reduce the price of exit or by which those who remain can compensate the exiters.

Cultural attitudes might also influence the number of exiters. As Hirschman notes, the United States in its national value system has long favored exit. The American nation was created by "exiting" from England; our founding father, George Washington, led the great "secession" of American history. Americans traditionally have more faith in the free market—an exit system—than in "politics." Indeed, the American nation is a product of "millions of decisions favoring exit over voice"—the countless migrants who left their countries of birth to come to the United States.[4] The American territories to the West also received many people who were exiting unhappy circumstances in the East. As Joseph Viteritti explains, the concept of secession from an unacceptable governing regime is founded on "the political concept of popular sovereignty. To assert that self-determination has a place in American political thought is an understatement. It is the very principle upon which the republic was founded"—literally as American as apple pie.[5]

However, the high regard in the United States for exit may be an anomaly in the history of the world. In many times and places, as Hirschman notes, exit has been "branded as criminal, for it has been labeled desertion, defection and treason." For centuries, those who sought exit from the Roman Catholic Church were branded as heretics and sometimes burned at the stake. Even in the United States, Hirschman expressed a "puzzlement" that a nation founded on exit could nevertheless in "a few key situations" take a much different view and exit could be "wholly proscribed."[6] While George Washington was a great secessionist, another one of America's revered presidents, Abraham Lincoln, died to save the Union.

New Exit Options

However, Hirschman thought that an easier option of exit might help the workings of American society in key areas. Indeed, he advocated a systematic review of situations where "an organization arouses but ignores voice while it would be responsive to exit." American society should seek ways to make exercising voice more effective but should also recognize that sometimes it's important to consider "appropriately redesigned institutions" that have the consequence of "making exit more easy and attractive."[7]

Government is an institution that often seems insensitive to citizen voice. Yet, exit from a government can be difficult. The prospect that voters will turn to other candidates motivates politicians to respond to public pressures. However, government agencies often face little or no threat of exit, and many are notoriously resistant to change. The Brookings Institution economist Anthony Downs comments that government "bureaucracies are basically monopolies, so their members—like all monopolists—come to focus on maintaining their own powers at the expense of the welfare of their clients." In large American cities, "the behavior of these bureaucracies tends to reinforce the dependence of their clients rather than liberate their clients' capabilities."[8]

Hence, it may be desirable to review systematically the institutional mechanisms that can provide an exit from local government. One obvious concern is to avoid any exclusive assignment of governing responsibility, as far as this is technically possible (it may be precluded in some cases by economies of scale or other physical supply considerations). The exit option will be promoted by a decentralized system that gives people a wide range of choice among alternative governmental jurisdictions. Other things equal, citizens will prefer more and smaller local governments to fewer and larger governments. This is an ancient and honorable principle of political philosophy; it is found, for example, in the principle of "subsidiarity" of the Roman Catholic Church.

Another important consideration is the cost of exit for a person who is already the citizen of a government. One way to exit local government is to buy a home in another location. However, this is not the only possible form of exit. If a large majority of the people living in a particular geographic area agree on the desirability of exit, it may not be necessary for them to move physically. Rather, it would be much less costly simply to withdraw as a group from their existing local government to form a new one. That is, the area could secede from the local government, a manner of exit likely to have lower transaction costs per person than physically removing one individual at a time.

The Nobel economist James Buchanan suggests that there may be inadequate "moral-ethical cement" in larger jurisdictions to prevent widespread "rent seeking" and other efforts to "seek private profit" by manipulating the actions of governments. The best hope might then be a constitutional revolution that involved "dramatic devolution" of governing authority. This might be accomplished by providing an option of secession, a useful means of pressuring larger governments even when the option is not actually exercised.[9] For this and other reasons, the new constitution recently proposed for the European Union includes an explicit guarantee of the right of each member state of the Union to secede.

Hence, following Hirschman's and Buchanan's recommendation, political theorists might explore new institutions and laws to facilitate local secession from local governments.[10] If no major problems or obstacles are found, a new legal option of local "free secession" might be provided in the law.[11] Viteritti suggests that "community self-determination at the local level" should be permitted, "so long as it does not jeopardize the larger public good, and the legitimate interests of concerned minorities are protected." Applying this standard to the movement within Staten Island in the late 1980s to secede from New York City, he concludes that the City and the State of New York had no legitimate grounds for preventing Staten Islanders from making their own choice in the matter.[12] As happened in the case of Staten Island, once the option to secede is available, the actual secession may not always be necessary. A realistic threat of secession may be a particularly powerful form of "voice" to alter the behavior of higher levels of government.[13]

Neighborhood Incorporation

At present, a neighborhood could secede from a local government through incorporating as a new municipality. The feasibility of this step, however, varies from state to state and according to the jurisdiction's legal status. Incorporating is easiest if the neighborhood is located in an unincorporated area. Although municipal and county governments often look similar, they are formed under very different legal regimes. Most states have had counties since their creation. In the United States, the county represents the default option in local government— absent any other option, the county government will assume the responsibility for delivering services and performing governance functions.

A municipal government, unlike a county, requires a formal act of municipal incorporation. Although the legal requirements for incorporation vary considerably, they often share the following themes. Citizens present a petition for incorporation to an appropriate government authority. If the petitioning area and group meet the state requirements, a referendum is held. A simple majority vote of the proposed municipality is generally required to approve the incorporation. However, county governments today frequently have a veto power. Some counties make this decision administratively, while others hold a referendum vote across the whole county. This referendum is generally decided by a simple majority of county voters—excluding the residents within the proposed new municipal boundaries.*

If an area has already been incorporated as a municipality, it is generally more difficult to satisfy the requirements for newly incorporating a subarea within the current borders. In some states, this requires two steps—the legal "detachment"

---

*There are three relevant local areas when considering a possible municipal incorporation and a referendum: the area of the proposed municipality, the area of the county minus the proposed municipality, and the combination of the two representing the entire county. Different state laws may require affirmative votes by citizens living in one or more of these three areas.

of the seceding area from the municipality, followed by a new act of incorporation. In California, the state legislature in 1977 effectively prevented almost any detachments by giving the city council the power to block proposed separations. Although this provision was removed in 1998, affirmative votes are needed from the proposing area as well as from the existing municipal residents as a whole.[14] Few if any detachments have been able to meet these requirements. Nationwide, given the legal hurdles created by states, the number of new municipalities that succeed in creating a new municipal jurisdiction within the boundaries of an existing municipality has been small.

There have been a few high-profile efforts—ultimately unsuccessful—to secede in recent years. In California, the state legislature created "local area formation commissions" for each county to review proposals for secession (and other important changes in local government structure). A group of residents from the San Fernando Valley within the City of Los Angeles met the requirements for a secession vote. In November 2002, the Valley residents voted narrowly in favor of secession, but the proposal was defeated when a large majority of voters elsewhere in Los Angeles opposed it.

While few neighborhoods historically have successfully seceded from cities, the laws of incorporation have permitted smaller communities to remain independent of central cities. In the 19th century, the general assumption was that the central city—itself usually an incorporated government—would annex the growing suburban communities. However, Brookline in the metropolitan Boston area in 1874 successfully fought off a proposal for annexation, described by urban historian Kenneth Jackson as "the first really significant defeat for the consolidation movement." As the trend spread, many suburban areas chose to incorporate as a means of heading off annexation. By the end of the 20th century, annexations were the exception; the general view was that "centralization and size are no longer seen as desirable objectives" in the metropolitan organization of local government.[15]

Private Secession

Creating a private neighborhood association is an act of local secession by an altogether different legal route.[16] In an undeveloped area where a new project is being built, this "private secession" is easier than a municipal incorporation. The developer needs merely to assemble the land, obtain regulatory approval, build the project, and file a declaration for the neighborhood association with the county government.

Admittedly, creating a new neighborhood association is not precisely equivalent to seceding. The neighborhood association still relies on the local public government to provide some services and it pays local property taxes. However, in the future, more complete forms of private secession may become possible. For example, if neighborhood associations become more numerous, the political pressures for substantial rebates from property taxes—for relief from the current system of "double taxation"—are bound to grow.

Indeed, in some existing neighborhood associations, the analogy to secession is even more appropriate. A gated community may control even temporary entry into the neighborhood area.[17] Although the geographic scale is small, one might say that in this respect at least such a private neighborhood resembles a tiny nation state with a "visa" requirement. A property owner—individual or collective—has wide discretion to exclude or to admit others from the use of the property and to control the precise manner of use. Indeed, within his or her domain, the historical prerogatives of a private owner might be said to resemble those of a "sovereign" authority.

Pro-Choice in Neighborhoods

In 1991, Allen Buchanan broke a long-standing unofficial sanction against serious discussion of secession among American political philosophers with the publication of *Secession: The Morality of Political Divorce from Fort Sumter to Lithuania and Quebec*.[18] In the United States, it was perhaps the first systematic treatment of the political legitimacy of secession since the efforts of John C. Calhoun and other Southern writers before the Civil War.* One factor making this possible was the end to official segregation in the 1960s, finally bringing the South into a more normal political relationship with the rest of the United States.

In more and more areas of American life, as traditional norms are increasingly challenged, the use of government coercion to enforce a uniform set of social norms has become less acceptable. What, then, can justify the use of coercion to compel one political jurisdiction to remain "married" to another jurisdiction? As Buchanan stated, "if we view political association, like marriage, not as an unalterable natural fact but as a human creation designed to satisfy the needs of those who live within it, there is no reason to assume that injustice provides the only justification for dissolution" of a political union as well. If America's divorce laws were made more liberal from the 1960s onwards by the adoption of no-fault standards, why not adopt no-fault laws for local government secession as well? At a minimum, rather than dismissing secession out of hand, Buchanan considered that "the absence of systematic thinking about secession is a serious defect in political philosophy."[19]

---

*The issue was of greater urgency in Canada, given the long-standing secessionist demands in Quebec. For example, Jane Jacobs addressed the option of secession, on the whole favorably, in *The Question of Separatism: Quebec and the Struggle over Sovereignty* (New York: Random House, 1980).

Indeed, people who took the principles of liberty seriously presumably had to be in favor in principle of secession.[20] Buchanan argued for the collective exercise of the freedom to "exit" from an unsatisfactory political jurisdiction:

> All arguments against recognizing a right to secede contend that secession threatens certain interests. But these arguments are incomplete and unpersuasive if they merely assume, without support, that these interests are of such moral stature that their protection justifies even the use of force to suppress secession. This assumption must be supported by argument, and in some instances the arguments turn out to be quite complex. . . . The general presumption in favor of liberty implies a presumption in favor of recognizing a right to secede in this sense: The burden of argument is on the opponents of secession to show that secession would cause not only harm, in some sense or other, but harm . . . of the moral seriousness required to justify the use of coercion to block secession.[21]

The rise of the private neighborhood association can be seen in this light. Though seldom described in these terms, it amounts to a powerful new movement of local secession in American life. As a form of private secession from an existing local government, it is consistent with the spread of pro-choice attitudes in marriage, abortion, and many other areas of American life.[22] In developing areas, a neighborhood association's exact boundaries are largely left to private choice. The internal covenants create new private options for the regulation of aesthetic, architectural details that traditionally have been outside the purview of local governments. And the basic form of a neighborhood association's governance is also open to wide constitutional alternatives because of its private status.

According to Buchanan, the burden should be put on those who would deny the option of secession—in this case a "private secession" by means of creating a neighborhood association.[23] If they seek to block neighborhood secession through government coercion, a compelling counterargument in terms of economic efficiency, social justice, or other core American principles and values must be made.[24] The need for a compelling objection, as part IV of this book argues, applies even in cases of older established neighborhoods where property owners may seek to create a new NASSEN.

Although the issue of private neighborhood secession is new to American public debate, a few writers have addressed the issue. The economist Fred Foldvary contends that, much as a consumer in the market can exercise choice among goods and services, in an ideal world "any person or organization having a title to land [could] withdraw the site from any government jurisdiction and create its own governance." Similar to Hirschman, Foldvary argues that such a regime of "legalized geographic exit" would make it possible for people collectively to "withdraw from a dysfunctional process as an alternative to [attempting] an infeasible reform of the system." Following Foldvary's reasoning, neighborhoods electing to withdraw could do so. Under a right of free local secession, as he proposes, they would not be required to provide "any substantive grounds to justify the secession" from an existing municipality or other local jurisdiction.[25]

Many neighborhood associations in the future may want to protect the surrounding immediate cultural and physical environment. In a fundamentalist Muslim neighborhood, all women might be required to wear a cover to protect their face from the view of strangers. Teenage girls could be required to wear a specific type of dress in a neighborhood Muslim school. Outside the neighborhood, no such requirement would exist in the interactions with the rest of American society. Many Arab women today live such a dual existence—dressing one way in Saudi Arabia or other home countries and another way on a visit to Europe.

Some may protest that such a dual existence inside and outside a neighborhood association's boundaries might induce cultural schizophrenia. As Mark Rosen notes, "scholarly opinion seems to be converging on the view that limiting [local] community self-governance is a good thing." It reflects a prevailing "deep skepticism about granting communities significant autonomy" in the United States.[26] Many people always seem to fear that forces of localism, parochialism, bias, ignorance, and prejudice may be lurking just below the surface of American life.

Nevertheless, as Rosen argues, for groups with strong commitments to their own value systems, denying the full right of self-governance undermines the "foundational liberal aspirations" of tolerance that have been a central element of "political liberalism" in the United States.[27] Most Arabs in America probably would not want to live in an Islamic fundamentalist neighborhood. The issue is not, however, whether such a neighborhood would appeal to a majority of Muslims. Rather, the question is whether such a neighborhood will legally be allowed to exist—including whether it may be formed by secession from local government.

Schools in Neighborhood Associations

Americans tend to think of education as learning how to read, how to write, and other practical skills. It is these things but much more. The school system is, next to the family, the most important means of instilling basic values in children. To teach American history is to communicate the meaning of the American national experience. When the United States occupied Japan, it quickly rewrote the history books (the Emperor was no longer a living god)—an act as important as writing the new Japanese constitution.

Freedom of association is therefore nowhere more important than in education. A neighborhood association that seeks to assert the values of a strong community may well want to operate its own schools. Indeed, the "exit option" is especially vital in education. Many well-off suburbanites have been exercising this option for some time. By clustering together in small homogeneous municipalities, they achieve the schooling benefits of a high-quality, private education system. If they do not like the existing local schools, they need only move a few miles away to another small municipality.*

It is much different, however, in the big cities of the United States, where there is no exit option for many parents who send their children to public schools. They cannot afford to move to the suburbs, and a monopoly public school system serves the entire city. Until recently, this school system required parents to send their child to one school that administrators determined with little or no parental consultation. It is not a coincidence that some big-city school systems have been among the poorest education providers in the United States.†

If neighborhood associations begin to provide schooling, educational considerations may well determine these associations' geographic size. An elementary school will probably have at least 20 students in each classroom from kindergarten through the sixth (or eighth) grade. At minimum, that would be a neighborhood school of about 150 children. If the neighborhood occupants are

---

*Citing work by Harvard economist Carolyn Hoxby and others, Howard Husock argues for greater decentralization of the provision of education in the United States. Large education systems, he finds, perform poorly in comparison to systems with greater independence from any central controlling authority:

> Between 1952 and 1992, even though consolidation bypassed America's municipalities, it did descend upon the nation's school districts, reducing their number by over 75 percent (from 67,355 to 14,422). At the same time, costs skyrocketed and quality plummeted—not coincidentally. Nor is it a coincidence that teachers' unions swelled in power: larger jurisdictions put average citizens at a disadvantage, since even the most zealous unpaid neighborhood activist is little match for the full-time paid staffs of public sector unions.
>
> In the same ways as government jurisdictions get larger, control gradually melts away from voters; realizing the difficulty of influencing officials, and increasingly impotent against the organized electoral power of public employees, individuals give up. . . . Voter participation is much lower in the San Fernando Valley areas that are part of Los Angeles than in those that are independent municipalities. See Howard Husock, "Let's Break Up the Big Cities," *City Journal* 8 (Winter 1998). Available at http://www.city-journal.org/html/8_1_a2.html.

†As Anthony Downs reports, "In general, big-city public school systems provide much lower quality education than suburban public school systems." Downs attributes this partly to concentrations of low-income students in big-city schools, and excessive regulation by the education bureaucracies in these cities. He finds that "most big-city schools are monopolistic bureaucracies dominated by a combination of teachers' unions and school administrators" who serve their own interests more than the students. In the future, it will be necessary, as Downs thinks, to "encourage competition as the most effective way to elicit maximum performance and maximum attention to the needs and desires of clients and customers" of big-city schools—including options for "charter schools, vouchers, competition with private schools, or other means." See Anthony Downs, "The Challenge of Our Declining Big Cities," *Housing Policy Debate* 8, no. 2 (1997), 391–92.

demographically representative of the United States, the total neighborhood population would have to be about 500 people in order to have enough children for an elementary school. This would require a neighborhood association of at least 150 housing units.

If a neighborhood association wanted its own high school, a considerably larger number of children would be needed. For example, assume the high school should be large enough to support physics and chemistry labs, a Spanish teacher, an advanced placement math teacher, and perhaps a football team. About 1,000 students might be the minimum size. This would require the neighborhood association to have a population in the range of 5,000 to 7,000 persons— corresponding to around 2,000 to 3,000 housing units. Many municipalities in the suburbs of New York, Boston, Philadelphia, and other Northeast and Midwest cities have about this number of homes. If America's suburbs have for most practical purposes been privatized, the size of the "private" municipality in the suburbs is often about equal to the minimum population needed to have its own high school.

The provision of elementary and secondary schools could be a major selling point for developers of future neighborhood associations. The profit motive of land developers—who might exhibit more education management skill than the average city school board—could be enlisted to improve the quality of American education. Neighborhood associations might relieve political jurisdictions of the fiscal burdens of building new schools. School construction costs would be reflected in the prices paid by the purchasers of new neighborhood homes.

Although developers might find it profitable to pay for especially attractive schools in new neighborhood associations (just as they now build Jack Nicklaus golf courses), financing their subsequent operation and maintenance would remain an issue. As political leaders increasingly hear complaints about double taxation, in the future, neighborhood associations may well receive rebates for education and other public services that they provide. The developer of a neighborhood association would pay for school construction and then look to the local government to finance operating and maintenance costs.

If school operating payments went directly to the neighborhood association, one might describe this as a system of "neighborhood association vouchers." Under the terms of such funding, the neighborhood might provide instruction in any religion or in any other basic system of values (within at least some broad limits) within the neighborhood. Twenty years ago, the idea of government vouchers for private neighborhood schools would have seemed radical. However, the "school choice" movement, the recent establishment in many states and cities of policies to encourage charter schools, and the increasing acceptance of public education vouchers for use at private schools may have opened the way for neighborhood associations to receive public funds for providing schooling.

Common Service Vouchers

A voucher system might be extended beyond education to other services such as garbage collection. Like an education voucher, a garbage collection voucher might be set to equal the current cost per household the municipality incurs for garbage collection. Moreover, neighborhood residents might be able to keep any "surplus." If they were able to provide garbage collection for considerably less than the current municipal cost, they could retain the extra funds for expenditure in another area—or even turn the money savings back to the unit owners. As law professor Eric Posner comments, private groups with strong shared values may do a better job supplying "collective goods that people otherwise demand from the state. Through policies of collective support, the state can effect increases in the supply of these goods more cheaply than it could supply them itself through direct or category-based regulation."[28]

There might thus be "street cleaning vouchers," "security patrol vouchers," "snow removal vouchers," "traffic management vouchers," and so forth. The neighborhood association in this way might take over many current responsibilities of the municipality or other local government. If economies of scale dictated operation on a larger scale than a single neighborhood association, the association might contract out to a private company that operates on a larger scale and serves many neighborhoods. It might also contract out to another neighborhood or local government that specializes in a particular service function.[29]

If local governments refuse to provide public money for neighborhood associations' operating expenses, there are other routes to the same end. The developers of neighborhood associations could cluster together in select municipalities. These municipalities would be distinguished by their minimal public services. Instead of public vouchers going to private neighborhood associations, the unit owners of neighborhood associations would pay for their own schools and other services with the savings realized in reduced property taxes in these jurisdictions.

Thus, to the extent that state law allows, such "public" municipalities might have few public services. Neighborhood associations would follow in the path of businesses that have gathered similarly in "public" municipalities that have few residents and thus little or no tax burden. Perhaps the most famous of these municipalities is the City of Industry in southern California (there is also a similar City of Commerce). The City of Industry was incorporated as a municipality and contains a large industrial park served by the Southern Pacific Railroad, but has never had more than 600 residents. To achieve even this number, the founders of the City of Industry had to set the boundaries to include a mental hospital whose residents "counted" for legal purposes of incorporation.

On visiting Industry, William Fischel describes the overall impression as one of "miles of large warehouse-style buildings and almost no houses."[30] Needless to

say, there is little need to collect any property taxes for schools or most other traditional local services. If local public governments do not find ways to coexist
amicably with neighborhood associations in the future, corresponding Cities of
Neighborhood Associations may be created across the United States. In such
places, services would mostly be delivered by private action, and municipal taxes
would be correspondingly low.

For the Purposes of Discussion

The principle of voluntary consent has increasingly become a central organizing
feature of American society. If the availability of no-fault divorce has contributed
to rising divorce rates, few people would advocate a return to the days when
divorces were difficult to obtain and required at least one guilty party. When it
comes to a larger "private family" of people living together in a neighborhood,
however, American governments still mostly deny the freedom to exit from the
local public government.

There is no good reason that the basic principle of voluntary consent should
not be extended to neighborhood exit. If a large enough supermajority of unit
owners in an established neighborhood wish to form their own neighborhood
association—and to assume the microfunctions of common service delivery
within their neighborhood—they should have the right to do so. Like free
speech and assembly, there should be a recognized "right of free private neighborhood secession." The secession would not be total in that some service
functions with significant economies of scale, such as water and sewer, would
require provision on a regional basis and would require wider local government action.

In newly created associations, most common services can be provided at the
neighborhood level; the private neighborhood association is the logical place to
put the responsibility for the delivery of these "micro" service responsibilities. It
would be consistent with long-standing American principles of federalism—
putting government functions at the lowest level of government where they can
be executed with the greatest flexibility and accountability. As this book has proposed, the right to create a new private association could be extended to older
established neighborhoods—resulting in a new NASSEN.

The same principle, allowing private secession of a subgroup of appropriate
size and configuration, should apply within an existing neighborhood association. The writers of new constitutions for private neighborhood associations
thus should include specific terms and voting requirements (presumably a
supermajority but less than unanimity) for the secession of a private subneighborhood group. Few neighborhood associations currently address the possibility
in their constitutions that a part of the neighborhood may want to withdraw to

form a new smaller association of their own. This is likely to become an important future issue for neighborhood constitutional revision.

In newly developing parts of metropolitan areas, farmers and other owners of undeveloped land should have the right to form a new neighborhood association—a farmer NASSEN—among themselves. They would then be able to develop this land according to their own assessment of market demands. As full-sized neighborhoods of metropolitan land were opened to development in a coordinated fashion, Americans could expect to experience major improvements in the efficiency and attractiveness of urban land use, including housing at lower prices, especially for middle-income buyers. The patterns of metropolitan land development would become more compact, as tight restrictions on uses of undeveloped land in suburban areas are loosened. There would be less incentive for suburban sprawl.

"Secession" really means "group freedom" to exit in matters of local governance and land use. In the modern age, much of the creative activity of society has necessarily occurred in groups. The legal instrument of the modern business corporation was created in the second half of the 19th century for managing and financing collective activity on an industrial scale. It is time now to give private neighborhood associations a similar legal authority and autonomy. A right of private neighborhood secession would follow after the revolution in business corporate law of the late 19th century. In a nation that has long revered "individual freedom," it is time to grant (logically configured) groups of land and property owners the collective rights to assert their "neighborhood freedom" as well.

NOTES

1. Chester E. Finn Jr., Bruno V. Manno, and Gregg Vanourek, *Charter Schools in Action: Renewing Public Education* (Princeton, NJ: Princeton University Press, 2000).

2. Albert O. Hirschman, *Exit, Voice and Loyalty: Responses to Declines in Firms, Organizations, and States* (Cambridge, MA: Harvard University Press, 1970).

3. Ibid., 38.

4. Ibid., 106.

5. Joseph P. Viteritti, "Municipal Home Rule and the Conditions of Justifiable Secession," *Fordham Urban Law Journal* 23 (Fall 1995), 25.

6. Hirschman, *Exit, Voice and Loyalty,* 17, 106.

7. Ibid., 106, 123.

8. Anthony Downs, "The Challenge of Our Declining Big Cities," *Housing Policy Debate* 8, no. 2 (1997), 384, 385.

9. James M. Buchanan, "Markets, States, and the Extent of Morals," *American Economic Review* 68 (May 1978), reprinted in James M. Buchanan, *What Should Economists Do?* (Indianapolis, IN: Liberty Press, 1979), 228–29.

10. Lee C. Buchheit, "The Search for a 'Right' to Secede," in Buchheit, *Secession: The Legitimacy of Self-Determination* (New Haven, CT: Yale University Press, 1978); and John McClaury, "Secession Now (Maybe)," *The Good Society* (Fall 1996).

11. David Gordon, ed., *Secession, State & Liberty* (New Brunswick, NJ: Transaction Publishers, 1998).

12. Viteritti, "Municipal Home Rule and the Conditions of Justifiable Secession," 68.

13. Thomas H. Naylor and William H. Willimon, *Downsizing the U.S.A.* (Grand Rapids, MI: William B. Eerdmans, 1997).

14. Leah Marcal and Shirley Svorny, "Support for Municipal Detachment: Evidence from a Recent Survey of Los Angeles Voters," *Urban Affairs Review* 36 (September 2000).

15. Kenneth T. Jackson, *Crabgrass Frontier: The Suburbanization of the United States* (New York: Oxford University Press, 1985), 149, 153. See also John V. Moeser and Rutledge M. Dennis, *The Politics of Annexation: Oligarchic Power in a Southern City* (Cambridge, MA: Schenkman Publishing Co., 1982).

16. Sheryll D. Cashin, "Privatized Communities and the 'Secession of the Successful': Democracy and Fairness Beyond the Gate," *Fordham Urban Law Journal* 28 (June 2001).

17. Edward J. Blakely and Mary Gail Snyder, *Fortress America: Gated Communities in the United States* (Washington, DC: Brookings Institution Press, 1997).

18. Allen Buchanan, *Secession: The Morality of Political Divorce from Fort Sumter to Lithuania and Quebec* (Boulder, CO: Westview Press, 1991).

19. Allen Buchanan, "Toward a Theory of Secession," *Ethics* (January 1991), 326.

20. See also "The Right of Free Secession," in Robert H. Nelson, *Reaching for Heaven on Earth: The Theological Meaning of Economics* (Lanham, MD: Rowman & Littlefield, 1991), Ch. 8.

21. Buchanan, *Secession,* 30.

22. Georgette C. Poindexter, "Collective Individualism: Deconstructing the Legal City," *University of Pennsylvania Law Review* 145 (January 1997).

23. See also Don Livingston, "The Very Idea of Secession," *Society* 35 (July/August 1998).

24. Possible objections to secession are explored in Cass Sunstein, "Constitutionalism and Secession," *University of Chicago Law Review* 58 (Spring 1991).

25. Fred Foldvary, *Public Goods and Private Communities: The Market Provision of Social Services* (Brookfield, VT: Edward Elgar, 1994), 206. See also Fred E. Foldvary, "The Completely Decentralized City: The Case for Benefits Based Public Finance," *American Journal of Economics and Sociology* 60 (January 2001).

26. Mark D. Rosen, "The Outer Limits of Community Self-Governance in Residential Associations, Municipalities, and Indian Country: A Liberal Theory," *Virginia Law Review* 84 (September 1998), 1060, 1059.

27. Ibid., 1144.

28. Eric A. Posner, "The Regulation of Groups: The Influence of Legal and Nonlegal Sanctions on Collective Action," *University of Chicago Law Review* 63 (Winter 1996), 193.

29. Gary J. Miller, *Cities by Contract: The Politics of Municipal Incorporation* (Cambridge, MA: MIT Press, 1981).

30. William A. Fischel, *The Homevoter Hypothesis: How Home Values Influence Local Government Taxation, School Finance, and Land-Use Policies* (Cambridge, MA: Harvard University Press, 2001), 224.

Conclusion

The Progressive Era set the stage for the development of the American welfare and regulatory state over the course of the 20th century. Like other areas of U.S. government, urban policies during this period reflected the trends of progressive thought. In 1916, zoning was introduced in New York City. The prospect of comprehensive city planning generated wide enthusiasm in the 1920s, influencing the Supreme Court in its approval of zoning in 1926. During the New Deal years, the federal mortgage insurance and public housing programs were created. Urban renewal and the authorization of the interstate highway system were the leading innovations in urban policy in the 1950s.

The 1960s, however, marked a turning point—not only in urban policy, but also for American government as a whole. Confidence in the federal government's ability to "expertly manage" the nation's affairs began a long-term decline. It was part of a general loss of faith in the role of professional expertise in America. People who had previously trusted their family doctor now sought multiple opinions. The place of science in American life was seen with a new ambivalence; as the Holocaust and other events of the first half of the 20th century had shown graphically, modern efficiency based on scientific knowledge could be used for very harmful purposes as well as beneficial ones.

The rise of modern science and industry had given human beings a new and unprecedented ability to control nature, but this new capacity could also mean introducing dangerous chemicals into the environment, endangering plant and animal species, releasing nuclear radiation, and potentially damaging natural processes of all kinds. In contrast to the confident progressive expectations of the early 20th century, modern "progress" was no longer seen as necessarily the path of the salvation of the world.

Such broader trends of thought were once again reflected in urban policy. The federal program of urban renewal, many major highways within cities, and other large-scale government projects were cancelled. Along with federal mortgage and housing programs, federal policies since the New Deal were now blamed for locking the poor into the inner cities. At the local level, zoning was widely employed for similar ends. The urban poor protested violently against their conditions in the 1960s, as riots broke out in many American cities. Even as the American economy continued to grow rapidly and prosperity spread, crime rates in urban America soared—contradicting the core tenet of the progressive "gospel of efficiency" that social dysfunction is rooted in adverse material conditions.

The progressive hopes for urban America had been based on greater centralization of authority in the hands of city planners and other professional experts. From the 1960s, however, a new generation of American intellectuals increasingly favored decentralization and local democracy. If scientific government by a professional elite had represented the application of "modern" thinking, "postmodern" trends were becoming visible in many areas. Even some "neoprogressives" expressed disillusionment with the efforts of their progressive predecessors; Gabriel Kolko wrote of the Progressive Era as in fact "the triumph of conservatism" that advanced powerful business interests in American society.[1] If still largely inchoate, the final decades of the 20th century would see the early appearance of a new political philosophy to replace the outmoded designs for American government that had been formulated in the Progressive Era.

The rise of the private neighborhood association in the 1960s coincided with the loss of faith in scientifically managed progress in America. Neighborhood associations represented a "private neighborhood movement" more important in practical terms than the more publicized efforts to decentralize big-city public governments. Private neighborhood associations substituted a neighborhood democracy of property owners in place of more centralized decisionmaking in the public sector. Instead of an American "melting pot," it now seemed that a diversity of senior citizen, Italian, Baptist, gay and lesbian, single adult, and other neighborhoods where people share similar lifestyles and cultural values might flourish over the long run.

The rise of the private neighborhood association thus can be seen as part of a newly emerging "postprogressive"—or as one might say, "postmodern"— project. However, the spread of neighborhood associations was not the product of any systematic design of postmodern intellectuals. The leading players were land developers and their attorneys, architects, planners, and other private consultants in urban affairs. Neighborhood associations also formalized the de facto private status of the small suburban municipality, as the politically autonomous American suburb had taken shape in earlier decades of the 20th century. Whatever the thoughts and intentions of the original Progressive-Era advocates, zoning in the suburbs had become in practice virtually a collective private property right.[2] And zoning had not been alone; the abolition of the Interstate Commerce Commission and the Civil Aeronautics Board, along with the deregulation of other industries, reflected a growing awareness that the progressive design for American government had often been used for private purposes.

The rise of the private neighborhood association, nevertheless, is not in itself a turn away from government power. Indeed, within their own domain, the powers of neighborhood associations exceed those of most other American governments—a system of "private socialism" at the small geographic scale of the neighborhood, as one might call it. The social significance of a neighborhood association is that it puts government control over land use and local services at the neighborhood level—the most decentralized level possible. Because of its private status, the neighborhood association has a much greater flexibility to experiment with new governing forms—even if few associations thus far have taken full advantage of this constitutional opportunity. Local governments in the public sector, by contrast, are today hemmed in by all kinds of legal precedents, public expectations, ideological commitments, and other constraints—many of them reflecting the Progressive-Era legacy that still retains considerable power in the judiciary and other branches of government, even as its intellectual influence erodes.

Admittedly, an enhanced role for the private sector in society is not altogether a rejection of the Progressive-Era vision. Indeed, the practice of contracting out the delivery of services to private firms can be seen as a new way of advancing the original progressive goal of separating politics from administration. The progressives of the early 20th century sought such a dichotomy as a main feature of their plan for American government. However, over the course of the century, democratic politics typically could not be separated from expert administration. Assigning a "public" task to a private contractor is a way of insulating the delivery of public services from politicians' routine meddling. Indeed, the widespread privatization of government functions in the last decades of the 20th century might be described as in itself a "neo-progressive" trend—a trend ironically most opposed by contemporary political groups that often label their own views as "progressive."

American intellectuals early in the 20th century sought to resolve a basic tension in society. The advance of scientific knowledge and modern technology had created important new administrative and technical possibilities, as seen in the extraordinary gains in economic productivity associated with the rise of the modern business corporation. Modern business expertise and efficiency should also be extended to the government, as leading progressives then argued. The application of new scientific methods to government tasks would require empowering experts to run large parts of the government. These experts would typically be recruited from professional schools of business and public administration as well as professional organizations such as the American Economic Association, the Society of American Foresters, and others created in the Progressive Era. The great dilemma for the progressives was the following: How could the experts be given the authority necessary to oversee a sleek and efficient American government without violating basic American principles of popular democracy? How could a government of administrative experts also be a government that was "of and by the people"?

In the end, the progressives and their successors never developed a satisfactory answer.[3] Their political theories merely papered over this basic tension between expert government and popular democratic government within American political traditions and constitutional forms. The events of the 1960s and subsequent political developments over the next few decades confirmed what had been evident by the 1950s—the old progressive solutions were unworkable, capable of surviving only with the invocation of a host of political and legal fictions.[4] It was not only that American democracy would not leave the professionals alone to administer the government on the basis of their technical skills. In many cases, the experts, as it now appeared, had been operating under exaggerated claims to specialized knowledge. As later events would show, the "expert" solutions had frequently been gravely flawed, even in concept, and often reflected powerful implicit value judgments of the technicians. Given substantial political autonomy, the scientific managers of society showed a distressing tendency to put government powers at the service of their ideological, religious, and other social objectives—and sometimes also for their private benefit as well.[5] The progressive plan for government seemed to require a disinterested "priesthood" of experts but the new professional classes that arose in the wake of the Progressive Era were much like other ordinary human beings throughout history.

As previous chapters have analyzed, the private neighborhood association is not a specific answer to a question of the desirable form of future neighborhood governance. Indeed, the neighborhood association is most significant for the wide range of governance opportunities that it provides. Private neighborhoods, as explored in part V of this book, might want to adopt a host of constitutional innovations. It would often be difficult or even impossible for a government in the public sector to adopt similarly innovative methods. The legacy of progressivism is still too powerful today, inhibiting the flexibility to make radical new departures.

A private neighborhood association thus stands for greater pluralism and choice in American life and governance. It increasingly seems likely that these will be essential elements of future communities. Robert Nozick captured this vision in *Anarchy, State, and Utopia*. Contrary to earlier utopian visions that saw one "correct" society for the whole world, Nozick reflected a new view that expected a long run pluralism of social values and corresponding social organizations. As he wrote, "the idea that there is one best composite answer, . . . one best society for *everyone* to live in, seems to me to be an incredible one. (And the idea that, if there is one, we now know enough to describe it, is even more incredible.)"[6]

However, each individual might plausibly have his or her own vision of an ideal society. Nozick thus proposed a "utopian process" in place of traditional efforts to define a "utopian end state."[7] Seeking the latter for the whole world was pure fantasy, but the former might actually be achievable. Each person would be allowed to join with others to try to create private ideal social arrangements of limited geographic scope. The "microorganization" of such small societies, nevertheless, would have to take place within the context of a "metaorganization" of the world that helped diverse utopian creeds flourish. But beyond this limited framework, no one grand utopian project would prescribe final social outcomes for the entire globe.

As the product of an age that worshipped science, progressivism reflected a modern rather than postmodern consciousness. The Progressive-Era experts subscribed to the idea that there was "one right way"—a way determined by the ever wider and more rigorous application of the scientific method. This propensity extended outside strictly scientific domains, as Americans looked more and more to the national level for a powerful sense of community and the national government increasingly regulated state and local affairs. Recall that it was in the Progressive Era that a nationwide prohibition on the sale of alcohol was written into the United States Constitution. The constitutional amendment in 1933 to abolish prohibition might well be seen as an initial "postprogressive" step—leaving public morality and policy in this area to the discretion of each state and locality.

The private marketplace has the unique feature that it allows for wide individual (and group) freedom, even while the forces of the market exert a powerful central coordinating influence that can extend even over the longest of distances. (International trade today works to coordinate closely the purchasing actions of American consumers with producing actions of Chinese workers.) While the postmodern era may be an era of pluralism, there cannot and will not be a return to autarkic patterns of social organization. A social system that relies on the free market allows for large grants of individual and group autonomy, even as the markets work to discipline this autonomy. In a market, you are free to do this or that according to your own wishes, but only if you are willing and able to pay the price (which often includes significant "opportunity costs" as well as money payments).

The private neighborhood association thus is a postmodern institution in American society in that it allows wider leeway for neighborhoods to define their future, even as it subjects these neighborhoods to market discipline. Yet, it does not answer the question of what that future may bring in each neighborhood. For those people who think they know the one answer for every neighborhood, this is perhaps the most objectionable feature of the private neighborhood association. It provides wide freedom for group life in the neighborhood that sometimes does not accord with the "best" values in the eyes of outside critics.

In a postmodern era it will be up to each neighborhood to decide its own fate (subject of course to certain limitations—no neighborhood can prohibit exit, for example). As a first step, it will be necessary to escape the many constraints and limits that the American judiciary and other branches of government—often acting in the name of the old progressive theories and values—imposed in the 20th century. If the American Progressive-Era intellectuals, in the end, sought one national church of "America," the future may offer much wider parish (neighborhood) autonomy.

A Postmodern Urban Agenda

The governance of neighborhoods will not be the only area in which a post-progressive or postmodern sensibility of market pluralism and diversity is likely to take shape in urban America. The development of postmodern designs, to be sure, will take time. It can occupy the attention of many thinkers and writers. A central feature, as I have suggested, will be new ways of balancing the imperatives of modern expertise versus the demands of popular democratic government. Needs for local autonomy will have to be balanced against requirements for central coordination. This balancing act will require a rethinking of the interaction of government with the private market. The trend, as I am arguing, is likely to be toward a greater market role and a diminished role for higher levels of direct political management and control. However, governments at lower levels, such as neighborhood associations, may become more powerful within their limited spheres, sometimes exceeding the authority to control individual actions of any previous level of government in American history.

Nevertheless, wider government bodies likely will continue to have a vital role in setting the institutional foundations, including the legal system, within which an urban marketplace of neighborhood associations and other forms of market pluralism will function. This book has focused on one aspect of a new setting of postmodern urban institutions—the rise of the private neighborhood association, which made official what suburban zoning had already significantly achieved in practice, the privatization of neighborhood government. As proposed in part IV, the trends toward local political autonomy that were strongest in the suburbs should now be extended into the bastions of centralized and Progressive-Era influence that remain in the center city. In order to accomplish this goal, new state laws could bring the institutional workings of the private neighborhood association (and the creation of NASSENs) to older established neighborhoods in big cities.

In the outer suburbs where land is being developed, the key step is to end local majoritarian confiscations of minority farmers' and other landowners' development rights. The willingness of the courts to look the other way as suburban local governments took away private development rights (for the benefit of other private parties) was a failure of the American judicial system in the 20th century. As Anthony Downs has recently summarized the continuing problem, most suburban governments "pass laws that require high standards of quality for new units, limit multifamily housing, prohibit manufactured housing, and so on," thus foreclosing the opportunity for many people to purchase desirable housing at a reasonable cost. As Downs therefore advocates, "Breaking this [political] impasse will require shifting some of the decision-making power over where housing is built to other levels besides suburban local governments."[8]

As proposed in this book, higher levels of government—or the courts—should intervene to limit the land use authority of suburban public governments over the use of undeveloped land. Unlike most previous proposals of this kind, however, the higher authority would open the way to greater decentralization, rather than centralization, of land-use management and control. The key unit of local land use would become the neighborhood and typically a private neighborhood. There are few instances in government and policy-making where the causes of economic efficiency, social justice, environmental protection, and individual liberty can all be advanced at the same time. In place of existing zoning, new legal authority for owners of undeveloped land to create private neighborhood associations of their own could promote such a "win-win-win-win" outcome.

Besides new legal institutions for the collective private ownership of neighborhood land and property, other key elements are likely to be part of a postmodern institutional setting for urban America. Such features of urban postprogressivism go well beyond the subjects addressed in this book. Nevertheless, it is possible to mention a few such directions in urban policy. They should be among the leading alternatives that deserve wide consideration in imagining a new urban America.

1. Highway Pricing. After the ownership system for land, the greatest need for major policy change in urban America is the pricing system for the use of highways. The technology for systematically pricing urban highways

according to market principles did not exist in the United States until recently. Proper pricing would align highway demands much more closely with the available supply of highway space, and thus greatly reduce traffic congestion in America's cities.[9] The net savings in commuter time and energy would be tens of billions of dollars per year. A related area in which new pricing policies are much needed is the current subsidized provision of free—or very low cost—space to park cars and trucks on city streets and lots.[10]

2. Public Service Pricing. The current pricing of urban public services in general exhibits large economic irrationalities. Many American cities base price on the average cost of delivering services. Instead, they should price according to the marginal cost of adding an additional unit of service delivery (which can admittedly require complicated calculations). The current pricing system for urban public services has subsidized the building of infrastructure, and therefore encouraged housing developments to spread over unnecessarily wide areas and to less economical sites.[11]

3. Educational Competition. Urban systems of water, sewer, major arterial roads, and other limited urban infrastructure may involve large economies of scale and require wide government coordination. Education, however, contains no natural elements that would require a monopoly. The original justification for the public school monopoly was the "melting pot" role that American schools were expected to serve. However, this concept no longer fits the requirements of a new century in which greater pluralism is likely to be a defining feature. Government should still pay most elementary and secondary education costs, but it should make its funds available to a wide range of school types; such a strategy is already seen in current programs for charter schools and a few examples of education vouchers.[12]

4. Freedom of Local Government Organization. Many urban functions can be performed in the private market. Some will, however, remain governmental. In the future, the structures of American urban government should have more flexibility to adapt to changing political and economic circumstances. The workings of local government should allow for wide trial and error. Local governments should be recognized as having businesslike functions that require more of the freedom of organizational experimentation and adaptation that now characterize American business corporations.[13]

5. Private Delivery of Public Services. In the original Progressive Era scheme, experts in appropriate professional fields were to administer government agencies with the efficiency of a business corporation. In practice, local governments have often been encumbered by rigid civil service rules, pay limitations, restrictions on hiring and firing, union job requirements, and a host of other barriers to efficient operation. Privately contracting out the delivery of public services can at least partially resolve these problems and, ironically, reassert in a new way the old Progressive-Era goal of separating politics and administration.[14]

6. Deregulate Subdivision Controls. Subdivision regulations of local governments today often require expensive building practices that are technologically and architecturally outmoded. As more and more land development occurs in large planned private projects, there will be less need for government oversight and control of design and construction details. Subdivision regulations should be limited to areas of clear potential for market failure because of factors such as a lack of homebuyer information concerning property defects that may not become apparent for many years.*

Toward a New Urban America

Tens of millions of Americans are today rightfully unhappy with their urban living conditions in the United States. Many of them spend hours each week sitting in traffic jams. Even when traffic flows freely, they often commit large parts of the day to long commutes. Dispersed urban development takes up millions of acres of metropolitan land that might better be left as parkland or green space. Despite large-scale building of new housing, many people cannot find an attractive home near their work at an affordable price. While property taxes continue to increase, the quality of schools and other public services remains low for millions of urban residents.

For decades, U.S. urban experts and political leaders have proposed solutions even as problems continued to fester. As one set of answers has failed, old ideas have been repackaged in new rhetoric. The old calls for "comprehensive land use planning" gave way to demands for "growth controls" in the 1970s, for "growth management" in the 1980s, and most recently for "smart growth" in

---

*In a 2003 survey, as described in a report prepared for the Lincoln Institute of Land Policy, developers "expressed their frustration with the excessive and often unwarranted nature of [required] physical improvements and standards associated with [traditional] subdivision development." Two-thirds considered traditional subdivision controls a "main culprit in prohibiting design innovation and increasing the cost of housing." For example, "lots are too standardized and streets use too much area" under many local rules. By negotiating with local governments, it was sometimes possible for developers of private communities to introduce innovative approaches. Because they could be more "flexible in their design solutions," such private neighborhood associations were typically "more agreeable to developers, consumers, and local governments." All in all, "in terms of design efficiency, utilization of space, and integration of social and environmental amenities, private communities illustrate the shortcomings of many standards applied to typical subdivisions." See Eran Ben-Joseph, "Land Use and Design Innovations in Private Communities," *Land Lines* 16 (October 2004).

the 1990s.* All of these ideas, to be sure, were in the tradition of the scientific management of the city according to progressive prescriptions originating early in the 20th century. The failures of urban America, it may finally be time to admit, reflect the failures of these original Progressive-Era theories and methods.

That is, the need may now be for a whole new postprogressive—a post-modern—approach. Today, urban America is a patchwork system that refuses to accept officially the basic inadequacy of the old principles on which it was built. Numerous fictions have been required to cover the tensions between official theories and actual practices. Current urban solutions are like bailing water from a boat with a large gash in its side. They may reduce some pain but will do little to resolve the core problems.

Before radical changes can be made, however, many more Americans need to envision a postprogressive and postmodern urban world. It will be a world of greater individual and small-group freedom, greater pluralism, a greater role for market forces, wider use of pricing, and more private planning. Although urban theorists have had little to do with it, the rise of the private neighborhood association has been in the vanguard of the creation of such a postmodern urban America of pluralism, freedom, and community.

---

*The U.S. Department of Housing and Urban Development recently issued yet another in a long line of government reports documenting the continuing harmful social consequences of the suburban land-use regulatory system. As HUD reported in February 2005, "Removing affordable housing barriers could reduce development costs by up to 35 percent." If this were done, "millions of hard-working American families would be able to buy or rent suitable housing that they otherwise could not afford." According to HUD, moreover, the adoption of "smart-growth" policies was often making the problems worse. As HUD found, many better-off suburban communities were now using "smart growth rhetoric to justify restricting growth and limiting developable land supply, which lead to housing cost increases" and suburban sprawl. See U.S. Department of Housing and Urban Development, *Why Not In Our Community? Removing Barriers to Affordable Housing, An Update of the (1991) Report of the Advisory Commission on Regulatory Barriers to Affordable Housing* (Washington, DC: U.S. Department of Housing and Urban Development, February 2005), 1, 5.

NOTES

1. Gabriel Kolko, *The Triumph of Conservatism: A Reinterpretation of American History, 1900–1916* (New York: Free Press, 1963).

2. Robert H. Nelson, *Zoning and Property Rights: An Analysis of the American System of Land Use Regulation* (Cambridge, MA: MIT Press, 1977).

3. Robert H. Nelson, *Reaching for Heaven on Earth: The Theological Meaning of Economics* (Lanham, MD: Rowman & Littlefield, 1991), Ch. 5.

4. I have previously explored the failures of the progressive-era vision in the federal management of the public lands. See Robert H. Nelson, *Public Lands and Private Rights: The Failure of Scientific Management* (Lanham, MD: Rowman & Littlefield, 1995); and Robert H. Nelson, *A Burning Issue: A Case for Abolishing the U.S. Forest Service* (Lanham, MD: Rowman & Littlefield, 2000). See also Robert H. Nelson, *The Making of Federal Coal Policy* (Durham, NC: Duke University Press, 1983); and commentary by A. Dan Tarlock, "The Making of Federal Coal Policy: Lessons for Public Land Management from a Failed Program: An Essay and Review," *Natural Resources Journal* 25 (April 1985).

5. Robert H. Nelson, *Economics as Religion: From Samuelson to Chicago and Beyond* (University Park: Pennsylvania State University Press, 2001).

6. Robert Nozick, *Anarchy, State and Utopia* (New York: Basic Books, 1974), 311.

7. Ibid., 332.

8. Anthony Downs, "Growth Management, Smart Growth, and Affordable Housing," in Anthony Downs, ed., *Growth Management and Affordable Housing: Do They Conflict?* (Washington, DC: Brookings Institution, 2004), 268, 269.

9. Robert W. Poole Jr., and C. Kenneth Orski, *Hot Networks: A New Plan for Congestion Relief and Better Transit* (Santa Monica, CA: Reason Foundation, 2003).

10. See Donald C. Shoup, *The High Cost of Free Parking* (Chicago: American Planning Association, 2005).

11. Jan Brueckner, "Infrastructure Financing and Urban Development: The Economics of Impact Fees," *Journal of Public Economics* 66 (December 1997); and John S. Adams et al., *Development Impact Fees for Minnesota? A Review of Principles and National Practices,* Report 99-04 (Minneapolis: Center for Transportation Studies, University of Minnesota, October 1999).

12. John E. Chubb and Terry M. Moe, *Politics, Markets and America's Schools* (Washington, DC: Brookings Institution Press, 1990).

13. Ronald J. Oakerson, *Governing Local Public Economies: Creating the Civic Metropolis* (Institute for Contemporary Studies, Oakland, CA: ICS Press, 1999).

14. *Privatization: Toward More Effective Government,* Report of the President's Commission on Privatization (March 1988).

About the Author

Robert H. Nelson is a professor at the School of Public Policy at the University of Maryland. His writings have appeared in many professional journals, and he is the author of seven books, including *Zoning and Property Rights* (1977), *Public Lands and Private Rights: The Failure of Scientific Management* (1995), and *Economics as Religion: From Samuelson to Chicago and Beyond* (2001). Mr. Nelson has written for the *Washington Post, Wall Street Journal, Los Angeles Times, Financial Times,* and many other publications. From 1993 to 2000, he was a columnist for *Forbes* magazine. Prior to joining the faculty of the University of Maryland, Mr. Nelson worked in the Office of Policy Analysis of the U.S. Department of the Interior—the principal policy office serving the Secretary of the Interior—from 1975 to 1993.

Index